Struggles for Justice

Struggles for Justice

Social Responsibility and the Liberal State

ALAN DAWLEY

THE BELKNAP PRESS OF
HARVARD UNIVERSITY PRESS

Cambridge, Massachusetts, and London, England
1991

This book is printed on acid-free paper, and its binding materials have
been chosen for strength and durability.

Library of Congress Cataloging-in-Publication Data
Dawley, Alan, 1943-
    Struggles for justice: social responsibility and the liberal state / Alan
Dawley.
        p. cm.
    Includes bibliographical references and index.
    ISBN 0-674-84580-3
    1. United States—Politics and government—1865–1933. 2. United
States—Politics and government—1933–1945. 3. Social conflict-
    United States—History. 4. Individualism—United States—History.
5. Liberalism—United States—History. I. Title.
E743.D345 1991
320.973—dc20   91–2102
                                                                    CIP

To
the late Herbert Gutman
in memory
and
Aaron and Evan
in hope

Preface

WHEN I BEGAN working on this project, the study of American history was coming apart at the seams. Pulled in a dozen different directions, it was turning into a loose patchwork of separate subjects with no coherent pattern. To be sure, aspects that had once been obscure, such as women's experience, slave culture, and industrial labor, were achieving a new brilliance. But it was hard to see how these revelations about everyday life fit into the larger historical process or how the new discoveries in social history were connected to the traditional topics of politics and diplomacy. It was as if the whole was less than the sum of its parts.

Dissatisfied with the drift toward fragmentation, I very much wanted a clearer image of the big picture. For several reasons, the period from the 1890s to the 1930s seemed like a good place to look. It had the right combination of pivotal events and deep structural changes. It contained vibrant social movements arrayed along the fault lines of class, race, and gender. And it sported a fascinating cast of characters. All of this promised a story full of excitement. Besides that, there was an embarrassment of riches in both primary and secondary source materials. The challenge, then, was to envision the evolution of American society in a way that did justice to its multicultural complexity.

In deciding how to proceed, I was able to rule out several approaches from the start. There was little vitality left in what had once been the two leading interpretative frameworks—conflict and consensus. Historians no longer cut their eyeteeth on disputes about whether the key to American history lay in the struggles of opposing social interests or in the wide acceptance of common values. As for newer ideas, theories of difference coming from linguistic and cultural studies seemed only to sanction the very fragmentation that had disturbed me in the first place.

One thing was clear: I would have to come to grips with the dynamics of change. I had always been intrigued by the incongruities in American history—liberty and slavery, poverty and plenty—and the more I burrowed into the subject at hand, the more it seemed that events were being driven by two sets of contradictions. One arose in the polarities of a social order divided by class, gender, and culture; the other in the imbalance between modern society and the existing form of the state. Once this framework was applied, things fell into place. Pivotal events linked up with structural changes; daily life merged with high politics; the struggle to reform state and society gave unity to the historical drama.

Having taken this turn, I could now examine the conflict/consensus debate from a new perspective. Instead of an either/or proposition, the question was how conflict forced changes in the forms of consensus. Clearly, the United States was able to hold itself together against its own internal contradictions, but only because it underwent a significant transformation. It seems reasonable to suppose that the same is true in other periods of social and political upheaval.

I also had to deal with the issue of who makes history. I began with the assumption that human agency cuts two ways: one person's freedom is another person's constraint. Too often it is assumed that the strong are able to control events, while the weak suffer what they must. The truth is that dominant and subordinate groups constrain one another at every turn. Time and again pressure from below—whether mass immigration, labor upheaval, or welfare demands—forced decisions upon elites that they would have preferred to avoid. Thus the destiny of modern America was in the hands of the meek as well as the mighty.

One final matter had to be confronted: the meaning of the past. I was originally attracted to the period in part because so many vital things were at stake: racial justice, sexual freedom, the right to dissent, war and peace. I was also fascinated by the conflict between individualism and social responsibility as it played itself out in a host of struggles around social welfare, government regulation, and the distribution of wealth. Although it was never a simple matter of good guys versus bad guys, there is no doubt that good and evil hung in the balance. In comprehending what happened, I have aspired to objectivity. But objectivity does not mean indifference. It matters very much how things turned out.

Acknowledgments

ALTHOUGH WRITING a book is a solitary labor, it is at the same time a collaborative one. During the decade in which this book took shape, I consulted a small library of monographs with the intention of weaving their findings into a general interpretation, and I frequently turned to colleagues for advice and criticism. Although the final result is my responsibility alone, and although it is impossible to thank everyone who helped, I want to single out several people who were especially generous. Katy Dawley offered the right kinds of advice at the right times. Herbert Gutman was helpful in a variety of ways and remained an inspiration after his untimely death in 1985. Eric Foner set a high standard in his own work and gave welcome support, as did colleagues at the Centre for Social History and the History Department at the University of Warwick, especially William Dusinberre. The same is true of Mari Jo Buhle, David Brody, George Fredrickson, Ellis Hawley, and Barrington Moore, Jr. In different ways, all were midwives to a somewhat protracted birth.

Along the way, a number of archivists and librarians tendered valuable services. Rudolph Vecoli shepherded me through collections at the Immigration History Research Center, which he directs at the University of Minnesota, and also provided advice on text and photos. Other assistance came from David Klaassen (Social Welfare History Archives), Dale C. Mayer (Hoover Library), Eva Mosely (Schlesinger Library), Michael Nash (Hagley Library), and the staffs of the Library of Congress and the National Archives. In addition, I could always count on the librarians of Roscoe West Library (Trenton State College) to track down an obscure reference or obtain an interlibrary loan.

As the chapters took shape, several colleagues offered the kind of detailed critiques that improved the text in both argument and accuracy. I am especially indebted to Ira Berlin, Nancy Cott, Gary Gerstle, Linda Gordon, J. H. M. Laslett, David Montgomery, and Martin Sklar for their keen observations.

Others who read smaller portions of the manuscript or responded to papers based on the research include Renate Bridenthal, Geoffrey Blodgett, Daniel Crofts, Leon Fink, David M. Kennedy, Moshe Lewin, William Preston, Mary Ryan, Theda Skocpol, and Eli Zaretsky. Here and there a commentator asked me, in effect, to write a different book, but most were indulgent—or realistic—enough to let it take its own path. Helpful questions were raised in various seminar presentations, particularly at the Cambridge University seminar in social history and the Oxford University seminar in American history. In addition, students in a variety of other classroom settings have provided much useful feedback.

As the project neared completion, Lloyd Gardner, Ellis Hawley, Kathryn Kish Sklar, and Stephan Thernstrom provided thoughtful evaluations of the whole manuscript. It was, indeed, gratifying to have readers engage the interpretation at such a serious level, and their extensive comments helped refine the argument and eliminate mistakes. The book is extremely fortunate to have been under the supervision of Aida Donald, editor-in-chief of Harvard University Press, who time and again pointed out the path to lucidity.

In days gone by, a scholar could not afford to prowl around dusty archives without the financial support of a wealthy patron. Nowadays, the historian of limited means requires the aid of a well-endowed granting institution. In this case, a good portion of the research and writing was made possible by a National Endowment for the Humanities Fellowship in 1986–87. In addition, smaller grants-in-aid underwrote forays to half a dozen archives; they included a Summer Stipend from the National Endowment for the Humanities, a Beveridge Grant from the American Historical Association, a Mellon Grant from Radcliffe College, and a grant-in-aid from Hagley Library, in Wilmington, Delaware. I am also obliged to the History Department and other parts of Trenton State College for secretarial services, released time, and the Distinguished Research Award in 1987–1989, under which the bulk of the manuscript was completed.

Contents

Illustrations

Struggles for Justice

Introduction

THE YEARS BETWEEN the Gilded Age and the New Deal were among the most tumultuous in American history. With seemingly boundless energy, the United States expanded in wealth and population to become the world's premier industrial power and went through bruising social conflicts at home, including the greatest strike wave and some of the worst race riots in a riot-torn history. Everything was in flux, from the mix of ethnic groups to the social relations of the sexes. And as if all this were not enough, there was still time to acquire an overseas empire, fight in the Great War, and endure the ravages of the Great Depression.

No wonder ruling structures and values were increasingly called into question. How could the existing form of the state, designed generations earlier for an agrarian-commercial society, withstand the brawling conflicts and relentless evolution of an urban-industrial way of life? How could such grave problems as poverty and unemployment be addressed within a framework of individual self-reliance? Certainly, to those who took seriously the Declaration's promise of equality, the time was fast approaching to make good on the pledge of "liberty and justice for all." The crux of American history in the early twentieth century, then, lay in the reckoning between a dynamic society and the existing liberal state. The story of that reckoning unfolded in three stages.

1. *The imbalance of state and society, 1890s–1913.* In the first period, lasting until the outbreak of the First World War, American society was on a collision course with its own political system. The dominant feature of the nineteenth-century political landscape was liberalism. Founded on the rock of opposition to tyranny, liberalism had long emphasized

constitutional checks and balances as against the arbitrary power of centralized authority. Then, by the time the Carnegies and the Rockefellers came along, the emphasis was on opposition to government intervention in the marketplace. Insofar as this laissez-faire liberalism was taken as a license for the accumulation of unlimited wealth, it underwrote the growing gap between urban workers and captains of industry. Whenever it came down to a choice between liberty and social equality in the Gilded Age, there was no doubt about which came first.[1]

Liberalism, then, was consistent with inequality, whether of class, gender, or race. Since women were denied the vote and other rights of citizenship, it could hardly be argued that the two sexes were equal in the eyes of the law or in the marketplace. The excuse was that women and men were supposed to inhabit "separate spheres"—she to home and church as the standard of selfless virtue, he to the market and politics in pursuit of self-interest. Similarly, the nation embraced white supremacy by accepting Jim Crow laws, disfranchisement, and the whole segregationist regime in the South under the Supreme Court doctrine "separate but equal." Thus was liberty reserved for white men only.

Whatever disturbed the social status quo was certain to pose a challenge to the traditional concept of liberty. There was certainly no shortage of disturbances in the early twentieth century, including the rise of corporate capitalism, the expanding role of women in public life, and the reshuffling of the ethnic deck. In fact, as polarities of class and culture intensified, struggles broke out on every hand—strikes and union drives, suffrage rallies, civil rights campaigns, and middle-class crusades against the evils of factories and slums.

In every case, reform struggles ran up against one aspect or another of the liberal state. Although giant corporations no longer played by the rules of family capitalism, laws devised in an earlier era made it hard to bring big business to heel. Despite the increasing influence of women in public life, male suffrage lay across the path of women's emancipation. Even though poverty on a mass scale made a mockery of the Protestant ethic of individual self-reliance, laissez faire prevented the community from addressing the needs of the urban multitude. In the face of new demands for civil rights, segregation held fast. Thus along every front and fault line of American life there arose a contradiction between the needs of society and the existing political system.

Another kind of contradiction appeared in U.S. foreign policy. Vaulting to the top of the world's industrial powers, the United States sent the products of its fiery furnaces and fruited plains to all parts of the globe. In the same burst of expansive energy, it startled the world by humbling one of Europe's great empires in the Spanish-American War. As a consequence of economic and diplomatic expansion, the United States became the colonial landlord of the Philippines and the effective overlord of much of the Caribbean and South America, particularly under the rambunctious Teddy Roosevelt and his Big Stick. The result was an inescapable contradiction between the new reality of world power and the liberal tradition. The more the United States assumed an imperial posture, the more it denied its own cherished principle of self-government.

2. *Confronting issues, 1914–1924.* Whatever brought the state into the act was certain to heighten these contradictions and force a confrontation with the new social realities. That was certainly the case in the boisterous years around the First World War. Before entering the war, the United States went through a short spurt of domestic reform under President Woodrow Wilson, marked by the creation of new regulatory machinery for banking and industry, plus modest social reforms. But all that was as nothing compared with the level of state intervention after the declaration of war in 1917. "War is the health of the state," warned one critic; and as if to confirm the warning, the Wilson administration mobilized, propagandized, regulated, repressed, and taxed the population as no government had ever done before.

In many ways, the level of state intervention increased during the immediate postwar years. A perverse twist of events turned laissez faire upside down in a series of actions from strikebreaking and the Red Scare to Prohibition and immigration restriction. In every case intervention hit the immigrant working population hardest, and the resort to repression represented a last-ditch effort by old-fashioned liberalism to stave off the consequences of social change.

In any event, the combination of acute emergencies and long-term social change subjected the liberal governing system to intolerable pressures. A governing system is defined to include, first, the state apparatus proper—army, police, courts, legislatures, electoral systems, and constitutional structures such as federalism and separation of powers. Second, it includes the means of access to state power, such as parties, elections, lobbying, and bribery. Third, it encompasses ruling ideas, patterns of authority in family, workplace, and community, and prevailing morality. In short, a governing system is the state embedded in society. Because state and society were linked in a dialectical relationship, it was impossible for one to change without affecting the other.

3. *Resolving the imbalance, 1925–1938.* The imbalance was finally resolved in the 1930s when the Great Depression triggered the same kind of national emergency as the Great War and called forth the same level of state intervention. Casting about for some way to restore balance to a system gone haywire, at first both Presidents Herbert Hoover and Franklin Roosevelt experimented with managerial controls. But when top-down state capitalism proved insufficient, Roosevelt devised new experiments to end the nightmarish spectacle of rampant poverty. Putting a bridle in the mouth of untamed capitalist empire-builders, Roosevelt's New Deal instituted a fledgling welfare state and imposed new regulations on industrial relations with the aim of restraining individual liberty for the good of society. If at the end of the decade America was still governed by a liberal state—and that is subject to interpretation—then it was liberalism with a social face.

This does not mean that the New Deal ushered in the happy reign of universal equality. Far from it. The overriding purpose of reform was captured in the name of one of the New Deal's major accomplishments: Social Security. If there was a watchword covering the reforms of the time it was neither liberty nor equality, but *security.*

In any case, the new social liberalism of the 1930s as consolidated in the next decade was a far cry from the preceding forms of liberalism. It differed from constitutional checks and balances in terms of its centralization of power and creation of new bureaucracies that became the "fourth branch" of government. It also differed from the liberalism of laissez faire in terms of its extensive regulation of the market. No doubt it would have dumbfounded the Founding Fathers and made Grover Cleveland turn over in his grave.

In summary, the crux of American history from the 1890s to the 1930s was the imbalance between a bustling society and the existing liberal state. The dynamics of social change and overseas expansion created contradictions that could not be contained within the political framework handed down from the nineteenth century. As a result of struggles between industrialist and worker, Victorian moralist and

New Woman, nativist and immigrant, the old governing system had to change.

Seeking to preserve their power in the face of change, elites devised a series of strategies to regain their legitimacy by reforming the system. Departing from the negative formulas of old-time liberals, they experimented with positive forms of state intervention, beginning with progressivism, ranging through managerial liberalism, and winding up with the social liberalism of the New Deal. The success of their experiments was proved by the longevity of the new system, which weathered the test of the Second World War and survived until the 1970s.

Given a choice, most Americans would probably have preferred some other solution. Shunning social obligations whenever possible, they display an inveterate attachment to personal liberty. They choose lone pathfinders as popular heroes, tolerate vast inequalities of wealth in the name of individual opportunity, and pay homage to the adage "That government is best which governs least." Down through the decades politicians could usually win favor with the voters by promising to get the government off their backs.

But history did not afford the luxury of a choice in this period. Given the dynamism and antagonisms built into American society, it was inevitable that state structures and ruling values would change. The only questions were how, and in whose interests? How would the state juggle conflicting demands presented by the host of social forces? How would it balance egalitarian demands against the preservation of a hierarchical social order? Driven by the necessity of circumstance, the United States shifted from the individual toward the social, from personal liberty toward social security, from less government toward more government. In short, Americans were dragged kicking and screaming toward social responsibility. The task of this book is to show why that shift took place.

A word or two on the underlying ideas at work in the following pages are in order at this point. To describe the transformation of the old liberalism into the new requires some vision of the historical process as a whole. It would be a fool's errand to attempt to cover everything and everybody; wherever omniscience may lie, it is not in the mind of the historian, at least not this one. But a satisfying account of any given period needs to embody a central problem. Usually, that problem originates in the balance of forces among the conflicting parts of the social whole. The task is not to present every last detail of daily life, but to comprehend what the office secretary and the secretary of state have to do with each other and how their common society was driven through time by its own internal contradictions.

To reconstruct that process requires, first, combining several sub-plots into a single narrative. There is no getting around it. To approach a cohesive understanding of our own world, we must pursue a cohesive understanding of the past. No doubt it is possible to extract a central theme different from the one presented here, and it is even possible to make *difference* itself the central theme. In fact, the prevailing mode for many years now has been the telling of separate stories about different social groups, each more fascinating than the next but without a unifying dramatic thread. So be it. Yet that does not deny the need to identify an overriding problem in any given historical period and to figure out how the separate subplots fit together.

Second, several threads of historical thought are drawn together to pose the problem of state and society. Interpretative arguments can provide clues to a culture's self-understanding, and surely it is a matter of broad importance that, for a long time, debate among historians turned on whether American history hinged on conflict or consensus.

During the reform-filled Progressive Era early in the century, histor-ians who were partisans in the political battles of the time began to write about the social and economic conflicts behind great political events. Even while rejecting the Marxist idea of history as class struggle, such leading works as Charles and Mary Beard's *The Rise of American Civilization* (1927) told a tale of continual conflict between creditors and debtors, industrialists and slavemasters, capitalists and workers. Introducing a vocabulary of interest groups, bargaining classes, and social forces into what had been a resolutely individualistic culture, their ideas have reverberated from that day to this. The dis-covery of contending social forces remains a vital key to unlocking what Walter Lippmann, an influential member of the progressive generation, called the "American difficulty."[2]

By the early 1950s, however, a powerful counterattack by so-called consensus historians had displaced conflict from the center of analysis. The new breed of counter-progressive historians pilloried their prede-cessors for economic determinism and, instead, argued the case for such cultural determinants as the Puritan mind and the myth of virgin land. Part and parcel of the decline of dissent during the Cold War, consensus history either celebrated the genius of American politics for escaping the ideological divisions of Europe, or else warned about the tyranny of the majority in a culture suffocating under an all-embracing liberal tradition. Either way, it rejected the idea of systemic conflict and portrayed America as a nation of exceptional unity.[3]

At its worst, consensus history was a one-sided glorification of American achievement in which there was economic progress without suffering, an ascent of organized labor without struggle, and leadership of the "free world" without imperial victims. At its best, in cases like Richard Hofstadter's *The American Political Tradition* (1948), it stripped public figures of sainthood and revealed the common capitalist values uniting seeming opponents. The fact that Hofstadter's *The Age of Reform* (1955) remains thought-provoking thirty-five years after its publication is attested by its use as a point of departure for the problem and periodization of this book.[4]

Since that time, a good deal of historical thinking has gone to shape a new problem. Attacking the consensus school at a vulnerable point, diplomatic historians in the 1960s revised accounts of the U.S. role in the Cold War and the Third World that overstated American benevolence. Pouring into the breach, a small army of social historians redressed the lack of attention paid to common people, including immigrant workers, plantation slaves, and southern women. The combined impact of revisionist and social history was to restore the role of conflict, resurrect a sense of change over time, and recapture a more democratic vista that had room for groups previously excluded by virtue of class, race, or sex. As a consequence, the drama of social conflict and the causative role of popular agency were restored to the center of American development.[5]

The trouble was, there was no center at the center. Social historians who laid the past under every possible grid of analysis—class, gender, race, region, sexual preference, religion, age, and so on—became trapped in a kind of analytic gridlock. By a cruel logic, the very multiplication of categories necessary for an inclusive history made the goal of writing such a history harder to attain. The proliferation of subdisciplines in politics, diplomacy, ethnic groups, women, labor, business, and so on, each with its own network of journals, conferences, old school ties, and mutually unintelligible dialects, only made things worse. The need to scale each of these mountains of scholarly literature seemed to condemn historians to an eternal labor of Sisyphus.[6]

Seeking to avoid gridlock, other historians undertook a search for order. Making a concerted effort to build a synthesis around the idea of modernization, several constructed broad narratives of twentieth-century history on the scaffolding of the large-scale organizations so prominent in modern life—corporations, interest groups, government bureaucracies, and the like. Using ideas rooted in the sociology of Max Weber, they demonstrated continuity in institutional development and a deepened understanding of the underlying structures of power.[7] Unfortunately, this attempt at synthesis had a hole where social history should have been. Instead of building popular agency and social dynamics into an account of change over time, it substituted the teleology of a bureaucratic search for order.

By the end of the 1980s—a decade as lean as the 1920s and 1950s for progressive social movements—grand theories of deep structures of domination were making great headway. Sensitive to the extraordinary sway of Western capitalism, one set of historians probed the centuries-long rise of the capitalist "world system," with its dominant core and subordinate periphery. Working in another vein, others insisted on reading history as a series of texts and emphasized the power of "discourse" to shape unequal social relations. The message seemed to be, contrary to Marx, that all history is the history of *text* struggle.[8]

There is no doubt that deep mental structures and long-term processes deserve attention. Whether these methodologies can encompass the actual historical process is another matter. The trouble with some of the history in vogue at the beginning of the 1990s that appeared under the labels "poststructuralist" or "postmodernist" is that, in some cases, it is just that, *post*history. It is what gets written after history has come to an end, when it no longer seems possible for people to mount the grand stage of historical events and play a central role in determining their own destiny.

The reason for focusing on (progressive) conflict or (Marxian) contradiction is not to portray a moralistic contest between good guys and bad guys, but to confront the question of why a society evolved through time. A number of approaches in anthropology, British and American social history, and French social theory emphasize internal contradictions. Again, the point is not to ask for some confession of faith but to develop a method adequate to comprehending the complex processes of actual events.[9]

As a result of the past quarter-century of historical writing, it is possible to set the earlier battles between progressives and counter-progressives in a new light. In fact, if the progressives are taken as the thesis and the counter-progressives as the antithesis, then it is possible to synthesize from them a third view, which may be stated in terms of a general problem: how was society held together (consensus) against its own inner contradictions (conflict)? In short, conflict and consensus are combined in the problem of *hegemony*.

That is to say, given the built-in antagonism among contending social forces, how was it possible to stave off some kind of breakdown in the system? Certainly, the ceaseless pressure of opposing forces posed questions about the place of women, the predicament of African-Americans, and poverty amidst abundance whose always-incomplete resolution moved America from one balance of forces to the next.[10] The question is, how did the United States survive the stresses and strains of massive social change, not to mention the acute pressures of the First World War and the Great Depression, without a change of regime? It appears that the evolution of New Deal liberalism out of its laissez-faire ancestor has a lot to do with the answer.

In addressing these matters, it is useful to set American development in the larger contours of world events. Transcending national boundaries, capitalist development reshaped class relations everywhere by boosting the great bourgeois families above the heads of ordinary commercial and industrial middle classes—more so in Rockefeller's America and the Germany of the Krupps, less so in late Victorian Britain and the French Third Republic. In the same process, the ranks of industrial workers swelled to the point that they were becoming the largest segments of the population in their respective countries. In England the milestone was passed in 1870; Germany passed it by 1895, the United States sometime before 1910, and France after the First World War.[11]

Meanwhile, changes in social reproduction were evident on every hand. Birthrates fell, literacy levels rose, and family life was transformed. Vast streams of cityward migration disrupted community relations, redefined national identities, and induced a backlash of racist and Social Darwinist ideas. The combined impact of these changes was to crystallize a set of grand historical issues by the beginning of the twentieth century as the Western world grappled with the "social question," the place of the New Woman, and imperial rivalry.

The existence of common forces and problems throughout the Western world establishes a framework for comparative analysis. Comparison is a way of asking "what if" questions using real alternatives, not mere conjectures or imaginary hypotheses. By juxtaposing the histories of actual societies, it is possible to determine with a reasonable likelihood what caused them to move in different directions. Since the historian cannot replicate past events in test tubes or particle accelerators, comparison becomes a kind of laboratory for conducting experiments in causation that, in the words of one practitioner, is "absolutely essential" to historical explanation.[12]

Two kinds of comparison are made in the following pages. First, within the United States, North and South are measured against each other as a means of exploring regional differences in industrial relations, race and gender, and ideas of liberty.[13] Second, within the international framework, the United States is compared with Germany. With respect to the evolution of corporate capitalism and bureaucratic controls over social reproduction, the United States and Germany were closer to each other than to Britain or France. Comparing the different ways the two countries handled the same issues—big business, the working class, gender, race relations, war, and depression—yields insight into the conditions that favored liberal or authoritarian states and the ideologies of liberalism, socialism, or fascism.[14]

One effect of the comparison is to call "American exceptionalism" into question. It is common for the United States and Germany to be treated as great exceptions, different not just from each other but from everybody else. Combining conventional treatments of the two countries produces a Tale of Two Exceptionalisms. It is an oft-told tale full of heroes (mostly American) and villains (mostly German) who work toward opposite destinies (the pragmatism of Roosevelt's New Deal, the fanaticism of Hitler's fascism) because of key absences in their respective histories (feudalism and socialism in one case, liberalism in the other). Indeed, to a great extent, the American and German aberrations have each been defined against the other. American exceptionalism has been defined against a model of Continental Europe, with its feudal legacy, class divisions, statist rule, and working-class socialist movements, while German exceptionalism has been defined against Anglo-American liberal capitalism, with its free-market individualism, fluid social boundaries, voluntarist politics, and anti-intellectual labor movements.

Taken separately, the two notions of exceptionalism have a certain plausibility. Let us allow that every country is unique, and that the

United States and Germany are no exceptions. But when they are put side by side, the logic chopping becomes apparent. First, logic breaks down in defining the two exceptionalisms against each other. How can the United States be the exception to the statist norm one minute and the norm for the statist exception the next? Second, both sides of the story rest on what might be called the *absence fallacy*, that is, the resort to absence as explanation. American development is explained in terms of absent feudalism, leading to absent socialism, which meant the absence of significant opposition to capitalism. German development, for its part, is explained in terms of absent liberalism, which failed to take power in 1848, failed to stop traditional elites from plunging the world into the First World War in 1914, and then failed to stop the Nazis from seizing power and plunging the world into the Second World War. The fallacy, of course, is that absent causes can produce no consequences whatever. Instead of trying to find the logic in it all, it is better to recognize that 1 American exception + 1 German exception = 2 misconceptions.[15]

Comparison aside, if the aim is to tell the story of whole societies in motion through time, then there are tried-and-true historical methods for doing so. Before rummaging about in the toolkits of other disciplines, historians should perfect their own techniques of analyzing cause and effect, choice among limited alternatives, and free will and determinism. Whatever else it is possible to avoid or ignore, there is no way of avoiding the inescapable reality of *time*. In the words of Marc Bloch, "Now, this real time is, in essence, a continuum. It is also perpetual change. The great problems of historical inquiry derive from the antithesis of these two attributes."[16]

Certainly, change-within-continuity characterized the evolution of laissez-faire liberalism into the social liberalism of the New Deal. In a more optimistic age, this transformation undoubtedly would have been called progress. The trouble with the nineteenth-century idea of progress is that it was too linear and self-serving, and, in any case, it did not survive the brutalities of twentieth-century history. Modern-day historians have learned to be more wary of the surprises the past holds in store—the unexpected turn of events and the unintended consequence. And they have learned to be sensitive to the puzzling paradox of will, in which history is the result of human will but is something no one individual or group willed. It is the result of conscious intent but is something no one intended.

Nothing is more basic to historical inquiry than a narrative of events.

Ages ago history started out with the telling of stories. Although it has come a long way since the days when it was linked with the myths of godlike kings and heroes, it is still a way of telling stories. The difference is that the complexity and mass literacy of modern society require that the stories be about more than mythical kings, or even real ones, for that matter. The modern narrative must range across all the levels of society, from material conditions of daily life through the forms of social organization to the structures of state power. It must come to terms with the role of human agency—ordinary as well as extraordinary people—and with the irreconcilable antagonisms that drive society from one state of unstable equilibrium to the next. In short, what is needed is a narrative of contradiction.

The level of historical consciousness, always low in the United States, seems to have sunk to new depths in recent years. The lament that "nobody reads history anymore" is all too true. This state of affairs is largely the fault of a culture drowning in a sea of meaningless information and obsessed with the immediate present to the point where the common phrase "It's history" has come to mean "You can forget about it." To anyone with a sense of the living vitality of the past, there can be no unkinder cut than this.

But it is also the fault of the loss of vision in academic writing. Dubious about progress, skeptical to a fault, caught up in the game of status, academics sometimes debate issues in a way that is all but incomprehensible to the educated reader. They have helped bring about their own isolation from the reading public by their very technical sophistication and professionalized discourse. If grappling with the dynamics of change helps restore a sense of the moving pageant of human affairs, it might help do something to reconnect scholarship to the real world. If a narrative of contradiction can help restore drama and passion to the story of human development, then it will serve a worthy purpose.

One might still ask what other purpose there is of telling the story of American history in the early twentieth century. After all, there is nothing the present can do to alter the outcome of those events. Maybe it is better just to accept the fact that "it's history." But although the past cannot be altered, what is thought and done today will inevitably affect the shape of things to come. When Franklin Roosevelt said in his 1936 reelection campaign that his generation had a "rendezvous with destiny," he put the matter exactly right. It was no longer possible for

Americans to put off the reckoning between individual liberty and social justice. Something had to give way.

Similarly, in our own time, the way the present generation handles questions of poverty, racism, gender identity, and war will determine the kind of world the future will inherit. Today's rendezvous with history, in turn, depends on how the present generation understands its own destiny. If new thinking about the past inevitably alters the course of future events, then we should admit that the overriding moral purpose of history is to guide humanity as it shapes the future. And since one is entitled to hope for a better one, memory and hope are linked together in the dedication at the front of the book.

I

THE PROBLEM:
STATE AND SOCIETY

·//·

1890s–1912

I

Gilded Age Liberty

WHEN THE STATUE OF LIBERTY was dedicated in New York Harbor on October 28, 1886, the nation was rife with industrial and farm discontent. There had been massive strikes in May leading to trials of Chicago's notorious Haymarket anarchists. Workingmen were running radical economist Henry George for mayor of New York. And in the South and the plains states, farmers were planting seeds that would soon grow into the Populist revolt, the largest agrarian reform movement in American history.

Faced with this upheaval from below, dignitaries from President Grover Cleveland on down who gathered for Miss Liberty's dedication ceremony were quick to seize upon her as a unifying national symbol, a goddess of republican virtue meant to evoke stability, antiquity, and maternity as much as liberty, equality, and fraternity. Among the orators at her unveiling was Chauncey Depew, railroad magnate and president of the Union League Club, who delivered an ode to self-government as the solution to the country's troubles: "the problems of labor and capital, of property and poverty will work themselves out under the benign influence of enlightened law-making and law-abiding liberty, without the aid of kings and armies, or of anarchists and bombs."[1]

To the Gilded Age upper crust, "law-abiding liberty" was the product of centuries of hard-won progress. Starting in the Dark Ages among Teutonic tribes, liberty had made its way through the England of Magna Charta to the newfound American republic to be enshrined in the Declaration of Independence and the Constitution. Then, having united the North against the slave South, it had reached its culmination in the Anglo-Saxon civilization of late nineteenth-century

America. Along the way, liberty had brought about a great devolution of power from hereditary rulers and their military and ecclesiastical establishments to self-made men like themselves.

Second only to liberty in the pantheon of American values was equality. Unlike European societies steeped in pelf and privilege, America was seen to be the land of opportunity, where anyone with talent and ambition could rise in status. Ceaseless mobility was supposed to ensure that the ladder of mobility did not harden into a rigid class hierarchy overgrown with the rank vegetation of titled nobility and hereditary monarchy. Novelist Henry James gently satirized this popular image of the self-governing republic: "No State, in the European sense of the word, and indeed barely a specific national name. No sovereign, no court, no personal loyalty, no aristocracy, no church, no clergy, no army, no diplomatic service, no country gentlemen, no palaces, no castles, nor manors, nor old country houses, nor parsonages, nor thatched cottages, nor ivied ruins."[2]

But not far below the surface was a half-hidden but equally potent set of hierarchical assumptions about property right, women's subordination, and white supremacy. In fact, these were no less foundations of the liberal state than nominal equality before the law. To scratch a defender of liberty was often to find a defender of *inequality*, as in the case of William Graham Sumner, the leading Social Darwinist of his day: "Let it be understood that we cannot go outside of this alternative: liberty, inequality, survival of the fittest; not-liberty, equality, survival of the unfittest. The former carries society forward and favors all its best members; the latter carries society downwards and favors all its worst members."[3] Sumner was only making plain what his fellow members of the elite felt deep down, that liberty and hierarchy went hand in hand in the progress of the race.

On occasions when the unfit became unruly, Miss Liberty put down her torch and called in the police. Among those to feel the full brunt of state power in the year of Liberty's enthronement were the Haymarket anarchists. Convicted in an Illinois court of conspiring to bomb a detachment of Chicago police, four of the eight defendants were hanged. Although they were subsequently pardoned by a courageous Illinois governor, this legalized lynching outraged many at home and abroad. Among the protestors was William Morris, English socialist and artist, whose satire of the homespun American republic was not so gentle: "a country with universal suffrage, no king, no House of Lords, no privilege as you fondly think; only a little standing army chiefly used for the murder of red-skins; a democracy after your model; and with all that a society corrupt to the core, and at this moment engaged in suppressing freedom with just the same reckless brutality and blind ignorance as the Czar of all the Russias uses."[4]

As these conflicting portraits attest, America was beset by puzzling contradictions. It was a country with no state in the European sense, yet it could suppress freedom as the czar did. Its citizens fervently believed in equal rights, yet they also accepted the inequality that went hand in hand with survival of the fittest. It was a stable regime, yet one racked by popular discontent. The Statue of Liberty, no doubt, would do its part as a unifying national symbol, but otherwise how was this unruly society to be ruled?

The Reign of the Middle Class

When Gilded Age America looked in the mirror it saw a society bulging at the middle. Especially if it was a circus mirror, rich and poor could almost disappear behind the distended image of the middling sort—the prosperous farmer, the bustling shopkeeper, and the rising industrialist. The image was captured for posterity in photographs, so popular in the Victorian era, of the whole family dutifully posing in their Sunday best, united for success in a heartless world. Idealized by Fourth of July orators as the very foundation of the republic, the family stood for the respectability and stake in society necessary to solid citizenship. As the junction point for things domestic and commercial, private and public, feminine and masculine, the propertied family was at the center of American life.[5]

No one was closer to America's heart than the family farmer. In 1900 there were perhaps 3.8 million farm owners in the United States, some 13 percent of the total labor force of 29 million, not counting another 2 million-odd tenant farmers. But after two and a half centuries of expansion, family farmers had reached a plateau, just barely holding their own in the afterglow of the frontier by mechanizing their operations to compete in national and world markets.[6] Social reproduction on the farm was closely bound up with the sexual division of labor, she in the house and he in the fields, with children of each gender working under close supervision of the respective parent. Since a successful marriage was directly related to the inheritance of the farm, the path to marriage was closely guarded around chastity for girls and self-denial for boys. Steeped in Protestant morality, rural families warded off the temptations of premarital intercourse and drinking by means of periodic crusades for purity and temperance, complete with the hoopla of public confessions and water-wagon parades.[7]

Urban proprietors were no less creatures of the competitive marketplace. While their rural counterparts were stuck on a plateau, industrialization was rapidly expanding the ranks of urban proprietors in manufacturing, distribution, and retail shopkeeping. The 1900 census counted some 1.7 million proprietors (including managers and officials), or about 6 percent of the labor force, plus another 1.2 million professionals. Facing intense competitive pressures, their enterprises failed in droves, particularly in the depressions of 1873–1878 and 1893–1896, even as their overall numbers were expanding. Industrialization transformed social reproduction in the cities by means of prepared foods, ready-made garments, and municipal water supplies, all of which reduced the role of unpaid household labor and set the stage for the expansion of women's paid employment. By the same token, bequeathing real estate had become less important than handing down a fat bank account and transmitting the kind of personal and educational skills that could keep the investments growing. Families could devote greater attention to rearing children for a business future, since the birthrate had plummeted from around 7 children per family at the beginning of the century to about 3.5 at the end, a demographic transition that was most pronounced among the urban middle classes.[8]

The shift of production from household to factory induced changes in the meaning of gender. The age-old separation between masculine and feminine had widened by midcentury to become a doctrine of God-given "separate spheres." Press, pulpit, and marital advice manuals all agreed: "Each has a distinct sphere of duty—the husband to go out in to the world—the wife to superintend the domestic affairs of the household." The self-made man moved in the heartless world of commerce and politics, animated by self-interest in the accumulation of sufficient wealth to become his own man, support his wife and children, and acquire a competence for old age. Along the way, if he was manly enough, he might somehow master the temptations of the saloon and his own appetite for the sordid pleasures of the flesh.[9]

Lucky the man who had a true woman to help him. Standing Genesis on its head, the Victorians made Eve the moral superior of Adam.

Instead of tempting man to fall, the true woman raised him up to her own higher moral plane by making her home a haven of domestic refinement away from the cares of the workaday world. Cleansed of degrading sensual passions, her chastity was the epitome of virtue. Instead of sex for pleasure, she had sex in monogamous (and ethnically endogamous) marriage for the sole purpose of procreation. Anything else was impermissible—premarital petting, prostitution, Mormon polygamy, and any interracial liaison, not to mention unspeakable "perversions." This "marital chastity," as popular marriage manuals referred to it, was a powerful impetus to family limitation and a sign of women's leverage in the home.[10]

In short, husband and wife were the perfect complement. Her disinterest complemented his self-interest; her self-sacrifice, his competitiveness; her absence of passion, his lust. Thus the doctrine of separate spheres was a perfect mask for male dominance in the sense that it presented the face of an egalitarian ideal: the true woman and the self-made man were each sovereign in their own sphere. They were separate, but equal.

Community activities cleaved along the fault line of gender. For women, there were the church social, the local women's club, and the Women's Christian Temperance Union; for men, the fraternal lodge, the local chamber of commerce, and the Young Men's Christian Association. Such voluntary associations operated in the public arena, the place where the structures of the state met and mingled with the private structures of authority in home and factory. Though less vital to public affairs than the patriarchal family of colonial times, the middle-class family retained certain public functions. When couples practiced, or at least preached, its virtues, they were likely to win the good reputation that was the ticket of admission to the women's club, the Presbyterian church, and credit at the local bank. And although the public sphere was dominated by men, the notion that true women were the epitome of virtue could be turned into a prescription for feminine influence that extended to church and community.[11]

Access to the public sphere was also determined by class. Supposedly, in a classless society everyone had equal opportunity to participate in public life. But in reality, prominent business and professional families played the dominant roles. Their boards of trade, benevolent societies, and Protestant churches were the recruiting grounds for civic leaders for most of the century. Although workers enjoyed some access to the public realm through political parties, their own class organizations and voluntary associations were kept at the margins. Except for an unusual moment such as the Knights of Labor's dash across the stage in the mid-1880s, trade unions, mutual benefit societies, and German *Turnvereine* lacked access to leadership, while secret societies such as the Irish Clan Na Gael were by definition excluded altogether.[12]

The reign of middle-class families was underwritten by the state. Among the welter of legal codes, conflicting court decisions, and overlapping jurisdictions can be found a common pattern in the evolution of laws governing both family and property. In colonial times, the family had been a "little commonwealth" whose patriarch embodied public authority, just as public corporations had embodied the larger commonwealth. In both cases, the distinction between public and private was blurred to the point that it was impossible to tell where one left off and the other began. After the Revolution, however, northern states began to define "public" and "private" as separate realms. Beginning in the 1830s, states passed general incorporation acts that left banking and manufacturing corporations free to conduct their business as private enterprises subject more to Adam Smith's laws of the market than to the laws of the state. Similarly, states increasingly treated marriage as a free contract between private parties and began to remove some of the legal disabilities of coverture, the doctrine that a married woman's legal existence was subsumed in her husband's. As a result, women began to gain rights to hold property within marriage. The rise of the free market in commodities went hand in hand with the rise of free contract in marriage. With the state presiding, cupidity marched down the aisle with Cupid.[13]

Freedom of contract in marriage and in business presupposed equality of the contracting parties before the law. As such, it was another example of the ruling myth of equality. Although women were a long way from full legal equality by the end of the nineteenth century, bit by bit they had gained many of the goals of the women's rights movement outlined in the Seneca Falls Declaration of 1848. Depending on the locale, they sat on juries, entered into contracts, retained control of their wages, and voted in school-committee elections. When it came to the marketplace, the courts expanded liberty of contract to the point where the poorest baker or candlestick maker was seen as fully competent to bargain individually with the richest employer. Echoing the laissez-faire doctrines of Herbert Spencer and relying on the constitutional rock of due process as expanded by the Fourteenth Amendment, the courts protected employers and individual wage earners from strikes, boycotts, union work rules, and state regulation. Since no person was to be deprived of life, liberty, or property without due process of law, unions had no right to deprive an individual of his or her liberty to contract with an employer, even if it meant crossing a picket line— *especially* if it meant crossing a picket line![14]

To describe "separate spheres," "the public," and "free contract" as ruling myths—masks to cover the reality of inequality—does not mean they were mere deceptions. To the contrary, the masks were a fundamental part of social consciousness; nowhere else in the world did the egalitarian myth define such a large part of lived experience. From the most mundane encounters of daily life to the grand events of high politics, Americans presumed that everyone was equal. Yet simultaneously and without sense of contradiction, they also presumed that some members of society were more equal than others. Even in the heyday of formal equality after the Civil War—in fact, especially then—authorities enforced hierarchical assumptions of property right, male dominance, and white supremacy. Let there be no misunderstanding: these, too, were ruling myths. What greater illusion could there be than the notion that by virtue of birth all whites were superior to peoples of color? The question remains how Americans could have had it both ways.

Gender, Class, Race

It took a different mirror for Gilded Age America to see inequality. Alongside the image of a bulging middle were images of dominance and subordination inscribed in the realities of gender, class, and race. To begin with gender, the separate spheres of men and women were anything but equal realms when it came to public life. Manhood suffrage rested on a series of invidious assumptions about the power and capacities of the sexes: only men of property could be truly independent of corrupt demagogues; only they could faithfully represent the interests of the entire household, including women, children, and other dependents. As her husband's dependent, a wife did not possess her own free will, as indicated by the legal barrier against compelling testimony against her husband in court and the assumption that there was no such thing as marital rape. Like children, imbeciles, and prisoners, she was, therefore, ineligible to participate in electoral politics.[15]

Her proper role was to be "the mother of the race," a status reinforced by state controls over procreation. Most states outlawed abortion, and many equated birth control with obscenity, as did the federal government after 1873 in the infamous Comstock laws, named after Anthony Comstock, purity crusader and special postal inspector. At the local level, police reinforced the double standard of sexual behavior by subjecting prostitutes only—not their clients—to harassment and arrest for lewd or disorderly conduct and, increasingly, criminalizing the act of prostitution. Along with statutes forbidding fornication and other forms of sexual activity outside monogamous marriage, the Comstock laws and the policing of prostitution reinforced the culture's split image of the "true woman" and the "fallen woman," the madonna and the whore.[16]

It was no accident that the idealization of feminine domesticity arose during the Industrial Revolution. Clearly, if propertied families could keep their women out of the labor market, they could set themselves above the burgeoning laboring population, whose women worked in clattering textile mills, smelly shoe factories, and stuffy garrets of the ready-made garment industry, not to mention the menial work of charwomen and laundresses. Working women fought a losing battle from the 1830s onward to make women's paid employment as honorable as men's by fending off the dual stigma of wage dependency and sexual mingling in the workplace. The first Bureaus of Labor took pains to refute the widespread notion that factories were promiscuous breeding grounds for the "infamous diseases" that led women into prostitution. Short-lived working women's associations and the Daughters of Labor of the 1880s proudly proclaimed the nobility of toil. But for all their pains, the defenders of women's labor did not prevail against the torrent of sermons and pamphlets that portrayed women's paid employment as a derogation of status. "Our men are sufficiently money-making," wrote Sarah Hale, the editor of the popular *Godey's Ladies' Book*. "Let us keep our women and children from the contagion as long as possible."[17]

By the end of the century, critics such as Charlotte Perkins Gilman were beginning to challenge what they called the "proprietary theory" of marriage, with its presumed exchange of the husband's support for the wife's services. In a critique that paralleled Thorstein Veblen's pointed attack on the leisure class, Gilman's *Women and Economics* (1898) described this kind of marital union—with its archaic labor process, sentimental "matriolotry," and "parasitic" femininity—as "the relic of a patriarchal age." Influenced by the ideas of reform Darwinism, Gilman believed that feminine domesticity had frozen women's labor at the lower stages of social evolution so that the housewife represented primitive "sex-labor" and domestic "slave labor." For society to progress, it would be necessary for industrial methods to revolutionize household labor and for women to follow men into industry. Would this not increase household efficiency, allow woman to claim her full humanity, and elevate marriage from a crass economic union to a higher spiritual union all in one fell swoop?[18]

Gilman's critique was too radical for most women of the age. Instead of worrying about how to abolish domestic "slave labor," they worried about how to find more obedient servants. It went without saying that nearly all the 1.6 million domestic servants employed in 1900 (5.5 percent of the labor force) were women. Until the 1870s domestic service acccounted for well over half of women's employment, and the assumption that girls would serve a few years before marriage was widespread, since it was easy to transfer a girl's subordination from one family to the next. Yet the pages of *Good Housekeeping* and other Yankee Protestant women's magazines were full of handwringing over "the servant problem." Catharine Beecher blamed the problem on "the spirit of democracy" that inevitably infected Irish and German servingwomen and led to protracted domestic battles between mistress and maid. The crux of the problem was that service attracted primarily the weakest competitors in the labor market—the famine Irish, Swedish peasants, rural Afro-Americans, and other young, poor migrants—whose culture clashed with that of the leisure class.[19]

The mistress-servant relationship illustrated the two-sidedness of middle-class families, egalitarian on one side, hierarchical on the other. Middle-class women displaced part of the load of "women's work" onto the poor, thus using class to ease a burden imposed by gender. But so long as they hired primarily women to do the work, they implicitly reinforced the link between women and household labor, thus confirming their own ties to the domestic realm and starting the cycle all over again. In all, the mistress-servant bond exemplified the fateful connections between women's and wage earners' subordination.

The growth of the working classes did not fit America's preferred image. No Western society has been more reluctant to acknowlege class in its midst. Whether insisting that the United States was a classless or a one-class society, Gilded Age notables did their best to blot out consciousness of built-in social antagonism. However, they could not alter the facts of production and reproduction. With the spread of the market economy, perhaps as many as two-thirds of the gainfully employed as early as 1870 were wage earners of all descriptions, more in the cities and towns, somewhat fewer in the countryside. Outside agriculture, by 1900 there were 10.4 million blue-collar workers, about 57 percent of the nonagricultural labor force.[20]

The very existence of so many wage earners was a standing contradiction to ruling values. The patterns of social reproduction of propertied and laboring families were different not just in degree, but also in kind. Instead of relying on income from property and the presumed independence that went with it, working-class families were dependent on the wage. Instead of cultivating feminine domesticity, working-class wives took in washing, kept boarders, and (less often) toiled for wages outside the home. Instead of hiring servants to do the housework while sending children to tutors and high schools, working-class families sent their daughters into service and their sons to the factories at an early age. Instead of accumulating an estate to pass on to their children, they were lucky to save up a meager competence against adversity and old age. Instead of giving charity, they received it. In the same way, the division in industrial production between workers and owners was not merely a functional difference between buyers and sellers of labor or a difference in the degree of earnings, but a difference in kind between producers of wealth and accumulators.

The refusal to recognize class division did not mean the state neglected to uphold it. Certainly, the massive web of property rights underwrote the subordination of the wage earner, as did the prevailing doctrines of liberty of contract and laissez faire. Starting with the *Slaughter House Cases* in 1873, the Supreme Court made laissez faire the law of the land by expanding the due process clause of the Fourteenth Amendment into an outright prohibition on state regulation of the market to protect wage earners. At the same time, the Court had no such compunctions about protecting property, for example, with high tariffs on imported goods. The overall tendency of case and statute law down through the end of the nineteenth century was to expand property right into proprietary absolutism.[21]

To the orthodox mind of the Gilded Age, the fact that wage earners teetered on the brink of poverty was a sign of their moral depravity. Combining the Puritan ethic of individual salvation with Manchester economics, Protestant economic doctrine held that responsibility for poverty lay not with the business cycle or the existence of a capitalist reserve army of the unemployed, but with the moral failure of the poor themselves to conduct proper family economy. According to one charity worker, the way to restore independence and prosperity was through "family rehabilitation." Moral regeneration was necessary before respectable labor could raise itself above the "dangerous classes" of criminals, vagabonds, and prostitutes who prowled the growing cities of the North.[22]

As if to confirm the worst upper-class fears, industrial violence broke out on a massive scale in the 1870s. After four winters of unrelieved hardship during the country's first great industrial depression, desperate workers mounted massive strikes in 1877. In what would become a pattern of labor wars lasting until the 1930s, workers rioted when authorities sent in troops to restore order and killed strikers instead. Consuming millions in property and dozens of lives, the "Great Riots" of Pittsburgh, Baltimore, St. Louis, and other flashpoints evoked ready comparisons with the bloody Paris Commune. Worried that workers were turning to "Socialistic and Communistic theories," a founder of Buffalo's Charity Organization Society wrote in 1878: "We shall have ourselves to blame if the poor, craving for human sympathy, yet feeling their moral deformity, should some fine day wreak their vengeance upon society at large." Yet even after further economic downturns and outpourings of discontent, orthodoxy held firm at the end of the century. Civic leaders refused to draw the lesson that the business cycle, not any outbreak of "moral deformity" among wage earners, lay behind acute bouts of poverty.[23]

The western frontier provides another illustration of how hierarchical attitudes grew from even the most fertile egalitarian soil. The frontier myth prescribed a specially favored destiny for the United States. Blessed with vast open spaces of "free land," successive generations of sturdy pioneers had taken advantage of unprecedented opportunity to build a classless society and a stable, democratic government defended by a citizen militia. Nestled between its two oceanic moats, and with no territorial ambitions overseas, the country was fortunate to escape European power politics and the late nineteenth-century scramble for empire, seeking only the fair commercial competition of the "Open Door."

This flattering self-image was sketched against a backdrop of opposing assumptions about the dark and tragic conflicts that wracked European countries. Hemmed in on all sides, Germans, for instance, were said to lack the opportunity to acquire small property or the freedom to dispense with a large standing army. These unhappy circumstances were seen to cause sharp class distinctions and belligerent *Machtpolitik*, a fateful combination that saddled Germany with an authoritarian government of Junker landlords and Prussian militarists under an emperor who prowled the world in search of colonial acquisitions.

No one did more to impart intellectual credence to the myth than Frederick Jackson Turner. Beginning with a lecture at the 1893 Columbia Exposition in Chicago, Turner argued his famous thesis that successive pioneer generations had adapted European cultures to the untamed North American environment to produce a uniquely American democracy.[24] Not far from the Columbia Exposition, Chicago's polar opposites of the Gold Coast and the stockyard slums were expanding apace. Yet social polarization, which should have raised doubts about equal opportunity, only heightened the appeal of the frontier myth. Even as the 1890 census was reporting that the frontier of white settlement had vanished as a point in space, the idea of the frontier as a point in *time* between present uncertainties and future opportunities seemed compelling to a generation anxious about its ability to regenerate a way of life based on the virtues of small property and the supremacy of a self-governing society over the state.

The frontier myth enjoyed a long vogue into the twentieth century because it struck so many resonant chords—individualism, competition, continental destiny, and, perhaps most of all, eternal egalitarian renewal. A far cry from the cosmic pessimism of Puritan damnation or Catholic original sin, the belief in secular redemption through economic expansion was close kin to the theological optimism that had suffused late nineteenth-century Protestant churches in the North. It expressed itself in the vulgar materialism of Reverend Russell Conwell's popular sermon "Acres of Diamonds," in which the Baptist minister preached a God-given duty to get rich. So strong was the grip of optimism that it pervaded even the "social gospel" of Christian reformers such as Washington Gladden and caused Christian Socialists such as Edward Bellamy to reject out of hand the idea of inevitable antagonism between capitalist employers and wage workers. Only blind faith explains this stubborn unwillingness to come to terms with the exploitative consequences of excessive opportunity. To this day a formidable fortress of egalitarian belief defends against the intrusion of ideas about class antagonism.[25]

Be that as it may, the West generated some of the most savage racial prejudices and plundering market practices on the continent. In the period when Yankee adventurers, grim sodbusters, and U.S. cavalry were dispossessing Indians of their "free land," all manner of villainy, treaty breaking, and massacre was justified by blaming the victim for not tilling the soil, abstaining from alcohol, or being an Anglo-Saxon. The conquering pioneers' idea of the West as a "white man's democracy" was kept alive by eastern intellectuals such as cowboy painter Frederick Remington, who boasted: "Jews, Injuns, Chinamen, Italians, Huns—the rubbish of the Earth I hate—I've got some Winchesters and when the massacring begins, I can get my share of 'em, and what's more, I will."[26]

With the end of the Indian Wars, the federal government turned from conquering to "civilizing" the tattered remnants of Indian cultures. Again, the mask of formal equality was placed over invidious assumptions about the propertyless. Prompted by eastern reformers such as Helen Hunt Jackson, Congress promoted the proprietary family as the standard of citizenship in the Dawes Act of 1887. Indians were forced to choose between tribal cultures, in which land rights were tied to complex kinship, and U.S. citizenship, based upon an individual allotment of land for private cultivation. Theodore Roosevelt, fresh from a stint in the wild West, welcomed nothing less than extinction for those who failed to attach themselves to a chunk of western real estate: "Give each his little claim; if, as would generally happen, he declined this, why then let him share the fate of the thousands of white hunters and trappers who have lived on the game that the settlement of the country has exterminated, and let him, like those whites, who will not work, perish from the face of the earth which he cumbers." Roosevelt was perhaps merely overstating what most of his Yankee countrymen felt. In any event, measuring Indians against the standard of the proprietary family consigned them to a purgatory somewhere between full U.S. citizenship and true national independence and hardly squared with the self-congratulatory vision of westward expansion as the onward march of liberty. It can be argued that the expropriation of Indian lands cleared the way for social progress, but what piece of land is worth the extinction of so many Native American cultures? Surely, it was a tragedy of epic proportions.[27]

True to its violent heritage, the West underwent intense industrial conflict. Spurred by government promotion in the form of huge federal land grants and generous local tax abatements, pioneer captains of industry rode roughshod over environment and workers alike. Galloping development of railroads, mining, and lumbering produced some of the most exploitative working conditions on the continent and unusually explosive industrial relations. Western workers played leading roles in all the late nineteenth-century railroad strikes, particularly in the 1885 strike against Jay Gould's Southwestern system, and in the depression conditions of 1894 they raised an industrial army under "General" Jacob Coxey and mounted what became the country's first mass protest march on Washington. In fact, social polarization was at its most extreme where frontier myth predicted it should be least.[28]

The plight of Asian immigrants in the West was closely bound up with the conflict between capital and labor. Originally imported by the Union Pacific and other transcontinental railroad companies, the Chinese had been abandoned by their capitalist patrons to fend for themselves when the job was done. Many white California workers regarded the poverty and cultural isolation of the Chinese as the features of an alien race and, especially after the depression of the 1870s, cheered anti-Chinese demagogues such as Dennis Kearney of the Workingmen's party and joined white businessmen in Chinatown race riots. Dispensable as far as employers were concerned and an "indispensable enemy" to demagogues in the labor movement, the Chinese were also the target of Congress, which prohibited future Chinese immigration by the Exclusion Act of 1882. When it came to sanctions on reproduction, nearly all western states prohibited marriage between whites and "Negroes, Mongolians, or Mulattoes." Oregon's statute went furthest in spelling out the prohibition against "any negro, Chinese, or any person having one-fourth or more negro, Chinese, or Kanaka blood, or more than one-half Indian blood."[29]

It was no accident that state-sanctioned racial exclusions went hand in hand with formal equality before the law. Although these exclusionary practices obviously violated the liberal creed of open competition on one level, in a deeper sense exclusion by race was its logical concomitant. The modern fiction of legal equality had no way of explaining the fact of social inequality comparable to the overtly hierarchical ideologies such as European feudalism and the Hindu caste system.[30] Therefore, the way was open to exempt oppressed groups from equal protection under the law, and racism supplied the groups. The concept of a white man's democracy allowed for the simultaneous holding of two contradictory ideas—that all were equal before the law, and yet that some were second-class citizens. In comparison with their European counterparts, American women undoubtedly benefited from the liberal atmosphere in law and manners, yet they nowhere enjoyed full rights of citizenship. Those wage earners who were inside the charmed circle of white men and enjoyed the same legal status as the employer found that the law upheld the absolute of right of property inside the factory gate. Thus, while the reign of the middle class was characterized by formal equality, it was precisely because of that ascendancy that property right and racial exclusions were so potent. It was not because the law was discriminatory, but because it was rooted in the fiction of evenhandedness that capitalists enjoyed greater freedom of action in the United States than anywhere else on the globe. Extreme liberty for some led to extreme constraints on others.

Capital and the Labor Question

The image of America as a classless society was dealt a heavy blow by the rise of a capitalist elite. Born in the rapid economic development at the end of the century, the new elite was associated with the fusion of investment banking and heavy industry known to contemporaries as finance capitalism. Popular vocabulary rang with derogatory terms for the Rockefellers and the Morgans—"plutocrats," "money-aristocrats," "robber barons"—as if the elite were somehow an outside imposition on the middle-class republic. In reality, they were its natural children. From one side, wide-open opportunity in the competitive market led to the concentration of capital in giant corporations and ostentatious displays of wealth that gave the Gilded Age its name. From the other side, hierarchical subordinations ensured an abundance of underlings to work the mills and tend the palaces of the elite. It was a triumph of high-flying entrepreneurs over the very market competition that had given them wings.

The new form of capitalism has been described variously as "corporate," "organized," or "monopoly." Whatever the term, it had its deepest impact on the United States and Germany. By the end of the century, both countries had outpaced Britain in all the major indices of industrial production. From 1887 through 1913, the United States increased iron output 368 percent to become the world leader at 31 million metric tons, although Germany's output rose even faster, by 480 percent to reach 19 million. Starting in 1870 German coal output rose an astounding eightfold before the First World War, but U.S. coal mines did even better. Partly as a result of this runaway growth, industrial capital became concentrated in oligopoly. In the years around the turn of the century, German coal operators consolidated in a regional syndicate, steel owners formed a loose confederation, and the newer technical industries such as electrical machinery and chemicals also formed cartels. In the same period, American industry moved toward the same oligopolistic structure along a somewhat different path. In part because of the antimonopoly tradition embodied in the Sherman Anti-Trust Act of 1890, U.S. businessmen steered away from loose cartels toward the tight form of direct ownership embodied in the corporation. Corporate concentration took a great leap in the wave of business mergers from 1898 through 1904 that reached its apex in the United States Steel Corporation, founded in 1901 with a capitalization of $1 billion.[31]

The trend toward big business was the result of several forces. Changes in capital markets made huge sums available for investment in expensive new technologies such as electrical equipment, leading to the formation of companies such as General Electric and its German counterpart. Control of product markets was important in the highly concentrated German coal industry, where there were no major technical innovations. In many cases, the key appears to have been vertical integration, that is, the linkage of mass production with mass distribution. Driven by relentless competition, entrepreneurs fought the free market in all aspects of their operations. They integrated backward toward supplies of raw materials and semifinished goods, as in the classic textbook example of Andrew Carnegie's steel operations, which formed the core of U.S. Steel. They also integrated forward toward consumers with brand names, sales forces, and franchised dealerships, as in the case of General Electric. Integration was especially effective in the United States, where the domestic market was large—76 million people in 1900, compared with Germany's 50 million—and relatively prosperous—U.S. per capita income was roughly double that of Germany. Corporate managers also created "internal" markets for labor, that is, personnel practices for recruiting inside the firm by means of loyalty, welfare plans, and promotion ladders, a good example being

American Telephone and Telegraph. To top it off, businessmen warded off international competition with tariffs against imports. As proprietary forms of ownership turned into corporate portfolios, competition into managed markets, and hit-or-miss methods into rationalized production, the competitive capitalism of the nineteenth century turned into the corporate capitalism of the twentieth.[32]

Wealthy parvenus had no respect for the middle-class ethic of self-denial. Instead of temperate displays of modest possessions, the *nouveaux riches* competed with one another in ostentatious displays of "conspicuous consumption" and "pecuniary emulation," to quote Thorstein Veblen's poisoned barbs in *The Theory of the Leisure Class* (1899). For the most part, the competition went on in woman's sphere, as business wives and would-be socialites outdid one another at dinner parties, charity balls, and home decoration to gain admittance to the select company of high society's upper "Four Hundred." The two areas in which Victorians allowed themselves uninhibited hedonism were the sartorial extravagance of bustle and lace and the architectural exhibitionism of castle turrets and gingerbread. A later age would be amused at this egregious flaunting of material wealth and would see Victorian spending of money as the result of sexual repression, indeed, as the unconscious substitute for sexual "spending." Be that as it may, husband and wife were yoked together on the treadmill of pernicious envy in pursuit of the things that money could buy.

Park Avenue mansions and Newport summer homes were reconciled with the ideal of equal opportunity through Social Darwinism. Justifying the avarice of the age, Social Darwinism linked the small businessman and the captain of industry in a common competitive struggle for supremacy, in which the very fact that railroad magnates such as E. H. Harriman and industrialists such as John D. Rockefeller had mounted the ladder of success was taken as proof that they were self-made paragons, not privileged parasites. Apologists for inequality proclaimed it a blessing. In a famous 1889 essay titled "Wealth," Andrew Carnegie wrote: "We accept and welcome . . . great inequality of environment, the concentration of business, industrial and commercial, in the hands of a few, and the law of competition between these, as being not only beneficial, but essential for the future progress of the race." That is exactly what William Graham Sumner had in mind when he linked liberty to inequality through survival of the fittest.[33]

Grasping for a noble pedigree, a handful of American heiresses mar-

Table 1.1   Sectoral distribution of gainful workers, 1880–1940

Year	Total (millions)	Agriculture (plus forestry and fishing) (%)	"Industry": mining, manufacturing, construction, transportation, utilities (%)	Other: service, retail, government, etc. (%)
1880	17.39	49	30	21
1900	29.07	38	37	25
1920	41.61	27	44	29
1940	53.30	17	39	44

Source: U.S. Bureau of the Census, *Historical Statistics of the United States from Colonial Times to 1957* (Washington, D.C., 1960), 74.

ried into the European aristocracy. But the link between money and blood in the American elite was as nothing in comparison with what happened in Germany. There a kind of fusion among notables took place in the late nineteenth century in which it was possible to speak of the "feudalization of the bourgeoisie." Although a few industrial magnates such as Alfred Krupp refused all noble honorifics and, instead, engaged in the same ostentatious display as his American cousins, most of Krupp's industrial peers coveted titles of nobility, purchased landed estates, and otherwise aped the gentry. At the same time, industrial wealth debased aristocratic notions of honor to a cash standard so that old-style princes took on modern values.[34] If there was anything comparable in the United States, it was the reconciliation between northern industrialists and southern planters under the umbrella of nationalism in the 1890s. But with no feudal tradition, there could be no talk of "feudalization."

The shift to corporate (or cartel) capitalism was accompanied by a major change in the occupational structure. Here the German pattern closely resembled the American one. The German industrial working class grew rapidly and surpassed the agricultural population in the 1890s; then, after the turn of the century, white-collar strata became the fastest-growing segment; the United States followed along at a distance of a decade or so. As indicated in Table 1.1, industrial employment, broadly defined, expanded to a peak of 44 percent in 1920, but then gave way to service occupations.

The greatest relative decline occurred in agriculture. Although the absolute numbers working on the farm did not fall until the 1910s, the relative percentage had been slipping throughout the century, a descent that now became extremely rapid. Whereas in 1880 agriculture accounted for 49 percent of all gainfully employed, it accounted for only 17 percent by 1940. In the agricultural sector, proprietors appear to have held their own, hovering at around a third of the total farm labor force. However, owing to the conversion to an urban-industrial way of life, farm owners (as distinct from tenants and laborers) steadily fell as a percentage of gainful workers, from 17.1 percent in 1880 to 6.2 percent in 1940.[35]

The causes of this turnabout were already evident in the late nineteenth century. Family farmers were caught on a treadmill of competition and debt. Selling cash crops such as wheat, corn, and hogs in international markets subject to glut, they had to buy equipment and fertilizer from increasingly oligopolistic manufacturers and ship produce on oligopolistic railroads. The downturn in commodity prices during the period hurt them as sellers of farm products, and although it moderated their costs of production, they had to buy increasingly elaborate and expensive steam tractors, threshers, and other equipment to raise output. In order to do that, they had to borrow from gold-standard banks, where currency deflation, always the bane of debtors, hit them hard.

Such pressures were the cause of persistent agitation for money inflation from the Greenback campaigns of the 1870s and 1880s to William Jennings Bryan's "free silver" run for the presidency in 1896. More substantive solutions came from the Populists, who proposed low-interest government loans through a subtreasury system, breakup of the trusts, and public ownership of the railroads, apex of big business. Though wedded to small property, the Populists attempted to assemble a coalition of small owners, tenants, and urban wage earners to turn the egalitarian side of proprietary values against the ethic of unlimited acquisitiveness. But the collapse of the Populist revolt by the end of the century left only the largely symbolic Sherman Anti-Trust Act to show for it.[36]

Challenging the capitalist dynamic from another quarter, industrial workers forced the "labor question" upon an unwilling country. In 1887 George McNeill, a labor intellectual with years of organizing experience, published a compendium, *The Labor Movement: The Problem of To-day,* in which he advanced the belief, common to labor leaders of his generation, that the protean struggles of short-hours leagues, boycott associations, cooperative societies, trade unions, labor parties, and the like were all tending toward the ultimate goal of the "abolition of the wages system." Casting this destiny in the Protestant terms of moral redemption, he avowed: "Then the new Pentecost will come, when every man shall have according to his needs."[37] The fact that history had a different destiny in store should not obscure the reality of the workers' challenge. From the cresting of the Knights of Labor in 1886 to President Cleveland's dispatch of troops to put down the railway strike of 1894, the country could not evade the labor question.

In the first instance, the problem presented itself as the day-to-day tussle for power on the shop floor between proprietors and skilled craftsmen. A host of craftsmen—iron puddlers, garment cutters, machinists, locomotive engineers—determined the pace and technique of the job and were also in charge of assorted helpers, assistants, and apprentices. Coal miners, for example, may have been subject to the dictates of coal barons in the company towns aboveground, but they were lords of the underground kingdom. The fact that miners were paid by the ton contributed to the belief that they sold products, not just their labor time. This stubborn bit of self-deception, plus their very real control over the work itself, inspired miners to defend their "freedom" against the slavery of the wages system.[38] To the extent that workers controlled the labor process, they exercised a check on proprietary absolutism. They also won a measure of public esteem by countering the pecuniary values of the marketplace with their own "producer" ethic. At every opportunity, they entered the public arena with labor newspapers, Labor Day celebrations (the holiday was created in 1882), and parade banners emblazoned with their deeply held belief that "labor creates all wealth."

If all this had the makings of a homegrown, anticapitalist ideology, there were also hierarchical elements in working-class culture. In the shop, craftsmen often exercised a kind of proprietary power of their own, particularly as "inside contractors" and subcontractors. "Boss" puddlers were paid for the number of balls of molten iron they drew from the iron furnace, and they exercised certain proprietary rights vis-à-vis fellow employees. According to James J. Davis, later secretary of labor in Warren Harding's cabinet, "Furnaces passed from father to son, so I could not hope to get one of the furnaces controlled by another family. My father was not ready to relinquish his furnace to me, as he was good for twenty years more of this vigorous labor." Under these circumstances, motivation came not just from the need for cash but also from a work ethic that included craft pride, a touch of heroism, and a large dose of masculine pride. As Davis crowed, "I have no more desire to be idle . . . than I have a desire to wear women's clothes." Indeed, families of skilled workers easily incorporated the reigning values of separate spheres and domesticity; it was a badge of respectability if the husband's wages were high enough to permit the wife to avoid paid employment.[39]

The day-to-day struggles for pay and power became most visible in a series of great strikes. Given the competitive pressures of the unregulated marketplace in a period of long-term price deflation, employers engaged in a Hobbesian war of all against all, cutting wages and increasing hours to win advantages over their competitors, especially during depressions. When workers retaliated by attempting to regulate the market, the stage was set for intense conflict, as in 1877, when wage cuts precipitated a massive railroad strike. As heirs to the popular tradition of direct action going back through wild-West vigilantes and Jacksonian mobs to the so-called Regulators of the American Revolution, working-class crowds often rose up in spontaneous mob actions, as in the Great Riots of 1877. Likewise, in the 1885 Southwestern strike, masked men hijacked trains and "killed" the engines; and again, Coxey's Army of the unemployed did not hesitate to commandeer trains for their 1894 march on Washington.[40]

At the same time, industrial regimentation was teaching wage earners a lesson in discipline. Combining union organization with militant direct action, workers mounted the general strike for the eight-hour day that began on May 1, 1886. With more than 250,000 participants, it was the first general strike on a national scale in world history. In Chicago, panicked authorities hanged four of the organizers after an unknown assailant killed several policemen with a bomb at a protest rally in Haymarket Square; whereas the violence hurt the labor movement, judicial overreaction only made international martyrs of the Haymarket anarchists and led to the immortalization of the strike in the workers' holiday May Day. Another form of working-class regulation of the market was the consumer boycott. Despite repeated court decisions outlawing the boycott as criminal conspiracy, the consumer boycott was in its heyday, as workers used it effectively against "foul" manufacturers of popular items such as beer and cigars. The most sig-

nificant attempts by workers to control the market involved unioniz-
ing. Workers' organizations made great headway in the case of the
American Federation of Labor, founded in 1881, and the Knights of
Labor, which peaked at 750,000 members in 1886, the largest worker
organization in nineteenth-century North America.[41]

As these events unfolded, many contemporaries regarded the relations between labor and capital as the most vital issue of the day. Edward Bellamy's highly popular novel *Looking Backward* (1887) envisioned a utopia in which the strife-torn, exploitative system of
industrial capitalism had been replaced by a harmonious, egalitarian
system that he dubbed Nationalism (to keep his distance from the socialists). Even a hard-boiled materialist such as Friedrich Engels could
get carried away in the rash of strikes for an eight-hour day, the growth
of the Knights of Labor, and the proliferation of local Workingmen's
parties to conclude that all this amounted to "the first levies *en masse* of
the great revolutionary war."[42] Prophecies of revolution were singularly inaccurate, but the fact remained that in asking the "labor question" America was coming to terms, however grudgingly, with the reality of class division.

The South and the Race Question

The South never fully accepted the myth of the middle class. The main
features of southern history—plantation slavery, the tragedy of race,
and the legend of the Lost Cause—gave the South a distinct culture. It
lived by a quasi-aristocratic code of chivalry and honor, disdained
money-grubbing Yankee traders, and placed racial hierarchy above
open competition. The key ingredient was the legacy of slavery. Slavery had implanted potent patriarchal traditions alongside the liberal
creed of formal equality. Despite stellar contributions to republican
thinking from illustrious sons of the South such as Thomas Jefferson
and James Madison, patriarchal ideas had not been effaced by the Revolution. They came to the fore again in antebellum defenses of slavery,
as in this view from Georgia in the 1850s: "The Slave Institution of the
South increases the tendency to dignify the family. Each planter is in
fact a Patriarch—his position compels him to be a ruler in his household. From early youth, his children and servants look up to him as the
head, and obedience and subordination become important elements of
education."[43]

The abolition of slavery gave a powerful push to equality. Going into the Civil War, the South held patriarchal and republican traditions in uneasy balance, but the Thirteenth Amendment and the force of Union arms seemed for a time to presage the dawn of a new era. Emancipation loosed a revolutionary whirlwind from below as freed slaves struggled to wipe out all traces of their former status. During the early phase of Reconstruction they received help from Radical Republicans in Congress, who wanted to build a southern wing of the Republican party by sending carpetbaggers and an army of occupation into the South.[44]

But Yankee support for free labor was not meant to overthrow the rights of property, and the North soon called a halt to experiments in land redistribution. Although the destruction of slavery carried off the Old South's more extreme patriarchal values, it by no means prevented hierarchical traditions from regenerating in the New South. Certainly, planters found ways to reimpose harsh forms of labor coercion. Some planters hired former slaves to work their estates under long-term labor contracts of dubious legality even after the Civil Rights Acts of 1866 and 1867 and the Fourteenth Amendment had outlawed the infamous Black Codes. But the prevailing solution was actually a compromise between the planters and land-hungry freedmen to ensure that the more fortunate tenants got the best land at money rent, while the great mass became sharecroppers. Paying between a third and a half of their crop to the planter, sharecroppers became a chronic debtor class, reduced in some cases to debt peonage and universally ensnared in a web of paternalist dependency.

Economists are right to point out that southern labor after the Civil War was no longer "bond labor" comparable to slavery or serfdom, but certainly the postwar plantation system contained far more compelling bonds of personal dependency and paternalist authority than did the family farms of the Midwest.[45] Planters exercised quasi-public police and judicial powers to a degree not possible in the North. Peonage was a prime case in point: ignoring an 1867 federal statute against peonage, some Deep South planters subjected debtors to involuntary servitude to work off their debt purchase and exercised the quasi-state authority of judge, jury, jailer, and, in more than one case, executioner. The very poverty of southern agriculture, imprisoned in cotton monoculture and ravaged by war, kept market incentives much less effective than in the more prosperous northern agriculture, so that, as the saying went, "It weren't no use climbin'.'" Whereas the work ethic in the North was linked to property accumulation through the frontier myth and the Darwinian ladder of success, the southern attitude toward work and property, especially among African-Americans, was connected to sheer survival and "freedom" from the web of dependency.[46]

Southern agrarian traditions shaped industrial class relations. Southern industrialists imported agrarian paternalism into their tobacco, iron, and textile mills. Posing as benefactors to benighted, poverty-stricken rural laborers, men such as William Gregg raised mills, built housing, and provided moral instruction to wage earners, who were expected to show deference and obedience in return. Although workers were far from being the docile servants of the bosses' reveries, it was true that mill owners reigned supreme. They won dominance in the mill and the mill town by means of integrated machine technology, family ownership, and paternalism. The closest analogues in the North were the closed company towns of Pennsylvania and West Virginia coalfields and some of the New England textile towns. The difference was that in the North personal paternalism had long been overshadowed by the impersonal "cash nexus," whereas in the South it was the other way around.[47]

Along with paternalist mediations of the cash nexus, southern industrialists took a leaf from the plantation system in deploying coercive labor disciplines, such as the convict lease system. When employers could not get enough cheap labor to work the worst jobs, they leased convicts from the state penitentiary and often drove them until they dropped. As many as 40 percent died on the job. One atrocity illustrates the brutality of the system: Mississippi leased men to cut a rail line through the Canay Swamps, where, according to a state legislative commission, they were chained together in knee-deep water, "their thirst compelling them to drink the water in which they were compelled to deposit their excrement." Though accounting for only a small number of workers at any given time, the system was an ever-present threat to wage workers, particularly, according to one defender, "the undisciplined young negroes who have grown up since the days of slavery." Partly as a consequence of workers' opposition, including a miners' revolt in Tennessee against convict lease, the system began to disappear in the 1890s, to be replaced by only somewhat less coercive prison farms and chain gangs in the twentieth century.[48]

One unintended consequence of the remarkable flux of Reconstruction was to make the laboring classes of the two races more alike than at any time since the establishment of slavery in the late seventeenth century. It is undeniable that white tenants received favored treatment under the reconstituted plantation system, while the most oppressed peons were likely to be African-American. Nonetheless, in contrast to the sharp demarcation before Emancipation, laborers and sharecroppers of both races sometimes bid for the same jobs and the same lands, while paying shares of the crop to the same planters and furnishing merchants. Indeed, a prime reason the South became an isolated, low-wage region was precisely that the common labor rate for poor whites was firmly anchored to the rate for black laborers.[49] Similarly, black families gained the same status under the law as white families after the abolition of the slave codes, which had not recognized slave marriages and, instead, had given the master legal claim to a bondswoman's child. Freed slaves moved quickly to legitimate their marriages in the eyes of the state, and the statistically typical Afro-American family in both rural and urban areas included husband and wife, just as the white family did.[50] What it came down to was that powerful forces were driving the landless poor of both races together, vertically in terms of their subordination to the planters, and horizontally in terms of the labor market and legal status.

The same thing was happening in industry. Propertyless laborers of both races were moving into perilously close circumstances. To be sure white wage earners monopolized favored positions, but the southern industrial work force was indelibly biracial. That was the case in lumbering, railroads, mining, tobacco, and all the other largest employers except textiles. Only New England before the Irish migration had hired such large numbers of native whites, and no other region hired so many Afro-Americans. Whereas first- and second-generation European immigrants dominated everywhere else, they were a small minority in the South. Thus the offspring of African slaves and the offspring of Confederate soldiers were thrown together in the same work sites under the same supervisors and, in some cases, in competition for the same jobs.[51] So industrial class formation paralleled the transformation of the plantation system in two vital respects: hierarchical forms of discipline predominated over marketplace ones; and the conditions of propertyless members of both races tended to converge.

To the extent that this convergence mitigated racial hatred, it became possible for the lower classes to find some basis for unity against the elite. In other words, it became possible to pose the "labor question." Although customary segregation ensured that urban workers would not organize interracial unions, it did not prevent cooperation between parallel organizations and even a tentative joining together under the single banner of the Knights of Labor. In Richmond, for example, thirty of the Knights assemblies were Afro-American and twenty-three were white. There were even a few episodes of racial solidarity, such as those among New Orleans dock workers, to relieve an otherwise sorry picture of racial strikebreaking.[52]

The more important challenge to paternalism arose in the countryside. In fact, from the Radical state legislatures of the late 1860s to the Populist upsurge of the early 1890s, no landlord, furnishing merchant, or regional banker was entirely safe from schemes for land redistribution, rural credits, and universal free public education. On its own, the Afro-American struggle for "freedom" posed a danger to authoritarian coercions. But what made the situation doubly threatening was the convergence of interests among lower-class members of both races. White tenants reaped a harvest in land, schools, and tax reform from Reconstruction measures intended initially to benefit the freedmen. And although it would be sentimental to pretend that racial harmony was widespread, it would be distortion to overlook examples of racial cooperation in the heyday of Radical Republicanism, from 1867 through 1869, and in the late 1880s with links between the Colored Farmers Alliance and its white counterpart.[53]

Most perilous to the planter elite, grass-roots liaisons between the races in both town and country sometimes blossomed into interracial politics that pitted laborers against landlords and financial interests. Examples came from Radical Republicans, Democratic Readjusters, and, above all, the Populists. Before his conversion to race baiting, Georgia's Tom Watson was perhaps the most eloquent exponent of lower-class insurgency: "You are made to hate each other because upon that hatred is rested the keystone of the arch of financial despotism which enslaves you both. You are deceived and blinded that you may not see how this race antagonism perpetuates a monetary system which beggars you both."[54]

As a measure of how far things had come, under the antebellum plantation system no southern political leader had ever imagined that Afro-American and white American labor suffered in the same way under a common oppressor. For a time, it seemed that rednecks and peckerwoods might latch onto the Afro-American message of "free-dom" to struggle against "financial despotism."

Unless the dimensions of this lost alternative are fully appreciated, it is impossible to understand the ferocity of the reaction against it. Pop-ular challenges to the elite were crowded off the stage by the savage Negrophobia of the 1890s. Speaking for a new generation of white rac-ists, South Carolina's Ben Tillman railed against "the nightmare of Ne-gro domination." The white-supremacy crusade of the 1890s was a many-pronged affair of lynching, disfranchisement, Jim Crow statutes, and paranoia aimed at halting the tentative steps toward interracial col-laboration that posed such a threat to planters and industrialists. The "black peril" became the anvil upon which white men of all classes hammered out their unity.[55]

Issues of gender and social reproduction were at the forefront. As with every reactionary movement in American politics, from the anti-Catholic Know-Nothings to the New Right Reaganites, the white su-premacists of the 1890s posed as defenders of women's virtue and fam-ily values. In this case, Negrophobes adopted a pernicious theory of "Negro retrogression," according to which Negroes had reverted to inbred "African" impulses toward promiscuity as soon as the "benevo-lent" influence of slavery had been lifted. As *The Plantation Negro as Freedman* (1889) put it, "Lasciviousness has done more than all the other vices of the plantation negro to degrade the character of their social life since they were invested with citizenship." In a cruel Victorian twist, blame was laid at the feet of black women for their supposed failure to live up to the commandments of true womanhood.[56]

Absent the restraining hand of feminine virtue, the black man was supposed to have turned into a creature known in racist cant as "the black beast." No one was better able to summon up this illusory mon-ster from the depths of the white psyche than Ben Tillman, who made it a central justification for the restoration of white supremacy: "So the poor African has become a fiend, a wild beast, seeking whom he may devour, filling our penitentiaries and our jails, lurking around to see if some helpless white women can be murdered or brutalized."[57]

In the minds of white southerners, racial and sexual stereotyping coiled around each other like the serpent around the apple tree in the Garden of Eden. In this fable of lust and degradation, white men dis-played their honor by protecting white women's chastity. There was no more devastating testimony on this point than lynching. Although sexual transgression was alleged in only a quarter of the lynchings in the South from 1882 through 1946, interracial rape was at the center of the mythology of lynching. Against the mythic "black beast," the brutally real white beast of a lynch mob went about the grisly work of defending the mythic southern lady. Newspaper descriptions of the social composition of lynch mobs reveal it was often the lower-middle and laboring classes that did the dirty work, suggesting the pervasive influence of the "protector" role among white men of all ranks. The fact that the incidence of lynching in the South peaked in the early 1890s sheds some light on the class composition of the mobs. White men who were being squeezed into wage-earning jobs and tenant farming may have felt a loss of prized independence and thus become easy prey for political demagogues who urged them to avenge their wounded honor in violently masculine use of rope and fagot.[58]

Another expression of the white South's obsession with race purity was legislation against miscegenation. Every southern state prohibited miscegenation in some fashion, going to great lengths to define how many drops of ancestral blood made someone a Negro, whether mulatto, quadroon, or octoroon. Georgia covered most of the bases by prohibiting marriage between whites and "all negroes, mulattoes, mestizos, and their descendants, having any ascertainable trace of either negro or African, West Indian or Asiatic Indian, blood in their veins." Southern planters, speaking through President Andrew Johnson's veto of the Civil Rights Act of 1866, had warned of the dire implications of allowing northern-style freedom of contract to govern race relations: "if Congress can abrogate all state laws of discrimination between the two races in the matter of real estate, of suits, and of contracts generally, may it not also repeal the state laws as to the contract of marriage between the two races?"[59] The doctrine of race purity required invasive public controls on the private institution of marriage.

The serpentine coils of race and sex fostered the subordination of labor, as well. A case in point was the southern solution to the "servant problem." Domestic service was overwhelmingly an occupation of black women: in 1900 the proportion of Afro-Americans among female servants in the South was over three-quarters, and climbing. One of the innumerable incongruities of the white-supremacist mentality was that the same women who were supposed to be the very font of immorality were entrusted with the care and feeding of white families from infancy to senility. In any case, the servant was subject to the authority of the white mistress, backed by the stern rule of the latter-day patri-arch. As the *Chattanooga Times* advised in cases of insolence, "The ne-gro girls who push white women and girls off the walks can be cured of that practice by the use of a horsewhip; and we advise white fathers and husbands to use the whip. It is a great corrective." [60]

The same fateful fear coiled around industrial workers. Textile-mill owners offered workers a paternalist bargain: if they accepted wage dependency, they could have race purity as a kind of psychic compen-sation. As a lily-white employer, the textile industry was the great ex-ception to the rule of biracial employment in southern industry. The prime reason textiles excluded black workers in the first place was that over half the labor force was female and another large contingent con-sisted of children. With these groups already on the premises, there was no need for black labor, and besides, the exclusion of Afro-Americans from the rooms where white women sweated was the nec-essary condition for winning white assent to the paternalist bargain. Owners also relied on paternalism to bend women to mill discipline, even to the extent of including feminine chastity in the disciplinary code: mere suspicion of loose behavior was grounds for dismissal. This does not mean that all was sweetness and harmony. Although the own-ers liked to present their mills as some kind of Anglo-Saxon benevolent society, they normally had a change of heart when white workers forgot their manners and went out on strike, whereupon Anglo-Saxon benev-olence gave way to Afro-American strikebreakers until the crisis passed. [61]

Otherwise, when both races were mixed together at a work site, pa-ternalists applied the rules of racial and gender subordination. Places at the top (owners and superintendents) were reserved for white men, while the bottom ranks of unskilled labor were occupied by black women. In between, owners did their best to maintain the ladder of inequality in a confused situation in which rules were often contradic-tory. The pattern was clearest in industries that employed workers of both sexes and both races, such as tobacco factories, but it left its im-print everywhere. [62] In these ways, the paternalist nexus carried New South industrialists into a more or less union-free environment in which strikes were all but sure to fail. Indeed, the southern solution to the "labor question" would become a model to open-shop employers in the North in the early twentieth century.

The southern solution required the strong arm of the state. Convict lease, peonage, and other coercive labor disciplines were ultimately state coercions, just as enforcement of the code of racial etiquette and the edicts of "Judge Lynch" required at least the connivance of the local sheriff. Beyond these, the 1890s witnessed a fateful array of laws and court decisions that created *de jure* segregation and the Democratic party's lock on the "Solid South." Responding to the threat from below, Democratic legislators enacted a spate of disfranchisement laws aimed at solidifying their power against Populist insurgency, conjuring up the specter of "negro domination" to carry their bills. To evade the equal protection clauses of the Fourteenth and Fifteenth Amendments, they usually did not use race per se, but followed the lines of the "Mississippi Plan" in imposing a poll tax, literacy test, and a requirement for interpreting the state constitution to the satisfaction of some petty official posing as an authority on the Constitution.

One consequence, intended or not, of purging the voter rolls in this manner was to strike off large numbers of lower-class whites. As a result, voter participation fell by roughly half from the 1880s, when more than 60 percent of adult males regularly voted, to the 1900s, when the figure was 30 percent. Because of the exclusion of African-Americans and poor whites, and because of the potency of race purity as a campaign battle cry, southern politics became a one-party system dominated by an oligarchy of planters and industrialists. The consequences were far-reaching. The party system solidified the dominance of elites inside the South, and because the Solid South was essential to Democratic capture of the federal government, it gave southern oligarchs veto power over the Democratic party's reform agenda all the way through the New Deal.[63] Southern conservatism became the tail that wagged the dog of northern liberalism.

A wave of Jim Crow statutes followed in the wake of disfranchisement. The long-standing custom of segregation was written into statutes governing railroads, streetcars, prisons, parks, and public accommodations generally. To efface the troublesome fact that all this squarely contradicted equal protection clauses in the Constitution, everybody pretended that that the rundown, segregated black school and the second-class black railroad coach were just as good as the white. The Supreme Court legalized the double standard in *Plessy v. Ferguson* (1896), reconciling racial hierarchy with the liberal tradition through the formula "separate but equal." Half a century would pass before there would be a reckoning with this judicial legerdemain; in the meantime, it invested the authority of the state in the folkways of segregation as enforced by every streetcar conductor, theater usher, and crazed vigilante who set about protecting his fragile superiority. Since this led to "an absolute identification of the stronger race with the very being of the state," as one liberal southern leader said, it no doubt offered some psychological compensation to the disfranchised white men who experienced only a vicarious sense of power.[64]

Once segregation and disfranchisement set the stage for one-party rule, elections became contests between rival cliques for control of the Democratic party, featuring two types of politicians strutting and fretting their hour upon the stage. On the one side, paternalists such as Wade Hampton of South Carolina espoused a kind of noblesse oblige, wasting no love on the masses over whom, they believed, it was their born duty to rule. On the other, demagogues such as James K. Vardmann of Mississippi and "Pitchfork" Ben Tillman of South Carolina cultivated a folksy image that belied their elite origins, and were not above summoning up a lynch mob. Most white men seemed to accept this sham democracy, so long as it flattered their pride at being "free, white, and twenty-one," and in the process poor whites lost contact for decades with the Afro-American tradition of freedom.

Meanwhile, Afro-Americans did their best to adapt to powerlessness. Folk culture was a treasury of wisdom and consoling humor on this score. Drawing on lessons learned on the plantation, that peerless school for survival, they sang "sorrow songs," as W. E. B. DuBois called the spirituals, and work songs that sometimes contained plaintive cries against the exploitation of sharecropping:

> The old bee makes de honey-comb,
> The young bee makes de honey;
> Colored folks plant de cotton and corn,
> And de white folks gits de money.

They retold trickster tales of Rabbit outsmarting the powerful Bear, and they raised children on cautionary tales about the white man's villainy. In one such tale, Rabbit wisely declines Brer Dog's invitation to dinner, even though a new law has been passed forbidding dogs to hunt rabbits: "De rabbits didn't go to school much and he didn't learn but three letter, and that's trust no mistake. Run every time de bush shake." And they bemoaned the denial of justice before the law: "White folks and nigger in great Co't [court] house/Like Cat down Cellar wit' no-hole mouse."[65]

The predicament of being the mouse having to face the cat with no means of escape constrained all political strategies. Booker T. Washington proposed a desperate bargain in his famous Atlanta Exposition address of 1895. If the gentlemen of the South would "cast down your buckets where you are" by giving employment to Negroes and reigning in the lynch mobs, then Negroes would respond by giving loyal service in fields, homes, and factories "without strikes and labour wars" and would abandon the "folly" of "social equality." He hoped that southern paternalists would be encouraged to follow the example of northern philanthropists such as Andrew Carnegie who had done so much for Tuskegee Institute. But without votes, organization, or coalition partners, Washington had no bargaining power with the paternalists, who, for their part, delivered nothing.[66]

In recognition of this failed compromise, W. E. B. DuBois proposed to do away with the cat and mouse game altogether by putting citizenship on an equal footing. Rejecting paternalist dependency, he countered "that voting is necessary to modern manhood, that color discrimination is barbarous, and that black boys need education as well as white boys." DuBois later came to support votes for women and radical social reforms, but at this stage in his protean career he was still hoping to complete the unfinished work of Radical Reconstruction by imposing the nation's ruling values of formal equality on the hierarchical South. At the same time, he knew that formal equality was not the same thing as freedom. In his classic statement of the dilemma of race in America, he wrote: "One always feels his two-ness, part American, part Negro."[67] Was it possible to embrace America's liberal creed without also embracing white supremacy? No one could say for sure. But the fact was that by the beginning of the new century, the South, with the complicity of the federal government, had answered the race question in a way that trapped African-Americans and the poor of both races in a system from which there was no apparent means of escape.

Empire of Liberty

With a great flourish at the turn of the century, the United States humbled the Spanish empire, reached for hegemony in the Caribbean and Central America, acquired Pacific colonies, and began contending with European powers for influence in East Asia. Seeing the United States as a brash David to the great-power Goliaths, American leaders genuinely believed they were extending the blessings of liberty to peoples benighted by a string of brutal colonial overlords and native tyrants. Speaking for diplomats and missionaries alike, President William McKinley said the United States had a holy mission to "uplift and Christianize" the backward peoples of the globe. But the imperial tide created an anti-imperial countercurrent. Anti-imperialists asked how the United States could become an empire abroad and still remain a republic at home. They wondered how self-government could be imposed from outside, particularly if the "natives" resisted its imposition to the death. Who, then, was David, and who Goliath?

Only the United States could enter the lists of imperial powers in precisely this way, posing as a champion of liberty against the old imperialism of Britain, France, and Spain. Yet it was motivated by the same kind of dislocations that attended the rise of large-scale industry and finance capitalism everywhere else. Like the other imperial latecomer, Germany, its economic dynamism was especially suited to the conditions of the new imperialism, in which the main aim was domination by the developed country over underdeveloped societies with or without direct territorial rule.

There was no denying the links between the outward thrust and uneven economic development at home. Rapid industrial expansion leading to excess capacity and unemployment during the so-called Long Depression of 1873–1896 caused industrial interests to press their governments for overseas markets and investment outlets to ease the crisis of overproduction. Although colonies were of trifling economic importance to Germany and the United States, overall foreign trade and investment were quite significant, and the larger the market, the more crucial were large enterprises. Who better than John D. Rockefeller to draw the connection? "It is too late to argue about the advantages of industrial combinations," he said. "They are a necessity. And if Americans are to have the privilege of extending their business in all States of the Union, and into foreign countries as well, they are a necessity on a large scale." In fact, Americans were making the country a net exporter of manufactured goods, boosting manufacturing exports 172 percent from 1895 to 1900, just as a great wave of corporate mergers washed over the economy. As for Germany, foreign investment absorbed perhaps 15 percent of German capital in the years before the

First World War, and although much of this flowed to other developed regions, the rate of investment often grew fastest in underdeveloped areas. That was also the case for the U.S. investments, which grew sixfold in the Caribbean and tenfold in Asia from 1897 to 1914, outpacing the rate of capital formation at home. There is too much evidence of economic imperatives to ignore theories of the new imperialism as a logical concomitant of capitalism (Hobson) or, indeed, as its "highest stage" (Lenin).[68]

Perhaps more important than balance sheets themselves was the new ideology of economic expansion. Whatever actual profits may have been drawn from overseas trade and investments, they became the stuff of which dreams were made. Just as Germans dreamed of domination in *Mitteleuropa* and hoped to make the Middle East an economic hinterland through the expensive Baghdad railway, so Americans periodically panted over the seemingly boundless China market. The acute depression of the mid-1890s convinced many that overseas markets were the answer to idle factories at home, and President McKinley was still talking, on the day before his assassination in 1901, of the need to look overseas to satisfy the "demand for home labor." In both countries political leaders linked imperialism to domestic political stability. Germans talked of "social imperialism," meaning, in part, the creation of jobs through armaments contracts and overseas trade, alongside the welfare system begun under Imperial Chancellor Otto von Bismarck. And Theodore Roosevelt, known as the American Bismarck, avowed the conservative purposes of his "large policy" overseas: "I wish that capitalists would see [that] what I am advocating . . . is really in the interest of property for it will save it from the danger of revolution."[69]

Meanwhile, old patterns of social reproduction were being ruptured in the worldwide expansion of industrial capitalism. As the agrarian way of life faltered, the peoples of eastern and southern Europe embarked on a great outmigration, sending Poles to Berlin factories, Czechs to Bavaria, and Italians to Pittsburgh. The fact that the ethnic composition of parts of Germany and the northern United States was changing at the same time that native birthrates were falling induced concerns about whether dominant ethnic groups would be able to reproduce themselves. By the first decade of the twentieth century, this concern would balloon into a full-scale panic over "race suicide" in both countries, and, in the meantime, racial nationalism fueled the outward thrust. Both Germany and the United States generated their own versions of the White Man's Burden, and both applied Social Darwinism to the global competition of races.[70]

In the United States John Fiske's notions of Aryan superiority enjoyed a vogue among Washington politicos, and Reverend Josiah Strong's *Our Country* (1885) began selling in the tens of thousands. Strong expanded Manifest Destiny from continental to global dimensions, writing of "the final competition of races for which the Anglo-Saxon is being schooled." Meanwhile, scholars such as J. W. Burgess and politicians such as Indiana's Senator Albert Beveridge expatiated on the duty of the English-speaking peoples, in league with democratic-minded Teutons, to govern "savages and senile peoples."[71] Just as many industrialists saw overseas expansion as a cure for domestic overproduction, so many among the Anglo-Saxon elite invoked imperial glory as a way of shoring up their prestige at home. Thus the 1890s engendered a sense of crisis that the national governing system might not be able to preserve existing privileges, and that both production and reproduction would have to be reorganized in a global context.

On the basis of such economic and cultural motives, the United States entered the high-stakes game of world politics in the 1890s. As a newcomer, it often acted out of crass economic motives or a missionary sense of American moral superiority, behavior later chastised by those who believed the rules of the game ought to hinge exclusively on "reason of state."[72] But realists take the international matrix of competing nation-states for granted, forgetting that it was itself a historical development closely related to the rise of capitalism, and that each nation-state was a crystallization of the governing system under the control of its own elites. Certainly, American elites constructed a foreign policy in part out of domestic materials, a fact that posed an acute problem: how could the United States impose the blessings of liberty on others without winding up an imperial overlord? How could it have both liberty and empire?

The story of the Spanish-American War of 1898 as the turning point in the creation of an American empire is well known. Seeking to defend American sugar interests in Cuba and spurred by jingoist cries from the Hearst press to "remember the *Maine*," the U.S. naval ship mysteriously blown up in Havana harbor, President McKinley issued an ultimatum that for Spain amounted to a choice between humiliation and war. Backed into a corner, the doddering Spanish empire fought to a quick and inglorious defeat in the Caribbean and in the Philippine Sea.

That left the United States in control of Cuba, nominally independent but dominated under the Platt Amendment, and of the Philippines, formally annexed as a U.S. territory. In the next eighteen years there followed the seizure of Panama, a spate of marine landings, control of certain Caribbean customs, and interventions in Mexico, all of which gave the United States genuine hegemony throughout the Western Hemisphere and a growing influence in Asia.

Although the events are straightforward, there is still a great puzzle in the 180-degree reversal in the U.S. position in the world. How could America move from anti-imperialist to imperial power virtually overnight? Anti-imperialists pointed out the contradiction at the time. William Jennings Bryan, for example, had campaigned for "free silver and free Cuba" in 1896, casting the United States as Cuba's liberator, and again in 1900 he condemned the United States as colonialist in the Philippines on the grounds that "a republic can have no subjects." Southern Democrats also worried that overseas empire would further subordinate the South as a kind of internal colony of northern capital and the Republican party. In addition, a small but articulate group of laissez-faire Republicans broke with their party to form the Anti-Imperialist League. One of the vice-presidents of the league was Samuel Gompers, head of the young American Federation of Labor, who denounced annexation in unmistakably pacifist terms and warned that if governments could not achieve peace, then "the workers will settle this question" through boycotts, strikes, and refusal to shoot down their fellow workers.[73] For the time being the question was settled by other methods. Although the election of 1900 was more a referendum on prosperity than one on imperialism, McKinley's resounding victory buried the anti-imperialists.

The turnabout of the 1890s appears less puzzling against the backdrop of the long history of middle-class expansion. Since the Napoleonic Wars, the United States had been following a twofold path of expansion. The first was *commercial*, supported by the anticolonial policy of the Monroe Doctrine and aimed at a hemispheric free-trade zone of formally equal buyers and sellers of commodities obeying the laws of supply and demand, not the dictates of a mercantilist government. It was the middle class browsing in the international marketplace, showing its benevolent, egalitarian face. The second path was *territorial*. Propelled by rail and mining investments, it was supported by Manifest Destiny, which claimed the entire continent as a patrimony for free white men and did not quail at the genocide of red and brown peoples who got in the way. It was the middle class, backed by aspiring farmers and nationalistic workers, making a malevolent, hierarchical face to shine upon Indians, Mexicans, and the propertyless.

Now, as the Spanish-American War pitched the United States headlong into world affairs, the country adapted both commercial and territorial expansion to the international arena. The Monroe Doctrine, as amended by the Olney and Roosevelt corollaries and the Platt Amendment, became a warrant for a U.S. protector role against the British and Germans in Latin America, as the realists emphasize. What realists forget is that the United States was at the same time subordinating underdeveloped Latin American societies to U.S. economic and military might and claiming the paternalist right to do so. Having compelled insertion of the Platt Amendment into the Cuban constitution, the United States secured the right to send troops into Cuba at its own discretion, and did so on three occasions. Again, as the realists point out, Secretary of State John Hay penned the Open Door notes not because American exporters might someday have economic interests to protect in China, but to put the other powers on notice that China must not be carved up into spheres of influence, at least not without consulting the United States. And American elites had dreams of their own regarding the China market and Christian missions. When nativist societies acting with the tacit connivance of the Manchu dowager empress threatened these interests in the Boxer Rebellion of 1900, the United States contributed a contingent of 5,000 troops to the international police force that suppressed it.[74]

The most telling evidence that U.S. action against dependent societies was not merely the reflex of great-power competition is the suppression of self-government in the Philippines. Admiral George Dewey's victory in Manila permitted the two-year-old Filipino insurrection against Spain to succeed, and on January 23, 1899, supporters of the insurrection's leader, General Emilio Aguinaldo, proclaimed the Republic of the Philippines. Perhaps in part to flatter U.S. authorities, with whom Aguinaldo had friendly dealings, a constituent assembly promulgated a national constitution that included representative government, individual liberties, and separation of church and state. President McKinley's decision to annex the Philippines, reportedly made after beseeching God for guidance on bended knee, led directly to military "pacification" of Aguinaldo's supporters. In reality, the United

States was not suppressing a new insurrection but making war upon a republican government brought to power as much by its own revolution as by U.S. defeat of the Spanish overlord.[75]

The closest parallel in the American experience was war with the plains Indians, insofar as U.S. soldiers fought not only an enemy army but also Tagalog institutions and culture. Especially when Aguinaldo's generals descended from mountain retreats to adopt hit-and-run tactics while relying on civilians for logistical support, the American military came to identify the enemy as the Filipino people. McKinley's unctious message about uplifting and Christianizing the natives often turned into vicious racism in jungle battlefields, where U.S. soldiers normally referred to their adversaries as "niggers." One American general vowed to turn a region into "a howling wilderness," instructing a subordinate, "kill and burn and the more you kill and burn the better you will please me."[76]

Until the Vietnam War, the U.S. record of colonial killing in the Far East was mild in comparison with the record of the Dutch in Indonesia or, later, of the Japanese in Southeast Asia. But the presence of racism among U.S. policymakers helps explain how they could have believed they were spreading liberty while they were devastating a popular republican goverment. This attitude fit in well with the mood of reconciliation between North and South that was also sweeping the country. As northern elites asserted the duty of Anglo-Saxons to govern the so-called darker races of the world, they came to be more sympathetic to white supremacy in the South. And as southern elites felt less threatened by northern liberalism, they became more comfortable with the imperial project. Southern-bred Woodrow Wilson piled up a record of intervention second only to that of New York patrician Theodore Roosevelt. So strong was the faith in Anglo-Saxon destiny to rule that onetime leader of the anti-imperialists William Jennings Bryan had no apparent compunctions about sending the marines to the Caribbean on several occasions once he became secretary of state in Wilson's cabinet.

As Caucasian elites in the United States made common cause around imperial conquest, Afro-Americans were driven still further into the political wilderness. Although most black voters probably remained loyal to the Republican party (as Frederick Douglass had warned, "The Republican party is the ship—all else is the sea"), a few campaigned against imperialist hypocrisy. One newspaper noted sarcastically,

One who steals a ham is a thief
One who steals a fortune is a financier
One who assists in stealing the Philippines is a patriot.

Revulsion against the new imperialism sparked the first Pan-African Conference in London, where delegate W. E. B. DuBois drafted an Address to the Nations of the World that included the prophetic words: "the problem of the Twentieth Century is the problem of the color-line."[77]

What has been aptly dubbed "the tragedy of American diplomacy" had no immediate counterpart in Germany. Because German imperialism began with authoritarian assumptions embedded in the country's governing system, there was never any betrayal of liberal principles in the colonies. Although there was talk of a civilizing mission to spread the blessings of German *Kultur,* there was no illusion about liberating hitherto-dependent peoples so that they could govern themselves. Indeed, that was precisely the tragedy of German diplomacy—that in seeking mastery in Europe, German elites plunged the world into the most terrible war in history. Meanwhile, in the years before the "war to end all wars," American leaders practiced what they believed was the imperialism to end all imperialisms.[78]

The Liberal State

The soldiers of the Spanish-American War died for the same liberal state that had been born in the fires of the American Revolution and reborn on Civil War battlefields. Outwardly, the whole panoply of liberal constitutional principles—consent of the governed, representative institutions, checks and balances, equality before the law, manhood suffrage, and civilian supremacy over the military—remained intact at the end of the century. What was more, America was steeped in the liberal values of individualism and equal opportunity and held open the gates to European immigrants, in the words of Emma Lazarus' poem on the Statue of Liberty, "yearning to breathe free." Quite rightly, all of this was the pride of American leaders and the envy of European liberals.

That does not mean that the liberal state had an easy transit through the Gilded Age. The reign of the middle class produced unintended polarizations, and from the loins of self-made men and true women unexpected social conflicts issued forth. Struggles between big business and family farmers shaped the political landscape around agrarian discontent, especially in the heyday of the Populists. At the same time, struggles between industrial capitalists and industrial workers placed the "labor question" squarely on the political agenda. Few affiliates of the American Federation of Labor, christened in 1886, and virtually no central labor union north of the Ohio was without its socialists and anarchists, and dissent also abounded in Bellamy Nationalism, Christian socialism, and women's rights.

There were also insurgencies at the ballot box. A prime example was the 1886 mayoral campaign of Henry George, apostle of the Single Tax, who proposed to confiscate the "unearned increment" of rising land values. Numerous independent labor parties campaigned for "gas and water socialism," and workers and middle-class elements came together to crusade against municipal corruption behind a new breed of municipal reformer and a politics of urban populism. Men such as Toledo's Samuel "Golden Rule" Jones and Detroit's Hazen Pingree co-opted working-class demands, campaigned against traction magnates and banking interests, and built "righteous" machines of their own.[79]

Both the independent laborites and the urban populists practiced a kind of democratic compromise; that is, they accepted the existing liberal state but turned egalitarian assumptions against the capitalist elite. They trained rock-ribbed, egalitarian beliefs upon the predatory "money-aristocrats" who had grown fat at the expense of the "producing classes" and were now threatening to transform the republic into a plutocracy. Adopting the language of the antislavery crusade, they proclaimed with George McNeill: "we declare that there is an inevitable and irresistible conflict between the wage-system of labor and the republican-system of government,—the wage-laborers attempting to save the government, and the capitalist class ignorantly attempting to subvert it."[80]

For all the faith in the republic, the liberal state was, after all, a *state*. It maintained itself, like any other state, by means of violence. Faced with the most disruptive labor struggles of all industrializing societies, American authorities drew their guns on numerous occasions, notably in suppressing the great railroad strikes of 1877 and 1894. The raw force of military power was evident in the flash of bayonets and whiz of bullets and accounted for dozens of deaths.

Yet the United States was no authoritarian regime. That fact was evident in the difference between American and German governing

Different groups put universal symbols of liberty to
widely divergent uses.

MARCH, 1912   PRICE, 10 CENTS

THE·MASSES

A·MONTHLY·MAGAZINE
DEVOTED·TO·THE·INTERESTS
OF·THE·WORKING·PEOPLE

ENLIGHTENMENT *vs.* VIOLENCE

THE MASSES PUBLISHING COMPANY, 150 NASSAU ST., NEW YORK

A radical version: the torch of freedom as a sign of enlightenment in a cover
illustration for *The Masses*, March 1912.

A conservative version: the Liberty Bell as a sign of national unity, formed by 25,000 soldiers at Camp Dix, New Jersey, 1918.

Cultural harmony: the Old World gazes adoringly upon the Statue of Liberty as
Abraham Lincoln presides at an Americanization pageant in Milwaukee, 1919.

IL CIBO VINCERÀ LA GUERRA!

Venite qui a cercare la libertà
Dovete ora aiutare a conservarla
Il PANE è necessario agli alleati
NON SPRECATE NULLA

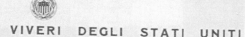

AMMINISTRAZIONE VIVERI DEGLI STATI UNITI

Patriotism: the U.S. Food Administration reminds Italian immigrants, "You came here seeking freedom, now you must help preserve it," in appealing for conservation on the home front during World War I.

systems, a contrast readily apparent in the different kinds of men chosen for the highest seats of power. The United States elevated commoners to the presidency, men such as hard-drinking, seat-of-the-pants General Ulysses S. Grant, who held the office from 1869 to 1876. Despite his long military career, no one could ever have said of Grant what was said of his contemporary Chancellor Bismarck, that he was "the pillar and standard-bearer of that mysterious quality, authority."[81] At the end of the century, the contrast was every bit as great between the homely "Sage of Canton" William McKinley and His Imperial Majesty Kaiser Wilhelm II.

Authority was the cornerstone of the German state. Under the constitution that unified Germany in 1871, the state was controlled at the very top by a hereditary monarchy, assisted by the nobility in the military and civil bureaucracies. Prussia was the predominant influence in the Reich—Prussian king and prime minister were automatically kaiser and imperial chancellor, respectively. Whereas the American president was a creature of party politics—of patronage, spoils, and scandal—the German chancellor was handpicked by the kaiser and was a creature of rank, privilege, and pedigree.

Authoritarian state structures in Germany reinforced the power of the great estate owners and the big industrialists, the notables who exercised a kind of joint command of "blood and iron." From the protective tariffs of 1879 down to the First World War, German politics is commonly presented as a delicate balancing act between these two groups called *Sammlungspolitik*. Like the English landed gentry before them, Prussian landlords, the Junkers, were becoming agrarian capitalists. All the main features of the old patriarchal regime had fallen to the capitalist ax: rule by the father, family lineage as the basis of the state, patrimonial inheritance, primogeniture, and personal obligation of the peasant to labor on the lord's estate.[82] The Junkers secured the equivalent of Corn Laws against grain imports from the American breadbasket. Determined to protect the agrarian way of life, they used the Conservative party as a mouthpiece to rail against the subversive effects of industrialization: dislocation of family life, the spread of Malthusian ideas, an invasion by Polish laborers, and a shift in the army's recruitment from loyal peasants to seditious urban workers. On the other side of the balance, heavy industrialists fought back against this economic isolation, demanding through the National Liberal party economic growth at home and exports overseas. Industrialists supported the outward reach for world power (*Weltpolitik*), which they argued would answer the problems of urban poverty and socialist agitation while shedding glory upon the nation.

Differences between landlords and industrialists were reconciled in the face of the common threat from below. Instead of democratizing the governing system to co-opt wage earners, whose numbers were growing day by day, notables held tight to one another in an embrace of top-down authority. Despite manhood suffrage for the lower house of the Reichstag and the appearance on paper of a constitutional separation of powers, elected representatives were impotent against the kaiser. Moreover, the Prussian three-class voting system accorded privileges to the Junkers, and envy of noble rank led to the feudalization of the bourgeoisie. Prominent spokesmen of big business who might have been liberals elsewhere came to accept an absolutist kaiser and an impotent Reichstag in return for the benefits of national unification, the promotion of exports, containment of the socialists, and fusion with the nobility.[83]

Against these aristocratic currents, bourgeois influence was spreading throughout German society, as it had in France and England. The constitution recognized civil equality and male suffrage, marking movement from a system of corporate estates (*Standestaat*) toward a system of contractual rights (*Rechtstaat*). That opened the gates to middle-class voluntary associations, bourgeois control of city government, and, after an unsuccessful period of cultural struggle (*Kulturkampf*), toleration of the Catholic Center party. Bourgeois standards of honor and taste spread outward from the middle classes. In the countryside, the advance of liberalism and industrial capitalism had brought peasant emancipation more or less to completion in the 1850s, making the late nineteenth century the twilight of the patriarchs.[84]

Nonetheless, the German middle classes played a subordinate role in the state. They certainly did not possess the power of their American cousins. German farmers were especially weak. Even after emancipation, East Prussian peasants tended to follow the lead of the great landowners instead of joining with Rhineland smallholders against the elite. Thus peasant "populism" made little headway. The lower middle classes of the cities and towns were more conscious of their self-interest, showing hostility to economic liberalism and forcing political parties to placate the middle levels. But butchers, bakers, and candlestick makers were too lightweight to make much of a dent in the governing system, and already they were scapegoating "Jewish capital" in their resentment against the Manchester economics of big capital, an adumbration of their pivotal role in the rise of Nazism a half-century later.[85]

The rule of authority excluded workers from a share of power, but at the expense of solidifying working-class organization. Using the carrot of social insurance to ameliorate the harsh conditions of industrial life, Bismarck also beat the young Social Democratic party with the stick of antisocialist laws, banishing the SPD as an enemy of the Reich. But because German social boundaries were more or less clearly inscribed in status levels (*Stande*), German workers tended to practice class politics, or, to be more precise, a politics of occupational status in imitation of agrarians and industrialists. Instead of putting the SPD out of business, Bismarck only radicalized the party, which adopted a genuine Marxist program at its Erfurt congress of 1891. As a result, when it regained legal standing, it was steeled by a revolutionary socialist ideology with the goal of seizing the state to abolish capitalist property. Ironically, the seeds of both German fascism and socialism were planted in the Bismarck era.

The similarities and differences between liberal America and imperial Germany do not add up to a Tale of Two Exceptionalisms but to a story of how two countries handled the rise of bourgeois (or market) society in different ways. The key differences were not in state structures alone—American liberalism versus German authoritarianism— nor in social organization—racial and ethnic factors in America versus occupational factors in Germany. Rather, the differences were more historical than sociological, more dialectical than structural, and had more to do with the different ways governing systems evolved over time than with the contrasts at any given moment. One implication was that no automatic link connected economy and polity. Imperial Germany and turn-of-the-century America had similar economic structures built around large-scale industry, but quite different forms of the state. Capitalist development could be accompanied by authoritarian rule as readily as by representative democracy.[86]

In any event, nothing like the German system was available in the United States. American elites had to find something similar in content—something that upheld a hierarchical social order increasingly attuned to industrial capitalism—but different in form—something that respected liberal traditions. One part of the solution was a tacit political bargain between northern industrialists and southern oligarchs. Following the instability of the Civil War and Reconstruction, elites had stabilized the system by striking a bargain against the threat from below, just as their counterparts had done in Germany.[87] Basically, there were two points to the bargain. First, northern industrialists acquiesced in the planters' solution to the "race question." That is to say, by the 1890s the Republican party ceased waving the "bloody shirt" and agitating for civil rights and, instead, welcomed the Supreme Court's "separate but equal" doctrine. In return, southern planters supported the industrialists' solution to the "labor question." For example, South Carolina Democrat Wade Hampton cast the issue in the railroad strike of 1894 as the very survival of civilized order, denouncing the strikers as "lawless mobs" who "blindly and madly struck at the very foundations of all organized society" and applauding Grover Cleveland's use of troops.[88]

Part and parcel of the bargain, a new party system emerged after 1896, with the Republicans conceding the Solid South to the Democrats, and the Democrats accepting minority status in the nation. This alignment discouraged partisan mobilization of working-class voters, and for this and other reasons, including outright disfranchisement in the South and antimachine campaigns in the North, workingmen's political participation declined. Meanwhile, a mood of sectional reconciliation came over the nation, and although southerners were dubious at first about colonial possessions, they soon rallied around the flag in support of U.S. interventions in Latin America.[89]

But unlike Germany, America could not get by with a simple deal between cotton lords and railroad magnates. Because they operated within a liberal state with representative institutions and open parties, American elites had to seek popular ratification of their leadership at regular intervals. The election of 1896 was a good case in point. Voters were offered two versions of the middle-class family. Democrat William Jennings Bryan spoke for those groups being "crucified" by financial interests "upon a cross of gold"—the temperate, Anglo-Saxon small proprietor, the discontented worker, and, above all, the self-reliant yeoman farmer and his chaste, pious wife. Republican William McKinley, on the other hand, spoke for the ambitious entrepreneur and his social-climbing wife, the large industrialist, and the wage earner who wanted "a full dinner pail" instead of the dregs of Democratic depression.[90] The differences between small property and large, between self-sufficiency and accumulation, between property as livelihood and property as investment were reconciled within the reigning values of the middle-class family.

The same liberal structures militated against a party system divided along the lines of economic interests. In contrast to the German pattern, fluid occupational and status boundaries in the United States allowed parties to become open, consensual associations that could honestly disclaim any direct attachment to one particular economic interest, permitting gold Democrats and big-business Republicans to find homes alongside their parties' respective urban, immigrant machines. For northern cities, the Gilded Age was surely the machine age if there ever was one. Because the machine was employment service, relief agency, sports club, and ethnic lodge all rolled into one, it was highly resistant to the civil service reforms of the Liberal Republicans in the 1870s and the Mugwumps in the 1880s. Genteel liberals more or less helplessly bemoaned the spectacle of plunder immortalized in Thomas Nast's cartoon portrayal of Tammany boss William Marcy Tweed as a bloated vulture. Well-bred foreign visitors were equally aghast at these democratic excesses. Lord Bryce's *American Commonwealth* (1888) held up municipal corruption as the worst blot on the shield of self-government in the United States.[91] The truth was that machine politics, corrupt or not, was but the adaptation of liberal self-government to the needs of the urban wage earner. It opened a channel into the system for the Irish laborer and German craftsman.

Even the more class-conscious workers could be co-opted by manhood suffrage. Samuel Gompers began supporting Democrats for president in 1896, although, in deference to Republicans and independents in the ranks, the AFL remained neutral. The vote proved useful to Illinois labor leaders, who were instrumental in securing Illinois Governor John Peter Altgeld's pardon of the surviving Haymarket anarchists. Even soon-to-be-socialist Eugene Debs supported Bryan as a way of repudiating President Cleveland's use of federal troops to break the 1894 railroad strike and destroy the fledgling American Railway Union that Debs headed. However feeble, a vote for Bryan was also a way of protesting the Supreme Court's invocation of the Sherman Anti-Trust Act not against the trusts it was intended to curb or against the Railway Managers Association for their collusion against the strikers, but against the railway union itself.

Voting trapped workers in an insoluble predicament. They were supporting a government that suppressed their own organizations. For perfectly good reasons, they attempted to use liberal structures of state power in their own interests, whether for patronage or for protest, through local labor parties, urban populists, or Republican and Democratic machines. But their participation only buttressed a governing system dominated by capitalist elites in which workers' organizations as such enjoyed little more legitimacy or real power than in Germany.

Elites were able to maintain their rule against popular discontent by holding fast to the liberal state. Embracing the common wisdom "laissez faire plus the constable," they found the deep structures of the Gilded Age state-in-society to their advantage. One pillar of the state rested on the bedrock of the competitive market and presumed a rough equality of opportunity among the bargainers. Likewise, it was supported by formal equality before the law, liberty of contract, and the ever-expanding frontier. And it appeared in the high politics of Supreme Court decisions and foreign relations based on the Monroe Doctrine and the Open Door.

The other pillar rested on the equally solid bedrock of actual social inequality. In different ways, it presumed the subordination of wage laborers, women, and nonwhites, as upheld by the myths of property right, male dominance, and white supremacy. And it was seen in the high politics of Indian wars and imperial hegemony in Latin America.

The fundamental institutions of the liberal state sat like a Greek temple on these twin pillars. The state was a system of self-government by formally equal citizens who elected representatives through open parties under an electoral suffrage that excluded women and Afro-Americans. In short, it was a white man's democracy. If Gilded Age America was a fit homeland for the Statue of Liberty, it was also a place where liberty was apportioned according to class, gender, and race.

2

New Workers, New Women

THE TWENTIETH century dawned auspiciously for Western elites. The engines of industrial expansion were humming at an ever-higher pitch, and corporate consolidations presaged boundless expansion for big business. Well-heeled men and women still moved in separate spheres by day, and showed off their finery at the opera by night. Nestled under Pax Britannica the world was enjoying a long period of peace, and the West bore the "White Man's Burden" without apparent shame. For good reason, the moment would always be remembered nostalgically as *la belle époque.*

But appearances were deceiving. A dozen years later, the world seemed to be turning upside down, or at least listing to one side. In Europe, Sigmund Freud was challenging Victorian morality, Albert Einstein was overturning the Newtonian universe, and Marxian socialism was threatening to upset the reign of property. Meanwhile, Japan had startled the world with its industrial and military prowess; revolutionary sparks had begun to fly in Russia, China, and Mexico; and rumblings of a great war could be heard as Germany looked for its "place in the sun." Even the United States was caught up in the changing currents. By 1912, self-styled "progressive" politicians (the term had just come into use) were outbidding each other in rhetorical attacks on the great trusts. Bohemians and sex radicals were lashing out against Victorian prudery, while painters were abandoning genteel sensibility for the urban realism that gave the "Ash Can School" its name. And somehow in the very Eden of private property, socialism was making astonishing strides.

These changes in politics and culture signaled deeper disturbances of two sorts in the dynamics driving the historical process. First, they pointed to significant realignments in the balance of forces between dominant and subordinate classes as industrial capitalism mounted toward its climax. Second, they hinted at disturbances in the relation between society and the state as new social forces—industrial workers, mass consumers, new immigrants, and the New Woman—more and more eluded the grasp of the old liberal governing system. These twin disturbances—one between social antagonists, the other between society and the state—gave rise to the great issues of the day as people became conscious of their differences and fought them out.[1]

Americans would spend the next four decades wrestling with the impact of social change. As a consequence of social evolution, there emerged a set of leading questions—the balance of power between corporations and industrial workers, the place of women in public affairs, the need for social welfare, the meaning of America as a nation of immigrants, and the role of the United States in world affairs. None of these questions could be answered within the framework of laissez-faire liberalism. Seeking a governing strategy more attuned to the realities of twentieth-century life, elites devised three new models. Progressivism, closely identified with Theodore Roosevelt and Woodrow Wilson, aimed at greater government regulation of society in the public interest. Managerial liberalism, which appeared in the First World War and was subsequently associated with Herbert Hoover, sought to avoid state bureaucracies by coordinating corporations and other large-scale institutions. New Deal liberalism, inseparable from the towering figure of Franklin D. Roosevelt, borrowed from both to lay the foundations for welfare state and Keynesian economic policies that finally restored balance and legitimacy.

What gave unity to the period that ended with the New Deal were the persistent efforts of elites to remake the liberal state in the context of the new social forces. As pioneer historian Frederick Jackson Turner—both a historian of pioneers and a pioneer historian—said in his 1910 presidential address to the American Historical Association, "Whatever may be the truth regarding European history, American history is chiefly concerned with social forces, shaping and reshaping under the conditions of a nation changing as it adjusts to its environment. And this environment progressively reveals new aspects of itself, exerts new influences, and calls out new social organs and functions."[2] As the new century opened, it was impossible to forecast what the new organs and functions would be a generation or two hence, but it was certain that modern American civilization would not be governed in the same way as its nineteenth-century predecessor.

Mass Reproduction, Mass Production

When America looked in the mirror in the morning of the twentieth century, it could not help but see the image of the multicultural urban masses. Certainly, that was the image seen even more frequently in literature and the arts. Instead of depicting prim nuclear families posing in well-appointed Victorian parlors, a new breed of socially conscious photographer such as Lewis Hine was shooting grizzled workers in grimy Pittsburgh foundries. A brash band of urban realist painters, appropriately dubbed the Ash Can School after their premiere exhibit in 1908, paid homage to the vitality of the immigrant masses perched on tenement sills and spilling out onto teeming streets in paintings such as George Bellows' *Cliff Dwellers*. In the same fashion, insurgent poets celebrated the workaday energy of manual laborers in cities such as Chicago, immortalized by Carl Sandburg as the "hog butcher for the world."[3]

What these images reflected was that daily life was lived more and more in the mass. Increasingly, the production of society's goods and the reproduction of its people, both biological and social, took place under conditions of mass production, mass transit, mass eduction, and mass culture. Crowded into Chicago meatpacking plants and Detroit assembly lines, the work force in the largest manufacturing firms eventually reached 50,000 and more, and in telecommunications the payroll at the supergiant AT&T was even higher. Stuffed into subways and electric trolleys, first- and second-generation immigrants made their way home to overcrowded, multistory tenements. From arts and letters to social policy, the impact of mass and masses was felt everywhere.

Reproduction in the mass inevitably changed family life. At the most elemental level, changes in biological reproduction began to weaken the family's control over its members. To begin with, the demographic transition moved inexorably toward lower birthrates so that, year by year, childbirth and child rearing consumed a smaller amount of time and energy. Falling from a peak in the early nineteenth century of some 55 live births per 1,000 population, the nation's birthrate had declined to 32 live births per 1,000 in 1900 and continued to fall toward the low point of 18 per 1,000 in the 1930s. Family size did not shrink as dramatically, but even when wide variations in socioeconomic background are taken into account, women were rearing significantly fewer children than their mothers had. For example, the number of children under five years old per 1,000 women in the childbearing years fell from 666 in 1900 to 506 in 1930 for the country as a whole, with rates still lower for the urban North. And household size edged downward from 4.48 persons in 1900 to 3.28 in 1930.[4] Such long-term, subterranean changes were preconditions for loosening in family controls on reproduction.

The weakening family was also evident in the shift of childbirth from home to hospital. A chorus of hygienists and physicians depicted midwives as superstitious old crones and advised women to abandon the "primitive" and "unhealthful" environment of home confinement for the "modern" and "hygienic" wards of the hospital. Despite well-founded fears that hospitals were unhealthy places—historically, the places the terminally ill went to die—increasing numbers of women followed the advice and chose the maternity ward of a general hospital, to be attended during delivery by medical professionals instead of a lay midwife. In doing so, they parted company with the community of women—female relatives, midwives, and neighbors—and passed out of women's "sphere" to be attended by a male obstetrician and his nurses.[5]

Child rearing was another activity in which family controls began to give way to professional ones. One sign was the emergence of child health centers, which multiplied from almost none in 1900 to 1,511 in 1930; another was the tradeoff between child labor and school attendance. The haggard, sorrowful faces of coal breaker boys, textile-mill girls, and garment porters that stared blankly from Lewis Hine's photographs were becoming the exception rather than the rule. Although the National Child Labor Committee was undoubtedly correct in contending that statistics understated the extent of the problem, there is no disputing the downward trend. The percentage of children aged ten to fifteen who were gainfully employed fell from a peak of 18.4 percent in 1910 to 4.7 percent in 1930. Predictably, school attendance increased very rapidly in the same period. From 1900 to 1930, there was an eight-fold increase in secondary school attendance, while the population did not even double; and schooling occupied more time, as well, rising from an average of 99 to 143 days a year.[6]

The technology of large-scale, rationalized production revolutionized the labor process.

Iron production on a gargantuan scale at Andrew Carnegie's plant at Homestead, Pennsylvania, dwarfs the human observer.

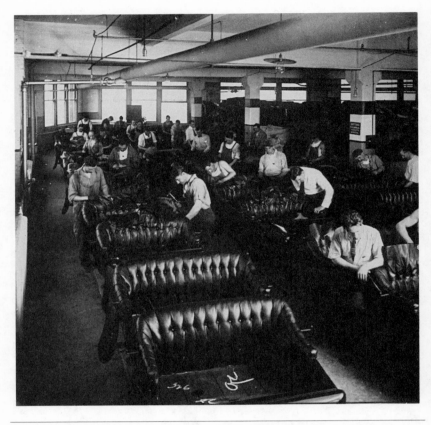

The assembly line at Henry Ford's Model T plant at Highland Park, Michigan: standardized parts and interchangeable workers, ca. 1915.

Certainly, when it came to foreign-language immigrants, there is no doubt that schooling weaned youngsters away from family controls. Increasingly, the good report card came to be seen as the essential credential for a fat pay envelope, the substitute for patrimony and dowry in a family economy no longer based on peasant property but on wage labor. Witness the appeal by a Czech newspaper editor: "By keeping your children in school you will do them the most good. You may leave them money, but it will be spent. You may leave them a fine residence, it may burn . . . You may leave them a farm, but a cyclone may turn valuable property into a desert. But give them an education, and there is nothing in the whole world that can take it away from them . . . Education is a most valuable dowry."[7] The idea that secondary schooling ultimately repaid the sacrifice of immediate income was becoming the accepted wisdom. And it made sense in an economy in which clerical, sales, and technical jobs were among the fastest-growing opportunities available, employers were demanding higher levels of numeracy and literacy, and states were boosting their investment in education as "social overhead" capital.[8]

No institution outside the family itself was more pivotal in social reproduction than the school. To John Dewey and his fellow progressive educators, democratic schooling in the new age required a trained corps of professionals. In place of martinet schoolmasters and shrewish schoolmarms, there should be college-trained superintendents, a trained teaching staff, plus a bevy of vocational and guidance counselors, social workers, and school psychologists. Against this battery of experts, parental authority could hardly stand intact.[9] The weakening of familial controls over the young was not just a top-down imposition of social control but a tug-of-war among parents, educators, and civic leaders over the running of the school. Whether intended or not, all sides furthered the expansion of formal schooling to the point that it eventually rivaled the parents as the primary agent for handing down the values of the culture at large.[10]

There was a similar trend toward mass entertainment. When the children grew up to court, they sought out the excitement of dance palaces, the delights of the nickelodeon and the movies, and the electrifying (and electrified) thrills at Coney Island amusement parks. In some respects, mass leisure parodied the frenetic pace and standardized experience of mass production, so that the high-voltage excitement of the roller coaster might give little more than a quick, impersonal escape from routine.[11] In any case, as the mass demand for leisure-time entertainment brought cash to commercial enterprises, the worlds of leisure and work—fun and profit—more and more overlapped.

The sum of all these changes was to make the reproduction of daily life more of a social affair. Altogether, they subverted genteel culture, diminished family controls, and knit together realms of production and reproduction—paid work and home life—that had once been pulled apart by the Industrial Revolution. Although the process was in its infancy before the First World War, it would eventually be possible to speak of the socialization of *re*production in the same sense that the Industrial Revolution had socialized production.[12]

But now the Industrial Revolution entered a second phase, characterized by the rise of science-based industries (electrical, chemical), so-called scientific management, and corporate rationalization of the productive process. Propagated by the gospel of efficiency, rationalization encompassed a whole complex of innovations aimed at reducing costs and boosting profits, including cost accounting, the assembly line, scientific management, and time-and-motion study. As a result, American industry was becoming famous for amazing feats of mass production and distribution. Henry Ford's Michigan assembly line was a veritable wonder of the world. Perfected at his famous Highland Park plant in 1914, the relentless routine of semiautomated machinery turned out tin lizzies at the rate of one a minute by 1920, thus bringing the cost of an automobile within reach of better-paid wage earners. One reason American workers had more meat on their tables than Europeans was that the assembly line at Armour & Company could process more than 20,000 head of cattle a day, and if machine tenders ever found time to smoke a Camel, they had no trouble buying a cigarette because Durham factories could turn out 10 million a day.[13] In all U.S. manufacturing, productivity almost doubled from the beginning of the century to 1930. As a consequence, the average American before the Crash enjoyed a per capita income some 50 percent higher than a generation earlier.[14]

These prodigies of production were made possible by new telecommunications and a new cultural sense of time itself. The web of telephone lines grew fast and thick after the turn of the century, soon taking over the burden of long-distance communication from the gossamer web of the telegraph. More astonishing was the electromagnetic magic of the wireless, which put the U.S. navy in direct transatlantic communication with the Allies by the end of the First World War. Soon thereafter radio broadcasts were being beamed across the country, so that by the time of Franklin Roosevelt's "Fireside Chats" in the 1930s, California and New York could listen to them at the same time. The existing time zones, which sliced the globe into equal-sized apple wedges, paid homage to the Newtonian world in which they had been invented by imposing regularized clock time upon the seasonal rhythms of earth, moon, and sun. In contrast, the new time frame was transcontinental, transoceanic, and soon global.

The ability to communicate instantly across vast reaches of physical space facilitated a new sense that time itself was relative to the observer. In fact, the new time sense was part and parcel of Western culture's emerging worldview of relativity. Modern art displayed the sense of relativity in paintings by Paul Klee and Joan Miró that depicted motion without the mover and in Pablo Picasso's blending of time and space in a work such as *Girl before a Mirror,* in which the subject is seen simultaneously in front and in profile. In the same vein, the invention of the motion picture made it possible to follow a subject through time and to define the observed in terms of the observer. Relativity, probably the most significant intellectual innovation of the twentieth century, also formed the basis of Einstein's famous theory. In any case, the Newtonian time sense of regular integers was fragmenting like a Cubist painting with its facets of overlapping solid and space, past and future.[15]

Just as the old time sense had been essential in the Industrial Revolution to maintain the regular work routines of the early factory system, so now the new sense of time's malleability hastened the spread of scientific management and the assembly line.[16] The industrial counterpart to the artists, filmmakers, and physicists was the efficiency expert. Hired by cost-conscious employers to raise labor productivity, experts such as Frederick W. Taylor, the founding father of scientific management, experimented with time-and-motion study, stopwatches, incentive payment, and assembly lines to see how the worker's normal time and motion could be rearranged to get maximum output in the shortest span of time. Frank Gilbreth, the pioneer of time-and-motion study, subdivided seconds into new units he dubbed "therbligs" (an anagram of his name) and, along with his wife, Lilian, used a contraption called a chronocyclograph with which to convert motion to a photograph of light tracings by means of time-lapsed photography.[17]

The new sense that time and motion were not fixed but fluid underlay the drive for efficiency. With the aim of increasing profit, industrial engineers speeded up the pace of work to cut back labor costs that went into everything from girders to flivvers. Control of machine technology gave employers control over the growing share of the work force that tended assembly lines in automobiles and electrical appliances, operated sewing machines in the needle trades, and ran rolling mills in steel plants. For good reason, the legions of semiskilled workers in mass production were sometimes called the "machine proletariat." And Henry Ford made no secret of the tendency of scientific management to reduce machine tenders to machinery: "The net result of the application of these principles is the reduction of the necessity of thought on the part of the worker and the reduction of his movements to a minimum."[18]

Mass production required legions of clerks. The lower-level white-collar workers who staffed corporate offices and retail establishments were both cause and consequence of the mounting productivity of semiskilled blue-collar workers. Some office staff merely kept tabs on the rising tide of wealth floating up from the factory floor, the same tide that provided profits for reinvestment and dividends for stockholders. But others contributed directly to rising productivity. In meatpacking, for example, among Gustavus Swift's 1,000 clerical employees at his Chicago headquarters were many who coordinated the timely arrival of cattle from suppliers and the efficient distribution of processed meat to distributors. They were as vital as hog butchers and were subject to similar bonus and incentive systems aimed at getting them to push their papers faster.[19]

Moving with glacial inevitability, mass production and mass reproduction ground away at nineteenth-century society. The more leisure and work became intertwined, the more the proprietary family broke down, along with its cultural supports in genteel respectability and the doctrine of separate spheres. Into the breach between inherited assumptions and new material conditions stepped critics such as Charlotte Perkins Gilman to condemn the customary sexual division of labor between husband-breadwinner and wife-homemaker as "the relic of a patriarchal age."[20] Certainly, these changes and the new thinking they engendered set the stage for the impending arrival of the celebrated New Woman. As she waited in the wings, mass production raised the prospect of universal abundance. Maverick economist Thorstein Veblen gloried in the new efficiency, but he believed that the en-

gineer's productivity was at war with the businessman's "price system."
His warnings about "parasitism," embodied in wasteful competition,
unproductive advertising, and military expenditure, exactly paralleled
Gilman's critique of the "parasitic" housewife.[21] When all the convo-
luted changes in the production and reproduction of social life were
added up, the consequence was an imbalance between the everyday
lives of working people and the liberal nexus of family, property, and
state that governed them.

The Working Class

The emergence of mass production/mass reproduction did not create a
"mass society," if by that is meant a society of interchangeable individuals horizontally integrated in functional groups under bureaucratic
structures of command.[22] Despite trends in this direction, the changes
in daily life did not automatically terminate class antagonism. Class has
been defined in many ways, whether as sociological layers, as economic
interest groups, or as warring armies drawn up in ranks and files ready
to do battle at the drop of a revolutionary manifesto. But if the goal is
to capture change over time, it is best to regard class as a dynamic
process of vertical antagonisms and horizontal liaisons. It might be
compared to a "field of force," something like the high school science
experiment with a magnet and iron filings in which the opposing magnetic forces are made visible by the characteristic pattern of filings between north and south poles.

Though borrowed from studies of preindustrial society,[23] the meta-
phor illuminates the polarities of hyperindustrial America in the early
twentieth century. The fact that some lived off the labor of others was
the key element in the opposition of dominant and subordinate. At one
pole were industrial-financial elites, mostly Yankee-Protestant, based
in the Northeast with headquarters in Wall Street; at the other were
those dependent on wages, especially industrial workers one or two
generations removed from the Old World, scattered in industrial districts and big cities throughout the country. Not all aspects of American life could be reduced to this field of force—race and gender
certainly had dynamics of their own—but no significant aspect of
life could escape the tension between corporate managers and wage
earners.

That was true, as well, for those who fell in between. The old pro-

Table 2.1 Occupational distribution, 1900–1930 (%)

Occupation	1900	1910	1920	1930
Managers, officials, proprietors	5.8	6.6	6.6	7.4
Professional, technical	4.3	4.7	5.4	6.8
White collar				
Clerical	3.0	5.3	8.0	8.9
Sales	4.5	4.7	4.9	6.3
Blue collar				
Craftsmen	10.5	11.6	13.0	12.8
Operatives	12.8	14.6	15.6	15.8
Laborers	12.5	12.0	11.6	10.9
Service	9.0	9.6	7.8	9.8
Farm				
Owners	19.9	16.5	15.3	12.4
Tenants and laborers	17.7	14.4	11.7	8.8
Total (millions)	29.030	37.291	42.206	48.686

Sources: U.S. Bureau of the Census, *Historical Statistics of the United States from Colonial Times to 1957* (Washington, D.C., 1960), 75–78, 278; Alba Edwards, *Comparative Occupation Statistics for the United States, 1870–1940* (Washington, D.C., 1943), 63–72, 187.

Note: Because of rounding, columns may not add to 100 percent in all cases.

prietary middle classes—family farmers and small entrepreneurs—remained numerically imposing but were losing ground; farm owners and tenants, in particular, fell from 19.9 to 12.4 percent of the gainfully employed (see Table 2.1). Meanwhile, the newer middle classes defined themselves less in terms of property accumulation than in terms of income, neighborhood ("good" or "bad"), language (the king's English or foreign accent), and education (college or grade school). Many of the new strata played a mediating role between wealthy philanthropists and the urban poor; among these were members of the new "helping professions" such as social workers and urban educators, who acted as cultural missionaries from Yankee Protestant high culture to the populace at large.

Class registered its impact in the changing social division of labor and, indeed, in the very *perception* of what that division was. The nineteenth-century census had grouped occupations according to horizontal function—agriculture, mining, manufacturing, transportation, trade, public service, professional service, domestic service, and clericals—but by the 1930s, occupations were being grouped along a vertical axis. A hierarchy had become visible, with managers, officials, and proprietors at the top, moving down through professionals and white-collar clerks, to blue-collar workers, with their own internal ladder of skilled, semiskilled, and unskilled.[24] Table 2.1 gauges the trends from 1900 to 1930.

Some inkling of the impact of mass upon class can be gleaned from the same statistics. The greatest gainers included those groups clustered around mass production/distribution: semiskilled operatives rose from 12.8 to 15.8 percent of the gainfully employed, and white-collar clerks increased faster than anybody else, from 3.0 to 8.9 percent. A further point of cardinal importance emerges from the statistics, namely that the social weight of industrial workers was never higher in the United States, before or since. With all blue-collar workers (craftsmen, operatives, and laborers) counted in mining, manufacturing, construction, and transportation, the combined total reached 40.2 percent of the work force in 1920. If ever there was an era of the industrial worker, it was now in the heyday of "carboniferous capitalism."[25] It is little wonder that when avant-garde intellectuals in Greenwich Village started up a magazine of irreverent commentary on the times, they called it *The Masses*.

The average American family in the early twentieth century cobbled together a livelihood from the same basic sources as before—women's unpaid household labor, the father's wages, plus the children's and the mother's incomes, loans in cash and kind, occasional charity, mutual benefits from parish and fraternal self-help, and, in a small minority of cases, union benefits. The received wisdom was that wage levels were higher in the United States than anywhere else in the world. Skilled workers defended the "American standard" against the "pauper labor" of Europe and the "pauper races" of Asia, and statisticians produced comparative figures that showed American workers lived, as German socialist Werner Sombart put it, "on shoals of roast beef and apple pie." Latter-day scholars confirmed that American industry tended to be capital intensive, in part because of high wages paid to scarce labor. Although the nineteenth-century notion of the ladder of opportunity emphasized escape from wage labor, the fact of high wages lent credence to the myth of success.[26]

Yet day-to-day experience hinged not on prosperity but on *insecurity*.

Certainly, the myth of success obscured hard realities of working-class life that labor radicals and Progressive reformers labored to expose. Robert Hunter's influential 1904 study, *Poverty*, conservatively estimated that 20 percent of the northern industrial population lived in dire want. The multivolume Pittsburgh Survey showed that Slavic unskilled laborers could not get by on the earnings of the husband alone, a fact confirmed by a barrage of family budget studies. Statistical comparison of Pittsburgh and Birmingham, England, confirms the received wisdom about shoals of roast beef for skilled Americans but also presents abundant evidence that unskilled Americans lived no higher off the hog than their European counterparts.[27]

What made this situation worse was the unpredictability of wage income. Industrial accidents deprived families of the major source of income with appalling frequency; Crystal Eastman's *Work Accidents and the Law* (1910) disclosed that 15 percent of the Slavic immigrants in midwestern steel plants were seriously injured each year. Unemployment stalked wage earners of all descriptions with seasonal, cyclical, and structural layoffs, which, according to Massachusetts statistics, afflicted one in five workers for a substantial period each year.[28]

According to orthodox economic doctrine, insecurity was not a bad thing but a positive incentive to work. Although scientific managers were modernizing Manchester economics around a productivity theory of wages, the prevailing view was still that of Adam Smith's law of supply and demand.[29] Likewise, public overseers of the poor and private charity organization societies still held to the nineteenth-century view that want was the consequence of moral failing. Charity workers worried that outdoor relief would corrupt its recipients and balked at the introduction of "mother's pensions," or payments to mothers of young children whose fathers had failed in their duty to provide, on the grounds they would sabotage self-reliance. Thus in the last great bastion of the Protestant ethic neither public relief or private charity filled the gap between income and need.[30]

Inadequate paternal income and the absence of state support drove working people back upon the family economy. From French-Canadians in Manchester, New Hampshire, to Italians in Buffalo and Poles in Pittsburgh, everyone relied on different combinations of income at different stages in the life cycle.[31] The very bedrock of family economy was not wage income at all but women's unpaid household labor, most of it still performed without benefit of the new household

technology. As budget studies make clear, a high portion of income
went for basic necessities of food, shelter, fuel, and clothing; perhaps a
fifth was left over for everything else, so that costly appliances, gas
stoves, or washing machines were totally out of reach.[32]

So long as women performed the unpaid labor of the household,
they encountered job segregation, low pay, and little power in the marketplace. That was certainly true for the young single women who
went into domestic service, which had once been the largest women's
occupation but was now in relative decline and was changing from live-
in to day work. In two important respects, however, service did not
change: it remained overwhelmingly a woman's job, and it recruited
disproportionately from groups with the least social resources. In the
nineteenth century that had meant Irish immigrants; now it meant
Afro-Americans. Second-class status was also the lot of women in factory work. Daughters were caught in a vicious cycle of low expectations and low-paid, dead-end factory jobs that they were only too glad
to abandon when the first bright marriage prospect came along, thus
beginning the cycle all over again. And it was true of wives' income.
Wives made their most significant contribution by looking after boarders, a practice especially widespread among Slovaks, Italians, and other
recent immigrants.[33]

The family economy was not complete without the labor of children, who apparently contributed on the order of a tenth of family
income before the First World War. Children as young as age ten were
expected to help out wherever possible, and were virtually required to
work when the father was incapacitated, although a child's work site
depended to a certain extent on parental preference—domestic work
for the Irish, needlework for Italians and Jews. In tenement industries,
food processing, textiles, and wherever a young helper could be attached to an adult, the tangible income from a young son or daughter
outweighed the uncertain returns of rote learning. As one child described his experience in a settlement school, "Gee, I humped myself.
I got three cards with 'excellent' on 'em. An' they never did me no
good. My mother she kept 'em in the Bible, an' they never did her no
good, neither. They ain't like a pay envelope." Failing to appreciate the
economic and emotional importance of the "pay envelope" in the
working-class family was one of the blind spots of middle-class benevolence in the crusade to abolish child labor.[34]

The same insecurity that produced child labor was the mother of working-class benevolence. Social surveys routinely turned up evidence of what Jane Addams described as "the kindness of the poor":

> the woman who lives upstairs will willingly share her breakfast with the family below because she knows they "are hard up"; the man who boarded with them last winter will give a month's rent because he knows the father of the family is out of work; the baker across the street, who is fast being pushed to the wall by his downtrodden competitors, will send across three loaves of stale bread because he has seen the children looking longingly into his window and suspects they are hungry.

Beyond kith and kin were formal institutions of mutual aid. No immigrant community was without its fraternal lodges for the men and parish societies for the women, and it is impossible to disentangle the purely economic from the social functions of the Odd Fellows and the Women's Benevolent Society. "None of us are so strong or so fortunately situated that there may not come a dark hour, when we will require assistance and sympathy. It is comforting to know that in such an hour we need not appeal for Charity, but we may command the kindly ministrations of our fraternal brothers—our 'Neighbors' of the Modern Woodmen of America." Mutual aid—"what goes around comes around"—was the working class answer to the indignity of a hand out.[35]

Mention must also be made of political machines. The nemesis of urban reformers, they were nonetheless primitive welfare agencies that bestowed patronage and emergency aid upon loyal constituents. One Tammany boss explained: "If a family is burned out I don't ask whether they are Republicans or Democrats, and I don't refer them to the Charity Organization Society, which would investigate their case in a month or two and decide they were worthy of help about the time they are dead from starvation. I just get the quarters for them . . . It's philanthropy, but it's politics, too—mighty good politics."[36] Some trade unions also offered mutual benefit within their meager resources, but the main contribution of the affiliates of the American Federation of Labor, whose ranks grew to around 2.5 million on the eve of the First World War, was the steady wages resulting from collective bargaining agreements.

Insecurity left its imprint on popular mentality. As would be expected of immigrants no more than a generation removed from patrimonial inheritance and dowered marriages, newcomers from southern and eastern Europe put a high premium on property ownership—so high, in fact, that the foreign-born were more likely than natives to own homes. Of the major new immigrant groups, Poles were the most likely to make a house the centerpiece of their aspirations, Italians somewhat less so, at least if comparisons of these two groups in Chicago and Pittsburgh can be generalized. These petty holdings were destined to remain petty, and they incurred opportunity costs that made them rather poor investments.[37] So the fact that workers bought houses and often became fiercely proud of their neighborhoods suggests that they placed a high value on security. Indeed, a new ideal was in gestation that was destined to displace the old proprietary ideal. In place of opportunity to accumulate wealth, there stood the quest for security. Bit by bit, the new ideal would be built into social policy until it was enshrined at the highest level of the state in the Social Security system in the 1930s, the cornerstone of the welfare state.

Corporate Rationalization

From the working-class perspective, corporate rationalization was something less than an exercise in pure reason. What the new breed of scientific managers liked to present as a rational system of efficiency and merit nonetheless contained all the irrationalities of class, race, and gender. The supposedly impartial bureaucratic hierarchy was also an axis of unequal power between managers and workers. What may have seemed perfectly reasonable to the efficiency expert was the height of irrationality insofar as it led to overwork, injury, and unemployment. Sitting in their mahogany-paneled offices in Wall Street, corporate executives regarded the drive for ever-higher productivity as a boon to society. But out among the clanging looms of New England textile mills, the blood-and-guts assembly lines of Chicago, and the heartless coal pits of the Rocky Mountains, the experience was something else again.

Race was another irrationality built into the system. The best scientific experts of the day could not get beyond prevailing ethnic stereotypes. To determine which ethnic groups were best fitted for particular jobs, they developed elaborate schemes and color-coded charts purporting to show that Afro-Americans were fit only for manual labor, Poles were best suited to lifting and hauling, and, not surprisingly, men of Scottish and English stock were born to manage.[38]

The same was true of gender. Graduates of the best business schools did not give a second thought to excluding women from all but low-paid, low-status jobs. Toiling in the veritable belly of the bureacractic beast, women quickly increased their share of clerical jobs; secretaries and telephone operators became more or less exclusively female.[39] Job opportunities in sales, factories, and the professions also increased, with the result that the percentage of women in the labor force edged up from 20.4 percent in 1900 to 24.3 percent in 1930 for the country as a whole and still more for women in northern cities. Whereas nineteenth-century male clerks had been treated as apprentice proprietors, the job ladder was now sawed off, and, instead of being groomed for command, female workers were commended for their willingness to follow orders without complaint.[40]

Rationalization introduced new forms of male dominance. As family constraints loosened, women were freed to enter the labor market. But because of women's socialization in subordinate family roles, employers took it for granted that they could be assigned subordinate roles in the bureaucratic hierarchy. As the husband was head of the proprietary household, so a male manager was head of the office. Unequal power in the family resulted in segregation in lower-paying jobs, as well as in lower pay at every job level; accordingly, women's income hovered at between 45 percent and 60 percent of men's.[41] Thus, like the Cheshire cat, gender inequality smiled and disappeared, only to appear again.

Rationalization also reformed the hit-or-miss system of industrial relations inherited from the nineteenth century. Under the old formula "laissez faire plus the constable," industrial relations had been left to the market, subject to state intervention only when public order or property rights were threatened. Work discipline was personal not bureaucratic, proprietary not managerial, and arbitrary not rationalized. The pivotal figure was the front-line foreman, often little better than a petty tyrant who collected tribute from favorites and laid off insubordinates and union activists with impunity. Under the "drive system," he cursed, threatened, and otherwise exacted production from his labor gang, as described by one Fall River textile worker: "The Board of Trade drives the agent, the agent drives the superintendent, he drives the overseer, and the overseer drives the operative. They drive us, and we drive each other."[42] As the turbulent history of the Gilded Age showed, this was not a recipe for industrial peace.

Scientific managers vowed to end the chaos. Frederick W. Taylor and his many imitators set out to subject the wage earner's every motion to managerial control, while a new set of personnel managers began to substitute internal labor markets for the uncontrolled markets and the drive system of old. Intruding on the foreman's domain, they hired and promoted according to résumé and performance, not nepotism and favoritism (in theory, at least). Imbued with the mystique of the expert, scientific managers approached industrial relations as a matter of social engineering: get the worker up to peak efficiency, and the problems of alienation, dehumanization, and industrial conflict would soon disappear.[43]

Be that as it may, the ultimate test of efficiency was always the same—did it boost profits? To stockholders and directors the question was whether saving time and motion also saved money. According to careful investigations conducted for the United States Commission on Industrial Relations, the aim was to raise output without a commensurate increase in wages. In fact, the most common of the new incentive pay schemes, the "sliding-bonus" system, severely restricted wage gains because the piece rate actually declined once output passed a certain quota. In the terms of classical economics, this meant that past a certain threshold of greater output marginal utility would decline. In Marxian terms, it meant that the lion's share of the gains in productivity went to augment surplus value, not wages. In either case, scientific managers were the latest in a long line of utilitarian rationalists going back to Charles Babbage, Jeremy Bentham, and the factory masters of the first Industrial Revolution.[44]

Given the built-in tension over pay and power, rationalization on the shop floor ran into stiff resistance of two kinds. From one quarter, opposition came from industrial craftsmen who had long since adapted to the industrial regimen and had developed their own constraints on the employer—the eight-hour day, union work rules, and "a fair day's work for a fair day's pay." Holding fast to these traditions of craft control and manly independence, the typographers' union prohibited a member from working under a "dead line" imposed by the employer, and the machinists' union mandated the expulsion of any member who accepted wages by the piece, premium, merit, or any other system geared to productivity. Railroad shop crafts conducted a long and bitter strike in 1911 against the introduction of time-study and other components of scientific management on the Harriman and Illinois Central lines, and it was at hearings on this strike that the public at large first heard about scientific management from an ardent defender, Louis

Table 2.2 Composition of selected occupations (male) in northern industry, 1920 (%)

Occupation	Illinois		Pennsylvania		New York	
	Native	Immigrant	Native	Immigrant	Native	Immigrant
Managers and superintendents	50	49	65	34	44	56
Manufacturers	30	69	47	53	35	64
Foremen and overseers	34	65	58	41	36	64
Machinists	29	70	n.c.		n.c.	
Semiskilled: blast furnace, rolling mill	25	72	39	55	27	69
Laborers: blast furnace, rolling mill	14	73	24	63	12	83

Source: U.S. Bureau of the Census, *Fourteenth Census: 1920* (Washington, D.C., 1921–1923), vol. IV, *Population*, 910, 911, 914, 980–982, 1004–05.

Note: Native = white native born of native parents; immigrant = foreign born or at least one parent foreign born; n.c. = not collected. Because of rounding and presence of data for whites only, columns may not add to 100 percent in all cases.

Brandeis. Eventually, most of the labor movement would come to accept incentive systems, with the AFL leading the way, but before the 1920s resistance was still significant.[45]

Resistance also arose from the ranks of immigrants who commonly filled unskilled slots in mining, textiles, and heavy industry in the North. As Table 2.2 indicates, first- and second-generation immigrants predominated in the lower occupational ranks. The large proportion of immigrant manufacturers reflects the inclusion of subcontractors and other petty operators in the census category rather than any dramatic upward mobility.

Unlike industrial craftsmen, most of the immigrant laborers were peasants once-removed who had no body of craft custom. Their resistance arose not from modern industrial experience, but from the lack of it. They clung to traditional work rhythms and seasonal calendars derived from the agrarian, sacramental cultures from which they came. The slow pace and irregular work habits of Jewish tradesmen or Italian *contadini* were an annoyance to many employers, as were the three-day wedding frolics of Slavic laborers and the dozens of festivals and saints days of Orthodox Greeks.[46] Likewise, the family life cycle, which turned on births, marriages, and funerals, conflicted with the strict requirements of efficiency. In New England textile mills, for example, mill superintendents had to bow to the customs of French-Canadian operatives who would send substitutes when the regular employee was attending to family obligations. In other cases, the migration of "birds of passage" back and forth across the Atlantic helped account for turnover rates that often exceeded 100 percent annually. In short, ethnic cultures clashed with the gospel of efficiency.[47]

Midwestern packinghouses were a closely watched test case of the new system. By the time Carl Sandburg dubbed Chicago "hog butcher for the world," the "Big Five" packinghouses had rationalized production through the famous "disassembly line." Prominent executives from the Armour and Swift companies joined the National Civic Federation to propagate the philosophy of corporate benevolence through efficiency. But rationalization could turn into chaos for the worker. Working at breakneck speed, 300 men performed a succession of minute operations that converted a lowing steer into mute hamburger with world-renowned efficiency. One superintendent explained how he reached his production quota: "If you need to turn out a little more, you speed up the conveyor a little and the men speed up to keep pace." Upton Sinclair recorded the result in *The Jungle* (1906):

> They worked with furious intensity, literally upon the run—at a pace with which there is nothing to be compared except a football game. It was all highly specialized labor, each man having his task to do . . . First there came the "butcher," to bleed them; this meant one swift stroke, so swift that you could not see it—only the flash of the knife; and before you could realize it, the man had darted on to the next in line, and a stream of bright red was pouring out upon the floor . . . It was let down to the ground, and there came the "headsman," whose task it was to sever the head, with two or three swift strokes. Then came the "floorsman," to make the first cut in the skin; and then another to finish ripping the skin down the centre; and then half a dozen more in swift succession, to finish the skinning.

Furthermore, intense work now meant no work later, and seasonal and weekly unemployment was common, especially among casual laborers, who were culled as needed by the foremen from the hundreds who normally gathered each morning at the plant gate.[48]

Against the chaos of corporate rationalization, industrial workers posed their own forms of rationalization from below. To minimize chronic insecurity, they demanded a shorter working day, stabilized employment through slack times, seniority, and an industrywide common labor rate. These perennial issues sparked repeated union drives among people who hoped trade unions and collective bargaining might be the rational answer to irrational bouts of overwork and idleness. A major strike occurred in 1904, and organizing resumed again during the First World War, when unions connected with the Chicago Federation of Labor mobilized to win the "basic" eight-hour day (that is, overtime pay after eight hours) through the federal mediation of Judge Samuel Alschuler. Given the babel of tongues in the stockyards, the union had to speak a language of rational toleration in order to succeed. It had to welcome all comers, as in this account of early union growth in meatpacking by a Lithuanian laborer: "The night I joined the Cattle Butchers' Union I was led into the room by a negro member. With me were Bohemians, Germans and Poles, and Mike Donnelly, the President is an Irishman . . . We swore to be loyal to our union above everything else except the country, the city and the State."[49]

Prejudice was the close ally of antiunion employers. Exploiting abundant ethnic tensions among working people, companies broke the 1904 strike with violence and minority scabs. Again, after the First World War, companies broke a general strike in the industry by pitting ethnic groups against one another and using police to protect strikebreakers. Nothing did more to destroy the fledgling labor movement than the racial hatred that boiled to the surface in the bloody Chicago race riot of 1919. Not until the Congress of Industrial Organizations found ways to bridge the racial gap in the 1930s did unions unite workers of both races and win concessions from management on the practice of rationalization.[50]

As the defeat in meatpacking suggests, the labor movement in the Progressive Era was, in some respects, less than workers' response to rationalization. None of the main centers of mass production—steel, autos, rubber, meatpacking, electrical manufacturing—achieved permanent union organization before the 1930s. Trade unions enjoyed greatest success in relatively well-paid craft preserves among railroad engineers and other labor aristocrats, and in fields such as the building trades that were furthest removed from rationalized factories.[51]

That was certainly the case with most of the affiliates of the American Federation of Labor, which had swelled to over 2 million members by the beginning of Wilson's presidency. Samuel Gompers, the battle-hardened autocrat of the AFL until his death in 1924, had long since stopped dreaming about ultimate ends and wished chiefly for a reform in liberal doctrine that would supplant individual bargaining with collective bargaining. Though pugnacious in defense of member rights, many AFL chieftains were conservative men with a business outlook who saw the labor market as a male preserve and often displayed nativism and ethnic prejudice. They commonly tapped into the sports clubs, saloons, and fraternal lodges of Irish and German workers but steered clear of the leisuretime networks of Slavs, Italians, and Jews, and totally ignored women's religious and neighborhood networks. They were sometimes associated with corrupt political machines, and when unions eventually did enlist the new immigrants, they commonly absorbed the old *padrone* system to become patrons themselves.[52]

Nonetheless, the labor movement was also more than a response to rationalization, in the sense that it sought to impose its own values on industry. In some cases, it acted through spontaneous revolts, as in the great 1912 textile strike in Lawrence, Massachusetts. Proclaiming a demand for "bread and roses," the strike began in response to wage cuts imposed after a state-mandated reduction in weekly hours for women and children (from fifty-six to fifty-four). Spontaneous work stoppages occurred when Italians at the American Woolen Company halted production at one of the largest mills in the world by slashing belts and yelling that they would not stand for a loss of "four loaves of bread." The temerity of Italians, Greeks, and French-Canadians striking in the land of the Puritans was compounded by the arrival of the Industrial Workers of the World. The IWW gave leadership to the protean movement of a dozen nationalities already intertwined through crisscrossing women's networks and interoccupational solidarities, now raised to a communitywide cohesion through continual pickets and mass parades. The owners fought back with an inept attempt to frame the IWW for a dynamite conspiracy (later exposed as the work of the American Woolen Company), and they sent in the cream of the Massachusetts militia to protect scabs, who received the blessing of Harvard's President Eliot as "the heroes of American industry." The turning point came when police beat up children being sent out of town for safekeeping, a vicious outrage brought to the attention of the nation by Margaret Sanger during congressional hearings. The strikers won wage increases from 5 to 21 percent and no doubt inspired a similar strike by silk workers in Paterson, New Jersey, in 1913.[53]

Lawrence and Paterson came and went without leaving any permanent organization. But they proved that immigrant laborers could endure long seasons of want in apparently stolid resignation, only to burst forth in some great protest. For a time they were the living nightmare of executives everywhere, as the "wretched of the earth" arose to demand "bread and roses" under an organization that disdained collective bargaining, advocated sabotage against rationalization, embraced unconventional sexual ideas, and aimed at proletarian revolution. What could possibly have been worse?

In the years around the First World War, workers massed on industrial battlefields in numbers comparable with the armies that fought on the plains of northern France. The strike of women shirtwaist makers in New York in 1909 was dubbed "the uprising of the 20,000"; Chicago clothing workers outdid that two years later in "the rising of the 50,000"; and in 1919 and 1920 strikers in steel and meatpacking were counted in hundreds of thousands. As a matter of fact, the United States may have had the most severe industrial relations problem in the Western world. Certainly, disorder in this period was more widespread than in Germany, which was passing through a similar phase of the second Industrial Revolution. On top of the American tradition of hard-fisted direct action, now the dislocations of mass production and mass immigration made for an unusually explosive situation. And so long as industrial workers had no home inside the governing system, the labor wars were destined to continue.[54]

The most thoroughgoing alternative to capitalist rationality was the socialist idea of a rational society. Socialists cast a third of the votes at the AFL convention in 1913, and they were especially strong among miners, machinists, and industrial craftsmen under siege by efficiency experts. In addition, they flourished among certain immigrant cultures, notably German and Jewish, and so-called new unions in the garment trades. In practical terms, they supported a whole panoply of piecemeal changes—the abolition of child labor and the sweatshop, hours and wages regulation, tenement inspection, "gas-and-water socialism," and so on down through the list of progressive social reforms. But their ultimate aim was to replace the existing system with a more humane and harmonious one. In a widely circulated pamphlet, *Unionism and Socialism* (1904), Eugene Debs lashed out at dehumanization under capitalism: "In the capitalist system the soul has no business. It cannot produce profit by any process of capitalist calculation. The working hand is what is needed for the capitalist's tool and so the human must be reduced to a hand." Against this soulless system, Debs offered a vision of a truly rational social order "in which every human being, in the full enjoyment of economic freedom, shall have full opportunity . . . to develop the best there is in him for his own good as well as the good of society at large." More than any other segment of the labor movement, socialists laid claim to the grand tradition of Enlightenment rationalism as it was handed down through the egalitarian ideals of utopians and Marxists. Against the rationality of scientific managers, they posed the rationality of scientific socialism.[55]

The New Woman

The years leading to the First World War rang with questions about relations between the sexes. Who was the New Woman? What was her destiny in a world of declining birthrates and increased work opportunities? What kind of moral values would govern sexuality if birth control separated sex from procreation? What would happen to the doctrine of separate spheres if women won the vote? No matter where people looked, from the intimacy of courtship to the public world of politics, and no matter whom they listened to, from sex radicals to social purists, there was no escaping what was called the "woman question."

The question arose, in the first place, because of myriad changes in everyday life. Certainly, women in the generation that came of age after the turn of the century had different expectations from their mothers. The impact of mass production/mass reproduction was weakening the family's hold on its daughters as education and the helping professions played a greater role in child rearing. Women's employment had doubled in the last two decades of the nineteenth century and now increased by another 50 percent in the first two decades of the twentieth thanks to a variety of new white-collar opportunities.[56] Every additional woman contributing a wage to the family kitty and every employment advance broke through the invisible boundary separating the masculine world of work, commerce, and vice from the feminine world of home, domesticity, and virtue.

Changes in sexuality could not be contained within the old boundaries, either. To the consternation of the elders, the rising generation launched an unprecedented assault upon chastity. Levels of premarital intercourse were rising to heights unknown in America since the eighteenth century. One survey found that the proportion of women who said they had not been virgins at marriage rose from 10 to 25 percent for the generation maturing in the 1910s, an upward trend confirmed decades later by the Kinsey report, which also showed that in the same period a growing number of young bachelors were turning from prostitutes to companions for sex play.[57] Since women's virginity had been the very citadel of virtue in the Victorian era, this mass assault weakened the whole constellation of inherited family values.

The trend toward freer sexuality was reflected in the world of high ideas. Writers such as Theodore Dreiser allowed their heroines to descend from the pedestals of the genteel tradition to become sympathetic working girls like the title character of *Sister Carrie* (1900), who turned concubine rather than endure the penury and confinement of a shoe factory. Tracing a similar story line, Dreiser wrote of a young man's headlong escape from the suffocating prudery of fundamentalist parents to the gilded squalor of city life in *An American Tragedy* (1925). Although American intellectuals had only a nodding acquaintance with the new ideas of psychoanalysis—penis envy, infantile sexuality, and the Oedipus complex—they pursued many of the same themes as Sigmund Freud and his disciples. Walter Lippmann, for example, rendered a scathing critique of "the old family, with its dominating father, its submissive and amateurish mother," which had pushed sexual repression and private acquisitiveness "to the point of morbidity."[58]

The trend was also reflected in popular culture. For immigrant youth, the point of departure was not the Victorian middle class but the patriarchal values of European peasant villages. Although such courting customs as chaperonage and strict separation of the sexes retained some vitality among Catholic Italians and Poles, as well as Jews from eastern European *shtetls*, the individualism of the American marketplace was a strong solvent for the folkways of the past. The young abandoned their parents' church festivals and fraternal galas and flocked to commercial dance halls—there were 500 in New York alone—where they dared to enjoy such "tough dances" as the turkey trot, bunny hug, and grizzly bear. They descended in droves upon picture palaces, where they watched titillating movies such as *Trapeze Disrobing Act* and followed the silent screen's first sex symbol, Theda Bara, through her seductive "vamping." They frequented Coney Island amusement parks and cheap eating parlors, where a few practiced the wiles of "charity girls," underworld slang for girls who were out to have fun and expected presents and attention, but not the prostitute's cash.[59]

Such mingling of the sexes confounded the rules of separate spheres. Adults typically worried that the young were creating confusion in the moral order and bringing ruination upon themselves. Records of juvenile courts, truant officers, and charity workers burgeoned with reports of dance-hall flirtations, cheap thrills in darkened movie theaters, and the seemingly unguilty behavior of "charity girls." What was promiscuity to the elders was sexual freedom to the young. Clearly, the pleasure domes of mass culture, were a staging ground of revolt against Old World Catholic and Jewish patriarchy and a challenge to the dominant Yankee Protestant morality, as well.[60]

Thus, from every side, the ground was being cut from under Victorian assumptions. Demographic changes, women's employment, rebel writers, mass culture, and the sexual revolt of youth all challenged the ruling norms of womanhood and manhood keyed to the old middle-class family. Every culture tolerates a certain amount of dissonance between norms and behavior, but given the centrality of the masculine/feminine identity, America could not tolerate so much dissonance indefinitely. The question was, what would replace the gender divisions of the Victorian era? Would the new social relations of the sexes undermine or reinforce male dominance?

One answer came from the New Woman. Appearing everywhere from birth control clinics to suffragist platforms, the new breed of independent women impressed all who met them. Randolph Bourne, one of the bright young iconoclasts of the *New Republic* and *The Masses*, encountered them busily overturning convention at Greenwich Village salons: "They talk much about the 'Human Sex,' which they claim to have invented, and which is simply a generic name for those whose masculine brutalities and egotisms and feminine pettinesses and stupidities have been purged away so that there is left stuff for a genuine comradeship and healthy frank regard and understanding." After decades of homosocial love and friendship, the idea of heterosocial comradeship was heady stuff. Rebel women thrilled to the inspirational leadership of Charlotte Perkins Gilman, the prophet of androgynous companionship who advocated the industrialization of housework and cooperative industrial production with the aim of simultaneously liberating women from "sex-slavery" and workers from wage slavery. They avidly read Olive Schreiner's *Woman and Labor* (1911), a manifesto of equal employment that proclaimed: "We take all labor for our province!" They appropriated the socialist idea "from each according to his [and now her] ability" and laid claim to Enlightenment rationalism in believing that the invidious divisions of humanity could be replaced by a rational social order. In fact, they stood forth as heirs to a great humanist tradition stretching all the way back to the Renaissance.[61]

If the New Woman was a humanist, she was still more a feminist. Indeed, the term *feminism* came into currency in this period to connote militant advocacy for women on all fronts. Recognizing the new terrain of social life, feminists broadened the nineteenth-century women's rights movement. They embraced the cause of wage-earning women and sometimes took their cues from such courageous struggles as the 1909 "uprising of the 20,000" in which Jewish and Italian needle workers defied all conventions of "true womanhood" to parade boldly in the streets, a spectacle repeated three years later in the dramatic textile strikes in Lawrence and Paterson. They were sympathetic to progressive labor organizations such as the Women's Trade Union League, supported protective legislation, and demanded women's right to labor for equal pay and freedom from sexual harassment. They supported women's suffrage, but the militant civil disobedience of the newfound Woman's party shocked the staider members of the National American Woman Suffrage Association. All feminists advocated votes for women, but not all suffragettes were feminists.[62]

When it came to sexuality, they boldly went where only a tiny few had gone before. Breaking Victorian taboos, they proclaimed with Havelock Ellis "the love rights of women," something no self-respecting matron of the nineteenth-century women's-rights movement would have dared embrace. To become fully human, they argued, women's erotic nature demanded recognition on the same plane as men's. Breaking sharply with the genteel tradition, women poets in little magazines such as *The Masses* and *The Liberator* broached the tabooed subject of sensual rapture, as in "Climax":

> I thought that I could sleep
> After I had kissed his mouth
> With its sharply haunting corners
> And its red.

> But now that he has kissed me
> A stir is in my blood,
> And I want to be awake
> Instead.[63]

However tame this would seem to later generations numbed by pornographic imagery, the publication of such explicit expressions connoted the awakening of erotic desire from the long night of Victorian prudery and seemed positively thrilling at the time.

In rejecting the double standard in favor of a "new morality," the sex radicals also rejected the madonna/whore dichotomy. No longer was a woman either an asensual damsel on the pedestal of respectability or a strumpet on the bed of shame. The always-brazen Emma Goldman attempted to break the mold single-handedly by trying prostitution to raise money for the anarchist cause. It didn't work. The next step was to envision new roles for men. At the very least, the new man was supposed to give up proprietary claims on wife or girlfriend and forgo prostitutes. Floyd Dell, an early champion of feminism for men, created a fictional hero who said, "I want a girl that can be talked to and that can be kissed, and I want it to be the same girl." Open marriages flourished in the bohemian world of Greenwich Village, where rebellious couples—John Reed and Louise Bryant, Max Eastman and Ida Rauh, Emma Goldman and Ben Reitman—kept their own names and their own company. Indeed, their letters and biographies suggest they sometimes thrived on the exquisite tortures of psychic dependence and betrayal, honing emotional torment to a fever pitch in which some relationships became cruel parodies of the worst in conventional marriage.[64]

Without stopping to count the casualties of wayward desire, these imperfect liberators kept up a drumfire of denunciation against bourgeois marriage. No one was more caustic or effective than Emma Goldman. A star of the lecture circuit, she excoriated Anthony Comstock and the whole purity crusade as "the Young-Men-and-Old-Maid's Christian Union, Temperance Union, Sabbath Union, Purity League, etc." Taking her cues from free-love anarchists and utopian socialists of the nineteenth century, she deliberately scandalized audiences with comparisons of bourgeois marriage and prostitution. "To the moralist prostitution does not consist so much in the fact that the woman sells her body but rather [in the fact] that she sells it out of wedlock. That this is no mere statement is proved by the fact that marriage for monetary considerations is perfectly legitimate, sanctified by law and public opinion, while any other union is condemned and repudiated." Goldman and her fellow anarchists went far beyond mainstream socialists such as Kate Richard O'Hare, who gamely promised that socialism would eliminate prostitution and redeem monogamy by ending capitalist exploitation of women. In refusing to grasp the nettle of changing sexuality, the staider socialists were less in tune with the deeper trends of modern life than the sexual radicals.[65]

The new morality gave birth to the modern birth control movement. The pivotal figure was Margaret Sanger. Sanger braided together the themes of women's "love rights" (leaving her lawful husband, she took Havelock Ellis to bed), the socialist condemnation of poverty, and the anarchist critique of marriage to argue for rational control over procreation. She wrote an article, "What Every Girl Should Know," for the socialist New York *Call*, but when the censor lowered the Comstock boom, the paper printed only one word—"Nothing!" Rounding up support from feminists and the IWW, she launched the *Woman Rebel* to blast away at the established order; emblazoned on the masthead was "No Gods, No Masters!" "I believe that woman is enslaved by the world machine, by sex conventions, by motherhood and its present necessity child-rearing, by wage-slavery, by middle-class morality, by customs, laws, and superstitions."[66]

It is true that sexual rebels were iconoclasts to a fault. Denouncing "mothers' pensions" as a "capitalist trap" was one thing, but for a time Sanger espoused the nihilism of Peter Kropotkin and defended the use of dynamite and even assassination in the cause of revolution. Later, when she made peace with the medical profession and linked arms with the Rockefeller Foundation around population control and eugenics, her radical views, which it was not necessary to pardon to understand, would seem like the excesses of an impressionable young woman. But the fact remained that radicalism tore away the scales of sexual mystification to permit the twentieth century to see with its own eyes that rational control of procreation might be not only a necessity, but a virtue. In their very audacity, rebels such as Goldman and Sanger grasped the awesome potential of social equality inherent in the rise of mass production/mass reproduction, in particular the growing separation of sexuality and procreation.

New Womanhood spread outward from its inchoate origins in the working class and among the educated social rebels to affect life-styles in the culture at large. Before the Roaring Twenties had even begun to mew, the flapper had already burst upon the scene. Her classic description was penned by H. L. Mencken in 1915: "She knows exactly what the Wassermann reaction is, and has made up her mind that she will never marry a man who can't show an unmistakable negative . . . This flapper has forgotten how to simper; she seldom blushes; it is impossible to shock her. She saw 'Damaged Goods' without batting an eye . . . She plans to read Havelock Ellis during the coming summer."[67] She was also abandoning the distended femininity of corset and bustle for plainer shirtwaists, bobbing her hair, and learning new dance steps.

The pace of popular entertainment quickened to the dizzying "spieling" of the fox trot and the rollicking syncopations of ragtime bounding up the Mississippi. Afro-American culture made a major contribution to the new mood. Out of the honkytonks of New Orleans and Memphis came W. C. Handy's "Memphis Blues" and the founding classics of jazz, the new sound that was winning praise from the *New Republic* as "the one original and indigenous type of music of the American people." White Americans loosened their straitlaces just enough to respond to Afro-American sensuality, or at least they listened approvingly to the strains of "St. Louis Woman," with all her diamond rings. Perhaps they may have even repossessed some of the female sexuality they had displaced onto the black woman. All in all, the 1910s were the pivotal years of modern culture, when the country turned away from the Sousa marches and cozy ice-cream parlors of the Gay Nineties toward the Charleston and speakeasies of the Twenties. If there was a "revolution in manners and morals," as is widely believed, it occurred before the war when thrill-seeking working-class youth, Afro-American musicmakers, and avant-garde bohemians came together in revolt against genteel, censorious Victorianism.[68]

It was more than conventional opinion could stand. How could feminist demands for real equality in everything from love life to citizenship be granted without a subversion of the entire social order? How could women and men become complementary sides of a common humanity without sowing confusion in the moral canon? What would remain to demarcate good from evil once the gender dichotomies—good girl/bad girl, female virtue/male vice, female continence/male lust—were gone? As if all that were not bad enough, the indiscriminate mixing of African and European, Protestant and Jew, Anglo-Saxon and Italian in the symbolic world of jazz music and the physical world of the dance hall compounded the confusion by dissolving the boundaries of endogamy. Who would lie with whom, and to whom would the uncertain issue of intermarriage belong? Although pioneer anthropologists such as Franz Boas were tearing racial stereotypes to pieces, ethnic parochialism combined with deep-seated gender dichotomies to arouse profound fears of pollution of bloodlines and the shattering of sexual taboos.[69] Indeed, to the extent that the feminist revolt overlapped working-class rebellion, conservatives were right to see it as a dangerous experiment subversive of the class, sexual, and racial foundations of Western civilization.

Thus it is hardly surprising that alongside the rise of feminism, there was a renewed push for social purity. Like their nineteenth-century forerunners, social purists were revolted by the unwanted consequences of bourgeois freedom—drunkenness, prostitution, obscenity, and promiscuous commingling of "races." They took the physical squalor of the city as a sign of moral impurity. A Massachusetts prohibitionist urged that the lower-class saloon be treated as "a typhoid-breeding pool of filthy water" and "a nest of rats infected with the bubonic plague." One Chicago philanthropist called upon patriotic men of wealth "to transform the environment, to make the houses and streets clean and wholesome" so that "the mind and soul are everywhere surrounded by pure, delightful, inspiring suggestions." Backed by business elites, prominent architects launched the City Beautiful campaign to purify gritty cities across the nation in the way that the Great White Way of the 1893 World's Fair had made Chicago physically and morally resplendent. Jane Addams, who took second place to no one in her admiration for immigrant cultures, could not abide rough working-class entertainments and strove to replace the illicit temptations of nickelodeons and dance halls with parks, playgrounds, and edifying orchestral music in public squares. The queen of social housekeepers, she called for a "new conscience" of scientific professionals to stand guard against the "ancient evil" of prostitution. The watchword of scientific environmentalists was *social hygiene*, and the head of the newfound American Social Hygiene Association (1913) proposed scientific sex education for those crammed into unhealthful, overcrowded tenements to purge them of their alleged "social vices and sordid communistic modes of living."[70]

America had traveled a long way from the sacramental society of seventeenth-century New England, but these latter-day Puritans *cum* social hygienists sought to moralize the marketplace in a knockout campaign against "commercialized vice." Beginning with New York City's Committee of Fifteen in 1900, civic leaders set up vice commissions to investigate what was euphemistically termed the social evil. True to the emerging progressive spirit, the commissions blamed immorality on social and economic conditions, unlike their forerunners in the nineteenth-century antiprostitution movement, who had blamed individual moral failing. The Chicago Vice Commission report of 1911 was typical: "The first truth that the Commission desires to impress upon the citizens of Chicago is the fact that prostitution in this city is a *Commercialized Business* of large proportions with tremendous profits of more than Fifteen Million Dollars per year, controlled largely by men, not women." Like the progressive regulation of the trusts, the target was not business per se, but greedy evildoers who profited from corruption through a nexus of saloons, sleazy hotels, low-class dance halls, and indecent picture shows. Local business elites and bigwigs such as John D. Rockefeller, Jr., a staunch Baptist, took command of the campaign to purge the marketplace of the purveyors of sin. Exhibiting new attitudes about social causation and the research methods of social science, by 1916 more than 100 cities had conducted vice investigations.[71]

Otherwise, progressive investigators preserved the old moral dichotomies. All the predators were men, and all the victims were women. Even though their own evidence revealed a more complex pattern of motivation, including entrepreneurial madams and gray areas between courtship and prostitution, the commissions preserved their concept of women's virtue intact: "Women do not seek lives of prostitution, except under economic pressure or economic expediency, or under the handicap of moral and mental defects resulting from previous family economic conditions." The stress on the virtue of victimhood was a clue to the deeper motives behind the drive to abolish prostitution. It was not so much a matter of how many country girls fell prey to pimps and venereal disease; rather, it was a question of upholding a set of gender ideals. Prostitution became a stylized set piece acted out to remind the larger audience of the dichotomy between (feminine) virtue and (masculine) vice. If the original sin was not Eve's but Adam's, then pure womanhood could still be held up as the standard of virtue. It amounted to a Victorian counterattack on the sex radicals.[72]

The campaign reached hysterical pitch over the alleged "white slave traffic." According to this lurid theory, international rings of vice merchants captured innocent girls to be sold into brothel captivity. As in the long-standing Protestant fables about nuns held captive by the pope, moral outrage masked pornographic fascination with sexual domination: the more taboos violated, the more enticing the tale. The epitome was a young virgin drugged and carried away by "cadets" to Chinatown to serve the fiendish perversions of her polyglot captors for the rest of her short life. According to a Boston suffragist, lifelong slavery always resulted because, "having been an inmate of a brothel even for a short time, they are forever debarred from normal association with right-minded people under wholesome conditions." (To which the *Woman Rebel* replied, "Could any more repulsive and foul conception of sex be given to adolescent girls as a preparation for life . . .?")[73] In contrived imitation of the antebellum Underground Railroad, missionaries such as "the good angel of Chinatown" made careers rescuing white women entrapped in vicious alien districts. The celebrity of rescue work attested to the larger meaning of the antiprostitution crusade. To bring back the fallen was a symbolic restoration of the established social hierarchy in all its aspects: it reclaimed a white skin from the clutches of darker races; it purified the market of illicit commerce; it reconverted whore to potential mother.[74]

Reformers turned more and more to the state to redeem a corrupt social order. The American Social Hygiene Association pushed for sex education in the public schools, and its head averred: "If the civilization of the white race is to survive, it must be saved through the diffusion and adoption of sound policies in regard to social hygiene." Surely, a goal as big as saving the white race was worth a little sex education, even if it meant going against the Comstock doctrine that any discussion of sexuality was obscene. Otherwise the motivation was repressive. Spurred by the vice investigations, several cities closed down their red-light districts, and the Mann Act of 1910 prohibited the transportation of women across state lines for immoral purposes and set up a Special Commissioner for the Suppression of the White Slave Traffic. If liberty meant freedom to traffic in vice, then, Jane Addams wrote, "hard won liberties must be restrained by the demonstrable needs of society."[75] In the battle between the new morality and social purity, between romantic innocence and moralistic guilt, the state weighed in on the side of repression.

The most celebrated prosecution under the Mann Act involved Jack Johnson, reigning heavyweight boxing champion of the world.[76] Whereas the legendary John Henry was a merely symbolic affirmation of Afro-American masculinity, Johnson was a living affront to white supremacy. Son of a former slave, Johnson made his start knocking down fellow youths to win pennies from white onlookers in a spectacle of humiliation known as a "battle royal." He went on to win big purses in prizefighting against a series of "white hopes" (the origin of the term). His tragic mistake was to try to fulfill the West Indian proverb "Money whitens." Money did, indeed, bring fast cars, lavish living, and an entourage of female companions. It somehow freed him to break the greatest of all racial taboos. Thrice he married white women, whom he alternately adored and abused.

To teach the country a lesson in race and sex relations, public authorities were determined to make an example of this "nigger who didn't know his place." While they ignored his abusive treatment of women—wives enjoyed no statutory protection against marital rape—they chose to prosecute his flagrant violations of racial taboos. Although the relations between Johnson and his consorts were voluntary, the newly created Bureau of Investigation twisted evidence to fit the technicalities of the law and won an easy conviction.

The prosecuting attorney held up Johnson's conviction as a public warning: "Money and fame . . . brought white women. One is a suicide, the others are pariahs. He has violated the law. Now it is his function to teach others the law must be respected." Speaking to the gallery of the House of Representatives, a Georgia congressman declaimed: "Intermarriage between whites and blacks is repulsive and averse to every sentiment of pure American spirit. It is abhorrent and repugnant to the very principles of a pure Saxon government. It is subversive to social peace." From across the Mason-Dixon line, the governor of New York concurred that it was "a blot on our civilization." The enormity of the transgression lay in the fact that Johnson's consorts had also shamelessly stepped out of their "place," a fact that Johnson's brutal mistreatment of them did not erase. For if white women were free to consort with black men, why did they need a male protector at all? And if they did not, what was the point of antimiscegenation statutes and the whole legal edifice of segregation, plus the racist customs and antipollution taboos of "a pure Saxon government"? Surely, to shore up the foundations of "white civilization," a little travesty of justice was a small price to pay.

Although the state was repressive with respect to sexual morality, political leaders were beginning to take the opposite tack with respect to suffrage. After stalling in the first decade of the twentieth century, the long march for woman suffrage resumed its advance: from 1910 through 1914, half a dozen states were added to the suffrage column, all but one in the West, with the result that women enjoyed equal suffrage in every western state except New Mexico. The victories in the West were something of a puzzle. Among suffragists themselves, most of whom were also progessives, the favored explanation was the progressive spirit of the frontier. It is easy to poke holes in this notion—Mormon Utah, the second in line, was hardly a hotbed of egalitarianism; and western commercial elites saw women as a civilizing influence on raucous miners and lumbermen; Protestant nativism also played a role. Even so, there is enough evidence of grass-roots support for suffrage, for example in Colorado and California referenda, to offset the evidence of top-down social control.[77]

Perhaps the more encompassing view takes into account the tension in the women's movement between equality and difference. If woman was seen as man's equal partner in a common humanity, then the stress fell on *equal* suffrage. Both sexes were entitled to the same democratic rights and positions of power, no matter how rough the political game turned out to be. However, if woman was seen as the possessor of special feminine virtues, then the stress fell on *woman* suffrage. Instead of accepting the existing rules, woman would purify a system corrupted by smoke-filled rooms. While the former tended toward a democratic distribution of power, the latter was often in league with elite reformers. The struggle for suffrage contained the same paradox that ran through other aspects of the woman question. In asserting their full claim to humanity, the prophets of New Womanhood nonetheless spoke in a feminine voice.

That tension was exemplified by the career of the National Women's party. In its early prewar days, trade unionists, social reformers, and society dames all found a home in the party, which supported a broad range of progressive issues while raising the stakes in the suffrage fight through militant protest. Feminists could successfully hold the two elements—human equality and feminine interests—in harmonious tension, battling male dominance for the greater good of humanity.

What made that possible was the larger reform dynamic of the times. So long as conservatives were kept off balance by the upsurge of reform, the twin currents of feminism and socialism reinforced each other, and it was possible for someone like Mary White Ovington (one of the white founders of the National Association for the Advancement of Colored People) to say that feminism and socialism were "the two greatest movements of today."[78] However, in the early 1920s, when conservatives regained the initiative and reversed the dynamic of reform, it became much more difficult to pursue feminine self-interest and social equality at the same time and in the same organization. Indeed, the National Women's party abandoned its former associations to wage a legalistic, single-issue battle for constitutional reform. Even that was unsuccessful in the face of resurgent ideas about woman's special role as wife, mother, and standard-bearer of moral purity, all of which came to the fore in the 1920s in reaction against the flapper.

That only made the achievements of prewar feminists all the more significant. The battle between New Womanhood and Victorian womanhood revealed an important fissure in American society. The values by which America had been governed in the nineteenth century were no longer compelling in the twentieth. Together with corporate capitalists and industrial workers, the New Woman was one of the major social forces of the modern age.

3

The Social Question

GIVEN THE increasing momentum of the forces of change, sooner or later there had to be a reckoning with laissez-faire liberalism. In the years from the turn of the century to the First World War, known as the Progressive Era, changes seemed to come from all directions at once—mass production/mass reproduction, Catholic and Jewish immigration, the growing social weight of the industrial working class, and the movements of women and labor. Indeed, the United States was caught up in changes that were worldwide in scope. In the capitalist heartland of western Europe, bourgeois elites had lost the initiative to social movements based in the working class, and from the agrarian hinterlands of Russia, Mexico, and China, where imperialism had torn asunder traditional ruling structures, revolution was already breaking out.[1] After more than a century of unremitting conquests leading to the snug bosom of *la belle époque*, the middle classes had less and less reason for complacency.

To be sure, the United States was the last candidate for violent political upheaval. Its fundamental state structures were intact; conservative ruling myths—nationalism, male dominance, white supremacy—all remained potent; and, given the proverbial mobility and fluidity of American society, it was not likely to break apart along the fault line of class. All the same, there was no escaping the growing imbalance between the inherited governing system and the way the society actually worked, a condition that posed the "social question" and dictated that voices would be raised against the laissez-faire policies of the existing liberal state.

Toward Social Justice

The most influential voice was that of progressive social reform. Rejecting the individualism of the marketplace, a generation of reformers called for a new *social* consciousness. The profession of social work, whose very name captured the shift, came into its own around such distinguished practitioners as Jane Addams, while many intellectuals joined John Dewey in pragmatist revolt against the formalism of nineteenth-century philosophy. Church leaders listened attentively to the "social gospel" preached by Walter Rauschenbusch, and among historians, Frederick Jackson Turner portrayed industrial workers and finance capitalists as the decisive new "social forces in American history." Even the polite euphemisms "social disease" and "social hygiene" implied in a backhanded way a kind of collective consciousness. In these myriad ways, progressives argued that their society was in the grip of forces they could not control as individuals but might influence through "social control" or "social reform." Truly, progressive reformers were "social"-ists. Their answer to the social question focused on government regulation of predatory private interests for the sake of the public interest. Through a cross-class alliance aimed at remaking the liberal state, they hoped to restore social harmony without overturning the foundations of private property or family life.[2]

Socialism was an answer to the same question from the left. A sprawling, protean movement almost as diverse as the population itself, socialism could be found in abundance among New York's Jewish garment workers, German-American brewery workers in the Midwest, native-born Christians, and onetime Oklahoma populists. When men such as Morris Hillquit, Victor Berger, and Eugene Debs brought these groups together to form the Socialist party in 1901, it rapidly surpassed the Socialist Labor party of Daniel DeLeon—called "the Pope" because of his self-proclaimed infallibility on Marxist doctrine.[3] Socialists held top offices in a third of the unions affiliated with the American Federation of Labor, despite Samuel Gompers' best efforts to keep them out of power, and at its prewar peak upwards of 1,200 socialists held office on the local level. The popularity of municipal ownership, or "gas and water socialism," proved that the ideology was both *in* the world and *of* it, while nearly 1 million votes for the party's inspirational leader Eugene Debs proved that significant numbers of Americans would respond to the millennial call for a new day.[4]

Buoyed by these rising fortunes and tutored by the "economism" of the Second International, American socialists did not regard with alarm the trend toward concentrated ownership. To the contrary, they believed they would one day reap the harvest of socialized production unwittingly being sown by the giant trusts. At the same time, they did not hold back on the message of socialism as salvation, a theme that runs through Upton Sinclair's *The Jungle* (1906), the quintessential muckraking novel of human exploitation and redemption. In their attitudes toward family life, leaders such as Kate Richards O'Hare were almost Victorian, commonly citing women's paid labor and prostitution as twin evils that socialists would abolish, although there was no holding back in support for women's suffrage.[5] Their view of history as progress, a legacy of Enlightenment optimism, inclined them toward the gradual, parliamentary strategy for gaining collective ownership. Certainly, Yankee Protestant socialists such as Charles Edward Russell and William English Walling were quite comfortable in polite company and proposed a gradual parliamentary road to socialism.

Denouncing this approach as "slow-cialism," anarcho-syndicalists in the Industrial Workers of the World called for workers' ownership and control of the means of production and proposed a general strike as the way to get it. Attuned to the cultural diversity of the American working class, Wobblies fought ethnic prejudice within the ranks and, unlike the AFL, went out of their way to organize both Afro-Americans and whites.[6] Meanwhile, anarchists such as Emma Goldman and, for a brief time, Margaret Sanger waged war on the sexual conventions of bourgeois marriage through journals such as the *Woman Rebel*. Such radical egalitarians counterposed brotherhood and sisterhood to masculine competition, collective ownership to class division, ethnic toleration to Social Darwinism, common frankness to bourgeois hypocrisy, utopian harmony to the contradictions of corporate capitalism. Like antebellum American communitarians, left-wing Jacobins of the French Revolution, and the Levellers of the English Revolution, they were mortal enemies of the system that had produced them and represented thoroughgoing opposition to the liberal governing system.

The left influenced progressives by both positive and negative example. Before the Great War, there was an open boundary between socialism and progressivism, and the list of people who straddled, crossed, and sometimes recrossed the line is long and impressive, including Florence Kelley, Robert Hunter, Walter Weyl, and Walter Lippmann. Their writings graced the pages of such leading journals of opinion as *The Survey* and the *New Republic*. Equally important as stealing socialist thunder, however, was progressive determination to dam up the socialist current behind moderate reforms. The Wisconsin labor economist John Commons worked hand in glove with Milwaukee socialists on specific legislative measures but devoted his career to refuting the class struggle and finding a place within the capitalist marketplace for collective bargaining. Herbert Croly's *The Promise of American Life* (1909) spelled out how socialism could be defeated by a new Hamiltonian nationalism that would interpose "the public" between organized capital and organized labor, stabilizing social hierarchy under the values of Jeffersonian democracy. In a higher register, philosophers such as John Dewey groped for a middle way between anarchic liberalism and state socialism.[7] In both the positive and negative sense, it was true to say: no socialism, no progressivism.

Especially when attention focused on family life and social reproduction, middle-class reformers presumed to speak for the working poor to the country at large. Social workers such as Mary McDowell drew attention to the slum conditions in Chicago's meatpacking district "back of the yards" and in countless hours of painstaking testimony to government commissions made the case for improving housing, reducing hours, compensating injured workers, and otherwise improving conditions to "conserve the home."[8] The "helping professions" showed a more sympathetic attitude toward disorderly families than had been common in the nineteenth century, when youthful criminals had been sent off to juvenile reformatories under the strict regimen of a stern warden. Instead, beginning in Illinois in 1899, reformers established juvenile courts, whose purpose was to help families control incorrigible children through supervised probation rather than incarceration. By 1930, forty-six states had such courts. Judge Ben Lindsey of Denver spoke for progressive criminologists in arguing that since crime had social causes, juvenile rehabilitation depended on ending the abuses of child labor, unemployment, and poverty, and this, in turn, depended on defeating "the big businessmen who commercialized political parties."[9] The pride of reform organizations was Florence Kelley's National Consumers League. A translator of Engels and a closet socialist, Kelley was an indefatigable crusader against the twelve-hour day in the steel mills, child labor in textile mills, and starvation wages for women homeworkers—the same outrages indelibly imprinted in Louis Hine's social-protest photographs.[10]

The prominence of women such as Addams and Kelley on the

battlements of reform was no accident. For all the glorification of domesticity in the nineteenth century, women were seen as performing vital public functions in church and school as guardians of respectability and sexual virtue. With the discovery of the realm of "the social," women reformers merely extended the boundaries of women's sphere to the realm of "social housekeeping."[11] They also carried over many conventional norms of gender ideology, particularly in arguing for protective legislation to shield women and children from abuse in the marketplace. Arguing for shorter hours and prohibition of night work, they invoked the special needs of woman as "the mother of the race" and portrayed women and children as vulnerable to greedy male predators. This ideological set piece reprised the standard nineteenth-century paired opposites of corrupt masculine commerce and virtuous feminine domesticity.

Thus women reformers pinned themselves on the horns of a dilemma. On the one hand, they brazenly violated the canons of "true" womanhood by marching into the public domain to run settlements, battle corrupt party bosses, and contend with male legislators in the proverbial smoke-filled rooms. But on the other, they accepted much of the prevailing family ideology, glorified motherhood, and argued that women's virtue would purify male corruption. The same contradiction ran through the campaign for women's suffrage and would bedevil twentieth-century feminism. The division was not between men and women, since most reformers of both sexes accepted the same assumptions about gender, but between the emerging values of equality between the sexes and the powerful conservative undertow of woman's special nature. Unwilling to make the kind of radical break with the past of the sort proposed by bohemian sex radicals and Wobblies, they were unable to resolve the dilemma.

A similar trap awaited reformers in the area of protective legislation. Responding to the very real exploitation of the most vulnerable denizens of the labor market, the National Child Labor Committee campaigned for protection from abusive parents and heartless employers, just as the National Consumers League worked toward regulation of women's hours and conditions. The American Federation of Labor also supported state regulation of the labor market for those supposedly at the margins—women, children, and "greenhorn" immigrants—although the AFL resolutely opposed regulation of men's hours and wages through fear that the antiunionism of the state would creep in. All these organizations accepted the ideal of the "family wage," or suf-

ficient income for a man to keep his wife and children out of the bruising world of work. Although most employers paid only lip service to
the ideal, Henry Ford paid some of his employees five dollars a day,
and made headlines doing so. Ford aside, as the air grew thick with
demands for government regulation, the argument was that the weaker
members of society needed protection from the strong.[12]

The argument for protective legislation was not always grounded on
women's weakness. Members of the Women's Trade Union League argued, instead, on the universal ground of justice for all wage earners:
first women, then men. And the famous "Brandeis brief" in *Muller v.
Oregon* (1908), written largely by Josephine Goldmark and the most
advanced example of sociological jurisprudence of the day, argued in
favor of recognizing biological difference without condoning the canard
of "the weaker sex." All the same, when the state adjudicated these
claims of the weak against the strong, it rejected more egalitarian demands in favor of reforms that underwrote inequality. In *Muller*, for
example, the Supreme Court was aghast at the tales of reproductive
horror resulting from overwork, including sterility, prolapsed uterus,
leucorrhea, fatigue leading to premature delivery, high infant mortality,
and congenital deformations. It held that the mothers of the race
needed paternalist protection: "her physical structure and a proper dis-
charge of her maternal functions—having in view not merely her own
health, but the well-being of the race—justify legislation to protect her
from the greed as well as the passion of man." The same pernicious
dyad—man as greedy and passionate, woman as eternal victim—
played a similar role in the Court's decision (later overturned) to uphold
a minimum wage for women.[13]

Progressive social reform gave birth to an infant welfare state. From
a mix of humanitarian and paternalist motives, a rash of states started
paying "mothers' pensions" beginning in 1910. Under nineteenth-
century poor relief, a widowed mother unable to support dependent
and neglected children had them sent to foster homes or orphanages.
This was thought to be a better solution than providing cash (outdoor
relief), which an official of New York's Charity Organization Society
deemed "the entering wedge towards State socialism." Now, however,
a 1909 White House conference on dependent children glorified the
home as "the highest and finest product of civilization," and soon states
began providing modest cash grants to permit fatherless children to
remain home.[14]

In a related innovation, northern states raced one another to enact workmen's compensation. Between 1911 and 1913, with Wisconsin taking the lead, twenty-one states set up various contributory insurance plans to provide a small income in cases of injury to the main breadwinner. In doing so they replaced the old "fellow servant" doctrine, which had placed the main liability for injury on the employee but at the same time had exposed employers to annoying litigation in the form of negligence claims.[15] At the federal level, Congress created new bureaucracies to look out for dependent members of society, including the Children's Bureau and later the Women's Bureau. These new federal bureaus cooperated with the Labor Department (raised to cabinet status in 1913) to conduct hundreds of well-publicized social investigations of child labor, factory conditions, industrial fatigue, and family budgets. Typical of the progressive approach to reform, the countless pages of scrupulously documented facts were supposed to mobilize public opinion for a scientific attack on social problems that required little government money or coercion.[16]

That was about as far as the welfare state got in the Progressive Era. By comparison with social insurance in Germany, these baby steps were a halting, penurious, and wholly inadequate response to the "social question." Despite pressure from the American Association for Labor Legislation, a well-connected reform lobby, for health insurance as "the next great step" after workmen's compensation, nothing was done on this front. The same was true of old-age pensions; all the lobbying by such groups as the AFL and the fraternal order of Eagles went for naught. The reasons had to do with the unusual hostility of American elites toward state intervention. True, there was widespread distrust of big government in many quarters, not excepting the AFL. But the decisive opposition to the welfare state came from an alliance of elites—northern businessmen, patricians, and southern merchant-planters (except, of course, when there was a direct benefit, as in the tariff or river projects). Unlike their European and especially German counterparts, they feared that state welfare would fall into the hands of democratic forces—in their view, raving demagogues and corrupt machines; and so, relying heavily on the institutional impediments of American federalism and the separation of powers, they invoked the ideology of states' rights and laissez faire to exercise a powerful check on reform.[17] Nevertheless, they could not stop every move toward state responsibility for private welfare, and the foundations had been laid for future expansion. Neither the interregional alliance among elites nor the alliance of working- and middle-class reformers had things entirely its own way.

If class is a fluid relationship, not a fixed group lined up in ranks and files ready to march off into history, then it is liable to take a variety of conscious forms. Consciousness was the result not only of the vertical antagonisms between workers and their employers, but also of the relations—both conflicts and liaisons—between workers and the middle classes. The love-hate relationship between progressive "social"-ists and true socialists depended on a cross-class alliance around the various issues comprising social reform. This common front was not the product of mimetic workers who absorbed middle-class consciousness or exhibited "false consciousness" of their true interests. Rather, it was a kind of consciousness in which workers' aspirations were no less important than middle-class aims in defining social justice. The United States was unusually fertile ground for such movements because, historically, class boundaries were so ill defined. No doubt the very possibility of engaging in a drawn-out process of reform co-opted many workers away from class struggle and collective ownership; no doubt, too, it legitimated the liberal state with all its built-in safeguards for capitalist property. In any event, through the alchemy of American politics, what would have been socialism elsewhere was largely transubstantiated into progressivism in the United States. It can be debated whether that changed gold into lead, or the other way around, but the fact was that wage earners, professionals, and urban smallholders found common ground in pursuit of "social justice." As Cleveland reformer Frederick C. Howe put it, "On the one side were men of property and influence; on the other the politicians, immigrants, workers, and persons of small means."[18] It was a loose shambles of an alliance, but it captured the political initiative down to America's entry into the Great War.

Toward Hegemony:
Imperialism and the New Nationalism

While the movement for social justice shifted power downward, imperialism and a renewed spirit of nationalism, close companions in the years of Theodore Roosevelt and William Howard Taft, had the opposite effect of shoring up the hegemony of governing elites. Unlike the great powers of Europe, the United States was an awkward competitor in the race for empire, because Americans felt compelled to justify their power over other peoples in terms of a democratic mission. No doubt America's new imperial proconsuls and expansionist ideologues were sincere in their intention to bring the blessings of liberty to peoples they regarded as benighted, feeling no contradiction in the notion that theirs was an imperialism to end all imperialisms. But just as Americans projected their egalitarian traditions overseas, so they also projected the hierarchical assumptions of Social Darwinism and white supremacy to justify taking the Philippines and other spoils of the Spanish-American War.

This Janus-faced foreign policy—one half looking to self-government, the other half to U.S. hegemony—had its counterpart in attitudes toward the large foreign-born population living in the United States. Masses of immigrants from the agrarian hinterlands of southern and eastern Europe had been uprooted by the same capitalist relations that were penetrating to the far-flung markets of Latin America and Asia.[19] Torn free from their age-old moorings, they were sent reeling to Milan, Warsaw, and Hamburg, and thence across the Atlantic to Ellis Island. Earlier waves of immigrants had already elbowed aside the cream of America's old families, the great names that had once inspired rapt devotion—Adams, Lowell, Livingston. And now Yankee Protestant elites worried that Old World peasants once-removed lacked proper respect for Anglo-Saxon traditions of self-government. If America's immigrants were the domestic counterparts of colonial subjects, what did the future have in store for liberal self-government?

Between the Spanish-American War and the onset of the First World War, the United States expanded its influence in Asia and established uncontested hegemony in the Western Hemisphere. Expansion overseas was inextricably tied to the rise of corporate capitalism. From one side, there was an escalating demand for raw materials and foodstuffs to feed and clothe the American population; from the other, the new techniques of mass production generated a plethora of commodities that required overseas outlets. Converting traditional cultures in Latin America to modern consumer ones required the spread of money economy, banking, mass communications, and, indeed, the culture of mass consumption. U.S. investments in what became known as the Third World started smaller and grew faster than anywhere else: sixfold in the Caribbean, ninefold in South America, tenfold in Asia, compared with fourfold in Europe and Canada. To be sure, the driving force was the search for profits in raw materials, commodity markets, and capital investments, but to abstract "the economy" from the larger way of life is to fetishize commodities. To make money, it was also necessary to spread the American dream.[20]

Part of the expansionist impulse derived from the ideology of Social Darwinism. All the so-called realists of foreign policy thought in terms of a worldwide struggle among races for survival of the fittest—from Brooks Adams brooding on the decay of the West to Admiral Alfred Thayer Mahan devising a global strategy of naval warfare, they believed in a hierarchy of races ascending from primitive Africans, barbaric Chinese, and backward Latins, through the barbarous Slavs, fickle French, and sturdy Germans, finally reaching the apex of fully civilized Anglo-Saxons. The sense of being destined to rule the world did not promote quiescence among these Darwinian imperialists but restless activity, because it gave them hope that if they struggled they were certain to prevail, a motivation akin to the attitude of Puritans toward Indians, communists toward capitalists, and other chosen peoples toward their adversaries. Thus they could not rest until they had gained control of Mahan's strategic naval chokepoints and won the economic competition of the Open Door.[21]

No small part in the struggle for supremacy was the "warfare of the cradle." Darwinists believed that the "lower races" were the more prolific, sending their surplus progeny swarming across the Atlantic to the North American domain of the Anglo-Saxon. No less a figure than President Roosevelt raised an alarm about "race suicide," a battle cry to rally Anglo-Saxon mothers to fill their cradles, lest leadership of the white race pass to the Germans and Slavs. These notions were deeply ingrained in the elite coterie of foreign policymakers that included John Hay, McKinley's secretary of state, and Elihu Root, Taft's secretary of war. Imperialism was not all markets and gunboats, but also a global biological struggle.[22]

When an assassin's bullet felled McKinley and elevated Theodore Roosevelt to the presidency in 1901, the pugilist/cowboy/Rough Rider had a chance to put these reproductive theories to work. Roosevelt's personal psychology—his obsessive preoccupation with spears, guns, and masculinity—went hand in hand with his phallic "Big Stick" diplomacy in Latin America. With Cuba safely subjugated under the Platt Amendment (1902), Roosevelt enlarged the American sphere of influence by supporting a revolt in Panama with troops, bribes, and hasty recognition of the new, pro-American regime. The pugnacious president boasted simply: "I took the Canal Zone." Later, in a dispute over collection of customs in Santo Domingo, Roosevelt added his famous corollary to the Monroe Doctrine, under which the U.S. would exercise "an international police power" whenever circumstances led to "chronic wrong-doing or an impotence which results in a general loosening of the ties of civilized society."[23] In playing the paternalist Uncle Sam, Roosevelt well represented the interests and worldview of the corporate elite, to whom the first test of civilized behavior was prompt payment of interest, and the second was having the right ancestors. Money, blood, and power went hand in hand to make Caribbean and Central American republics into U.S. protectorates.

There was to be no such American hegemony in Asia, however. Possession of the Philippines did not make the Pacific an American lake, nor did ritual insistence on the Open Door in China succeed in giving U.S. investors a large share of the China market or in keeping the great powers at bay. That was plain in the peace settlement at the end of the Russo-Japanese War (1905); Roosevelt's mediation did not prevent the victorious Japanese from grabbing a chunk of Chinese real estate formerly controlled by the Russians, despite a pro forma reaffirmation of the Open Door. Roosevelt's healthy respect for Japanese prowess in the manly art of war overrode his racial prejudice, and in return for Japanese acceptance of U.S. control of the Philippines, he recognized Japanese "suzerainty" over Korea. He also rebuked the "idiots of the California legislature" for enacting anti-Japanese laws that gave insult to a needed friend, and tried to smooth injured Japanese feelings with a so-called Gentlemen's Agreement, by which Japan promised to restrict emigration to the United States. But Roosevelt was no more above using racism in power politics than Kaiser Wilhelm, with whom he competed in warnings about the "Yellow Peril." In fact, once he had completed his negotiations with Japan, he promptly sent an American fleet on a world cruise mainly to impress the Japanese "that there were fleets of the White races which were totally different from the fleet of poor Rodjestvensky" (the defeated Russian admiral).[24]

With the election of William Howard Taft in 1908, the tenor of U.S. policy changed, but not the substance. Taft and his secretary of state, Philander Knox, are known for having practiced "dollar diplomacy," a kind of vulgar liberalism for underdeveloped countries. Indeed, they supported the efforts of U.S. bankers in China to corral an equal share

of the proceeds of railroad and other concessions to the point of allowing China's nearest predators, Russia and Japan, in on the spoils, a mistake that contributed to the 1911 Chinese revolution against the ineffectual Manchu dynasty. Likewise, in Latin America, where dollar
diplomats had a freer hand, Taft did not hesitate to send in the marines
when U.S. investments seemed in jeopardy, as in Nicaragua in 1912.
Having been governor-general of the Philippines, he firmly adhered to
the Social Darwinist tenets of rule by the Anglo-Saxon races. Handpicked by Roosevelt to carry on his work, he frequently intervened in
Latin America and strengthened the paternalist assumptions of the
Roosevelt corollary.[25]

U.S. entry into the big-power game inevitably had consequences for
the governing system at home. The same White Man's Burden projected upon Chinese and Filipinos overseas also applied to Asian-
Americans and African-Americans. The same consular and business
emissaries who doubted that Asian and Latin American peasants were
capable of self-government also had their doubts about immigrant
workers coming to the United States. Race consciousness pervaded the
elite, from New York Republican patricians such as Teddy Roosevelt
to southern-bred Democrats such as Woodrow Wilson; never mind the
fact that the American branch of the Anglo-Saxon "race" crumbled at
first touch into Welsh coal miners, Cornish tin miners, Scotch-Irish
farmers, plus true-blue Englishmen.[26]

The concept of race gained added credence from the new "science"
of eugenics. Using distorted ideas of Darwinian evolution and Mende-
lian genetics, eugenics proposed to do for human beings what the
American Breeders Association had done for livestock: build better
germplasm through selective breeding. It attracted a large number of
eastern bluestockings whose three-name signatures—Henry Fairchild
Osborne, Henry Pratt Fairchild—attested to the interweaving of pedigreed family lines. Their earliest legislative triumphs were the immigration statutes of 1903 and 1907, which denied entry to defectives of
the mental and political kind—the insane, the feebleminded, and anarchists. With the nation immunized against the virus of genetic pollution from abroad, a dozen northern states soon enacted laws authoriz-
ing public officials to sterilize the feebleminded. Although courts
recognized the danger of abuse and few sterilizations were actually performed, eugenics had a wide ideological impact through popular magazines and college textbooks, which issued ominous warnings: "From

the rate at which immigrants are increasing, it is obvious that our very life blood is at stake."[27]

In the decade before the First World War, an average of almost 1 million newcomers arrived each year, roughly 70 percent of them from southern and eastern Europe, adding new patches of color to the crazy-quilt of American culture. Ethnic neighborhoods such as the Jewish Lower East Side and various Little Italies and Polonias, dotting the country from Boston to San Francisco and rich in Old World sights and smells, were the most visible signs of separate cultural identity. In addition, peasant migrants such as the *contadini* from Italy's Mezzogiorno transplanted in modified form their code of family honor and other patriarchal traditions ranging from the Holy Father to the godfather and stubbornly maintained cultural continuity through ethnic endogamy in the second generation.[28]

Another sign of continuity was parochial education. Not only did a large proportion of Catholic children attend parochial schools, but most of these little citadels of tradition were key parts of the ethnic community, as in Chicago, where a majority of Catholic pupils attended ethnically separate schools. Among groups such as the Poles that were riven by factional rivalry between secular nationalists and clerical leaders, the parish school was one thing both sides could agree on. The reasons were clearly summed up by *Dziennik Zwiazkowy*, a Polish newspaper which argued that knowledge of the Polish language, literature, and history "will be a shield against loss of our national identity and submergence in the boundless sea of Americanism."[29]

The irony of immigrant nationalism was that it was an American invention. In fact, since nationalism was a modern phenomenon, immigrants had to make up national "traditions" as they went along. Polish nationalists were trying desperately to find a homogeneous culture upon which to construct an independent nation, but emigrants from the Congress Kingdom not far removed from serfdom adjusted to urban America differently from longtime denizens of Warsaw and Łodz. Initially, *paisano* did not necessarily mean a fellow Italian but a countryman from Lombardy, Sicily, or the Abruzzi. When Russian Jews began arriving in America, many resident German Jews would have nothing to do with them. In each case, a new basis for tradition had to be invented. Behind the shield of modern nationalism were the elements of parochialism, as embodied in patriarchal values, Old World kinship, the Catholic church, and the Jewish synagogue. Parochialism ran counter to the forces of mass reproduction and bolstered tradition against the buffeting individualism of the American marketplace.[30]

That was exactly the reason Yankee Protestant elites took offense at this carnival of immigrant customs. They realized they could not exercise cultural leadership over people who were Catholic or Jewish, who had no compunctions about alcohol, and many of whom did not even speak English. Instead of supporting "good government," they were likely to fall in with the ethnic political machines, once the mortal enemy of Gilded Age liberals, now the nemesis of their Yankee Protestant descendants. In their overheated imaginations, they saw barbarians at the gates. One prohibitionist editor warned that human waves from "besodden Europe" had already toppled the republic:

> with all their un-American and anti-American ideas of morality and government; they are absorbed into our national life, but not assimilated; with no liberty whence they came, they demand unrestricted liberty among us, even to license for the things we loathe; and through the ballot-box, flung wide open to them by foolish statesmanship that covets power, their foreign control or conquest has become largely an appalling fact.[31]

Yankee Protestants also scared themselves with lurid fantasies of immigrant sexual practices. In the moral cosmology of Yankee Protestants, the very admixture of nationalities was a kind of pollution, and even some Wasps who sympathized with the plight of the poor were viscerally revolted by what they could not help but see as sexually promiscuous mingling of peoples. The progressive author of *Poverty* wrote: "In our American cities Negroes, Whites, Chinese, Mexicans, Half-breeds, Americans, Irish, and others are indiscriminately housed together in the same tenements and even in the same rooms."[32] These poor immigrant districts were seen as breeding grounds of all manner of vice—saloons, gambling dens, nickelodeons, dance halls, and other dangerous resorts of sexual congress.

Nativism was the irrational outgrowth of these irrational anxieties. Anglo-Saxons coexisted in uneasy alliance with older immigrant groups from Germany, Ireland, and Scandinavia under the rising banner of nativism. The boundary line of "true" Americanism ran between native and foreigner, and more precisely, between the "old" immigration from northern and western Europe and the "new" from southern and eastern Europe. That distinction gained wide currency as a result of Vermont Senator William Dillingham's well-publicized hearings on immigration, which were billed as an impartial, scientific investigation of the "problem" of immigration but which produced the famous Dillingham Report, a forty-one-volume manifesto for restricting the new immigration. Critics were quick to complain of the aspersion cast upon recent arrivals, but soon Congress attempted to add illiterates (those unable to read and write in any language) to the list of excluded aliens, although it would take the atmosphere of war in 1917 to generate enough votes to pass the Literacy Act over President Wilson's veto.[33]

In theory, nativism was an ideology of native solidarity against the 15 percent of the population who were foreign born. But in reality the nativist alliance contained a cartload of contradictions. Many of the old immigrants who had grown up in German or Norwegian households felt their parents' nationality pulling against assimilation to Anglo-Saxon norms, and class hostility divided Irish Catholic hod carriers from Boston brahmin bankers. In the face of such cultural tensions, nativism was not likely to become the kind of cohesive ruling ideology in the North that white supremacy was in the South.

Drink was another prime fault line in the nativist alliance. Urban members of the Anti-Saloon League and legions of rural teetotalers were every bit as alarmed about German and Irish beer-swilling as they were about the "new" immigration. In fact, much of the alarm about the "foreign conquest" of America rested on the centrality of liquor as a symbol of evil in American Protestantism. To partisans of "old-time religion" such as revivalist preacher Billy Sunday and the Women's Christian Temperance Union, succumbing to the wiles of "Satan in a bottle" was a sign of the fall from grace, just as surely as total abstinence was proof of being "a good Christian." A prohibitionist congressman in full cry before the galleries denounced liquor dealers as "the parasites that clothe themselves in the proceeds of women's shame, the inhuman ones that bathe themselves in the tears of little children, the wastrels who wreck and ruin material things while they contaminate childhood, debauch youth, and crush manhood."[34]

The belief in a pernicious link between commerce and vice came to the fore in the middle-class, Yankee Protestant encounter with the city. Despite the dominance of urban commerce in American life, or perhaps because of it, Puritan and Jeffersonian hostility to the city had made commercial vice a perennial issue. There was nothing new in moral revulsion against what Lincoln Steffens called "the shame of the cities," and there were plenty of nineteenth-century precedents for the shocking exposés of corruption that filled the pages of journals such as *McClure's* and *Outlook*.[35] As always, old-time Protestants thrilled to the stock tales of saloon keepers and party bosses fattening on the profits of sin, and nativists fumed again, as they had in the 1850s, about alien ways overwhelming true Americanism.

The temperance crusade was given a new twist, however, by progressive social engineers. Instead of an eternal battle between God and Satan for possession of the individual soul, they envisioned a battle between urban corruption and civic virtue. When it came to the crusade against drink, instead of blaming inebriation on the demon rum and staging revival meetings and street parades to beat the devil, they blamed it on "commercialized vice" and conducted sober surveys to expose the social underpinnings of evil through a spate of urban vice commissions. Through careful social engineering, they believed, it would be possible to replace the corrupt nexus of real estate interests, traction magnates, ward bosses, and public officials united by the bonds of greed and power with a new nexus of civic virtue. Though outwardly secular, they cannot be understood apart from their Protestant heritage. Although they cut the sacramental heart out of religion and replaced it with the authority of science, they retained such Protestant moral values as temperance and self-control in secular form. They took *Pilgrim's Progress*, the Puritan exemplary tale of individual regeneration, and translated it into progress for society as a whole through social regeneration.[36]

Whatever moral impulses were on the loose, urban elites bent them to their own interests. In city after city, civic leaders connected with the chamber of commerce and exclusive social clubs turned corruption scandals to their own advantage in their running battle against immigrant-based political machines. With a large segment of the native-born middle class in tow, they set out to take control away from the ward bosses by implementing "good government," defined as at-large elections, city managers, and reform commissions, all of which were supposed to put urban administration on a businesslike basis, susceptible to the expert advice of college-educated professionals. Frequently, it came down to a battle for control of the police. Big-city cops were part of the urban underworld they policed. In an environment of rackets, shakedowns, and strong-arm tactics, they ran legalized rackets of their own. They did not attempt the impossible task of eradicating crime, but instead tried to regulate it through raids and shakedowns targeted at brothel keepers and loan sharks who had fallen out of favor with the machine. Unhappy with this spectacle, urban patricians resolved to smash party bosses and police corruption on the anvil of civic righteousness. They established nonpartisan crime commissions and introduced scientific police methods such as fingerprinting and espionage. Together with the Society for the Suppression of Vice and similar legions of decency, to which they lent their prestige and money, they made middle-class moralism the servant of elite power.[37]

The most potent ideology of all was nationalism. Whereas nativism was crippled by its lack of cohesion, nationalism had a broad, simple sweep. The spirit of nationalism had celebrated the rise of the American nation-state every step of the way from the War of Independence through the triumph of the Union to the burst of imperialism in the 1890s. As class conflict (strikes, trade unions) and ideologies of class (socialism, syndicalism) intensified in the early twentieth century, a new nationalism arose. One sign was the popularity of the word *national* in the names of organizations founded around the turn of the century—National Association of Manufacturers, National Child Labor Committee, National Consumers League, National Women's Trade Union League, National Association for the Advancement of Colored People . . . the list went on and on.

The perfect embodiment of what Herbert Croly in *The Promise of American Life* (1909) dubbed the "new nationalism" was the National Civic Federation. The aim of the NCF was to combat class ideologies by bringing together the likes of J. P. Morgan and Samuel Gompers through the mediation of social engineers such as Ralph Easly in a tripartite structure of capital, labor, and the public that would bargain as corporate entities to resolve their differences peaceably within the overarching solidarity of the nation. What was new about this nationalist explosion was that in every case, the new organizations proposed to ride herd on social forces, so that America's destiny would no longer be the haphazard result of inchoate forces such as Manifest Destiny, the westward movement of the frontier, or the "unseen hand" of the free market. Instead, destiny would be in the hands of social organizations that were conscious and purposive expressions of human will.[38]

The Americanization movement was an important component of the new nationalism. Fearing that American identity was being "balkanized," Americanizers proposed a rigorous program of immigrant assimilation, in contrast to the exclusionary plans of the nativists. "Nativism is no substitute for Americanism," wrote Frances Kellor, head of the National Americanization Committee, which spearheaded the drive for Americanization after 1914 in cooperation with Roosevelt and Croly. Addressing the problem of industrial discontent, Kellor blamed disorder on radical agitators appealing to "un-Americanized" immigrants in their own languages and warned that the country would be racked by violence until it Americanized them: "The road to American citizenship, to the English language, and an understanding of American social and political ideals is the road to industrial peace." A number of big employers, including International Harvester and U.S. Steel, adopted Americanization plans, and Henry Ford staged Americanization pageants around a giant melting pot into which workers dressed in Old World costume descended and out of which they marched dressed as ready-made Yankees carrying Old Glory and supposedly brimming with loyalty to the captains of industry.[39]

Americanization received support for a variety of motives. Wealthy donors such as Mrs. E. H. Harriman, Felix Warburg, and T. Coleman du Pont, president of the National Americanization Committee, no doubt sought to shore up the status of old money. Besides, insofar as nationalism prevailed over class consciousness, they could have their cake of cheap immigrant labor and eat it too. It also appealed to social engineers and scientific managers—Herbert Croly and Walter Lippmann joined the committee—because it promised industrial efficiency by boosting the skills and morale of immigrant workers. Provided they proved their absolute loyalty to the United States, these newcomers might even be enlisted in the global "warfare of the cradle." President Roosevelt was groping toward a larger purpose than mere nativism when he told the National Congress of Mothers that a woman's duty to bear children for the nation was no less than the soldier's duty to defend it.[40]

Nationalism was intimately linked to America's overseas expansion. Certainly in Roosevelt's case, the militant and martial spirit of the new nationalism provided the link between progressivism and imperialism.[41] Teaching "chronic wrong-doers" how to behave involved imparting the national virtues of the United States, which, not surprisingly, the Yankee Protestant policymaking elite took to be their own values: free enterprise, Darwinian hierarchy, and self-government. After the defeat of the anti-imperialist opponents of the Spanish-American War, only a handful of dissidents were on hand to point out the contradiction—that imposing self-government upon an unwilling people was a contradiction in terms. That lack of self-examination, in turn, left the United States ill prepared to deal with the two major challenges it was about to face, one from the revolutionary hurricane sweeping through Mexico, China, and Russia and the other from great-power politics at the outbreak of the world war.

The new nationalism had much to contribute to a new mythos of national identity in a society divided by class and race. Unlike nativism, it did not exclude the new immigrants; unlike Anglo-Saxon race consciousness, it did not stigmatize the half of the population that was not of British ancestry. If hegemony in capitalist democracy required elites to win consent from subordinate groups, then the purely rational test of loyalty to the republic was the most likely to win broad popular consent. And to the extent that working people gave their loyalty to the state, it could be said that they consented to their own subordination. That was the beauty of nationalism. It presented itself not as class consciousness, but as the opposite; not as the consciousness of the dominant class, but as all-class consciousness. It was the perfect answer to the socialist ideology of class conflict, the ideal mask for dominant interests.

The South as Counterweight

The South felt the same social forces remaking the nation at large, but not in the same way. Even as cities grew and corporate capital expanded, southern traditions left their distinctive mark. For instance, agrarian paternalism guaranteed that the hold of family authority would be greater than in the North. Although southern birthrates were declining, particularly in urban areas, the South was at the tail end of the demographic transition. In the South Atlantic states, for example, as late as 1930 there were 593 children under five years of age per 1,000 white women of childbearing age, a high rate that had not been known in the Middle Atlantic states for some four decades. In addition, the existence of a large servant class made up mostly of black women recalled the old master-servant bond. Although domestic service was in decline everywhere, southern cities had three times the proportion of servants as northern. Life in Atlanta and Birmingham was not merely life in New York and Pittsburgh plus magnolias and mint juleps.[42]

Race was still the anchor of the southern way of life. Occupation and sex were closely linked to race, as evidenced by the fact that African-Americans accounted for upward of four-fifths of southern servants. The genteel matrons of Atlanta's Peach Tree Street escaped the traditional burdens of household labor by employing lower-class women. But southern lower-class women were also divided by race, and although many white women of the working class experienced the dependency of wage labor, few also worked in another woman's kitchen; some even used race to escape some of the burdens of their class by hiring black washerwomen. Constrained by the triple subordination of poverty, sex, and race, black women were no longer slaves, nor were they yet free, and their experience was a harsh commentary on the southern way of life.[43]

This knot of gender, blood, and property underlay the white South's obsession with so-called race purity. Well into the twentieth century, the white Southern lady was chained to her pedestal, an object of chivalrous worship by her gentlemen protectors. Her maidenhead and marital fidelity were the very foundations of the social order, to be protected from the supposed advances of black men. At the opposite extreme were the fleshpots of Memphis and New Orleans, the object of moral condemnation by Presbyterian elites and Baptist fundamentalists alike. The lower-class saloon came in for heavy criticism because it broke all the taboos at once on sex across racial and class boundaries.

> The saloon is a place of rendezvous for all classes of the low and vulgar, a resort for degraded whites and their more degraded negro associates, the lounging place for adulterers, lewd women, the favorite haunt of gamblers, drunkards and criminals. Both blacks and whites mix and mingle together as a mass of degraded humanity in this cesspool of iniquity. Here we have the worst form of social equality, but I am glad to know that it is altogether among the more worthless of both races.

Whereas in the North the crusade against the saloon was couched in terms of commercialized vice, in the South it was couched in terms of race purity. In fact, it was the South that placed Prohibition on the national agenda in 1907 when a Georgia law kicked off the national drive that culminated in the Eighteenth Amendment.[44]

This white fear of lower-class sexuality was not merely a projection of repressed libido. Southern folklife was just then giving birth to jazz, a decidedly sensual revolt against Victorian propriety that remained America's most distinctive contribution to music until the arrival of rock and roll, another largely southern contribution. The main sources of jazz were Afro-American—the heavy emotional strains of the blues and the lighter rhythms of ragtime—but in the uniquely rich confluence of New Orleans, it also drew from French quadrilles, Spanish rhythms, and old-fashioned marches. Respectable recording artists such as W. C. Handy, "the father of the blues," drew their inspiration from the likes of Jelly Roll Morton and from lyrics loaded with double-entendre—"If You Don't Like my Potatoes, Daddy, Why Do You Dig So Deep?" It would not be long before jazz and blues traveled up the Mississippi to reach white audiences through Louis Armstrong's flaming trumpet and Harlem nightclubs.

The gap between the doctrine of race purity and the fact of race mixing in such tenderloin districts as New Orleans' Storyville and the Memphis Levee made hypocrisy the stock in trade of white moralists and politicians.[45] Nevertheless, so long as race purity held sway, the mere hint of premarital dalliance between a black man and a white woman, not to mention interracial marriage, was enough to raise a lynch mob. For instance, rumors of sexual assaults upon white women triggered the Atlanta race riot of 1906. Newspapers and politicians inflamed the climate of racial hatred, and progressive Governor Hoke Smith and ex-Populist Tom Watson united as champions of the Anglo-Saxon in a tough electoral campaign, for which a plague of rapes was a convenient invention.[46]

Race purity deeply affected southern industry, even as paternalism went into slow decline. In the face of the presumptive equality of all white people, paternalism had justified the subordination of white male wage earners, offered "protection" to white women as they mingled with men outside their own families, and was certainly consistent with the family system that continued through the First World War, under which family life was incorporated into the world of the cotton mill.[47] However, paternalism did not work well in the biracial setting typical of most southern industry. In fact, every industry except textiles hired Afro-Americans in significant numbers—a majority in tobacco, about half in lumber mills, half in iron and steel works, and about a quarter in railroads. The trouble was that the mingling of the two races at the same work site confounded paternalism. If all employees were dependents of the owner—in a symbolic sense his "children"—then theoret-

Table 3.1 Composition of occupations (male) in selected southern industries, 1910–1930 (%)

Occupation	1910 Black	1910 Native white	1920 Black	1920 Native white	1930 Black	1930 Native white
Proprietors						
Managers and superintendents[a]	.9	93.6	—	89.3	—	96.2
Manufacturers, officials[a]	4.1	83.2	.6	85.2	2.2	93.4
Mine managers[a]	n.a.	n.a.	—	84.2	n.a.	n.a.
Rail officials and superintendents[b]	—	75.9	—	79.0	—	96.4
Operatives and semiskilled						
Blast furnace, rolling mill[a]	45.3	40.4	49.3	46.0	38.0	59.1
Saw mill[c]	41.2	51.2	36.3	38.4	41.2	58.4
Coal operative[a]	53.9	37.3	53.8	41.5	53.2	45.3
Laborers						
Blast furnace, rolling mill[a]	78.8	11.2	83.9	11.9	81.3	17.4
Saw mill[c]	64.3	30.3	67.1	29.3	67.8	31.4
Railroad[b]	36.9	31.4	25.8	21.4	28.1	25.9

Sources: U.S. Bureau of the Census, *Thirteenth Census: 1910* (Washington, D.C., 1912–1914), vol. IV, *Population*, 434–435, 521; idem, *Fourteenth Census: 1920* (Washington, D.C., 1921–1923), vol. IV, *Population*, 874–876; idem, *Fifteenth Census: 1930* (Washington, D.C., 1931–1933), vol. IV, *Population*, 118, 625, 1211, 1528.

Note: Native white = native born of two native parents; N.A. = not available.

a. Data from Alabama only.

b. Data from Texas only.

c. Data from Louisiana only.

ically black and white employees were siblings, and the line between the races was in danger of being blurred. Instead, to preserve the racial distinction, paternalism had to be abandoned.

With paternalism in decline, racial segregation came to the fore. Segregation was no mere horizontal separation of the races, but a vertical hierarchy in which blacks were totally excluded from management and were heavily concentrated in low-paid laboring slots.[48] Evidence that a biracial work force was the norm and that race played a major role in shaping the occupational hierarchy is presented in Table 3.1. While African-Americans were virtually absent from the highest levels, whether Texas railroad superintendents or Alabama manufacturers and mine owners, blacks predominated among laborers at the opposite end, whether in Alabama blast furnaces or Louisiana lumber mills. Between these extremes, blacks and whites were more evenly balanced in semiskilled jobs in manufacturing. Likewise, a slight majority of coal operatives in Alabama, the most important southern mining state, were black; most of the rest were native white.

The biracial pattern left little room for European immigrants. In the leading industries, first- and second-generation immigrants from all sources normally accounted for no more than a tenth of the managers, and rarely as many as a fifth of the wage earners. Thus the new immigrants were peripheral in the South.[49] Comparison with the North, where blacks were all but absent from manufacturing, while first- and second-generation immigrants were omnipresent, suggests the critical importance of race in shaping employment patterns, work discipline, and the whole culture of southern industry.

How did industrial segregation come about? Jim Crow laws said nothing about reserving places at the top of the job ladder for white men, in contrast to South Africa, which underwrote segregation in its biracial industrial work force with so-called kaffir laws reserving the higher positions in diamond mines and other industries for whites.[50] The fact that such statutes were absent in the South testifies to the lasting impact of the Reconstruction Amendments, which effectively eliminated the Black Codes, the would-be equivalent of kaffir laws. But the bargain between North and South that had ended Reconstruction in 1877 said nothing against segregation, and so long as southern legislators paid lip service to the *Plessy* doctrine of "separate but equal," they were free to segregate at will. Southern industrialists did not need statutes to segregate their work force; they relied instead on the custom and ideology of race purity (as, indeed, northern industrialists did).

Southern industrialists combined race with gender in constructing the ladder of inequality. In textiles, for example, women made up more than a third of the labor force on the eve of the First World War but held none of the skilled jobs as loom fixers, despite a generation of factory experience; and black men were still excluded from work inside the factories, finding jobs only as laborers in the yards.[51] In the tobacco industry, jobs were allocated in such a way that all supervisors from foremen on up were white men, and most black women were consigned to unskilled jobs stripping tobacco leaves. In the middle ranges, white men monopolized the strategic work of machine "making," while a handful of black men, but no women of either race, occupied skilled positions.[52] It came down to a simple rule that no white man ever took orders from a black person, and no black man from a black woman.

Segregation was a brutally effective strategy of divide and conquer. Reflecting on the "aggressions of exploiting capitalists," W. E. B. DuBois wrote, "So long as white labor must compete with black labor, it must approximate black labor conditions—long hours, small wages, child labor, labor of women, and peonage. Moreover, it can raise itself above black labor only by a legalized caste system which will cut off competition and this is what the South is straining every nerve to create."[53] The strategy created a dilemma of class and culture for southern labor organizers far more complex than the cultural divisions within the northern working class. If unions were going to become a potent force in the South, it would be necessary to organize workers of both races; but that meant at least an implicit challenge to white supremacy, which, in turn, brought down the full force of southern authorities against the unions.

Few unions were willing to meet the challenge. Instead, most, like the machinists, either bowed to local custom and organized only white craftsmen or, like the railway brotherhoods, prohibited Afro-American members outright or, in the majority of cases, simply abandoned the southern field altogether. The redoubtable socialist Oscar Ameringer described the bloody ironies of the racial dilemma on the New Orleans docks:

> When the Negroes struck, the cry went up from the white man's sanctum, rostrum and pulpit: "White men, assert your supremacy, rescue your jobs from the niggers," and the white dock workers asserted their supremacy by scabbing and breaking the strike. This went on until both whites and blacks got down to sow-belly wages. In one of the last of these affairs, the white-supremacy strikers killed some ninety black strike breakers, whereupon the white-supremacy militia of white-supremacy Louisiana shot hell out of a similar number of white-supremacy strikers.[54]

With a handful of bright exceptions such as the United Mine Workers, unions did not seriously tackle the problem until the Congress of Industrial Organizations mounted interracial drives in the 1930s; but even then, in contrast to their success among meatpackers, steelworkers, and other multiethnic populations of the North, CIO unions continued to be frustrated by segregation in the South.

Partly because of segregation, the South continued to be cursed with low productivity and consequent poverty as it entered the corporate era. In the initial stages of industrialization, leading industries depended on local raw materials, low-wage labor, and labor-intensive technologies that did not generate the sort of profit margins attractive to large-scale outside investment. Moreover, southern industries were not as productive as their counterparts in other sections of the country. For example, in 1910 southerners accounted for 38.4 percent of employment in cotton textiles nationwide but for only 30.8 percent of value-added. In fact, every southern industry except tobacco products created less than its share of value-added, whether it was labor intensive like lumber or capital intensive like iron and steel. Even as the South industrialized, the burden of past generations weighed like an incubus on the present.[55]

As a consequence of low productivity, the South did not generate sufficient wealth to sustain a robust middle class. The same forces that made domestic service the largest employer of women kept women's clerical employment the lowest in the nation. For example, in the South Atlantic states in 1930 (the earliest date for which comparative statistics are published), clericals accounted for 16 percent of women workers, compared with 34 percent in the Middle Atlantic states. In the same vein, southern states invariably had the lowest proportion of professionals and the highest proportion of proprietors in the nation, owing to the inclusion of sharecroppers and tenant farmers among the proprietors.[56] If these landless farmers are excluded, however, the net result was a small middle class whose paltry ability to consume left the South with the lowest per capita income in the nation. As early as 1919, when statisticians began to gather data on the subject, per capita income for the South stood at $405, compared with $614 for the nation as a whole, and the gap actually widened in the 1920s.[57] High-volume mass production was confined to steel mills and tobacco factories, and mass consumption made little headway, leaving the South as the caboose on the consumer gravy train that was about to leave the station in the 1920s.

The fact that every economic index was low relative to the North does not mean the South was twenty years behind on the same path of modernization. In truth, it was still walking a different path. Southern time was not merely slower; it was in a different frame. Southern productivity was not merely lower; it was part of a web of feedback links among low productivity, racism, chivalry, limited education, and poverty, which returned to haunt the region whenever it seemed to be making progress. What the law of slavery and agrarian paternalism were to the antebellum plantation economy, and what coerced labor and factory paternalism were to the early stages of industrialization, segregation and a less chivalrous male authority were to the emerging corporate order in the South. Not until the first stirrings of the civil rights movement in the 1950s did the South begin to break this vicious cycle, and in the meantime, as southerners recognized more than most, there was no escaping the past. The sins of the Old South were visited upon the New.

Worse yet, the South bore the added burden of "colonial" dependency. As its development fell increasingly under the influence of the great corporations of the North, it became an internal analogue of Latin America, producing raw materials and profits for absentee owners. The South's top two industrial employers—textiles and lumber—were closely tied to cash-crop agriculture and forestry; the region imported most of its finished manufactured goods; and much of the wealth it produced was accumulated in New York banks and Pittsburgh corporations. In fact, it seems that wherever mass production could be linked to mass distribution through integrated firms, the South fell under outside control, notably in the case of Birmingham steel mills under the mammoth U.S. Steel Corporation. Yankee firms had their southern agents, retainers, and branch executives, plus an elite corps of bank executives who answered to Wall Street firms. Even where native southerners seemed to reign, as among the fabled Texas oil millionaires, they were often indirectly subordinate to a few integrated firms such as Gulf Oil and Standard Oil, which controlled the strategic pipelines. With its "comprador bourgeoisie," its "colonial" exports, and its rendering of tribute to absentee owners, the South fit the case of an underdeveloped economy filling the coffers of a developed one.[58]

The illustrious career of tobacco king James Buchanan Duke is a revealing case study of the gravitational pull of northern capital. Starting with mills in Durham, North Carolina, Duke built his empire on the twin foundations of mass production, made possible by the Bonsack cigarette machine, and mass marketing through branch sales offices. By the turn of the century, profits generated by annual sales of 3–

5 *billion* cigarettes financed mergers with four other firms to form the American Tobacco Company, whose centralized management operated from its own office tower at 111 Fifth Avenue in New York. Although the Supreme Court ordered the company broken up in 1911 under the terms of the Sherman Anti-Trust Act, the Court's edict proved to be a license for oligopoly, not a commandment for competition; the four corporations that emerged from the breakup still controlled 80 percent of the market. Meanwhile, the Duke family extended its investments into textile mills in North Carolina, the Duke Power Company, and global ventures such as the British-American Tobacco Company. Driven by ambition remarkable even among his cupiditous contemporaries, Duke helped usher in the corporate era that eventually pushed aside swashbuckling robber barons like himself.[59]

There was opposition to corporate wealth. Smallholders and rural laborers did not bury all their hatred of monopoly when they interred the Populist party, and on occasion their anger boiled to the surface in acts of vigilantism, the most dramatic example of which was the Black Patch War of 1906–1908 against Duke's American Tobacco Company. Masked night riders of the Planters Protective Association in western Kentucky and Tennessee used dynamite against the tobacco trust's warehouses and factories, resurrecting a vigilante tradition that went back through nineteenth-century "whitecappers" all the way to the Regulators of the Revolutionary era, and it took considerable military force to stop them. In a few places, raw anger translated into socialist politics; in Oklahoma, coal miners and tenant farmers were so hospitable to socialism that the Sooner state boasted the highest concentration of socialists in the country.[60]

Even more remarkable were the occasional examples of interracial organizing, in the face of incredible odds, among Gulf Coast longshoremen and Louisiana lumber workers. In 1912–1913 a bold strike by the multicultural Louisiana Brotherhood of Timber Workers, loosely affiliated with the Industrial Workers of the World, occasioned an extraordinary display of solidarity described in a statement issued by the strikers:

> It is a glorious sight to see, the miracle that has happened here in Dixie. This coming true of the impossible—this union of workers regardless of color, creed or nationality. To hear the Americans saying "You can starve us but you cannot whip us"; the Negroes crying

"You can fence us in, but you cannot make us scab"; the Italians singing the *Marseillaise* and the Mexicans shouting vivas for the Brotherhood.

"Miracles" like this were extremely rare in Dixie. When they occurred,
they were likely to have been performed by the United Mine Workers,
an industrial union that made unusual efforts to organize miners of
both races. Though no paradise of biracial unionism, the UMW was
vulnerable to racist condemnation for promoting "social equality,"
which gave mine owners another stick to use in driving the UMW from
the main southern coalfields for a decade after an unsuccessful strike in
1908.[61]

In the main, working-class rebels could do little more than snap at
the heels of corporate capital, and southern traditions kept them on a
short leash. There is no better illustration of the influence of racism,
honor, and xenophobia on attitudes toward the factory than the tragic
events surrounding the murder of Mary Phagan. Mary was a thirteen-
year-old mill girl whose strangled corpse was found in 1913 in the base-
ment of the National Pencil Factory in Atlanta. Her murder aroused
deep-seated anger toward the factory system for all its offenses against
the family—the exploitation of child labor, the sexual dangers faced by
women wage earners, and the inability of male wage earners to act as
women's protectors. Moral revulsion exploded in southern pulpits and
newspapers, and Tom Watson, the ex-Populist who had become one of
the most powerful men in Georgia and editor of *The Jeffersonian*, loosed
a torrent of moralistic clichés, calling the victim "a daughter of the
people . . . who in so many instances are the chattle slaves of a sordid
Commercialism that has no milk of human kindness in its heart of
stone." In the same vein, the Atlanta *Journal of Labor* mourned her as "a
martyr to the greed for gain which has grown up in our complex civilization, and which sees in the girls and children merely a source of exploitation in the shape of cheap labor."[62]

If Dixie's daughters were going to be martyred to commercial greed,
someone had to pay for it. But who? The demands of race purity normally would have called for the blood of a black assailant to atone for
the soul of a white girl, particularly since stories were circulating that
Mary had died for defending her honor against a sexual assailant. True
to form, initial suspicion fell upon the night watchman who first reported her body, but on second thought it seemed unlikely that the

perpetrator would have disclosed the deed himself. When another black employee named Jim Conley came forward to say he had placed the victim's body in the factory cellar, attention might well have shifted to him. Instead, authorities arrested the man Conley accused of the crime—factory superintendent Leo Frank.

Therein lies a puzzle. Why was a black wage earner invited to play the role of accuser instead of accused? Why was a member of the rising New South elite hailed into court as an attempted rapist and murderer? The answer held important lessons in class and culture. In the first place, factories were seen to be "places of grossest immorality." The fear was widespread that "to let a girl go into a factory was to make a prostitute out of her," and a stock character of popular culture was the lascivious boss who compelled sexual favors from female subordinates. The popular code of honor took offense at the sexual transgressions of the rich, as in typical complaints from a Nashville preacher about "the sharpness in business which condones successful dishonesty," "the lax sense of honor," "the looseness of the marriage bond," and, finally, "the sexual immoralities of the social leaders." In the case at hand, the evidence showed Leo Frank to be a devoted family man, the very opposite of the profligate, whisky-swilling, southern colonel. But Frank had two things going against him: he was Jewish, and he was a Yankee. Anti-Semitism and xenophobia combined with the masculine code of honor to become Frank's ultimate undoing. Normally, deference to men of property ruled out a frontal attack on factory owners, but since Leo Frank was an outsider twice over, he automatically forfeited some of the immunity ordinarily enjoyed by the men of his rank. Popular passion could slake its thirst for vengeance against a symbol of economic and sexual predation without menacing the capitalist class as a whole. As Mary's Baptist pastor said, a black worker "would be poor atonement for the life of this innocent girl," but a rich Jewish Yankee would be "a victim worthy to pay for the crime."[63]

Frank was duly convicted in an Atlanta court and sentenced to death. But the matter did not rest there. The mob atmosphere of the trial did not sit well with respectable opinion, already embarrassed by the Atlanta race riot of 1906, and a host of southern governors, senators, and state legislators, plus 10,000 Georgia petitioners, called upon Governor Slaton to grant clemency. Because he believed Frank's accuser to be the real guilty party, the governor commuted the sentence to life imprisonment. But the crowd was not to be denied its vengeance.

As long as there had been Regulators, whitecappers, Klansmen, and night riders, the trigger for vigilantism had been the belief that authorities had failed in their duty to uphold the moral order. Whether the issue was moral economy, white supremacy, or female chastity, "Judge Lynch" normally took the law into his own hands to teach established authority a lesson, not to overturn it. In keeping with the time-honored pattern, a lynch mob took Frank from his poorly guarded cell and hung him from a tree on August 16, 1915, until he was dead. Within a few weeks, an enterprising devotee of the Lost Cause named William Simmons took the so-called Knights of Mary Phagan and turned them into the second incarnation of the Ku Klux Klan.[64]

The rebirth of the Klan was a telling end to the story of Mary Phagan, because it illustrated the conversion of class tensions into racist actions. Governor Slaton and Tom Watson personified the two main political styles in the years after disfranchisement, the one representing the progressive views of the "best men," the other the demagogic passions of the rednecks, but neither posed a serious challenge to the reign of New South industrialists. That did not mean the North always found the way to social justice. Only two years before Mary Phagan met her sad end, more than 100 young women employed at the Triangle Shirtwaist Company in Manhattan had died in a factory fire, some of them trapped in the inferno because the doors leading to escape had been locked to make sure no one left work early, others crushed when they hurtled to the pavement eleven stories below. Despite a public outcry, legislative hearings, and a trial, the owners incurred no criminal punishment. If the North could fail to render social justice, southern politics had a way of avoiding the question altogether. While progressives promoted business outright, demagogues launched misguided attacks in the name of race purity and southern honor that channeled anticapitalist feelings into irrelevant emotional catharsis.

In the dialectic between the South and the nation, colonial dependency did not mean that the South simply tagged along behind the northern mastern. Deep-seated southern traditions shaped corporate development. Racial segregation in industry hemmed in the labor movement on all sides, so that unions were even less of a foil to big business than in the North. The disfranchisement of Afro-Americans and poor Anglo-Saxons fostered two political styles, progressive and demagogic, neither of which was really responsible to sharecroppers or factory workers. The organizational weakness of popular movements, in turn, denied social-justice reformers the social bases they needed for winning government regulation of the market in the interest of wage earners—hours laws, protective legislation, and public welfare. And because state governments were unresponsive to popular interests, poor whites took out their class hatreds on targets constructed by racism and xenophobia as popular vigilantism became a substitute for authentic popular protest. Consequently, New South industrialists—regional capitalists as well as those who fronted for northern absentee corporations—encountered little sustained opposition. And the combined effect was that the South made its influence felt in the nation as a counterweight to progressive social reform.

Why Progressivism?

Progressivism was an attempt to reconcile state and society that drew in varying degrees upon each of America's leading political traditions—liberal, republican, populist, and socialist. Its ranks ranged from leaders in the American Federation of Labor and reformers in the National Consumers League to social engineers such as Herbert Croly and patricians such as Theodore Roosevelt. Prodigious intellectual efforts from that day to this have gone into hunting down the "social origins" of progressivism. Progressive intellectuals themselves got things started by inventing a new methodology (at least new for the United States, where political economy was weak) of tracing political institutions back to their social and economic origins. The method was exemplified in Charles Beard's explanation of the Founding Fathers in terms of competing economic interests, the "new history" of James Harvey Robinson and Frederick Jackson Turner, and the historical jurisprudence of Oliver Wendell Holmes, Jr.[65]

Once the problem was defined as "the social origins of politics," virtually all schools of analysis got into the hunt for economic interests, class conflict, ethnocultural factors, and so on. The social origin of progressivism itself has been hunted down in lairs ranging from the top to the bottom of the social scale, from the Yankee Protestant urban elite, through the status-panicked middle class, to the working-class milieu of "urban liberalism."[66] The very plausibility of each of these rival views demonstrates the need for a more comprehensive interpretative framework; otherwise, they merely cancel each other out. In the face of such confusion, some historians denied that anything so amorphous as progressivism could be called a cohesive movement and abandoned the idea altogether.[67] Yet it is likely that if the concept of progressivism disappeared, something else would have to be invented to replace it. For the present, there is no better term to encompass the protean efforts to remake the liberal state in the early twentieth century.

The fact that self-described progressives could be found in all classes marks progressivism as a characteristically American phenomenon; in European party politics, openly cross-class political alliances were a sideshow, not the main act.[68] Certainly in Germany, class was clearly inscribed in occupational status. Although there was considerable individual mobility, the boundary lines between the layers of status and occupation were apparent as one descended from the upper middle class (*Burgertum*) and lower middle class (*Kleinburgertum*) through white collar (*Angestellen*) to blue collar (*Arbeiter*). Obviously, similar boundaries were present in the United States, but the sense of rank was far less apparent.

The importance of these national differences was brought home around the "woman question." Similar issues arose in both countries around women's employment, suffrage, family roles, and sexuality, and there were transnational affinities between various kinds of feminists, including supporters of women's suffrage, as well as the small bands of sexual radicals epitomized by Margaret Sanger and her German counterpart Helene Stocker. Radicals in both countries combined sympathy for the poor and a utopian vision of sexual freedom, opted for free marriage in defiance of bourgeois family norms, and ran birth control clinics in defiance of the law. They were among the prophets of the "new morality," which transcended national boundaries and promised a new stage in human emancipation.[69]

Or so they thought. Disciples of Sigmund Freud had a different idea of the prospects for sexual liberation. After a visit to the United States in 1909, Freud began to attract a small, devoted band of intellectuals on both sides of the Atlantic who struck a blow for liberation in breaking Victorian taboos, but who also believed that the psychosexual dynamics of the (bourgeois) family—"penis envy" and Oedipal conflicts, in particular—left women subordinate to men. In any case, sexual repression was the necessary concomitant of civilization.[70]

Economic and demographic trends were moving in the same direction in both countries, in terms of their impact on women in the home and the labor market. The trend in women's paid employment was upward in both cases. In fact, German women went out to work in considerably higher proportions than their American sisters: on the eve of the First World War women made up more than a third of the German labor force, compared with less than a fifth in the United States, and women's share of employment as retail clerks was at least 42 percent, considerably higher than the 30 percent in the United States. In most other respects, the occupational position of women was virtually the same in the two countries—job segregation by sex in domestic service, garments, and textiles; exclusion from the skilled trades; and low wage rates.[71] In the face of rising women's employment and shrinking families, the reassertion of family subordination did not confine women to the home, but helped justify the "double burden" of keeping house while also ensuring their subordination in paid work outside the home. Birthrates were also declining in both countries, prompting outcries against "race suicide" and fears expressed in similar terms by Kaiser Wilhelm and Teddy Roosevelt that the Teutonic and Anglo-Saxon races were losing the "warfare of the cradle" to Slavs, Asiatics, and others low on the Social Darwinist totem pole.

It is because there were so many similarities in gender between the two countries that the contrast in the women's movement is so illuminating. In its organization and ideas, the women's movement reflected the different notations of class in the two societies. The sharp delineations of German life clearly divided middle-class and working-class women's organizations. The premiere women's group was the Federation of Women's Associations, which started out with an impeccably feminist program calling for the elimination of gender discrimination in suffrage, marriage, pay, and education. However, that changed in reaction to the growing strength of the socialist movement. So as not to be confused with the socialist women, middle-class feminists of the federation toned down their demands and embraced the existing Wilhelmine state. Infiltrated by right-wing women of the Imperial League against Social Democracy, the federation more and more emphasized the conservative theme of woman as the mother of the race, calling for "racial hygiene," the acceptance of Prussian three-class voting, and nationalist ideas of the *Volksgemeinschaft* above party or class. Thus German feminism was more thoroughly bourgeois in membership and orientation than American, and its proponents were more isolated from working-class women. Although Social Democratic women supported equal pay and protective legislation, their main effort lay in building a movement of working women through their own women's bureaus, arguing that the exploitation of women was a special case of capitalist exploitation in general.[72]

To be sure, there were class and cultural divisions in the American women's movement. The largely middle-class National American Woman Suffrage Association reflected the status prejudices of its members in giving nativist and racist justifications for women's suffrage as the cure for lower-class corruption of American politics, and its single-minded focus on votes for women earned it the scorn of socialist women such as Mother Jones, who barked, "You don't need the vote to raise hell." But the broader impulse for women's uplift as represented by the National Women's Trade Union League, the National Consumers League, the child labor crusade, and the settlement movement cut across class lines. That is to say, women reformers in the United States harbored *within* their organizations the same class tensions that divided German women's organizations against one another.[73]

The same national differences are apparent in the linkage between class and party. Politics in the United States was a free-for-all in which parties represented competing economic interests only in the vaguest of terms, and even then they did not divide so much along class lines as between metropole and periphery. The northern heartland of corporate capitalism was led by the Republican party, while the periphery of small property and the "colonial" South was led by the Democratic party. After the electoral realignment of 1896, the Republicans were the dominant party.[74] In Germany, by contrast, class and party were much more tightly tied. In general, the leading parties could be paired with their respective occupational groups—Conservatives with great estate owners, National Liberals with big industrialists, and Social Democrats with blue-collar workers. Other parties were harder to pigeonhole but gravitated toward the middle class. The confessional bonds of the Catholic Center party cut across occupational lines to a certain degree, but it tended to be middle class in orientation. The middle-class bent was even more apparent in the case of the Progressives, the liberals of principle who were the custodians of the failed revolution of 1848. To find the parliamentary majorities necessary to vote appropriations, the chancellor normally first tried to join the interests of Conservatives and National Liberals in the balancing act of *Sammlungspolitik*, literally, the politics of togetherness, but when that was not possible, he reached down to the middle-class representatives of the Center or the Progressives.[75]

This middle-class collaboration with what remained an authoritarian state provides ammunition for the theory of German exceptionalism, in which German history is portrayed as a recurring nightmare of middle-class failures—1848, 1871, 1918, 1933. It is true that German liberals kowtowed to militarism and higher authority and failed to lead a bourgeois revolution along the model of the Atlantic republics Britain, France, and the United States. The difficulty is that capitalist development did (and does) not necessarily bring liberal democracy, as Germany itself proves. So the German middle classes were inclined to look to capitalist elites and estate owners for leadership. In any event, in comparison with the whirligig of American politics, this system was a model of clarity and order. Parties normally stood for class interests, and everyone knew his or her place in the hierarchy.[76] The explanation for this state of affairs will not be found in the internal characteristics of any one class or even in the purely economic relations among all of them, but in the ways in which the entire social order was linked to state power. The difference between the two countries on that score can be described as "loose coupling" in the United States versus "tight coupling" in Germany.[77]

Given the different party systems, it was only natural for the "social question" to be posed in different ways. Industrial development and urbanization were even more rapid in Germany, than in the United States, bringing more than 60 percent of the population of 65 million in 1910 into towns and cities such as Berlin, a center of metalworking, and the great coal and steel complexes of the Ruhr. Like workers everywhere, both German and American workers were conscious of antagonism with their employers. The difference was that it was possible to speak without awkwardness of a German working *class* in the singular. The growing number of German industrial wage earners entered into a rigidly stratified social order in which worker and employer moved in different worlds, and it is hardly surprising that party cleavages came to reflect the hard lines between the National Liberals, the party of big business, and the Social Democrats (SPD), the party of the industrial proletariat. This is not to deny other cultural influences, such as religion. Catholic workers often supported the Center party; Lutherans were more likely to support the SPD, especially secular ex-Lutherans, for whom socialism became a kind of substitute religion. Yet, all in all, the Social Democrats adopted a Marxist program at the Erfurt conference of 1891 because of the close fit between Germany's class-conscious society and Marxian analysis of class struggle.

Germany's Social Democratic party was the pride of the Socialist Second International. It had the largest following, the purest Marxian doctrine, the premiere theoretician of the movement in Karl Kautsky, and, in theory, it posed a serious threat to the existing order. By 1912 the SPD counted nearly a million members and garnered over 4 million votes, one-third of the total cast, to become the largest party in the Reichstag, and absent the rigged electoral system, it would have been even larger. In practice, it followed a reformist, parliamentary strategy, accepted the autonomy of trade unions in pursuit of piecemeal economic advances, and pursued limited constitutional reforms. Its demands for universal male suffrage against the Prussian three-class voting system and its call for a chancellor responsible to the Reichstag, not to the Kaiser, only showed how far behind Germany was in the struggle for democracy.[78]

Since the SPD had quite visibly repudiated the revisionist doctrines of Edward Bernstein, its electoral triumph could be portrayed as both a confirmation of revolutionary faith and a stunning vindication of the parliamentary strategy of pressing for limited democratic reforms. Meanwhile, the labor movement displayed renewed militancy as the number of workers involved in strikes rose above 1 million in 1912 for the first time. The fact that this tension and ferment did not break through to the surface only confirms the dangerous rigidity of German politics. No prewar government ever stooped to bring Social Democrats into a governing coalition. Instead, many highly placed figures came to believe that the only way to preserve their power and privilege against social change at home was war abroad.[79]

Given its power and prestige, the prewar German Social Democratic party was the yardstick against which working-class politics of other countries was measured. Certainly, that was the case when Werner Sombart, a German economist, hurled his famous question against American workers: "Why is there no socialism in the United States?"[80] To Sombart, the answer lay in the exceptional affluence of the American wage earner, in the memorable phrase "shoals of roast beef and apple pie." From that day forward, American "exceptionalism" became an *idée fixe* under which the history of the American working class was but a litany of failure to form a Social Democratic party on the German model, a Labour party on the British model, or some other party on some other model. The failure was chalked up to a variety of causes—prosperity, racial and cultural divisions, upward mobility, consensus values, or the absence of class consciousness. The other side of this coin is the strength of American pragmatism—business unionism, ethnic politics, and preference for voluntarism (private collective bargaining) over state intervention.[81] There are many kernels of truth here, but, ground together, they do not bake bread.

The trouble with the question "why no socialism?" is that it asks about an absence and is usually answered in terms of other absences. The weakness of the socialist movement is explained in terms of absent class consciousness, absent poverty, and even absent feudalism. The fallacy is that absent causes cannot explain real events. The question should be turned around to ask, "Why did American progressives win such a large role in translating working class needs into social policy?" Much has already been said in answer to that question in the discussion of movements for social justice. The remaining issue has to do with the way those cross-class movements affected party politics. In particular, how did the broad movement for progressive social reform crystallize into the Progressive party of 1912? Although the American Progressive party bears some resemblance to its German namesake, the two were as different as the American and German party systems. Whereas the German liberals of principle appealed to a self-conscious middle class, the American Progressives represented a cross-class alliance.

No one better personified that hybrid mix of elite conservatism and grass-roots progressivism than Theodore Roosevelt. Soon after taking office as president in 1901, Roosevelt was confronted with a bitter anthracite coal strike in which the United Mine Workers squared off against the leader of the coal barons, George Baer. Posing as God's gift to the working man, "Divine Right" Baer averred that wage earners would be protected by "the Christian men whom God in his infinite wisdom has given the control of the property interests of the country." Roosevelt was furious with the owners and intervened by appointing J. P. Morgan to mediate the strike because "I was anxious to save the great coal operators and all of the class of big propertied men, of which they were members, from the dreadful punishment which their own folly would have brought on them if I had not acted." By 1910 the willingness to mediate industrial disputes, root out municipal corruption, enact protective legislation, and expand public welfare was being called progressivism, and Teddy Roosevelt was ready to be its standard-bearer.[82]

Hankering for the White House again, Roosevelt pushed aside Robert La Follette, the quintessential insurgent and rightful leader of the progressive forces. When Roosevelt became angry with his chosen successor, William Howard Taft, for prosecuting U.S. Steel under antitrust statutes for a business deal that bore his approval, the die was cast for a run for the Republican nomination. When that failed, Roosevelt bolted to form the Progressive party. Reformers of many stripes gravitated toward this obsessively masculine man, who, in his inimitable way, said he felt as strong as a bull moose, a label that immediately stuck to the party. The Bull Moose platform incorporated many of the social-reform initiatives of the past dozen years, ranging from Jane Addams' brand of social justice to Herbert Croly's protocorporate regulatory state, animated throughout by an awakened middle-class conscience. As William A. White wrote, "Some way, into the hearts of the dominant middle class of this country, had come a sense that their civilization needed recasting, that their government had fallen into the hands of self-seekers, that a new relation should be established between the haves and the have-nots . . . because we felt that to bathe and feed the under dog would release the burden of injustice on our conscience." White added: "But Roosevelt's under dog was not proletarian. He was a middle-class, white collar dog." Ever one to sound off in some "bully pulpit," Roosevelt roused the middle-class men and women of good conscience at the founding convention to "stand at Armageddon and battle for the Lord."[83]

Socialists had their own reasons for rejecting the two major parties. As Eugene Debs liked to say, whether workers voted Republican or Democrat they wound up with the same capitalist masters. Although the Socialist party had a fair share of middle-class writers and reformers, along with one or two wealthy philanthropists such as A. G. Phelps Stokes, the party stood unequivocally with wage earners. Socialists explained the imbalance between emerging social forces and the existing form of the state in terms of a contradiction between the forces of production (technology, division of labor, skill, and so on) and the relations of production (property rights, ideology, state power, and so on). Those with a smattering of Marxist education gleaned from Laurence Gronlund's *Cooperative Commonwealth* (1884) or Friedrich Engels' *Socialism: Utopian and Scientific* (1880) contended that industrial capitalism had socialized household production in giant factories while leaving the ownership of property in the same private hands as before, with the result that unparalleled abundance was accompanied by growing poverty. The solution was to bring property relations into conformity with the forces of production by socializing ownership, starting with the banks, railroads, and mines. Indeed, many scientific socialists agreed with prophets of scientific management that an ever-greater concentration of wealth only hastened the day when capital would fall like a ripe fruit into the hands of the people. In the meantime, the Socialist party was poised to make its greatest electoral advance, giving Debs nearly a million votes in 1912, carrying some 1,200 socialists to local and state offices, and eventually bringing Victor Berger and Meyer London to Congress. With its demands for minimum wages and maximum hours for workers of both sexes, noncontributory pensions, and unemployment compensation, it also set much of the agenda for twentieth-century social reform.[84]

Progressivism *contained* socialism, in both senses of the word. In one sense, the social-justice planks in the Progressive platform incorporated watered-down socialist demands on wages, hours, and working conditions, and Roosevelt himself was convinced beyond a doubt that if conservatives did not come forward with reform, the masses would turn to socialism. In the other sense, progressives saw socialists as the enemy. Campaigning under the banner of the New Nationalism, they invoked the potent force of national unity against the ideology of class struggle. Their campaign documents, such as Walter Weyl's *New Democracy* (1912), argued that "democracy" could triumph over "the class war." In the remarkable 1912 election, some 3 million people voted the Progressive ticket, some merely because they adored the ebullient Roosevelt, but most, no doubt, because they saw him as a safe road to reform. He got three times as many votes as Debs. Even President Taft, who had donned the purple robes of conservatism for the election, had supported, or at least not opposed, such progressive measures as trust-busting, the income tax, and a new Commission on Industrial Relations. By diverting socialist ideas into safe channels, and then posing as the only alternative to cataclysm, progressives succeeded in outflanking socialists.[85]

Victory, however, belonged to the Democrat Woodrow Wilson. Wilson was less concerned with answering Debs than with answering the New Nationalism, and he engaged Louis Brandeis, a Boston lawyer prominent for his support of both scientific management and social reform, to put together the New Freedom, a vague summons to moralize the marketplace so that big business would not be able to collude against small. Brandeisan rhetoric about fair competition for "men on the make" attracted Bryan Democrats, who believed that the New Freedom embodied their fantasies of a return to the competitive world of smallholders promised by the Sherman Anti-Trust Act, a misimpression that Wilson did not bother to correct until he became president and unveiled the Clayton Act and the Federal Reserve System. In fact, much of Wilson's 1912 electoral program would have been congenial to a nineteenth-century pillar of free trade and sound money like Grover Cleveland, and there was nothing in his few halfhearted gestures toward social reform that disturbed the sleep of Bourbon Democrats. Wilson captured the spirit of reform but not the substance, and as a result of division in Republican ranks, he was elected more as a late Victorian liberal than as a twentieth-century progressive.[86]

In terms of its impact on conservative elites, the outcome of the election was no Armageddon. Wilson was constrained by conservatives in his own party, including a large contingent of southerners whose support was essential to Democratic victory and who could be counted on to oppose social legislation and any federal intervention that had the slightest hint of disturbing segregation or overturning disfranchisement. North of the Mason-Dixon line, business elites took comfort from the influence of nativism, which divided workers against one another, and of nationalism, which fused all ranks in a common ideological bond. This does not mean that the social dynamics derived from the class "field of force" ceased to drive the historical process through successive states of unstable equilibrium. To the contrary, the perpetual clash of strong and weak persisted throughout the Progressive Era, even when government regulation of the market seemed to advance the interests of the weak—of impoverished mothers, child laborers, and wage earners. That was because, at the same time, the state did not neglect to build in protections for the strong. Women's protective legislation, for example, redefined the legal form of male dominance by substituting state regulations for family paternalism, forecasting the rise of the welfare state in the 1930s. In adjusting the claims of both sides, the state was seen to be evenhanded—in some respects, it *was* evenhanded—a fact that helped maintain the hegemony of a system based on inequality.

Nevertheless, it would be a mistake to regard the election as a triumph of conservatism.[87] It registered the impact of popular demands for social justice through the Progressive and Socialist parties and

showed that forces arising from the working classes had gained the political initiative, challenging elites to remake the liberal state in accord
with emergent forms of social life. The response included a host of
social reforms and protective laws at the municipal and state levels,
plus direct election of senators, an income tax, and new business regulations at the federal level. In proposing to construct a new governing
system that went beyond the formal equality of nineteenth-century individualism to reach toward *social* equality, they prepared the ideological ground for reforms during Wilson's first term, the First World War,
and ultimately the New Deal.

Keeping the balance between egalitarian and hierarchical forces in
mind helps shield posterity from the self-satisfied complacency of its
own hindsight. New forms of state power and social hierarchy had to
be fought for and imposed against resistance; they were not a forgone
conclusion, as if history were merely palingenesis—the exact genetic
replication of the past. What would grow up to become the bully of an
inevitable outcome was born into the world as the mere babe of contingent possibility.

II

CONFRONTING
THE ISSUES

//.

1913–1924

THE PERIOD *beginning with Woodrow Wilson's assumption of the presidency saw the first major efforts to rectify the imbalance between state and society. One solution was the progressive statecraft of the first Wilson adminstration. In response to popular clamor for reform, Wilson created a set of government regulations of the market that form the starting point in the long process of rebuilding the liberal state around conditions of twentieth-century life.*

A second solution was the managerial liberalism of the First World War. Given U.S. imperial involvements and strong European ties, no amount of twisting and turning could have allowed the United States to escape a role in the fighting. And given the press of war, no compunctions about centralized power could have prevented a new breed of managerial liberals from hastily assembling public-private machinery to manage the economy and mobilize civilians.

After the war, however, both progressive and managerial strategies foundered on the shoals of social conflict. Unwilling to go further on the path of reform, in part out of fear of revolution, they were unable to prevent liberal reaction. The trouble was that laissez-faire liberalism could be restored only by force, evident in troops, Prohibition, or Red Scare. The glaring incongruity of imposing the doctrine of minimal state intervention through heavy-handed state repression was a sign that the liberal state was not in tune with American society. Having moved from old-fashioned liberalism to progressivism and back again, the period ended without a solution to the problem.

4

Progressive Statecraft

AFTER YEARS of social ferment it seemed to Walter Lippmann, perhaps the most discerning social critic of the day, that American civilization was coming apart at the seams: "the sanctity of property, the patriarchal family, hereditary caste, the dogma of sin, obedience to authority,—the rock of ages, in brief, has been blasted for us."[1] Lippmann's catalogue of disintegration was a clear sign that on the eve of the First World War American culture was breaking free from nineteenth-century orthodoxies. Newspapers rang with popular clamor about predatory practices by the "money trust," landlord abuses in tenement slums, and the cruelties of child labor. Mass meetings convened to hear sexual radicals foretell the dawn of erotic delight and social radicals extol collective ownership of wealth. City streets were exotic, open-air bazaars of Russian Orthodox peasants, Jewish pushcart operators, and Italian anarcho-syndicalists, whose raw energy was celebrated by the new breed of urban realist painters. Arts and letters were a veritable kaleidoscope of bright new ideas and sentiments from the poets of the Chicago Renaissance, the irreverent cartoonists of *The Masses*, and avant-garde artists saluting the iconoclasm of the Cubists. Against the prevailing chaos of "drift," Lippmann urged what a growing chorus of contemporaries demanded, a commanding strategy of "mastery."

No longer could Yankee Protestant elites be complacent about their place atop the social hierarchy. The unwanted children of nineteenth-century American society were in revolt against the parent, and their revolt called into question the existing relation between state and society. From 1912 through 1916 the key battles were fought out around the trust, industrial democracy, and social justice, all of which were forced upon an otherwise unwilling national leadership by popular movements originating in the working and middle classes. In response, elites developed two new strategies with a view toward reconstructing the liberal state under the conditions of twentieth-century life. One was managerial liberalism, in which corporations were seen as the cornerstone of public affairs in everything from social welfare to foreign policy. The other was progressive liberalism, in which the state would regulate private interests in the public interest. As the pace of politics quickened in the years before U.S. entrance into the First World War, progressive statecraft gained ascendancy with the presidency of Woodrow Wilson.

Wilson and the Trust Question

The trust question dominated Wilson's first two years as President. The rise of the giant corporation threw a huge monkey wrench into the inherited governing system. Corporations as big as United States Steel did not play by the same competitive rules as small proprietary firms. They did not link up with family ownership and inheritance in the same way as individual entrepreneurs. They did not hire or supervise their thousands of employees in the same way as the on-site boss in his own shop. Yet they continued to be governed by the same legal rules that applied to the competitive marketplace. This underlying contradiction between the actual relations of production and the ideological-legal form of property came to the surface in political battles around the trust in which nearly every economic group had a stake. Wall Street wanted a private central bank; shippers wanted lower freight rates; farmers wanted cheaper credit; small manufacturers wanted competitive advantages; technocrats wanted efficiency; and workers wanted greater leverage. Out of this tangle of competing interests, a daunting possibility arose: what would happen if all those who had been gored by the plutocratic ox made common cause? The pursuit of social justice had already brought workers and middle-class elements together; could the same groups draw upon the legacy of the Knights of Labor and the Populists to forge a new antimonopoly alliance against the trusts?

The term *trust* was a holdover from nineteenth-century populism, and it came freighted with faintly evil connotations. It was easier to define the enemy in rhetoric than in fact. Contemporaries applied the term to everything from monopolies such as the American Telephone and Telegraph Corporation to oligopolies such as the handful of giant meatpackers and, for that matter, to just about any other big business. Though imprecise, it reflected the need for some generic term to cover the emergence of large-scale enterprise whose characteristic industrial structure was neither monopoly nor competition, but something in between named oligopoly. The rise of industrial goliaths such as U.S. Steel, Armour, and the American Tobacco Company was the result of convergence of changes at several levels, including the emergence of mass-production techniques and mass consumption, along with the legal prohibition on cartels embodied in the Sherman Act.

In terms of the mode of production, the key was vertical integration, that is, the linkage of mass production with mass distribution. Integration was both a matter of new technologies, such as the integrated steel mill, which turned iron ore into steel girders, and business reorganization, in which a single firm took control of purchasing, production, and marketing. Coordinating these complex operations called forth an elaborate internal managerial apparatus in each of the giant firms. Where once separate firms had bought and sold, now functional divisions, each under its own vice-president, coordinated purchasing, production, and marketing. In short, the corporation turned the competitive markets of the proprietary era into their opposite, managed markets.[2]

Mass production and distribution would not have been possible without changes in social reproduction. To move beyond the pioneering stage of illustrious inventors such as Thomas Edison toward the systematic exploitation of scientific discoveries, it was necessary, particularly for new electrical and chemical industries, to have at their disposal an expanding corps of engineers and scientists coming from the Massachusetts Institute of Technology and other polytechnic training grounds. By the same token, to manage markets properly required a corps of college-educated planners whose decisions were recorded and communicated by legions of high-school-trained office clerks, the same feminized work force that also made mass distribution possible through their low-paid work as telephone operators and sales clerks. Mass education inculcated the skills and work habits that prepared the rising generation for the discipline and tedium of the office routine. Absent these changes in the reproduction of daily life, the evolution of twentieth-century society with the giant corporation at the hub simply could not have gone forward.[3]

Presiding over these wide-ranging developments, investment bankers and big stockholders were converting proprietary ownership into corporate ownership. The advantages of limited liability quickly proved themselves in manufacturing, where 87 percent of wage earners toiled for a corporate employer by 1919. Although most of the several million employers in the United States were small, a large share of corporate property was being concentrated in a few hands. By 1914 a mere 2.2 percent of all establishments produced more than $1 million worth of goods, but these same firms employed 35 percent of all wage earners in manufacturing, and the proportion rose to more than half after the First World War. No nineteenth-century coal baron or railroad tycoon could match the $1 billion capitalization of U.S. Steel, and soon other manufacturing combines, investment banks, and insurance companies surpassed railroads as the largest concentrations of wealth. An increasing share of this wealth was owned by corporations that purchased shares of other corporations, whether as holding companies, investment trusts, or simple owners. Individual ownership of public stock issues was also highly concentrated; although data are astonishingly sparse, there is no mistaking the uneven distribution. One investigation disclosed that the richest 1 percent of individuals in 1929 held 65.6 percent of corporate stock and 82 percent of corporate bonds. All in all, proprietary forms of ownership were turning into corporate portfolios.[4]

Such were the agglomerations of wealth that came under attack for being "trusts." Seen as standing conspiracies against the public interest, the trusts gained notoriety in the great merger wave of 1898–1904, when hundreds of horizontal competitors were consolidated into a relative handful of large corporations a few of which controlled over 70 percent of their markets (Du Pont, International Harvester) and others over 40 percent (U.S. Steel, American Smelting and Refining, National Biscuit).[5] Maverick economist Thorstein Veblen contended that these mergers were a parasitic incubus on the underlying productive system, and in *Theory of Business Enterprise* (1904) he pressed the case for a conflict between the technical efficiency of the modern machine process and the "pecuniary motivation" of property owners. Damning the corporate investor with faint praise, he wrote, "the captain of industry works against, as well as for, a new and more efficient organization."[6] In a more popular vein, Upton Sinclair indicted the Beef Trust for its careless disregard of public health and brutal exploitation of immigrant workers in *The Jungle* (1906). In defending supposedly "soulless corporations" against "demagogues" and socialists, John Moody ironically gave ammunition to the critics in *The Truth about the Trusts* (1904), which depicted a steep pyramid of wealth topped by two rival groups of finance capitalists around the Rockefeller and Morgan interests. The Wall Street Panic of 1907 only confirmed public anxiety about the machinations of high finance.[7]

In this highly charged atmosphere, government efforts to resolve the contradiction between the corporation and the legal tradition of antimonopoly only succeeded in further politicizing the issue. President Roosevelt won a reputation as a "trustbuster" largely on the strength of a single successful prosecution under the Sherman Anti-Trust Act of the Northern Securities railroad empire. His successor, President Taft, initiated more prosecutions but left the deciding influence in the hands of the Supreme Court. For its part, the Court tried to take the trust issue out of politics in announcing the "rule of reason" doctrine in 1911, under which only "unreasonable" combinations in restraint of trade would run afoul of the law.[8] Although the Court actually struck a blow against monopoly by breaking up Standard Oil and the American Tobacco Company, the result tended to promote not free competition but oligopoly. In political terms, the "rule of reason" had the opposite effect of the one intended, by inflaming public opinion against the Court. At a much lower temperature, its impact can be compared to the Dred Scott decision of 1857, when the Supreme Court had attempted to put the slavery issue above partisan politics but only wound up inflaming the kind of passions that led to the Civil War.

By the election of 1912, antitrust feeling was running high. Eugene Debs resolved to bring the system of property ownership into line with already socialized production through nationalization of big capital, while "Bull Moose" Progressives talked about thoroughgoing government regulation under their New Nationalism. Woodrow Wilson, for his part, solemnly announced with Delphic ambiguity, "I am for big business and I am against the trusts." To the consternation of conservatives, the atmosphere was reminiscent of the great battles of the Gilded Age over money inflation and the protective tariff. There was no guarantee that a Congress susceptible to democratic enthusiasms would not do something drastic such as taking public control of the banking system or putting teeth into the Sherman Act. The trust question, broadly defined, was the most pressing business faced by the incoming Wilson administration, and it was clear that a solution would require statecraft of the highest order.[9]

There is enough conflicting evidence about the president to suggest that upon coming to office he simply did not know what he was doing, or at least he did not know exactly how to proceed. He fully accepted the rise of big business as "normal and inevitable" and in common with progressive opinion believed that some middle way in the law would have to be found between extreme individualism and public ownership. Yet he had also accepted Louis Brandeis' prescriptions for restoring competition and had campaigned as a Victorian liberal devoted to free trade and what he called "the men who are on the make rather than the men who are already made." [10] Such rhetoric placated the Bryan wing of the Democratic party and other legatees of the nineteenth-century antimonopoly agitation, who were also gratified by Wilson's first major action as president in support of the Underwood Tariff, which reduced import duties from 40 percent to around 25 percent. [11]

Having shown his gentlemanly independence from the bribery and intrigue of high-tariff lobbies, Wilson next tackled the thorny problem of currency and banking. The popular clamor for "people's money" had revived after lying dormant since Bryan's defeat in 1896. Agrarians of the Southwest and militant midwestern followers of Robert La Follette, plus the handful of surviving inflationists who had once wept with Bryan to see mankind crucified upon a "cross of gold" all demanded public currency and public control over private bankers. Even Teddy Roosevelt had been heard to denounce "the malefactors of great wealth." The revival of the antimonopoly hatred for the "money power" received a big boost in 1912 from the Pujo Committee, named after a Louisiana congressman, whose investigations of the "money trust" were condensed by Louis Brandeis into a muckraking classic, *Other People's Money* (1914). These attacks indicted finance capitalists for a vast conspiracy of interlocking directorates and behind-the-scenes banker control of industry. [12]

Money trust or not, Wall Streeters sought to insulate themselves against just this sort of "agrarianism," not to mention socialism. They came forward with the Aldrich Plan under what amounted to a revival of the old Bank of the United States, which they also hoped would prevent a recurrence of the Panic of 1907. That was too much centralized banking for Carter Glass, a Virginia senator who was thoroughly conservative on every point except his antipathy to New York banks. Although Glass was the principal author of the administration's bill, Brandeis contributed the key progressive innovations—government currency and a Federal Reserve Board to oversee private banks. In its final form, the bill contained only weak antimonopoly provisions, which enabled a large body of big bankers to support it in the expectation that real power would lie not in the Federal Reserve Board but in the officers of the member banks themselves.[13]

What emerged as the Federal Reserve System in 1913 was an exquisite political compromise that satisfied advocates of both centralized and decentralized banking, as well as supporters of private and public control. It created a dozen federal reserve banks with New York as the first among equals; banks could issue Federal Reserve notes in small denominations backed by the U.S. Treasury; the system was overseen by a federal bank board appointed by the president but presumably drawn from the leading men of the banking community. It also created the statutory basis for U.S. branch banking overseas. In all it was a remarkable balancing act that expanded the federal government's regulatory role without resorting to statist control and built on decentralized, federal structures congenial to small property while recognizing the primacy of New York banks and their leadership in foreign investment.[14] It edged away from the "drift" of laissez faire while lodging "mastery" not in a public bureaucracy but in a regulatory-corporate complex that left the main decisions in private hands. As a consequence, currency and banking disappeared as major issues until the Great Depression.

With respect to giant industrial combines, progressive statecraft followed the same lines of finely balanced compromise. The most drastic proposals came from latter-day populists, Bryan Democrats, and southwestern agrarians who wanted nothing less than destruction of oligopoly itself in the name of free enterprise. To that end they called for strict government regulation of the stock exchange, abolition of the "rule of reason," and outright prohibition on corporate interlocks of the sort uncovered by the Pujo investigation. By comparison, the socialist prescription for public ownership of concentrated capital, though a radical transformation in property relations, would have resulted in less disruption in the actual day-to-day processes of production and distribution. Keeping both of these drastic remedies at bay became the first aim of progressive policy. Taft's preferred method had been to refer the trust question to the courts, the branch of government most shielded from popular influence. In Roosevelt's case, the preference was for hands-on administrative regulation through a commission that would police the activities of big business, a position that accorded well with the tripartite, protocorporatist proposals of the National Civic Federation. Wilson, on the other hand, was more elusive. As a professor of government at Princeton, Wilson had accepted the big corporation as a legitimate fact of life, but as a presidential candidate he had talked like a latter-day Jeffersonian about a New Freedom in support of small property and against monopoly control.[15]

In the event, progressive statecraft was based not on campaign rhetoric or presidential whim but on the balance of political forces. It was clear that the socialist proposal for government ownership fell beyond the pale of liberal ideology and that the agrarian proposal for dissolution of the trusts was also unacceptable. Both were ruled out when Wilson reassured businessmen at the start of the 1914 legislative session that "the antagonism between business and government is over."[16] At the same time, the government could not simply continue drifting on a laissez-faire course, because doing so had only raised the popular temperature to a fever level. In the end, the administration and Congress charted a course between radical change and the status quo. They established the Federal Trade Commission (FTC), which was empowered to set rules for fair competition, issue cease-and-desist orders against infractions, and collect information on trade conditions.

This compromise was enough to placate both the New Nationalists, who welcomed clarification of the rules of oligopolistic competition, and New Freedomites, who hoped that small competitors would be protected against monopoly pricing. Even Taft conservatives were mollified by having FTC decisions made subject to judicial review in courts that were well beyond the reach of the people's elected tribunes. To guide judicial decisions, the Clayton Act defined "unfair" competition in terms of price discrimination, tying contracts, and some kinds of interlocking directorships and stockholding. When all was said and done, business leaders were in agreement with Wilson that antagonism between business and government was over. The U.S. Chamber of Commerce spoke for most in supporting the new arrangements for what it called industrial "self-regulation," a necessary euphemism cloaking the reality of expanded government regulation. A Missouri senator was closer to the mark in saying that the Clayton Act started out as "a raging lion with a mouth full of teeth. It has degenerated to a tabby cat with soft gums, a plaintive mew, and an anemic appearance."[17]

Wage earners had an immense stake in the trust question. Their ability to organize for self-protection was deeply affected by the way property relations were being redefined to keep up with the rise of the corporation. President Cleveland's use of the Sherman Act against the American Railway Union in the 1894 railroad strike was the opening gun of the era of the injunction, which lasted until the Norris-Laguardia Act of 1932. Although courts had long since stopped holding unions and strikes to be illegal per se, the broader forms of worker solidarity ran afoul of antitrust law, including the industrywide strike (*In re Debs*, 1895), the consumer boycott in support of a strike (*Loewe v. Lawlor*, 1908), and publication of a list of "foul" employers (*Bucks Stove*, 1911). In fact, most of the early prosecutions of "illegal combinations in restraint of trade" went against unions, no matter how much the American Federation of Labor invoked the free speech protections of the Bill of Rights.[18]

With the National Association of Manufacturers crowing over this string of courtroom victories, the AFL set out to break the potent alliance between business and the judiciary. AFL strategy was geared to the system of constitutional checks and balances and was aimed at electing "friends of labor" to Congress and the White House. Gompers supported Wilson in 1912 and used every ounce of his rather puny congressional muscle to win exemption for unions under the Clayton Act. For all his pains, the only outcomes were a pious reiteration of common legal doctrine that unions were not illegal and an eloquent but empty proclamation that "human labor is not a commodity." Grasping for any straw of legitimacy, Gompers nonetheless embraced the new law as "labor's Magna Carta." He lived to eat those words. In the ensuing fifteen years, the courts handed down more antiunion injunctions than in the twenty-four years before Clayton. Although open-shop industry enjoyed steady injunctive relief from trade unionism, it was not until the Great Depression that the balance was partially redressed and unions got some relief.[19]

In purely political terms, the progressive answer to the trust question was a masterful compromise. It gave just enough to Bryan Democrats and "friends of labor" for them to stand with conservative Democrats, Taft Republicans, and Bull Moosers behind the new regulations on banking and corporate practices. It harmonized the three branches of government insofar as Congress gave a statutory basis to the executive's Federal Trade Commission and Federal Reserve Board, while providing for judicial review of FTC decisions. It tended toward centralized control, but it left enough regional autonomy, for example, in the dozen Federal Reserve districts, for continuity with federalist tradition. It modified the liberal state in the direction of government regulation of the market, but instead of erecting a state bureaucracy, it lodged real power in a kind of parastate, that is, a nexus of private-public authority that combined corporate management with government regulation. As a result, it took the trust question out of politics in both senses. That is, it silenced much popular clamor, removing trust-busting as an issue in the next presidential election; and it referred future issues of corporate malfeasance to "nonpolitical" bodies of experts.[20]

This harmonious political resolution of the trust question should not be mistaken for a resolution of social antagonism. Contrary to the aims of social-justice advocates at the grass roots, progressive statecraft at the national level favored capital against workers and large capital over small. The consequence of federal action at the height of progressive influence was to reshape property relations by helping to redefine the legal norms of ownership. The formal cartel arrangements among oligopolistic firms of the sort common in German industry—price fixing, exclusive contracts, direct government promotion—were put out of bounds, and true monopoly was discouraged. But the tight oligopoly of a handful of separate corporations was fully accepted, so long as they refrained from "unreasonable" collusion.[21] The Supreme Court made it official in 1920 by upholding the legality of the United States Steel Corporation under the "rule of reason," leaving the steel industry in possession of a few firms that preferred stability to competition and were therefore willing to follow the lead of Judge Elbert Gary and his "Steel Trust." It was crystal clear that the new balance favored open-shop employers in their battle against the unions, a fact that would be resoundly confirmed in the defeat of the great 1919 steel strike. Thus the progressive corporate-regulatory complex altered the relation between state and society in ways that helped transform the corporate elite into the dominant class and legitimate their leadership in society at large.

Progressive Liberals versus Managerial Liberals

In the early morning of the corporate era, as industrial disorder spilled over into the public arena, it was clear that "laissez faire plus the constable" would not be enough to restore public order and protect property. But what would? The problem confronting the Rockefellers, Mellons, and Morgans was not how they might secure better policing of this or that isolated industrial community, but how they were going to legitimate their considerable property before the country at large. Because of a long tradition of democratic struggles beginning in the Revolution and running through the labor and populist revolts of the late nineteenth century, popular forces probably had more influence in the state than anywhere else in the world. Why else were elites in the United States so frightened of state intervention, whereas conservatives everywhere else invariably championed state power? As soon as the question of legitimacy was broached, corporate magnates ran into the same difficulty their forerunners had encountered with labor republicanism and agrarian populism in the late nineteenth century: how could capitalist inequality be reconciled with democratic values?

Although the rich were in no imminent danger of being relieved of their fortunes, they were obliged to operate within a field of force in which the working and lower middle classes traditionally had significant access to the levers of political power and cultural authority. Having succeeded in defeating insurgent workers and farmers in the 1880s and 1890s, they were now faced with renewed initiatives from the movements for social justice behind people's lawyers such as Clarence Darrow and Louis Brandeis, social reformers such as Jane Addams and Florence Kelley, and hell-raisers such as Mother Jones and Big Bill Haywood. So it was clear that the inherited liberal governing system would have to change, that subordinate groups would have a hand in changing it, and that the outcome was not a foregone conclusion.

That was the lesson learned at considerable cost in human life from the most dramatic industrial confrontation of Woodrow Wilson's first term—the Ludlow Massacre. When the massacre occurred, on April 20, 1914, Colorado was already notorious for the ferocity of its labor wars fought out over two decades. Battle lines had been drawn in company towns such as Telluride and Cripple Creek, where miners and their families, assisted by unions such as the Western Federation of Miners and the Industrial Workers of the World, were pitted against absentee owners, Citizens' Alliances, private police, state officials, and the militia. Official tolerance for antiunion vigilantism made for legalized lawlessness, and after one especially brutal reign of mob rule, miners asked: "Is Colorado America?"[22]

That question hung like a dark cloud over the property of the Colorado Fuel and Iron Company, a Rockefeller subsidiary located in a barren, mountainous region near the Purgatory River, during the strike-torn winter of 1913–14. The strike had erupted when the company refused to deal with the United Mine Workers and, instead, imported private detectives and sheriff's deputies, along with a motorized Gatling gun nicknamed the Death Special. With bullets flying in both directions, the governor sent in the militia, which was gradually taken over by company guards to become a strikebreaking force. "Bullet bargaining" culminated on April 20, 1914, when militiamen attacked a tent colony of miners' families who had been evicted from company housing, killing sixty-six men, women, and children, including eleven incinerated in a pit below the blazing tents. The infamy of the Ludlow Massacre raised a cry of outrage throughout the country, and telegrams flooded the White House, many demanding that President Wilson withdraw the troops currently occupying Vera Cruz, Mexico, to keep an eye on Standard Oil interests and send them, instead, to defend Colorado miners. At last, Wilson sent in federal troops who restored public order on terms that permitted the mines to reopen on a non-union basis.[23]

Was Colorado America? No, not insofar as the West's unusually violent social antagonisms rapidly escalated into great political battles over property rights and state power. One reason for this politicization was the high profile of the federal government in the West. Because the frontier era had barely passed, many westerners still remembered when U.S. cavalry had suppressed Geronimo's revolt and put down Sioux tribes at the 1890 Battle of Wounded Knee. Having pacified the rebellious tribes, government agents dealt with reservation "nations," the largest of which, the Navaho, lay astride four southwestern states, and direct federal control of Arizona and New Mexico did not end until statehood in 1912. In addition, the federal government played an unusually large role in the economic development of the region, originally through railroad land grants and later in river and irrigation projects, forerunners to the lucrative military contracting of the late twentieth century.[24]

The military also played an exceptionally large role because of chronic tension on the Mexican border. U.S.-Mexican relations were the closest analogue in North America to the border tensions among the proximate and often warring states of western Europe that did so much to promote large military establishments and labyrinthine state bureaucracies. During the reign of Porfirio Diaz (1877–1911), the United States maintained garrisons at a number of border points from Brownsville, Texas, to Nogales, Arizona, even though the Mexican dictator was determined to win favor with U.S. mining companies by using the murderous *rurales* against bandits and unruly workers. The Mexican Revolution inflamed smoldering conflict, and twice the United States invaded Mexico (Vera Cruz, 1914; the Punitive Expedition, 1916–17), and twice more mobilized the national guard at the border in anticipation of full-scale war. For all these reasons, federal rifles and flags were close companions to the dollar in the transition from frontier industrialization to the corporate era in the West. In fact, most of the episodes of federal troop use in industrial disturbances took place in western mining districts, including Coeur d'Alene, Idaho (1892, 1897); Morenci, Arizona (1903); and Goldfield, Nevada (1907).[25] In short, state repression was the crux of the western solution to the problem of public disorder.

Sure to be on hand when the going got rough were the Industrial Workers of the World. The Wobblies emerged from the rough-and-tumble of western metal mining and lumberjacking, where they experienced raw exploitation of people and nature first hand in hard-fisted mining camps and rough-hewn bunkhouses. Founded in 1905 at the "Continental Congress of the working class," they gained notoriety with "Free Speech Fights" in the West, and burst upon the East in the famous Lawrence textile strike of 1912. In espousing direct action, industrial unionism, and sabotage they showed a violent streak that was very much in the American grain. They resurrected the revolutionary tradition of the Declaration of Independence, invoked the Bill of Rights in their frequent court appearances, and gave the labor movement its twentieth-century anthem "Solidarity Forever." Though described by Big Bill Haywood in a moment of conciliation as "socialism with its working clothes on," the Wobblies' brand of revolutionary unionism was similar to French syndicalism, Italian anarchism, and British industrial unionism.[26] And it showed the depth of the problem in American industry.

If the West was an extreme case, it was not unique in posing the conflict between property rights and worker rights, between capitalism and democracy. Violent class warfare raged in other parts of the country, notably the West Virginia coalfields and the textile mills of Lawrence and Patterson, and western disorder was properly seen as a national problem. Certainly, the eyes of the nation were upon a Los Angeles courtroom in 1911 where the McNamara brothers, two trade unionists accused of bombing the antiunion *Los Angeles Times*, were on trial for their lives. The case ended when Clarence Darrow, the noted defense attorney, entered a guilty plea that astounded their supporters but saved their necks. But clearly, the cycle of violence and repression that brought such cases in the first place cried out for new remedies.

In fact, progressives were ready with an answer: let labor and capital work out their differences through collective bargaining under the watchful eye of an impartial public. With the goal of mediating industrial disputes before they escalated to lethal confrontations, progressives urged Congress to create a Commission on Industrial Relations. When intellectuals and social workers associated with *The Survey* magazine proposed a scientific investigation of the causes of industrial violence, President Taft embraced the idea in the hope of remedying the status quo, under which "industrial disputes lead inevitably to a state of industrial war." After intense lobbying by the AFL, Congress created a commission on Industrial Relations, composed of equal numbers of representatives from labor, capital, and the public to conduct investigations and file reports that would enlist public opinion against the parties to violent industrial disputes. Congressman William B. Wilson, soon to be the first secretary of labor, promised that the commission "will tend to show the employer and employee alike the necessity of getting together and thrashing out their differences over the table instead of in the industrial battlefield of strikes." The public would play umpire; that is to say, social workers, journalists, lawyers, educators, and other middle-class opinion makers were supposed to represent some disinterested general will, as if the middle classes did not have interests of their own in industrial peace. Although the lack of coercive power kept the commission squarely within the liberal tradition, the recognition of labor as a corporate entity coequal with capital reworked liberalism to conform more closely to the emerging corporate system.[27]

Within these limits, commission chair Frank Walsh made the most of it. A St. Louis labor lawyer and loyal Democrat, he portrayed industrial disputes as a conflict between capitalism and democracy. Laying the blame for disorder squarely at the feet of open-shop employers who refused to deal with the legitimate grievances of their employees, he turned the Commission on Industrial Relations into a platform for "industrial democracy." The most dramatic moment in the commission's five-year history came in hearings on the Ludlow Massacre, when Walsh inflicted humiliation upon John D. Rockefeller, Jr., by disclosing that Rockefeller, contrary to his pious protestations of innocence, had been in close touch with the situation in Colorado. Walsh laid into Rockefeller for his intransigence in refusing to deal with employees at Colorado Fuel and Iron and for the corporate callousness that had led to so many deaths. By the time he was finished, the blood on Rockefeller's hands was there for all to see. The final report, issued in 1916, warned employers to cooperate with labor voluntarily or face moves toward compulsory bureaucratic paternalism of the sort that existed in Germany. It counterposed the existing regime of "industrial feudalism" to the promise of "industrial democracy" and warned that the continuation of high levels of conflict posed a mortal threat to the republic. It concluded, "political democracy can only exist where there is industrial democracy." [28]

The story of the Commission on Industrial Relations illustrates a recurrent feature of American politics—the tendency to conduct politics as public theater in congressional hearing rooms and public courtrooms. In the absence of ideologically polarized parties or a great state bureaucracy to adjudicate disputes, the courts carried an unusually heavy load in attempting to legitimate the regime of corporate property. The annals of labor history from 1900 to 1916 are filled with celebrated cases of defendants facing criminal charges for union or political activity: witness the IWW "free speech" fights, Clarence Darrow's defense of Big Bill Haywood on a trumped-up murder charge, the firing-squad execution of Wobbly bard Joe Hill. [29]

Did such celebrated cases promote faith in the legal system? Unlike the everyday workings of local courts, which were often linked to working-class political machines, the more spectacular courtroom dramas probably did little to inspire popular confidence in the majesty of the law. On some occasions, anti-Red hysteria and ethnic prejudice got the best of the sober men in black robes, as in the executions of the Haymarket anarchists in 1887 and of Nicola Sacco and Bartolomeo Vanzetti in 1927. As passions cooled and these individual cases came to be perceived as miscarriages of justice, they hardly vindicated the legal system per se, any more than did the barrage of antiunion injunctions. The most that can be said is that the labor movement's running encounter with the courts probably reinforced middle-class perceptions of organized labor as a pariah and did not contribute much to winning workers' assent to their own subordination within the regime of private property. Not until the 1930s, when much of workers' collective action was decriminalized, did the law unequivocally exercise a hegemonic function.[30]

In the meantime, the Wilson administration took a few tiny steps toward labor reform. Ignoring the call for "industrial democracy," the administration nonetheless elevated the Department of Labor to cabinet rank and worked with Congress to set up nonbinding mediation machinery under the Newlands Act of 1913 on the model of a dozen such state commissions. It was not as if the AFL wanted much more than that, certainly nothing resembling government-supervised collective bargaining of the sort that emerged in the 1930s. To the contrary, the AFL wanted to reduce the state's role in labor relations to win relief from the devastating effects of antiunion court injunctions, a goal that still eluded the movement despite the Clayton Act. Otherwise, Samuel Gompers was in tune with the ideas of labor economist John Commons, intellectuals such as Herbert Croly, and the National Civic Federation, who proposed to resolve class conflict through stable collective bargaining and the mediation of permanent government commissions. As one of the fledgling industrial relations experts defined the problem: "How can the discipline and efficiency of the shop be maintained, yet the workers be granted a larger share in the management of industry?" That question would not be answered until the Wagner Act of 1935 underwrote collective bargaining; in the meantime, the fact that these changes took place reflected the growing strength of industrial workers; but their minimalism reflected the still-impregnable inner fortress of property right in the workplace.[31]

Since a frontal assault on property right proved impossible, progressives came forward with protective legislation, a back-door attack on laissez faire. In areas that were out of the direct line of collective bargaining, the AFL could abandon its voluntarist philosophy to call for increased state intervention. Indeed, motivated by notions of manly independence, craftsmen were eager for government to exclude their dependents from the labor market altogether; similarly, for both economic and nativist motives they demanded state intervention to cut off the influx of foreign labor.[32] As the experience of wage earners in modern industry more and more contradicted the norm of the self-regulating middle-class family, public authorities looked to police powers for the legal warrant to regulate the market, under which a number of states instituted factory inspections for health and safety. The issue that excited the most outrage was child labor. From Dickens' *Oliver Twist* (1838) to Lewis Hine's heartbreaking photographs of exploited children, nothing moved a stricken conscience to tears more quickly than an impoverished waif, innocent of all crime yet condemned to suffer. Tapping these humanitarian wellsprings, the National Child Labor Committee won a spate of state restrictions on child labor and, with some cynical support from northern manufacturers troubled about southern competition, pushed the Keating-Owen Act through Congress in 1916. Although the federal law failed to pass constitutional muster before the Supreme Court, even in a subsequently modified version, many state laws against child labor remained on the books.[33]

At the same time, states were putting curbs on hours for adult workers. The Supreme Court had little trouble upholding an eight-hour limit in hazardous occupations such as mining, or even time-and-a-half after ten hours for male workers in *Bunting v. Oregon* (1917), although the Court took only the health, not the wealth, of workers into account. Where women workers were concerned, regulation of the market went still further, and after *Muller v. Oregon* (1908) courts routinely upheld women's maximum hours and prohibitions on night work. Minimum wages for women were more troubling, and the Court reversed itself on the matter in a span of six years.[34] Even so, some federal barriers were starting to fall. Pressed hard by the AFL, Congress adopted the eight-hour day for federal employees and, after similar pressure from the railroad brotherhoods, passed the Adamson Act in 1916 imposing the eight-hour day on the railroads. Thus on the eve of U.S. entry into the First World War, a cross-class alliance of middle-class reformers, social feminists, and labor advocates was successful in building a few social-justice planks into the governing system.

The more progressives chipped away at the edifice of laissez faire, the more corporate leaders recognized that unless they embarked on self-regulation, they would be subject to further unwanted government regulation. Knowing they needed to answer the arguments for industrial democracy and protective legislation with a positive program of industrial self-government, the Rockefellers and the du Ponts hired public relations men such as Ivy Lee to spruce up their images. Meanwhile, an executive from General Electric named Magnus Alexander rounded up half a dozen manufacturers' associations to create the National Industrial Conference Board (NICB) in 1916 as an ideological clearinghouse and publicity bureau for industrial corporations. The NICB held up welfare capitalism, scientific management, and employment management as examples of corporate benevolence that benefited worker, consumer, and stockholder alike. Undoubtedly profit and power were the prime movers in the corporate drive for efficiency, but enlightened businessmen also recognized the need to legitimate big business to the public at large.[35]

Welfare capitalism was another managerial initiative. For their own self-interest and to keep the state at bay, corporations began to experiment with programs that addressed the economic and social needs of family life. For loyal employees, they instituted pensions, health plans, and stock ownership, and they drew social engineers, Americanizers, and the Young Men's Christian Association into the vortex of industrial relations in the hope of making the fearsome factory environment seem more like the kind of happy families depicted in company magazines such as the *American Sugar Family*. In a few cases, companies supplied coal at cost, built housing, and provided garden plots, as well as clubs for "little mothers," lectures on infant hygiene, washrooms, and lunchrooms. They hired sociologists to ferret out moral evils and visiting nurses to weed out malingerers.[36]

The railroad branch of the YMCA set the pace with leisure-time clubs, smoking and reading rooms, and gospel meetings, all of which were intended as edifying alternatives to the low theater, gambling den, and saloon. Executives hoped that a self-disciplined Christian worker would be both more efficient and loyal. As one Pennsylvania Railroad executive noted, "The fact that the Company is interested in his welfare . . . should convince the thoughtful employee that he is not working for the proverbial 'soulless corporation,' but is an integral part of a mutually conducted industry."[37] Moved by the same goal, the National Civic Federation established a Welfare Department under Gertrude Beeks, who helped conduct celebrated welfare work at International Harvester and National Cash Register on the principle that it was not enough to weed out socialists and labor agitators; management also had to cultivate positive loyalty from its subordinates. In all these aspects, welfare capitalism was an attempt to circumvent unions, a fact proved by the growth of welfare programs from 1916 to 1922 in the face of the most rapid union growth and the biggest strike offensive in American history. At the same time, it was an attempt to bond the working-class family to corporate management that recognized the failure of the cash nexus as a basis for stable industrial relations.[38]

In many ways, the main target of welfare capitalism was not the industrial worker but the middle-class public. In other words, welfare capitalism was the answer not just to unions, but also to protective legislation and the whole range of social reform. That was certainly the case with the most famous welfare plan of the period, the Colorado Industrial Plan. When the gruesome details of corporate malfeasance in the Ludlow Massacre came to light in the hearings before Frank Walsh and the U.S. Commission on Industrial Relations, Rockefeller brought in the big guns of the YMCA and Canadian industrial relations expert MacKenzie King to improve labor (and public) relations. The Colorado Plan included such welfare capitalist measures as YMCA recreation, subsidies to the Boy Scouts and Campfire Girls, and improvements in housing; it introduced such measures of employment management as employee representation on committees to deal with sanitation, safety, and working conditions; and it even set up grievance machinery.[39]

In all, it was a model managerial solution to worker discontent, right down to the one thing it did not do—recognize the union. In fact, the parties involved were quite candid about their aims in developing employee relations plans: they sought to build "unity of interest" and to avoid insubordination of the sort they believed arose from "third-party" meddling among otherwise "loyal" employees.[40] More important, management had to combat the public image of the soulless corporation if it was going to rebut the ideologies of class struggle and repulse the movement for social justice. Although prewar welfare capitalism had only a marginal impact on industrial relations, it marked a change in the ideology by which capitalists sought to legitimate their dominance.

Scientific management was another route to the same end. Frederick W. Taylor and his disciples introduced the science of management with much fanfare about harmonizing the interests of employer and employee. As Taylor said, "both sides take their eyes off the division of the surplus until this surplus becomes so large that it is unnecessary to quarrel over how it shall be divided." Hard-boiled economics wrapped in the mystique of science provided an answer to class struggle. Wages did not depend on collective bargaining or a redistribution of the fruits of labor, but on efficient production calculated with stopwatch precision and rewarded by incentive and bonus. That was how Louis Brandeis presented the case for scientific management in public testimony before the Interstate Commerce Commission in the Eastern Rate Case of 1911. He put an efficiency expert on the stand to tell an eager, gullible audience that instead of charging higher rates, railroads could save $1 million a day by cutting labor costs, which would benefit all concerned—stockholders, railway workers, shippers, and consumers.[41]

A battery of progressive intellectuals were soon waving Taylor's magic wand as a cure for profiteering and discontent. Whereas nineteenth-century critics such as Edward Bellamy had indicted the capitalist system for wasting monumental amounts of labor, capital, and resources, Herbert Croly and Walter Lippmann contended that efficiency entailed eliminating waste, and Josephine Goldmark held up efficiency as the remedy for overwork, long hours, and the employment of women in unhealthful conditions.[42] Efficiency, or "the elimination of waste," became a kind of anal-compulsive battle cry in the latter-day Puritan war on nature, outflanking the egalitarian rallying call for industrial democracy.

Another reason social reform did not make any greater headway was the counterweight of the South. In the first place, the South continued to be cursed by a vicious cycle of poverty and racism. It was possible for dogged optimists to find auguries of economic progress in the narrowing gap of regional wealth: in 1912 the South's per capita income was about half the national average; by 1940 it had risen to 65 percent.[43] But on balance, what stood out were the differences. On the eve of the First World War, the South was still burdened by the legacy of inequality bequeathed from plantation slavery to agrarian paternalism and then to industrial segregation. Although a few brave crusaders raised their voices in favor of labor laws, protective legislation, and women's suffrage, the South lacked the key ingredients for a successful social-justice coalition. Working-class organization was unusually weak, in large part because of the influence of racial segregation, and middle-class conscience was no stronger, in large part because of the paucity and timidity of the new urban professionals whose careers were bound up with social uplift. Where they did exist, it was often to operate the local franchise for national organizations such as the National Child Labor Committee and the Young Women's Christian Association.[44] Thus the social basis did not exist for the kind of cross-class alliance for social justice that made northern states such as Wisconsin and New York models of reform.

Southern politics was part of the problem. Progressive officeholders came largely from the ranks of planters, mill owners, and bankers and were more likely to be boosters than knockers of business. Several southern governors such as Hoke Smith of Georgia and Braxton Comer of Alabama won reputations as progressives by building roads and schools, aiding commercial banking, and otherwise promoting industrial development. Such factory and railroad regulations as existed had even fewer teeth than similar measures in the North. Thus, in the main, southern progressivism was a conservative version of its northern counterpart confined to "whites only," and it caused barely a ripple in corporate offices.[45]

Populism was no longer a threat, either. Having given a great scare in the 1890s, populism had become a grotesque caricature of its former self. Elites had taken advantage of demagogic ferment around the "race question" to disfranchise virtually the entire black electorate and, by means of the poll tax, residency rules, and literacy tests, had also effectively excluded as many as half the white voters. In some cases, this evisceration of democracy had been carried out in the name of progressive reform, as in Virginia, where the turnout of the potential electorate dropped from 59.6 percent in 1900 to 27.7 percent in 1904 after the new measures went into effect. Cut off from their popular voting base and thoroughly poisoned by white racism, former Populists such as Georgia's Tom Watson and out-and-out demagogues such as South Carolina's Cole Blease clung to power by posing as champions of the little guy against the rich. Playing out the farce, what had been a vibrant reform tradition in the days of the Populists degenerated into a choice between elite progressives and populist impostors.[46]

The effect was felt all the way to Washington. The Democrats' control of the White House and Congress under President Wilson, an adopted son of the South, gave southern elites greater weight in the scales of national power than they had enjoyed since the antebellum period. The names of southern legislators were affixed to every major piece of New Freedom legislation, including the Underwood Tariff, the Clayton Anti-Trust Act, the Glass Federal Reserve System, and the Adamson Railway Act. In keeping with the spirit of southern progressivism, the region's representatives supported federal aid for farm loan credits, agricultural education, highways, and boll weevil eradication, in effect writing a preface to southern support for the Sheppard-Towner child health bill in the 1920s and federal aid to agriculture under both Hoover and Roosevelt. Where capitalist development and commercial agriculture were concerned, the South supported federal action.[47]

However, the southern delegation brought not just a glass of tepid progressivism to Washington, but gallons of the entire Dixie elixir. Having embraced the scholarly canon that Reconstruction had been a ghastly mistake, Wilson now appointed a raft of southern segregationists to the cabinet. Postmaster General Albert Burleson and Treasury Secretary William McAdoo promptly segregated previously integrated government facilities, a move Wilson supported over the vehement protests of Afro-American leaders such as William Monroe Trotter. Meanwhile, he waxed enthusiastic about *Birth of a Nation* (1916), D. W. Griffith's epic masterpiece of white supremacy in which the Ku Klux Klan is lionized as the redeemer of the white South from the lecherous and corrupt rule of blacks and carpetbaggers. As a Presbyterian gentleman, Wilson abominated mob rule, but he turned a deaf ear to the mounting demands from the National Association for the Advancement of Colored People for national action against lynch mobs. In fairness, the North also took *Birth of a Nation* to heart and was preparing to greet southern black migrants with a spate of vicious race riots from 1917 through 1919, which strengthened white supremacy as a national phenomenon.[48]

The South acted as a potent counterbalance to feminism and social justice. The South was the most reliable bastion of opposition to women's suffrage. Southern advocates of suffrage were few and far between, and for every Jessie Daniel Ames arguing the case against paternalism on grounds of equal rights there were many others such as Belle Kearney who argued that white men of power ought to see "Anglo Saxon women as the medium through which to retain the supremacy of the white race over the African." Left to the South, women's suffrage would never have been enacted; only four southern states eventually ratified the Nineteenth Amendment.[49]

The same could be said for the social-justice legislation that squeaked through in Wilson's first term, such as labor laws pertaining to seamen and federal workers. In the case of child labor, the Keating-Owen Act of 1916 met intense opposition from the Carolinas, where the textile industry was centered, and if two Border states are excluded, a slight majority of the South's representatives voted against it. Where federal intervention threatened both racial segregation and property rights, southern gentlemen were among the staunchest defenders of laissez faire. Heeding the warnings of the National Association of Manufacturers, they opposed an eight-hour law for federal employees on the grounds that it "would upset everything in the towns, would bring the Negro in in great numbers."[50] The one point on which the South joined forces with progressive social reformers was Prohibition; beginning in Georgia in 1907 and running through Wilson's presidency, every state in the region eliminated the saloon, and southern representatives were a leading force in passage of the Eighteenth Amendment. But Prohibition was not only a repressive measure that gave authorities a club over blacks, poor whites, and immigrants alike; as the country was soon to discover, it caused more crime than uplift.[51] As southern politics counterbalanced the budding alliance of urban workers and new middle classes around social reform, it was not only southerners who paid the price of the South's peculiar institutions, it was the whole country.

National elites had to look elsewhere for models of how to govern. In fact, they experimented with three models. The first was old-fashioned liberalism—a state of courts and parties, a policy of laissez faire on social issues, the use of troops to police industrial disturbances, and the ruling myths of private property right, separate spheres, and white supremacy. Still the dominant model, it hardly presented an innovative path to the future. The other two models—progressive and managerial—were rival attempts to resolve the contradiction between emerging social forces and the existing liberal state, and they would compete with each other through the First World War into the New Era and all the way to the New Deal. They represented alternative revisions in the American liberal tradition of self-government. Managerial liberals redefined it to mean self-government in industry, emphasizing the public benevolence of the private corporation. Progressives redefined it in social terms, emphasizing government as the benevolent influence balancing the claims of selfish private interests. At the end of Wilson's first term in 1916, progressives held the initiative at the national level, and social reformers, social feminists, and the labor movement were notching victories, however small, for social legislation. For the moment it seemed as if the walls of laissez faire were going to fall.

Progressivism versus German Statism

The completion of Wilson's 1916 legislative program in time for the fall election rang down the curtain on the progressive period in American history. It was a time when the old order of laissez-faire liberalism began to die, while a new order struggled to be born; when family capitalism gave way to corporate capitalism; when the first Industrial Revolution of factories and steam power gave way to a second phase of mass production and electric power; when small farmers took a back seat to rising industrial workers; when a nation of immigrants from northern Europe tried to decide how to react to the mass influx of southern and eastern Europeans. There was drama enough in these epic social changes; yet always the most compelling part of the story was the way people became conscious of the tensions in their daily lives and fought them out in public life. For some dozen years, insurgent forces at the grass roots had taken the initiative, carrying their campaigns for reform to the camp of Yankee Protestant elites, never marching in a single column but repeatedly throwing the enemy on the defensive. Unwilling to rest content in the face of social injustice, they threw down the gauntlet of reform whenever the New Woman demanded equal suffrage and birth control, or the labor movement demanded industrial democracy and social welfare, or socialists called for nationalization of the giant corporations. This was progressivism at the grass roots, and ever since, the term *progressive* has been applied to the junction point between liberalism and the left.

The ultimate threat in these restive social movements was that they would somehow be able to turn democratic political traditions against the reigning elites. Ever since the first age of reform, in the time of Andrew Jackson, the democratic idea that the people should rule themselves packed a potentially subversive punch, especially in combination with the antiauthoritarian implications of universal suffrage and consent of the governed. If these great myths could be put into practice in the actual life of the society as well as in the realm of formal political rights, then the upper classes, from Wall Street investors to Chicago parvenus, might well tremble. In the absence of a ruling establishment—no bishops, no king, no hereditary privilege, no bureaucracy, no great standing army—dominant and subordinate groups coexisted in an uneasy compromise between hierarchy and democracy.[52] In the past, business elites had shielded themselves from democratic use of the state by the doctrine of laissez faire, and laissez faire remained the most adamant enemy of social reform all through the period.

However, it was plain that a society of corporate planning and mass welfare needs could not be governed by the precepts of nineteenth-century liberalism. And if grass-roots progressivism was going to be checked, there had to be modifications of the liberal state. Among the growing number to recognize these imperatives were the managerial liberals. Refusing to play King Canute with the tide of reform rising all around, pioneer organizations of enlightened capitalists began to offer positive programs of their own. Determined to keep their shops and communities out of the hands of trade unions and social reformers, the National Civic Federation and the National Industrial Conference Board promised to bring a modicum of security to modern industrial society. They invented welfare capitalism as the alternative to state welfare, touted scientific management as the solution to waste, proposed corporate philanthropy as the alternative to public expenditure, and argued that the cure for poverty was raising productivity, not redistribution of wealth. In short, they held up big business itself as the source of social reform, and thus transformed nineteenth-century laissez-faire liberalism into modern managerial liberalism.

Recognizing the same imperatives, elite progressives at the national level charted a course between grass-roots reform and corporate business, between democracy with a "social" bent and managerial liberalism. Some of their achievements were in reform of the political process, notably the direct election of senators, made possible through the Seventeenth Amendment. Others were in economic policy. The Wilson administration performed a virtuoso balancing act as it built reforms into the liberal state. The Federal Reserve System, for example, combined the element of private banker control with the element of public oversight through the presidentially appointed board affectionately known in Wall Street as "the Fed." Likewise, the Federal Trade Commission combined private control of business with public regulation through cease-and-desist orders. Wilson was more timid about intervening in industrial relations, but the Commission on Industrial Relations, the new federal mediation service, and the Adamson Act represented the first institutional recognition that the government should mediate between labor and capital. These were the first steps in the creation of a corporate-regulatory complex, a permanent private-public structure whose respiratory cycles of expansion and contraction would carry on through wartime expansion, contraction in the 1920s, expansion again in the Great Depression, and so on down to the late twentieth century.

To understand why America's corporate-regulatory complex took the shape it did, comparison with Germany is useful. Both countries were in the grip of similar world-historical forces—mass production/ mass reproduction, corporate or "organized" capitalism, the "social question," changes in the relation between the sexes, and the ideological and political struggles that these social forces engendered. The point of departure for understanding German development is the inverse of liberal America—not the supremacy of society over the state, but the opposite. On the eve of the First World War, the constitutional pyramid of power fashioned by Bismarck for the Wilhelmine empire remained intact, with the imperial chancellor responsible not to elected representatives in the Reichstag, but to the emperor and his army. Industrial-financial elites supported this system as strongly as traditional landed and bureaucratic elites; the middle classes had given up their quarrel with monarchy after the failed revolution of 1848; and even working-class leaders accepted a centralized regime upon which they projected their own future rule. The welter of medieval free cities, petty principalities, and the great kingdoms of Prussia and Bavaria remained united into one state, federal in form but monolithic in fact.

In an effort to explain this authoritarian system to American readers, the pro-German journal *The Fatherland* insisted on recognition of Germany's imperiled geopolitical position: "National existence among close, hostile and powerful neighbors depends on power as a nation. The individual must always place the state before himself."[53] As a consequence, social relations were immediately seen in political terms, in contrast to the American system, in which the long sway of the market tended to separate social relations from state power. Just as Germany's foreign entanglements had helped crystallize the two great international blocs that had plunged into war in 1914, so government at home was a matter of interparty negotiation to form governing blocs, of which the alliance of Conservatives and National Liberals was a longstanding example, and the "Bulow bloc" a short-lived one. Not even defeat in war and the founding of the Weimar Republic would dislodge this system of parliamentary blocs, which continued to be the rule in the precarious circumstances of the 1920s.

The contrast to the United States is obvious. No such formal blocs existed, and the reason was, at least in part, geopolitical. In contrast to central Europe, the United States was spared the pressures of international diplomacy by virtue of its isolation across the seas, a circumstance that permitted the supremacy of society over the state and the divorce of mass-based parties from particular social interests. Instead of the multiparty system with complex negotiations among the parties to form a government, the two-party system did not offer programmatic or ideological combat between Republicans and Democrats. In fact the parties were essentially loose electoral machines, not tight governing institutions. The contrast between German and American parties shows, in short, how the relation between state and society was shaped by the international relation of forces.

In further contrast, German society was thoroughly integrated at the level of the state, whereas American society was not. The difference between the two can be described as "loose coupling" in the United States versus "tight coupling" in Germany.[54] There were only indirect connections in the United States between occupation, status, access to education, religious belief, party identity, social welfare, civil service, and state power. By contrast, in Germany the links among all these things were tightly drawn. Although the links were severely strained by social change and individual mobility, boundaries between hierarchical levels were quite distinct, political parties were clearly based within occupational levels, and nothing moved without affecting some aspect of state power. In other words, the modes of social production and social reproduction were visibly tied to the governing system.

That was certainly the case at the highest levels of the state, where politics was the province of an oligarchy of notables. For example, the upper house of the federal legislature was composed of "the greatest executives of large enterprises and trusts, the most noted lawyers and professors, statesmen of the highest repute, financiers and bankers of the first rank, great land and realty owners, and prominent manufacturers and merchants." A post in the higher civil service depended on passage through an elite training school; social insurance was provided through different channels according to blue-collar or white-collar occupation; parties openly represented different economic interests; cities were governed by a self-selecting bourgeois oligarchy, even in centers of heavy industry such as Dusseldorf, where a top-down alliance of local industrialists and Catholic notables ran things to the exclusion of industrial workers. Even the German reputation for discipline and order was an accurate reflection of the sociopolitical hierarchy in the sense that from the time of Bismarckian social insurance down to 1914, nothing moved in society without being registered in the delicate balance of social interests represented in the state.[55]

Paradoxically, the proclivity for order ensured that social antagonism would be more or less openly represented in politics. That was certainly true of class conflict. Polarization between industrial workers and industrialists was measured in the rise of the Social Democrats to become the largest party in the Reichstag by 1912. It was widely believed that the schism between Social Democrats on one side and Conservatives and National Liberals on the other posed a direct threat to the Wilhelmine regime. It was also true in respect to social welfare. When Germans debated the social question, they took it for granted that answers would be worked out at the level of the state. It was even the case with religion. Bismarck's war against the pope (*Kulturkampf*) had been no more successful than his war against socialism and only guaranteed the formation of the Catholic Center party to look out for the confessional interests of Catholic citizens in a country in which Lutheranism was an established church in most of the federal states. Heirs of Luther, Marx, and Bismarck, Germans could not have escaped even if they had wanted to the direct representation of social antagonism in the state.[56]

The importance of the state was brought home in the fact that prominent differences in women's experiences in Germany and the United States derived in many instances from different forms of the state. Whereas patriarchal traditions had withered in America, going the way of patrimonial inheritance and paternal autocracy, they remained extremely potent in Germany, where they were inscribed in the legal code. Until revision of the Prussian civil code in 1900, husbands reigned supreme and could legally prohibit their wives from working outside the home. Even after revision, although wives controlled their own wages, husbands still controlled all family property. Domestic servants were still subject to quasi-feudal obligations depriving them of rights vis-à-vis their employers. In addition, citizenship inhered in gender: women were denied the vote and, in a realm where the military counted heavily, were excluded from military service. Most strikingly, until the 1908 Law of Association, women were barred from even forming public associations.[57] The importance of Germanic state traditions is suggested by a comparison with Norway and Sweden, every bit as Lutheran as Prussia, but where proprietary marriage was rapidly decaying.[58] Whatever the ultimate reason, patriarchal and paternalist forms of male dominance were especially strong in Germany. Denied access to public life and subject to severe constraints in marriage, women were not supposed to stray beyond children, church, and kitchen (*Kinder, Kirche, Küche*).

German men and women lived in the shadow of the state, for good and for ill. Foreign travelers reported German homes to be as well kept and well ordered as German factories, and linked the reputed efficiency and discipline to the habit of subordination to the state. The idea of the authoritarian family was already taking root well before the National Socialist party arrived on the scene. However, the other side of the authoritarian coin was the paternalist welfare state. With the aim of reducing infant mortality, the state added maternity insurance to accident and health benefits and gradually expanded eligibility and coverage to include all female wage earners. Thanks to the feminist Federation for Mother Protection, unmarried mothers also gained coverage.[59]

In America the balance was reversed. Foreign travelers from Alexis de Tocqueville to Harriet Martineau to Lord Bryce could not help commenting on the independent spirit of American women. It would have been too much to say, as one observer did in 1905, "In Germany women are 'subordinate,' that is they take orders from men; in America they are dominant and give orders to men."[60] But there was a kernel of truth in the idea that American women enjoyed greater individual liberty, because that was true of the whole society. The unwelcome companion of personal liberty was economic insecurity. American women enjoyed less security than German women, because the German state was geared to provide it, while the United States was not. Although "mothers' pensions" and workmen's compensation were introduced in the Progressive period, there was nothing to compare with arrangements under the German welfare state.

Advanced social insurance was one thing some American progressives found attractive in Germany. New Nationalists such as Herbert Croly touted Germany's unity of national purpose, educational efficiency, and military strength. Elite urban reformers admired the clean, efficient administration of German cities as a decided improvement over America's urban machines, what one called an "infinitely divided system of 'democratic' powers preying upon the public." But to most progressives, Germany represented an undesirable extreme of state control over society, the opposite pole to the equally undesirable extreme of laissez-faire individualism. Seeking a middle way between the two, John Dewey warned that in rejecting "atomistic empiricism" reformers should know that "the remedy is not to be found in recourse to a philosophy of fixed obligations and authoritative law such as characterized German political thinking." That fear of the state lurked behind everything progressives did, even as they expanded the sphere of state intervention.[61]

Wilsonian statecraft brought to a close the first chapter in the emergence of twentieth-century liberalism. The social movements of workers, women, and middle-class reformers had forced their issues into the public arena around calls for industrial democracy, feminism, and social reform, many of which were embodied in the spirited Progressive and Socialist party campaigns of 1912. But campaigning is not governing, and although American parties were responsible for putting people into elective office, they were not responsible for running the country, at least not in the same way as British, French, and, after 1918, German parliamentary parties. That cardinal difference gave President Wilson the flexibility he needed to include elements outside his own party in fashioning a program of reform. Elected as a Victorian liberal who advocated free trade and open competition, he adroitly stole regulatory and social justice planks from Roosevelt's Progressive party, thereby co-opting the social-justice wing of progressivism and, much more distantly, co-opting socialism. And if his program *contained* socialism and social reform in the inclusive sense, it also did so in the exclusive sense, making sure that there would be no significant experiments in state paternalism. Certainly, the southern wing of the Democratic party in conjunction with Republican business conservatives set severe restrictions on how far he could go toward aiding the poor.

Thus even at its highwater mark, progressive statecraft at the national level stopped far short of the kind of statist authority found in Germany. Instead of a German-style welfare state, President Wilson supported women's protective legislation on the state level and the federal child labor act, but scarcely anything more. Instead of full-scale federal mediation of industrial relations, he supported the exercise in public relations known as the Commission on Industrial Relations and the Adamson Act, but, again, little else. Instead of extensive state controls on central banking, Wilson set up the Federal Reserve System under private management with minimal federal oversight, and he appointed friends of business to the Federal Trade Commission. In short, instead of a statist bureaucracy, he constructed a corporate-regulatory complex within the liberal state that left society supreme over the state. As a consequence, the most powerful element in the market—that is, big business—remained supreme in society.

The corporate-regulatory complex pointed the way toward a new governing system in which corporate property and a new form of the nuclear family oriented toward consumption instead of production might be better secured than in the increasingly outmoded shell of laissez-faire liberalism. Certainly, the Federal Reserve helped legitimate Wall Street's finance capitalists at a time when their trusts had come under strong public censure. Likewise, protective legislation came to the support of the family ideal of husband-breadwinner/wife-homemaker, which legitimated women's subordination at a time when radical voices had been raised in favor of equality between the sexes. In addition, the new corporate order increased inequalities of wealth and income to the point that a higher share of income went to the top than ever before in American history; several combined studies show that inequality of income distribution peaked in 1916.[62] In sum, the achievement of Wilson's progressive statecraft was to remake the liberal state so that liberalism could continue as the dominant tradition in altered form, and also as a tradition that upheld the dominance of rich, white men.

This does not mean that social antagonism was adjourned, or that the great questions of the day had been answered, or that there would never be another attempt to remake the liberal state. But it did mean that progressivism would never get another chance; for even as the Wilsonians were putting the finishing touches on their work, a new dynamic took command of events as more and more the United States was drawn into the vortex of the Great War in Europe.

5

The Dynamics of
Total War

WHEN THE GUNS started booming on European battlefields in August 1914, the sound was just distant thunder to most Americans. Unable to conceive any course but neutrality, no one called for U.S. intervention, not Anglophiles or Germanophobes, missionary diplomats or imperial realists, President Wilson or ex-President Roosevelt. Yet over the next five years, the United States would reverse direction 180 degrees, not once, but twice. In the first reversal, Congress declared war on Germany and Austria-Hungary on April 6, 1917, at Wilson's urgent request with only a handful of dissenting votes. The federal government mustered all the economic, military, and psychological resources at its command for total war. Vowing not to stop until the enemy was driven to surrender, Wilson called for "force, force to the utmost, force without stint or limit."[1]

Then, after the guns fell silent, the country reversed course once again. Refusing to join the League of Nations, it came to regret ever having gone to war, renounced the use of force in formal treaties in the 1920s, and passed neutrality laws in the 1930s. This erratic behavior was brought on, in part, by internal divisions between the forces of reform and the forces of order. In 1917 and 1918 there was no more important question on the home front than how the dynamic of war would affect the dynamic of reform.

The dynamic of war was foisted upon the United States from the outside, in the sense that the country was not a party to the twin crises in domestic and international affairs that caused the outbreak of war in 1914. On the eve of war, each of Europe's great powers was racked by internal division that threatened the dominant position of its ruling classes. Because imperial Russia and Austria-Hungary were the most antiquated, their ruling classes were the most threatened; conversely, the most liberal regimes, Britain and France, were the least imperiled. Germany lay somewhere in between. It has been argued that German elites—landed, bureaucratic, and military—unilaterally plunged into war in a desperate attempt to fend off the rising power of working-class Social Democrats, and certainly they believed there was much to be gained from the national unity and internal discipline that inevitably came with war. In the international arena, two decades of economic expansion following the late nineteenth-century race for empire had produced two great international alliance systems—the Triple Alliance of Germany, Austria-Hungary, and Italy; and the Triple Entente of Britain, France, and Russia. The extremely delicate balance between the two blocs was revealed at every diplomatic flashpoint—the Morocco crises, revolution in Turkey, and war in the Balkans in 1912 and 1913. Add an arms race, nationalist passions, and military strategies that depended on rapid and total application of force, and the result by August 1914 was a world war waiting to happen.[2]

Decision

Although the outbreak of war in Europe had the air of tragic inevitability, that was not the case with the U.S. decision to intervene. Happily excluded from the two great alliance systems, the United States had no diplomatic promises to keep, and so from 1914 through 1916 a series of diplomatic crises came and went without consequence. A great public outcry over the German invasion of Belgium, fueled by British depictions of Prussian militarists bent on rape, booty, and conquest, passed without consequence. More serious was the sinking of the "unarmed" passenger liner *Lusitania* by a German U-boat on May 7, 1915, with the loss of 128 American lives, in part as a result of the explosion of munitions hidden deep in the hold. Although Wilson declared that the United States was "too proud to fight," he took the opportunity to protest the sinking to the German government, which promised to be more careful about civilian lives in the future. This exchange prompted Secretary of War William Jennings Bryan to resign in protest against the double standard that condemned Germany but ignored British violations of neutral rights on the high seas in enforcing its blockade of Germany. The next major crisis followed a similar script. A German U-boat sank an unarmed channel steamer, the *Sussex*, in March 1916, prompting U.S. protests and a German pledge to warn merchantmen before attack. Thus through 1916 U.S. diplomacy sidestepped the snares of belligerency.[3]

Much had changed, however, in the two years since war began. The labor and social reform movements together made inroads upon laissez faire as more and more states enacted protective legislation, workmen's compensation, mothers' pensions, and tenement inspection, while Wilsonian reforms such as the Federal Reserve System, the Clayton Act, and the child labor law had given just enough ground to placate popular demands for public control of the trusts. American culture blossomed forth with bright new ideas in iconoclastic magazines such as *The Masses* and the *New Republic*, in Carl Sandburg's *Chicago Poems* (1916), and in freewheeling discussions of the "new morality." Margaret Sanger returned from her European sojourn to court arrest for defying the Comstock code by opening a birth control clinic. Charlie Chaplin was making some of his finest silent movies, including *The Pawn Shop* (1916), depicting the ragamuffin workingman who was a thorn in the side of authority but a hero who always found true romance. Although Socialist party growth had slowed, there were still hundreds of socialist officeholders, and the prairie socialist newspaper, *Appeal to Reason*, reached 100,000 subscribers. In addition, the period saw the foundation of the militant National Women's party, the rise of "new unionism" in mass production, and the first ripple in what was to become a major strike wave in industry.[4]

With every new diplomatic crisis, social reformers turned more of their attention to the issue of peace. Shortly after the outbreak of fighting, luminaries such as Paul Kellogg and Florence Kelley founded the American Union against Militarism to inveigh against militarism as a mortal enemy of social progress. Jane Addams and sister activists organized the Women's Peace party and sent delegates to a 1915 pacifist conference at The Hague, which planted many antiwar seeds, one of which became the Women's International League for Peace and Freedom. The American Socialist party, for its part, held fast to the antiwar internationalism that its European comrades had forsaken in 1914, and a considerable body of AFL trade unionists believed that the only ones who stood to gain from U.S. participation in the war would be profiteering munitions makers. Alarmed by proposals to expand the military, the president of the United Mine Workers told its 1916 convention that he hoped "that the plans to make our country an armed camp which may be used to extend commercialism abroad and exploit labor at home will be defeated." Thus as the issue of the European war worked its way into the American body politic, the great majority of advanced progressives and socialists were Cassandras who warned that war would be the undoing for all the causes they held dear. So long as a decision on intervention could be put off, their call for peace and justice commanded the moral and political high ground.[5]

There is no doubt that a majority of the population opposed U.S. entry into the war at least through the November 1916 elections. Their motives, however, did not always square with the aims of the reformers. To isolationists of the small-town Midwest and jingoists of the big city press, the Monroe Doctrine, with its rigid separation of Western and Eastern Hemispheres, was holy writ. Such traditional liberals had no compunctions about sending the marines to Latin America, but the idea of sending troops to Europe was sheer heresy. For different reasons, Irish-Americans opposed any aid to Britain, their ancient passion rekindled by the bloody suppression of the 1916 Easter Rebellion; and there was a similar fear in German-American communities that the United States would enter the war on the wrong side. Neutrality was popular with voters in both the West and the South, but although large numbers of western voters combined peace and progressive principles, very few southern voters did, and they were the most solidly Democratic.[6] The fact that many who supported neutrality harbored no principled opposition to war and saw no incompatibility between war, once it came, and their own domestic agendas helps explain why the country could reverse directions so abruptly in the spring of 1917.

On the opposite side of the fence, a small band of eastern patricians beat the drum for preparedness. Just as the progressives attached world peace to their reform program, so the cream of the Yankee Protestant establishment made military buildup an integral part of their campaign for national unity. The growing ranks for preparedness came from the arch-Republican members of the Union League, the "swallow-tailed" Democrats of the posh Manhattan Club, a bevy of Ivy League presidents, the *New York Times*, and a number of New Nationalists itching for a return to power, including General Leonard Wood, Elihu Root, and Teddy Roosevelt. All of these were prominent in the League to Enforce Peace, had close ties to the military through the Navy and Army Leagues, and were identified with the managerial reforms in the military begun during Root's tenure as secretary of war a decade ear-

lier. As the war on Europe's western front settled into bloody stalemate, they took some satisfaction in congressional appropriations for
new battleships, but had to settle for less than they hoped in the National Defense Act of June 1916. Disappointed because the national
guard, reserves, and regulars were not integrated into a massive "continental army" with universal military service, Secretary of War Lind-
ley Miller Garrison resigned in protest. All the same, the act increased
the regular army to 175,000 and the national guard to 475,000 and established machinery for civilian mobilization under the Council of National Defense.[7] Clearly, the warmakers were gaining ground.

Besides beating plowshares into swords, the militants of preparedness countered social justice with social discipline. Teach the manly
virtues of martial discipline to the unruly multitudes of immigrant
workers, and the problems of popular ferment and industrial discontent would be solved. They founded such organizations as the National
Security League and the American Defense Society to preach "Absolute and Unquestioned Loyalty to the State," in the words of the lead
banner in a giant New York City parade, and they proposed 100 percent Americanism and universal military training as "the only way to
yank the hyphen out of America." Frances Kellor, hard-headed leader
of the National Americanization Committee, began to describe her
work as "the civilian side of national defense" and called for universal
military service in her aptly titled *Straight America: A Call to National
Service* (1916). It was no accident that Senator Henry Cabot Lodge and
Congressman Augustus P. Gardner, leaders of preparedness in Congress, were also among the most prominent immigration restrictionists;
nor is it surprising that many of their cohorts were attracted to the
racist theories of "Nordic" supremacy that had begun to make the
rounds of elite social clubs and Ivy League universities.[8]

The preparedness movement was also viscerally antiradical. When
an unidentified bomb-thrower attacked a preparedness parade in San
Francisco, local authorities pinned the blame on prominent labor radical Tom Mooney, whose innocence it took twenty years to vindicate.
As the social-justice wing of the 1912 Progressive party went over lock,
stock, and barrel to Wilson, New Nationalists around Roosevelt shed
the trappings of reform to emerge as the first American incarnation of
the twentieth-century right. New Nationalists always had an authoritarian streak—not for nothing was Teddy Roosevelt called "the American Bismarck"—and now they marched toward the netherworld of

authoritarian domination, restrained only by the liberal traditions of civilian supremacy and checks and balances, which prevented American nationalists from going the route of ultranationalist movements in Europe toward fascism.

The saber-rattlers of the eastern establishment were a potent influence for war, but they did not get exactly what they wanted. They did succeed in polarizing the presidential election in November around the question of war, but they lost the decision, in part, because their support for the Republican candidate, Charles Evans Hughes, was, at best, a mixed blessing. Wanting to avoid the appearance of a warmonger, Hughes shilly-shallied on preparedness and lost several northern states, while Wilson was able to ride to a narrow victory on the unequivocal slogan "He kept us out of war." Democratic victory came in the middle of an era of Republican dominance, and, aside from the anomalous election of 1912, the only time Democrats won the presidency between 1896 and 1932 was when they combined the issues of peace and justice. Eventually, when war came, the most prominent men of the Big Stick did not even get to wage it—Theodore Roosevelt was denied command of a volunteer regiment, Leonard Wood was denied command of the American Expeditionary Force, and Henry Cabot Lodge was excluded from the councils of power.[9]

Although Republican militarists did not get their way, pressure from northern elites was highly influential in the final decision for war. Certainly, there was no groundswell of popular enthusiasm to join the fighting. Even after the resumption of Germany's unrestricted U-boat warfare on February 1, nothing happened to compare with the jingoist outburst that erupted after the sinking of the *Maine* in 1898. But if the common people did not beat the war drums, more and more of the people in power did. To understand why neutrality became intolerable to governing elites, it is useful to examine the one place where American troops were already engaged on foreign soil—Mexico.

A decade and a half after the Spanish-American War, the United States was well on its way to hegemony in the Western Hemisphere. Although Britain and, increasingly, Germany maneuvered for influence among the unstable republics of Latin America, they were no match for U.S. investment, the Platt Amendment, the Olney and Roosevelt corollaries to the Monroe Doctrine, and repeated marine landings. The keystone of Latin America was Mexico. The same extractive and banking corporations that were coming to dominate the economy of the southwestern United States were growing increasingly potent in Mexican affairs—Daniel Guggenheim's American Smelting and Refining Company, with copper mines in Arizona and in Chihuahua; the Southern Pacific Railroad, with lines on both sides of the border; and Standard Oil, with wells in California and Tampico. Altogether, U.S. interests owned an astonishing 43 percent of all Mexican wealth, more than the Mexicans themselves![10] Seeing Mexico through the distorting lens of dollar signs did not help Yankees understand the historic differences between their country and Mexico. With great landed estates, patriarchal authority, and a Catholic establishment, nineteenth-century Mexico had not seen the growth of a large middle class of businessmen and family farmers upon which liberal forms of government could bite; instead, a corrupt, autocratic regime had grown up under the iron rule of Porfirio Díaz.

By 1911 leading families decided they had had enough of Díaz, and they ousted the dictator in a typical palace coup. But events soon took a more profound turn. Rapid and uneven economic development had generated great extremes of wealth and poverty, and under the leadership of men such as Emiliano Zapata and Pancho Villa, the submerged mass of dispossessed peasants, landless peons, and manual laborers began to stir. Their demands for redistributing the latifundia and for humanizing industrial conditions threatened to overturn the whole governing system, including the centuries-old network of special privilege, quasi-feudal estates, and the established church, as well as the more recent nexus of industrial and financial power. Though roughly contemporary with revolutions in China and Iran, the Mexican revolution was the first in the world to link a change of government with mass social upheaval.[11]

The Wilson administration plunged into this vortex of social revolution with painfully little understanding of the forces at work. Although Wilson was no fan of Taft's "dollar diplomacy," he operated within the same nexus of interests and assumptions—large-scale corporate investments, paternalist attitudes, and a closed mind on the superiority of liberal self-government. For the same reason that Yankee elites could not sympathize with dictators, *caudillos*, and corruption, they could not sympathize with peasant armies and the invasion of property rights. In the fall of 1913 Wilson persuaded the British government to follow the U.S. lead with a policy that was intended to "teach the South American Republics to elect good men" who would establish a government "under which all contracts and business and concessions will be safer than they have been." One of Wilson's key emissaries to Mexico was Franklin K. Lane, who publically invoked the White Man's Burden in justification of U.S. intervention: "There is a great deal of the special policeman, of the sanitary engineer, of the social worker, and of the welfare dictator about the American people . . . It is one of the most fundamental instincts that have made white men give to the world its history for the last thousand years." Lane would later describe the revolutionary leaders as "naughty children who are exercising all the privileges and rights of grown ups."[12]

To teach the Mexicans how to behave like good Americans, Wilson twice sent in troops. In April 1914, after the Tampico incident involving Mexican arrest of a U.S. naval officer and the discovery of an impending shipment of German arms, Wilson ordered a small detachment of U.S. troops to shoot their way into Vera Cruz. The stated purpose of extracting an apology from Victoriano Huerta's government, which the U.S. did not recognize, barely masked the real hope that Huerta would fall. And so he did, to be replaced by the Constitutionalist leader Venustiano Carranza, a man more in line with liberal principles but no more amenable to taking orders from Washington. Wilson was not to be mollified by only apparent success, and no sooner had "the First Chief" marched into Mexico City than the United States was casting about for someone to replace him. That it chose bandit-turned-revolutionary Pancho Villa to be the standard-bearer of stability lent an air of comic-opera unreality to the whole Mexican imbroglio. As the balance of forces in Mexico shifted toward the Constitutionalists, Villa made a desperate gamble to draw the United States into combat on Mexican soil and thereby weaken Carranza's claim to authority by crossing the border and attacking the U.S. garrison at Columbus, New Mexico, on March 9, 1916. Wilson took the bait. He ordered up the Punitive Expedition under General "Black Jack" Pershing, sent it into Mexico to hunt down Villa, and mobilized all 100,000 national guardsmen to defend the border. When Pershing blundered into a battle with the government's regular troops, the two countries stood at the brink of a full-scale war.[13]

Yet war did not come, even though the social revolution was reaching its crest. Radical influence reached high tide in the new constitution, in which article 123 established advanced social-welfare and labor regulations and article 27 provided for appropriation of latifundia for the purpose of creating smallholdings, as well as reserving all subsoil resources to the nation. The new constitution took effect February 5, 1917, the same day the last U.S. forces were evacuated. The puzzle is why the United States withdrew at the very moment corporate interests seemed most imperiled. The answer is that a larger threat was looming in Europe. In the same weeks Wilson was deciding on withdrawal from Mexico, he was attempting to mediate the war in Europe and could ill afford a war at his back while presenting himself to Europe as a peacemaker. He had already pulled back from the brink in Mexico on another occasion in the summer of 1916 because "it begins to look as if war with Germany is inevitable. If it should come, [and] I pray God it may not, I do not wish America's energies and forces divided for we will need every ounce of reserve we have to lick Germany." [14]

What sealed the decision to let Mexico go its own way was the growing fear that a German victory in Europe would upset the balance of power in Latin America. Since the United States was getting along well under British control of the high seas, and since Britain was cooperating with American policy in Mexico, the United States had reason to worry about a British defeat at the hands of Germany. Just five days before U.S. withdrawal from Mexico was complete, Germany had resumed unrestricted submarine warfare, and in anticipation of a probable U.S. declaration of war in response, German Secretary of State Arthur Zimmermann proposed a secret alliance in which Mexico would be encouraged "to reconquer its former territories in Texas, New Mexico, and Arizona." A flagrant affront to the Monroe Doctrine, the Zimmermann note burst like a bombshell upon Wilson's cabinet on February 25. Now, it must have been apparent to all concerned that Germany was in no position to make good on its promise to help Mexico regain territory lost to the United States seventy years earlier; Germany could not even contemplate a cross-Channel invasion, let alone wage transatlantic war. But the expression of intent was enough to convince the cabinet that the war in Europe was threatening U.S. interests throughout Latin America. The irony was that in preparing to defend the Monroe Doctrine, the United States was getting ready to violate one of its cardinal precepts—that the affairs of Europe should remain separate from those of the Western Hemisphere. But conditions had changed since the doctrine was originally formulated in the 1820s, and now U.S. hemispheric hegemony required action on a global scale. Much the same idea governed the favorable U.S. response to revolution in Russia, which broke out in March just as Wilson was making up his mind about intervening in Europe; that is, the precondition for incorporating revolutionary Russia in a liberal world order was the defeat of German autocracy.[15]

Wilson would not have dared turn the Monroe Doctrine inside out without compelling reasons. The first was American economic interests in Europe, a stake that grew with every increase in trade and credit to Britain and France. Owing to the effective British blockade, U.S. trade with Germany fell to a trickle while the tide of food, cotton, manufactured goods, and munitions going to the Allies rose to a flood. Above all, J. P. Morgan and other big Wall Street bankers were already financing the Allied war effort to the tune of more than $2 billion. It was not a calculation of short-term profits that tipped the balance; after all, neutrality had been good for business; for example, export-oriented cotton and wheat farmers remembered 1915–1917 as bonanza years to be used as the standard for determining "parity" between the prices of agricultural and manufactured commodities. Rather, it was the long-term worry about what would happen if America's biggest debtors and best trading partners went down to defeat.

The second reason was the Anglo-American cultural bond. To a generation raised on Tennyson, Kipling, and Shakespeare, England was still the Mother Country. From the earliest days of the war, there was little doubt that U.S. elites were largely Anglophilic, something the preparedness movement played to the hilt, since a decision for war seemed to promise a renewal of Anglo-Saxon cultural leadership in the face of "balkanizing" cultural influences. Germanophiles such as Sylvester Viereck were few and far between; Anglophiles were legion, and none was more devoted to English ways than the president. The New York patriciate and the first families of Virginia aped the mores of Britain's faded aristocracy, not those of German barons, and despite the impact of German scholarship in certain American universities, the Ivy League looked to Oxbridge more than to Heidelberg for its curriculum, architecture, and social values. Somehow identification with German, Polish, Italian, or Russian roots was the mark of undesirable "hyphenates," whereas worshiping at the feet of English aristocracy was the mark of a true American. In the same vein, the decision for war rallied Yankee Protestants, southern Anglo-Saxons, midwestern Wasps, and western Anglos around the White Man's Burden. Even as Wilson postponed a final decision through the agonizing days of March, he told

Secretary Robert Lansing that "'white civilization' and its domination over the world rested largely on our ability to keep this country intact as we would have to build up the nations ravaged by war." [16]

The third and final reason was Wilson's realization that he would have no voice at the peace table unless he put armies into the field. In December 1916, seeking a middle way between peace and preparedness at home and between Britain and Germany abroad, Wilson tried a hand at peacemaking by asking the belligerents to state their war aims. When the responses to his messages made it clear that despite the military stalemate, both sides still sought victory, he took it unto himself to define the basis for settlement in his famous "Peace without Victory" message of January 22, 1917. In it he proposed freedom of the seas, equality of nations, moderation of arms, and consent of the governed as the basis for a lasting peace. Given the strength of the great powers even as they tore each other apart, there could be no assertion of U.S. hegemony over Europe. Instead, American diplomacy presented its egalitarian face, as it always did when checked by equal or greater power. Ignoring the fact that the Monroe Doctrine had become a warrant for U.S. domination in the Western Hemisphere, Wilson pretended that it stood unambiguously for self-determination and recommended that all nations "adopt the doctrine of President Monroe as the doctrine of the world." Having failed to mediate between the belligerents, he was, in effect, proposing to go over their heads and guarantee peace among equals by "the organized force of mankind," a beautiful and grandiose notion that was the germ of the League of Nations. [17] Taken together, these were the basic ideas of the Fourteen Points.

Even as Wilson called for "peace without victory," Germany had decided upon resumption of unrestricted submarine warfare, to begin February 1. This was the decision that lit the fuse that eventually ended in the U.S. declaration of war two months later, but only after the application of a diplomatic double standard. British violations of freedom of the seas and neutral rights with the intention of starving the Central powers into submission did not provoke humanitarian outcries and diplomatic protest in the United States of the same magnitude as German U-boat sinkings of merchant and passenger ships. Nor did the fact that Britain and Japan had already picked clean the carcass of Germany's overseas colonies in Africa and China. In other words, Germany would be held to strict account for violations of liberal principles, whereas Britain would be excused. In any event, when a small group of determined neutral senators blocked the president's request to arm U.S. merchantmen, Wilson scorned them as "a little group of willful men" and went ahead and armed the vessels anyway under obscure executive authority. Armed neutrality, not war, was the immediate response to U-boat warfare, and for a short time it kept the U.S. on the middle path between peace and preparedness.[18]

With each step toward belligerency, more segments of American opinion came to accept full-scale war as preferable to armed neutrality. In mid-March the entire cabinet, including southern Democrats such as Albert Burleson and progressives such as Josephus Daniels and Newton Baker, recommended the warpath. Traditional liberals in the Republican party swung around to a prowar stance alongside the New Nationalists, as did southern Democrats and even many Bryan Democrats and *New Republic* progressives.[19] This shift in the internal balance of forces was accompanied by a shift in the international balance as a result of the Russian Revolution in early March, which seemed to make it a clear fight between democracy and autocracy (provided, of course, British and French imperialism were ignored). Thus on April 2, his conscience clear, Wilson could finally ask Congress for a declaration of war.

The speech was a masterstroke of national unification. In the first place, its spirit of crusading liberalism fused the main segments of elite opinion—the bellicose nationalists of the eastern establishment, the traditional liberals of the Midwest, and the leading men of the New South. After noting the outrages of submarine warfare, Wilson reiterated the main points of his "Peace without Victory" message—freedom of the seas, self-determination, and a concert of nations opposed to militarism. But even more significant was his appeal to the common people through the single most memorable phrase of the entire war, the ringing pledge "to make the world safe for democracy." Confronted by a lack of popular enthusiasm for war, he reached out to the laboring masses in town and country with the one thing that might inspire a passion great enough to overcome revulsion for the mass slaughter going on in the trenches. He said that world order depended on all people becoming "really free and self-governed," not subject to autocratic governments dominated by little groups of ambitious men and outmoded dynasties. Thus the United States would make war on Germany in order to rid the world of tyranny on behalf of "the liberation of its peoples," adding with remarkable audacity, "the German peoples included."[20] Wilson's vision of America leading a world crusade was a tour de force that united elites and masses, liberalism and democracy.

It was true that antiwar sentiment persisted. It could be found in many working-class precincts of northern cities, where the socialist vote increased; among farmers of the high plains who followed the Non-Partisan League; among some midwestern progressive backers of Wisconsin's Robert La Follette and Nebraska's George Norris, both of whom joined Claude Kitchin of North Carolina to lead Senate opposition to the war resolution. Warning that belligerency would benefit only bankers and munitions makers, Norris spoke fervently against the resolution in the populist tones of Bryan's "cross of gold" speech: "We are going into war upon the command of gold . . . I feel that we are about to put the dollar sign on the American flag." Whatever its effect on prairie populists and discontented workers, such dire warnings otherwise fell on deaf ears. Jeremiads against big business no longer incited anger among what Randolph Bourne called "the worried middle classes." Those who had been through the crusades against the trusts and industrial abuses "were only too glad to sink back to a glorification of the State ideal, to feel about them in war the old protecting arms, to return to the old primitive sense of the omnipotence of the State, its matchless virtue, honor, and beauty, driving away all the foul old doubts and dismays."[21]

When the vote came, only six senators stood opposed. Victorious at home, Wilson was free to embark on the high seas of world power, not as a Machiavellian power broker, but as a crusading liberal, indeed, a New World revolutionary who would redeem the sins of the Old. Truly, Woodrow Wilson was the last of the Founding Fathers.

War Nationalism

Having chosen to fight, there was no alternative but to wage total war. Europeans had already shown the way. In 1914 the spirit of nationalism had overwhelmed domestic political squabbles, uniting each country in collective hatred for the enemy. Germans sang a "Hymn of Hate" for the ancient Slavic enemy; France came together around the spirit of revenge for defeat in 1870; Britons of all ranks rushed to defend Britannia against the Prussian marauder; and even the doddering empires of Russia and Austria-Hungary felt a wave of national pride that temporarily washed away internal conflicts. Such were the enthusiasms that turned Europe into a charnel house. The casualties at the siege of Verdun in the spring of 1916 reached 350,000 French and 330,000 German dead, and that summer an even more staggering 1 million died on both sides in the protracted Battle of the Somme.[22]

Thus, by the time the United States began to gear up for war, the diabolical path to fear and loathing was clearly marked. The extraordinary thing is that the American public, which must have had some inkling of this immense slaughter, still marched off to war in a spirit of jaunty confidence. Never were soldiers so perky while entering the death house. Singing the popular ditties "The Yanks Are Coming," "Over There," and "Mademoiselle from Armentiers," American doughboys set out to test their mettle, blithely ignoring what the young men of Europe had been finding out—that the muck and barbed wire of trench warfare was a sorry place to practice the manly art of war.

Evidently nationalism had the capacity to make sane men mad. This was but the latest of America's periodic binges of patriotic fervor. Particularly around moments of national expansion in the Mexican and Spanish-American wars, the country went into fits of Manifest Destiny and jingoism, spasms that soon passed in an extreme, up-and-down emotional cycle. Now, once again, the declaration of war in the spring of 1917 put the United States into a manic mood. In the conjurings of an overheated imagination, no image of "the Hun" was too barbaric, no depiction of Prussian militarism too bloodthirsty, no account of the "rape of Belgium" too repulsive. Such mass pathology was what Randolph Bourne had in mind when he warned, "War is the health of the state."[23]

The fact was that in the age of democratic warfare, it would have to be fought by the masses *with their consent*. And where consent was not freely given, the state was ready to enforce it by fostering what Tocqueville had long before called the "tyranny of the majority." Wilson agonized about it the night before he asked Congress to declare war: "Once lead this people into war and they'll forget there ever was such a thing as tolerance. To fight you must be brutal and ruthless, and the spirit of ruthless brutality will enter into the very fibre of our national life, infecting Congress, the courts, the policeman on the beat, the man in the street." Nationalism brooked no domestic enemies. Needless to say, everything German was suspect. There had been much alarm about "German intrigues" during the neutrality period, and now federal authorities interred some 6,000 enemy aliens, while the Bureau of Investigation mobilized some 250,000 volunteer sleuths under the American Protective League who pretended to ferret out German spies. Authorities at all levels of government were determined to expunge German influence in American culture by prohibiting German-language instruction, impugning the loyalty of people with German names, and going to the absurd lengths of renaming sauerkraut "liberty cabbage."[24]

Other immigrant nationalities also fell under the shadow of suspicion, regardless of their position on the war. In particular, Slavs and Jews from the Russian and Austro-Hungarian empires, along with Italian immigrants became the target of an increasingly virulent nativism; it did not seem to matter that Italy had switched to the Allied side, and most South Slavs yearned for the breakup of Austria-Hungary. Such nice distinctions mattered little to the growing chorus of nativists who identified foreign birth itself with disloyalty. Although President Wilson opposed immigration restriction, he had given aid and comfort to the nativists, unintentionally perhaps, in his warning about "hyphenated-Americans pouring their poison into our veins." Now in the first rush of nationalism, Congress enacted over Wilson's veto a literacy test designed to exclude unlettered and supposedly ignorant immigrants from southern and eastern Europe.[25]

The deepest prejudices were reserved for African-Americans. Under the stress of war, contradictions between nationalism and racism quickly came into the open. The cutoff in European immigration created a demand for unskilled labor that was met in part by some 500,000 African-Americans who moved north in the Great Migration. As a consequence, northern cities were rife with racial tension, and white youths unleashed a brutal race riot in East St. Louis in the summer of 1917. The same contradiction could be found in the military itself. There were black American soldiers in every war fought by the United States, and this was no exception, as units like the notable 92nd Regiment made their contribution on the battlefield. But African-Americans served in segregated units with mostly white officers and were relegated for the most part to logistical operations. These indignities, compounded by mistreatment by local police, led to a bloody mutiny of black American soldiers stationed in Houston on August 23, 1917, which left twenty-one dead, mostly whites, and resulted in courts-martial and hangings for the rebels. Not since the end of Reconstruction had the country seen African-Americans in armed rebellion, a spirit of defiance kindled by the promises and betrayals of wartime nationalism that would soon give birth to the race-proud New Negro.[26]

Wartime flag-waving unleashed a new round of vigilantism. The West had its share of antiwar dissidents, such as the Central Labor Union of Miami, Arizona, which denounced the "purely commercial war brought about by the concentration of wealth," and the draft resisters of Oklahoma's Green Corn Rebellion, which took its name from the proposal to forage on ripening corn along a protest march route to Washington. But on the whole, the IWW and other opponents resisted conscription with words, not arms. Supporters of the war were considerably more violent. When industrial disputes broke out in the summer of 1917, Anglo residents along the border with Mexico had already organized paramilitary squads to deal with border raiders from Mexico and rebellious copper workers, in the belief that Mexican revolutionaries such as Pancho Villa were collaborating with the IWW. In Bisbee and Jerome, Arizona, vigilantes conducted infamous "deportations"; on July 12 copper company officials and Citizens Protective Leagues rounded up over 1,000 strikers and sent them in sealed boxcars into the desert heat. The hapless deportees wound up in what amounted to military confinement at the army post in Columbus, New Mexico, site of the notorious Villa raid a year earlier. In a similar episode on August 1, vigilantes in Butte, Montana, put a rope around the neck of Wobbly organizer Frank Little, cut off his genitals, and flung his beaten and mutilated body off a railroad trestle to dangle until he died. No southern lynch mob could have done more.[27]

One of the heaviest ironies of the war was the suppression of dissent in the name of democracy. The fact that elites had closed ranks around the declaration of war did not automatically translate into universal popular support. The worst fear in Washington was that somehow vocal opponents of the war would tap into the mass of disgruntled farmers, workers, and Irish- and German-Americans. Indeed, in the fall 1917 elections socialist candidates increased their percentage of the vote over their prewar totals in a number of cities, vindicating the decision of the Socialist party to defy the government, the only member of the Second International to do so. In addition, Quaker pacifists and Wobblies raised dissident voices, and some labor progressives, immigrant socialists, and single taxers set up the People's Council (with a friendly eye toward the councils of workers and soldiers in revolutionary Russia). Given the possibility that antiwar sentiment might fuse with social reform, Washington could not afford to ignore it.[28]

With the "ruthless brutality" Wilson had predicted, his own administration moved to silence dissent. Armed with the Espionage Act (June 1917) and the Sedition Act (May 1918), Postmaster General Burleson excluded *The Masses, International Socialist Review,* and all other left-wing publications from the mails, except those that followed minority Socialists in recanting their party's position. Seeking to silence its most vociferous working-class critics, the Justice Department moved to outlaw the IWW altogether. In the first of many raids, agents swooped down on IWW offices in September 1917, scooping up tons of evidence to be used in the prosecution of more than 100 top leaders of the embattled organization. Indictments charged the IWW with deliberate violation of the Selective Service and Espionage Acts and with seditious conspiracy for its strikes and sabotage against war producers, even going so far as to criminalize syndicalist ideas in prosecutions for use of the motto "An injury to one is an injury to all." The antiradical campaign reached absurd heights on the western slopes of the Rockies when the army sent in Colonel Bryce Disque, veteran of the campaign against Aguinaldo in the Philippines, to pacify recalcitrant timberworkers by enrolling them in what amounted to an antiunion closed shop christened the Loyal Legion of Loggers and Lumbermen.[29]

The loyalty campaign spread far and wide. The Justice Department's fledgling Bureau of Investigation gave encouragement to the amateur gumshoes of the American Protective League in their surveillance of labor radicals and their vigilante-style "slacker raids" directed largely against unemployed workers. Meanwhile, official spies from the Justice Department attended socialist rallies against "capitalist war" to collect evidence for use against scores of socialist leaders, including Eugene Debs, who was convicted and sent to the Atlanta penitentiary. Debs's lawyers objected that the suppression of liberty in the name of liberty did not make a very pretty sight, but that did not impress the Supreme Court, which upheld book banning and the convictions of dissenters. One case involving a Socialist party leader yielded one of the most significant doctrines in American jurisprudence, the "clear and present danger test." In the *Schenck* (1918) decision, Justice Oliver Wendell Holmes opined that free speech could be punished under circumstances such as war where there was "a clear and present danger" that speech could lead to illegal acts.[30]

The first six months of war confirmed Wilson's dire prediction about the spirit of intolerance. Once loosed, the dogs of war could not be restrained from attacking immigrants, racial minorities, pacifists, radicals, and, in general, anyone who did not conform to the superpatriots' notion of true Americanism. It did not take long for the political impact to be felt. First, war nationalism drove a fatal wedge into the fragile coalition from below that had made 1916 a banner year for social reform and had elected the peace candidate president, sealing the once-open border between socialism and national progressivism. One illustration of the end of cooperation between the left and the progressives was the fragmentation of the American Union against Militarism, an organization that had grown up on the border between socialism and progressivism, so to speak, but that now shattered into three opposing parts—the antiwar People's Council (hounded out of existence), the forerunner of the American Civil Liberties Union (put under surveillance), and prowar supporters of the Wilson administration (welcomed into the fold). Although the left was the immediate sufferer, the whole progressive reform project was dealt a crushing blow. Second, the ability of the patriotic societies to wrap themselves in Old Glory revitalized old-fashioned liberalism, with all its racial and nativist assumptions. After suffering a decade of criticism from the reformers, the worried middle classes of British-American descent could at last reestablish the claim for their own small-town verities—self-made men and true women, Anglo-Saxon preeminence, and the rights of property—as the only true 100 percent Americanism.

Mobilizing Masses

If there was madness in nationalism, there was also a method to it. Total war involved a devastating combination of rationality and irrationality, modern efficiency and atavistic hatreds, the machine gun and war hysteria. Because society had evolved elaborate structures of rationalized production and mass reproduction, the United States could not fight the kind of "splendid little war" it had waged against Spain in 1898. Instead, it would have to fight as Europeans had learned to fight, not by daring cavalry maneuvers or bold Schlieffen Plans, but by systematically mobilizing all available forces and hurling them against the forces on the other side, mass against mass. By the time it was over some 10 million had died, and the killing power of modern mechanized warfare was linked to the rapid growth of heavy industry. Pig iron output in Germany grew from 1.3 million tons in 1870 during the Franco-Prussian War to 14.7 million tons in 1914, and there were similar increases elsewhere. Once the Industrial Revolution was harnessed to war nationalism, the potential for destruction was virtually limitless.[31]

The Wilson administration used modern mass communications to mobilize every bit of emotional and material energy in the country. All the agencies of government used the mass media for their own purposes—the Treasury sold Liberty Bonds, the Food Administration sold conservation, and the War Department sold patriotism. The prime minister of high-power salesmanship was George Creel, head of the Committee on Public Information (CPI), who boasted about "how we advertised America" through three dozen propaganda films such as "Pershing's Crusaders," 1 million four-minute speeches in movie theaters by "4-Minute Men," and 75,099,023 pieces of patriotic literature. Unlike out-and-out nativists, the Creel Committee accorded immigrant cultures a certain respect through its Division for Work with the Foreign Born, which used the foreign-language press as a multilingual megaphone to advertise Red Cross subscriptions and Liberty Bonds. Government agencies mobilized ethnic benevolent and religious societies for prowar celebrations, such as a big Kosciusko Day rally in Chicago that brought together the Polish National Alliance, Polish Falcons, and Roman Catholic Union.[32]

The aim, of course, was to foster not immigrant nationalism but American nationalism. Toward that end, the U.S. Bureau of Education endorsed the National Americanization Committee's proselytizing in the public schools and private business for Flag Day ceremonies and other patriotic rituals on the factory floor. The Creel Committee tried to impart reverence for the old republic to recent immigrants by staging patriotic festivals, including a Fourth of July pilgrimage to Mount Vernon in which prominent figures from thirty-three immigrant nationalities sailed up the Potomac aboard President Wilson's yacht *The Mayflower* to lay wreaths at the grave of the Father of Our Country, serenaded as they went by a band playing the "Battle Hymn of the Republic." This historical mishmash of Pilgrims, Founding Fathers, and Civil War anthems showed a decided awkwardness in government efforts to Americanize their Old World brethren. Nevertheless, these Americanization activities hastened the emergence of Polish-American, Italian-American, and other immigrant-American identities.[33]

The martial spirit was evident in both peacetime social protest and wartime mobilization.

May Day: the regiments of socialism march behind quasi-military banners in New York, 1909.

Liberty Bond drive: led by a marching band, columns of navy men encourage
patriotic contributions to the war effort, New York, ca. 1918.

Women's suffrage: disciplined ranks of women parade in the white uniform of the suffrage campaign, New York, 1915.

The New Negro: convention delegates of Marcus Garvey's Universal Negro
Improvement Association show their militance in a Harlem parade, 1920.

Government sponsorship of Americanization attested to the role of the state as "educator" in cultivating a hegemonic set of values and beliefs among its citizens. But who would educate the educator? Immigrants were not merely empty vessels into which the state poured its propaganda. They imparted their own meanings to Americanism—freedom from Old World restraint, the American standard of living, the right to join a union, or cultural pluralism.[34] Once immigrants themselves were included in the equation through official toleration of cultural diversity, the path was open for winning consent of the governed. Insofar as the state established a rational—rather than religious or ethnic—test of republican citizenship, it became possible for America's heterogeneous peoples to find common ground within the liberal framework of the Constitution.

By the time the United States began to make its influence felt on the battlefields of Europe in the winter of 1917–18, the western front had long since become a grueling war of position. After General Alfred von Schlieffen's sweeping offensive had been halted at the First Battle of the Marne in 1915, the two sides settled into the stalemate of trench warfare that converted the gentle rolling fields of northeastern France into a vast graveyard. Massed land armies backed by great industrial machines and superheated civilian emotion had proved impotent when confronted with the equivalent sum of civilian and military forces on the other side. By contrast, the eastern front was a war of maneuver along a boundless battlefield that stretched from the Baltic to the Dardanelles upon which the mechanized discipline of the armies of the German emperor prevailed over the demoralized forces of the Russian czar. Just as Russian armies disintegrated on the battlefield, so the Romanov dynasty collapsed in the revolution of March 1917 (February in the old calendar), and after a second revolution in November, the Bolsheviks made a separate peace at Brest-Litovsk on March 3, 1918.

The collapse of the eastern front made U.S. weight all the more important in the scales of power. War weariness on both sides was undermining the will to fight; French mutinies, British munitions strikes, and German food protests signaled popular disenchantment, which prompted socialist and labor leaders to lay plans for a people's peace conference that would bring together delegates from both sides in Stockholm. Wilson did his best to foil this effort. Since gaining influence at the peace conference was one of Wilson's main war aims, he forgot about "peace without victory" and bent every effort to keep the war going until U.S. troops could make their weight felt in the total defeat of Germany. To bolster workers' fighting spirit, Wilson sent his "labor ambassador" Samuel Gompers to Europe to head off the Stockholm plan. Shortly after Wilson issued his own Fourteen Point peace proposal, members of the influential League to Enforce Peace were writing in private, "We must not forget that the statements of our peace terms mean not peace but war until Germany is beaten into accepting them." To great U.S. relief, peace did not break out before American soldiers arrived in significant numbers, thus getting the opportunity to die by the thousands for every foot of ground at obscure places such as St. Mihel, Chateau-Thierry, and Belleau Wood. All told, 112,000 doughboys were killed.[35]

If U.S. influence tipped the balance, it was not because of stunning battlefield victories, but because the United States possessed a seemingly inexhaustible reserve of troops, food, and war matériel that bolstered Allied resolve in the face of German submarine warfare and the last German offensive in the spring of 1918. Drawing from a population just over 100 million, the United States raised an army of some 4.8 million men, of whom almost 2 million eventually served in the American Expeditionary Force in Europe. Propaganda promised that the AEF would deliver a "bath of bullets" to the enemy, made possible by "the man behind the man behind the gun" working in munitions plants, garment factories, and increasingly mechanized farms. Men and matériel moved about on a rail network that had grown eightfold since 1860 to its alltime peak of 254,251 miles of track in 1916; factory furnaces burned coal whose output had risen fivefold since 1890 to a peak of 579,000 tons in 1918; steel output increased tenfold in the same period, reaching 42.1 million tons in 1920.[36] The hyperindustrialism of the First World War marked the culmination of trends that had appeared in the Civil War, the first modern war fought with large conscript armies transported on steam railways bearing arms made with interchangeable parts. The democratic and industrial revolutions that had made this possible by the 1860s continued to influence the American way of war half a century later.[37]

In debating how to pay for the new military machine, wartime finance reached an impasse between progressives, who wanted to tax high incomes and excess profits, and managerial liberals, who wanted to tax mass consumption. The first round went to the progressives in the Revenue Act of 1916, which significantly increased the income tax, imposed new taxes on corporate profits, and hiked estate taxes. To the delight of farmer and labor groups, this system moved several notches toward shifting the federal tax burden from customs and excise taxes—that is, taxes on popular consumption—to personal income, corporate profits, and estates—that is, taxes on the rich. It did so by setting the personal exemption high enough to exclude all but the well-to-do from the obligation to pay. Although it stopped far short of the conscription of wealth, which many advanced progressives were calling for, it marked a step toward fulfilling the redistributive goal of the original Populist income tax of the 1890s, and it was a benchmark in aligning government financing to fit twentieth-century society.

The second round, however, went to federal bondholders. With expenses outrunning all predictions at $1 million per month, the government had to find other sources of funds. It relied on bonded debt and price inflation, both of which tended to cancel out any redistributive effects from taxes on high incomes. Besides hawking Liberty Bonds to the general public, Treasury Secretary William McAdoo sold certificates of indebtedness to banks through the Federal Reserve System. That fueled inflation because banks used the debt they accumulated as reserves, which rapidly expanded the money supply, and along with the inevitably inflationary effect of military purchases, these factors caused consumer prices to double. Since inflation amounted to an indirect tax on mass consumption, and since wealthy bondholders would collect the lion's share of future interest payments, the system of war finance took back with one hand what it had given with the other.[38]

The military mobilization of 1917–18 would have seemed strange to Abraham Lincoln and even to William McKinley. Gone were the days of citizen soldiers when a national army could be patched together from local regiments connected to state politics. The rise of corporate capitalism and modern management had induced a managerial revolution in military methods begun by Secretary of War Elihu Root during the Taft administration and continued in the National Defense Act of 1916. The organizational reforms paralleled scientific management in industry and, under the army chief of staff, created a more efficient bureaucracy capable of shouldering the immense logistical burden of equipping and transporting nearly 5 million men in arms. To make that possible the navy, meanwhile, commissioned 300 destroyers in an expansion that would soon bring it up to parity with the mighty British fleet. Facilities such as the Watertown, Massachusetts, arsenal were veritable proving grounds for scientific management, and the new contingency planning of the Army War College represented a stab in the same scientific direction, although, as with much bureaucratic planning, prognostications often went far astray. For example, the Black Plan for war with Germany envisioned the kaiser ferrying troops to the East Coast but made no provision for an American Expeditionary Force of the sort that embarked in the opposite direction. Riddled with faulty assumptions, the contingency plans had to be left on the shelf.[39]

The reorganization of American society to make room for mass production and mass reproduction altered civilian mobilization, as well. Gone were the days when the isolated household could be left to look after its own affairs; now, with all the urgency and fanfare that accompanied the war emergency, federal agencies wrapped the home in the flag. Herbert Hoover's Food Administration exhorted housewives to patriotic service in the home through "victory bread" made with cornmeal, "wheatless Mondays" and "meatless Tuesdays," and even distributed pamphlets on "garbage utilization." Likewise, the Girl Scouts and Boy Scouts who joined Uncle Sam's Home Garden Army saved food by rooting around in backyard "victory" gardens. Lacking a centralized bureaucracy to allocate resources, Hoover relied instead on the channels of mass communication and the pressure of community conformity—the tyranny of the majority—to make the message stick. Just as the Creel Committee's propaganda taught commercial advertisers a thing or two, so the Food Administration's campaign for efficient consumption helped shape a new ideal of the family—one that would be oriented toward consumption rather than production, the acquisition of consumer durables rather than the accumulation of property.[40]

The same set of social changes altered the methods of industrial mobilization. Gone were the Civil War days of competitive capitalism, when the quartermaster had merely gone into the open market to purchase needed supplies. Although many purchases were still made in this old-fashioned way, now the government had to deal with a relative handful of corporations that had come to manage their respective industrial markets. To coordinate the complex war economy, the Wilson administration had set up the Council of National Defense in 1916, comprising, for the most part, such paragons of the corporate world as Charles Schwab of Bethlehem Steel and Julius Rosenwald of Sears & Roebuck. During the war itself, responsibility shifted to the War Industries Board (WIB) under the flamboyant financier Bernard Baruch. The fact that the WIB set prices of industrial products, allocated market shares, and otherwise intervened in the market was evidence of how much things were changing. None of the prewar corporate-regulatory machinery, not even the Federal Trade Commission, had dared penetrate this far into the sacred preserve of private property. No wonder many progressives believed the war was a great opportunity to advance their reform agenda; as the *New Republic* said, it would serve "as a pretext to foist innovations upon the country."[41]

In the end, however, the center of "war collectivism" lay closer to the giant corporations themselves than to the new Washington bureaucracies, or perhaps somewhere in between. Stripped to the essentials, the WIB was a constellation of industrial leaders hammering out their own cooperative policies under the aegis of the state, a fact Baruch recognized in admitting he lacked the authority to dictate terms to a recalcitrant firm. Likewise, Herbert Hoover relied heavily on personal powers of persuasion and the pressure of public opinion to bring giants such as Pillsbury and Swift into line and to stimulate an association of prosperous farmers that eventually grew into the American Farm Bureau Federation. The two exceptions to this rule were the railroads and telegraphs. Owing to their strategic importance the government took direct control of rail transportation and communication, making Secretary of the Treasury McAdoo the only government official who actually got to boss corporate presidents around. But even here the owners had little to complain about, since the government paid a guaranteed 6 percent profit, and, in any case, they repossessed their lines shortly after the war ended.[42] Indeed, business, in general, made out rather well. Corporate profits showed such substantial gains that Congress investigated the steel and copper companies amid charges of wartime profiteering, and the Du Pont corporation had so much money at the end of the war that it was able to buy controlling interest in General Motors, later held in violation of antitrust.[43]

How did the mobilization affect business-government relations? Since the new government bureaus came to life during an emergency lasting less than two years, there was little in the way of a permanent institutional legacy. Yet even these short-lived growths revealed long-term imperatives. Forced by an emergency such as war (and later the Great Depression), one way or another the United States had to go beyond laissez faire to coordinate the workings of a society increasingly attuned to mass production and mass reproduction and dominated by corporate capitalism. The great corporations themselves were taming the wild horses of free-market competition, and their managerial liberalism thwarted any attempts to create statist bureaucracies for the control of industry. Instead, what emerged was a nexus of private institutions keyed to the corporation and clothed in the raiment of public authority. In marked contrast to Germany, where business was subject to far greater state control under a state of emergency where something approaching martial law prevailed, the United States mobilized under what might be called a parastate, representing a compromise between still-dominant liberal institutions and the imperatives of modern management.

Nationalism in Industry

As the biggest industrial machine in the world wheeled into action, it was unclear what impact wartime nationalism would have on the balance of power in industry. On the one hand, the captains of industry were sure to gain added leverage as a result of their command over war production. "War means autocracy," President Wilson confided to a friend. "The people we have unhorsed will inevitably come into the control of the country, for we shall be dependent upon the steel, oil, and financial magnates. They will run the nation." And so they did, in a way, in the Council of National Defense, the War Industries Board, the Food Administration, and at scores of other para-state junctures where the state and the great corporations meshed together. But there was another side to the conflict. Working people were equally sure to gain advantages through the improvement in the labor market and the absolute need to win their cooperation in production. What was more, fighting a war to make the world safe for democracy would inevitably raise their aspirations for true democracy at home. Even the skeptical Walter Lippmann was temporarily swept off his feet by the glorious possibilities: "we shall stand committed as never before to the realization of democracy in America . . . We shall turn with fresh interest to our own tyrannies—to our Colorado mines, our autocratic steel industries, our sweatshops and our slums." Either the autocrats of big business were going to run things, or the laboring masses were going to get industrial democracy. Which would it be?[44]

The European experience from 1914 through the end of 1916 had proved that nationalism could override industrial conflict, at least temporarily. The spirit of national unity that broke out everywhere in 1914 rang down the curtain on a mounting crescendo of discontent.[45] Under "war collectivism," all belligerent governments had suppressed dissent and subjected society to unprecedented bureaucratic regulation. In Germany, industrialists and industrial workers concluded a formal "fortress truce" (*Burgfrieden*) at the beginning of the war, a peace pact that held up through 1916 even in the face of mass slaughter and severe privation. Beset by growing labor shortages, Germany conscripted much of its industrial working class into a civilian counterpart of compulsory military service under the National Service Law of December 1916, with only Minority Socialists and the free-market National Liberals dissenting.[46]

In Britain, where Conservatives and Liberals alike frowned upon such extreme government intervention, the truce between labor and capital was informal and state regulation more limited. Under the Munitions Act of July 1915, the ability of workers to protest was curtailed by a "leaving certificate," a kind of good-conduct pass regarded as a potential blacklist, but under the circumstances all parties, including Labour, accepted it. In France workers were determined to defend the nation against the force of German arms and showed loyalty to the tricolor throughout. Although privation and war weariness caused food demonstrations and wage protests on both sides by 1917, they were on a limited scale, so that industrial relations within the western powers resembled the stalemated war of position on the western front.[47]

Equally eager for labor peace, the Wilson administration had fewer levers by which to obtain it. Typically, it made full use of its powers of persuasion. Wilson appointed Samuel Gompers and other AFL leaders to various government posts, in return for which Gompers issued a much-publicized "no-strike" pledge, and no one noticed when the AFL Executive Committee quietly repudiated it. The importance of public relations in winning workers' consent was attested by the unprecedented appearance of President Wilson at the September 1917 AFL convention, and by the Creel Committee's "4-Minute Men" who spoke to movie audiences in hopes of inspiring "the man behind the man behind the gun" with a patriotic work ethic. All this ballyhoo showed the weakness of federal bureaucracy under the American liberal state and the consequent need to ply the channels of mass culture to reach the laboring masses.[48]

At the same time, the war emergency put such a high premium on harmony in the factory that authorities relaxed their liberal inhibitions about state intervention and began to experiment with corporatist bureaucracies. As early as March 19, 1917, the day Wilson's cabinet unanimously recommended war, the president had told feuding railroad executives and union leaders that they had to accept the mediation of the Council of National Defense on the issue of the eight-hour day, because "the peace of the whole world makes accommodation absolutely imperative." Without doubt the most significant piece of mediation machinery was the War Labor Board. Chaired jointly by former president Taft and feisty labor attorney Frank Walsh, the War Labor Board was the most advanced national progressive solution to industrial disputes to come forward at any time before the New Deal. It was created at the instigation of the National Industrial Conference Board, itself a brand-new organization composed of flagship corporations and employer associations, which won the privilege of appointing business representatives to the board. The AFL got to select the labor representatives, eagerly grabbing the opportunity to appear as the equal of business, and the board was rounded out by presidential appointments supposed to represent the public. Too much should not be made of this departure from the norms of the liberal state. The board lacked strong coercive powers, leaving some important awards unenforced, and it was an emergency creation that quickly went out of business at war's end. All the same, the fact that it incorporated the two great estates of the realm, business and labor, in a tripartite structure unknown to the Constitution clearly marks the War Labor Board as an American counterpart of similar corporatist agencies in Europe.[49]

As Gompers' vigorous support of the War Labor Board implies, the AFL chief was determined to make the most of wartime opportunities. Beginning with his service on the Council of National Defense, Gompers' extensive collaboration with the government marked a dramatic rupture with the past practice of AFL voluntarism. Ever since Grover Cleveland had crushed the railroad strike of 1894, top AFL leaders had based their strategy on the twin assumptions that organized labor could not win a battle with the giant corporations as long as they were backed by state power. The contrast between the success of craft unions in the building trades and the virtual absence of unions from mass production was evidence to bolster what had become self-fulfilling prophecy. But Gompers was quick to recognize that total war changed the rules of the game. With 2.5 million members, AFL unions had something the government badly needed—skilled war workers, many of whom were German and Irish union officers who could bolster support for the war in the very ethnic communities where it was weakest. Under these conditions, it might to possible for unions to win benevolent neutrality from the executive branch to balance the resolutely hostile Supreme Court, which upheld the yellow-dog contract in the 1917 *Hitchman* case, and an unreliable Congress, whose Clayton Act had miserably failed to fulfil Gompers' wish that it be "labor's Magna Carta." As proof of AFL loyalty, Creel and Gompers set up the American Alliance for Labor and Democracy. As the loyal alternative to the People's Council, the AALD became the main bridge over which the minority of prowar socialists, including John Spargo, Charles Edward Russell, and Rose Pastor Stokes, could cross into the two-party mainstream. Gompers actually became more loyal than the National Security League and the American Defense Society, elite loyalty leagues that were honeycombed with carping Republicans.[50]

If the aim of war nationalism was to stifle industrial discontent, it did not succeed. The evidence of wartime strikes is eloquent on that point: the number of workers on strike shot up in 1916, and, although it dipped the next year, it remained well above prewar levels through the end of the war.[51] Skilled machinists fought quick, sharp battles over work rules; operatives and laborers in the heavily female garment trades obtained wage increases to offset rising prices; and coal miners braved fierce employer resistance to increase membership in the United Mine Workers to 400,000, turning some sectors of West Virginia into what was described as "civil war." Riding the wave, union membership doubled from 2,607,000 in 1915 to 5,110,000 in 1920, and strikes crested in the extraordinary year of 1919, when more than 4 million workers hit the bricks. It was a remarkable working-class offensive the likes of which had not been seen since the 1880s, nor would be seen again until 1946. In contrast to the situation in Europe in 1914–1916, the war did not close the floodgates of industrial discontent; it opened them.[52]

One reason for the discontent was the pinch on working-class consumers. The mobilization disrupted the delicate balance of family economy, particularly among immigrants in mine patches, steeltowns, stockyards, and garment districts whose reliance on multiple incomes from children and boarders was thrown off kilter. Worse, runaway inflation seemed to devour whatever income was left: all the available price indices concur that consumer prices roughly doubled between 1914, when the Bureau of Labor Statistics index stood at 42.9, and 1920, when it registered 85.7.[53]

The experience was nothing like the absolute impoverishment in Europe, of course, but insecurity was rife, against which halfhearted regulation did little. Indeed, government sometimes made things worse, as in New York City, where municipal rationing of meat caused food riots in 1917 when Jewish women from New York's Lower East Side turned American nationalism into a justification for protest against wartime price inflation. Fusing new expectations of an American standard of living with Old World notions of moral economy, they rioted when the city tried to substitute rice for the traditional chicken, carrying banners that read:

> We American Can Not Live on Rice.
> We Want All Food Stuffs to Come Down in Price.
> Speculators and Robbers Will not Survive
> By Lowering the Standard of American Live.[54]

Fortunately, for the first time in decades workers were in a position to do something about insecurity. Thanks to an influx of war orders at the same time immigration was falling to a trickle, workers experienced the tightest labor market they had ever known; unemployment fell precipitously from upward of 15 percent in 1915 to an unprecedented 2.4 percent in 1918. Given the unusual shortage of unskilled labor, employers began hiring women and southern migrants and engaged in something of a bidding war for skilled and semiskilled labor, with the result that average hourly earnings in manufacturing increased 137 percent from 1915 to 1920, compared with a 44 percent increase over the previous twenty-five years. For the same reason, average hours declined substantially. Short hours had been a prime demand of the labor movement since the 1830s. In the twenty-five years before 1915 the average work week fell from 60 to 55 hours; in the four years after 1915 it plunged rapidly to 51.[55]

For all the political and economic gains notched by workers, there was a darker side to wartime industrial relations. The war brought a dramatic expansion in the repressive machinery of state. Newly expanded police forces tightened work discipline as they ferreted out disloyalty, stopping just short of equating loyalty to the nation with absolute obedience to the employer. Although nothing like Germany's

Auxiliary Service Law was ever contemplated, Selective Service chief General Enoch Crowder issued a well-publicized "work or fight" order threatening to draft the unemployed. Armed with the Espionage Act and the Sedition Act, the Bureau of Investigation infiltrated into war plants industrial spies who commonly equated protest against overwork with apologies for the kaiser. Intertwined with existing law-and-order leagues, these new loyalty police collaborated intimately with private labor spies at such corporations as International Harvester, U.S. Steel, and Ford. Additional help came from Military Intelligence and its subsidiary, the Plant Protection Service, which spied on civilians through its Negative Branch MI-4 under doubtful constitutional warrant.[56]

Repression reached its apogee in the West, where industrial relations displayed the sharpest point/counterpoint anywhere in the nation. Absentee corporations and their local minions squared off against a ragtag assortment of hard-living industrial workers, migratory "bindlestiffs," and pugnacious tenant farmers among whom socialists, Wobblies, and assorted other labor radicals had wide-ranging influence.[57] In the customary western response to industrial discontent, authorities cracked down on labor radicals, only now on a far grander scale than ever before. Under the logic of total war, any production site with even a remote connection to the war effort could be defined as a "public utility," so any disruption of production could be taken as a threat to the national interest. In the past, the use of the army as a domestic police had been constrained by the "insurrection" doctrine which prohibited use of the army unless state authorities could not "guarantee a republican form of government" as stipulated in Article IV, section 4 of the Constitution.[58] Now such constraints were swept aside as the War Department hastily improvised a new "public utilities" doctrine under which Army Department commanders were authorized to supply troops directly upon request of the governor, and soon soldiers were guarding West Coast lumber yards, orchards, and wheat fields against merely "threatened" strikes and the perceived "danger" of sabotage.[59]

When actual strikes hit copper camps from Bisbee, Arizona, to Butte, Montana, in the summer of 1917, the Wilson administration was ready with the iron heel of troops in the velvet sock of mediation. Whereas a hastily assembled President's Mediation Commission did little to dampen conflict, the military was more effective, sometimes in tacit collaboration with local vigilantes, as in the infamous Bisbee deportation, in which three people were killed on deportation day, yet the Military Intelligence officer on the scene calmly cabled his superiors: "Everything orderly." In fact, U.S. troops would continue to keep labor peace in the copper districts at both ends of the Rocky Mountains until 1921.[60]

It would be a mistake to visualize a monolithic state conspiring with a nefarious network of night riders to suppress worker discontent. Indeed, the Justice Department prosecuted the Bisbee vigilantes all the way to the Supreme Court (where the vigilantes won), and cries were heard from congressional representatives such as Jeannette Rankin, the nation's first congresswoman, in protesting anti-IWW lynch mobs. There were checks and balances even within the federal bureaucracy, as evidenced by the obstinate refusal of the Labor Department to accept mere IWW membership as grounds for deportation of aliens.[61]

Yet it would be a still greater mistake to believe that in its own discordant, pluralistic fashion the Wilson administration did not play a major role in winning the West for big business and, in general, securing a political-legal order congenial to corporate capitalism. In extreme cases, the federal government even went so far as to collaborate with vigilantes. The Loyal Legions and Citizens Protective Associations of western industrial districts were establishment vigilantes who sought the restoration of accepted rules of the marketplace against usurpers, not the overthrow of constituted authority. That fact helps explain why so many authorities from the local to the national level held a double standard toward violence: strikes of immigrant workers, especially with the IWW present, were disorder, whereas vigilante raids on private homes and union offices, deportations, terrorism, and even lynchings were indications that everything was "orderly."[62]

And what of the balance in industry between autocracy and democracy? Did nationalism favor one over the other? In many respects, wartime nationalism boosted the preferred progressive solutions to industrial discontent. That much was clear when the War Labor Board and its companions went much further than any prewar institution in mediating industrial disputes. Likewise, insofar as they incorporated "labor" as one member of a tripartite body, they redressed the balance of power somewhat in favor of industrial workers. And there was no doubt that the ideology of "making the world safe for democracy" boosted the idea of democracy in industry. Frank Walsh used the War Labor Board as a platform to broadcast the message: "The country, I promise you, is beginning to understand that we may have 100 per cent democracy in the form of our political government and yet autocracy of the most despotic type in industry." Workers filled Americanism with democratic content, and their support for the war grew the more they held Wilson to his promise to make it a war for democracy.[63]

But the price of nationalism was acceptance of the state's right to define what was and was not legitimate. That was fine for the AFL so long as it was the "legitimate" organization, as against the "illegitimate" IWW.[64] But did Gompers think he could dictate the terms of labor's bargain with the government? What would happen in peacetime when the nation-state had less need of labor's loyal service? The entire labor movement—conservative and radical alike—was about to find out. After the war, the tables were turned rapidly as national loyalty became equated with the open shop in the "American Plan" and as the western solution became the blueprint for suppressing industrial discontent. In response to the unprecedented level of strikes in 1919 and 1920, all the features of suppression reappeared writ large, including the use of troops as domestic police, military spying on civilians, deportation of alien radicals, and the coordination of Loyalty League vigilantes with local police and federal troops. And further, the wartime experience with enforced consent—that is, loyalty as defined by the state backed by legal coercion—prepared the ground for the Red Scare looming just over the horizon. While protecting wage earners from autocratic employers, the weak from the strong, the state also took care to protect the strong from the weak.

War between the Sexes

Total war politicized relations between the sexes, though not quite in the way anyone intended. The messages from most government publicity bureaus traded heavily on sentimental conventions of femininity and masculinity. It was time to end the battle of the sexes and pull together—women and men alike—for total victory in Europe. In the saccharine iconography of propaganda posters, wives with husbands away at the front were urged to keep the home fires burning for the eventual homecoming, and the image of saintly motherhood was milked for every drop of patriotic sentiment it held. Recruiting posters artfully played on masculine themes: the famous "Uncle Sam Wants You!" challenged men to be *real* men from one direction, while Howard

Chandler Christie's fetching band of coquettes challenged from an-other: one poster with a pert blond decked out in Navy blues was cap-tioned, "Gee!! I wish I were a man; I'd join the Navy—Be a man and do it." Gone was the identification of manhood with being "too proud to fight"; gone was the message of the most popular song of 1916, "I Didn't Raise My Boy to Be a Soldier." Instead, the country harked to the message of the preparedness movement that the strenuous life under army discipline would convert callow youth into sturdy defend-ers of family and nation. The same martial spirit that would make boys into men would also make a young nation into a world power; going to fight would mark the end of innocence and the beginning of national maturity. Thus were psychosexual energies drafted to serve the ambi-tions of the nation-state.[65]

Yet the gulf between these conventional images and the changing relations of the sexes was only widened by the war. There were so many points at which the formerly separate spheres overlapped, so many objections to the Victorian double standard, so many more women in the labor market, and so many women voting in the fourteen states that had enacted female suffrage that it was impossible to put the genie of change back in the bottle. The fact that there was no going back did not make clear which was the way forward. Unfortunately, the war confronted the women's movement with agonizing choices. Should they support the war in hopes of making gains for women's suffrage and women's protections, or should they risk these advances in principled devotion to the pacifism that had long been an integral part of their cause? Was there a way between the Scylla of opportunism and the Charybdis of marginalism?

To many suffragists and social feminists, the opportunity to grab a seat at the table of power and thereby legitimate their cause was too great to pass up. Well-connected matrons of the civic clubs and genteel suffragists of the National American Woman Suffrage Association se-cured appointments to many state Councils of National Defense, capped by the appointment of Anna Howard Shaw to head the all-volunteer Women's Advisory Committee. Long thorns in the side of the male power structure, women such as Shaw put aside their pro-fessed pacifism and busied themselves with the kind of charitable and philanthropic work benevolent ladies had always done, only now clothed in the kind of public authority that would weaken the antisuf-fragist argument that women's place was in the home.[66] Others in the movement, however, were not so quick to compromise. Crystal East-man was among the sturdy band of feminists who helped establish the People's Council in a vain effort to link opposition to the war with social reform. The division between Shaw and Eastman roughly paralleled the division in the labor movement between AFL chief Gompers, who also won a coveted seat on the CND, and Eugene Debs, who wound up in jail for making antiwar speeches.

The militant feminists of the National Women's party followed a very narrow third path between the rocks of prowar and antiwar opin-ion. Declining to take any position on the war, they also refused to abandon militant tactics. Having vowed to oppose the party in power as long as it failed to support equal suffrage, they were not mollified by a mild pledge from the president to consider suffrage; instead, they took his promise to "make the world safe for democracy" and threw it back in his face with a campaign of civil disobedience that included hunger strikes, pickets for "Kaiser Wilson," and the burning of "watch-fires" across from the White House. Like a number of labor leaders who walked a similar tightrope by leading strikes in war industries, they earned the enmity of the authorities, but they also kept the suf-frage question on the front pages alongside news from the war front.[67]

Social reformers beat a path to Washington in the hope of expanding the toehold they had already won for protective legislation at the state level. The clearest sign of their success was the newfound Women in Industry Service, soon rechristened the Women's Bureau, which took up the aspirations of the the National Women's Trade Union League for women's hours and wage regulations and prohibitions on night work and heavy lifting. As always, it was easier to get special protec-tion for women than to implement equal protections for workers of both sexes. Although "equal pay for equal work" became the official government policy, there was virtually no enforcement, since that would have meant hard battles with industry.[68]

The path of least resistance was the family wage. All the main play-ers in the regulatory game—male bureaucrats, private employers, middle-class allies of working women, and trade unionists—supported the idea that a man should earn enough to support wife and child. Be-fore the war, the government had begun to implement the concept in a halting fashion as the basis for wage standards in railroad arbitrations, industrial commissions, and family budget studies. Now, in the rush to mobilize industrial workers, Felix Frankfurter's War Labor Policies

Board drew up a presidential proclamation setting the family wage as official government policy.[69] Though commonly honored in the breach, that meant the state was, in effect, putting its authority behind the old saw that women's place was in the home. Progressive reformers thus ran into the same dilemma that had bedeviled them before the war. They had to choose between special protections for women, which curtseyed to the conventional notion of the "weaker sex," and equal protections, which had little chance of being effective.

This was not the only breach in the barrier between the state and family welfare. Congress had already lent support to the principle by outlawing child labor at the height of the prewar progressive tide, an act the flinty-hearted Supreme Court now deemed unconstitutional in *Hammer v. Dagenhart* (1918) on the grounds that Congress had overreached its authority over interstate commerce by invading the private preserve of manufacturing, not to mention the sanctity of the family. Without wasting a moment, Congress enacted a new law that outflanked the Court's laissez-faire decision by laying a heavy tax on the interstate products of child labor, although that too would be thrown out in a few years. The list of social-welfare innovations did not stop there. For the first time, the federal government sponsored dozens of housing projects at war production sites and set up a social insurance fund to which soldiers were required to contribute. At the state level, inhibitions about government regulation of family affairs were falling even faster as social reformers won expanded tenement inspection, milk provision, and juvenile courts. The sum of these innovations was not a greatly expanded welfare state under anything like the "war collectivism" in Germany but a few more small steps on the road away from laissez faire.[70]

The principle of the family wage was severely tested by the need to attract women to fill jobs vacated by men. There is evidence that women workers made gains during the war in the entrance of half a million new workers into the job market and the promulgation of "equal pay for equal work." Certainly, Mary Anderson, a veteran trade unionist, had some reason for optimism as she assumed her post at the helm of the newly created Women's Bureau. But closer examination reveals that these gains for equal treatment were overridden by other decisions upholding women's second-class status. Even as bureaucrats and employers enticed women into such nontraditional lines as machine shops and streetcar conducting, the prevailing attitude was that these women were only temporarily filling in at men's jobs and could be properly discharged at the end of the war. For its part, the War Labor Board sometimes violated its own stated policy of equal pay in awarding differential pay on the basis of gender. The clearest test of government influence was the railways. Precisely because Uncle Sam was a relatively good employer, people expected a minimum of discrimination under the Railway Administration, but such was not the case. At the end of federal control, just as at the beginning, women were segregated by sex into lower-paying jobs with virtually no supervisory responsibility. Despite flirtations with the outer limits of opportunity, women remained overwhelmingly concentrated in "women's jobs," even though the jobs might have changed.[71]

Government regulation of sexuality was still more conservative. Social hygienists marched into Washington upon the outbreak of war, determined to expand their crusade against commercialized vice. The efficiency-minded social engineers of the American Social Hygiene Association advanced in seven-league boots, according to the head of the organization in a letter to its principal financial backer, John D. Rockefeller, Jr.: "In the early years, the problems of social hygiene were carefully studied and public opinion molded in such a way as to prepare for the wonderful opportunity which came to the Association at the outbreak of the war."[72] The "wonderful opportunity" arrived when the Social Hygiene Association beat out the YMCA in competition for control of the Commission on Training Camp Activities (CTCA), the most important command post for the government's campaign against venereal disease and prostitution. With a faith that surpasses understanding, the CTCA set out to combat venereal disease through continence. The same idea had also seized the Social Hygiene Division of the Council of National Defense, which officially adopted the principle "that continence is compatible with health and that it is the best means of preventing venereal disease." To spread the word, the CTCA lecturers produced the first film ever made by the U.S. government, *Fit to Win*, warning of the dire consequences that awaited a man who consorted with diseased women.[73]

To end all temptation in that direction, the CTCA switched off the lights in every major red-light district in the nation. Just as national Prohibition would win its first victory in a military regulation excluding drink from the area around military cantonments, so the CTCA shut down red-light districts on the grounds that they were making

American servicemen unfit to fight, a claim buttressed by the shockingly large percentage of enlisted men tested positive for VD. One after another the citadels of vice fell to the attack. Most dramatic was the closing of New Orleans' fabled Storyville, "the Gibraltar of commercialized vice." Altogether, the agency claimed credit for putting 110 red-light districts out of business. Wrapping repression in the flag, the American Social Hygiene Association dubbed this work the "American Plan": "It did not try to make the rattlesnake harmless by extracting its fangs. It chose rather to kill the snake outright as an enemy to national efficiency and welfare."[74]

Unfortunately, there were a lot of rattlesnakes in Uncle Sam's army. When Samuel Gompers got wind of the policy of continence, he no doubt spoke for the prevailing attitude among enlisted men in objecting that "real men will be men." Secretary of the Navy Josephus Daniels was initially aghast at the prospect of recommending continence during shore leave, and army and navy officers merely ignored the exhortations of the social hygienists and handed out condoms to the troops instead. Once the American Expeditionary Force began arriving in Europe, French officials found the policy totally incomprehensible, and Premier Georges Clemenceau reportedly offered to furnish the doughboys with medically certified prostitutes. Clemenceau may have seen nothing unseemly in offering to be chief procurer to the American army, but when Raymond Fosdick, a CTCA officer on loan from Rockefeller, took this proposal to the secretary of war, Newton Baker exclaimed, "For God's sake, Raymond, don't show this to the President or he'll stop the war."[75]

In case the recruits failed to heed the call of continence, social hygienists were there to protect the young girls who might become their victims. The main federal agency charged with this task was the Committee on Protective Work for Girls, which boasted the patronage of society dames such as Mrs. John D. Rockefeller, Jr., and whose matrons of virtue saw themselves as surrogate chaperones to the urban masses. They were especially vigilant toward unescorted girls who congregated in dance halls, movie theaters, and other haunts of popular entertainment and supposedly vicious commerce. Not ones to curse the darkness without lighting a candle, they went about literally putting lights in darkened movie theaters, and they were on high alert against low forms of dancing:

1. No undue familiarity, exaggerated or suggestive forms of dancing will be tolerated.
2. Partners must be at least three inches apart, including heads. Hands must not be placed below the waist, nor above the shoulder, nor across the breast. Clasped hands must not be less than six inches from the body.

They functioned as a kind of chastity police.[76]

If social engineers took the fun out of vice, they also took the vice out of fun. To rear up a generation worthy of the Boy Scout oath to be "cheerful, brave, thrifty, clean, and reverent" required the substitution of wholesome recreation for commercialized vice. The CTCA enlisted the services of the Playground Association, the Russell Sage Foundation, and the ubiquitous YMCA to bring edification and fitness to the troops through baseball, community sings, and university extension courses. The U.S. Public Health Service was not far behind in recommending uplifting literature, including *Treasure Island* and *Tom Sawyer*, a list modified in a special exhibit for young black men to include Rudyard Kipling's *Kim* alongside W. E. B. DuBois's *The Negro* and Booker T. Washington's *Up from Slavery*. Public health officials also campaigned for cleanliness in mind and body with a traveling exhibit, "Keeping Fit," that urged men to honor their mothers by protecting the honor of all women and girls: "Take no liberties with any girl that you would not have another man or boy take with your sister or sweetheart."[77]

The modern sex hygienists did not so much overturn Victorian conventions as reformulate them. They actually carried to an impossible extreme the either/or image of the madonna/whore. Pamphlets such as *Keeping Fit to Fight* contrasted all-American sweethearts at one extreme with the diseased prostitute, every one an enemy agent, at the other; and visual exhibits counterposed wholesome family scenes—mother and sister waiting patiently for the soldier's return—to a blindfolded soldier's lascivious reverie of titillating nudes titled "Is Your Mind Diseased?" They also relied on old-fashioned concepts of male honor that presented woman as the sexually passive helpless victim. To foment hatred for the enemy, propagandists appealed to the male protector of feminine virtue in relentlessly invoking "the rape of Belgium" and asking: "How would you like to have twenty Prussian beasts, one after another, indulge their lusts upon your sister?"[78] So long as the moral reformers played out this script, they could only rework the idylls of the proprietary family—feminine chastity and masculine chivalry— around the theme of scientific efficiency. But they could not develop a new morality suitable to the coming age.

The wartime triumphs of social purity ended commercialized vice as a major issue in American politics. It marked the culmination of efforts to moralize the marketplace by drawing a hard and fast legal boundary between virtuous and vicious commerce. Exulting in their victories, the purity crusaders never stopped to ask whether state coercion was the best way to resolve contentious issues of private morality. Critics rightly objected that it was futile, at best, to try to run a multicultural twentieth-century society as if it were a Puritan theocracy, or even a secularized utopia fit only for efficiency experts. By the law of unintended consequences, the suppression of commercialized vice only led to the criminalized vice of bootleggers, gangsters, pimps, and procurers in the Roaring Twenties. If sexual purity won a pyrhhic victory during the war, other ostensible gains for women were quickly offset. The victories of female reformers in getting the Women's Bureau and of female workers in gaining job opportunities were also offset by new forms of subordination in which war nationalism played a prominent part in terms of patriotic motherhood and patriotic housewifery. Although the democratic ideology of Wilson's war aims probably made women's suffrage inevitable, it still had a long way to go when the fighting stopped. Thus the overall impact of the war on the relations between the sexes was by no means wholly or even primarily in the direction of equality.

Consequences

By the time the guns fell silent on November 11, 1918, the balance of forces in American life had changed considerably from what it had been when Wilson had made his fateful decision a brief twenty months earlier. Most important, the state loomed larger than ever in the workings of society. Never before had federal officials dumped so much patriotic gore into the channels of mass communication, silenced so many voices of dissent, intervened in so many labor disputes, coordinated so many business activities, sold so many government bonds, or collected so many tax revenues. For the first time, federal bureaucracies intervened in the market on a large scale through the War Industries Board and the War Labor Board, while the permanent bureaucracy expanded as the Treasury Department sold Liberty Bonds, the Justice Department conducted domestic surveillance, and, of course, the War Department mobilized millions of men and policed industrial disputes. The heavy features of state power—nationalism, suppression of dissent, military and secret police—were all much in evidence. Had the country been mobilized for four years instead of a year and a half, these centralizing influences undoubtedly would have evolved further in the direction of a more statist system.

But the contrast with the Continental European regimes remains striking. In Germany, for example, the heavy hand of the state was present at the outset and only grew stronger during the war. The statist tradition derived partly from the persistence of authoritarian elements from the old regime—landed and bureaucratic elites, hereditary princes, the army officer class, and the aristocratic ethos—none of which, of course, had any provenance in the liberal republic of the United States. To be sure, Germany was no medieval kingdom in 1914. The rise of the bourgeoisie had left an indelible mark on civil society through the preeminence of industrial over agrarian wealth and on the state through the principle of equality before the law. As opposed to the old regime, in which assent was secured through deference under patriarchal, monarchical, and military hierarchies, the integration of liberal elements into the German empire by 1914 obliged elites to secure active consent in some fashion from the governed. Indeed, historians have shown that elites grew increasingly alarmed about the advancement of the lower and middle classes, and may very well have consciously chosen a path for war in the hope of resolving domestic conflicts. If socialists insisted on asking the "social question," the answer of industrialists and landlords would be war.[79]

Whatever the reasons, once war was chosen the chancellor had to submit his military budget to the Reichstag, where it was permitted to pass only by the abstention of the main opposition Social Democrats. Ever afterward, their action was rightly remembered as the triumph of nationalism and the betrayal of socialist internationalism. It permitted Germans of all parties to march off to war in lockstep. Under "war collectivism" the government coopted civil society wherever it could, securing a "fortress truce" in industry, spreading the mythology of the *Volksgemeinschaft*, calling upon housewives to make patriotic sacrifices in the face of the food blockade, and putting the middle-class women's movement to work on home relief. In sum, German mobilization on the home front cannot be understood solely in terms of the persistence of the old regime, but must also take into account modern industry, mass communication, and the political integration of subordinate groups.[80]

That granted, the comparison between Germany and the United States is not one between a traditional and a modern system, but between a statist and a liberal one. Germany fought total war under a hierarchical chain of command that reached its apex at the kaiser. Under his authority, the government immediately imposed a state of emergency, abrogated all civil liberties, rationed food, and subjected civilian workers to military discipline. As the war dragged on, more and more of civilian life came under military control, so that by the end of 1916 the country was under a virtual military dictatorship by Generals Ludendorff and Hindenberg. Nothing like this was possible in the United States. Liberal inhibitions on centralized power, civilian supremacy over the military, the sanctity of private property, reverence for the self-reliant family, opposition to public welfare—in short, the supremacy of society over the state—made for a business-dominated system that instead relied heavily on voluntarism and high-power advertising.

Paradoxically, these very liberal restraints on state power turned into their opposite in federal restrictions on drink and sex. Taking advantage of the wartime need for discipline, the century-old temperance movement seized the levers of power in the fond hope of delivering a knockout blow to alcohol. The most enduring element in the antiliquor impulse was evangelical Protestantism. With roots in the stern religious discipline of Methodist camp meetings and Lutheran self-denial, the Women's Christian Temperance Union and revivalist preachers such as Billy Sunday embodied an unforgiving attitude toward the pleasures of the flesh, small-town hostility toward the sinful city, and a large dose of feminine anger toward ne'er-do-well husbands. Having watched with growing alarm the rising tide of immigrant "wets," they found in the martial discipline of the war an opportunity to scratch the evangelical itch to make everybody a saint. Another prime impulse originated in the South, where New South elites seeking to master the poor of both races led a campaign that succeeded in shutting the saloons in every southern state by 1919. An added impetus for national Prohibition came from women reformers and social engineers, who grasped the "wonderful opportunity" provided by wartime discipline to remake the urban masses in their own image of self-respecting efficiency.

Prohibition became the law of the land in a series of ever-widening decisions. First, the War Department encircled military encampments with a kind of *cordon sanitaire* across which the Army Section on Vice and Liquor Control allowed neither sex nor drink to pass. This purity zone was repeatedly expanded under the doctrine of military necessity until it encompassed a complete prohibition on the manufacture of all liquor, a position reaffirmed by the postwar Volstead Act. Meanwhile, Congress had sent the Eighteenth Amendment out to the states, whose ratification in 1919 finally made it the law of the land. Because of the absence of a strong regulatory tradition, when teetotaling morality seized control of the state, its aim was not to regulate vice but to abolish it. Thus laissez faire turned into its opposite, absolutist state control of private life.[81]

Prohibition cannot be understood apart from the class field of force. In the name of regeneration and efficiency, middle- and upper-class elements set out with the intention of completely reforming, in the literal sense, entire ethnic cultures whose customs were profoundly opposed to Yankee Protestant temperance, individualism, and self-denial. Unlike the nineteenth-century working class, which was honeycombed with temperance movements of its own, twentieth-century working people floated on the high seas of alcohol. Needless to say, that was more the case with men than with women, who all too often suffered abuse at the hands of drunken husbands. But even so, Italian women who may have despised the saloon for stealing bread from their table would not have dreamed of giving up wine at Communion or their daughter's wedding; Polish Catholic families toasted health at Sunday afternoon picnics; and the inebriated uncle was a necessary fixture of the legendary Irish wake.

Thus the Prohibitionist exercise in social uplift was condemned to become in equal measure an exercise in repression. Whether Prohibitionists represented a majority of the country is doubtful, but it is certain they did not win over a majority of the urban working class, who simply turned to bathtub gin, rum runners, and bootleggers. Perhaps more than any other single governmental act, Prohibition earned the undying enmity of working people. Not one to overdramatize class consciousness, Samuel Gompers described Prohibition as a class law against workers' beer, and in the same vein, one urban congressman undoubtedly spoke for the majority of wage earners in denouncing the howls of malicious joy issuing from rural America in "inflicting this sumptuary prohibition legislation upon the great cities. It preserves their cider and destroys the city workers' beer." [82]

Prohibition had a close parallel in the regulation of sexuality. Like drinking, prostitution bore a moral stigma but was not in itself illegal until the early twentieth century when it came under a widening ban culminating in the wartime closure of the red-light districts. The same combination of evangelical Protestants and social hygienists was behind the abolition of prostitution, and in the absence of a regulatory tradition, the only alternative to laissez faire was its exact opposite, total suppression. That was also the case with public discussion of sexuality, which was proscribed from the mails on grounds of obscenity, defined as whatever Anthony Comstock, special inspector for the Post Office, said it was. A more distant parallel lay in the suppression of dissent; again, liberal openness turned into its opposite.

Upper-class control of drink also had a parallel in the regulation of courtship. Most of the patriotic protectors of prostitutes, juvenile girls, and the poor came to the government from organizations such as the Rockefeller-backed American Social Hygiene Association or the Juvenile Girl's Protective Association, run by a wealthy Chicago philanthropist. Outlets for the upper-class impulse to remake the urban poor appeared in such Protestant reform agencies as the Salvation Army, YWCA, Red Cross, and women's clubs. At the same time they totally neglected such working-class institutions as extended families, ethnic benevolent societies, and parochial schools, which they shunned as too closely tied to "the swarm of petty politicians" buzzing around urban political machines. Although the social hygienists protested affronts to womanhood in the criminal justice system, they believed working-class youth had to be protected from their own dating customs, risky sexuality, and popular amusements, an attitude that was less sisterly than matriarchal. [83]

The war left an indelible imprint on the contest among progressive, managerial, and laissez-faire liberals for national leadership. At the outset, it looked as if progressives might overtake laissez faire. The dynamic of reform had been building for a decade, the war would inevitably bring federal regulation of the market, and a host of veteran leaders took up command posts in Washington, including Felix Frankfurter in the Labor Department, Anna Howard Shaw at the Council of

National Defense, and Newton Baker in the cabinet. Small wonder that progressives believed with Lippmann that the moment of "mastery" was at hand. Sure enough, the government created new machinery for adjusting social conflict in the War Labor Board, the Women's Bureau, and the Federal Employment Service, and, what was more, the air rang with high ideals of crusading liberalism and industrial democracy. By the end, the expansion of corporate-regulatory machinery had marked a milestone in the transformation of nineteenth-century laissez faire into twentieth-century regulatory liberalism. But in the excitement of the moment, progressives mistook the spirit of nationalism for crusading reform. Heedless of dark warnings about superpatriotism and little troubled by the crushing blows that fell upon radical dissenters, they went their optimistic way under the illusion that somehow they could encompass the dynamic of war within the dynamic of reform.

Laissez-faire liberals made no such mistake. With no hidden reform agenda, they had no illusions that the war would permanently redress the balance of power between the weak and the strong. Instead, their illusion lay in believing the war would restore the fast-disappearing world of Victorian America. Intolerant of "hyphenates," feminists, radicals, and unionists, they held fast to a vision of a self-governing republic of sturdy Anglo-Saxons scattered in self-reliant families who revered the old verities of respectability, property, and motherhood. Though overshadowed in Washington, they dominated the court system and state legislatures, flourished as the shock troops of "100 percent Americanism," and exulted in Prohibition. Their menfolk identified with self-reliant Sergeant Alvin York, the sharpshooter who single-handedly wiped out enemy machine-gun nests to become the prime hero of the war; and their womenfolk, prompted by the Daughters of the American Revolution and the Women's Section of the Navy League, believed it their duty to support the boys overseas through the Red Cross and "victory bread." Although most historians continue to regard the First World War as an advance for women, the fact remains that enemies of the women's movement, male and female alike, used superpatriotism to strengthen their networks at lower levels of the bureaucracy and in the Republican party that would serve well the conservative cause of antifeminism after the war.[84] Along with the business defenders of laissez faire, they would soon discover champions in Calvin Cooldige, Henry Ford, and the Ku Klux Klan, and they would return with a vengeance in the early 1920s to reverse the dynamic of reform.

In the meantime, managerial liberals were closest to the real centers of power. They had no intention of redressing the social imbalance of power and no illusion about restoring the lost world of Victorian liberalism. Instead, their illusion lay in believing that they could somehow surmount all the forces of war, bureaucracy, and social conflict making for the growth of massive state structures in the twentieth century. Since American participation in the war was relatively brief, they were spared an unwelcome confrontation with the truth, and had much to cheer about in the way the government mobilized for war through a parastate. The key wartime agencies of civilian mobilization—the War Industries Board, the Food Administration, and the like—were prime examples of the nexus of public-private authority under the nominal control of "dollar-a-year men" such as Bernard Baruch and Herbert Hoover. In addition, the federal government sanctioned the war work of a host of private organizations, including the American Social Hygiene Association, the National Americanization Committee, the Playground Association, and the omnipresent YMCA, all of which owed their budgets, personnel, ideas—in short, their very existence—to business philanthropy. The character of the parastate was brilliantly illuminated at war's end when most of the new federal quasi-bureaucracies simply disappeared. To the extent that scientific, managerial minds imagined the future, they saw a utopia fit for efficiency experts, with workers subordinate to managers and consumers responding to the ploys of mass advertising. They would eventually find their champion in Herbert Hoover.

The war heightened the influence of the state, and especially of the federal government, in American society. Certainly, at war's end public regulation of private enterprise and private life in general was greater than ever before. In fact, it is possible to see agencies such as the War Industries Board and the War Labor Board as examples of corporatism, a far-reaching development in twentieth-century capitalist societies defined as rule through quasi-public institutions based on large-scale producer groups such as business, agriculture, and labor rather than through elected officials. If so, the American state had a good deal less corporatism than the European states, where war collectivism had been more extensive.

Whatever the form, corporatist or liberal, mediating or repressive, state intervention only sometimes protected the weak from the strong. In the main, it was the other way around. That was the opposite of what most progressives had intended, but the fact that history did not turn out as they intended does not absolve them of the blame or burden of making history. That is to say, progressives in the Wilson administration, and certainly Wilson himself, supported the parastate machinery and, more fatefully, the new repressive machinery of state. Not only did the suppression of dissent deny national progressives their most vital source of new ideas; they also lost vital links to the industrial working class and discontented farmers, the only groups big enough to stand up to big business. If the progressives were knocked out of the running, it was in part by their own hands. Taken as a whole, the dynamic of war doomed the dynamic of reform to defeat.

A few of Wilson's progressive supporters saw the turnabout coming in late 1918. Frederick Howe, for example, was custodian of immigrant radicals held for deportation, many of whom he personally knew to be innocent, and he deeply regretted becoming a jailer "not of convicted offenders but of suspected persons who had been arrested and rail-roaded to Ellis Island as the most available dumping-ground under the successive waves of hysteria which swept the country." Racked with guilt, Howe suffered a nervous breakdown. Another prominent progressive, George Creel, was too much of a self-booster to admit culpability for the sins of his own propaganda machine, but he was a perceptive political soothsayer who saw ominous signs in the 1918 election results. Writing to Wilson just three days before the November 11 armistice, he said: "All the radical or liberal friends of your anti-imperialist war policy were either silenced or intimidated." Democrats were "afraid of raising the class issue" against big-business Republicans, who had wrapped themselves in the flag ever since the preparedness campaign. Unless this electoral verdict was reversed, Creel predicted, "the reactionary patrioteers will defeat the whole immediate future of reform and progress." Rarely has a prophecy proved more accurate.[85]

6

Response to Revolution

WHEN WOODROW WILSON sailed for Europe to attend the Versailles Peace Conference, he sought to shape a postwar world that was "safe for democracy." That is, he wanted to create a world order around America's liberal ideals—self-government, open diplomacy, free trade, and national self-determination. He seemed eager to pick up the gauntlet thrown down by the Bolshevik Revolution in 1917, confident that liberalism could best bolshevism in a fair contest for world opinion. If that meant promoting revolutionary changes in European politics, so be it. As he said while crossing the Atlantic, "Liberalism is the only thing that can save civilization from chaos—from a flood of ultra-radicalism that will swamp the world . . . Liberalism must be more liberal than ever before, it must even be radical, if civilization is to escape the typhoon."[1]

To fend off "the typhoon," Wilson looked to America's own revolutionary heritage. The symbolism of his ocean crossing aboard the *George Washington* did not go unnoticed, and he received a tumultuous welcome from the people of Paris, akin to the welcome given Franklin and Jefferson a century and a half before. The torch of liberty Wilson carried had been lit in the revolutionary fires of 1776, and revolutionary liberalism continued to burn in the great crusade against slavery. It inspired American support for liberal revolutions from 1789 through 1848 and for the independence of Latin American sister republics. It appeared in the rhetoric of 1898, when Americans said they went to war to free Cuba and the Philippines from Spain's imperial yoke. It ran through the great political testaments from the Declaration of Independence to Lincoln's Gettysburg Address. Buoyed by the Spirit of '76, Americans rightly took pride in their New World experiment as a shining example of opposition to tyranny.

Wilsonian diplomacy epitomized this crusading liberalism. During the period of neutrality from 1914 through 1916, Wilson had called for "peace without victory," asking both sides to put aside centuries of power politics and to renounce all territorial claims and indemnities. He had welcomed the overthrow of the czar in March 1917 because it enabled him to portray the struggle with Germany as a pure conflict between "democracy and autocracy." He had summoned warring nations to lay down their arms on the basis of his Fourteen Points of liberal doctrine—freedom of the seas, neutral rights, national self-determination—and he announced his peace plan independently of the Allies in January 1918 in order to be free of the taint of imperial designs. Yet, as Wilson himself recognized, crusading liberalism was about to run into another crusading force no less potent.

The Specter of Bolshevism

The Bolshevik Revolution of November 1917 finally made palpable the specter that had been haunting Europe ever since the *Communist Manifesto*.[2] Thereafter the Allied struggle against Germany became ever more deeply entangled with a struggle against the Bolsheviks, and the question of what to do about the infant Soviet Union hung over all the deliberations at the 1919 Versailles Peace Conference. By the time Wilson arrived in Paris, he was in a race with Lenin for leadership of revolutionary forces in the world. The first act of the new Bolshevik government upon seizing power had been a Peace Decree appealing to "all belligerent peoples" and especially "class-conscious workers" to demand that their governments make peace, with "no annexations, no contributions, no punitive indemnities." To beat Lenin at his own game, Wilson used virtually identical language of "no annexations or indemnities," adroitly appealing to peoples of the world over the heads of their governments. Portraying the war in his Fourteen Points address as "the culminating and final war for human liberty," he countered the revolutionary eschatology of the Bolsheviks with liberal millennialism.[3] By raising the ideological stakes to this cosmic plane, Wilson ascended to the level of a revolutionary liberal in the grand tradition of the Founding Fathers.

In general terms, revolution happens when a governing system undergoes irremediable crisis: when its fiscal, military, and bureaucratic structures collapse; its symbols and ceremonies no longer command allegiance; its legal and moral justifications for hierarchy in daily life lose their legitimacy; its rulers fall out among themselves; and its ruled take things into their own hands. Depending on circumstances, the causes of revolution may be located in state breakdown, class antagonism, popular resistance to oppression, or some combination of all three.[4] By this definition, all the countries suffering defeat underwent some kind of revolution at the end of the war. Austria-Hungary saw the overthrow of the Hapsburg dynasty, dismemberment of the imperial administration, and the creation of a set of new nations—Austria, Hungary, Czechoslovakia, Poland, and the Balkan nations. The Ottoman Empire saw the cession of imperial territory to the same new nations, the growth of Turkish nationalism, and a paper constitution.

Germany had the Revolution of 1918. Severe economic hardship had caused strikes, and massive demonstrations of upward of a million in January 1918 included demands for democratization of the empire. On top of this discontent on the home front, sailors mutinied at the great Kiel naval base after the failure of the last German offensive in the summer of 1918. These events prompted the kaiser to grant parliamentary reforms in October, which only further diminished the emperor's mystique. In truth, there was nothing the government could do to extricate itself from the class polarization that had gripped the country in the final year of the failing war effort. Intensified discipline only spurred popular resistance; reforms only betokened weakness. The result was that the Wilhelmine empire became the victim of its own excess, first, in suffering the military defeat that was the consequence of its own imperial overreach, and, second, in reaping the harvest of blame for its failure to prevent privation or profiteering at home. Wilsonian diplomacy gave the *Kaiserreich* a final nudge toward the brink. In a famous appeal to the German people over the heads of their government on October 23, 1918, Wilson said he could not deal "with any but the veritable representatives of the German people who have been assured of a genuine constitutional standing as the real rulers of Germany." With that, the imperial regime constructed by the great Bismarck collapsed in early November 1918, to be replaced immediately by a liberal republic.[5] The war that had begun in 1914 by submerging social conflicts wound up four years later intensifying the dynamic of social revolution. It was a lethal irony to the dynastic princes and conservative elites who had gone to war to stave off just this outcome.

If that was all there was to world revolution, it would easily have been contained within the framework of the Fourteen Points. But the principles of eighteenth- and nineteenth-century revolutions—liberalism, nationalism, representative government, constitutionalism—were being superseded by land redistribution, workers' councils, collective ownership—in short, by twentieth-century social revolution. To everyone's surprise, social revolution first came to power in Russia. Before the war, revolutionaries had focused their attention on Germany, because it had a highly developed capitalist economy and the strongest socialist party in the world. Marxists regarded the idea of socialist revolution in czarist Russia as heretical, because the Russian proletariat was but an island in a sea of peasants. Right down to the final moment, Lenin faced potent opposition to insurrection not only from the Mensheviks, his social-democratic rivals, but also from other Bolshevik leaders. Be that as it may, it was hard to argue with the fact that at the first blow, Kerensky's provisional government fell to a bloodless coup in November 1917—the famous storming of the Winter Palace in St. Petersberg—that installed the Bolsheviks in power.[6]

Unexpected or not, the Bolshevik seizure of power took place in a context of great changes sweeping through eastern Europe as a result of the war. The eastern front had experienced a "war of movement," as battle lines shifted back and forth over vast stretches of territory, and political changes of a similar scope arrived with the collapse of the Russian, Austro-Hungarian, and Ottoman empires. Observers drew a contrast to the "war of position" in the West, where rival armies immobilized each other in trench warfare, and where no such political collapse occurred. From this perspective the war may have been a catalyst of social revolution in the East, but just the opposite in the West. That is, in Germany, at least, the war may have been a delaying and distorting influence in a process that might otherwise have seen a revolutionary outbreak.[7]

Whatever the underlying causes—social conflict, military defeat, political breakdown—most Americans refused to accept the fact of the revolution. At first, most liberals from Wilson on down pretended the Bolsheviks were some kind of grotesque historical mistake. From the beginning, the Wilson administration withheld diplomatic recognition and maneuvered with the Allies to restore Russia's will to fight the Germans. The fact that the policy became bankrupt as soon as the Bolsheviks capitulated to the Germans at Brest-Litovsk in early March 1918 did not prevent the Allies from launching military expeditions at opposite ends of Russia's mammoth land mass, one of Archangel and the other at Vladivostok, with the professed intention of reopening the eastern front.

However, the Allied intervention soon became entangled with the efforts of Admiral Aleksandr Kolchak and the White Russians to overthrow the Bolsheviks. The fact that Allied troops fought Bolsheviks, not Germans, was excused by the invention of a "German-Bolshevik conspiracy." This fanciful idea was fomented by propaganda arms of the U.S. government, particularly by the Committee on Public Information, which distributed a set of documents purporting to show that "the Bolshevik Revolution was arranged for by the German General Staff and financed by the German Imperial Bank." Although the November armistice removed any military justification for being in Russia, U.S. and other Allied troops remained there for another year and a half in the vain hope of finding a way to kill the Bolshevik infant in the cradle.[8]

The greater fear was that bolshevism would spread to central Europe. There was good reason to be concerned. Feeding on postwar dislocation, Red revolution was a real possibility because governments were unable to provision the civilian population; nationalist enthusiasm had given way to cynicism; promises to workers and women went unfulfilled. Thus strikes and food protests erupted everywhere, factory occupations were rampant in Italy, a Bolshevik government briefly took power in Hungary, and the belief was widespread that a second revolution on the Bolshevik model loomed on the horizon in Germany.[9]

That threat was taken quite seriously by top U.S. officials. On the eve of the German Revolution of 1918, Secretary of State Robert Lansing mused on the future of central Europe: "There are two great evils at work in the world of today. Absolutism, the power of which is waning, and Bolshevism, the power of which is increasing . . . The possibility of a proletariat despotism over Central Europe is terrible to contemplate." Lansing voiced the belief of many conservatives that the greatest peril to world order was an excess of democracy:

> Democracy without education and Autocracy with education are the great enemies we have to face today. But I believe the former is the greater evil since it is destructive of law and order. How can we best utilize the hostility of these two principles, which are at opposite poles of political thought, so that both will be weakened? How much

encouragement should we give radicalism in Germany in the effort to crush out Prussianism?

When Prussianism was finally driven to its knees, most of the effort went to bring radicalism to heel. Herbert Hoover administered food relief in postwar Germany with the intention of securing political stability and thus thwarting "Bolshevist committees." President Wilson was equally anxious that his efforts to encourage the overthrow of "the military masters and monarchical autocrats" not push Germany into a second revolution. He warned against squeezing the fledgling Weimar Republic too hard in the peace settlement: "We owe it to the cause of world peace to save Germany from the temptation to abandon itself to Bolshevism." Invoking the canard that the kaiser had been the real author of Russian bolshevism, he added: "we know only too well the connection betweeen the Bolshevik leaders and Germany." [10]

The Social Democratic leaders of the infant German republic held the same fears. On the eve of their ascension to power, they were already obsessed with the threat from the left. As Philipp Scheidemann told the cabinet on November 2, "The central question is not the Kaiser's abdication, but whether we shall have Bolshevism or not." Indeed, there was much cause for alarm. Workers' and soldiers' councils had grown up in the wake of the mass demonstrations late in the war, and it was in their name that the Council of Berlin arrogated to itself the right to ratify the new government on November 10, the day after it was proclaimed. Local workers' councils wielded considerable power for the next several months, and although the Social Democratic leadership loathed the councils as an uncontrolled dual power, they paid homage to them by dubbing the new government the Council of People's Commissaries. Meanwhile, the Independent Social Democrats, who had championed an early end to the war, now pressed for a fundamental change of government; and they were flanked on the left by the Sparticists, who staged an ill-prepared insurrection in January 1919 in which their top leaders, Rosa Luxembourg and Karl Liebknecht, were assassinated. Revolutionary winds continued to blow for several years in the Communist party, Kurt Eisner's leftist government in Munich, the agitation of industrial workers, and the organization of a Red Army in the Ruhr. [11]

That Germany did not plunge headlong into a second revolution was the result of political bargains designed to shore up the infant Weimar republic. Unlike their Russian counterparts, German workers had won legal recognition for trade unions in return for union support of the war, and now Carl Legien and Hugo Stinnes, the heads of the largest trade union and industrial federations, respectively, concluded a postwar pact that promised support to the republic. Another prop was the granting of women's suffrage, enabling a number of women to be duly elected to parliament, just as professional women passed through newly opened doors in the bureaucracy. At the same time, conservative forces remained a formidable obstacle to revolution. Obedience to authority in family, workplace, and state was an ingrained tradition, and although patriarchal values were in decline, they were far stronger than the values of radical equality between the sexes, as advocated by some German Communists. Moreover, unlike the Russian peasantry, Germany's small farmers and peasants were in no mood to redistribute estates.[12]

In the end, the key to preventing the second revolution was probably the unwritten pact between Social Democrats and the army. The Social Democratic leaders of the new republican regime were moderate reformers desperate to avoid the kind of collapse that had befallen Kerensky in Russia. In fact, they were so desperate that they did not mind being rescued by Germany's military leaders. The military dictatorship of Hindenburg and Ludendorff was gone, but the German military machine remained intact and had no intention of imitating the czar's disintegrating army. So General Wilhelm Groner cut a deal with the new regime whereby the army agreed to support the republic against left and right, so long as the republic did not dismember the army. Faced with a choice between the palpably democratic institutions of workers' and soldiers' councils, most of which were under Social Democratic control, and the undeniably authoritarian general staff, the Social Democrats chose authority. Although the Weimar Republic was the product of a revolution of sorts, it was equally intended to be a bulwark against social revolution from below. Thus, in a popular saying, "The Kaiser went, the generals remained."[13]

The Versailles Treaty itself dealt cruel blows to crusading liberalism. Instead of "peace without victory" it was a peace made by the victors. Germany was excluded from the conference and bore the entire burden of "war guilt." Wilson was able to pare French demands for reparations but was forced to concede on virtually every other point. With respect to national independence, the treaty granted self-determination to European minorities within the vanquished empires but withheld it for the colonial possessions of the victorious British, French, and Japanese empires. Instead, "secret treaties" dividing up the colonial spoils were written into the settlement, a world-class land-grab covered over with a verbal fig leaf called a "mandate system." In the end, all that remained of Wilson's Fourteen Points was Article X, creating a League of Nations to guarantee the peace through collective security against an aggressor nation. The trouble was that instead of being the guarantor of a sound treaty, the League now had to stand as the savior of an unsound one.[14]

Finally, all was lost when the U.S. Senate blocked ratification. At one level, the ratification fight was merely a battle of political will between an uncompromising president and a band of Senate "irreconcilables." There was little doubt that a substantial majority of the country supported U.S. membership in the League when the treaty first came to a vote in November 1919. But first it had to get through a two-thirds vote in the Senate. As a result of the 1918 congressional elections, Republicans controlled the Senate, and their leader, Henry Cabot Lodge, attached "reservations" guaranteeing American sovereignty against the collective-security provisions of Article X. In addition, a small group of mostly Republican senators stood opposed to the League in any form. These "irreconcilables" included progressives such as Robert La Follette, who had been opposed to the war at the outset, and William Borah, who cast an eye toward Irish votes in arguing that the League would freeze Ireland's subjection to British rule.[15]

It was true that voting rights for British dominions and the mandate system were a boon to European colonialism, although that did not prevent a few Senate opponents from casting racist aspersions. For example, James Reed, a Missouri Democrat, defied Wilson's party leadership to object that "this is a colored league of nations," a tribunal on which "a nigger from Liberia, a nigger from Honduras, a nigger from India, or an unlettered gentleman from Siam each [has] votes equal to that of the United States of America." Demagoguery aside, most southern Democrats stuck by Wilson, and a large majority of the Senate favored ratification, with reservations attached. But Wilson now refused to compromise. In contrast to his exquisite ability to forge political majorities behind reform in the prewar years, he now could not muster the necessary two-thirds vote either in November or in March

1920. Wilson's obduracy alongside Lodge's obstructionism doomed the treaty to defeat.[16]

At a deeper level, U.S. rejection of the League of Nations revealed the limits of American liberalism in a revolutionary world. Not even Woodrow Wilson could bridge the contradiction between the United States' long-standing hemispheric isolation and its recent entrance onto the world stage; not even the great progressive leader could fuse domestic reform to permanent overseas entanglement; not even the most eloquent spokesman of crusading liberalism could persuade his countrymen that they had won "the final war for human liberty."[17] Already, the treaty itself was a travesty of liberal hopes for "no annexations, no indemnities" in its support of colonialism and in its Carthaginian reparations. Worse, the treaty seemed powerless to check the spread of bolshevism. Despite Western intervention, the Bolsheviks still held power, while social revolutionaries of various ideological stripes remained active from central Europe to Mexico. Bested by their wartime allies, frustrated by their postwar adversaries, most liberals were ready to give up the effort to remake the world in America's self-image. There was something tragic in the utter collapse of crusading liberalism. Not only was Wilson in part the author of his own downfall, but the fact that the United States broke faith with the pledge to collective security helped make for a weak response to the rise of fascism in the 1930s.

Could the United States have escaped this fate? Could American liberalism have played a more fruitful part in its first major role in world affairs? There is no shortage of hindsight on the question. According to the school of thought known as liberal realism, if Americans had been more realistic and less moralistic in appraising their national interests, and if they had not waited until 1917 to throw their weight into the scales of warfare, then the Great War might have ended before the cataclysmic breakdowns of European states in 1917 and 1918 and before the Bolshevik Revolution.[18] There is undoubtedly some truth in the criticism that American feelings of moral superiority contributed to the extreme reversals in U.S. policy—first refusing to fight, then plunging head over heels into the fray, then refusing to uphold collective security.

It is, however, highly unlikely that the United States could have dodged the question of revolution under any circumstances. Twentieth-century history has been dominated by revolution of one sort or another, whether liberal (middle-class), social (working-class, peasant), or national. In a world that between 1910 and 1920 saw liberal revolutions overturn age-old dynastic houses in Europe, social revolution in Mexico and Russia, and the stirrings of anticolonial revolt in China and India, there was simply no place for the United States to hide. Realism itself would have done little to help the country come to terms with the economic aspirations of peasants and workers or the desire in Latin America for national liberation from U.S. hegemony.

If some understanding of the revolutionary dynamic was required for a more rational and humane U.S. foreign policy, where would it come from? Most of the leading shapers of public opinion were blindly anticommunist. These included supposedly reliable newspapers such as the *New York Times*, which, as one critic noted, "reported the fall of Petrograd six times . . . burned it to the ground twice . . . and had it in revolt against the Bolsheviks six times, all without the slightest foundation in fact. Tamerlane never treated a conquered city worse than Petrograd has been treated in the columns of the 'Times.'" At the grass roots, there was general enthusiasm for the overthrow of the czar and a good deal of labor support for the Soviets, but precious little solidarity with the Bolshevik party. American Communists were hardly in a position to influence the State Department, and only a handful of pro-Soviet progressives even tried. Among the most important was Raymond Robins, a progressive Republican who returned from Russia on a Red Cross mission to urge cooperation with the Soviets because they represented the only force that enjoyed the support of the Russian masses. This assessment was certainly closer to reality than the wild fantasies of the supposedly sober national press.[19]

Unlike most of their liberal compatriots, this minority of progressives kept faith with the Spirit of '76 and retained their faith in revolution as the path to progress. Unlike American Communists, they did not believe that the dictatorship of the proletariat was either possible or desirable for the United States, but they did believe that American liberalism had to reform itself before it could seriously compete with bolshevism for world leadership. Although progressive reformers proposed plans along these lines for thoroughgoing "reconstruction" after the war, their ideas remained pinned to the drawing board because old-fashioned liberals, managerial liberals, and true conservatives entertained little sympathy for serious social reform. However, history was about to show that foreclosing this option had unfortunate consequences. By cutting themselves off from their own revolutionary heritage, Americans minimized their relevance to popular movements in the developing world and turned their crusading zeal inward in the Red Scare, with devastating consequences for liberty at home.

Postwar Reconstruction

When the fighting stopped in November 1918, American progressives were positively gleeful about the prospects of postwar reconstruction. Margaret Drier Robins evoked the mood of hope and promise in her keynote address to the Women's Trade Union League: "The war has created new values. Men and women are conscious that as citizens they must . . . share in the management of industry and the administration of government." The same spirit animated John Dewey's *Reconstruction in Philosophy* (1920), which charted a third path for reform between the Enlightenment idea of "atomistic" individualism and the Hegelian "monistic" theory of state supremacy. Striking an unmistakably Madisonian chord, Dewey argued that economic interest groups had become the real social units and the role of the state was that of orchestra conductor to "harmonize" these competing groups. Even as staunch an advocate of voluntarism as Herbert Hoover recognized the new role for large interest groups—business, labor, farmers—and prophesied that government-sponsored cooperation among them would yield "a new economic system, based neither on the capitalism of Adam Smith nor upon the Socialism of Karl Marx." [20]

Labor reformers were also hopeful that the war had solidified public acceptance of a permanent role for government in industrial relations. Industrial relations expert Gordon Watkins credited the War Labor Board with pacifying wartime labor unrest and predicted an expanded role for federal mediation, which would "make unnecessary a dictatorship by the proletariat and put an end to the autocracy of capital." Although prominent figures such as Frank Walsh, cochair of the War Labor Board, harbored no illusions that wartime regulatory machinery would be preserved intact, they took seriously their own speeches about "industrial democracy" and fully expected some kind of government mediation to persist. Similarly, social reformers felt they were riding a worldwide tide. Left out of key positions at Versailles, women trade unionists called the first International Congress of Working Women in Washington, which embraced the eight-hour day, abolition of child labor, and other protections dear to the U.S. sponsor, the

Women's Trade Union League. In addition, there was much talk about "the endowment of motherhood," or public welfare payments to mothers of young children; and the National Child Labor Committee notched a gain in the form of a second federal child labor law, revised to circumvent Supreme Court objections to the first Keating Act. (Ultimately, it, too, was overturned.) Thus labor and social reformers believed they were gaining the upper hand in their struggle against laissez faire.[21]

There is no denying that the postwar atmosphere was electric with radical ideas. Socialists in the garment unions joined midwestern labor progressives and latter-day prairie populists to form short-lived Labor and Farmer-Labor parties, which called for nationalization of certain industries, short hours, and the restoration of First Amendment rights that had been trampled during wartime repression. Having benefited from government control of the railroads, the normally conservative railway brotherhoods got behind the Plumb Plan for government ownership and became the backbone of the Conference for Progressive Political Action in 1922. Finally, in a last hurrah, labor and agrarian progressives launched a new Progressive party in 1924 behind the candidacy of "Fighting Bob" La Follette, garnering 16 percent of the vote, the largest third-party percentage (excluding the Bull Moose campaign) of the twentieth century.

Reformers were understandably jubilant when women's suffrage went over the top with the ratification of the Nineteenth Amendment in August 1920. The women's movement must be credited with providing the main impetus behind the victory after a struggle that went back to the Seneca Falls women's rights convention of 1848. The fact that suffragists such as Susan B. Anthony had been crusading for so long raises the question of why the "Anthony Amendment" finally triumphed now. Sectional differences provide part of the explanation. The strongest support for suffrage came from the West, where all but one state had adopted it before the First World War, sometimes out of a desire to civilize the wild West, but more often in response to popular—and often populist—pressures. The strongest opposition was lodged in the South, where no women voted. The South's bitter-end opposition casts strong doubt on the notion that suffrage was an effort of a native, Anglo-Saxon, Protestant elite to expand its power at the ballot box. No one was more xenophobic than the arch-Protestant white men of the South; yet they fought suffrage to the bitter end, because they feared that the quick overthrow of paternalist conventions would not only undermine male privilege but also subvert white supremacy. The fact that Russian Bolsheviks and French Catholics were implementing suffrage at the same time casts additional doubt on the Yankee-Protestant "social control" thesis, which relies too much on the fact that Protestant Scandinavian nations had been the first to adopt women's suffrage before the war.[22]

The North's delegation was the swing vote in Congress. Mobilizing against Republican patricians and Catholic political machines, the National American Woman Suffrage Association rallied support in a growing number of states that had adopted suffrage, including Illinois and New York. In addition, genteel suffragists such as Carrie Chapman Catt conducted polite interviews with the president, while the militants of the National Women's party hit upon the brilliant publicity device of burning "watchfires" in Washington until the antisuffrage enemy—which before 1918 included the president himself—was defeated.

In the end, it was the impact of the war that counted most. It was true that suffrage was nowhere adopted as a war measure, but certainly Wilson's call to battle on the lofty ideological plane of "democracy versus autocracy" probably doomed male-only suffrage to extinction. In this respect, Wilson's "safe for democracy" speech was analogous to Lincoln's Emancipation Proclamation, which did not actually free any slaves but probably made freeing them inevitable. Wilson finally came around to accept the logic of universal democracy, and by repudiating the southern antisuffrage forces of his own party he gave a mighty push to the cause in the Democratic-controlled House, which passed the amendment in January 1918. Although enough diehard Republicans in the Senate joined the sons of southern patriarchs to postpone the measure for another year, it was only a matter of time before thirty-six states ratified in time to allow the New Woman to cast ballots in the 1920 presidential election.

Meanwhile, the New Negro was also astir. The Great Migration from the South to the freer air of northern cities plus the experience of Afro-American soldiers in Europe engendered militant defiance of Jim Crow. The new mood also fed on anticolonial agitation in faraway places such as South Africa and India, giving hope to fledgling organizations such as the African Blood Brotherhood that the world's color line was beginning to come down, while the collapse of Europe's Continental empires caused the *Amsterdam News* to ask: "Security of Life for Poles and Serbs—Why Not for Colored Nations?" Watching the upheavals of the world's workers, Socialists such as A. Philip Randolph and journals such as *The Messenger* called for "absolute and unequivocal *social equality*" through common cause with the working classes. Every advance for the New Woman gave added impetus to racial equality because it encouraged black women such as author Zora Neale Hurston to develop their talents and because race relations could not remain fixed while relations between the sexes changed. To the extent that women emerged from their "protected" status, they no longer needed male protectors of their own family, class, or race.[23]

It was also the springtime of the Harlem Renaissance. This was the effloresence of social thought and literature by the likes of W. E. B. DuBois and Langston Hughes, to which white intellectuals paid homage by trooping uptown to drink in the jazz tones of chic after-hours clubs while talking art and poetry. There were also signs of political awakening in the rapid growth of organizations such as the NAACP, which attracted large numbers of southerners to double its membership. Most important, progressives of both races grappled with the idea of the New Negro, an effort to confront the conundrum DuBois had posed years earlier around the "two-ness" of the African in American, a race apart yet inextricably American. One thing was certain—there could be no American democracy that excluded African-Americans. Alain Locke, one of the key figures of the Renaissance, put his finger on the problem: "So the choice is not between one way for the Negro and another way for the rest, but between American institutions frustrated on the one hand and American ideals progressively fulfilled and realized on the other." No one from Alexis de Tocqueville to Gunnar Myrdal better expressed the crux of America's racial dilemma.[24]

Another bright star in the "reconstruction" constellation was the "new morality," now emerging from wartime eclipse. In books such as *Our Changing Morality* (1924), social critics resumed their attacks on Victorian morality and "the proprietary theory of marriage" wherein the husband was entitled to the wife's conjugal attention and household labor. Shrewdly assaying the forces undermining proprietary marriage, Elsie Parsons pointed to the employment of women, the corrosive effect of urban life on old-fashioned sexual mores, and the impact of birth control in separating mating from parenthood. The result was that "reciprocity in passion, emotional integrity, and mutual enhancement of life might share in the approval once confined to constancy, fidelity, and duty, virtues that are obviously suggested by the hit or miss system of mating and reproducing our social organization has favored." Parsons did not quail at the implications of "reciprocity in passion" or "mutual enhancement"; she endorsed what became known as "companionate marriage," an idea whose most prominent champion was social reformer Judge Ben Lindsey, wherein companionship and lovemaking would take precedence over legal bonds and moneymaking as the bases for marriage.[25]

A small band of sexual radicals launched a campaign to repeal those sections of the Comstock laws that defined birth control as obscene. Unlike the prudish social engineers of the American Social Hygiene Association, the radicals behind Mary Dennett's Voluntary Motherhood League distributed educational materials that portrayed sex-play as a garden of sensual delights for both sexes.[26] Of course, that only provoked the censors, but banning books did not stop petting in movie theaters and rumble seats any more than petulant tongue-wagging stopped flappers from going to their infamous parties. Heaping guilt upon premarital sex-play and autoeroticism did not end those practices, either, as sober social hygienists learned from scientific surveys subsequently confirmed by the Kinsey reports.[27]

As significant as the new courting rituals was the growing separation of sex from procreation among married couples. Families had been limiting births since the early nineteenth century, but largely through abstinence, withdrawal, and similar practices that inevitably rested on the denial of desire. In contrast, the diaphragm and the condom were at least theoretically consistent with marital eroticism, and one implication of the increase in divorce rates, from 20 per 1,000 married people in 1900 to 36 per 1,000 in 1930, was that people were beginning to search for sexual compatibility in their mates. Terminal monogamy was on its way to becoming serial monogamy.[28]

These changes in family and property harbored a potential for a more egalitarian future. Combining sex for pleasure and companionate marriage—equal love rights and equal property rights—held dangerous implications for social hierarchy. Feminist author Suzanne La-Follette drew the ultimate conclusion: "The ultimate emancipation of woman, then, will depend not upon the abolition of the restrictions which have subjected her to man—that is but a step, though a necessary one—but upon the *abolition of all those restrictions of natural human rights that subject the mass of humanity to a privileged class.*"[29] Such critics of sexual convention glimpsed the hidden potential for social equality embedded in the everyday separation of sex from procreation.

In this highly charged atmosphere, the boldest sounded the tocsin of revolution. The first manifesto of the newly founded American Communist party in September 1919 began: "The world is on the verge of a new era. Europe is in revolt. The masses of Asia are stirring uneasily. Capitalism is in collapse. The workers of the world are seeing a new life and securing new courage. Out of the night of war is coming a new day."[30] As the pall of wartime repression was lifted, the left wing of the Socialist party and the foreign-language federations, in particular, took inspiration from the idea of revolutionary councils (soviets) of workers and soldiers and split away to form the core of the Communist party. Meanwhile, a smaller group around John Reed, author of *Ten Days That Shook the World* (1919), proclaimed themselves to be the true American revolutionaries and founded the Communist Labor party. Soon to be driven underground by the Red Scare, the two factions would re-emerge in 1921 united and disciplined as a Leninist party pursuing the dictatorship of the proletariat. If being a vanguard party in a formally democratic society proved to be a recipe for isolation, the fact remained that in a world in which Bolsheviks had wrested power from the czars, anything seemed possible.[31]

Looking at the world through red-colored glasses, revolutionaries easily mistook the social upheavals of 1919 and 1920 for the harbingers of mass revolt. In Seattle, shipyard workers won the backing of the entire labor movment for a general strike that briefly translated the IWW doctrine "solidarity forever" into class-conscious reality. Labor militancy was at an all-time high as some 4 million wage earners hit the bricks, more than in any other period of American history. The spirit spread from steelworkers to the Boston police and infected even lower-level managers and efficiency experts such as Frank Gilbreth, who briefly lost his scientific composure to hail the idea of a "soviet of technicians."[32] Afro-Americans, too, displayed a new militancy. In Chicago, they retaliated with unexpected ferocity against rampaging white youth gangs in the largest race riot of the era. Some of the thirty-nine dead were white victims of young men from the South and returning veterans asserting a militant form of black manhood. Jamaican-born Claude McKay captured their defiant spirit in an oft-quoted poem, "If We Must Die," published in the left-wing journal *The Liberator:* "Like men we'll face the murderous, cowardly pack,/ Pressed to the wall, dying, but fighting back!"[33]

Although revolutionaries such as John Reed, Crystal Eastman, and Claude McKay disagreed vehemently with mild progressives such as Felix Frankfurter and Margaret Robins, both sides of the revolution/ reform dynamic shared a conviction that laissez faire was historically obsolete. Both knew that the old liberal concepts of private property and the proprietary family did not comport with a world of mass production, women's employment, and trade unions. Both wrestled with the conundrum of a society that was egalitarian and racist in equal measure. Both recognized that the boundaries between public and private, men's and women's "spheres," state and society were dissolving. As archrivals in a race to reshape the relation between society and the state, both professed to be the true twentieth-century antithesis to nineteenth-century liberalism. And both dared to hope for redemption from social evil and war. With the United States riding a worldwide progressive tide, Chicago social worker Agnes Nestor recalled the expectant mood: "We were living in a time of great dreams—dreams of co-operation between the working peoples of the world, dreams of dignity and plenty for all, dreams of lasting international peace."[34] It is a tribute to American optimism, or naïveté, that upon waking from the nightmare of 10 million dead in the Great War, it was still possible to have "great dreams."

Progressive Paralysis

The dynamic of reform/revolution came to grief on the shoals of social conflict. At every turn, America was splitting into opposing camps— the New Woman and antifeminists, the New Negro and the old racism, the new immigrants and the native born. Most stunning was the conflict between workers and employers. The immediate postwar years bucked and heaved with the most acute industrial unrest the nation had ever known. More than 4 million workers were involved in strikes and lockouts in 1919—365,000 in steel, 400,000 in coal; altogether, perhaps one in five industrial workers, the highest proportion before or since. Basil Manly, the last chairman of the War Labor Board, explained: "The workers of the Allied world have been told that they were engaged in a war for democracy . . . They are asking now, 'Where is that democracy for which we fought?'" Ironically, Wilson's wartime administration was a prime cause of the postwar upheaval. The propaganda of democracy raised workers' expectations; mediation of industrial disputes legitimated workers' grievances; wartime nationalism helped override cultural divisions among the myriad ethnic groups whose cooperation was the precondition for working-class collective action. Spurred by postwar inflation, workers struck to obtain the American standard of living, and for "industrial democracy"—a share of power—that might bring it about.[35]

Their challenge was all the more potent because by the time of the 1920 census, they were reaching the peak of their social weight. As the country turned the corner to become more than half urban, a third of the gainfully employed toiled in mining and manufacturing, and altogether blue-collar workers amounted to 59.7 percent. There were more miners, railway workers, and cotton textile workers than ever before or since. It was the historic climax of the gritty complex of coal, steel, and rails that Lewis Mumford dubbed "carboniferous capitalism," and it contained enormous explosive forces.[36]

While a working-class army was amassing, captains of industry did not stand idly by. To forestall further union growth and head off dangerous experiments such as the Plumb Plan for government ownership of the railroads, industrialists went on an open-shop offensive of their own. Wrapping the open shop in the flag as the "American Plan," they resolved to roll back wartime gains in union membership. Denouncing collective bargaining as a violation of the sacred canons of American individualism, garment manufacturers locked out thousands, while U.S. Steel, the largest industrial employer in the country, took the largest strike in American history in September 1919 rather than hold a conference with the steelworkers' national committee.[37]

Employers of all descriptions gathered in the revival tent of free-market ideals. Southern industrialists, midwestern Rotarians and Kiwanians, 1,400 chambers of commerce, and Wall Streeters all found their natural leader for the open-shop drive in the National Association of Manufacturers. NAM had launched the first open-shop drive in 1903 and now coordinated activities through its New York office, publicizing the struggle through its *Open Shop Bulletin*, which first appeared in November 1920. Never wavering from its free-market ideology, NAM continued to preach the message of its president, David Parry: "The Open Shop means liberty and liberty is the life of industry." Though often pretending neutrality on workers' right to join a union, the kind of unions they had in mind was summed up by Mr. Dooley, the fictional cracker-barrel philosopher and mouthpiece for Peter Finley Dunne: "No strikes, no rules, no contracts, no scales, hardly iny wages, an' dam few mimbers."[38]

Under the constitutional warrant of the *Hitchman Coal* decision (1917), which validated the yellow-dog contract in a West Virginia case brought by the United Mine Workers, newly formed open-shop associations urged employers to remove the gloves and fight unions with strikebreakers, private police, and federal troops. Many employers did not hesitate to bring in thugs and gunmen from professional strike-breaking outfits such as the infamous Bergoff, Corporations Auxiliary, and Baldwin-Felts detective agencies, whose "nobles" (guards) and "finks" (strikebreakers) frequently touched off a melee of riot and killing.[39] So it had been in the nineteenth century, and now, again, imposing the open shop required the country to pay for the maldistribution of wealth and power with the coin of violence.

The adamant antiunion stance of American employers revealed much about the distribution of power in the United States, particularly in comparison with Europe. American employers had a freer hand in dealing with their employees because the market was subject to much less regulation. The facts that the market ruled so much of American society and that society was supreme over the state established the long reign of the businessman. In Europe, employers did not have such a free hand in dealing with their subordinates because society in general and the market in particular were subject to greater state regulation. Thus the way was open to corporatist experiments after the war. Whereas America's War Labor Board was sacrificed at the altar of laissez faire, in Europe interest-group bargaining and tripartite machinery comprising capital, labor, and government expanded rapidly. German industrialists accepted collective bargaining within the framework of the Weimar Republic under the Stinnes-Legien Agreement, and they accepted an expanded welfare state. They saw these compromises as a positive path to social stability and, in any case, as far preferable to much more serious inroads on property that might have come through working-class revolution under Communist leadership. Although Britain faced less of a revolutionary threat, enlightened industrialists pinned their hopes for labor peace on government-sponsored Whitley Councils, tripartite machinery that accorded unions the status of an equal bargaining partner.[40]

American industrialists would have none of this class collaboration. Heir to generations of free-market ideology, the American businessman believed it a fundamental prerogative to control his own shop free from government or union interference. All the segments of the business community united behind the open shop, from the medium-sized employers of the National Association of Manufacturers to the corporate magnates of the National Industrial Conference Board (which had supplanted the National Civic Federation as the main clearinghouse of big business opinion). Standard Oil, Du Pont, and a dozen other leading corporations, most of them linked to the Rockefellers, formed the Special Conference Committee in 1919 to coordinate policy on labor and other matters. This committee recommended against any plan resembling the Whitley Councils that "introduces into labor discussions representatives of outside organizations," noting that "it would be distinctly un-American to force here such unionization as the English Plan requires." In place of unions, it recommended a management-controlled employee representation plan along the lines developed for Rockefeller after the Ludlow Massacre. American business of any stripe, large or small, rarely accepted collective bargaining except when forced to, and corporatist experiments were rarer still.[41]

Employer intransigence in the face of worker upsurge confronted Wilsonian progressives with extremely hard choices. Had the United States undergone four years of war instead of a year and a half, the War Industries Board and the War Labor Board might have become permanent agencies with coercive powers, but, as it was, the "dollar-a-year" men in charge saw no alternative but to return to the liberal status quo ante bellum. Actually, progressive "reconstruction" plans were not so bold as might have been expected from men such as Bernard Baruch and Felix Frankfurter, who so recently had been standing up to corporate executives such as Elbert Gary and Daniel Willard. In fact, the entire Wilson administration envisioned a speedy return of the railroads to private hands and a rapid dismantling of the Federal Shipbuilding Corporation, the Food and Fuel Administration, and other bureaus that had sprung up to handle war production. Having completed their trust-busting agenda before the war began, the Wilsonians now could envision little more than maintaining existing corporate-regulatory machinery, overseeing the railroads, and creating new commissions as circumstances might require.[42]

Since progressive hopes for finessing industrial conflict had always

depended upon voluntary cooperation, they stood paralyzed as cooperation was crushed between the jaws of worker insurgency and the
open-shop offensive. There is no better illustration of the collapse of
progressive policy than the fate of the Industrial Conference in the fall
of 1919. Resurrecting the old progressive commission idea, the Wilson
administration staked its all on a tripartite body of business, labor, and
"the public" in the vain hope for labor peace. The conference came to
grief October 14 around the steel strike when "the public" delegation,
including of all people Elbert Gary and John D. Rockefeller, Jr., vetoed
Gompers' urgent proposal for a panel to adjudicate the strike. That left
the tried-and-true method of federal troops as the only alternative to
mediation. As a matter of fact, at that very moment U.S. troops under
the command of General Leonard Wood—Rough Rider, Governor of
the Philippines, army chief of staff, and aspirant to the Republican
presidential nomination—were sweeping the streets of steel towns
clear of strike demonstrations.[43]

In another test of the progressive strategy a few weeks later, Secretary of Labor William Wilson tried unsuccessfully to settle a dispute in
the coal industry that had idled almost 400,000 miners. Here again,
Attorney General A. Mitchell Palmer was ready with a court injunction outlawing the strike under the Lever Act. Although Gompers
fumed that the move betrayed a promise from the administration not
to use this war regulation as the basis for breaking strikes, United Mine
Workers chief John L. Lewis asked his uncooperative men to go back
to work and shrugged off defeat with the comment, "You can't fight the
government."[44]

All told, the Wilson administration used the army as a domestic police more than any other administration since military Reconstruction
after the Civil War. On top of the continued military occupation of
western copper and lumber districts, and alongside the widespread industrial use of Military Intelligence, the War Department sent federal
troops marching into strikes, race riots, and mob disturbances on
twenty occasions from June 1919 to the following June alone, and the
threat of troops hung over every major industrial dispute. No one in
the administration had a purer progressive pedigree than "pacifist" Secretary of War Newton Baker, but Baker had no compunctions about
using troops against unruly strikers. Attempting to calm the nation as
President Wilson lay incapacitated by a stroke in October 1919, he proclaimed that he had put the army's department commanders under orders to "respond instantly" to any governor's request for troops.[45]

As a final blow to the progressive strategy, government machinery actually began to trigger disorder, not prevent it. The Railway Labor Board was by far the best-established federal mediation service. Chartered in the 1916 Adamson Act, it was absorbed into William McAdoo's wartime railroad empire and then reconstituted in the Transportation (Esch-Cummings) Act of 1920. When the board imposed a 12 percent pay cut on shop craftsmen in 1922, a quarter of a million men walked out, exceeding even the number involved in the great railway strikes of 1877 and 1894. In imitation of their nineteenth-century forebears, shopmen in western Missouri and northern Texas conducted a riot wrapped in a strike. According to Attorney General Harry Daugherty, it was an unremitting catalogue of horrors: "kidnappings and abductions, followed by tar and feathers or whippings and beatings . . . sending of letters and circulars containing threats, abusive and insulting language; picketing . . . forcible entrance into the railroad shops, whereupon they destroyed and damaged engines and railroad property." It took a small army of some 3,500 federal marshals, plus thousands more local police and railroad detectives, to suppress the rebellion.[46]

In sum, class polarization pinned progressives on the horns of a dilemma. Siding with insurgent workers meant joining forces with the Farmer-Laborites, or even in some fashion with the socialists, and burning the bridges of liberal reform. On the other hand, siding with entrenched capital meant using the iron fist of troops instead of the velvet glove of commissions. Either way, they wiped out the very premise of class compromise on which they preferred to stand and forfeited the philosophy of the middle way. In the face of force used by strikers and employers alike, plus the *force majeur* of U.S. troops, it is no wonder that progressive reformers lost heart. For the first time in years, the *New Republic* felt impotent: "Between organized labor, on the one hand, and organized capital on the other, the large class which lives by rendering services to both stands an excellent chance of being crushed as between the upper and nether millstones."[47]

What was in fact being crushed was not the middle class per se, but the links between the broad middle class and industrial wage earners. And the consequence of disrupting that cross-class alliance was to remove the necessary condition for progressive social reform. Accordingly, no new reform legislation emerged at the state or federal level after 1919 until the Great Depression once again established a more favorable balance of forces. In the meantime, state intervention favored big business. That does not mean the state was a mere cats-paw. Despite the way things no doubt appeared to a trade unionist looking down the barrel of a rifle, the immediate motive in sending troops into industrial disputes was not to restore corporate profits, but to establish public order, protect the rights of property, and defend the Constitution against "subversion." Be that as it may, the end result was to uphold a set of property relations in which corporations flourished and wage earners foundered. It goes without saying this is not what Wilsonian progressives had intended by "reconstruction," but given the decisions they made in the unwanted circumstances of 1919 and 1920, they could not help but become the authors of their own downfall.

Progressives were no better able to handle the race question. Their failure to confront the issue during their prewar heyday came back to haunt them in the polarized racial climate of the postwar years. The massive Chicago race riot of 1919 revealed the dramatic pattern. It began when white youths attempted to enforce social boundary lines that appeared to be crumbling with the influx of African-Americans. White bathers at Chicago's lakefront stoned a black swimmer for straying onto a segregated beach; the Ragen Colts and other Irish street gangs attacked those who wandered across the racial perimeter; immigrants intimidated black workers in the packinghouses; realtors and property owners, such as Chicago's Hyde Park–Kenwood Association, warned of the Negro's "evil design against the white man's property." Masculine values fueled racial hatred as white men engaged in a kind of tribal competition over turf, jobs, opportunity, and status with men of the rival group. Such rivalry differed markedly from the kind of sexual issues at stake in the South, where lynch mobs enforced white supremacy through male supremacy, and vice versa. There, the fiction that black men lusted after white women provided the justification both for women's submission to a male protector and for savage victimization of black men. The sadistic ritual of lynching reconfirmed the social hierarchy through reaffirmation of the taboo on interracial sex.[48]

One thing that white vigilantes had in common, North and South, was the belief that by taking the law into their own hands they were defending legitimate authority against usurpers. And authorities behaved in such a way as to confirm the belief. Instead of enforcing equal access regardless of race, police preferred to enforce segregation. For example, instead of arresting the Chicago whites who stoned the bathers, police arrested blacks who protested the incident. Instead of upholding fair housing and equal job opportunity, Democratic party leaders accused Republicans such as Chicago Mayor Big Bill Thompson of "colonizing" southern blacks in white jobs and neighborhoods. When the Illinois national guard was called in to suppress disorder, it sometimes shot black victims instead of white rioters.

As a consequence of racial polarization, African-Americans remained isolated from the struggles of industrial workers. Although their concentration in still-unorganized service occupations played a part in that isolation, even in industries such as steel and rails, where they labored in significant numbers, segregation had done its work so well that they took no part in organizing. In the case of meatpacking, in which some blacks stuck by the union while others scabbed, the Chicago riot foreclosed interracial organizing for more than a decade.[49]

In contrast to their frustration in industrial relations and helplessnes in race relations, progressives felt a surge of triumph with the victory of women's suffrage. Nothing made reform hearts beat faster than the Nineteenth Amendment. Dubbed "the jewel in the progressive crown," it marked the culmination of a long series of steps toward women's legal emancipation, including married women's property acts and the abandonment of the doctrine of coverture. The combined effect of these emancipations was to shatter the symmetry of "separate spheres." Winning the right to vote proved that wives and daughters were themselves public actors in the drama of consent of the governed and would no longer be the silent subjects of paternalist will.[50]

For all that, gaining the vote proved to be more significant than using it. Contrary to expectations on both sides, women did not vote disproportionately for social reforms of the sort backed by the newly founded League of Women Voters, successor to the main suffrage organization. If anything, they shied away from welfare reforms such as the "endowment of motherhood" that seemed to license irresponsibility for husband-breadwinners by shifting the burden of support to the state. This cautious conservatism reflected women's continuing subordinate social position in the home and workplace, plus the stabilizing consequences of gaining the suffrage. Just as white male suffrage had given nineteenth-century male workers and distressed farmers a stake in the existing political system, so co-opting women into the state pacified their protest. Being part of the machinery of consent was not the same thing as having a proportional share in state power, let alone holding anything like equal sway in the entire complex governing system, with all its parastate institutions for regulating the market and the family and its myriad ramifications into the hierarchies of daily life. Having won a nineteenth-century battle, the women's movement was slow to adapt its strategy to twentieth-century terrain and was therefore unable to capitalize on its moment of greatest triumph for the cause of broader social reform.

The state was no neutral broker when it came to the norms of family life. Though no mere tool of the upper classes, it enforced standards for social reproduction in home, school, and community that were congenial to middle- and upper-class practices and inimical to working-class morale and self-improvement. From federal agencies such as the Public Health Service and state boards of charities and corrections came battalions of genteel Anglo-Saxon matrons and college men to tell immigrant women how to scrub their floors, feed their infants, honor Old Glory, and keep their daughters away from dance halls. From the Bureau of Immigration and the Justice Department came calls for immigration restriction, bolstered by dubious IQ testing and the pseudo-science of eugenics claiming to show that "inferior races" produced more than their share of deviants and feebleminded. From Congress came the Prohibition Amendment, a clear-cut victory of Yankee Protestants and southern elites over the laboring population, for whom drink was an integral part of the weddings, wakes, and festivals that made up community life. Although progressives were not the main impetus for these top-down controls on social reproduction, many looked favorably upon these elements of "social hygiene." Insofar as they cut themselves off from the realities of working-class life, progressives further eroded the alliance that had made social reform possible.[51]

Thus progressivism became increasingly paralyzed. Like the president himself, who lay stricken for weeks after suffering a disabling stroke in September 1919, progressives could summon neither will nor intellect to guide postwar politics to a higher plane. Part of the reason for their paralysis was the impact of the First World War on American politics. When the Wilson administration decided to suppress all wartime dissent, it set such a rigid standard of political orthodoxy that socialists and pacifists were tainted with disloyalty. The political dialogue between the left and moderate progressives that had generated so many new reform ideas until 1917 came to an end. Once the left was shut out of national debate, respectable Republican and Democratic hearts were frozen against reform from below, leaving labor radicals, socialists, populists, feminists, and communists to launch various third parties—Labor, Farmer-Labor, Communist, and Women's.

Yet it is hard to escape the conclusion that the progressives' plight was partly of their own making. They were confronted at the end of the war by choices between change and stability, progressive reform and orthodox liberalism, egalitarian social forces and the hierarchies of class and race. This was by no means the way Wilson and his progressive advisers would have wanted it, but as guardians of the progressive trust they were compelled to choose. In suppressing labor discontent with injunctions and troops, evading the issue of race, shunning the new morality, and joining in the repression of popular customs, progressives blocked the very path of slow and steady reform they preferred to tread. If they were unable to find a progressive way to resolve postwar polarizations, it was, in part, because they themselves made it impossible.

Red Scare

Absent rational solutions to social problems, Americans succumbed to the irrationalities of the Red Scare. The trigger for obsessive fear of the "Red menace" was disillusionment with the outcome of the war. In the first place, most Americans were fast losing their zeal for any further overseas crusading. Turning their backs on their own revolutionary heritage, they grew mistrustful of a world rife with working-class and peasant upheaval that had already singed Uncle Sam's whiskers in the Philippines and Mexico and now was spreading bolshevism in eastern Europe. The Bolshevik Revolution set up a new polarity in international politics between communism and liberalism, the Third International and the Western powers, that was to last (except for the decade 1935–1945) until the end of the Cold War in the late 1980s. But initially most Americans refused to accept this bipolar structure. Although some members of the foreign policy elite, such as Secretary of State Robert Lansing, were ready to gird their loins for battle from Siberia to Seattle, most felt it was better to shun the Soviets and seal the borders against radical foreign influences.[52]

As if that was not enough, further disillusionment came in the Versailles Treaty itself. As word filtered back from the peace conference, it became clear that Old World cunning was defeating New World innocence at every turn, erasing one after another of the Fourteen Points until all that remained was the League of Nations. Even the League had become tainted as the guarantor of imperial spoils and a Carthaginian peace. Alarmed about a possible sacrifice of American sovereignty, the Senate rejected League membership, and with that, U.S. diplomacy turned turtle and withdrew into the hard shell of the Western Hemisphere. Wilson, who had gone to Versailles as a revolutionary liberal, the last of the Founding Fathers, turned into the defender of a lost cause. The same worried middle classes who had clasped 100 percent Americanism to their bosoms during the war, now lost faith in any crusade to remake the world in America's image. Instead of making the world safe for democracy, they chose to make democracy safe for America.

They felt a special urgency because the forces of democracy were advancing at every hand. The root causes of the Red Scare were buried in the polarizations gripping American society. The labor movement chalked up 5 million members, the most in history, while the great strikes of immigrant workers sent shock waves from Main Street to Wall Street. The New Woman was rolling the suffrage bandwagon toward victory and increasing the power of reform lobbies in Congress for the task of social reconstruction. Meanwhile, newspapers in 1919 were full of reports of mounting public disorder—the unabashed radicalism of the Seattle general strike; the misbegotten attempts by persons unknown to mail dozens of bombs to prominent figures timed to detonate on May 1; the bloody Chicago race riot in July; the shock of the Boston police strike; and the massive steel and coal strikes in the fall.[53]

It was all too much for middle Americans. Small businessmen and Protestant ministers who might have warmed to trust-busting and Christian charity before the war now grew cold toward the mobilization of the urban masses. Small-town editors and educators schooled in liberal individualism and steeped in Protestant morality lacked the intellectual machinery to comprehend the social forces welling up from heavy industry and tenement districts. What could they possibly make of industrial democracy, except to see it as an assault on private enterprise? What was the new morality, if not an insult to feminine virtue? Who was the New Negro, if not an impudent affront to traditional privileges?

Unable to fathom the homegrown causes of discontent, they concluded that America must have been poisoned by foreign ideologies.

The superpatriots of the right treated bolshevism as a kind of social disease against which people could be vaccinated by large doses of 100 percent Americanism. In fact, the entire battery of superpatriotic loyalty leagues merely substituted Russian bolshevism for Prussian militarism and went on beating the foreign devil. Antiforeign, anticommunist paranoia surged out of control in the spring and summer of 1919. Antiradical vigilantes stormed peaceful May Day demonstrations in several cities, including Cleveland, where, in the company of police and army tanks, they left 2 dead and 100 wounded. With the tempo of fear closely attuned to the patriotic calendar, the prophets of counterrevolution in the Federal Bureau of Investigation called upon local police to mobilize in advance of a supposed July Fourth insurrection. The fact that no revolt occurred did not staunch the panic, because the mass psychology of fear fed on itself. By September, even President Wilson was saying that "the poison of disorder, the poison of revolt, the poison of chaos" had forced their way "into the veins of this free people." Understood in anthropological terms, the Red Scare was a ritual of purification, an effort to cleanse the sacred days of the republic and bleed poison from the veins of the American body politic. Pervaded by superstition, it aimed at uniting the community through the expulsion of filth.[54]

That compulsion held countless elected officials in its grip in 1919 and 1920. New York State set up the Lusk Committee on "revolutionary radicalism" to probe the supposedly Russian origins of subversion in the public schools. Following suit, the Senate committee dealing with bolshevism in the United States, chaired by Senator Lee Slater Overman, took lurid testimony about the imaginary "German-Bolshevik conspiracy" from a parade of anticommunist witnesses. One of these, Archibald Stevenson, made a career of the Red Scare by shuttling back and forth as a professional witness before various investigating committees. Explaining industrial discontent in terms of Bolshevik influence on foreign workers, Stevenson counseled: "We must remember, Senator, that the American people—and by that I mean the really American people—are not present in very large numbers in industrial centers." To give the appearance of a balanced investigation, the committee also heard from a small band of progressives, including Raymond Robins, on the importance of reconciling American liberalism to the Bolshevik Revolution, but toleration for radicalism was exactly what was being purged. The main effect of these investigations was to strip radicalism and discontent of their legitimacy before the public at large. Given America's liberal inheritance, political purges in the United States normally came through voluntarist channels rather than state dictates, and that is exactly what was provided by presidential speeches, congressional hearings, the press, and the other organs that molded public opinion.[55]

The purge extended to "improper" notions of gender. Given the traditional symbol of woman as the guardian of virtue, purification inevitably trenched upon the relations of the sexes. The grand inquisitors in Congress gave Louise Bryant, comrade in arms of John Reed, the toughest grilling of all its witnesses. When she objected to "the third degree," Senator Overman fairly dripped paternalist contempt: "You are a woman and you do not know anything about the conduct of an examination such as we have in hand here. We are going to treat you fairly and treat you as a lady." Not to be intimidated, Bryant shot back: "I do not want to be treated as a lady, but I want to be treated as a human being." Trying to rebut the falsehood that Bolshevik commissars such as Aleksandra Kollontai had ordered the "nationalization of women," she taunted the senators for their gullibility in mistaking a news article in a provincial anarchist paper for a decree of the Bolshevik government. The canard about the "nationalization of women" was central to the Red Scare, because it posed the ultimate threat of destroying the middle-class family. Senators made much of the phantasmagorical "bureau of free love" and the news from Moscow that educated ladies of property were reduced to selling magazines in the street to earn a living. What better proof of the bourgeois world turned upside down than tales of free love and ladies of leisure forced into manual labor?[56]

Patriotic societies warned that changing the position of women subverted the Constitution and disfigured property relations. Since the old liberals could not conceive of the family apart from private property, in their superheated imaginations the nationalization of property automatically led to the promiscuous nationalization of women. The *Woman Patriot*, organ of the Sentinels of the Republic, proclaimed itself "Dedicated to the Defense of the Family and the State AGAINST Feminism and Socialism." Such superpatriots believed that the "endowment of motherhood" and even mild reforms such as the abolition of child labor were the entering wedge of family disintegration. The problem was not their linking of family, property, and the state—on this score they were on the right track; rather, it was their red-baiting of social reform. They attacked not only John Reed and Louise Bryant for their open support of the Bolshevik Revolution, but also moderate reformers such as Carrie Chapman Catt, the National Child Labor Committee, and the League of Women Voters, all of whom were said to be "organizing revolution through women and children." Obviously, what was at stake was not the family per se, as if the family had been some eternal, inviolate institution until the Bolsheviks came along, but the kind of family dear to the hearts of old-fashioned liberals, in which self-made men were enshrined as the protectors of "true" women.[57]

Though mostly middle-class in origin, anticommunism was also present in the working class. To the extent that working people fell under the influence of Catholic family doctrine and the strong patriarchal values of immigrant cultures, they were likely to be receptive to the idea that bolshevism meant the communism of women. In fact, many ethnic communities were ideologically polarized, as between Red and White Finns, Communist and Fascist Italians, Socialist and Orthodox Jews.[58]

As for the labor movement, the one segment that joined heart and soul in the anti-red crusade was the American Federation of Labor. Samuel Gompers had had years of preparation for combatting the "red menace." Having vanquished many a socialist over decades of power plays, he had conjured up the American Alliance for Labor and Democracy to convert socialists to the Allied cause during the war and had worked tirelessly with the government's wartime campaign to destroy the rival IWW. Now, as labor insurgencies broke out at every hand, he redoubled his efforts to defeat the labor left, win a measure of political legitimacy for the AFL, and use superpatriotism as a shield against the "American Plan." In the narrow view, anticommunism served all these ends so well that it would have been amazing if Gompers had not taken up the cudgels. That he did so with unsurpassed fervor is a measure of the Americanization of Gompers, a Dutch Jewish immigrant who had once had socialist convictions, and of the many Irish and German workers he led. However, it was not the miniscule power of Communists that employers were determined to curb, but the growing power of organized workers. U.S. Steel had no compunctions about red-baiting the steel strike, and the National Association of Manufacturers' *Open Shop Review* landed telling blows with the slogan "Unionism is nothing less than bolshevism." Employers had no trouble whatever beating Gompers at his own superpatriotic game.[59]

The state was no mere umpire in the Red Scare; it was the single most important player. Authorities fomented the Red Scare for reasons of state, especially for the maintenance of law and order in domestic disturbances. Secretary of War Newton Baker, for example, in speeches widely reported in the press, justified sending troops into the 1919 steel strike on the grounds of "violent agitation by so-called Bolsheviki and radicals counselling violence and urging action on behalf of what they call social revolution." The fact that William Z. Foster, former Wobbly and future Communist, headed the AFL committee to organize the steelworkers was taken as proof positive that left-wing agitators were out to cause disorder for the sake of destabilizing the government.[60]

On the same theory that strikes were the result of insidious Bolshevik infiltration from overseas, Attorney General A. Mitchell Palmer conducted a series of red raids in the fall of 1919 under authority of recent revisions in the immigration statutes that made mere membership in a revolutionary organization a criminal offense. Rounding up members of the Union of Russian Workers and other foreign-sounding organizations, he did what the theory of foreign origins compelled: he packed them aboard the *Buford* with foreign-born anarchists such as Emma Goldman and Alexander Berkman and sent them on "the Soviet Ark" back where they had come from. The fact that they were being punished for their ideas, not for any overt act, raised the hackles of civil libertarians, who no doubt agreed with the cartoon in *The Liberator* showing the *Buford*'s smoke besmirching the Statue of Liberty as the ship sailed out of New York Harbor. Ritual purgation, of course, did nothing to stop discontent, so Palmer tried again on January 2, 1920. Putting the young J. Edgar Hoover in charge of the Justice Department's Anti-Radical Division, he mounted a nationwide dragnet that collected some 4,000 members of the two Communist parties. Those who escaped the roundup took Palmer's agents to be the American equivalent of the czar's secret police and went underground.[61]

The Palmer raids brought the panic to its peak, but the purge continued through the spring and summer of 1920. New York legislators expelled five duly elected members of the state assembly solely because they were socialists, and California prosecutors indicted Wobblies who had somehow escaped wartime arrest under "criminal syndicalism" statutes. From the Anti-Radical Division came a steady drone of warnings about bombings and general strikes supposedly slated for May 1, amplified by sensational headlines such as "Terror Reign by Radicals, Says Palmer," and "Nation-wide Uprising on Saturday!"[62] In the self-enclosed logic of the true believer, the failure of the predicted uprisings to materialize only proved that the crusade was victorious. To doubters it appeared that hysteria had triumphed over reason.

Irrational or not, reason of state lay behind one of the more intriguing aspects of the whole episode—War Plans White. Defending the Constitution against revolution was the professed aim of the Army War College's top-secret, color-coded, counterrevolutionary war plans. Their central assumptions were not those of the professional warrior or of the crazed superpatriot but of the armed progressive. After a scientific survey of American society and politics that drew heavily on the latest sociological scholarship on group behavior, Military Intelligence divided the population into friends and enemies of the Constitution. Friends included Protestant voluntary organizations, the National Security League, Rotarians, YMCA, and the like. The host of enemies included everyone from the Communist and Socialist parties through the Amalgamated Clothing Workers and the International Association of Machinists to the Women's International League for Peace and Freedom, the American Civil Liberties Union, and the NAACP.[63]

The list of enemies also included all ethnic groups from southern and eastern Europe, plus Jews and Afro-Americans. The Third Corps Plan summed up the last: "Their class consciousness, racial instincts, poverty, instinctive hostility to the white race and susceptibility to propaganda, makes [sic] this group a fruitful recruiting field for radical agitation, arousing the race to organization and union with the communistic cause under assured promise of that Utopian dream of social equality." Illiterate immigrant workers were of special concern to Military Intelligence, since they accounted for a disproportionate share of industrial discontent. The same worry led several states to establish their own iron-disciplined state police built on the military model whose purpose was to be "the State made visible" to the "unassimilated foreign element."[64]

By the time of the November 1920 election, the fires of the Red Scare were burning themselves out. With Wilson's policies paralyzed by events even though Wilson himself had recovered from his stroke, Democratic progressives had no clear champion. When A. Mitchell Palmer's presidential ambitions collapsed in the excesses of the Red Scare, and the seeming heir apparent, William McAdoo, Wilson's son-in-law, could not muster a majority of delegates, the Democrats chose lackluster Ohio governor John Cox. For their part, the Republicans at first lined up behind General Leonard Wood, the darling of the right-wing, which had come together in the prewar preparedness movement. Many members of the American Legion, the spy-struck American Protective League, and the vigilante Loyalty Leagues looked with favor on General Wood, as did many New Nationalists after their champion Teddy Roosevelt died in 1919. The emerging right—with its worship of the state, links to the military, and notions of male majesty and Nordic superiority—represented an authoritarian, if not, indeed, a nascent fascist response to the postwar discontent.[65]

However, such flirtations with militarism and glorifications of the state got the fledgling right in trouble with popular traditions of civilian supremacy and business aims for a free hand in running the economy. To be sure, corporate managers wanted a certain amount of government assistance; but they feared to build up a state bureaucracy that might become a power center rivaling their own. On that score, a man on horseback such as General Wood was a dangerous risk, while a dark horse such as Warren G. Harding was an amiable and harmless alternative. Having secured the nomination as everybody's acceptable second choice, Harding struck a responsive chord in campaign speeches when he said the country needed "not heroism, but healing, not nostrums but normalcy, not revolution but restoration . . . not submergence in internationality but sustainment in triumphant nationality." Such platitudes, which William McAdoo aptly described as "an army of pompous phrases moving over the landscape in search of an idea," proved soothing to the voters, who gave Harding the largest popular majority since before the Civil War.[66]

The Death of Revolutionary Liberalism

The election of a mild-mannered moderate and the waning of intense fear lent credence to the interpretation of the Red Scare as a passing spasm of political paranoia. To be sure, a great troupe of demons danced on this Walpurgis Night of political unreason—psychosexual fear, pollution taboo, class hatred, anti-Semitism, xenophobia, and racism. Undoubtedly, such demons always lurk just beneath the surface of even the most complaisant and otherwise hardworking, God-fearing community, bursting forth in witch hunts from Puritan Massachusetts to McCarthyite America. But the eruption of unreason did not spring from wholly irrational causes. Indeed, like the snake swallowing its tail, irrationality sprang from the grandest of all rationalisms, *raison d'état*. The most important consequence of anticommunism was to help legitimate the state. By the time the conflagration burned itself out, anticommunism had become the credo of millions at all points on the social scale, a consensual bond between Elbert Gary and Samuel Gompers, the Daughters of the American Revolution and the Sons of Italy, progressive Democrats such as A. Mitchell Palmer and conservative Republicans such as General Leonard Wood. To Americans adrift in an insecure world and divided internally by class and culture, communism was a convenient enemy against which they could unite in defense of God and country, private property, and the family. Although the hysteria of the Palmer raids and the *Buford* deportations soon passed, the legacy of this episode of enforced consent was to transform the antiradical strain in American politics into a cornerstone of twentieth-century hegemony. As such, it was a solid bulwark against any further reform that might displace woman from the center of the moral universe as wife and mother or disturb the inner sanctums of corporate power.

Was there an alternative? Was there something the Frankfurters, Catts, and Deweys might have done to guard the free flow of ideas and keep the dynamic of social reform from going under? A handful of the most advanced reformers embraced the Bolshevik Revolution along the lines of Lincoln Steffens' famous remark after returning from the Soviet Union: "I have been over into the future, and it works." Whether the future actually worked in Russia or not, those who believed that the dictatorship of the proletariat could not work in America tried to develop a progressive alternative to both communism and anticommunism. Reformers such as Raymond Robins and E. A. Ross believed that the Bolsheviks had won power because they spoke to the genuine yearnings of the masses for social revolution, not because of German intrigues or Allied betrayals, and that American progressives should pick up the gauntlet thrown down by Lenin and his comrades. Walter Weyl, a onetime Bull Mooser, spoke for this group of left liberals in saying that the West did not need or want a dictatorship, proletarian or otherwise, but it did need to institute "economic democracy." The reason was that political democracy alone was "a democracy with as many holes in it as a Swiss cheese, but in which the holes are the essence of the cheese." Such arguments were the forerunner of the social-democratic answer to communism, the idea that only by humanizing capitalist society was it possible to compete ideologically with communism in the world arena. That this was a real historical option, not a mere pipe dream, was vouchsafed by the experience of an open boundary between socialism and progressivism before the First World War and, later, by U.S. recognition of the Soviet Union and by New Deal reforms in the 1930s.[67]

In the present circumstances, however, liberals who wanted also to be revolutionaries faced a seemingly impossible predicament. Since Russia was the only place in the developed world where revolutionaries held power, revolution itself was closely identified with bolshevism. Since the Communist Third International branded all manner of radicals, reformers, anarchists, and socialists as "objective" counterrevolutionaries, left liberals stood little chance of obtaining revolutionary credentials. Thus, as Wilson found out, it was impossible to be a mere liberal in a revolutionary world.

It was equally impossible to be a revolutionary within the framework of American liberalism. For all the upheaval in American society, politics remained a war of position in which the basic structures of the liberal state suffered no breakdown. Basking in victory and safe behind the great moat of the Atlantic Ocean, American elites were spared the fate of Continental ruling classes who watched as brittle structures came crashing down in the German Reich, czarist Russia, the Hapsburg realm, and the Ottoman Empire. Despite Wilson's crusading zeal, American elites were losing confidence in liberalism as a revolutionary cause—that was precisely the implication of the "scare" in the Red Scare. Instead, they did their best to halt progress toward social reform at home. Once the ideological White Terror of 1919–20 had tarred even mild reforms with the brush of bolshevism, it was impossible to revive the prewar reform drive. In short, the Red Scare delivered the coup de grâce to progressive "reconstruction."

The Red Scare also held an important implication for foreign policy. American elites seemed to lose their nerve about fomenting liberal and national revolutions, for fear that they could not control the outcome. Soon stabilizing the capitalist economy became the order of the day, and American foreign relations fell increasingly under the sway of corporate diplomacy. That was true not only in Europe, but also when the United States was confronted with revolution in Latin America. Instead of siding with revolutionaries such as Nicaragua's Augusto César Sandino and El Salvador's Farebundo Martí, it supported landed oligarchs and military elites, because the alternative was thought to be communism.

Thus the dilemma: American liberals could not be world revolutionaries; revolutionaries and even reformers could not find space inside American liberalism. Liberalism and revolution became contradictions, liberals and revolutionaries, enemies. The agony of the American left impaled on the horns of this dilemma was evident everywhere in the paralysis of progressivism, the enmity beween socialists and progressives, the compulsory underground status of the Communist party, and the absence of new initiatives in social legislation. Undoubtedly, the ultimate causes of the dilemma lay beyond the control of American progressives. Yet they were not without a share of responsibility. Having chosen to support Prohibition, sexual repression, troops, and injunctions, they set themselves against the forces of movement and held back the very changes that would have given them room to maneuver against the old-fashioned liberals. In short, they helped create the dilemma upon which they themselves were impaled. Their unhappy experience was a standing challenge to twentieth-century reformers, leftists, and liberals alike to find a way out of this predicament by promoting social revolution within a liberal framework—or, to turn it around, by promoting liberalism within the framework of social revolution.

7

§

Restoration by Repression

FROM THE VERY moment of the birth of the nation, Americans had been asking themselves: "Who are we?" With every new influx of immigrants, every westward advance, every generational revolt against the ways of the parents, the question was posed anew. And always there was a reassuring answer: Americans were citizens by choice. Ever since the American Revolution had put into practice what was only imagined in Enlightenment philosophy, citizenship had become a matter of rational choice. Unlike European regimes, steeped in privilege, the United States held open the door to all comers, respected equality before the law, and allowed common men of uncommon ability access to power. Indeed, by the late nineteenth century the image of America as an open society was a fundamental part of national identity. What was the United States, if not an immigrant asylum, a moving frontier, a land of opportunity? What could be more appropriate as a symbol of the republic than the Statue of Liberty, welcoming all who would freely choose America as their homeland?

At the same time, just beneath the surface of this sunny self-image, there was a darker side to American identity. Instead of an open republic, the United States was seen to be a closed country of chosen people. The Puritans had posed as God's elect, and Virginia planters reigned on the assumption that Indians and Africans were unfit to govern themselves. Even as the democratic ethos took shape in Andrew Jackson's Age of the Common Man, even as citizenship was extended to slaves after Abraham Lincoln's Emancipation Proclamation, and even as European immigrants poured in to do the hard work of the Industrial Revolution, full citizenship was granted only to white Anglo-Saxon Protestants. Racial segregation, Asian exclusion, and Social Darwinism all showed the persistent tyranny of race.

On the surface it would seem that the rational republic and the racial republic were as different as light and darkness. Certainly, the idea that superior races were destined to rule inferior ones was the exact antithesis of Enlightenment rationalism, with its concept of universal citizenship. But at a deeper level, race was a logical, if perverse, resolution of the contradiction between formal equality and the reality of social hierarchy. The doctrine that all men are created equal could apply only at the very beginning of the "race of life," when all might reasonably be seen to start at the same place; it could not account for the fact that some groups always wound up ahead of others at the finish line. Race was too convenient an explanation to have been ignored.[1]

It was no accident that race consciousness returned once again in the early twentieth century, as the gap between vast accumulations of corporate wealth and squalid immigrant slums called forth renewed efforts to perpetuate that difference and give it some sanction. The fact that great changes in gender relations were taking place along with massive infusions of new immigrants heightened consciousness around issues of racial and sexual "purity." Thus it was not at all surprising to find a motley collection of "old-stock" Americans in the early 1920s invoking racist and nativist definitions of Americanism in the face of threats to their privileged position.

One Hundred Percent Americanism

The problem of finding a unifying myth of American identity was complicated by the real diversity of the American people. According to tabulations prepared under the 1924 Immigration Act, no single ancestral group could claim a majority. Perhaps 42 percent could trace their heritage to Britain, but other lines were also strong—Germans accounted for some 14.5 percent, and the Irish for 10 percent. When these three groups were combined with Scandinavians and other northwestern Europeans, the peoples of the Atlantic predominated. But Italians, Greeks, and other peoples of the Mediterranean were also significant, as were those of eastern Europe—Slavs and Jews from Poland and Russia—so that altogether southern and eastern Europeans contributed some 12.6 percent. African-Americans, the most visible refutation of the notion of the melting pot, were just under 10 percent.[2]

The swirling tides of international and internal migration kept the ethnic mix constantly in flux. In 1920 large-scale immigration resumed after a brief reverse flow, when the number of emigrants had approached the number of immigrants for the first time on record.[3] Now, as more and more newcomers from southern and eastern Europe poured into the burgeoning industrial cities of the North, they ran into another current of internal migration flowing from the farms and small towns of rural America. Beginning in tiny rivulets in the "hollars" of Appalachia, the Mississippi Delta, the flatlands of the middle Border states, and the gentle valleys of Wisconsin, myriad tributaries joined to form the swelling stream flowing to St. Louis, Detroit, and Milwaukee. These same two currents—European immigrants and rural-urban migrants—had collided across a century of conflict, and once again southern drawls and midwestern twangs clashed with Italian, Yiddish, and other foreign languages over Sunday "blue laws" and political patronage. All the folkways that governed the pivotal events in the life cycle—birth, marriage, death—were at issue. When was it proper to baptise a child? If a dutiful Catholic daughter brought home a Protestant boy, was an Italian father supposed to give his consent?

If every ethnic group had been distributed evenly up and down the social scale, it is likely that the most intense ethnic hatreds would have run off into the sands of cultural pluralism. As it was, because ethnic groups occupied different niches in a hierarchical social order, cultural differences were magnified by class antagonisms. In the upper reaches of wealth and prestige, the overwhelming majority of the business and governmental elite came from British backgrounds: people of British ancestry accounted for a disproportionate three-quarters of the top businessmen in the early part of the century.[4] The line of presidents from British backgrounds (English, Scottish, Welsh, or Scots-Irish) was unbroken, and hybrids such as Theodore Roosevelt (English and Dutch) were usually thoroughgoing Anglophiles. The ranks of the Ivy League and prestigious metropolitan social clubs were liberally sprinkled with Germans, Dutch, and Scandinavians, but there were precious few Poles or Italians, and Jews were stopped at the door by a rigidly exclusive quota.

At the opposite end of the scale, immigrant workers had long occupied a disproportionate share of the lower rungs of industrial jobs. In fact, there were few blue-collar occupations in the North in which first- and second-generation immigrants made up less than two-thirds of the total: together the foreign born and their children accounted for 76 percent of the operatives in Pennsylvania coal mines and virtually the entire work force in Massachusetts textile mills—92 percent of the men and 93 percent of the women.[5] Ethnic enclaves were commonly located close to commercial and manufacturing districts, whether they were Jewish garment workers in New York's Lower East Side, Lithuanian packinghouse workers "back of the yards" in Chicago, or Italian laborers on "the Hill" in St. Louis.

What kept cultural and class tensions in check was the overriding force of nationalism. Three myths of national unity—three versions of Americanism—vied to determine the meaning of the motto "E pluribus unum." From the turn of the century until the early 1920s, the myth of America as a republican melting pot had prevailed. In the mood of optimism before the First World War, the United States was seen to be an asylum for the "huddled masses yearning to breathe free," according to Emma Lazarus' poem inscribed on the Statue of Liberty. Most progressives had supported Americanization in the belief that republican institutions—open competition, equality before the law, self-government—would take care of assimilating the newcomers. Examples of optimism could still be found after the war in the settlement houses and the Carnegie Endowment's sympathetic studies of immigrant life. The only test of loyalty was a willingness to undergo naturalization and to pledge allegiance to the flag "and to the republic for which it stands, one nation, indivisible, with liberty and justice for all."[6]

To the progressives, the republican melting pot applied to female citizens, as well. The leading women's reform organizations identified the cause of women with the Enlightenment spirit of rational citizenship. Nearly all included "national" in their names and stressed equal rights under the Constitution. The National League of Women Voters captured the spirit in the title of their journal, the *Woman Citizen*. When Margaret Drier Robins, head of the National Women's Trade Union League, cast her first presidential ballot in Illinois, she predicted that the day would come when "we will have fitting halls of citizenship symbolic of our dream and adventure of Democracy," a day that came closer when the Nineteenth Amendment was adopted in 1920.[7] The National Women's party reduced equal citizenship to the formula embodied in the Equal Rights Amendment, first introduced in Congress on December 10, 1923: "Men and women shall have equal rights throughout the United States and every place subject to its jurisdiction." Since the ERA seemed to threaten the legal status of women's protective legislation, it caused a rift in the ranks of women reformers.

Nevertheless, everyone accepted the idea of women as full and equal citizens.[8]

A second myth of national identity held America to be a "nation of nations." Voices representing the ethnic working class took up the idea in rebuttal to the concept of the melting pot. One editor of an immigrant newspaper argued that America was "a gathering of peoples in the family of one nation," a formula repeated in Horace Kallen's classic statement of cultural pluralism *Culture and Democracy in the United States* (1924). Kallen presented a rich vision of democracy whose essence and vitality derived from cultural diversity. He had a kindred spirit in John Dewey, who argued that the American was both international and interracial: "He is not American plus Pole or German. But the American is himself Pole-German-English-French-Spanish-Italian-Greek-Irish-Scandinavian-Bohemian-Jew-and so on. The point is to see to it that the hyphen connects instead of separates."[9]

Some of the greatest support for this pluralist idea came from the labor movement. Although workers may not have been any less prejudiced than other segments of society, the labor movement of necessity had to hold up the values of cultural toleration in order to unite the polyglot rank and file. Indeed, it was the connection among Irish, Italian, Polish, Jewish, and other "hyphenates" that permitted wage earners to mount mass strikes in industry after industry. Unions such as the United Mine Workers published their literature in Italian and Polish, and foreign-language speakers (many of them socialists or anarchists) were often brought in during organizing drives. In a few cases—very few—they even rejected outright the prevailing view that democracy was for whites only.[10] Insofar as the "nation of nations" myth was attached to the cause of wage labor, it might have transcended the built-in contradiction between equality of opportunity and social hierarchy by pushing America toward equality of condition. But it did not get the chance. Just as collaboration across ethnic boundaries was the precondition for working people to discover their own solidarity, so the reverse was also true; that is, the fate of pluralist democracy was bound up with the popular social movements from which it sprang. It thrived when the labor movement mobilized the lower ranks in industry, and it withered when immigrant wage earners suffered defeat. With the repulsion of the labor upsurge of 1919–1922, the idea of America as a nation of nations was driven underground for a decade.

That cleared the way for the third alternative—100 percent Americanism. To Yankee Protestants of high and middling rank, pluralist democracy was exactly the "balkanization" they feared. Losing confidence in the capacity of republican institutions to transform the newcomers into true Americans, they saw raging industrial discontent as irrefutable proof of the inability of immigrants to assimilate. At the height of the Red Scare, the Lusk Committee, for example, devoted half of its four-volume report, *Revolutionary Radicalism*, to Americanization, drawing special attention to the failure of the public schools to inculcate a sufficiently patriotic spirit and calling for teacher loyalty oaths and training in Americanism. Likewise, the federal government shifted the main burden of Americanization from the more positive Bureau of Education to the narrow-minded Bureau of Naturalization. Coercive Americanization became the order of the day, and just as many states outlawed "criminal syndicalism" and created state police to discipline immigrant workers, so a number of states enacted coercive prohibitions against the teaching and, in a few cases, even the speaking of foreign languages.[11]

The roots of 100 percent Americanism ran deep. Already by the turn of the century, Yankee Protestants in New England had launched a nativist campaign behind the Immigration Restriction League; anti-Catholic, antiradical nativism had made gains in Congress behind Massachusetts' Senator Henry Cabot Lodge and Vermont's Senator William Dillingham; and the same values had found an outlet in the preparedness movement of 1915 and 1916. Had it not been for the momentum of prewar confidence, it is likely that the 100 percenters would have triumphed over the more tolerant, progressive version of Americanism during the war. But now their turn finally came. As the wartime wave of national pride crashed upon the breakers of the Versailles Treaty and the Bolshevik Revolution, Yankee Protestants were gripped by status panic. It was the same loss of confidence at home and abroad that engendered the Red Scare, and the same compulsion to purify the nation that motivated deportations of alien radicals now appeared in the effort to purge the nation of "alien" cultures. American Legion vigilantes attacked "un-American" demonstrators; California legislators whipped up anti-Japanese hysteria; lynch mobs attacked foreigners.[12] If America could not remake the world in the image of "true Americanism," at least it might remake itself.

The myth of the true American fed on status panic wherever old-stock Americans were found in the social scale. At the top, regional elites from New York's old money to Georgia's planter-merchant oligar-chy wailed: "The man of the old stock is being crowded out of many country districts by these foreigners, just as he is to-day being literally driven off the streets of New York City by the swarms of Polish Jews." Family wealth and patrimony meant less in an era of corporate prop-erty; deference to the "better sort" meant little in an era of immigrant political machines; genteel culture had already lost the respect of younger artists and writers such as Theodore Dreiser and Ernest Hem-ingway. No wonder eastern bluestockings from the brahmins of Boston to the faded gentry of Charleston felt a combination of class and ethnic anxieties and lamented the decline of the patricians: "In America we have nearly succeeded in destroying the privilege of birth . . . we are now engaged in destroying the privilege of wealth." [13]

Among middle ranks, newspaper editors in the Border states and real estate agents in the Midwest felt threatened by the great move-ments of immigrant workers. In response, they lionized self-made men such as Henry Ford, flocked to the Rotary and the Women's Club, and subscribed to middle-brow literature such as the *Saturday Evening Post*, in which they read homilies to their own kind: "Not yet has enough stress been laid upon the importance of the story of the middle class. Wherever this class has grown in numbers and enlightenment, the course of history has been upward." They were the stuff out of which Sinclair Lewis fashioned *Babbitt* (1922), his scathing satire of middle-class mediocrity. [14]

The layers between the middle and lower ranks also contributed their share. The nondescript men and women who were not quite suc-cessful, economically insecure, and lacking in social graces envied those above them only slightly less than they feared those below. If they could not get into the Chamber of Commerce or the prestigious Wom-en's Club, at least they might join the American Legion, the Loyal Or-der of Moose, or the women's circle at the Methodist church and thereby turn away the hot breath of competition from upwardly mo-bile second-generation immigrants, especially the Jews, against whom anti-Semitism barred the door.

Seeking escape from impotence, the same little man who became a mock potentate in the red silks of the Shriner could easily slip into the white sheets of the Ku Klux Klan. Unlike the infamous night riders of the Reconstruction, the Klan of the 1920s was as popular in the North as in the South, directed intolerance as much against Catholics and

Jews as against Afro-Americans, and was as strong among urban small businessmen and skilled workers as among farmers.[15] Reborn in 1915 after the lynching of Leo Frank, the Klan was taken over by high-powered salesmen who transformed the group from the original vigilante defender of southern womanhood to a quasi-fraternal organization of Imperial Wizards and Grand Dragons with a national membership in the millions devoted to "native, white, Protestant supremacy." The Klan was white man's democracy incarnate. According to its chief proselytizer, Hiram Evans, "liberalism" had committed treason against the "plain people" for failing to suppress the influence of Catholics, Jews, foreigners, and Negroes. But once these groups were safely excluded from the charmed circle of democracy, the Klan supposedly stood for traditional liberal virtues, including "equal opportunity, religious liberty, independence, self-reliance."[16]

The country was taking a lesson from the South—race and religion worked well in uniting people across class lines. The Klan was a low-brow expression of principles shared by such highbrow patriotic societies as the National Security League, the American Defense Society, and the Daughters of the American Revolution. Even Madison Grant, who liked to think of himself as some kind of Nordic archduke, could reach down the class ladder to say, perhaps in jest: "The great hope of the future here in America lies in the realization of the working classes that competition of the Nordic with the alien is fatal, whether the latter be the lowly immigrant from Southern or Eastern Europe, or the more obviously dangerous Oriental, against whose standards the white man cannot compete."[17]

No would-be ruling myth is complete without some word on the family. Where gender was concerned, the 100 percent philosophy clung to the nineteenth-century doctrine of separate spheres, carried forward the wartime notion of patriotic motherhood, and accorded women's suffrage only the most grudging acceptance. The Sentinels of the Republic, for example, had fought hard against the Nineteenth Amendment, and now refined their message in their journal, aptly titled the *Woman Patriot*, to say that woman served the nation better as self-sacrificing wife and mother than as active citizen in the rough-and-tumble of politics. Clinging to the double standard like a drowning man to a life raft, Yankee Protestant patriots and social purists grew ever more out of touch in their idealization of woman, chaste and true, paired with the self-made man struggling against his own inner weakness. According to the president of the National Security League, "Manhood means ambition, self-denial, thrift. These ideals can spring only from the right of property—the right of individual possession of property as guaranteed by the Constitution. He who does not believe this cannot be an American."[18] Thus the superpatriots restored the old constellation of values built around the proprietary family—masculine headship, mother worship, the sanctity of private property, patriotic intolerance. They aimed at restoring the fast-disappearing world of family capitalism and laissez-faire liberalism. And they hoped to rebuild a pristine republic set atop the "inferior races" by means of native-born, white, Protestant supremacy.

Latter-day Victorians had their mirror opposite in the exotic forms of patriarchal family economy that grew up during Prohibition. By the unwritten law of unintended consequences, successful suppression of "commercialized vice" only resulted in the proliferation of *criminalized* vice. It did not take much more intelligence than that of a snub-nosed .38 for enterprising racketeers such as Chicago's Johnny Torrio to deduce that Prohibition was a golden opportunity for bootlegging, or that the closing of the red-light districts afforded a potential fortune in the form of illicit sex. One sharp-eyed journalist noted: "The unpleasant truth is that the racketeer has simply taken an American economic, political, and social ideal—*wealth*, and tried to achieve it in a minimum of time and according to his peculiar lights." And scholars have incorporated underworld gangs into the saga of immigrant success, showing how the drive for upward mobility was channeled into criminal activity "when the opportunities to success are barred or limited in a community in which economic success is the ultimate goal." In short, gangsters gave a perverse twist to the motto of the age, "The business of America is business."[19]

Insofar as underworld networks such as the mafia derived from immigrant adaptations to American life, they were mutations of Old World patriarchy. The gang boss or *don* played the patriarch in a family economy based on extreme sexual division between the masculine business world and the feminine home. The ancient code of family honor demanded loyalty from subordinates, and the sexual double standard, along with the split image of woman as either madonna or whore, permitted gangsters to pose as good husbands even as they pimped for prostitutes. The legendary Al Capone's first big break depended on family ties to his godfather, Johnny Torrio, who inducted him into Chicago's rackets and acted as his patron until Capone took over himself.[20] Thus did Catholic patriarchal traditions (and, to a lesser extent, Jewish ones) enter into a bizarre unity of opposites with traditional Protestant family values. If ever history played a cruel joke on the Yankee Protestant establishment, it was the Prohibition-era gangster.

Superpatriots of the 1920s, like the Know-Nothings of the 1850s and the McCarthyites of the 1950s, sought to protect a privileged position that was being eroded by social change. They appear reactionary because they sought to hold back the tides of history that had given rise to the industrial working class, corporate enterprise, the New Woman, and the "new" immigration, not to mention the greatly expanded regulatory machinery of the progressive and wartime state. That was why the attempt to restore Yankee Protestant privileges drew energy from the dark side of the American myth to become a nasty nest of "antis"—antiunionism, anti-immigration, antifeminism, anti–New Negro, and anticommunism. One of its most acute critics, Horace Kallen, railed against this reincarnation of Know-Nothingism: "The witch hunting of the Quaker Attorney General Palmer, the czaristically inspired Jew-baiting of the Baptist automobile maker, Ford, the malevolent mass mummery of the Ku Klux Klan, the racial mumblings of Mr. Madison Grant, Mrs. Gertrude Atherton, the *Saturday Evening Post*, are all, ultimately manifestations of this Know-Nothingism."[21] But in the climate of the early 1920s, such impassioned pluralist protests against bigotry were to no avail. Imbued with class hatreds and ethnic prejudice, 100 percent Americanism seemed for a time as if it might become one of the ruling myths of the twentieth century.

The Biological Republic

The case for 100 percent Americanism came to rest more and more on biology. The proponents of race consciousness argued that race and sex, not reason and culture, were the keys to civilization. They used the term *race* for broad divisions of the human family—African, Caucasian, Mongoloid—but more often for what later came to be called ethnic groups. Since heredity supposedly outweighed environment, they believed that only certain races (ethnic groups), notably Scandinavians, Teutons, and Anglo-Saxons, were capable of self-government. Having decided that biology was the basis of civilization, they were forced to link race and sex. Taking their cue from animal stockbreeding, they argued that the purity of the line depended on the purity of female reproducers, whose sexual behavior therefore had to be carefully controlled. If biology was destiny for the race, it was also destiny for women. Thus even when 100 percenters accepted the values of liberty and equality—and that was not always the case—they reserved the exercise of full citizenship to the biologically elect.

Not that the defenders of race over reason had an easy time agreeing on who was supreme. Madison Grant, scion of a wealthy New York family, touted the notion of Nordic supremacy in his widely read jeremiad *The Passing of the Great Race* (1916). Borrowing from the same ideas of Houston Stewart Chamberlain that were soon to inspire Nazi ideology, Grant wrote of ancient Aryans and modern Nordics as the creators of high civilization, and he displayed open contempt for Rousseau, the Enlightenment, and the French Revolution. However, his Nordic notions and aristocratic proclivities rubbed many Anglo-Saxons the wrong way. The partisans of Magna Charta and Agincourt found a wide audience in the pages of leading journals of opinion such as the *Atlantic Monthly* and in the genteel literature of Gertrude Atherton, and they had many followers in the inner sanctums of the federal government. For example, the army's top-secret, counterrevolutionary contingency plans were aimed at suppressing the polyglot working population and betrayed the defensive mentality of the besieged Anglo-American.[22]

Whether Nordic or Anglo-Saxon, racialists feasted on the theory that "mongrelization" had always been the downfall of civilization. Lothrop Stoddard, a disciple of Grant, put the case for a new blood-aristocracy in terms of "the Iron Law of inequality" in a book whose Nietzschean title captured much of what the movement had to say: *The Revolt against Civilization: The Menace of the Under Man* (1922). Others argued a theory of cultural "reversion" akin to the "Negro regression" theory propounded by southern white supremacists under which "lower races" represented a primitive form of human existence. By some implacable Gresham's law, bad blood supposedly always drove out good, and so half-castes were said to embody a "reversion to a primitive and savage condition," and racial mixing inevitably dragged down the standard of civilization. As the author of the popular text *America: A Family Matter* (1922) put it, "The result of the marriage of an educated and refined white man with a beautiful South Italian peasant girl would probably be to put the children back in the stage of intellectual development many hundreds of years."[23]

Eugenics made a vital contribution to the case for biological determinism. At every opportunity, eugenicists held up the results of army
intelligence tests administered to First World War recruits, which they
said demonstrated the shockingly low mental ability, or IQ, of the
American population at large. They claimed that this was the result of
the debasing influence of mentally deficient ethnic groups, because
large numbers of Slavs, Italians, and Negroes fell into the lowest
"grades," while the majority of Anglo-Americans wound up in the
highest. (Outraged by the the inhumanity of the ranking system, Al-
dous Huxley made it the subject of savage satire in *Brave New World*.)
Turning a blind eye to the gross cultural biases built into the test instrument, eugenicists trumpeted the results as vindication of the theory
that the cultural level of the United States was being debased by the
"new" immigrants.[24]

Eugenics also blamed "lesser breeds without the law" for all manner
of vice. Whereas progressive reformers had once emphasized the envi-
ronmental causes of social evils, antireformers now trotted out biology
to explain crime, poverty, urban squalor, disease, and sexual transgression. The rector of New York's Grace Episcopal Church accepted a
portion of the argument of the prewar vice commissions in noting "the
unmistakable and disgusting alliance . . . between the saloons and the
liquor trade behind them, on the one hand, and commercialized vice,
the seduction of women and girls, and the wide network of police corruption and sordid politics on the other." But his explanation of why
Prohibition was not working came to rest on race; he quoted a 1927
study prepared by the National Federation of Settlements:

> Wherever there is a Nordic-American population which for several
> generations has not been in close contact with the newer immigra-
> tions or the cosmopolitanism of the great cities, there prohibition
> works. This is true in general in the South and in Maine and in parts
> of the Mississippi Valley. Wherever there are large unassimilated for-
> eign populations accustomed to the making and use of alcoholic
> drinks and also an eager market for their product, as in the great ports
> and the industrial cities, there the law is halting and . . . difficult to
> apply.[25]

Undoubtedly, it was true that the scorching sun of the Eighteenth
Amendment had failed to dry up the lakes of alcohol on which Irish,
Polish, and Italian recreation floated so merrily. But the teetotaling

prejudice of the "drys" was hardly convincing proof of the biological inferiority of the "wets."

Once the notion was accepted that true Americanism issued not from the head but from the loins, logic dictated expanded controls on sexuality. For the "better class" of workers who aspired to middle-class status, eugenicists proposed birth control education. But for the "dysgenic classes," they had no compunctions about compulsory sterilization. Indeed, in response to fears of biological contamination, a number of states began to permit courts and medical authorities to sterilize various categories deemed mentally defective—criminals, idiots, the feebleminded, and rapists; by 1931 twenty-seven states had some form of mandatory sterilization. It may be that sterilization was the extreme case of state control of reproduction, but by the 1930s forty-one states prohibited marriage among the same groups. The question of how to define the biologically "unfit" did not seriously trouble the Supreme Court, either; writing for the majority in 1927, no less an authority than Oliver Wendell Holmes, Jr., upheld sterilization on the dangerous doctrine that "it is better for all the world, if instead of waiting to execute degenerate offspring for crime, or let them starve for their imbecility, society can prevent those who are manifestly unfit from breeding their kind." Embracing the notion that crime was congenital, he added: "Three generations of imbeciles are enough." [26]

The key to race purity was feminine virtue. When it failed, "mongrelization" was sure to follow. Speaking to a congressional committee on behalf of the Eugenics Record Office, H. H. Laughlin warned in 1920 that "whenever two races come in contact, it is found that the women of the lower race are not, as a rule, adverse to intercourse with men of the higher." [27] Whether lewd women degraded the lower races, or the other way round, the view of low-caste women as slatterns was commonly associated with campaigns for social hygiene. Indeed, the very idea of female eroticism was seen as a degradation of true womanhood. Leading professors of gynecology found the notion of women's delight in sex to be "pornographic," and leading ministers lambasted "the superficial philosophy of our time that translates liberty into license." The pastor of New York's Calvary Baptist Church warned that if sex was allowed to escape the sacred bonds of matrimony, then barbarians would be at the gate threatening the ruin of American civilization: "No stream can rise higher than its source and no race can be greater than its womanhood. The greatest danger to our country is the breaking down of the sanctity of the marriage vow, the consequent increase of the divorce evil and sex relationships that result in disease. It is a fundamental truth of history that every great civilization of the past has decayed first and fastest precisely at this point." [28]

To preserve feminine virtue, Methodist ministers and the Women's Christian Temperance Union joined the literary guardians of the genteel tradition and the Society for the Suppression of Vice to attack the "new morality." They succeeded in banning distribution of everything from abstruse novels such as James Joyce's *Ulysses* to sober sex education manuals such as Mary Dennett's *The Sex Side of Life*. (All that did not prevent far more salacious silent movies from escaping the censor's eye until the late 1920s.) Dennett's pamphlet showed the influence of the sexual radicals in setting erotic experience in the context of love rather than marriage, refusing to condemn masturbation, and describing heterosexual intercourse as "the very greatest physical pleasure to be had in all human experience," for women as well as for men. For such turpitude, the pamphlet was banned and the author jailed. [29]

Biological determinism was inimical to democracy. Even while speaking in the idiom of republicanism, Henry Fairfield Osborn, H. H. Laughlin, and other leaders of the eugenics movement preached an elitist gospel. In a distant echo of the Puritan self-image as God's chosen people, Osborn held up Anglo-Saxon New Englanders as the true foundation of self-government and warned the Second International Congress of Eugenics in 1921 of the political consequences of race suicide: "The purest New England stock is not holding its own. The next stage is the no-child marriage and the extinction of the stock which laid the foundations of the republican institutions of this country." [30] Once it was accepted that the instinct of liberty was inborn, no amount of education could rescue the benighted races allegedly incapable of self-government. Within the twisted framework of this logic, the only way to preserve liberty was to purge the body politic of what Lothrop Stoddard called the "under-man." As the well-respected mouthpiece of establishment opinion, the *Atlantic Monthly*, put it: "Indeed, we may have to admit that the lower-grade man is material unusable in a democracy, and to eliminate him from the electorate, as we have the criminal, the insane, the idiot, and the alien." Distinguished midwestern universities heard another eugenics expert praise the "inborn" spirit of freedom in the United States: "Such a democracy can, in the last analysis, spring only from good blood." [31]

The idea that nature had endowed some Americans with good blood and others with bad was a recurring theme in American culture. It appeared first among the Puritans, God's chosen people for subduing the heathen; it justified the pioneers' genocide of Native Americans; it explained white supremacy over African-Americans; it appeared in the Social Darwinist notion of the triumph of the "fittest" races over the "unfit." The spread of Nordic and Anglo-Saxon race consciousness was but another chapter in the history of bigotry written in "blood."

The idea of biology as the basis of human destiny had its enemies. H. G. Wells's *Outline of History,* which made the best-seller lists in 1921, gave full credit to non-European civilizations; and Charles and Mary Beard, in the most popular history text every published, cast *The Rise of American Civilization* (1927) in terms of a succession of titanic struggles between great economic interests, not racial groups. In addition, American Marxists studied the philosophy of historical materialism (not to be confused with economic determinism) and learned from Marx that "men make their own history, but they do not make it just as they please . . . but under circumstances directly encountered, given and transmitted from the past."[32] Such views may have been elbowed aside for the time being, along with scientific rationalism, Whitmanesque democracy, and cultural pluralism, but they were never eclipsed.

Even within the racial definition of Americanism there was little internal cohesion. How could there be, when a hodgepodge of Anglo-Saxons, Britons, Teutons, and Nordics all claimed the highest "cephalic index" and the bluest blood? There was also an implicit contradiction between racial nationalism, which implied transnational loyalties, and the machinery of the nation-state. Given time, a more cohesive myth of the superrace might have developed along the lines of Aryans versus Slavs and Jews, as in Germany, although the wide ethnic assortment in the United States makes that outcome seem unlikely. In any event, it is chastening to recognize that the United States escaped some of the worst consequences of the Aryan myth because of the overriding influence of white racism. Whatever cultural gap divided northern and southern Europeans, all Euro-Americans could see themselves drawn as one race as against the "darker races."

Race Purity, North and South

White supremacy was the ultimate expression of biological Americanism. Whatever internal divisions there were among whites, they were secondary to the gulf between Caucasians, on one side, and Africans and Asiatics, on the other. As W. E. B. DuBois had written years earlier, "The problem of the twentieth century is the problem of the color line." Of course, from the dominant perspective it was the other way around—not the restrictive ceiling on opportunity but, in the title of one prophecy of doom, *The Rising Tide of Color.* Either way, race was a powerful cultural construct. The mentalities of race consciousness and racism had long since become a material force. They had entered into the structure of society and played a role in determining where and how people lived and worked, and how they handed down their way of life from one generation to the next. Race shaped both production and social reproduction. Again, DuBois put his finger on the main point: "To be a poor man is hard, but to be a poor race in the land of dollars is the very bottom of hardship." [33]

Given the pervasive legacy of African slavery in the South, that region had long been the most important source of race consciousness. In the twentieth century the South continued to be the most significant counterweight to the ideas of both pluralist democracy and melting pot assimilation. Although the Democratic party's defeat in 1920 had cut off southern access to the White House, southern elites, often with other white southerners in tow, had pushed to the front of the nation's march toward Prohibition, immigration restriction, laissez faire, and the open shop. In addition, the South's obsession with race and sex was very much in step with the national trend toward race consciousness. Although the psychic pathologies of race hate and vigilantism bore the outward marks of backward-looking resistance to modernization, the fact remained that the whites busy constructing the New South, whether textile owners or urban shopkeepers, were no less likely than the old planters to carry the banners of racial purity. Indeed, racial segregation was deeply embedded in the emerging urban-industrial social order. To be sure, more than any other region the South felt the dead hand of the past, but in adapting its traditional myths to a new era it was also helping to construct the scaffolding of American society as a whole. [34]

A clear case in point was industrial relations. After the First World War a small flurry of industrial disputes took place in southern mines and mills. For instance, serious strikes occurred in Carolina textile mills in the context of organizing by the United Textile Workers, which chartered some forty new southern locals and raised membership in North Carolina to more than 40,000. But despite these efforts, trade unions made no long-term headway against the implacable opposition of southern employers and their allies. In a fit of rhetorical froth, a Georgian inveighed against "that unholy, foreign-born, un-American, socialistic, despotic *thing* known as *labor unionism.*" Tarring unions with all these alleged evils was a means of winning over small farmers, shop-keepers, and even wage earners to the bosses' side, and the rapidly expanding Ku Klux Klan provided an important staging ground for this interclass alliance. Unlike its Reconstruction counterpart, the revived Klan was stronger in the cities than in black-belt counties ruled by the planters' courthouse gang. In between defending the purity of southern womanhood and celebrating the death of "King Barleycorn" in a massive temperance parade through Atlanta, the Klan fought labor organizers in Mobile shipyards and Birmingham steelworks.[35]

The cardinal principle in southern industry was the open shop, and southern manufacturers placed one of their own, Tennessean John Edgerton, at the helm of the National Association of Manufacturers from 1921 to 1931, during the height of the national open-shop campaign. As a result, the *Manufacturers' Record* could boast in 1924 with little exaggeration: "The 'solid South' means security for every manufacturer trembling under the whiplash of the anarchistic labor leaders."[36]

Similarly, conventional ruling norms of family life came on strong after the war through Protestant fundamentalism. It was true that religious fundamentalism was by no means confined to the South. As a broad countercurrent to biblical "higher criticism" and Darwinian evolution, it gained national influence with the distribution of 3 million copies of the 1910 pamphlet series *The Fundamentals,* compelling denominations such as the Northern Presbyterian General Assembly to reaffirm the fundamental "Five Points" of doctrinal orthodoxy—biblical infallibity, the virgin birth, atonement, the Resurrection, and the Second Coming.[37] However, only in the South did this doctrine become an integral part of the regional governing system. Smarting under the ridicule of H. L. Mencken and other northern critics, southern legislators defended the Bible's infallibility as a matter of regional pride: "Go back to the fathers and mothers of Mississippi and tell them that because you could not face the scorn and abuse of Bolsheviks and Anarchists and Atheists and agnostics and their co-workers, you turned their children over to a teaching that God's Word is a tissue of lies." This tender sentiment toward the younger generation revealed the obsession of fundamentalists with issues of social reproduction. For example, they saw the virgin birth as a parable of family honor and Christian identity: "The Modernist juggles the Scripture statements of His deity and denies His virgin birth, making Him a Jewish bastard, born out of wedlock, and stained forever with the shame of His mother's immorality."[38] To such minds, the doctrine of immaculate conception did double duty, first, as an anti-Semitic rebuttal to the fact of Jesus' Jewish ancestry, and second, as a restatement of feminine chastity.

Fundamentalists entered politics primarily for the purpose of controlling public education. In 1923 Oklahoma became the first state to proscribe the teaching of evolution and other "atheistic" doctrines. Florida followed close on its heels with a similar law drafted by William Jennings Bryan, and eventually North Carolina, Texas, Tennessee, Mississippi, Louisiana, and Arkansas passed laws or regulations on the teaching of evolution. Although disfranchisement had severely limited the number of eligible voters in these states, clearly, fundamentalism was popular with those who remained on the rolls.[39] Why was it so important to defend a literal interpretation of Genesis against Darwinian biology? Since many theologians and laymen in the North were abandoning this doctrine, why did it hang on in the South?

The answer may very well lie in the South's obsession with race purity. In the first place, as a political phenomenon religious fundamentalism was lily-white. To be sure, Protestants of both races shared key points of doctrine, including a belief in divine creation, but virgin birth and Darwin were simply not big issues in the black churches. To white Protestants, on the other hand, the idea that man "descended from apes" seemed an intolerable pollution of bloodlines. The concept of evolution was in itself unclean, because it corrupted the otherwise pure minds of young innocents and made them unfit to reproduce their racial and familial lineages. It was literally a piece of filth. Thus it was necessary to prevent the teaching of evolution "to save our dear school children from the mental and moral defilement of this 'Mud Philosophy.'" Governor Miriam "Ma" Ferguson of Texas supported a ban on the grounds that "I am a Christian mother, and I will not tolerate this rot in the schools." Bryan's Florida statute pronounced it unlawful to teach anything "that links man in blood relationship to any other form of life." The governor of North Carolina personally undertook to censor biology texts because "I don't want my daughter or anybody's daughter to have to study a book that prints pictures of a monkey and a man on the same page."[40]

As the country at large wrestled with the impact of emerging social forces on inherited liberal state structures, the South made a significant contribution in unashamedly restating such hierarchical values as employer absolutism, white supremacy, and women's subordination. These values played important roles in rationalizing the newly emerging forms of authority—corporate managerial prerogatives, racial segregation, and privileged access for men to the highest positions of pay and power. If the reactionary politics of the 1920s were crucial in securing a new form of social hierarchy against opposing egalitarian potentials, then, surely, the ruling values of the South played a major part.

Northerners who normally gagged on openly hierarchical values made an exception for white supremacy. As hundreds of thousands of southern black migrants poured into the North, the question inevitably arose how they would be inducted into northern life. Would northern states imitate their southern counterparts by enacting Jim Crow statutes? Would they, instead, treat the new arrivals as just another group of immigrants left to fend for themselves in the pluralist marketplace? If Washington stood foursquare behind *de jure* segregation in Dixie, would it do the same in the liberal North?

One thing was clear. The rapid expansion of the black population required abandonment of the exclusionary practices common in the nineteenth century, when a number of northern states had excluded African-Americans from legal residence and full citizenship; when manufacturers had all but excluded African-Americans from employment, quite the reverse of their southern counterparts; and when most trade unions, including the railway brotherhoods and the machinists, had prohibited black members by constitution or initiation rites.[41] Now as the tide of migrants to the North rose ever higher, outright exclusion became untenable. It was equally clear that Afro-Americans were not going to be treated as just another ethnic group. First of all, they were the most thoroughly dispossessed of the migrants to northern cities. Almost none accumulated significant business capital, and relatively few could afford home ownership. In northern cities such as Chicago, the foreign born were four times more likely than black families to own a home.[42] In terms of both individual and intergenerational mobility, the evidence is overwhelming that whatever differences existed among European-Americans, all fared better than African-Americans. None of the Polonias and Little Italies that dotted the urban landscape were as impermeable as the emerging racial ghettos of

South Chicago and Harlem. Whereas a shift in the relative position of, say, Poles and Norwegians affected little else, a shift in the color line affected the entire social order. In short, the Afro-American experience was unique.[43]

All this suggests that race carried far more weight than ethnicity did, not because of genes or skin color but because it stood as a fundamental element of social hierarchy in the supposedly egalitarian North. De facto segregation made the black ghetto a basic part of every major northern city. Although the driving forces behind the creation of the ghetto were economic and cultural, the role of the state cannot be gainsaid. Authorities refrained from prosecuting white rioters, overlooked employment discrimination, sanctioned restrictive covenants and other practices that led to segregated housing, and tolerated the second-class schools, hospitals, and services that became the standing outrage of everyday life. Insofar as all this underwrote the job ceiling, inferior schooling, and the whole cycle of poverty, northern municipal and state governments became the official guarantors of inequality.

Segregation may have set the limiting conditions, but it did not determine what Afro-Americans would do with them. They determined that for themselves, and for a time the leading force in the black community was Marcus Garvey and his Universal Negro Improvement Association (UNIA). From his Harlem base, the charismatic Jamaican immigrant spread his message throughout the country—"Up, you mighty race, you can accomplish what you will." He captured hope, not despair, and his identification with Africa was not an escapist fantasy but a search for historical identity to instill race pride.[44] Unlike intellectuals who never got outside isolated circles of pan-African agitation, Garvey bridged the gap between the Afro-Caribbean elite and the native black masses, and he did it while rejecting the typical prejudice within the black community in favor of light skin. Just as national leaders in other ethnic groups reacted to Anglo-Saxon scorn with prideful presentations of their own national cultures, so Garvey turned white civilization inside out with the aim of constructing a great black civilization.

Like other forms of ethnic consciousness, Garvey's racial nationalism came on strong with the fragmentation of working-class protest after the defeat of the great strikes. It swelled in the face of frustration both for socialists such as A. Philip Randolph, who ran into the same Red Scare brick wall as his white comrades, and for liberals such as DuBois, who fell victim to the same reversal of hope as his fellow progressives. With trade unions in decline and the NAACP at a plateau, as many as 2 million flocked to the UNIA at its peak from 1920 to 1922, making it the biggest mass organization in Afro-American history outside the churches and fraternal/sororal organizations.

In its economic doctrines, the UNIA combined capitalism and nationalism, personal wealth and racial progress. It sought to pool the meager resources of sharecroppers, beauticians, and schoolteachers in investment schemes such as the Black Star Line, an international shipping company. Garvey's agents sold shares by the thousands in what was billed as the UNIA "navy." What distingushed this venture from the numbers racket, proliferating in the ghettos at the same time, was the fact that the line's ship, the *Yarmouth*, actually made voyages in the hope that, one day, the venture would be the sea bridge to Liberia. As a poor person's investment trust, it sought to address the material privation of the black community through the values of family capitalism. In his twin message of race pride and individual accumulation, Garvey was in perfect accord with the restoration of race consciousness and old-fashioned proprietary values in the culture at large. He was right in step with the prevailing idea that "the business of America is business," and, in fact, he supported Calvin Coolidge in 1924.[45]

But the same factors that created the UNIA made it impossible for it to succeed. Garvey's numerous critics included the socialist editors of *The Messenger*, who wrote: "Negroes are the easy marks of the sharpers, having as it were some vague idea that they can make millions like Ford, Rockefeller, and Morgan by buying stocks." DuBois in this stage of his protean career was less averse to black capitalism, but as an implacable opponent of segregation he saw Garvey's racial separatism as merely white supremacy turned upside down. Garvey himself gave his critics fatal ammunition by praising the separatist message of the KKK after meeting with one of its leaders.[46]

Deeply embroiled in controversy within the black community, Garvey was unable to forge a unified defense against the federal government's attempt to put him behind bars. Military intelligence and the Bureau of Investigation had already put him under surveillance during the war, and the growth of Garvey's following convinced J. Edgar Hoover and his bureau boss, William Burns, that it was time to rein in this "dangerous agitator." Disguising their political motives, they secured a criminal indictment against Garvey, who went on trial for mail fraud in May 1923. Instead of building a politically principled defense, Garvey fell into the government's trap by proclaiming his innocence and blaming his associates, which only gave credence to charges against the organization he ran. The trial itself had heavy racial and class overtones: Judge Julian Mack was an elite jurist of German-Jewish ancestry who had contributed to the NAACP but who could not comprehend Garvey's street-wise self-help schemes as anything but personal greed. Garvey actually lived quite modestly for all his public pomp, but he let fly anti-Semitic remarks about his Jewish persecutors, along with diatribes against DuBois. Through this haze of class and racial prejudice, no one focused clearly on the political purpose of the trial, which was accomplished by Garvey's conviction, jailing, and, in 1927, his deportation to Jamaica.[47]

This effort by the oppressed to cope with their predicament embraced fundamental values of their oppressors. There is nothing unusual in that phenomenon. What is surprising is Garvey's faith in a judicial system that was determined to convict him regardless of his innocence. He spoke favorably of American justice even as he portrayed himself as the victim of a conspiracy, apparently because he believed in universal standards of justice so compelling that even white men might adhere to them. In the same light, Garvey appealed to the universal aspiration for liberation, to which all who opposed racism and colonialism could adhere. That higher appeal set him off from his many venal contemporaries, including the high-placed merchants of greed in Harding's Ohio gang, and plain racketeers such as Al Capone, to whom there was no social movement, only loyal followers or enemies; no impartial standard of justice, only the law of the strong and weak; and no universal yearning for freedom, only the desire for money and power. But an important ambiguity remains in the Garvey movement: at times, it gave vent to the same kind of intolerance that helped create it. Hate turned back hate. And that ambiguity was passed along to Garvey's closest successor, the Nation of Islam and its successive leaders W. D. Fard, Elijah Muhammed, and Louis Farrakhan.

Black nationalism was not just a reaction to white supremacy. It gave expression to authentic impulses within the Afro-American community—esteem, discipline, organization, self-improvement—and it inspired national anticolonial movements in Africa and cultural revival in the Caribbean. But it was inescapably paired with its opposite, because the myth of white supremacy was a fundamental ruling structure of American life. The pretense of a common Caucasian community could unite the elite and, more important in a democratic culture, bond otherwise social inferiors to their superiors. By contrast, the fictions of Nordic superiority or Anglo-Saxon "good blood," besides their mutual exclusions and inner confusions, could not embrace the majority of the country. Anti-Semitism served that purpose, but white racism served it best.

For that reason, black nationalism was the most significant and most tenacious of the ethnic nationalisms embedded in American culture. Irish nationalism lost its sting with Irish independence; Polish-American, Greek-American, and all the other American-immigrant cultures were rapidly becoming what the moderate Americanizers hoped—colorful ethnic variations on a central theme, fully compatible with mass culture and dominant marketplace values. Only African-American culture posed an indigestible alternative, because even when it did not adopt nationalist forms, it refused assent to the ruling structures of white supremacy. Locked in a fateful embrace, the opposing myths of black nationalism and white supremacy were doomed forever to a dance of death. Transcendence would have to come from other aspects of Afro-American culture—the tradition of freedom going back through Reconstruction to emancipation; but that was not reborn until the civil rights movement of the 1950s and 1960s. In the meantime, racism performed its labors of division and thereby denied progressive and radical social movements the necessary social base from which to compel a hearing for social justice.

Fundamentalist Liberalism

A yearning to restore a bygone age gripped Washington in the Harding-Coolidge years. Capitalizing on disenchantment with progressive reform at home and crusading liberalism abroad, old-fashioned liberals raised the banner of 100 percent Americanism and rewrote public policy with the aim of restoring such liberal fundamentals as family capitalism, laissez faire, male headship, and the presumptive superiority of white, Anglo-Saxon Protestants. Wresting the liberal legacy away from the progressives, the men in power called a halt to the effort to modernize the liberal state, at least for the time being. For this reason, plus the affinity of Protestant fundamentalists for these values, it is fitting to dub this a period of fundamentalist liberalism.

There is no use looking for a governing blueprint for the years 1921–1924. Unlike the progressives before them and the Hooverians who followed, not to mention the New Deal "brain trusters," the men who came to Washington in the Harding-Coolidge years had no grander design than to restore "normalcy." President Harding carried normalcy to the point of permitting his "Ohio gang" to act like nineteenth-century spoilsmen, notably when his secretary of the interior Albert Fall collected handsome sums for lavishing Teapot Dome on the Sinclair oil interests; and he imitated Grover Cleveland by sending the army to break the 1922 railroad strike. Upon Harding's death in 1923, Calvin Coolidge entered to the White House, a perfect embodiment of the old verities. It was all a far cry from the reform zeal and crusading spirit of the Wilson years.

Initiative came not from the corporate titans of Wall Street, but from older regional elites who had felt elbowed aside in the years of progressive ascendancy and war: urban patricians in the Northeast who felt threatened by "the rising tide of color"; manufacturers in the industrial heartland worried that social legislation would crimp their profits; southern men of property worried that women's suffrage and the New Negro threatened the entire "southern way of life." In addition, elites collected support from lower ranks through the channels of Protestant fundamentalism, nativism, and racial solidarity, by which small men of property, native-born white workers, and country folk could identify with successful businessmen and planters. Standing outside the emerging corporate hierarchy, this amorphous collection of self-appointed "true" Americans still harbored the values of nineteenth-century proprietary families. Resenting the fact that the rock of ages was coming to pieces and convinced that white Protestant men of British ancestry were the most "fit" to run things, they attempted to impose their values on the rest of the population.

Precisely because their values did not win universal assent, it was necessary to use state coercion. If Prohibition was the best example of enforced consent, next came immigration restriction. Outwardly, the emergence of a highly restrictive immigration policy was fairly straightforward. When it became clear that the Literacy Act of 1917 would do little to hold back the tide of postwar immigration from southern and eastern Europe, nativists put together an overwhelming bipartisan congressional coalition around the Johnson Act of 1921, named after Albert Johnson of Washington, a zealot for Nordic solidarity, who had the help of Massachusetts Republican Henry Cabot

Lodge, mouthpiece of the Immigration Restriction League, and Georgia Democrat Tom Watson, champion of the Anglo-Saxon cause. The act set up a quota system that limited admission of any nationality to 3 percent of the foreign born counted in the 1910 census. When this arrangement did not stanch the tide, the same forces pushed through the National Origins Act of 1924, which temporarily reduced the quotas to 2 percent of the foreign born in the 1890 census and mandated a statistical determination of the national origins of the American population as of 1920 to become the basis for proportional representation of quota countries up to a limit of some 150,000. Behind these dry calculations, restrictionists had three main objectives: to immunize American sovereignty against "balkanizing" influences; to regulate the labor market in the interests of native-born skilled men; and to preserve Anglo-Saxon Protestants' cultural predominance.

The new pieces of legislation marked the culmination of decades of nativist agitation going back to the Know-Nothings of the 1850s. What finally pushed it over the top was the shock of U.S. participation in what was called "the European War." The same fear of losing national sovereignty that made Article X of the Versailles Treaty so unpopular also worked against the "new" immigration. The wartime campaign for 100 percent Americanism played into the hands of nativists who argued that "hyphenates" were really foreign agents loyal to their home governments, which no amount of evidence of faithful service in the U.S. army was sufficient to disprove. According to nativist propaganda, foreign voters were stripping America of her sovereignty: "Tending to cohere, and increasingly to become organized into racial and cultural groups, our aggressive foreign voters not only transfer the political and social system of Europe to America, but also they denationalize and 'de-Monroeize' American foreign relations."[48]

Immigration restriction was equally a matter of foreign and domestic policy. That was proved by the close association between immigration restriction and Prohibition. Both measures started out with strong southern support in Congress, gained western support, and finally pulled the North along. Analysis of voting records shows that 80 percent of eastern congressmen who voted for Prohibition also voted for the 1917 Literacy Act.[49] In both cases, Yankee Protestants, not big business, took the lead. Corporate lobbies such as the National Industrial Conference Board would have preferred an immigration commission to regulate the international flow of labor according to the needs of

American industry. Likewise, the National Association of Manufacturers, the American Mining Congress, and the U.S. Chamber of Commerce fought rearguard actions every step of the way against tightening restrictions and were pleased when the final bills exempted Canada and Mexico from the quota system. At the same time, business lobbyists gave away much of the game by conceding the need to exclude "undesirable" groups, and in any event, they put up only a mild opposition. In fact, businessmen were really of two minds. A number of prominent industrialists and Wall Street lawyers bankrolled patriotic societies such as the American Defense Society and the National Security League, which were ardent restrictionists.[50]

Working people were also of two minds. Some—chiefly the recent immigrant nationalities and the unions, settlement houses, and big-city congressmen who catered to their interests—favored the open door for continued immigration. But these voices were drowned out by the leaders of the American Federation of Labor, whose opposition to the open door was as ardent as that of the most intense nativist. In Samuel Gompers' view, immigration was the number one problem of the postwar era, alongside taxes and bolshevism, and he did not hesitate to join the Ku Klux Klan and the American Legion in calling for a temporary suspension of *all* immigration.[51]

The reason the AFL stood shoulder to shoulder with some of the most militant enemies of organized labor (which included the leader of the restrictionists, Albert Johnson) had to do, in part, with the desire to reduce competition in the labor market. But it also had to do with attitudes toward family life. To men such as Harding's Secretary of Labor James J. Davis, a second-generation Welshman, and to skilled German carpenters and Irish ironworkers, proper family life rested on the conventional division of labor between the sexes—husbands should earn a "family wage" while wives kept house. Adding a racial component, they defined the American standard of living around family respectability. "The American laboring man demands and deserves a full dinner pail, refinement in his home, sanitary surroundings, respectable wearing apparel for his family, education for his children, and a few occasional luxuries; and these things cost money. On the contrary, give an Asiatic and most of the European workers a hovel to live in, some spoiled pork, beans, and cabbage, and such like, and he is perfectly content."[52]

The combination of economic and cultural motives accounts for the successive campaigns against ethnic newcomers: the anti-Chinese agitation of the 1870s, prewar resistance to Slavs and Italians, and now the exclusion of the "pauper races" of Europe.[53] Like the businessman's laissez faire, the supposedly apolitical voluntarism of the AFL presuppposed a hefty amount of state regulation of the labor market. To protect the American standard, the AFL argued, it was necessary for the state to regulate the labor market to keep out "unfair" competitors, which meant anyone compelled by circumstance to work for low wages, whether children, women, or immigrants. From the AFL's point of view, state controls were necessary for some semblance of equal bargaining power between workingmen and their employers.

From the point of view of the AFL's socialist critics, of course, equal bargaining under capitalism was an impossibility. Moreover, as feminists pointed out, this kind of state regulation only reinforced male advantages in the workplace. A handful of labor and sexual radicals had learned the lesson that using race or sex to solve class problems might rearrange groups on the ladder of social hierarchy but did not dismantle the ladder itself. In any case, those radical critics who had somehow avoided being silenced by the Red Scare were effectively muffled by the resurgence of fundamentalist liberalism. And it was the force of fundamentalism—the residual power of old-time elites and the support of the forgotten men and women of the middle classes—that accounts for the change in U.S. immigration policy, not the clout of the AFL.

In fact, organized labor had no clout in Washington. The years 1921–1924 were a rout for trade unionism and a reversal for such political influence as workers had managed to acquire during the war. Although workers could count on a few supporters on Capitol Hill, the other two branches of government were busy refurbishing the old formula "laissez faire plus the constable," which had done so much to weaken labor in the past. The Supreme Court uphold severe restrictions on picketing and secondary boycotts, while the Harding administration took a hard line against strikes.[54] Whatever the intention, the effect was to strengthen the hand of employers in their battle for the open shop, the bare-knuckled power play sanctified by the label "American Plan." The fact that immigration restriction was the only major piece of legislation from 1918 to the 1926 Railway Labor Act in which the AFL came out on the winning side suggests that that victory was more coincidence than anything else.

Immigration restriction elevated the invidious assumptions of the biological republic to the level of national policy. Already, the immigration laws of 1903, 1907, and 1917 had banned those deemed "unfit" by the eugenicists—the feebleminded, paupers, criminals, prostitutes, and illiterates.[55] Like the campaign for sterilization of the same groups, the drive to exclude "undesirable" foreigners played on irrational psychic fears of "polluting" the race. Orientals had been excluded already; now the aim was to exclude southern and eastern Europeans. Eugenics expert H. H. Laughlin held Congress in thrall to charts of ethnic ranking by cultural stereotypes and wartime IQ test results, inspiring congressmen such as Georgia's Carl Vinson to expatiate on "the Aryan race." So firm was the grip of these views that even the target groups could invoke their invidious categories, as in the pathetic petition of Yugoslavs in Ohio for favorable treatment on the grounds that Laughlin's statistics "give people of our nationality a very favorable record, and class them as desirable immigrants."[56]

The federal bureaucracy and foreign policy apparatus were dominated by men in the grip of the same racial stereotypes. For example, in 1919 the State Department submitted a survey of the views of consular officers in Europe to the Senate Committee on Immigration, according to which the typical prospective immigrant was an illiterate anarchist or Bolshevik, mentally unfit, and otherwise "undesirable." An especially bigoted view came from the consul in Warsaw, who depicted the prospective Polish emigrant as "stultified," "illy educated," lacking in patriotic spirit and "mentally incapable of acquiring it," and then the coup de grâce: "At the moment, 90 percent may be regarded as a low estimate of the proportion representing the Jewish race."[57]

Immigration restriction was at one with the Red Scare in seeking to purge America of evil foreign influences. Restrictionists conjured up an older, racially homogeneous America in which self-government had flourished. This link between racial homogeneity and liberal government was a common theme in testimony to congressional immigration committees: "we must strive for homogeneity among the citizenship. Therein lies the strength of a republic." The aim of immigration policy should be to eliminate "mongrel communities with discordant views and aspirations," since "America can not exist with a large number of communities where a foreign language is spoken and where foreign ideas prevail." Calvin Coolidge subscribed to a watered-down version of racial Americanism in this widely quoted message to Congress:

"American institutions rest solely on good citizenship. They were created by people who had a background of self-government. New arrivals should be limited to our capacity to absorb them into the ranks of good citizenship. America must be kept American." What Coolidge seems to have meant is that national leadership must be kept in the hands of old-stock Americans. That impulse to restore cultural dominance to the Wasp elite is what finally closed the door upon the open republic of reason.[58]

By a perverse logic, the same constellation of old-fashioned liberal values that militated in favor of strong state controls on drink and immigration, in other respects worked in favor of laissez faire, especially when it came to regulating the market in the interests of working people. That was certainly the case with child labor, over which a fierce battle raged. Under the promptings of the National Child Labor Committee and a host of other progressive reformers, Congress had twice enacted prohibitions on child labor. But laissez faire held sway at the Supreme Court, and twice the Court had overturned the legislation, first in *Hammer v. Dagenhart* (1917) and then in *Bailey v. Drexel* (1922).[59] Unbowed, progressive reformers returned in 1924 to win congressional passage of a constitutional amendment that would have tied the hands of the Court.

As the battle over ratification heated up, interest groups divided into two camps roughly along progressive-fundamentalist lines. On one side were the usual progressive lobbies: the National Child Labor Committee, the National Consumers League, the League of Women Voters, and the American Federation of Labor, who felt that the only way to end the abuse was through state action. They were still seeking a path between laissez faire, with its constitutional barriers to regulating the market, and German-style paternalism, with its statist enforcement machinery.

On the opposite side, the National Association of Manufacturers, the Farm Bureau Federation, the Southern Textiles Association, and the Catholic hierarchy mobilized their respective constituencies against a supposed conspiracy to turn all children into wards of the state. Their appeals rang with the old standbys of nineteenth-century liberalism—freedom of contract, the sanctity of the family, and the work ethic. Celebrating the virtues of industrial discipline, NAM flooded key states with pamphlets warning that preventing boys from working was "taking away their manliness and self-respect, and making them into weaklings, and taking away the liberties of the parents." Contending that a child labor amendment would lead to all manner of federal regulation, the archliberal Sentinels of the Republic described it as "an assault against individual liberty" that would surely bring about the "nationalization of children." To such extreme liberal fundamentalists, laissez faire and paternal authority were indivisible; federal regulation of the family was, therefore, nothing less than the entering wedge of socialism. [60]

For related reasons, the Catholic hierarchy mounted an equally spirited campaign. Fearing that any federal regulation of children threatened parochial education and patriarchal values, the *Boston Pilot* charged that the idea was an atheistic scheme hatched in the Soviet Union, and Massachusetts church leaders denounced it in similar terms at specially summoned conventions of the League of Catholic Women. Under such pressures, Massachusetts gubernatorial candidate James M. Curley withdrew his support, and Massachusetts referendum voters swamped the amendment by a two-to-one margin, which all but killed hopes for national ratification. [61]

Fundamentalists triumphed over progressives on every other battleground of laissez faire. The National Association of Manufacturers joined with the Women's Harding-Coolidge Clubs to stop any extensions of protective legislation for female workers. Standing foursquare on "liberty of contract," NAM's Women's Bureau, comprised mostly of female personnel officers, contended that protective laws actually curtailed women's opportunities for employment and promotion. As if to prove that politics makes strange bedfellows, this argument cropped up almost verbatim in the platforms of the National Women's party, and the Supreme Court accepted the same view in *Adkins v. Children's Hospital* (1923), which threw out minimum wages for women on Fifth Amendment grounds of due process. Justice Holmes took vigorous exception, protesting the translation of "liberty of contract" into constitutional dogma, and even Chief Justice Taft, perhaps remembering his experience on the War Labor Board, dissented against the patently false assumption that women competed equally in the marketplace with men. But to no avail. In the end, women workers wound up with the worst of both laissez faire, which withheld redress for their unequal condition, and state paternalism, which in *Muller v. Oregon* had granted special protections, but only on the grounds that women were the weaker sex. [62]

Similarly, laissez faire returned as the order of the day with respect to public provision for the poor. When the state of Wisconsin began talking about unemployment insurance in the depression of 1920–21, business lobbies moved to stamp out the virus before it spread. The National Industrial Conference Board waged a small pamphlet war upon the "Wisconsin idea," and the Special Conference Committee reassured its corporate members that unemployment insurance was "as chimerical as insurance against unhappiness."[63] With respect to old-age pensions, some corporations experimented with company retirement plans, but, on the whole, industry was perfectly in step with NAM in allowing only for the almshouse beyond private charity. Indeed, even after the onset of the Great Depression, NAM still dared to assert that the best course was "thrift, forethought, frugality, and individual initiative."[64] The lone exception to the revenge of laissez faire in the early 1920s was the Sheppard-Towner maternity act of 1921, a precedent-setting measure that provided public health advice and nutrition to expectant mothers. A congressional sop to a coalition of reform lobbies named the Women's Joint Congressional Committee, it survived apparently because of farm support for its nutrition program.

In the prevailing climate, the notion of America as a classless society was restored to its former glory. Close companion to the free-market philosophy, the idea that America had escaped the ravages of class warfare received a boost from the diplomacy of isolation from things European. In an exemplary work of the period, *American Individualism* (1922), Herbert Hoover spelled out why the United States was different: "We have a distaste for the very expression of 'class,' but if we would use European scales of 'classes' we would find that above their scale of 'lower classes' we have in equivalent comfort, morality, understanding, and intelligence fully eighty per cent of our native-born whites."[65]

As Hoover unwittingly demonstrated, the key to preserving the notion of American exceptionalism was the exclusion of all but "native-born whites" from the equation. By pretending that immigrants from southern and eastern Europe, African-Americans, and Asian-Americans were not "true" Americans, nativism and racism made a mighty contribution to the fiction of the classless society. Thus for the time being, the clock was turned back to the nineteenth century, as if the old liberal state of courts and parties and the old ideas of laissez faire could actually govern a modern society. Except for a handful of national leaders including Hoover himself, no one at the top stopped to ask whether the almshouse really addressed the need for economic security or whether an excess of liberty for corporate oligarchs under conditions of modern mass production harbored hidden dangers for the country at large.

The Diplomatic Challenges

It is impossible to say whether full U.S. participation in the League of Nations or a cordial U.S. welcome for Europe's tempest-tossed emigrants would have made much of a difference, but the years after Versailles were stormy ones. Weimar Germany was most in danger of being dashed on the rocks. The new Weimar government was the first parliamentary regime in German history and had barely enough support to survive. Industrialists and the military went along with a liberal republic only because they saw it as a shield against a left-wing socialist republic. Though foiled in their attempt to stage a second revolution in 1919 on the Bolshevik model, Communists were still a force to be reckoned with in industrial districts. The urban middle classes had got along with authoritarian regimes for so long that they felt no deep loyalty to the current regime, especially after skyrocketing inflation ate up their savings; and the peasantry felt left out of the Weimar settlement altogether. Only the Social Democrats and their trade union allies were principled supporters of the republic. In the crisis year 1923 the whole system nearly collapsed when the French occupied the Ruhr to press for payment of reparations, and the mark fell so low that people trundled worthless paper money about in wheelbarrows.[66]

Out of this chaos emerged fascism. Whereas the old right in Europe had been aristocratic, monarchist, and traditionalist, the new right was mass-based, popularist, and, in its own way, modernist. Whereas the old had aimed at restoring a world of hereditary privilege and military caste, the new intended to bring forth a folk community (*Volksgemeinschaft*) of an Aryan superrace; whereas the old held upper-class women in highest esteem, the new esteemed women of the masses devoted to children, kitchen, and church; whereas the old Conservatives were contemptuous of capitalist parvenues, the new Brown Shirts of the National Socialist Workers party (Nazis) were resentful of capitalist wealth; whereas the old right was reactionary in opposing both liberalism and communism, the new was counterrevolutionary.[67]

Americans did not understand the seriousness of counterrevolution in Europe. For the most part, they looked the other way when Hitler staged his half-comic beer-hall putsch in 1923. What good was a Europe rife with revolution, coup d'état, untamed militarism, and paramilitary "bully boys"? Another reason they did not regard the rise of fascism as a momentous threat to the liberal values of Western civilization was that many Americans were sympathetic to fascist aims. The Red Scare had implanted a visceral hatred of communism in many quarters, and 100 percent Americanism had brought new popularity to patently racist ideas. The myth of the Aryan race had strong defenders in the United States; Anglo-Saxon eugenicists proclaimed racial kinship with sturdy Teutons; vicious anti-Semitism blotted the pages of some of the most popular magazines and newspapers in the country; and white supremacy ruled, North and South.

The Harding administration was in step with leading opinion at home when it extended diplomatic recognition to Mussolini, expecting him to be a bulwark of law and order against bolshevism. Perhaps the American ambassador in Berlin during the 1923 crisis was likewise in step when he supported a temporary military dictatorship as a better obstacle than Weimar to the establishment of a "Red Republic."[68] Prime reasons for American policymakers' readiness to accept authoritarian regimes in both a wartime ally and a wartime enemy were the loss of confidence in the liberal republic of reason and the advance of racial republicanism at home.

Conversely, the United States achieved diplomatic success in upholding liberalism abroad precisely where the influence of 100 percent Americanism and isolationism were weakest. By all accounts, the greatest U.S. diplomatic achievement in this period was the Washington Naval Disarmament Conference of 1921–22, a feather in the cap of Secretary of State Charles Evans Hughes. Though no friend of bolshevism, Hughes was no paranoid anticommunist, either. He had laid his prestige on the line as a former presidential candidate and member of the Supreme Court in speaking out against the expulsion of five duly elected socialist members from the New York legislature. Responding to a disarmament resolution sponsored by Senator William Borah, the leader of the "irreconcilable" opponents of the Versailles Treaty, Hughes invited Britain, Japan, and a number of other interested powers to Washington.

His aim was to win parity with Britain, break up the Anglo-Japanese alliance, and placate domestic opponents of militarism. The conference succeeded on each count. In a series of multilateral treaties, the participants set the ratio of battleships at 5:5:3 for Britain, the United States, and Japan, respectively; required international consultation—but not military force—before changing concessions in China and elsewhere in the Pacific; and set caps on the naval forces of the signatories. The treaties were a remarkable synthesis of realism and disarmament. Insofar as there were provisions for consultation and disarmament, they marked a signal triumph for the principles of Wilsonian internationalism and, at the same time, notched a victory for the informal imperialism of the Open Door in Asia because they limited the action of Britain and Japan.[69] The Washington conference proved that the United States might spread liberal principles when it did not act on the isolationist spirit of 100 percent Americanism.

Internal Contradictions

By the election of 1924, fundamentalist liberalism blanketed the Republican and Democratic parties. Prohibition seemed a "noble experiment"; the National Origins Act unified political will as nothing had since the declaration of war; laissez faire had returned as the order of the day; and organized labor's opposition to the "American Plan" was rapidly dwindling into insignificance. The two men at the top of the 1924 Republican ticket embodied a bargain between the middle classes and the corporate elite. Calvin Coolidge stood for the small manufacturer and the individual entrepreneur for whom the path to wealth lay with the middle-class family of olden days. By contrast, the vice-presidential nominee, Charles G. Dawes, embodied the new corporate businessman, the large-scale industrialist, the finance capitalist—in short, the corporate future. A leading Chicago banker, Dawes got the nomination as a reward for renegotiating German reparations payments under the international financial agreement of 1924 that bears his name. Both men had well-deserved reputations as opponents of organized labor, Coolidge because he had first gained national prominence as governor of Massachusetts by breaking the Boston police strike in 1919, and Dawes because he had advised the Harding administration to get tough with striking railroad workers. They were not the first (or the last) national leaders to garner support by appealing to (middle and upper) class hatreds, all the while denouncing unions and labor radicals for fomenting class division.

As for the opposition, it was deeply divided. The Democratic convention was polarized for more than 100 ballots between urban wets, who presented a resolution condemning the Ku Klux Klan and favored Al Smith, governor of New York; and southern drys, who beat back the anti-Klan resolution and favored former railroad czar William McAdoo. In the end, delegates gave the worthless nomination to John Davis, a House of Morgan lawyer with dry sentiments. What was left of serious opposition to laissez faire and the open shop lined up behind the Conference for Progressive Political Action, spearheaded by the railroad brotherhoods, and then rallied for one last hurrah around the one-shot Progressive party and its standard-bearer "Fighting Bob" La Follette. The 16 percent showing of the indomitable Wisconsin insurgent was far too small to throw the election into the House of Representatives, as some of his managers had hoped, but was large enough in key states such as New York and California to take electoral votes from the Democrats, suggesting for the future that the route out of Democratic paralysis lay through labor reform.[70] But in the meantime, prosperity had returned after the 1920–21 depression, and Calvin Coolidge had the good luck to be a sitting president when it did, so that "Silent Cal" barely had to utter a word to be elected by a margin almost as large as Harding's.

Calvin Coolidge was not so much a symbol of the age as a mask for its contradictions. Coolidge stood for the stern New England virtues of temperance and self-denial, lived in a modest home in the Berkshires where square dancing was as much excitement as a person could stand, and seemed to have stepped out of a Norman Rockwell cover painting for the *Saturday Evening Post*. Against this life-style, the smart set drank bootleg liquor, danced the Charleston, and started hanging modern art on the walls of their Park Avenue penthouses. The incongruity of Calvin Coolidge's presiding over the Roaring Twenties was not lost on midwestern journalist William Allen White, who titled his biography of Coolidge *A Puritan in Babylon* (1938). The clash of cultures—wet and dry, flapper and mother, urban sophisticate and country hick—was fixed in popular imagination at the time and has defined the twenties ever since. Coolidge's election represented the revenge of the "true" Americans against the forces remaking their way of life.[71]

This cultural tension provides a clue to the larger historical process, in which other, deeper contradictions were at work. A prime example was the celebrated case of Sacco and Vanzetti. Nicola Sacco and Bartolomeo Vanzetti epitomized the immigrant working class filling the crowded, wooden tenements of the red-brick factory towns that had taken over much of the New England landscape during the Industrial Revolution. Speaking English with thick Italian accents, the "good shoemaker" and the "poor fish peddler" identified with the workers' cause and with the philosophy of anarchism, and thus saw themselves—and certainly were seen by the authorities—as enemies of the state. The opposition between radicals and authorities intensified during the Red Scare, with its spate of anarchist bombings, including one on Attorney General A. Mitchell Palmer's doorstep, and its repression of the left, including members of the anarchist group around the newspaper *Crònaca sovversiva.* As members of the group, Sacco and Vanzetti were known to police and became understandably alarmed when a comrade died after "falling" from a window while in police custody. Their fear helps explain their use of false names and their possession of revolvers when Massachusetts authorities arrested them for robbery and murder in May 1920 in connection with a payroll robbery in Bridgewater and another in South Braintree in which two had been killed.[72]

Caught up in the antiradical climate, officials developed a theory of anarchist involvement in the crimes. Whether the accused had any involvement or not, there is little likelihood that Sacco and Vanzetti would have been arrested if they had been, say, churchgoing Yankee Republicans. Once in court, ethnic stereotyping came into play in the testimony of witnesses, one of whom identified the accused on the grounds that he "looked Italian," and nativism and antiradicalism undoubtedly influenced the conduct of the presiding Judge Webster Thayer, who was reported to have boasted about what he did to "those anarchist bastards." In his charge to the jury, Judge Thayer told the twelve good men of Norfolk County that they represented "the spirit of supreme American loyalty" against alien enemies. In the climate of the Red Scare and 100 percent Americanism, the jury did its patriotic duty and in May 1921 handed down a guilty verdict with the death penalty.

Immediately, Sacco and Vanzetti became a worldwide *cause célèbre.* With the weight of the Yankee Protestant establishment coming down on radical immigrant workers, it seemed to writers such as John Dos Passos that society had cracked into "two nations," just as it seemed to a handful of eminent jurists, including Felix Frankfurter, that American justice was itself on trial. World opinion was revolted by the spectacle of class and ethnic prejudice condemning two humble men widely regarded as innocent (and whose innocence has been upheld by the preponderance of subsequent historical investigation). As the date for the execution neared, large-scale demonstrations erupted from Paris to Australia, even as a distinguished panel that included the presidents of Harvard and the Massachusetts Institute of Technology cleared the way for Sacco and Vanzetti to die in the electric chair shortly after midnight on August 23, 1927.[73]

The victims immediately became martyrs. The funeral procession turned into a protest march beneath banners reading "Remember Justice Crucified." Upton Sinclair treated the martyrs as modern-day Christ figures in his novel *Boston* (1928), where he wrote: "It was the mysterious process of blood-sacrifice, by which through the ages salvation has been brought to mankind." State police, nicknamed Cossacks, caused more blood to flow when they rode their horses into the line of the mourners. The furneral orator, an Irish Catholic woman, denounced the betrayal of American ideals of liberty and equality. And Sinclair contemptuously referred to the use of clubs as "the process known as 'Americanization.'"[74]

The fact that so many sectors of opinion—progressives such as Frankfurter, socialists such as Sinclair, communists, Italian Catholics—found common grounds for protest suggests, at the very least, that "the spirit of supreme American loyalty" was not a valid basis for meting out justice. In a "government of laws, not of men," the law must seem to be impartial, above mere prejudice and partisan ideology. In this case, the law seemed to have been captured by bigots of the Yankee Protestant upper crust who were unwilling to give fair treatment to political dissidents because they were poor Italian laborers. The executions, far from promoting the hegemony of the law, revealed polarizations of class and culture; instead of vindicating Anglo-Saxon jurisprudence, it brought 100 percent Americanism into contempt.

The same could be said of immigration restriction. Although the National Origins Act remained the law of the land, the assumption behind its passage, that the United States was a biological republic governed by Nordics, did not square with the character of American society. No amount of Anglo-Saxon ancestor worship or eugenics fantasy could erase the fact that America was a multiethnic society in which descendants of British Protestants were in a minority. That is why the logic of immigration restriction was self-contradictory; intending to preserve a fictional homogeneity, it froze the actual heterogeneity. The notion that "America must be kept American" was the problem, not the solution. The contradiction stands out in a House Immigration Committee report in defense of the shift to the more restrictive 1890 census base: "It is used in an effort to preserve, as nearly as possible, the racial status quo in the United States. It is hoped to guarantee, as best we can at this late date, racial homogeneity in the United States."[75] Indeed, as the committee's apologetic tone suggests, it really was too late. To preserve "the racial status quo" was to guarantee there would be no "racial homogeneity." Such an internally contradictory policy was a shaky platform from which to govern the country.

In practice, it was also a leaky dike. To be sure, the National Origins Act held back the "undesirable" Italians, whose quota dropped from 42,057 to 3,845, and the "inferior" Poles, who went from 30,977 to 5,982. But it soon became clear that others would take their place in the supposedly overpopulated cities of the North and West. Whereas southern and eastern Europeans had accounted for over 70 percent of the immigration in the decade 1901–1910, they represented only 29 percent of the smaller total in 1921–1931; meanwhile, Canadians increased from 2 to 22.5 percent, and Mexicans jumped from 0.6 to 11.2 percent.[76] If Catholic French-Canadians fit uncomfortably in the Nordic category, Mexicans did not fit at all. In fact, as Mexicans streamed across the Rio Grande into the agricultural valleys of California and Texas, the Bureau of the Census performed a miracle of eugenics and lifted them out of the "white" category, where they had been until 1920, and reclassified them as "non-white." The unintended consequence of restriction was to increase the ethnic diversity of the United States.

Restriction backfired in one other way. Insofar as the stigma of exclusion rubbed off on the immigrant groups already present, ethnic stereotyping actually encouraged Little Italies and Polonias to unify against assimilation. Instead of fostering the melting pot, nativist prejudice fostered the spirit of ethnic "tribalism" that characterized the 1920s.[77] The same environment that heightened Anglo-Saxon race consciousness and Garveyite black nationalism also promoted a strong national identity among Greek, Croatian, and Czech immigrants. Another contributing factor was the diminished ability of the labor movement to bridge the gaps among ethnic sectors in the laboring population, and labor's retreat, in turn, enhanced the fortunes of the storekeepers, community leaders, and foreign-language publishers who had the most to gain in keeping their respective national causes alive. Still, as permanent parts of the American landscape they had to accommodate themselves to the larger culture, and a new pattern of immigrant Americanism was beginning to emerge. Old World cultures were adapting to the American environment to produce Italian-American, Polish-American, or Jewish-American communities led by their own middle-class "race leaders"—whether Italian *prominenti*, Polish priests, or Jewish lawyers—who also stood as ambassadors from the ethnic enclave to the world outside. Besides, the immovable racial theories of the restrictionists simply could not contain irresistible social forces.

Another illustration of outmoded ideas was the infamous Scopes "monkey trial." For a few exciting days in July 1925, the mass media riveted the nation's attention on sleepy Dayton, Tennessee, where biology teacher John Scopes was on trial for violating the state's recently enacted prohibition on the teaching of evolution. Scopes's conviction was a foregone conclusion, but the small army of reporters portrayed the trial as a contest between religious fundamentalism and modern science, with William Jennings Bryan and Clarence Darrow acting out the respective roles. Ever the Great Commoner, Bryan rejoiced that the trial was taking place in "a Christian state" before a jury of "the yeomanry." Taking a shot at the modern deification of science by "the little irresponsible oligarchy of self-styled 'intellectuals,'" he argued that the Great War had proved that you could build wondrous machinery, but without Jesus' love you could not prevent its misuse. Had it not been for Darrow's withering cross-examination, this might have stood as a telling critique of the modern idolatry of science and technology; instead, it turned into an exhibition of sanctimonious bigotry. Bryan said he was perfectly content with the absolute truth of Genesis, and was ignorant of alternative explanations of creation because he "never felt it necessary to look up some competing religions."[78]

In the presidential election of 1896, Darrow had voted for Bryan, and their parting of the ways hints at underlying social transformations. In the 1890s Bryan's beloved yeomanry was still the largest occupational grouping, and the values of self-discipline, chastity, and property accumulation associated with Yankee Protestant small proprietors were still cherished above all others. But as these old middle classes declined in relation to professional groups and industrial workers, new ruling values of consumer accumulation and socialized reproduction came to the fore. Meanwhile, cultural heterogeneity destroyed the easy assumption that the United States was a purely Protestant country. Certainly in the North and in the nation at large, the mystique of science was proving more potent than the metaphysic of fundamentalist Christianity. Fundamentalists may have won the battle, but they lost the war for hegemony.

In conclusion, the fundamentalist liberals of the Harding-Coolidge years were unable to reconcile state and society. Since the 1890s, the United States had been evolving toward a modern industrial society in which class tensions appeared most visibly in the polarity between the great bureaucratic corporations and the multicultural industrial working class. The emergence of this new social order undermined the position of pedigreed Yankee Protestants from many sides at once: in the shift from family to corporate ownership, in the rise of managerial-technical elites, in the emergence of independent women, and in the influx of Catholic and Jewish immigrants. Attempting to shore up their declining status, Yankee Protestants of old wealth and lineage reached out to other old-stock Americans, reasserted the principles that had once made them great, and called upon the state to enforce them. With so much at stake, they turned away from the rational republic and, instead, dredged up from the dark side of the American myth the hierarchical principles of the biological republic—white supremacy, Anglo-Saxon nativism, "America for the Americans."

These internal contradictions made fundamentalist liberalism an inherently unstable governing strategy. Instability was partly the result of Coolidge's failure to dislodge the regulatory machinery left behind by the progressives, including the Federal Trade Commission, the Railway Labor Board, and the Federal Reserve Board, all of which the fundamentalists were singularly ill equipped to administer. Otherwise, instability was a consequence of fundamentalism itself. Foisting Prohibition, the Red Scare, laissez faire, and immigration restriction on the country only widened the gap between state and society. Impeding welfare legislation only threw wage earners back upon the inadequate resources of family economy. Squelching what would later be called "countercyclical" measures only deepened the gulf between the economy's capacity to produce and its capacity to consume. Restricting European immigration only promoted ethnic diversity from other sources. Attempting to impose conformity to the Anglo ideal only engendered a spirit of ethnic "tribalism"; Prohibition only gave birth to Al Capone.

In the end, liberals of the 100-percent-American stripe only wound up deepening the contradictions—between state and society, and between dominant and subordinate groups—that drove historical events. No more capable of resolving those twin tensions than the Wilsonian progressives before them, they were destined to be overwhelmed by the flow of events. It was only a matter of time before other strategies of rule came forward, of which the first was managerial liberalism, represented by Herbert Hoover.

III

The
Resolution
//.

1925–1939

REDUCED TO ITS *essentials, the overriding historical problem of the early twentieth century hinged on the incompatibility of modern society and the old liberal state. Despite the best efforts of progressives, managerials, and old-fashioned liberals, the problem remained unsolved as the sounds of war gave way to the Roaring Twenties. It was left to the period beginning in the late 1920s and culminating in the New Deal to resolve the imbalance by synthesizing the modern system around corporate property relations, the middle-class consumer family, and extensive state intervention in the market.*

True, the prosperous Twenties and the depression Thirties seem at first to be as different as night and day. The decade of bathtub gin, extravagant prosperity, and Coolidge conservatism seems forever set off from the decade of legalized whiskey, hard times, and Roosevelt liberalism. But the more historians have examined the origins of the modern governing system, the more it has become necessary to look at the late 1920s and early 1930s inside the same framework. Below the surface, social hierarchy remained surprisingly intact through the Depression; at least, the structures of corporate power, male dominance, and white supremacy were little disturbed. And despite glaring differences between Herbert Hoover and Franklin Roosevelt, there was a considerable degree of overlap in their governing strategies. No one would deny that the United States had changed by the end of the 1930s, but the links between Hoover's New Era and Roosevelt's New Deal were more extensive than at first appear.

8

The New Era of Corporate Capitalism

Corporate Feudalism

By the mid-1920s, the great corporations stood forth as central institutions of modern life. The likes of General Motors, General Electric, and Procter and Gamble presented themselves as benefactors of the consumer, patrons of the wage earner, and protectors of the modern woman. They proclaimed mass consumption as the alternative to the redistribution of wealth, and welfare capitalism as the alternative to the welfare state. They wrapped the open shop in the flag as the "American Plan" and presented it as the patriotic alternative to trade unions and industrial democracy. They plied the New Woman with vacuum cleaners and refrigerators, as if household conveniences were the route to liberation. They even privatized foreign policy; international bankers and corporate executives became the key architects of international financial stability. Not content to remain leaders in the business world, corporate capitalists aspired for the first time to become a ruling class for society as a whole.[1]

In what was undoubtedly the most significant study of big business since the Progressive period, *The Modern Corporation and Private Property* (1932), Adolf Berle and Gardner Means described the "Corporate system" as the modern equivalent of feudalism. They noted that corporate leaders were being called upon "to accept responsibility for the well-being of those who are subject to the organization, whether workers, investors, or consumers." Although Berle and Means were by no means blind to the dangers of oligarchical wealth and power, they recognized that the lords of big business were widely seen as benefactors, not as parasitic plutocrats. And in any event the corporate system "bids fair to be as all-embracing as was the feudal system in its time."[2]

Ironically, the notion of corporate capitalism as the equivalent of feudalism had been invented by the archenemies of big business, and it was not intended as a compliment. Critics from Edward Bellamy and Thorstein Veblen to Clarence Darrow and Eugene Debs portrayed big businessmen as oppressors of the little guy. In the populist folklore of the late nineteenth century, the People's party and the Knights of Labor had fought coal and railroad barons on behalf of yeoman farmers and industrial "serfs." In the Progressive Era, labor leaders had counterposed industrial democracy to the evils of "industrial feudalism," while Christian socialists and social reformers had played Robin Hood to the robber barons.

Now all these critics lay vanquished. The victory of corporate capital was, in the first instance, a matter of sheer economic power. After a generation of breaking Adam Smith's rules of competition, big business had ushered in the reign of oligopoly. Outside the highly concentrated world of high finance, the 200 largest nonfinancial corporations controlled almost half of all corporate wealth and some 22 percent of the entire wealth of the nation. Most industries were dominated by a handful of giant firms—U.S. Steel, Bethlehem, and a few other steel producers; General Electric and Westinghouse in electrical equipment; General Motors, Ford, and Chrysler in automobiles; the Pennsylvania, New York Central, and a few other rail systems. No individual tycoon could rival these firms, the largest of which was the monopoly American Telephone and Telegraph, a giant among giants worth $4.2 billion with almost half a million employees in the late 1920s.[3]

Owing to the wide dispersion of stock ownership among as many as 7 million stockholders, the nominal owners of the corporation did not control it. Instead, Berle and Means estimated that a tiny knot of some 2,000 among the hundreds of thousands of business owners wielded vast power through minority control, holding-company pyramids, and management proxy-voting. Although ultimate power remained with minority stockholders who owned the controlling interest, day-to-day decisions rested with salaried managers. Hailed as the new heroes of prosperity, modern managers were said to be driven by an organizational imperative to raise output, not by a market imperative to maximize profit.[4]

From the pages of the *New York Times* to the pamphlets of the National Industrial Conference Board, prophets of the New Era touted the advent of "self-government in industry." The corporate system was said to have brought stability out of the chaos of old-style competition through internal planning and external coordination of the sort represented by trade associations such as the Cotton Textile Institute. Under what he called "the association idea," Herbert Hoover lent the Department of Commerce to the promotion of industrial cooperation. With government support, capitalist planning was supplanting laissez faire.[5]

Even some onetime Robin Hoods came to believe that the rise of management marked a progressive turn in capitalist development. Although Walter Lippmann retained the Marxist idea that capitalists had "socialized" production, he rejected the socialist prescription of public ownership. And in place of Veblen's conflict between the engineers and the price system, Lippmann posited a harmonious division of labor between managers and owners. The organizational genius of the corporate system was evident in "that growing use of experts and of statistical measurements, and that development of trade associations, of conferences, committees, and councils with which modern industry is honeycombed. The captain of industry in the romantic sense tends to disappear in highly evolved industrial organizations."[6] This idea of a managerial revolution that made socialist revolution obsolete would reverberate through twentieth-century economic doctrine in both conservative (James Burnham) and social-democratic (John Kenneth Galbraith) versions.

The corporate elite could hardly claim the right to rule society at large if they could not keep their own subordinates in line. The first order of business under industrial "self-government" was to control their own shops. Given the weakness of unions, especially in mass production and the rising service sector, managers had virtually a free hand in managing labor markets within their own firms. AT&T set the example with its well-publicized personnel policies. It established clear ladders for promotion and pay, which, of course, were separated by gender—all telephone operators and most lower-level clerks were women, while virtually all blue-collar linemen and installers were men. It also introduced incentive plans, time study, and the new twist in scientific management known as "human relations," made famous by the discovery of the "Hawthorne effect," that workers' productivity varied according to the amount of interest supervisors showed in their work.[7]

The fact that managers held the upper hand did not eliminate shop-floor tussles over productivity. As far as management was concerned, the problem was how to raise productivity without a commensurate increase in pay. General Motors was typical in experimenting with everything from simple piece rates to the elaborate Wennerlund group bonus plan, while other firms tried out Taylor's task-and-bonus system, the Bedaux system, and Gilbreth's time-and-motion study. These high-pressure productivity schemes drew a mixed reaction from workers. From the weakened ranks of organized labor, AFL head William Green called upon members to cooperate in implementing incentive systems. At the same time, unorganized opposition was widespread on the shop floor. Skilled workers grew particularly adept at resisting rationalization by deceiving the time-study man, "banking" extra pieces, or even throwing the proverbial monkey wrench into the works.[8]

There is no doubt about who won this uneven contest between managers and workers. Productivity in manufacturing leaped by 32 percent from 1922 to 1929, while average wage rates rose by only 8 percent.[9] Ignored at the time, the gap in these figures harbored a hidden time bomb. If productivity was increasing so much faster than wages, how could wage earners afford to buy back their extra output? Sooner or later there had to be a reckoning between the capacity to produce and the capacity to consume.

The fact that industrial relations were conducted on decidedly unequal terms did not mean that employers could forget about the fealty of their subordinates. In effect, managers offered workers a modern version of the feudal compact: the company would be the worker's lord and protector if, in return, the worker rendered loyal service. Under the terms of this unwritten corporate-feudal contract, many firms cultivated worker loyalty through the various features of welfare capitalism. Pension plans and health insurance were touted as a "stimulus to efficiency" and an "incentive to reduced turnover." Employee stock ownership was even hailed as the answer to socialist redistribution.[10]

Employee representation was another device to forge harmony between management and labor. International Harvester, Standard Oil, and other leading corporations set up works councils and company unions as alternatives to trade unions and collective bargaining.[11] As the National Industrial Conference Board pointed out, the astute manager stood to gain by heading off discontent before the union came knocking at his door. "Beyond the settlement of grievances and, better, their prevention, is the broader and more constructive accomplishment of employee representation in welding together management and working force into a single, cohesive productive unit." [12]

Forging a single, cohesive unit required that managers take workers' needs and desires into account. Even when the rule of the strong appeared to be unchecked by opposition from below, there was an element of reciprocity between dominant and subordinate groups. In cultivating worker loyalty, management incurred the obligation to provide security against unemployment, illness, injury, retirement, and want. In the cold, antiunion climate of the 1920s, immigrant workers but one generation removed from agrarian paternalism looked to property owners for redistributive justice. They commonly accepted favoritism as a form of patronage, as in the case of a Pennsylvania worker who said: "And if you were the friend of a boss, or if you had a friend who was the friend of a boss, then you had a possibility of getting priority when a job would be opened." Just as the feudal landlord should not engross grain in times of famine, so the industrialist should not forget his obligation to provide jobs, holidays, and light work to oldtimers. [13]

It is not inconceivable that the informal corporate-feudal contract might have evolved into a permanent system of industrial relations. Molders' union leader John Frey lamented the success of welfare capitalism in creating habits of dependency: "So many workmen here had been lulled to sleep by the company union, the welfare plans, the social organizations fostered by the employer . . . that they had come to look upon the employer as their protector, and had believed vigorous trade union organization unnecessary for their welfare." [14]

Far from the dreams of labor radicals for reorganizing society, or even the aims of "pure and simple" trade unionists for a share of economic power, the desire for security was the very bedrock of the mass mind. Certainly, the influence of Catholic social teaching upon the largely Catholic immigrant working population reinforced the corporate-feudal contract, both in its fervid combat of socialism and in its own substitute doctrines. Ever since Pope Leo XIII's *Rerum Novarum* (1891), the Catholic hierarchy had preached a modern version of medieval corporatism, and the majority of bishops and priests undoubtedly took it as axiomatic that capital and labor were duty-bound to each other, the former to command, the latter to obey. Although there was a Catholic reform tradition, as embodied in John A. Ryan and the American bishops' 1919 Program of Social Reconstruction, the burden of Catholic influence in the 1920s fell on the conservative side. [15]

The one thing that kept the feudal system of industrial relations from becoming solidly entrenched was management's deeply ingrained habit of looking first, last, and always for a bigger bottom line. Instead of meeting the legitimate needs of wage workers for security across a broad front, management institutionalized only those welfare schemes that repaid indirect dividends to the owners. For example, because work accidents undercut productivity, safety campaigns to reduce the costs of industrial accidents were virtually universal. Otherwise, welfare was most evident by its absence.

Plans that paid out cash benefits were as scarce as hen's teeth. Group accident and health insurance plans might be commended on the grounds that "proper health supervision of workers pays in terms of return upon the investment, besides fulfilling broad humanitarian considerations." But even so, only a small minority were actually enrolled.[16] Even low-cost benefits such as profit sharing and stock ownership did not get very far. At least a million employees did own stock, but only a tiny fraction owned stock in the company they worked for, and employee ownership appears to have leveled off even before the Crash made it a complete mockery. Few companies added new welfare programs after 1925, and many dropped existing ones. With all the various company benefits, from health plans to pensions, added together, perhaps one in seven industrial workers was covered. The bottom line was that benefit expenditures amounted to a scant 2 percent of corporate payrolls.[17]

The most glaring absence was unemployment assistance. Although the wolf of unemployment stood at the door even in relatively good times, every business organization opposed all forms of public unemployment insurance. Most accepted the common wisdom that it would reduce "incentives toward individual industry and thrift" and, therefore, reduce "industrial efficiency." In other words, it would drive up labor costs. Their alternative was "employment stabilization," that is, planned production schedules that minimized seasonal and cyclical layoffs. But despite a brief flurry of attention after Secretary of Commerce Hoover's 1921 Unemployment Conference, interest flagged when the business cycle picked up, with the result that employment stabilization remained pinned to the drawing boards until 1929.[18]

When all was said and done, the apostles of corporate benevolence were mistaken. The separation of ownership from control did not lead to a new era of managerial responsibility for worker security. Had big businessmen fulfilled their obligations under the unwritten corporate-feudal compact, they might have converted worker resignation into loyalty, the fact of subordination into its willing acceptance. They might even have legitimated the corporate system as something akin to the feudal system. Whether that would have been historical progess, particularly in view of the rise of fascist corporatism in Europe, is another matter. But even as they tried out new corporatist experiments, they anointed their program with a telltale liberal label, "self-government in industry," and for the most part reneged on their promises. Shackled by their own obsession with reducing costs and raising profits, fortified by the postwar victory of the open shop, and trapped in a process of exploitation of their own making, they could not become the enlightened ruling class they aspired to be.

The Middle-Class Consumer Family

Although big business failed to institutionalize benevolence toward workers, it succeeded far better with the middle-class. The stereotype of the modern consumer couple emerged in the 1920s. In typical portayals, a day in the life of Mr. and Mrs. John Q. Citizen began with Mr. John Q. cranking up the family car for his pilgrimage to the downtown office, where he might manage the housewares division of a department store. Meanwhile, after sending the two children off to their suburban school, Mrs. John Q. busied herself managing the household, cleaning the new gas stove, and ordering groceries over the telephone. At midday, they attended their respective club luncheons, Rotary for him, Sorosis for her. After being reunited for dinner, the family settled in for its evening relaxation, he with the papers and radio, she with the latest women's magazine. After making plans for the weekend drive in the country and the summer vacation and switching off the new electric light, "dear" and "honey" said their goodnights.[19]

This homely image of the middle-class couple surrounded by consumer goods is too deeply ingrained in portraits of the 1920s to be sheer fantasy. It is found everywhere—in the *Saturday Evening Post*'s fond evocations of the family circle, in Sinclair Lewis' scathing satire of the self-righteous in *Babbitt* (1922), and even in Frederick Lewis Allen's sophisticated cultural retrospective *Only Yesterday* (1931). The emergence of a consumer ethic is a central theme of the single most influential book on the decade, Helen and Robert Lynd's *Middletown* (1929), which argued that automobiles, home appliances, and the cinema became consolations for the declining satisfactions of work. Though well aware of differences between the "business class" and the working class, the Lynds emphasized the growing addiction to consumer goods as a major transformation in the American way of life.[20]

Certainly, consumption transformed middle-class family life. In contrast to the old orientation toward work, production, and accumulation, the new orientation was toward leisure, consumption, and income. A presidential commission on recent social trends stressed the importance of consumption with data on the mechanization of the home, showing rapid increases in per capita consumption of washing machines (65 percent), gas (40 percent), and electricity (135 percent). Madison Avenue played on family themes in its come-ons for home appliances. A typical ad for General Electric depicted a Christmas-morning scene with Mother still in her dressing gown receiving a surprise refrigerator from Father dressed in his business suit while one child of each sex gleefully looked on.[21]

Turning the pages of *Good Housekeeping*, readers gazed upon a veritable cornucopia of General Motors cars ("a car for every purse"), Radio Corporation of America Victrolas ("his master's voice") and Kotex sanitary napkins ("the new way"). Madison Avenue modernized traditional values; democracy became the "democracy of goods," popular sovereignty became "consumer sovereignty," and the notion that an abundance of material possessions was the outward evidence of salvation—once a religious heresy—became accepted doctrine. It was not even considered blasphemy when Bruce Barton portrayed Jesus Christ as an advertising-minded businessmen; to the contrary, *The Man Nobody Knows* (1926) was an instant best-seller.[22]

The central consumer icon of the age was the automobile. From Henry Ford's humble flivvers to Al Capone's sleek limousines, the car was everywhere, even turning up in Hoover's presidential slogan "A car in every garage." No wonder—in 1925 a new Ford leaped off the assembly line every ten seconds. This rising tide of production threatened to make Ford and his fellow manufacturers into sorcerer's apprentices turning out more cars than the market could absorb. The sage of Dearborn himself coined one of the key aphorisms of the age: "Mass production requires mass consumption." Accordingly, to increase the number of car buyers Ford had already introduced the famous five-dollar day, and he kept car prices low through efficiencies in production and a network of franchised distributors. But even the hero of mass production could lose step with the times. A cranky, anti-Semitic busybody at heart, he embodied the pinched vision of smalltown values. He proclaimed that the customer could have any color "so long as it's black." It was with great reluctance that he finally caved in to the advertising mania in 1927 and introduced model changes and color preference.[23]

More and more Americans packed up their Fords and Maxwells and moved to the suburbs. Whereas railroads had tended to concentrate population in cities, the growing latticework of highways tended to disperse it to commuter suburbs. Organizations such as Better Homes preached the gospel of the suburban bungalow, and everyone from the Federation of Women's Clubs to the Bureau of Home Economics promoted the detached, single-family dwelling as the ideal home for the American family. By giving the nuclear family a stake in society, the modest suburban house was to be the modern replacement for the vanishing family farm and artisan workshop, the substitute for Jefferson's yeoman ideal. As Hoover said, "There can be no fear for a democracy or self-government or for liberty or freedom from home owners no matter how humble they may be."[24]

Hoover had a point. To the extent that a house chock full of gadgets became the measure of social status, the source of psychological satisfaction, and the index of economic well-being, consumers fell under the thrall of the great corporations. Unlike workers, whose daily contacts with management often had the palpable sting of exploitation and who could feel the compulsion to labor as a form of coercion, consumers were likely to feel the urge to buy as an exhilarating exercise in free choice. Oblivious to the psychological manipulations of advertising and the mental chains of compulsive shopping, they saw the market as a realm of freedom. It was not as if corporate managers had a hidden agenda—all they wanted was to sell their products. All the same, to the extent that the worship of consumer goods became a vital part of the culture, it was an important ideological prop of corporate power.[25]

All the eager consumer needed was money, the more the better. Consumer markets were based on the fiction of equality—everyone's dollars were the same. In the aggregate, these dollars constituted what economic sages began to call "purchasing power," and the key to a healthy economy was said to be "America's capacity to consume." Of course, the reality was that not everyone had the same number of dollars. It was left to pioneering statisticians such as W. I. King and W. C.

Mitchell to teach the twentieth century how to think in terms of national income distribution, whose reality was that the top 5 percent received between a quarter and a third of national income. The fact that some people had a lot more dollars than others was disclosed in a Brookings Institution study estimating that the top 0.1 percent of American families in 1929 had combined income equal to that of the bottom 42 percent. As more people felt the need to "keep up with the Joneses," the income ladder began to displace occupation, religion, and pedigree as the prime measure of status. In all, the level of income became the means of establishing two opposing standards: on the one hand, the equality of all income receivers regardless of gender or cultural background; and, on the other, the rank order among them.[26]

Gender roles shifted along with the new middle-class life-style. Instead of bringing home profits from selling products, the ideal husband brought home a steady salary to be deposited in a checking account from which the wife would withdraw to meet something called installment payments. Instead of following the hit-or-miss customs of her mother, the ideal housewife was supposed to be a professional homemaker. Elite women's colleges such as Vassar offered courses on "The Family as an Economic Unit"; home economists such as Christine Frederick wrote textbooks on *Household Engineering: Scientific Management in the Home* (1920); and expert product testers assisted the careful shopper by bestowing the Good Housekeeping Seal of Approval.[27]

Academic social science joined in the effort to redefine marriage in the consumer era. The key was companionship. Sociologist E. W. Burgess argued in influential works that "semi-patriarchal" marriage among native farmers and immigrant workers had broken down under the influences of premarital sex, women's emancipation, democratic values, and mass culture. He contended that a new marital bond based on egalitarian companionship had arisen to take its place. Although there was much concern about marital stress—the divorce rate reached one in six marriages by 1930 (with rates as high as 50 percent in some cities), contemporaries took comfort in high rates of remarriage. There was a flurry of interest in the idea of "companionate marriage," a purely voluntary bond that either partner was free to break at will. Although few middle-class couples went that far, the fact that they expected emotional and sexual companionship from each other marked a new norm. Instead of finding emotional support in homosocial separate spheres, couples were supposed to find it in their mates.[28]

Photography documented the grimy realities of industrial labor,
while advertising focused on middle-class leisure.

Working class: the tenement sweatshop created opportunities for male subcontractors
to exploit underpaid seamstresses, New York, ca. 1910.

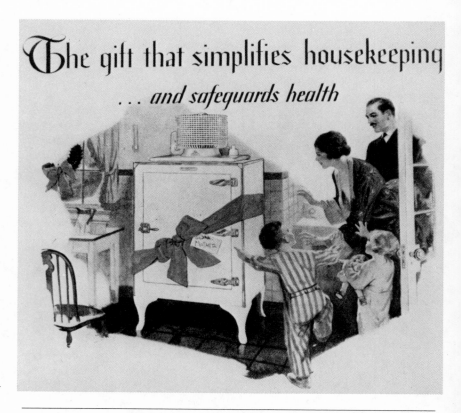

Middle class: the ideal family as portrayed by Madison Avenue in a General Electric ad from *Good Housekeeping*, December 1928.

For all the talk about equality, the consumer family locked women into a double bind. On the one hand, the housewife was a bird in the gilded cage of the modern home. Obliged by law and custom to labor at home in return for the husband's financial support, she was both chief cook and bottlewasher and chief consumer. For a generation, social reformers had been predicting the industrialization of housework, but the actual process was not their dream of liberation. Instead of taking shape in the kind of cooperative dining and cleaning arrangements envisioned by Charlotte Perkins Gilman and Edward Bellamy, it was taking place in isolated private homes under the auspices of privately owned corporations. No doubt, modern conveniences lightened the drudgery of housework; but it was also true that becoming dependent on General Electric washers, Hoover vacuums, and Procter and Gamble soap made housewives into pawns of marketing strategies under the ultimate control of corporate executives.[29]

On the other hand, the very advertising imagery that portrayed consumption as the route to freedom lured housewives into the job market. As one astute observer noted, "In an age [in which] the emphasis is on consumption, women need wages, want wages, to keep themselves afloat on the tide . . . As our pleasure philosophy takes deeper hold, as the demand for luxuries, artificially stimulated by advertising, mounts giddily higher, there is no help for it—women have to go to work." For those who did go out to work, the consequence was the double burden of housework on top of paid work, a form of exploitation in which both husbands and employers reaped advantages.[30]

Among the working classes, wives were increasingly substituting wage labor for in-home employment. The proportion of married women in the labor market edged up from 5.6 percent in 1900 to 11.7 percent in 1930; altogether, about a quarter of the adult female population took paid jobs by 1930, as women's employment continued to surge in sales and clerical jobs. Although economic compulsion was still the main motive, increasingly wives went out to work to boost family status.[31]

In truth, women faced the dilemma of choosing between the frying pan of the household and the fire of the marketplace. Picking up where Gilman had left off, feminists argued that the modern woman could not remain content as a parasitic housewife. According to Alice B. Parsons, "if the twentieth century woman is to live happily and fully she must let go the daily repetition of her housekeeping tasks and find a job outside the home."[32] But once in the outside world of work, they were shunted into lower-level "women's jobs," kept below the ceiling of 60 percent of men's earnings, and subjected to the command of an invariably male-headed bureaucracy.[33] For example, in the field of education, one of the largest employers of women, the top administrative positions were reserved for men. Likewise, in health care, the base of the occupational pyramid was composed of female nurses and kitchen staff and the bureaucratic apex of all-male hospital administrators, drug company executives, and foundation directors. Women's dependency was even built into modern medical technology; the parturient woman who rejected the "confinement" of a home birth found herself lying flat on her back on the delivery table, legs stuck awkwardly in stirrups, swooning under total anesthesia. Clearly, bureaucratic forms of social reproduction transformed but did not overthrow male dominance.[34]

Bureaucratic institutions were taking over much of the work formerly done by the family in reproducing hierarchies of class and gender. As trusts, holding companies, foundations, and other forms of corporate ownership expanded their sway, family inheritance appears to have become less important in preserving accumulated wealth. Among the middle classes, an inherited estate was taking second place to a professional education, and even immigrant workers made less use of the home as capital to generate income through boarding. Nor was the family any longer the key site for reproducing the occupational structure. In the massive shifts of population from agriculture to industry and service, plus the whirlwind of occupational mobility, most sons (70 percent in one study) did *not* follow in their father's footsteps.[35]

The nuclear family was also ceding authority to professional experts. Three or four generations earlier, when the family had been the fulcrum of social life, outside influence was more or less limited to the prying eyes of church and state. But with the ever more complex social division of labor came a growing battery of professionals—physicians, educators, child psychologists, juvenile court judges, and a host of others—to supervise social reproduction from cradle to grave. For example, the scientific sex educators of the American Social Hygiene Association provided information on human biology and planted seed money for veneral-disease education through the League of Women Voters, parent-teachers' associations, and the YWCA. Funded by the Rockefeller Bureau of Social Hygiene, these professional sex educators were a vital link between the managerial elite and mass reproduction.[36]

As the case of social hygiene suggests, the arrival of the professional expert did not involve merely a horizontal separation of social functions, but also a vertical division between elites and the mass of the population. The American Child Health Association was a case in point. Founded in 1909 by physicians and public health advocates, it worked through public schools and mass propaganda to teach proper hygiene for children to uneducated parents. With strong support from the American Medical Association and Herbert Hoover, it campaigned for the "elimination of waste" through the eradication of childhood diseases. In addition to teaching the supreme virtue of efficiency, it struggled to recapture May Day from the reds by revitalizing the ancient Anglo-Saxon festival of May 1, complete with May queens, maypoles, and prancing fauns. The culmination was a White House Conference on Child Health in 1930, the first such event on child development since 1909.[37]

Contrary to the conservative notion that the family has an eternal and universal form, human families have always displayed remarkable variety—nuclear, extended, patrilineal, matrilocal, and so on—depending on time and circumstance. By the time of the New Era, the old middle-class family was well on its way to being transformed into the new consumer family. As the necessary link between mass production and mass consumption, the consumer family was an essential element in the development of corporate capitalism. It was both the consequence of technological and economic changes and the necessary condition for those changes to go forward. It was also a key site for the transformation of relations between the sexes after the waning of separate spheres.

Instead of a smooth teleology of universal modernization in which everyone somehow gained, the evolution of the new family was full of built-in conflicts beneath the surface. For one, the rising importance of the family as a consumer unit conflicted with its declining importance in social reproduction. For better or for worse, parents increasingly had to share authority over the young with college-trained professionals whose loyalties usually extended to the strata above rather than below them. For another, the housewife may have been gaining stature as the queen of consumption, but she was losing the esteem once paid to her as the queen mother. A generation down the road, the contradiction came to a head in middle-class housewives' revolt against the "feminine mystique."[38]

Another conflict arose from the unequal distribution of income. Although a fair number of the 3 million cars sold each year eventually went to workers, few wage-earning families enjoyed the advantages of ample discretionary income.[39] At the lower rungs of the income ladder, economic insecurity remained an inescapable fact of life. Not until a portion of industrial workers won a modicum of economic security in the 1950s and 1960s did the consumer couple occupy center stage as the typical American family. For the most part, then, the consumer family of the 1920s was still a middle-class phenomenon. Amounting to no more than a quarter of the population (see table 2.1), the middle classes had the requisite level of income to buy a ticket on the treadmill of consumption, where, like the proverbial donkey chasing the carrot, the more they bought, the more they wanted to buy. Whereas the bonds of "feudal" dependence between workers and managers snapped like straws with the onset of hard times, the bonds of consumption between the middle class and the corporate elite survived the Great Depression with ease.

The Modern Ethos

From Art Deco skyscrapers to Hollywood extravaganzas, modernism increasingly set aesthetic and moral tastes. Modern paintings began to decorate Park Avenue penthouses, and a new magazine called the *New Yorker* appeared in 1925 as the weekly bible of the smart set. Modern couples practiced family planning, and modern critics applauded when books such as James Joyce's *Ulysses* (1914) finally triumphed over obscenity statutes. Modern heroes of popular culture such as baseball legend Babe Ruth and romantic film stars Mary Pickford and Douglas Fairbanks made their debuts. Modern intellectuals championed Darwin's evolution against religious superstition, and cosmopolitan values against parochial prejudice. Certainly, by comparison to 100 percent Americanism, modernism was more consistent with the material conditions of mass production/mass reproduction and was better able to bridge elite and popular culture.

Given that modernism came to be the culture of the establishment, it is ironic that its origins lay in the revolt against bourgeois convention. In the effervescent years before the First World War, avant-garde exhibitions of modern art—the Ash Can School, Cubism at the Armory Show, and the architectural iconoclasm of Frank Lloyd Wright—were nothing if not unconventional.[40] Writing for *The Masses*, harbingers of modernity such as radical siblings Max and Crystal Eastman relished every opportunity to *épater le bourgeois* on behalf of the social-justice movements of labor and the New Woman. If these movements had not suffered defeat after the war, modernism might well have remained an insurgent philosophy laced with bohemianism and peppered with radical ideas for universal equality. Even as the rebels lost their mass audience, they succeeded in forever deflating the stuffed shirts of Victorian gentility. After the biting cartoons of *The Masses*, the earthy poetry of Carl Sandburg, and the free love of Emma Goldman, it was impossible for American culture to be stuffy and complacent in the same way ever again.

With the country unable either to accept radical egalitarianism or to return to Victorianism, the stage was set for a new cultural synthesis. Elites increasingly adopted the modern sensibility as their own. They sanitized the down-and-dirty elements of lower-class culture, patronized toned-down versions of New Orleans jazz, and commercialized popular sports such as football and baseball. Abandoning Victorian certitude, they embraced the doubt and anxiety of modern art. Wealthy collectors such as Abby Aldrich Rockefeller poured their money into the Post-Impressionist and Cubist paintings that found their way into posh Manhattan galleries and eventually to the walls of the Museum of Modern Art, founded in the late 1920s. The transition did not always go smoothly. In one case, the Rockefellers destroyed a Diego Rivera mural they had commissioned for Rockefeller Center because it contained a flattering portrait of Lenin. Who said modern art was not political?[41]

The modern synthesis bridged the downtown office tower and the lower-class tenement through mass culture. Beginning with the same kind of unsavory associations as the burlesque hall, movies quickly became the prime example of mass culture, arguably a more important artistic expression than modern architecture. Like Cubist paintings, movies fractured time and space, recombining them according to the whim of the director. Although the end product gave the illusion of traditional narrative, the medium was a collage of multiple "takes," the result of countless remakes and outtakes, and, of course, it was all a fake. But then, illusion is exactly what fascinated movie audiences. Shopgirls and delivery boys may not have appreciated Picasso, but they could not get enough of Charlie Chaplin.[42]

The commercial entertainments of mass culture drew heavily upon lower-class cultures. Long before it became the national pastime and Babe Ruth became a national hero, baseball had been a workers' sport played in neighborhood sandlots. Likewise, modern recorded music drew upon the lower classes of the South. Victrolas and vacuum tubes smoothed out the rough edges and amplified the humdrum experience of family ties, lost loves, and hard traveling into something larger than life. Heroes such as Stagolee and John Henry crossed the barriers of race, and Jimmy Rogers, "the Singing Brakeman" who was the first authentic star of country music, played with black backup bands and learned to sing "The blues ain't nothing but a good man feeling bad."[43]

There was even a certain awkward attempt to include Afro-American culture in the modern synthesis. Tin Pan Alley and Broadway producers sweetened the bitterness in folk experience with the syrup of commercialization, as in the romanticized life of Afro-American street vendors portrayed in George Gershwin's ever-popular opera *Porgy and Bess* (1935), which had been a best-selling novel and then a Broadway show. The Harlem Renaissance was very much in vogue, giving a platform to writers such as Alain Locke and Zora Neale Hurston, whose names were synonymous with the New Negro. Drawing less on African roots than on American experience, writers such as Langston Hughes lamented the legacy of "a dream deferred" and won over white arbiters of taste such as Carl Van Vechten. Otherwise, it was hard for whites to drink from the bitter cup of the Afro-American experience. The fashionable white audiences who took in the all-black revue at Harlem's Cotton Club did little to disturb racist conventions. The great Irish-American dramatist Eugene O'Neill intended *Emperor Jones* (1920) as a blow against racism, but when black audiences saw his grotesque portrait of an African potentate, they laughed it off the stage.[44]

Despite such tensions, modernists of all descriptions made common cause against old-fashioned Americanism. People up and down the social scale could unite against the Know-Nothings of 100 percent Americanism, the bigots of the Ku Klux Klan, and the prudes of the Comstock code. Just as Protestant elites were expected to soft-pedal their age-old prejudices and allow a few Catholics to sing in the choir (Jews, on the other hand, were still largely excluded), so the working classes were expected to play down the parochial loyalties of the urban neighborhood, with its tangled kin networks, sports clubs, street gangs, and parish churches.[45] By the same token, regional and ethnic cultures were expected to fuse in the melting pot. Modern Americanism was becoming as homogeneous as mass advertising and as faceless as the gray stone facade of the modern skyscraper.

Yet the very consensual and functionalist elements of modernism implied the opposite. The blending of highbrow and lowbrow implied some starting point of mutual antagonism. The melting down of parochial cultures left behind the raw emotions of tribal feeling. The question of who/whom? remained fundamental wherever managers bent workers to their tasks, masculine authority presumed upon feminine subordination, and the corporate elite lorded it over the common people. For all its resonance with modern life, modernism was a mask of harmony over an internally divided society.

Take the modern view of gender. It was true that modernism blurred the boundaries between separate spheres. With the younger generation in the vanguard, the two sexes increasingly socialized together at dance halls, picture palaces, and other mass entertainments. Their unchaperoned courting rituals—jazz dancing, petting parties, and premarital sex—elicited horrified disapproval from their elders and marked the waning of the old double standard. Within marriage, the old verities were also coming apart. Social surveys confirmed what advice manuals counseled—that married couples expected erotic satisfaction from their partner. Marital sex for pleasure threw the quaint notion of "marital chastity" out the window. If, as a result, wives were more like men, the reverse was also true; that is, husbands were more like women insofar as their sexual appetites were domesticated.[46]

Another reason the old boundaries blurred is that women were undeniably in the public sphere to stay. Every time a woman voted or took part in the vast array of voluntary associations from the YWCA to the League of Women Voters, it became harder to hold the fort of feminine sentimentality. Although Maude Wood Park of the League of Women Voters, Alice Paul of the National Women's party, and Florence Kelley of the National Consumers League did not see eye to eye on many issues, their appearance in the public eye indubitably subverted notions of women's domesticity.[47] Thus in both private and public life, the modern ethos advanced toward equality between the sexes.

At the same time that it rejected Victorianism, however, modernism also rejected the radical New Woman in favor of a more docile creature who would make a home for her husband and accept her employer's commands at work. Indeed, the very meaning of masculine/feminine was being redesigned to fit corporate specifications. Edward Filene, the department store magnate, announced that the "ancient prerogatives of the patriarch" were gone because women and children were ultimately dependent not on their husbands but on great industrialists for their welfare, and because they looked for wisdom "not to their fathers but to the truths which science is discovering." Among these "truths" was freedom through consumption. Assured by a leading psychologist that modern women regarded cigarettes as a symbol of emancipation, advertising genius Edward Bernays (Freud's son-in-law) staged a "freedom march" down Fifth Avenue on Easter Sunday 1929 featuring ten young women lighting up their "torches of freedom." It was hardly the notion of freedom the New Woman had in mind.[48]

Modern views were also undoing the work of a generation of liberators in the realm of sexuality. Once a tocsin of erotic revolt to sexual radicals, Freudian psychology was now busy spinning webs of psychosexual development around male-dominated monogamy. Floyd Dell, who had once celebrated the varieties of sexual experience, now became a drum major for heterosexuality and monogamy. Under Freud's influence, he dismissed sexual experimentation as "infantile" and commended lifelong monogamy as the only really legitimate form of *Love in the Machine Age* (1930).[49] Working under similar assumptions in *Plea for Monogamy* (1923), Wilfrid Lay coined the term *hologamy* as the ultimate in erotic matrimony. To be sure, both husband and wife were entitled to sexual gratification, but since "women are unable to control or direct their own development in the erotic sphere up to the point of greatest exaltation," Lay argued, it was necessary for the man to "control the erotic sphere." Thus, under the Freudian canopy the eroticized marriage bed became a key site for reproducing gender inequality. So it would be until the sexual revolution of the 1960s came along and overthrew the "myth of the vaginal orgasm."[50]

Behavioral psychology may have harbored less of a masculine bias, but it offered little in the way of truly humane values. Setting out to chart the stormy seas of desire, sexologists from the Rockefeller Bureau of Social Hygiene probed the intimate lives of 2,200 college women. The results showed startlingly high rates of everything from masturbation (two-thirds) to homosexuality (one-quarter). A decade later a team of researchers led by Alfred Kinsey, an expert in the biology of gall wasps, quietly began the painstaking investigations that eventually produced the infamous Kinsey report. Counting up every imaginable orgasmic "outlet," from bestiality to extramarital affairs, the Kinsey team helped demystify the myth of "normal" sex as a married couple in the missionary position. But by reducing sexuality to a numbers game of counting orgasms—a kind of orgasmetrics—the early sexologists dehumanized the subject and totally ignored questions of gender and power.[51]

Modern women more and more adapted themselves to the corporate-dominated social order. The pioneering professionals who had been the prime purveyors of prewar protest were now content to consolidate past gains. Organized feminism declined as fast as organized labor. Although the National Women's party carried on the fight through the proposed Equal Rights Amendment to abolish all legal distinctions based on gender, this one-issue lobby was unable to get a complacent country excited about the "woman question." No one dared confront the issue of birth control. The League of Women Voters, the Federation of Women's Clubs, and other middle-class reform organizations evidently preferred hypocrisy to scandal; they steadfastly opposed any tinkering with the Comstock code. Neither organized women nor organized labor nor middle-class reformers backed Mary Dennett's proposed national bill to repeal legal sanctions on birth control information; it died a quick and inglorious death.[52]

Otherwise, many onetime sexual radicals abandoned a frontal attack on the old morality and sought elite support for their cause. Margaret Sanger, for example, courted the ultraestablishment American Medical Association and was soon accepting financial support from the Rockefellers, a 180-degree turnabout for the former supporter of the Industrial Workers of the World. The strategy failed to win congressional passage of a "doctors only" bill, which would have removed Comstock penalties on physicians who gave out birth control in the privacy of their own chambers. But it did underwrite the narrow, one-issue focus of Sanger's Planned Parenthood. The name of the organization was a telltale sign of the times. Couples should imitate corporate managers and put planning before passion. Thus alienation set in once again. Either sexuality was trivialized in the decadent abandon of the speakeasy, treated as an unimpassioned matter of social hygiene, or reduced to a matter of orgasmetrics. Any way one looked at it, the sexual revolution was over.[53]

By the end of the 1920s, modernism was fast becoming the leading cultural style. In the first place, it displaced old-fashioned American-ism. As the fundamentalist mood of the early years of the decade waned, there were fewer incidents of nativist violence; race riots dis-appeared; less was heard of eugenics; the Red Scare waned; and the panic over sexual anarchy passed. Second, modernism deflected the cultural insurgencies of the 1910s by moving avant-garde art from bo-hemian garrets to uptown penthouses and taming the sexual revolu-tion. As a result, the outward face of American culture grew increas-ingly impersonal. A host of signs—functionalist architecture, commercialized sports, mass entertainment, behaviorist psychology, and planned sex—pointed in that direction. America took off the mask of tribalism and put on the mask of science.

But not in the South. With demagogues such as Theodore Bilbo of Mississippi and Tom Watson of Georgia churning the waters of intol-erance, hostile critics such as H. L. Mencken had a field day denounc-ing "the Sahara of the Bozart" (that is, the desert of the *beaux arts*). Dixie's per capita income of 55 percent of the national average severely curbed mass consumption. With state government revenues averaging only thirty-three dollars per capita annually, less than half the average in the rest of the nation, education was, without question, the worst in the nation.[54] Such dismal facts provided the backdrop to the stereotype of southern backwardness: "The South—so the tale runs—is a region full of little else but lynchings, shootings, chain-gangs, poor whites, Ku Kluxers, hookworm, pellagra, and a few decayed patricians whose chief intent is to deprive the uncontaminated spiritual-singing Negro of his life and liberty."[55]

Wounded by ridicule, a small group of self-described "agrarians" re-belled against modernity altogether. Resurrecting regional pride in Confederate gallantry and Jeffersonian pastoralism, a dozen writers tried to reclaim southern honor in the famous agrarian manifesto *I'll Take My Stand* (1930). Rejecting Ford's automobiles, Dewey's philoso-phy, and Hoover's idea of progress, they wrapped themselves in a fan-tasy of eighteenth-century English-gentry life. Little wonder they were unable to mount an effective critique of modern capitalism. Ac-cording to Lillian Smith, a southern-bred writer, they failed "to recog-nize the massive dehumanization which had resulted from slavery and its progeny, sharecropping and segregation." Even their purported agrarianism was fraudulent, since they stood aloof from the actual farmers' movements of the period, which flourished in the great plains and midwestern cooperatives.[56]

Not all the southern critics of modernism were escapist. For William Faulkner, sole resident of the mythical Yoknapatawpha County, Mississippi, there was nothing worth escaping to, neither the cupidity of the New South nor the futility of the Lost Cause. Instead, Faulkner adopted a romantic pessimism in which all causes were lost. His saga of the fall of the Compson family was an allegory of the fall of the South in which romantic honor and rational pursuit of gain alike led to utter ruin. Cursed from the moment of its founding, the Compson lineage suffered irreversible decline after the Civil War. As if to prove that the whole tale signified nothing, the final collapse in *The Sound and the Fury* (1929), a title taken from a soliloquy in *Macbeth*, is a tale told by an idiot.[57]

Paradoxically, the sharpest critiques of the modern way of life came from some of the giants of modern literature. To writers steeped in humane or religious values, the worship of science amounted to a dangerous cult of hyperrationalism. One of the first to sound a warning was T. S. Eliot. Although Eliot's austere style set a tone for much of modern poetry, he rejected the core values of modernism. Having abandoned his native America for England on the eve of the First World War, he spurned science and rationalism to find solace in the medieval metaphysics of Catholicism. The modern world had become *The Waste Land* (1922) where hollow men with "headpieces filled with straw" lived in a man-made spiritual desert. Although such avowed critics of pure reason produced some immortal literature, they did not constitute an antimodern movement. To the extent that their vision was encrusted with obscurantist philosophy and paralyzing pessimism, they could hardly nurture oppositional thought.

As other critics pointed out, modernism was weak in the ways of the heart. Without the capacity for love (or hate), it lacked passion for social justice and the gift of spiritual inspiration. To fill the void, large numbers of people turned a deaf ear to the siren song of science and mass culture and, instead, harked to the offbeat notes of family and ethnic community. Parochial cultures flourished in Appalachia, the Deep South, the rural Midwest, the Hispanic Southwest, the Jewish Lower East Side, and the multitude of Little Italies and Polonias. The holiday calendar in such ethnic enclaves turned around Rosh Hashanah more than the advertisers' invention Mother's Day, around the feast of the Blessed Virgin more than Valentine's Day, around Christmas worship more than Christmas shopping.

The most significant and self-sustaining ethnic culture was African-

America. Its roots ran to the rural South, where pentecostal beliefs and evangelical fervor inspired people to "get happy" and talk in tongues, hardly the language of mass culture. Instead of carefully engineered progress, people aspired to freedom; but since overt protest against white supremacy was all but ruled out, aspirations flowed in the underground channels of folklore and religion. Trickster tales of Brer Rabbit, heroes such as John Henry, and stories of Long John's remarkable escape from the authorities kept hope alive, as did the Lord's deliverance of Daniel from the lion's den and Moses' leading the Jews into the Promised Land.

The opposite side of hope was despair. If life was mean, "bad niggers" were meaner still. Railroad Bill had no compassion for his victims, no Robin Hood intentions, or any other redeeming features: "Railroad Bill so mean an' so bad/Till he tuk ev'ything that farmer had." Likewise, Stagolee, the most famous of the bad men, killed out of wounded pride, spurning his victim's plea for mercy: "What do I care fo' yo' children, what do I care fo' yo' wife,/you taken my new Stetson hat, an' I'm goin' to take yo' life." And the best known of the female avengers, Frankie, killed Johnny for no other reason than because "he done her wrong." There was no attempt to right the wrongs of the world, only a cosmic vengefulness.[58]

Ethnic cultures gave vent to feelings that the modern ethos could not comprehend. In taking the scientific spirit to an extreme, modernism threatened to make the New Era a "brave new world" that threatened to stifle the human spirit. In taming erotic emotion, modernism sided with reason against desire. In commercializing lower-class sports and folk music, it chose packaging over authentic experience. In erecting sterile towers of glass and aluminum, it sacrificed human personality on the altar of efficiency. In every respect it was becoming the value system of the corporate establishment, and it had a far greater capacity for unifying elites and masses than did old-fashioned Yankee Protestant values. That outcome was ironic in light of the fact that modernism itself had begun as a revolt against Victorian ruling conventions, but for better or for ill, to call something "modern" was to bestow the highest of compliments.

Corporate Statecraft

To an increasing number of public figures in the New Era, the main business at hand was reshaping the state around the modern corporation. The manager-politicians and corporate diplomats who came to prominence by middecade were something of a new breed in Washington. Clearly, they differed from Wilsonian progressives, who had lost control of their regulatory agencies to the very corporate interests supposed to be the objects of regulation. But they also differed from Warren G. Harding's old-style Republicans with their laissez faire and 100 percent Americanism. Instead, they took the corporation as the key institution of contemporary life and proposed, in effect, to make the state into a kind of giant accounting firm for capitalist planning. In that they modified the liberal tradition of limited government to use the corporation as a chosen instrument of public policy, they represented a new kind of managerial liberalism.

Herbert Hoover was their hero. Having made his fortune as an industrial engineer and his reputation as the efficient organizer of wartime food production and famine relief, Hoover took up the effort to transform the liberal state where Woodrow Wilson had left it. Writing in his *American Individualism* in 1922, he argued that the key to avoiding a battle between "revolutionaries and reactionaries" was to find a middle way between laissez faire and statism. The answer lay not in the old "rugged individualism"—Hoover was quite explicit about this—but in a combination of modern, large-scale organization and traditional free-market individualism, a synthesis of managerial and liberal thinking that he called "the association idea."[59]

As a kind of unofficial prime minister, the secretary of commerce pressed his association idea upon Coolidge's cabinet. As Hoover saw it, the role of the state was to coordinate organized social groups—farmers, consumers, workers, and so on—under the umbrella of corporate enterprise. The key was to promote "self-government in industry" so that big business would take responsibility for the general welfare. Toward that end, the Federal Trade Commission gave out free advice on how to avoid antitrust prosecutions, and Hoover brought businessmen and economists to Washington in 1921 for a first-of-a-kind Conference on Unemployment. This became the model for literally hundreds of similar conferences on everything from efficiency in wood products to standardized bedsheets. Hoover also helped carve out a subordinate role for organized labor in the Railway Labor Act of 1926, which revitalized the Railway Labor Board, a tripartite organization for guaranteeing industrial peace on the railroads.[60]

The obeisance of public authorities to private businessmen had its predatory aspects. Andrew Mellon came to the Treasury from the top of a corporate empire ruled from the Pittsburgh offices of the Mellon Bank, and his name was forever linked with the flagrant return, mostly to the corporate rich, of $3.5 billion in tax rebates. This act in itself was roundly criticized as barefaced piracy that handsomely benefited the Mellon interests; but the larger issue was the dismantling of the progressive tax structure that had been erected in 1916. Reversing progressive policy, Mellon took the state out of the business of redistributing wealth downward and, instead, gave free rein to the market on its proven course of upward distribution.[61]

Otherwise, much of what the Coolidge administration did was merely negative. Coolidge himself had learned nothing of the new managerial ideas and opposed anything that smacked of state intervention. He opposed government running of the Muscle Shoals power project in the Tennessee Valley, which became the core of the Tennessee Valley Authority under Roosevelt. He twice vetoed bills pushed through Congress by the farm bloc that provided for government grain purchases to restore parity between agricultural prices and industrial goods. The parity proposal, known as McNary-Haugenism after its main congressional sponsors, enjoyed wide support in the Midwest ranging from hardscrabble farmers to manufacturers of agricultural implements. Although the idea had some business support, as the battle was played out it was reminiscent of the populist wars of the 1890s, with Coolidge playing McKinley to the farm bloc's Bryan.[62]

Long on negative stands, managerial liberalism was short on major accomplishments, but among the most important were in foreign affairs. Deep economic and cultural involvements with the rest of the world hardly made for U.S. isolation. It is true that the refusal to join the League of Nations amounted to a repudiation of Wilsonian internationalism and a costly rejection of collective security, for which the bill would come due with the Second World War. But historians have shown that abstention from the League did not mean a reversion to nineteenth-century isolation. Instead of high-profile diplomacy, the State Department preferred to work through "chosen instruments" such as the Federal Reserve Board and corporate chieftains such as Charles Dawes, Benjamin Strong, and Owen Young, who carried no formal diplomatic appointment but represented the United States just the same. Young saw the invisible hand of economic inevitability in this: "whether the United States will sit in the court of great economic movements throughout the world is not a question which the Senate, or even all of our people combined can decide. We are there . . . inescapably there."[63]

American businessmen not only sold American-made commodities in record amounts overseas, but also spread the American dream of individual achievement and mass consumption. During the war, the Creel Committee had inundated Europe with the gospel of Americanism, and Wilson had seized the new invention of radio to broadcast his appeal for peace directly to the German people over the heads of their government. Now American popular culture influenced European lifestyles. There were imitation flappers in Paris and "girl *Kultur*" in Berlin. The German version of the New Woman resembled the American woman's supposed independence, and while Freudian psychology was delving into American libido, a similar study of sexuality was under way at Magnus Hirschfeld's Institute for Sexual Science in Berlin.[64]

No aspect of American popular culture was more influential than the movies. Hollywood obtained a near monopoly on the world's consumption of motion pictures, accounting for almost all the films shown in Britain and 70 percent of those shown in France. A perceptive French critic measured the American impact: "whether as missionaries loaded with Bibles or producers well supplied with films, the Americans are equally devoted to spreading the American way of life."[65] Hunger for things American translated into demand for American commodities. According to the National Geographic Society,

> Travel where you will you can't escape American customs and fashions. Berlin flocks to its first elaborate soda fountain for nut sundaes, served by snappy soda "jerkers." American movies, automobiles, dental schools, typewriters, phonographs, and even its prize fights lead in spreading American fashions and customs throughout the world. American automobiles have spread the gospel of mass production.

Although Europe's need for American foodstuffs declined, demand for manufactured goods grew apace, helping to make the United States the world's leading exporter. By 1929 the United States accounted for 15.6 percent of all world trade. Pittsburgh steel lorded it over Essen and Birmingham, Detroit assembly lines were the model for Turin autoplants, and American electrical equipment had no trouble competing with Allgemeine Electrik Gesellschaft. The United States had replaced Britain as the workshop of the world.[66]

Wall Street was also superseding the City of London as the center of world finance. As a result of the war, the United States reversed its debtor status and became the world's largest creditor. Already by 1919, the United States enjoyed a credit balance with the rest of the world of some $3.7 billion, partly as a result of burgeoning direct investment and partly as a result of some $10 billion in loans to the Allies. Until the Depression stanched the outflow of funds, American banks continued to pour out billions in loans, a large chunk of which went to Germany so that she could pay for reparations and imports.[67]

The "diplomacy of the dollar" also superseded gunboats in Latin America. In contrast to Roosevelt, with his Big Stick, and Wilson, with his liberal crusades, the Republican presidents of the 1920s did little to expand direct American control over the hemisphere. Uncle Sam kept a paternalist posture, however, as the colossus of the North supervised several Caribbean protectorates, while Chase Bank, United Fruit, International Telephone and Telegraph, and other transnational corporations expanded their Latin American operations. The prime exception to the rule of nonintervention was Coolidge's 1927 invasion of Nicaragua, which led to the puppet dictatorship of Anastasio Somoza.[68]

As the flag followed the dollar overseas, American influence was felt in Europe as never before. The best example of corporate diplomacy was U.S. rescheduling of German reparations. Twice Germany teetered on the brink of default, and on both occasions the United States was the key player in restoring the flow of funds. In the first crisis, France had occupied the Ruhr to enforce the Versailles Treaty in the face of Germany's threatened default. To break the impasse, in 1924 the U.S. State Department gave its blessing to a team of international financiers led by Charles Dawes. A Chicago banker and get-tough industrialist, Dawes had founded the Minute Men of the Constitution to crush labor unions in his home state. Forced to be more evenhanded with foreign governments, he was able to reschedule German payments on terms acceptable both to the French and even to many arch-conservatives in the German Nationalist party.[69]

By the time the Dawes Plan ended the worst international crisis since the war, international capital flows had settled into a well-worn circular pattern. American loans enabled Germany to pay reparations that Britain and France used to offset their war debts on American accounts. The lesson was that international financial and political stability depended on continuous infusions of American loan capital.

When Germany threatened to default again in 1929, once again the State Department tacitly gave approval for Owen Young, former chief executive at GE and RCA, to reschedule reparations. For the time being, the Young Plan resolved another grave international crisis.[70]

The main reason Europeans had to listen when America talked was that Wall Street had them by the bank ledgers. Because Congress refused to cancel Allied war debts, prime lenders such as J. P. Morgan & Co. were more or less able to dictate terms to the British and French. It was not uncommon for Wall Street to act as surrogate for the U.S. government. For example, when France and Germany reached an impasse during negotiations to stabilize international trade, Benjamin Strong, chairman of the New York Federal Reserve Board, held a promised $100 million loan hostage until the French came to terms.[71]

The fact that privatized foreign policy helped stabilize postwar Europe was a tribute to the power of the American purse. But it was not a triumph of diplomatic realism. In one decision after another, the United States limited the scope of its own diplomatic action and held aloof from big-power politics. Having rejected membership in the League, it refused to participate in the World Court or to recognize the Soviet Union. Domestic politics contributed its share to the world of illusion. Because U.S. governments were not carefully balanced party blocs that rose or fell on great foreign policy questions, the American public was not forced to educate itself on world realities. For all its hard-nosed economic influence and potential diplomatic power, the United States seemed more like Alice in Wonderland.

That is the backdrop to the intense pacifism of the postwar period. Even conservative Republicans embraced progressive and, in a few cases, pacifist ideas. Popular revulsion against the senseless carnage of the Great War led to a White House Conference on the Cause and Cure of War in 1925. Initiated by women progressives such as Carrie Chapman Catt who were passionate supporters of Wilson's League, the conference was backed by the National Council for the Prevention of War and won the blessing of none other than Calvin Coolidge. Despite White House sponsorship, the final communiqué was distilled essence of progressive thought. It located the causes of war in psychological insecurity, imperialism, social inequality, profiteering, secret treaties, and nationalism, and it recommended such remedies as the outlawry of war, economic cooperation, and public education.[72]

The culmination of this feminization of foreign policy was the

Kellogg-Briand Peace Pact of 1928. Conceived by American Secretary of State Frank Kellogg as a ploy to sidestep a bilateral treaty proposed by French minister Aristide Briand, the pact was eventually signed by scores of governments, all of which solemnly pledged themselves to renounce war as an instrument of foreign policy. After the Second World War, such pacifism was mocked as a mushy-headed attempt to repeal in one fell swoop centuries of *Realpolitik* summed up in Clausewitz's dictum that war is "diplomacy by other means."[73]

Yet if blame is to be fairly apportioned, progressive internationalists were not the authors of the world of illusion in which they operated. It was self-described realists such as Henry Cabot Lodge who were chiefly responsible for keeping the United States from assuming the big power role that by rights it should have played. Nor were the illusions of the peacemakers as dangerous as those of the warmakers. Time and again during the Great War the generals of both sides had concocted grandiose plans for "final" offensives, only to see the troops bog down in the trenches. A peace pact may have been a harmless exercise in futility, but when nations chased after the chimera of glory, the consequence ran to millions of corpses. It was somehow fitting that the nightmare of war produced the dream of peace and that the calamities produced by the supremely masculine institutions of war engendered a feminine search for collective security.

As it was, the combination of corporate diplomacy and popular pacifism created an interlude of relative stability in Europe from 1924 to 1929. Business and government elites pinned their hopes for stability not on the contentious wrangling of divided parliaments but on extra-parliamentary, corporatist bargaining. Germany was the critical test of stability, and the newborn Weimar Republic started out as an uncertain combination of infant liberal institutions and untested corporatist arrangements. Given the tight linkage in Germany between social interests and the state, survival of the new parliament depended on a compact between capitalists and workers. In fact, at the end of the war, heavy industry and social democratic workers had forged a bargain of steel and muscle in support of the new regime against enemies of both the right and the left. Eventually, that bargain produced such social legislation as an eight-hour day and unemployment benefits, plus government support for export industry. Although the exclusion of peasants and of the urban lower-middle class created aggrieved groups that posed future dangers, for the time being the Weimar Republic appeared to have weathered its worst challenges.[74]

Common features of social evolution make it possible to compare Germany and the United States. The rise of corporate or "organized" capitalism and the weakening of familial and patriarchal structures posed similar questions in both countries. Both had to find a place for the industrial working class, and both wrestled with the changing relation between the sexes. By the mid-1920s, the question was not whether there would be class and gender subordinations but what form they would take. For example, in both countries women's suffrage and protective legislation had been converted from liberating reforms into props of stability in an unequal social order.[75] But although there were other similarities, what stand out are the political differences. Liberalism was fragile in Germany, but solidly entrenched in the United States. The antiauthoritarian aversion to statism plus the closely related strength of the market as against the state insulated American capitalists against corporatist bargaining. Thus instead of state-supervised bargaining between heavy industry and organized workers, managerial liberals relied on the corporations themselves to regulate the market. Instead of corporatism, the United States got *corporation*ism.

For the same reasons, the American middle classes enjoyed greater power and status than their German counterparts. In the first place, the burgeoning spirit of consumerism—consumer identity, compulsive shopping, brand loyalty—drew America's middle and lower-middle classes in city and suburb into a tacit alliance with the corporate elite as the great providers of goods and exemplars of taste. Unlike German shopkeepers and small producers, they did not feel aggrieved at being left out of corporatist bargaining between industrialists and industrial workers.

Professional segments of the middle classes also found common ground with the corporate elite. Although the very concept of professionalism supposedly implied independence from higher masters, more and more professionals became vassals of the great corporations and corporate-linked foundations. Leading universities such as Wisconsin and Chicago that had once spawned impertinent crusaders for social reform settled into training conformist cadres for the bureaucratic machine. Engineers who had prided themselves on scientific independence slid comfortably into the ranks of middle management. Economists who had once aimed at curbing corporate power sidled up to the Carnegie Corporation and the Rockefeller Foundation. With such funding sources and a boost from Commerce Secretary Hoover, the National Bureau of Economic Research began a massive study of "recent economic changes." Ostensibly nonpolitical, the purpose was to teach business how to rationalize itself, so that state intervention would be unnecessary.[76]

Even the helping professions were going hat in hand to corporate donors on a regular basis. Before the Red Scare, to scratch a social worker was to find a social reformer, but now more and more social workers sought to adapt the "maladjusted" individual to the existing environment regardless of how much injustice there was in it. At its best, the method recognized with Miriam Van Waters' *Youth in Conflict* (1925) that individual breakdown was the consequence of unbearable stresses built into modern life, the prescription for which was sympathetic probation, psychological counseling, surveillance by the juvenile court, and referral to a child guidance clinic.[77] It is certainly understandable why, in the absence of public funding, social workers of the National Social Work Council sought to open regular funding channels to Millbank, the Commonwealth Fund, and the Rockefeller Foundation. But the temptation to truckle to power raised eyebrows among the keepers of social conscience. Near the end of her career, first lady of reform Jane Addams warned a 1926 convention against looking at the profession "too steadily from the business point of view."[78]

Apart from the farm protest generated by the agricultural depression, there were no visible signs of middle-class discontent. Even in the countryside, larger farmers learned to live without parity and otherwise hankered for the same automobiles and electric lights as city folk. Consumerism and professionalism forged new links between the middle and upper ranks, tying small property tightly to the governing system. The significance of these bonds would become apparent in the Great Depression. In contrast to the alienation of the German middle classes from the republican institutions of Weimar and their readiness to embrace the fascist alternative of the Nazis, the American middle classes enjoyed a certain privileged position, which they were not ready to risk by supporting a right-wing party, let alone an entire change of regime.[79]

The position of workers in the two countries was also different. Unlike their German counterparts, U.S. industrial workers had no place at the table. Although they had a certain minimal impact on "corporate feudalism," their unions were impotent, their drinking customs were outlawed, and their immigrant origins were held in contempt. Their internal divisions by race and gender as well as by ideology and culture mocked the very idea of class solidarity. As cultural issues often were in the forefront of national campaigns, at the level of local party organizations economic issues were posed in the narrowest of bread-and-butter terms. Thus as a Democrat or Republican, the wage earner could be a full-fledged citizen and yet in his or her capacity *as a wage worker* remain a political pariah.[80]

In the absence of significant opposition, Hoover and his associates were free to modify the liberal state around the great corporations. Insofar as they preferred to coordinate the work of otherwise private citizens in preference to creating new state bureaucracies, their efforts were well within the broad liberal tradition as it came down from the nineteenth century. But insofar as they brought government into the market, they consciously abandoned laissez faire. To call this strategy of rule managerial liberalism is not to deny the conservative intent of upholding the power of corporate elites, but to capture the balance between the old ruling structures and the new forms of organized social life.

The Spirit of Utopian Capitalism

Through most of modern history, utopians and capitalists stood as mortal enemies. From the communitarians of the 1830s to the populist radicals of the 1890s, generations of utopians denounced the evils of private property in the name of the brotherhood of man. Their apocalyptic visions in which the first became last and the last became first repeatedly turned capitalist society upside down. Meanwhile, defenders of capitalism gave as good as they got. From the pioneer factory masters of the Industrial Revolution to the railway tycoons of the Gilded Age, they hailed the spirit of capitalism as the engine of human progress. Invoking Social Darwinist justifications for the status quo, they defended inequality as the best environment for the survival of the fittest.

Now during the ascendancy of the great corporation, a strange thing happened. Capitalists themselves began to sound like utopians. Normally stolid bankers such as Charles Mitchell, president of the National City Bank of New York, started talking like revolutionaries: "A revolution in industry has been taking place that is raising all classes of the population to a more equal participation in the fruits of industry, and thus, by the operation of economic law, bringing to a nearer realization the dreams of those Utopians who looked to the day when poverty would be banished."[81] One after another, apologists for capitalism looted the socialist tradition of its millennial aspirations. Walter Lippmann, a former Harvard classmate of John Reed and onetime adviser to a socialist mayor, quoted no less an authority than Lord Keynes to say that corporations themselves were waging "the battle of socialism against unlimited private profit." Going one better, Edward A. Filene said, "What the socialists dreamed of the new capitalism has made a reality."[82]

Casting aside the Social Darwinist belief in the virtue of inequality, the prophets of utopian capitalism argued that equality was both desirable and attainable. According to economist Thomas Nixon Carver, "Neither state socialism, guild socialism, sovietism, nor the ordinary cooperative society [presents] a plan of organization so well suited to the needs of the workers who desire to own their own plants as does the joint-stock corporation." With the advent of "people's capitalism," who needed socialism? In fact, "It is just as possible to realize equality under capitalism as under any other system."[83]

With capitalists waxing idealistic, social critics hardly knew what to say. For the first time in a generation, plutocrats were exempted from mainstream attack. The sharpest barbs in the Twenties were aimed not at the big bourgeoisie, but at what H. L. Mencken called the "booboisie." Sinclair Lewis sharpened his wits on middlebrow mediocrities like the hapless George F. Babbitt and the hypocrite Elmer Gantry. The most that Princetonian F. Scott Fitzgerald could muster against wealthy Jay Gatsby and his peers was that "they smashed up things and creatures and then retreated back into their money or their vast carelessness." That Fitzgerald shared the anti-Semitism, white racism, and avarice of the *nouveaux riches* whose self-destructive binges of profligacy and alcohol he imitated was a sign of the poverty of criticism in the Jazz Age. With their homeland in the grip of an acute spasm of philistinism, many intellectuals simply packed their bags and quietly stole away to sip absinthe with Gertrude Stein and Ernest Hemingway in the cafés of Montmartre.[84]

Only the most committed and toughened radicals survived the anticommunist purges early in the decade. For John Dos Passos the execution of Sacco and Vanzetti in 1927 in a case growing out of the Red Scare was a declaration of class war. For Theodore Dreiser the excesses of the period only proved the inability of tepid reform to rein in predatory wealth, preparing him for a turn toward communism in the Depression, along with luminaries such as W. E. B. DuBois. The Communist party itself went through an intense internal struggle over the issue of "American exceptionalism," which was resolved in the Comintern by the expulsion of Jay Lovestone as a heretic for espousing it. As good internationalists, the Communists believed that the survival of socialism was bound up with the survival of the Soviet Union, a fateful attachment that keyed their thinking to the interests of Soviet foreign policy and caused wrenching twists in their politics. Meanwhile, significant numbers of Jewish and Finnish immigrants remained devoted to the socialist ideal, just as a handful of unrepentant feminists with left-wing convictions, including Suzanne LaFollette and Mary Van Kleeck, kept going against all odds. But until the Depression turned things topsy-turvy, all such radical ideas survived only at the margins.[85]

Nor did the South offer any significant resistance to corporate dominance. A generation earlier, southerners would have thrown up populist objections to managerial liberalism, but now Dixie was just as hot in pursuit of the main chance as anyone else. Southern leaders spurned attacks on railroads and monopolies to indulge in the same business boosterism as the rest of the country. No one could top the Old South credentials of Harry F. Byrd, a scion of one of the first families of Virginia and governor of the Old Dominion, but he made no bones about emulating business: "The administration of government should be efficiently conducted along the lines of well organized business enterprises." Southern leaders hungered for progress, defined as industrial development and the rising real estate values of the great Florida land boom. They also improved southern schools after the war, exceeding the national average of growth in per capita expenditure; and they lent their support to crusades against the distinctively southern debilitating diseases hookworm, malaria, and pellagra. Against the backdrop of regional backwardness, such achievements moved the South toward convergence with the North.[86]

So did the impact of modern corporations. The more southern industry expanded and rationalized, the more the labor disciplines of paternalism and extreme coercion disappeared. Although the chain gang persisted in some states, not to mention in song and legend, by 1920 only one state had failed to abolish its convict lease system. Although mill owners still liked to pose as Big Daddy, paternalism was going by the boards as tobacco companies sold off their mill villages, and textile firms moved away from the old family-based employment system and toward the impersonal disciplines of incentive schemes, personnel offices, and labor spies. Flagship companies such as Dan River Mills, which had pioneered a full-scale welfare system complete with company-sponsored employee representation, relied more and more on the "stretch-out," whereby workers were forced to tend more machinery. Burlington Mills, soon to be the largest textile operation in the world, turned to college-trained supervisors and efficiency experts to bring in time study. In every respect, they trod the same path as northern industrialists.[87]

Resistance was all but ruled out for the southern Afro-American. Segregation wrapped its coils so tightly around the South that the New Negro barely showed his face in the years after the collapse of the Garvey movement and the postwar labor unrest. The NAACP's campaign against lynching bogged down and would not revive until the 1930s. The terrors of white vigilantes, Klansmen, and the chain gang were vividly portrayed in stories by Richard Wright. Although the hero of "Down by the Riverside" performs a string of noble deeds in the great Mississippi flood of 1927, he kills a white man in self-defense and is shot down like a rabbit while trying to make his escape. Like the Mississippi-born Wright, tens of thousands fled poverty and racism along the escape routes of the Great Migration, and the northward flow quickened in response to the cutoff in European immigration.[88]

Poor whites had somewhat more room to maneuver. Prominent women writers broke with the genteel tradition and the cult of the Lost Cause to write about the dogged strength of unlettered sharecroppers in such works as Ellen Glasgow's *Barren Ground* (1925). White mill hands found a chink in the owners' armor by hurling old community values against the speedup, the stopwatch, and short wages. Their protest culminated in the "revolt of the Piedmont," the most significant industrial unrest anywhere in the country in the late 1920s, which lasted until the textile workers' general strike of 1934. The men and women who fought the series of desperate and bitter strikes buried the remnants of mill-owner paternalism, while the prominence of women rebels challenged the paternalism of male workers. The presence of Communists at Gastonia and elsewhere showed that the South was not immune to modern radicalism, and the example of struggle against all odds in the midst of depression undoubtedly inspired protest elsewhere. Nonetheless, there was little permanent union organization to show for it, and segregation ensured that the poor of both races rarely made common cause under the banner of populism or any other brand of radicalism.[89]

In the absence of significant opposition, the mood in the country at large reached new heights of capitalist utopianism during the 1928 election. Once Coolidge bowed out with the terse remark "I do not choose to run," attention quickly turned to Herbert Hoover, the perfect embodiment of the aspirations of the New Era. In his speech accepting the Republican nomination, Hoover boasted in the seventh summer of prosperity: "We in America today are nearer to the final triumph over poverty than ever before in the history of any land. The poorhouse is vanishing from among us."[90] His Democratic opponent, Al Smith, did nothing to challenge the idea that the economic interests of the working poor were secure in the hands of big business. If anything, Smith outdid Hoover in kowtowing to great wealth. As governor of New York, the wiley Irishman had learned how to straddle immigrant districts and Wall Street by playing up his opposition to Prohibition while remaining solidly conservative on financial matters. His selection of John J. Raskob to chair the Democratic National Committee represented the same balancing act; Raskob was both a Catholic opponent of Prohibition and a prominent Wall Streeter. A corporate officer at General Motors, Du Pont, and Bankers Trust Company, Raskob was the epitome of everything progressive reformers and agrarian populists detested. Even so, there was nothing really surprising in Smith's choice; except for Wilson's 1916 campaign, the Democrats had not fought an election on economic reform since the Bryan crusade of 1896.

During the campaign, Hoover defended Prohibition as a noble experiment and appealed especially to small-town Protestant "drys," while Smith tried to capitalize on discontent with Prohibition by appealing to urban Catholic "wets." If Smith challenged the cultural predominance of the old Yankee Protestant elite, it was not in the name of wage earners seeking to redress the balance of power but in the name of Catholics seeking a place at the rich man's table. In the end, prosperity made the election of the Republican heir apparent a foregone conclusion. Even the normally Democratic Solid South cracked apart, with Florida, Texas, North Carolina, and Virginia going to the Republican for the first time since Reconstruction. The one hopeful sign for the Democrats was an expanded base among northern urban industrial workers, a harbinger of Democratic strength in the 1930s. But for now

Hoover's landslide was a personal triumph for the man who personified the utopian spirit of New Era capitalism.[91]

As if to avenge their humiliating defeat, Smith and Raskob decided to build the tallest building in the world. With its Art Deco design and bold vertical lines soaring 102 stories above Manhattan, the Empire State Building was intended as the crowning symbol of modern capitalism. With financial backing from the du Ponts (also the prime investors in General Motors) and Metropolitan Life Insurance, the towering skyscraper was linked to chemicals, automobiles, and insurance—the glamor industries of the era. To make way for modernity, a grand symbol of Gilded Age capitalism had to be torn down. The Waldorf-Astoria, an ornate hotel in the elaborate German Renaissance style, had hosted many a lavish event of New York high society. But just as the Astors and Livingstons were giving way to the Raskobs and Smiths, so a pleasure palace of the leisure class had to make way for an office tower of corporate bureaucrats.[92]

Demolition began in the still-flush days of August 1929, and construction took place in record time. Steel girders were set in place a mere eighty hours after being cast in Pittsburgh; each story in the central spire was an interchangeable part set atop the last; the gleaming chrome-nickel strips bracketing the windows reduced the time required for cutting the stone facing. *The Nation* exclaimed that these modern methods made the Empire State a monument to "Organization! Speed!" The developers took pains to make construction workers feel they had a stake in the project. They hired Louis Hine to photograph the "poet builders," and instead of focusing on exploitation, as in his earlier industrial photographs, he focused on heroism. In a similar vein, Al Smith flattered the craftsmen by promising to erect a tablet in their honor. No doubt the 3,000 workers employed on the project were glad enough to be working at all, but 14 men gave their lives in satisfying the demands of "speed."

By the time it was finished in 1931, the Great Depression was in full swing and only one-quarter of the building was rented. Speaking at the dedication, Franklin Roosevelt, who had replaced Smith as governor of New York, brushed aside wags who called it the "Empty State Building" and hailed it as a bright expression of faith for dark times. The *New York Times* pronounced it one of the "permanent notations of a great surge of prosperity." As the tallest building in the world, it was to New York what St. Peter's was to Rome and the Eiffel Tower was to Paris.

Hollywood could not resist appropriating such a magnificent prop for the 1933 beauty-and-the-beast classic *King Kong*. When pushy photographers seem to threaten the beauty, Kong breaks the chains of his commercial exploiters to go on a rampage that winds up atop the Empire State. In the climactic scene, Kong is killed by airborne machine-gunners and tumbles to the pavement below, coming to rest at the foot of the 102-story tombstone. The symbolism of the colossus of stone and steel towering over all else in the modern city was brought home by comparison with the Statue of Liberty; looking down from atop the observation deck, a *New Yorker* writer said that the Statue of Liberty seemed puny, like "something to throw at a cat."

It was somehow fitting that a symbol of liberty was overshadowed by a symbol of empire. The faceless megaliths rising skyward were monuments to the dominance of the modern corporation in American life and the preeminent weight of the United States in the world economy. Against such power, what was the point of utopian dreams? Great architecture, whether the amphitheaters of imperial Rome, the pyramids of the Maya, or the cathedrals of medieval Christendom, always symbolizes the dominance of ruling elites over the common run of humanity. In impressing construction workers, office workers, and common passersby with the overweening power of financiers and industrialists, the Empire State Building was no exception.

The New Era anchored American civilization firmly to corporate property and the consumer family. Whatever doubts the middle classes had once harbored about big business were overwhelmed by consumerism. Once-vital sources of working-class opposition melted away as industrial workers became dispirited and disorganized. Trivialized as the flirtatious flapper, domesticated as the queen of home consumption, and segregated on the job, the New Woman was so thoroughly tamed that the issue of equality between the sexes went underground for a generation. The South, once the great antagonist of industrial capitalism and the nursery of agrarian discontent, subdued its own lower classes and increasingly aped the business boosterism of the North. For better or for worse, not even the Great Depression or the New Deal would overturn the dominance of the great corporation.

9

Managing the Depression:
Hoover and Roosevelt

THE GREAT DEPRESSION of 1929–1939 is justly remembered as one of the watershed events of the twentieth century. It was an archetypal historical drama full of villains (Hoover and the superrich) and heroes (Roosevelt and the New Dealers). It had the pathos of Dust Bowl victims, the courage of rebel sit-down strikers, and the escapism of Hollywood musical extravaganzas. It was a reservoir of popular folklore about stockbroker suicides and Depression soup (hot water plus ketchup). Like wars and revolutions, it even changed the way people marked time. To anyone living when all the indexes hit bottom in 1932, hobo jungles and breadlines made the Roaring Twenties seem like ancient history. To anyone who survived it, the hard times of the 1930s were a psychic scar carried to the grave.[1]

Unfortunately, the mystique of the Depression obscures understanding. There is no denying that dramatic changes occurred from 1929 to 1932, but three years is simply too short a span to permit any major transformation in the fundamental life processes of a great civilization. Although capital and labor stood idle, industrial capacity and worker skills remained about the same. Although families had to make do with a third less income, basic family structure did not change. Even as corporate profits turned to losses, large capital remained intact. Given the continuities, the problems that appeared by 1932 must have arisen from social dynamics already existing in 1929. If maldistribution of wealth and social injustice existed at the depth of the Depression, they must have existed beforehand in the period of prosperity.

The Crisis of Corporate Capitalism

Perhaps the most riveting aspect of the Depression was the contradiction between poverty and abundance. Responding to Hoover's callous boast that "no one has starved," none other than *Fortune* magazine admitted that starvation had been a factor in certain cases of urban mortality, and it sent a reporter to cover the poor who were dining at garbage dumps: "As soon as the truck pulled away from the pile, all of them started digging with sticks, some with their hands, grabbing bits of food and vegetables." While people went hungry, farmers in the Midwest burned corn for fuel because marketing it did not pay. The collapse of markets for food, housing, clothes, automobiles, and radios did not mean that industry could no longer produce these commodities, but that people lacked the money to buy them. If there was a gap between capacity to produce and capacity to consume, the forces creating it had not emerged after the collapse, but before. That is what British economist John Maynard Keynes had in mind when he said, "this is not a crisis of poverty, but a crisis of abundance."[2]

The fact that there was something rotten in the state of American capitalism was utterly incomprehensible to neoclassical economists. Although Adam Smith's law of supply and demand had long since been modified to make room for the business cycle, it could not explain why this particular downturn went so deep and lasted so long. Modern-day monetarists single out a supposedly shrinking money supply as the cause, but in fact the period was one of severe price deflation and a real increase in money supply. Likewise, dogmatists of supply-side economics posit government intervention in the otherwise efficient free market; but in fact state intervention was relatively limited.[3]

One contemporary theory blamed the foreigners. President Hoover was the most prominent advocate of the idea that the United States was the victim of a "financial hurricane" that had originated in the dislocations of the First World War and then blown westward across the Atlantic. A stronger case can be made that the cessation of U.S. loans in 1931 pitched Europe over the brink. After all, in addition to becoming the world's biggest lender during the war, the United States had already developed the largest economy in the world before 1914 and was now the largest trading partner. It is hard to escape the conclusion that the United States itself was the source of the hurricane.[4]

Although the spectacular stock market crash in the fall of 1929 looked like the trigger to many at the time, in retrospect it was seen to be more symptom than cause. Sooner or later the speculative bubble had to burst. The fact that market values plunged 40 percent in a month of "Black Tuesdays" and "Black Thursdays" contributed to the rush for liquidity that marked the devastating collapse of credit, but it was not one of the deeper forces at work. The same can be said of the other events said to have triggered the Depression, such as the sharp decline in housing construction in 1928, the price deflation in agricultural commodities, or the economic nationalism of the Smoot-Hawley Tariff of 1930. Nor is it likely that all these unfortunate coincidences together caused the Depression.[5]

It took a truly original thinker in the person of John Maynard Keynes to step outside the boundaries of classical economics and to deduce from the crisis that modern capitalism lacked any built-in self-righting mechanism. It was quite possible, even probable, said Keynes, that underinvestment and low aggregate demand could continue indefinitely in a state of permanent stagnation. In the long run ("In the long run, we are all dead," he quipped), Keynesian ideas became the basis for building a new balance wheel into the capitalist economy in the form of massive state intervention through countercyclical fiscal policies and deficit spending.[6]

The only theory not taken by surprise at the time was Marxism. To the Marxists, crisis was the inevitable concomitant of capitalism. Inner contradictions in the process of capital accumulation between the forces of production (technology, skills, division of labor) and the relations of production (property, law, ideology) led to a crisis of accumulation when profits were choked off. Put another way, there came a point at which capitalists could no longer squeeze more surplus value (profits) out of wage labor. Such ideas informed a good deal of the most advanced thinking of the day even among those who refused a Marxist label.

Ever since the Depression, economists have conducted a bustling commerce in explanations borrowing from the broad traditions of neoclassical, Keynesian, or Marxian economic theory. For purposes of historical analysis, the important thing is to understand the Depression in terms of the larger flow of events. Previous depressions, from the panic of 1819 to the Long Depression of 1873–1896, had originated in the older milieu of commercial agriculture, the "first" Industrial Revolution, and dislocations in a system of international finance whose hub

was the City of London.[7] By contrast, the Great Depression of 1929–
1939 originated in seismic disturbances in the corporate economy of the
"second" Industrial Revolution, whose biggest engine was the United
States and whose financial center was Wall Street. Since the United
States was the center of the world capitalist economy, it was also the
vortex of world depression.

In the years before 1929, many Americans were so beguiled by prosperity that they imagined they had become immune to depression.
Caught up in their own rhetoric about "people's capitalism," they believed that a relatively even distribution of wealth had eliminated im-
balances between production and consumption, capital and labor, savings and investment. Under a modern version of Say's Law (supply
creates its own demand), business economists saw "purchasing power
growing out of production." Giving this theory the highest official
stamp of approval, the President's Commission on Recent Economic
Changes, which included General Electric executive Owen Young and
Wall Street Democrat John Raskob, boasted that the old-fashioned tendency toward overproduction had been eliminated by the almost insatiable appetite for goods and services from 1922 to 1929: "For the seven
years under survey a more marked balance of production-consumption
is evident." Stock prices rose in the summer of 1929 to what Irving
Fischer, head of the American Economic Association, called "a permanently high plateau." Talking like utopians, luminaries from Hoover to
Walter Lippmann argued that capitalism had already accomplished
what socialism could only promise.[8]

Never had men of such high repute had to eat their words so fast. As
conditions went from bad to worse, chastened observers took a second
look at the prosperity decade. Economists such as Stuart Chase and
George Soule began to point out that whereas wages had risen on the
order of 1 percent a year, profits had leaped 9 percent annually, with
most dividends going to the already well-to-do. Turning the hucksters
of "people's capitalism" on their head, they argued that instead of a
balance among the various parts of the economy, the years 1923–1928
were characterized by just the opposite. Soule described "a fatal lack of
balance between industrial production and popular purchasing power."
Although notions of overproduction and underconsumption were popular on the left, they were also found among engineers and industrialists who had taken to heart Henry Ford's dictum that "mass production
requires mass consumption." Among them was oil executive J. N. Pew,

who said, "If a larger share of prosperity's profits had gone to wages, there would have been more consumption and less speculation."[9]

Instead of high wages, mass production generated immense riches for giant corporations and big investors. According to a Brookings Institution study, the richest 1 percent of the population reaped a bountiful harvest of corporate dividends and tax rebates that combined with other sources to increase their disposable income nine times faster than that of the population as a whole. Subsequent research has confirmed the study's conclusion that "income was being distributed with increasing inequality, particularly in the later years of the period." What was true for income was also true for accumulated wealth. The richest 0.5 percent of individuals owned 32.4 percent of all wealth by 1929, and the 200 largest nonfinancial corporations, a scant .07 percent of all corporations, controlled half of all corporate wealth and 22 percent of national wealth. This tiny knot of giant firms grew faster in 1924–1929 than did business in general, partly through a minor merger wave. The peak year 1929 was truly the Mount Everest of inequality.[10]

So long as the corporate rich found profitable investment outlets, the economy could expand. A good part of their investment went to pay the costs of rationalization—expensive capital goods, high-priced engineers, and increased layers of supervisory personnel. Rationalization, in turn, was usually accompanied by rising productivity; output per worker in manufacturing jumped by a minimum of 43 percent across the decade. Partly for that reason, gross national product measured in constant dollars rose from $710 per capita in 1919 to $857 in 1929. That was obviously good news.[11]

The problem was what to do with the proceeds. Thanks in part to the bonanza in productivity, corporate profits rose 62 percent and dividends 65 percent in the same years 1923–1929. Unfortunately, given the maldistribution of income, it was getting harder to find profitable investments in plant and machinery to produce yet more consumer goods. When hourly wages were going up by only 8 percent and weekly earnings by even less, workers were constrained in what they could buy back from what they had produced. Middle-class consumption also had its limits, particularly given chronic farm distress, and the boundary of economic expansion was reached when markets for homes and automobiles became saturated in 1928.[12]

So it comes as no surprise that by the end of the period, investors were shifting their money from productive capital to what Hoover aptly damned as "an orgy of speculation." Huge paper empires piled up in holding companies, investment trusts, leveraged buyouts, and stocks of questionable worth bought on margin. Swindlers bilked the greedy and the gullible alike for millions in Florida swampland, and bankers of impeccable reputation paid exorbitant fees to middlemen in Latin American loan deals and pretended it was not bribery. After the slump, investment opportunities of all types—productive, speculative, or otherwise—rapidly disappeared, with the result that profits turned into net losses by 1931, and total investment fell from 16 percent of GNP in 1929 to a mere 2 percent in 1932. Keynesians stress the overriding importance of this blockage in the flow from savings to investment, and economists of all stripes concur that such a bottling up of profits (or surplus) is a knife at the throat of the capitalist system.[13]

It was certainly fatal to the capital of thousands of individuals. Actuaries worked overtime to record the failure of 4,000 banks in one twelve-month period and of 32,000 enterprises in 1932 alone. Mostly smaller firms, the casualties included shaky investment pyramids such as Samuel Insull's utilities empire, which collapsed like a house of cards. Yet virtually none of the great industrial corporations disappeared. In fact, even as profits turned to losses, corporations cannibalized assets to pay dividends. The $2 billion paid out to stockholders in 1933 was a lot less than the peak of $5.8 billion in 1929, but the fact that dividends now came out of reserves caused many to wonder about what Harvard Professor Sumner Schlichter dubbed a "dole for employers." The irony was that what was bad for the system as a whole was not necessarily bad for dominant corporations, which seemed capable of surviving like huge dinosaurs in the swamp of general stagnation.[14]

As for industrial workers, hard times were like good times, only worse. It was true that wage earners shared in the general prosperity, once the 1920–21 depression passed. Yet throughout the decade, turnover and unemployment were persistent problems, recognized by the President's Commission on Unemployment in 1921 and by the corporate promoters of employment stabilization. Hardship was especially severe for the Mexican immigrants and southern blacks who replenished the supply of common laborers after immigration restriction reduced the flow of newcomers from Europe, but virtually no wage earner was immune to insecurity. Even in the best years, 1–2 million were out of work at any given moment, and some 4 million got the sack even in the "good times" of 1928. Wage poverty was not limited to marginal workers or to minority and female victims of discrimination but afflicted millions of fully employed wage earners.[15]

Their problems were compounded by a structural shift from industry to service. Industrial capitalism was receding from its high tide after the war. Occupational statistics tell part of the tale. During the 1920s, the percentage of workers in manufacturing and mechanical jobs fell from 31.1 to 29.0 percent of total U.S. employment, and the absolute number of workers in the coal, rail, and factory nexus of the first Industrial Revolution declined on the order of 100,000 each for coal mining, steam railroads, and cotton textiles, never to recover. Coal production reached a ceiling during the First World War and was increasingly displaced by oil and gas. Pittsburgh and sister cities of the Industrial Revolution grew slightly, but they ceased to be boom towns. Although the number of blue-collar workers of all types rose in absolute terms, from 16,974,000 in 1920 to 19,272,000 in 1930, their percentage of the work force remained unchanged. (See Table 2.1.)[16]

In a society that relied so heavily on the market to allocate resources, there was no effective way to meet the welfare needs of working-class families. For all the hoopla surrounding welfare capitalism, a scant eleven firms, including General Electric and Procter and Gamble, had unemployment plans, and only a tiny segment of the better-paid workers were eligible for profit sharing and private pension plans. Worst of all, most of these schemes were jettisoned as the Depression deepened, just when they were needed most. Private charity and public relief operated on the principle that able-bodied workers should seek work, not a "dole," and this moral filter guaranteed—and was *intended* to guarantee—that need would always substantially exceed aid.[17]

Workers' own devices were no more successful. Constructed out of localized and patriarchal traditions, they were incapable of meeting the conditions of modern life. Voluntary restriction of output, for example, had become a common tactic in the shop-floor guerrilla war between worker and efficiency expert. Skilled workers believed that by slowing the pace they would increase the availability of work; as one Indiana machine operator said, "By holding back we were able to avoid the layoff." But individual and localized resistance to rationalization could not prevent structural unemployment.[18]

Harking back to a time when patriarchal families were the very center of survival, many immigrants hoisted the burdens of capitalism onto the shoulders of the family economy. The poor tended to have larger families in part because the labor of children contributed to family resources, a fact that caused much hand-wringing among charity officials and social reformers. At the most primitive level, families bartered pigs and vegetables for goods or services in a crude struggle for survival. In some cases the catch-as-catch-can system shaded over into an underground economy of working off the books and selling moonshine. "We sold a couple of quarts," said a woman from the Pennsylvania coal regions, "and got a little money that way. My mother was also the midwife for the area. She got paid in food—chickens, ducks." Corner storekeepers were drawn into the system when customers arranged to be "trusted" for delayed payment, and ward bosses granted patronage jobs, notary services, and other favors to the party faithful. In addition, backyard borrowing of food, clothing, and money was conducted on the folk principle "What goes around, comes around." Said one social worker: "the primitive communism existing among these people was a constant surprise to the visitors."[19]

Beyond kith and kin, community networks did their best to provide aid. Fraternal lodges such as the Odd Fellows provided assistance to their members in preference to the dishonor of having to take private charity or "go on the county." Mutual benefit clubs and sickness and death societies attached to ethnic parishes tried to sustain their flocks. But the combined resources of voluntary self-help paled beside the need arising from mass unemployment. However vital they were in maintaining morale, in the end these parochial institutions were more appropriate to the localism and small-scale production of the nineteenth century than to the mass production of the twentieth.

The result of all these elements combined—overproduction, maldistribution, speculation, inadequate welfare—was a crisis waiting to happen. The crux of the problem was that the laboring masses had too little income to purchase the fruits of their rising productivity, while the corporate rich had too much capital to invest profitably. As the gap between capacity to produce and capacity to consume grew ever wider, the Depression yielded a fearsome picture of the fateful connections between progress and poverty. Although the plunging indexes of economic decline gave the appearance of an abrupt fall from grace, the crisis stemmed from deep-seated problems in the world capitalist economy. Keynesians put the matter in terms of an inbred tendency toward stagnation that only government intervention could correct, while the tiny knot of Marxists posed it in terms of the internal contradictions of a system geared to production for profit, not use. As economist Lewis Corey wrote, following Marx, "Abundance creates scarcity because abundance becomes relatively unprofitable. Thus under capitalism production appears as a malevolent fate: man is enslaved and tormented by his own material creations."[20] Under either interpretation, the causes were built into the capitalist system, and it was no accident that the two most advanced economies, those of the United States and Germany, were the two hardest hit. Clearly, there was a dangerous imbalance between the increasingly socialized forms of mass production/mass reproduction and the still-private forms of ownership and control.

Whatever the causes of the Depression, the main long-term consequence in the United States was to compel a reckoning with liberty. From the American Revolution on, liberty and property had been linked as nowhere else, and the relationship was reconfirmed with every turn in the evolution of the liberal state: liberty of contract and laissez faire in the Gilded Age, liberty and empire in the Spanish-American War, liberty and the Fourteen Points in the First World War. Despite inroads on the reign of profit in the Progressive Era, the New Era handed leadership over to the great corporations.

The worse the Depression became, however, the more Americans began to wonder whether unbridled liberty for private enterprise had not resulted in a denial of liberty for the majority. Certainly for the millions who lost jobs, homes, and farms, it was a wrenching and cruel experience that forever set off the Depression generation from preceding ones. At the extreme, the contrast between *rentiers* clipping dividend coupons and the unemployed rummaging through garbage dumps presented an obscene spectacle that pierced the armor of New Era business boosterism, punctured America's self-image as the land of equal opportunity, and punched holes in the theory of laissez faire. To a small but growing band of social critics, the time had come to change the basic relation between state and society. In *Tragic America* in 1931, Theodore Dreiser wrote that "the haphazard anarchy of the whole regime of Capitalism" required "a fundamental change in our government."[21] Few went that far, but increasing numbers of the elite came to realize that if they were to preserve their power, if stability was to be achieved, if continuity with the past was to be maintained, then, paradoxically, the liberal state would have to be modified. Otherwise, who knew what worse things lay in store?

The Ordeal of Herbert Hoover

Before the Depression had run its course, American government would have changed more than it had since Reconstruction. Centralization of power in Washington, establishment of the federal bureaucracy as the "fourth branch" of government, unprecedented state regulation of the economy, the beginnings of the welfare state, and recognition of business and labor as great estates of the realm—all this amounted to a significant restructuring of the liberal state. Most of the credit for this great transformation has gone to the New Deal, for which Franklin Delano Roosevelt has been permanently enshrined in the pantheon of national heroes. Herbert Hoover, meanwhile, has languished in political purgatory for being the president who fiddled while America burned.[22]

Folk memory is undoubtedly correct in remembering Roosevelt for his bold initiatives to aid the poor family on relief and in remembering Hoover for his careful stratagems to aid the rich family on dividends. For these reasons Roosevelt is the patron saint of modern liberalism, while Hoover is a founding father of modern conservatism. But surely, so great a transformation must have been the result of more than the accident of presidential personality. The pressure to change came from historical tides a president could swim with or against but could not escape. Major structural changes in the relation between state and society depended on institutional and ideological factors beyond the control of whoever happened to occupy the White House.

From this perspective, it appears that both men have been poorly served by folk memory. Roosevelt got more credit than he deserved for managing the Depression, which did not end until the Second World War, and Hoover got too little credit for his unprecedented interventions in the economy. Despite glaring differences between the paternalist Democrat and the self-made Republican and between the political coalitions behind them, both recognized the urgent need for changing state structures and policies. Their different solutions fall well within the frame of saving capitalism by changing the liberal state. Both men must be recognized in some measure as architects of the modern system of government.[23]

The irony of Hoover's consignment to purgatory is that, at the outset, no one seemed better prepared to cope with the Depression. Having just won the presidency by one of the largest margins in history, the man who had built a mining empire in Asia, fed Europe's starving war victims, and sponsored the 1921 Unemployment Conference seemed perfectly positioned to chart the best course around economic dislocation and human suffering. The key to the ordeal that followed— to Hoover's few successes and his many failures—lies in the two political traditions he represented.

One was modern managerial liberalism, a governing strategy of which Hoover himself was the prime architect. No one better represented the idea of state assistance to capitalist planning. From his expert management of the wartime Food Administration to his promotion of trade associations as secretary of commerce, the energetic engineer did more than any other single official to align government policy with an increasingly bureaucratic, mass society. The other tradition was nineteenth-century self-government, into which Hoover was born in West Branch, Iowa, on August 11, 1874. The orphan son of a Quaker evangelist mother and a blacksmith-merchant father, he was raised by relatives in the West, but he never forgot the small-town ideal of Protestant self-reliance. As president he was still talking about "the vision of the millions of homes of the type which I knew as a boy." [24]

As the Quaker small producer grew into the organization man, he developed a dogmatic faith in American innocence. Rejecting the Christian evangelical belief in original sin, he embraced the frontier myth of original innocence, the belief that a man could always start from scratch and achieve independence, provided he had initiative and ambition. Unlike members of the class-ridden societies of Europe, Americans were not held in the bondage of wage poverty, and they had "a distaste for the very expression 'class.'" [25] Indeed, independence was a critical part of what it meant to be a man. Moving in the all-male worlds of engineering and government bureaucracy, Hoover fully accepted the conventional view of woman's place. His wife, Lou, the daughter of a modest Iowa banker, remained almost invisible as First Lady.

To Hoover and his associates, the challenge of the Depression was to preserve the spirit of independence in an age of bureaucratic organization. To keep America's imperiled innocence from falling victim to either autocracy or communism, the New Era administrators almost welcomed the opportunity to modernize the American system of self-government by enlisting corporations, trade and professional associations, mass media, and other aspects of modern life in the battle for what Hoover had called in his 1928 campaign "the final triumph over poverty." [26]

The evolution of federal farm programs provided the best example of that transformation under Hoover and the strongest evidence for bracketing him with Roosevelt. Before Hoover, there was scarcely any federal aid to farmers, notwithstanding five decades of farm protest stretching back to the populists and the Grangers. After Roosevelt, the federal government was a silent partner in virtually every successful farm enterprise in the land.

State intervention developed against the backdrop of the protracted decline of the family farmer. The golden age of the wheat, corn, and dairy farmers of the Midwest and great plains came to a dreary end with the collapse of the wartime boom in food exports. As European production resumed, American agricultural exports fell from an index peak of 253 in 1921 to a dismal 94 in 1929. With increased competition in world markets, the price of a bushel of wheat fell from $2.19 in 1919 to $1.05 in 1929, and a similar decline affected corn, cotton, and other export crops. Beset by these devastating price declines, the farm economy settled into chronic depression.[27]

Struggling to hold on to their way of life, family farmers turned to a relatively new source of energy—petroleum. In the forms of fertilizer and gasoline, petroleum fueled farm mechanization (the number of tractors and trucks increased tenfold from 1918 to 1930). The result was increased production that depressed prices still further. Even worse, it required debts and mortgages that put farmers at the mercy of implement firms and banks. Similarly, the eagerness for automobiles to break out of rural isolation only increased farmers' dependence on the city.[28]

The intensification of the vicious cycle that had afflicted agriculture since the late nineteenth century made a mockery of the goal of family independence. The dreams of countless Yankee, German, and Scandinavian pioneers in the western Great Lakes states, the middle prairies of Iowa, and the high plains of the Dakotas went sour as the proportion of tenants among farm proprietors in the midwestern heartland of the yeoman rose above 40 percent. With tenants already a large majority in the South, the ratio rose to almost 1:1 for the country as a whole in 1930. Having peaked during the First World War at over 32 million, the farm population declined thereafter in absolute terms for the first time in American history. Every foreclosure and every departure of a son or daughter for the city was another drop of blood in the slow hemorrhage of the Jeffersonian ideal.[29]

The Depression accelerated the dispossession of the small farmer.

Despite the temporary return of recent migrants unable to find work in the city, structural trends quickened. Collapsing corn prices and mounting bank failures were compounded by a crippling drought. Fleeing the South, many black sharecroppers whose families had been established on their little plots since Reconstruction now pulled up stakes and headed North along with Richard Wright's autobiographical *Black Boy* (1945), while thousands of poor whites joined the westward stream of "Okies" and "Arkies" like the fictional Joad family in John Steinbeck's *Grapes of Wrath* (1939). Some remained behind to be immortalized in Walker Evans' haunting images of haggard tenants in *Let Us Now Praise Famous Men* (1939).

In the preindustrial era, such men and women would have swelled the ranks of the rural proletariat. In fact, wage labor had become crucial to such up-and-coming sectors as the fruit and vegetable enterprises in California's San Fernando Valley, where large-scale agribusinessmen paid notoriously low wages in labor-intensive operations to migrant workers, many of them of Latino extraction. Lincoln would have been shocked to find that hired hands in Illinois accounted for a third of male farm labor. But outside the Deep South and the western agribusiness valleys, the agrarian middle class was dug in deep. Owing to the lack of jobs and mechanization, the number of agricultural wage earners in the country as a whole actually dropped during the Depression.[30]

One route to survival popular among Scandinavians of the Midwest was to pool their capital in cooperatives. At a time when trade union membership fell precipitously, farm co-ops boomed to the point that combined membership reached some 3 million in the late 1920s, jumping fivefold from 1915. Otherwise, farmers obeyed the old law of the market, "Grow or die." Their main strategy was increased capitalization of the family enterprise. While the number of middle-sized farms declined, the number of large ones increased for highly capitalized farmers well connected to rural banks, close to agricultural extension services, and able to afford the increasingly costly farm machinery.[31]

It was these farmers who benefited most under both Hoover and Roosevelt. The Agricultural Marketing Act of 1929 was Hoover's answer to agrarian populism. For decades farmers had put forward a string of proposals for farm credits, free silver, state-owned railroads and granaries, and, in the 1920s, the system of government price supports known as McNary-Haugenism. All these measures were intended to bolster the independent producer against the overweening market power of large-scale capitalist enterprise—railroads, food-processing firms, farm implement corporations, mortgage companies, and banks. Now at last, the country had a president ready to use state power in the marketplace.

To the disappointment of the small farmer, however, Hoover used his power to align agricultural marketing with corporate practices. He prevailed upon Congress to set up the Federal Farm Board, which spawned a set of semipublic corporations to spend $500 million on open-market purchases of surplus commodities. Just as the wartime Food Administration had looked to the corporate world for organizational models, so now Hoover appointed the president of International Harvester as head of the Farm Board. By 1930 one of its subdivisions, the Wheat Stabilization Corporation, was buying a quarter of the U.S. wheat crop to the cheers of the conservative leaders of the American Farm Bureau, who hoped the government would lead the farm cooperatives toward the paradise of higher prices. The cheering stopped when it became apparent that the Farm Board was unable to halt the downward plunge of food prices.[32]

All the same, Hoover had opened a door for Roosevelt's Agricultural Adjustment Act. Insofar as both Hoover and Roosevelt treated "Agriculture" as a monolithic bloc to be balanced with "Industry," and insofar as they set up state bureaucracies outside the control of Congress and alien to the Constitution, both administrations took steps toward corporatism. To the small farmer, it was a bitter irony that when state intervention arrived after two generations of struggle, it favored the larger farm enterprises over the small and hastened the integration of the farm economy into the corporate-dominated world of agribusiness.[33]

A second example of corporatist continuity was the Reconstruction Finance Corporation (RFC). When Hoover became convinced in 1932 that a credit shortage prevented recovery, he asked Congress to set up the RFC with authority to loan public money to financially strapped banks, railroads, and insurance companies. By the end of the year, it had loaned out almost $2 billion in what one wit described as "feeding the sparrows by feeding the horses." Also dubbed "trickle-down" economics, it proved a spectacular failure. It was not credit that the economy needed as much as profitable investment opportunities, and, in any case, the loans were too little too late to stave off the virtual collapse of the banking industry. Bank failures occurred at the rate of ten per day in the winter of 1932–33, and as a means of protecting remaining assets, the entire banking system had closed down by the time Roosevelt took office in March. Undoubtedly, that was the single worst moment in the entire history of American capitalism. Given the failure of the RFC to prevent the banking crisis, the remarkable thing is that FDR did not kill the RFC the way Jackson had killed the "monster" Bank of the United States. To the contrary, the Roosevelt administration expanded the RFC until it became what amounted to the biggest bank in the world.[34]

Hoover also used federal powers to help corporations manage their way to recovery. Although this approach was justified under the euphemism "self-government in industry," it depended on federal government acting as a clearinghouse where corporations could coordinate their response to collapsing markets in order to restore the balance between mass production and mass consumption. Prominent industrialists trooped to well-publicized White House conferences and emerged uttering solemn pledges to maintain wages and employment against the deflationary tide. Broadcasting the message of confidence through all the channels of modern mass communication, Hoover embodied the modern ethos and went further toward state intervention than any of his peacetime predecessors.

None of this pleased acolytes of the old orthodoxy. Laissez-faire liberalism found advocates in "liquidationists" such as Secretary of the Treasury Andrew Mellon, who believed in letting the depression run its own course, and in blueblooded financiers at the International Chamber of Commerce and the National Foreign Trade Council, where hopes for recovery were pinned on the gold standard. Objecting to any new departure, a Chase Manhattan banker stubbornly invoked Say's Law against the inconvenient fact of overproduction: "The old economics saw purchasing power growing out of production, and it held that a good equilibrium among the various elements of production meant large aggregate purchasing power, which would take care of large aggregate production." In the early stages of the Depression, the old economics still commanded a majority in Congress, whose Republican leaders resorted to a tried-and-true method of protecting American industry by pushing through the highly protectionist Smoot-Hawley Tariff in 1930.[35]

Nonetheless, the Hoover administration forged ahead with its managerial innovations. As construction of residential property fell by 95 percent, foreclosures rose fivefold above a typical pre-Depression year to the point that fully half of all home mortages in the country were technically in default by the spring of 1933. Hoover made his typical response of calling a White House conference, and the resulting twelve-volume technical report on home building and home ownership drummed home the notion that "the scientific method must be brought to bear on housing and homemaking."[36]

The closest Hoover actually came to building houses was the creation of the Home Loan Bank Board. Signed into law in July 1932, the Home Loan Bank became the first federal housing assistance effort. Believing that direct government aid to needy people would destroy individual initiative, the board did not assist homeless families but, instead, loaned money to building and loan associations, banks, and mortgage companies through the RFC. Rent subsidies, public housing, and a moratorium on mortgage foreclosures were all out of the question. In the New Era, what came first was assistance to financial institutions in their effort to accumulate capital.[37]

The same dogma of individual self-reliance prevented Hoover from giving direct relief to the poor. Winning the battle against poverty had been the New Era's greatest boast, and, appropriately, Hoover's relief policy was its greatest failure. Ironically, Hoover initially seemed to have exactly the right combination of humanitarianism and organizational ability, especially when he overruled "leave-it-alone liquidationists" to take vigorous preemptive action against the unemployment everyone knew was coming. But it was not until 1932 that he secured the Relief and Construction Act, and, even then, small-scale aid came in the form of RFC loans to states, not direct relief to individuals. When he did take direct action, it was sometimes punitive and shot through with ethnic prejudice. To ease the glut of labor, for example, he summarily deported 400,000 Mexican-Americans, many of whom had only recently been welcomed as braceros. Among these were 80,000 involuntary deportees, some of whom were U.S. citizens by birth.[38]

Hoover's biggest mistake was to place his main hope in corporate self-management. He had no trouble securing pledges from industrialists to avoid strikes and lockouts, maintain wage levels, provide employer relief, and share the work. The trouble was that the promises were largely meaningless. Welfare capitalism proved to be a cruel disappointment as companies jettisoned their meager unemployment payments, pensions, and health benefits. In the case of wage maintenance, a few companies with well-developed internal labor markets held the line on wages for a year or two, but U.S. Steel's abandonment of the practice in 1931 was a signal for a general retreat.[39]

As unemployment exceeded 12 million in 1932, the campaign to "Share the Work" gained increasing prominence. Championed by Standard Oil executive Walter Teagle, the six-hour day or the four-day week won the endorsement of a host of business organizations, including the National Association of Manufacturers and the U.S. Chamber of Commerce. Although businessmen talked to the public at large about combatting unemployment, all the talk among themselves was about efficiency. *Business Week*, for example, argued in favor of reducing hours on the grounds that it would lead to increased return on investment through elimination of meal periods, increased rate of operation, labor efficiencies, and greater unit productivity. To the extent that firms actually rationalized the labor process, they heaped structural unemployment atop cyclical unemployment. Although production would finally recover its former level in 1937, unemployment remained at the Depression level of 15 percent.[40]

Hoover did his best to avoid federal responsibility for relief. Determined to "maintain the sound American tradition" and shun the statist paternalism of European bureaucracies, he promoted corporate paternalism instead. He appointed the head of the Rockefeller Foundation and the head of American Telephone and Telegraph to run volunteer relief committees that had no money to give to the poor but instead sponsored social surveys, recommended ideal family budgets, and appealed to the benevolence of women's clubs, garden clubs, and the Business and Professional Women's Association. The volunteer committees put efficiency expert Lillian Gilbreth on the radio to urge the nation's 30 million housewives to hire handymen to "spruce-up-the-home." During one fundraising drive cosponsored by the Community Chest, the head of Hoover's relief organization said: "America will feel the thrill of a great spiritual experience." The mix of old-fashioned self-reliance and modern management was proving a cruel dogma.[41]

Holding fast to that philosophy did more than anything else to destroy Hoover's leadership. Besides squandering his popularity with the people, it loaded the guns of congressional opponents. Expressing outrage that the Department of Agriculture was providing millions of dollars for farmers to buy cattle feed but nothing to feed hungry people, Nebraska progressive George Norris quipped: "Blessed be those who starve while the asses and mules are fed, for they will be buried at public expense." Another senator mockingly invoked Hoover's former relief work in the Russian famine to suggest that America's unemployed might be better fed if they moved to Russia.[42] Hoover's response to depression measured exactly how far liberal ideas had come since the heyday of laissez faire; although his efforts were dismissed as too little too late, in fact no other president had done so much so soon. But his failure by 1932 measured how far liberal ideas still had to go.

Changing of the Guard

By the 1932 election, the country had endured three years of ever-worsening depression, and everywhere the ranks of the poor were growing. As the army of the unemployed swelled to more than 12 million, the worm of fear turned ever deeper in the soul. A steelworker from the Edgar Thompson plant reminisced: "Even the engineers were laid off, the plant guards were laid off. There was no work. They were down completely. And the plant guards' positions were taken over by the supervision. There was no security, absolutely none!"[43] Cast adrift, migrant workers "rode the rods" between hobo jungles. Poet Stephen Benet described the plight of the young drifters

> Who ride the blinds and the box-cars from jail to jail,
> Burnt in their youth like cinders of hot smokestacks,
> Learning the thief's crouch and the cadger's whine,
> Dishonored, abandoned, disinherited.[44]

In the battle against poverty, it looked as though poverty was winning.

With people reduced to selling apples or begging for work, the increase in poverty made a mockery of the consumer family ideal. A growing number of families consisted of male breadwinners who could not afford bread and female homemakers who could not make a home without relief. As evictions drove thousands from their homes, squatters set up housekeeping in shantytowns they dubbed "Hoovervilles." *Fortune* magazine reported that after welfare cuts in St. Louis, "large numbers of the destitute have been living in refuse dumps along the river where they build shacks and dig in the dump for food." Visiting the dump in Youngstown, Ohio, a journalist reported that, in the stench of decaying garbage, "I found that there were more women than men—gathering food for their families."[45]

Though a great annoyance to authorities, marginal men and women were no force of revolt. Drifters, tramps, and garbage pickers were easily dispatched by the railroad "dick" and the mean old judge of the Woody Guthrie song "Hard Travellin'" who liked to hand out "ninety days for vagrancy." To the Irish scrubwoman, Italian street sweeper, and Afro-American sharecropper, poverty seemed an implacable fate, not the sort of thing to be overcome by joining some radical organization. Contrary to romanticized notions about the radicalism of people with nothing left to lose, the most destitute were least likely to revolt.

Industrial workers were not in a rebel mood, either. Shell-shocked by unemployment, they remained for a long time in the supine position in which the 1920s had left them. Having suffered devastating defeats in 1919–1922, trade unions had lost ground until they enrolled fewer than 3 million members. Attracted from opposite sides by ethnic tribalism and mass culture, workers grew less conscious of class interests, which led to a decline in radicalism and a cessation of third-party ventures after 1924. Once-bold AFL chieftains grew passive under the leadership of William Green, who preached efficiency and cooperation with management. Typically, the panjandrums of organized labor treated their offices as lucrative sinecures, or else lapsed into outright racketeering. Either way, they appeared complacent and corrupt even to a prolabor writer such as Louis Adamic, who found them "prosperous-looking, Babbitt-like . . . vast-bellied, with gold watch-chains across their paunches and stickpins in their ties."[46]

One of the rare bright spots for unions was the passage of the Norris-Laguardia Act in 1932. The legislation significantly restricted court injunctions against striking and picketing and outlawed the yellow-dog contract. Although the act fulfilled the AFL's long-sought objective of reducing state intervention, the intent of Congress was not to promote trade unionism per se, but to encourage labor stability in industrial relations as an aid to economic recovery. In any case, the general picture was bleak, indeed. Thoroughly defanged and all but absent from mass production, organized labor retained strength only in the building trades, where the precipitous decline in construction jobs all but ruled out strike action. Accustomed to chronic insecurity, working-class families simply tightened their belts a notch and somehow made do.[47]

By the third year of want, however, people were running out of notches. The first signs of protest came from the farmers of the Midwest. As commodity prices plummeted in 1931, the simmering discontent of the distressed 1920s boiled over in open protest. Adhering to a radical populist tradition, midwestern branches of the Farmers Union began to withold products from the market and foment a farm strike:

> Let's call a Farmer's Holiday
> A Holiday let's hold.
> We'll eat our wheat and ham and eggs
> And let them eat their gold.

The tide of direct action rolled outward from Iowa across the upper great plains, where crowds blocked roads, stopped trains, halted foreclosures, and issued the old populist war cry, "Raise less corn and more hell."[48]

Conditions caused even the American Farm Bureau to back away from its corporate connections, and all the major farm organizations came to support federal action to inflate prices. By March 1933, the more radical Farmers Union was calling for a moratorium on debt repayment and an alliance with organized labor because both were "exploited by the capitalistic owners of the means of production and distribution." The traditions of agrarian socialism and prairie populism embodied in the Non-Partisan League were also evident in Minnesota's moratorium on farm foreclosures and North Dakota's creation of a state bank. The specter of agrarian class conflict was appearing once again.[49]

Meanwhile, workers were also beginning to stir. The most convincing sign of discontent was the Bonus March of 1932. The idea for a veterans' march on Washington came out of an abortive hunger march in which Communists had played a leading role. As with their organization of unemployed councils at the same time, Communists failed to generate a large following of their own, but their militancy proved infectious. When unemployed war veterans in Portland, Oregon, vowed to march across the continent in the spring of 1932 to demand early payment of a promised bonus for wartime service, they captured the imagination of workers everywhere, and the Bonus Expeditionary Force was born.[50]

As the Bonus Marchers rolled across the Continental Divide in commandeered boxcars, they gained support from a wide array of disgruntled workers ranging from American Legionnaires to Communists.

Their claim to a public pension was modest enough, but their tactics harked back to the radical army of redressers who marched in 1894 under "General" Jacob Coxey. Ultimately, their roots ran back through the Whitecappers and vigilantes of the nineteenth century to the Stamp Act rioters and backcountry Regulators of the Revolutionary era. But far from seeking to overthrow the Constitution, they marched under the protection of the Bill of Rights, lawfully petitioning Congress for a redress of grievances. When the legislators failed to pass a bonus bill, many marchers vowed to remain in Washington until their demand was met.[51]

Peaceable intent did not stop jittery officials from treating them as incipient revolutionaries. Among the more ludicrous reports out of the army's counterintelligence division G-2 was one from Fort Sam Houston blaming the march on a Communist-Jewish conspiracy financed by the head of the Metro-Goldwyn-Mayer movie studios! Federal authorities interpreted the vow to remain in the capital as radical defiance of the law and began desperately trying to get rid of them. Washington's chief of police called upon the army to take its secret counterrevolutionary War Plans White off the shelf and prepare to put down the purported threat to the Constitution.[52]

As a siege mentality increasingly gripped official Washington, a scuffle in which police killed two marchers triggered the president's decision to end the encampment. On advice from the secretaries of war and treasury, Hoover summoned up the might of the U.S. Army, and in a matter of hours "the battle of Anacostia Flats" was over.[53] If there was a threat to the Constitution, it came not from the veterans but from the government itself. The spectacle of General Douglas MacArthur astride a white horse leading a bayonet charge against men who wore the uniform of the United States did not look much like defense of the people's liberty. In the end, the episode only deepened the crisis of confidence in the ability of Hoover's government to respond to the mass suffering of the Depression.

Government overreaction was one sign of the spasm of red scare that gripped conservatives in the hard winter of 1932–33. Adopting a crude economic determinism, many reasoned that bread lines meant barricades, and the War Department was nervous enough to dust off its counterrevolutionary war plans and issue instructions to military commanders and national guardsmen on how to put down race riots and demonstrations by the unemployed. At the local level, authorities mistook tramps for political insurgents, confused Communist-led unemployed councils with revolutionary cells, and worried that Communist involvement in the defense of the Scottsboro Boys, Negro youths accused of rape, presaged a Negro revolt. As one veteran Socialist ruefully quipped, "You have more Bolshevism among the bankers to-day than the hod carriers, I think."[54]

Despite anticommunist alarm, there was no revolution on the horizon. Not only was working-class protest weak, but the other grand questions of social transformation—equality between the sexes and between the races—were simply absent from the agenda at the onset of the Depression. Nor were fundamental matters of family life and property relations under attack. Since the essence of revolutionary consciousness is a sense that an old order is giving way to a new—that everything is up for grabs—then failure to confront the absence of these social issues precluded a mass radical response to depression.

But conservative paranoia was well founded in one respect—popular faith in existing authority was wearing thin. Never mind workers' revolution; people were fed up with Prohibition. By criminalizing liquor, the Eighteenth Amendment had only ensured that everyone who visited a speakeasy or patronized a rumrunner was violating the Constitution. As gangsters fought for control of the illicit traffic in liquor, the 1929 St. Valentine's Day Massacre (Al Capone's way of eliminating rivals from his crime empire in Cicero, Illinois) gave an object lesson in the amendment's failure to improve the nation's morals. Worried that if widespread lawbreaking continued much longer "our whole system of self-government will crumble," Hoover appointed the Wickersham Commission to study the problem. The commission concluded that as long as the law was "enforced against the insignificant while the wealthy enjoy immunity," the double standard would cause disrespect for the law.[55]

Seeking to salvage their moral leadership from the wreckage of Prohibition, members of the elite began to campaign for repeal. Wealthy Catholics such as John J. Raskob and the du Ponts had for years bankrolled the Association against the Prohibition Amendment and had supported "wet" Al Smith in the 1928 election. The Women's Organization for National Prohibition Reform, founded by New York society matron Pauline Sabine in 1929, soon grew to be the largest of the repeal groups. By the time of the 1932 campaign, the issue of repeal outweighed the fact of the Depression at both the Republican and Democratic conventions. Wedded to what Hoover called "the experiment noble in purpose," Republicans promised to improve the system, whereas Democrats called for its abandonment. In total exasperation, John Dewey wrote: "Here we are in the midst of the greatest crisis since the Civil War and the only thing the two national parties seem to want to debate is booze."[56]

Of course, that was only normal for American presidential elections. Unlike European parliamentary elections, the purpose of America's quadrennial rites of November is not to choose between alternative strategies of governing but to find the center point of national consensus. Even by these low standards, the election of 1932 was remarkable for blurring the issues. Despite growing popular disaffection, neither party offered any bold new vision of economic recovery. Hoover steadfastly held to the theory of the depression's foreign origins and to the dogma of self-reliance, while Roosevelt made speeches denouncing the incumbent for reckless spending. Calling for a 25 percent cut in federal outlays—a pointed irony in light of his future deficits—he said: "I accuse the present Administration of being the greatest spending Administration in peace times in all our history."[57]

Confusion over program tended to highlight the importance of symbolism and personality. As a self-made man of the midwestern small-town middle class, Hoover had raised himself up by dint of intense self-discipline and a degree from Stanford to become a wealthy mining engineer. Awkward in front of crowds, he felt most at home in the upper reaches of the corporate and government bureaucracies. Cautious to a fault, he believed that the times required prudent planning, so as not to crush the already-fragile state of business confidence. Instead of emphasizing the radical departure of his unprecedented Reconstruction Finance Corporation, he said: "The essential thing is that we should build soundly and solidly for the future." Instead of invoking the revolutionary heritage of the Declaration of Independence, he made a pilgrimage to Valley Forge on May 30, 1931, where he recalled "these men who in adversity and in suffering through the darkest hour of our history held faithful to an ideal." When he said the country now faced "the same test of steadfastness of will, of clarity of thought, of resolution of character, of fixity of purpose," he only sounded like an overbearing schoolmaster.[58]

The contrast with Franklin Roosevelt could not have been more striking. Roosevelt's youth was a study in privilege—a stable of ponies, frequent trips to Europe, an exclusive private school, capped by a Harvard degree. His family's money came from railroads and banking, but he affected the manners of an eighteenth-century Hudson River patroon. Having chosen politics as a vocation appropriate for a gentleman of leisure, he received appointment as assistant secretary of the navy. Although a bout with polio chastened the somewhat supercilious youth and left him crippled for the rest of his life, he never lost his jaunty smile or the *bon vivant* style symbolized by his rakish cigarette holder. Unlike Hoover, he equated manhood not with steadfastness of will but with experiment and innovation, and as governor of New York he had supported social reforms, while his presidential campaign sounded the theme of "a new deal." He said: "The country needs and, unless I mistake its temper, the country demands bold, persistent experimentation."[59]

But the campaign gave no hint of what kind of experiments lay in store. Although he was harsher than his opponent on "economic oligarchy" and spoke of "driving the money changers from the temple," Roosevelt also ran as a fiscal conservative. If he had any philosophy, it was close to the managerialism of the New Era, but without the boosterism. Believing that the heroic age of capitalist expansion had ended, he spoke of the dull tasks "of meeting the problem of underconsumption, of adjusting production to consumption, of distributing wealth and products more equitably, of adapting existing economic organizations to the service of the people." When he announced that "the day of enlightened administration has come," there was nothing to distinguish his philosophy from Hoover's.[60]

The difference was that Roosevelt was a consummate politician. He believed that the test of a policy was not whether it was sound economically, but whether it worked politically. With popular discontent on the rise, he knew that government had to do something: "If it fails, admit it frankly and try another. But above all, try something. The millions who are in want will not stand by silently forever while the things to satisfy their needs are within easy reach." Thriving on public acclaim, he knew how to speak directly to the millions of forgotten men. When Hoover plied the channels of mass communication, they seemed to silt over, but when Roosevelt later delivered his "fireside chats" over the radio, they overflowed with optimism.[61]

Although his campaign ignited no great enthusiasm or increase in voter turnout, it did show Roosevelt to be adept at holding together southern Bourbons, Wall Street Democrats, and urban political machines. He received 22.8 million votes to Hoover's 15.8 million, or about 60 percent of those cast, one of the biggest margins in history. There were also lopsided Democratic majorities in the Senate (59–37) and House (312–123). Although the Communist and Socialist parties increased their counts, their combined total was no more than the 900,000 Socialist votes in 1912 at a time when the electorate was smaller and prosperity reigned. In all, the election was more a repudiation of the party of depression and Prohibition than a shift to the left or an endorsement of the charming but elusive Roosevelt.

And what of Hoover's place in history? The great reversal in Hoover's fortunes from one of the most respected to probably the most despised president in American history might seem to have the makings of an American tragedy. One commentator wrote: "The history of H[oover]'s administration is Greek in its fatality." Certainly, that is how Hoover saw it. His telling memoir *The Ordeal of Woodrow Wilson* is easily read as an autobiographical account of his own painful ordeal. He wrote of Wilson: "With his death ended a Greek tragedy, not on the stage of imagination, but in the lives of nations."[62] One does not have to look far to find tragic figures in American history—Lincoln, Nat Turner, Sitting Bull, and perhaps Wilson, whose best-laid plans went sadly awry. But there was nothing of the tragic personality in Hoover—no Faustian struggle between good and evil, no Hamlet-like doubt, no Oedipal guilt. In holding fast to the dogma of self-reliance in the face of events grinding it to pieces, he represented not tragedy but obstinacy. Steeped in the frontier belief in limitless progress, Hoover was innocent of the Puritan notion of original sin and devoid of the Founding Fathers' distrust of self-interest.

What Hoover defended at all costs was the myth of American innocence. America had escaped the dark and guilty fate of Europe's divided, warring nations by the happy providence of limitless opportunity. Since all that was pernicious came from outside—war, famine, the Bolshevik Revolution, the "financial hurricane" that caused the Depression—there could be no recognition of the unsound condition of the corporate system and no guilt at giving money to banks but not to people. The steadfast defense of American innocence against the menace of class division and state paternalism was the secret of his few successes—such as government management of agricultural marketing—and of his colossal failures—such as the adamant refusal to provide direct relief to the poor.

There is no way of knowing whether an acquaintance with the evil ingrained in American history—slavery, the annihilation of Native Americans, exploitation—would have better prepared him to cope with the tragedy of poverty amidst plenty, because his moment on the historical stage had come and gone. Ironically, he had done more than any of his peacetime predecessors to involve the state in administering the economy, and he certainly prepared the way for the more thoroughgoing reforms of the New Deal. As fate would have it, Franklin Roosevelt took credit for reforms made possible by Hoover, while the latter bore the blame for the Depression.

The Legend of the First Hundred Days

No story in American politics is more gripping than the legend of the Hundred Days. After a fourth winter of despair, the country was close to collapse. Capital investment had ceased, labor stood idle, farmers were desperate, and popular confidence in the system of self-government was waning. When all the banks shut down in early March, it seemed as if the very heart of capitalism had stopped beating.

Enter Franklin D. Roosevelt. Dr. New Deal immediately gave the banking system the kiss of life, put industry on the road to recovery, doled out jobs and relief, stabilized agriculture, and, most important, restored confidence in government. Having worked themselves into a small panic, many Americans heaved a great sigh of relief. From disgruntled conservatives on Wall Street to anxious little men on Main Street, the "Roosevelt revolution" was hailed as the answer to proletarian revolution. The honeymoon between Roosevelt and the corporate elite rested on the conviction that, as one elderly conservative confided, "This fellow Roosevelt may not be sound, but he has certainly taken the wind out of the radicals' sails." Years later, the view was still common that Roosevelt began such a revolutionary change in the affairs of state that his ascension marked the dawn of a new age.[63]

Like any other enduring myth, the legend of the First Hundred Days has a certain basis in fact. The outlines of the economic calamity are clear beyond dispute: corporate profits turned to losses in 1931 and continued to slide; gross national product fell from $104 billion in 1929 to $56 billion in 1933; and unemployment rose to almost 13 million. When the entire banking system closed its doors to avoid more runs on deposits, the effects were devastating. Akron, Ohio, was typical: "On Saturday morning all business came to a complete halt . . . Thousands and thousands of men, still employed despite the Depression, were sent home from work 'temporarily laid off.' Money nearly disappeared from circulation. Pay rolls were not met. Checks were not honored." The inability of the Hoover administration to stem the apparent collapse of capitalism undermined confidence in the federal government. Faced with farmers revolting, unemployed workers marching, relief rolls mounting, and banks crashing, Hoover was gripped by a paralysis of will.[64]

By all accounts, the advent of Roosevelt certainly brought a breath of fresh air. The new president fulfilled his campaign promise of "bold, persistent experimentation" with a vengeance. No other administration, before or since, took so many landmark actions in so short a time—the Bank Holiday, the National Recovery Administration, the Agricultural Adjustment Administration, the Federal Emergency Relief Administration, to name only the highlights. It is not a gross exaggeration to say, in the words of an early acolyte, "More history has been made during these fifteen weeks than in any comparable peacetime period since Americans went into business for themselves on this continent."[65]

But the notion that the First Hundred Days marked the beginning of a revolution is not credible, at least not if the word *revolution* is to retain its real meaning. To most contemporaries the aim of the New Deal was just the opposite—to save liberal capitalism from revolutionary overthrow. At a time when memories of revolutions elsewhere in 1917–1919 were still fresh, it seemed as if great changes might be in store. Donald Richberg, a prominent New Dealer, warned that the country stood at the brink of "the collapse of our financial and industrial system, and the political revolution which would inevitably follow." And as everyone in the administration agreed, the task was to prevent that from happening.[66]

Actually, most New Dealers were sensible enough to recognize that the threat of revolution from the left was remote. There was a sense of crisis, to be sure, but there was to be no hysterical replay of the Red Scare. Roosevelt had so little fear of the "red menace" that before the year was out he reversed fifteen years of diplomatic policy and accorded recognition to the Soviet Union. There was also to be no return to the populist-progressive tradition, at least not in the first phase of the New Deal. Nor was laissez faire a viable option—Hoover himself had seen to that.

Instead, Roosevelt turned to managerial ideas from the First World War and the New Era. Although he never put forth a coherent theory of the New Deal, he subscribed in a vague way to the idea of an administrative state. In a key campaign speech he had said: "Our task now is not discovery or exploitation of natural resources, or necessarily producing more goods. It is the soberer, less dramatic business of administering resources and plants already in hand." In constructing an administrative state, Roosevelt and his advisers compared the economic emergency facing them with the war emergency facing the Wilson administration, and they consciously modeled the New Deal's "alphabet agencies" and semipublic corporations on the War Industries Board, the Food Administration, the War Finance Corporation, and other wartime institutions.[67]

It is not surprising that Roosevelt relied so heavily on the wartime experience. What is extraordinary is the extent to which he also borrowed from the New Era. Given the depth of the depression, Wall Street's loss of prestige, the huge electoral mandate for change, the radical difference in personalities between Hoover and Roosevelt, and the feeling that the First Hundred Days was a breathtaking departure—given all this, the surprising thing in retrospect is how much the first stage of the New Deal relied on managerial ideas that came out of the New Era.

The fingerprints of the Hoover administration were all over the Emergency Banking Act, the very first piece of New Deal legislation, rushed through a special session of Congress in a few hours on March 9. The act provided legal authority for the Bank Holiday Roosevelt had proclaimed three days earlier shortly after taking office. Although Hoover had balked at the idea of a holiday, the new legislation was actually drafted in his administration. The idea was to rebuild confidence in the banking system by putting the federal government behind the nationwide bank closure, giving more solvent institutions time to reorganize on a sounder footing. The daring rescue did a lot to restore business confidence, prompting the famous boast by Raymond Moley, a key member of the Brain Trust, "Capitalism was saved in eight days."[68]

The same gave the Reconstruction Finance Corporation a new lease on life. Instead of junking Hoover's RFC for its manifest failure to prevent the collapse of credit, Roosevelt expanded it. Under the energetic "business Democrat" Jesse Jones, the RFC "virtually took over the great bulk of the work normally done by Wall Street," according to Adolf Berle, another Brain Truster. In addition, it bankrolled virtually every New Deal program from Harry Hopkins' Federal Emergency Relief Administration (FERA) to the Home Owners Loan Corporation (HOLC). Although it operated beyond legislative control, nearly all members of Congress were indebted to it for projects in their districts. Further state support for banking came in the Glass-Steagall Banking Act, which separated investment from commercial banking and created the Federal Deposit Insurance Corporation to secure the savings of small depositors. Together Hoover and Roosevelt fashioned new instruments of state capitalism, setting precedents for capital accumulation in the hands of the state and for federal bailouts of financially troubled corporations that would hold up through the last decades of the century.[69]

To be sure, there was far more gut instinct than grand strategy in all this. Not one to dwell on the fine points of economic theory, Roosevelt felt that the economic crisis was first and foremost a crisis of political legitimacy. The main thing was to "try something," and he was perfectly capable of trying opposite things at once. Having sided with orthodox bankers in his clarion call for a balanced budget, he then aligned himself with congressional inflationists by taking the country off the gold standard. In June 1933, following Hoover's economic nationalism, he further disappointed ultraorthodox international bankers by scuttling the World Economic Conference in London.[70]

Roosevelt also used the managerial ideas of the New Era for his industrial recovery plan. As the mood grew increasingly desperate, capitalist planners began to follow the logic of state assistance, begun under Hoover, in the direction of state coercion. All the leading solutions to "overproduction" or "underconsumption" embodied some form of state-assisted capitalist planning to restore the balance. The U.S. Chamber of Commerce got behind a plan to give legal status to trade associations, while many other business leaders backed the more drastic Swope Plan. Named after Gerard Swope, the chief executive at General Electric, the Swope Plan proposed to give trade associations sweeping authority to regulate production, prices, and trade, and it gestured toward full-scale corporatism in proposing social insurance and labor-management committees to handle industrial disputes.[71]

Progressive intellectuals became equally enamored of a planned economy. Forgetting that capitalists themselves had dominated the government administrations of the First World War, they took the War Industries Board as a model for public control of private enterprise. Prominent figures such as Stuart Chase, Charles Beard, and George Soule debated the form it should take, whether a peace industries board, a national economic council of "industrial syndicates," or a national economic board of civic leaders. They often looked favorably upon economic planning in the Soviet Union, which had escaped unemployment and the business cycle through its five-year plans. Eventually, they would realize a small portion of their hopes in the creation of the Tennessee Valley Authority (TVA), a semipublic corporation that owned a system of hydroelectric dams and power stations.[72]

The most popular alternative to corporate-backed recovery plans, however, was not full-scale state planning but limited state regulation in the tradition of progressivism. As flagship corporations abandoned efforts to stem the tide of unemployment, the National Industrial Conference Board (NICB) had to admit that work-sharing had not worked. In fact, the entire antidepression program of "industrial self-government"—welfare capitalism, managed labor markets, work-sharing, trade associations, and White House conferences—had proved a crashing failure. When paragons of corporate paternalism such as the great Amoskeag Mills of Manchester, New Hampshire, cut payrolls while imposing the stretch-out, the result was an eruption of wildcat strikes and plant gate protests in favor of a thirty-hour week. Given the failure of private enterprise, the Senate turned to the progressive regulatory tradition and passed a bill introduced by Senator Hugo Black of Alabama for a compulsory thirty-hour work week. Even the lethargic leadership of the AFL rediscovered its roots in the short-hours movement and reversed decades-old opposition to state regulation of men's hours to support the Black Bill.[73]

Although Roosevelt was not above populist flourishes about ousting the money changers from the temple, the last thing he wanted was to make an enemy of business by dictating the hours of work. Instead, he chose business-government cooperation, embodied in the National Industrial Recovery Act. Using the Swope Plan as a blueprint, Secretary of Labor Frances Perkins and the Brain Trust crafted a strategy around a network of committees empowered to establish industrial codes for prices, wages, and trade practices. Antitrust statutes were shelved to permit the committees to function as legalized cartels. In a culture steeped in the folklore of free enterprise, it was necessary to cover over state intervention with some kind of fig leaf, so the system was said to be aimed at "fair competition." To promote industrial stabilization, the act included a sop to organized labor in section 7a, which acknowledged workers' right to organize and bargain collectively. The strategy was similar to that of wartime labor mediation, and it came nowhere near treating organized labor as a producer group on a par with agriculture, finance, and industry, which had won recognition in the Agricultural Marketing Act, the RFC, and the National Recovery Administration (NRA), respectively. If the New Deal was moving toward corporatism, it had a long way to go.[74]

From the start, the NRA walked a tightrope between free enterprise and state capitalism. Recognizing only too well that business was on the slippery slope of state coercion, the National Industrial Conference Board warned: "It is clear that industries that fail to govern themselves will be subjected to government regulation." In the actual workings of the code committees, technocrats who had hoped for state planning along the lines of the TVA were quickly outmaneuvered by the blustery head of the agency, General Hugh Johnson, who was perfectly content to let the Iron and Steel Institute, the Electrical Manufacturers Association, and other trade associations enforce their own codes. There was enough self-regulation that leading industrialists of the NICB and the National Association of Manufacturers could pretend that nothing had changed and that the goal of the NRA was "to provide self-government for industry."[75]

They were kidding themselves. In reality, government supervision of industry was not the same as industrial self-government. As in the First World War, government bureaucrats preferred to coordinate voluntary decisions rather than coerce involuntary ones, but in the end it was the authority of the U.S. government, not of U.S. Steel, that stood behind the codes. Architects of the NRA such as Donald Richberg recognized the difference. Since the Constitution prevented direct government price and wage fixing, it was necessary to rely on "voluntary cooperation," but there also had to be "public supervision." Thus did the NRA demonstrate how "the principles of self-government may be extended to bring order and security into the anarchy of modern industrial operations." Richberg's logic perfectly recapitulated the history of industrial regulation; starting with self-government, it wound up with state intervention.[76]

The NRA took another leaf from the wartime experience in its campaign for patriotic consumption under the sign of the Blue Eagle. As in the Liberty Bond and food conservation drives of the war, the NRA used the techniques of mass advertising, relying on the symbol of the national bird to generate enthusiasm. General Johnson kicked off the campaign with a mammoth parade in New York, followed by the biggest propaganda blitz since the Creel Committee had hawked patriotism during the First World War. Only firms that susbcribed to the codes were allowed to display the Blue Eagle in their windows; the idea was to boost consumption and reward participating companies at the same time. There was a heavy irony in the federal government's sponsoring what amounted to a nationwide consumer boycott: when trade unionists boycotted "foul" employers, they were threatened with jail; but no such punishment awaited good citizens who did their duty to the nation by patronizing NRA-approved companies. Again, as in banking, Roosevelt followed up on Hoover's initiatives; drawing the connection, Walter Lippmann pointed out that "in all its essential features, the substance of N.R.A. existed before the Blue Eagle was hatched."[77]

In its efforts to revive purchasing power, the New Deal took the modern consumer family as a given. It carried over the assumption from the New Era that the ideal family was composed of an efficient housewife, who took care of shopping and child rearing, and a male breadwinner, upon whom wife and children were dependent for support. As average family income fell from $2,300 in 1929 to $1,500 in 1933, the aim of federal work relief was to put able-bodied men to work to restore family finances. (One public opinion survey found 80 percent of respondents opposed to the employment of married women.) By the same token, advertisers continued to portray the American dream in terms of the accumulation of consumer goods. Encouraging "feminine longing and feminine envy," one company told its salesmen to play up the feeling that owning a vacuum cleaner made the ordinary woman feel she was "on a plane of equality with the wealthiest woman in the world."[78]

One reason the Depression era did little to disturb gender relations is that feminism had fallen to its lowest level in decades. Women reformers looked to the indefatigable Eleanor Roosevelt to carry the banner of humanitarianism, but for the most part her husband's government was able to duck the once-vital "woman question." Secretary Perkins kept faith with the fast-fading Women's Trade Union League by appointing Rose Schneiderman to watch over the interests of female workers, and Perkins joined the Women's Bureau to press for equal pay regardless of sex. But NRA codes provided lower women's rates in almost a fourth of all cases, made no move against job segregation, and excluded domestic service, the largest female occupation, from any protection. Thus by its various enfeeblements and exclusions, the New Deal threw the mantle of legitimacy over industrial practices that gave men privileged positions. Although it fulfilled many of the objectives held by women reformers since the Progressive Era, the issue of sexual equality per se would have to wait until the 1960s for a rebirth.[79]

New Deal farm policy was no great departure from Hoover's policies, either. Worried about the votes of rebellious farmers, Roosevelt knew he had to "try something," but he drew on the same corporatist ideas as Hoover. With help from Hoover's Department of Agriculture, the American Farm Bureau was already at work on a plan for crop limitation, which the Brain Trust made into the centerpiece of Roosevelt's farm program. The newly created Agricultural Adjustment Administration, dubbed the "Triple A," aimed at raising prices by taking land out of production through an allotment system, and it provided subsidies to make up for lost income. Although the Supreme Court soon held such extensive federal intervention in the market to be unconstitutional, the key provisions were subsequently reenacted.[80]

Like his predecessor, Roosevelt treated farmers as a single phalanx of propertied producers. The only recognized internal division was by commodity—wheat, corn, cotton, and so on—not by class. The New Deal completely ignored the 3 million agricultural wage earners, and, instead of dealing directly with tenants and sharecroppers, it funneled allotments and subsidies through the larger landowners. The result was to underwrite the nexus of highly capitalized farmers, local merchants, regional bankers, and manufacturers of fertilizer and farm implements. Thus policies justified as a way of shoring up the independent farmer wound up making the farmer dependent on big business and federal largesse.[81]

If there was an exception to the rule of continuity between the New Era and the First Hundred Days, it was federal relief to the poor. Although private donations for cash assistance rose fivefold from 1929 to 1933, and total government spending more than doubled, actual want increased faster still. Most people were able to keep their heads above water only because of the informal networks of family redistribution—taking in relatives, handing around old clothes, extending "loans" to poor cousins—supplemented by ethnic benefit societies and religious charity. All in all, the combined forces of family self-help, private charity, public outdoor relief, welfare capitalism, and Hoover's voluntarism—the institutional sediments of decades of liberalism—were wholly inadequate.[82]

Roosevelt went further than all his predecessors in spending federal money directly on relief and job creation. To restore purchasing power and to win votes, the New Deal launched a series of relief agencies, including the Federal Emergency Relief Administration, the Public Works Administration (PWA), and the Civilian Conservation Corps, that culminated in the legendary Works Progress Administration. By 1935 $3 billion in government relief of one form or another reached some 8 million households, or 22 percent of the population, not counting public works projects such as TVA. Not that the old Protestant-liberal affection for individual initiative disappeared. None other than Harry Hopkins, the progressive social worker at the helm of FERA, counseled: "Give a man a dole, and you save his body and destroy his spirit. Give him a job and pay him an assured wage and you save both the body and the spirit." Nor was there a total break with Hoover's approach. Roosevelt's measures simply extended the relief operation begun by Hoover with $300 million in loans to the states. The difference was that Roosevelt was willing to spend a lot more in cash grants and to become the employer of last resort.[83]

The repeal of Prohibition was a major shift from Republican policy. With Democratic majorities in both houses, repeal was approved overwhelmingly in the final month of Hoover's presidency, and by the end of 1933 the Twenty-first Amendment had been rushed through the ratification process. Opposition, strongest in the Carolinas and the Dakotas, could not stand against the popular tide. Repeal was a delayed vindication of Al Smith's 1928 "wet" campaign rather than a New Deal measure, but the political gains redounded to the Democrats. A popular ditty went:

> Since Roosevelt's been elected,
> Moonshine liquor's been corrected
> We've got legal whisky,
> Beer, wine, and gin.

The popularity of repeal and relief enabled Democrats to make gains of historic proportions in the election of 1934. Although discontent on the left accounted for the election of ten Progressives and Farmer-

Laborites, when the dust settled Democrats outnumbered Republicans in the House by the enormous margin of 322 to 103, and the Senate had the largest imbalance in its history.[84]

Assessing Managerial Liberalism

Five years after the Crash, no one doubted that irrevocable changes had occurred. Beginning under Hoover and quickening under Roosevelt, leading elements of the corporate elite and a growing corps of public administrators combined to create new structures and ideas of rule keyed to joint business-government management of the market. The cumulative result of the new initiatives, especially under FDR, was that public power expanded. Power also gravitated toward Washington the more individual states ceded power to the central government. And as Congress bowed to presidential leadership, the system of checks and balances tilted toward the executive branch.

With laissez faire a thing of the past, it seemed in 1934 as if a new administrative state was taking its place. With the proliferation of "administrations" (NRA, AAA, FERA, PWA), "authorities" (TVA), and semipublic "corporations" (RFC, FDIC, HOLC), it appeared that America would resolve the crisis of depression through a nexus of public-private authority based in the boardrooms and bureaus of New York and Washington. These institutional changes were not without precedent. In the Wilson years, progressive statecraft had erected the Federal Reserve Board, the Federal Trade Commission, and other corporate-regulatory machinery that interwove public and private authority. A more direct precedent lay in the various boards and administrations of the First World War. The fact that the Great Depression induced another round of similar innovations demonstrates that the changes were not merely some hothouse growth in response to a short-term emergency, but the long-term result of a still-incomplete evolution in the organic relation between state and society.

Contemporaries were divided on what all of this meant. To unreconstructed liberals, the New Deal was sheer apostasy. The Supreme Court struck a blow for liberal orthodoxy in the *Schechter* decision of 1935, knocking out the legal underpinnings of the NRA in a unanimous decision on two counts: first, Congress violated the separation of powers by devolving legislative authority upon the president in the industrial code committees; and second, in any case the federal government had no power under the interstate commerce clause to regulate the kind of local manufacturing done by the Schechter Poultry Company. In a similar vein, the Court threw out the Triple A in the *Butler* decision, holding that agriculture did not come under the purview of interstate commerce either; it might be fit for state regulation, but not for federal regulation. The old liberalism, with its federalism and checks and balances, still carried a good deal of weight.[85]

So did self-government. To Herbert Hoover, the Swope Plan and the NRA were blueprints for an intolerable statism. Reacting against proposals for central planning, Hoover lagged behind corporate managers for the first time in his career. He warned against adopting "a state-controlled or state-directed social or economic system in order to cure our troubles. That is not liberalism; it is tyranny."[86] The NRA had barely begun to function before many businessmen came to the same conclusion. They realized belatedly that state intervention inevitably limited their own freedom of action. Standing on a platform of free enterprise, states' rights, and federalism, the Du Ponts and the National Association of Manufacturers joined Al Smith to found the Liberty League in 1934. This turn of events was pregnant with long-term political significance. Opposition to the New Deal was the touchstone around which extreme laissez-faire liberalism transformed itself into modern ultraconservatism.

Meanwhile, the Communists saw the NRA as a harbinger of fascism. The party argued that the fusion of monopoly capital and the state, plus the quasi-military insignia and mass marches for the Blue Eagle, was a desperate attempt by a dying system to resuscitate itself through state power. Most on the left were less harsh. Antitrust progressives saw the NRA as the tool of big business, and from the bowels of the NRA bureaucracy itself, Clarence Darrow, the old warhorse of dissent from the Wobblies to the Scopes trial, issued a controversial report that condemned the NRA for creating "monopoly sustained by government." What most social reformers wanted was not complete socialized ownership and control but some sort of "planning for the masses" in place of existing planning for the capitalists. No one worked harder to reconstruct twentieth-century liberalism around such mild socialist ideas than John Dewey. Carrying the progressive tradition to new lengths, he argued that social planning "is now the sole method of social action by which liberalism can realize its professed aims."[87]

New Dealers, of course, were not about to abandon the liberal tradition to their critics. The one element that unified the scattershot experiments of the New Deal was the mission to save liberal capitalism. The common refrain in New Deal speeches and writings was the twofold goal of saving liberalism from fascism and saving capitalism from communism. Arguing that nothing less than the Constitution and the "economic system based on private profit making" were at stake, Donald Richberg described the NRA as "a new advance in the age-old struggle for self-government." Gripped by an apocalyptic mood, Walter Lippmann warned that "the barbarians are again at the gates" and urged: "It is imperative that we find a true balance between liberty and authority in the modern state." [88]

Groping for new ruling values, New Dealers knew that they had to go beyond liberty as it was traditionally understood. It was readily apparent that untamed liberty had led to the vast inequality so painfully exposed by the Great Depression and to the anarchy of competition that prevented private enterprise from ending it. Although the whirlwind of the Hundred Days had done much to restore confidence, it had not resolved the contradiction between liberty and equality. Virtually none of the key New Dealers, certainly not the president, believed that the solution was to move toward an equal distribution of wealth. Instead, they tried to find ways of providing economic security in an unequal environment—security to business through stabilization of prices and production, security to farmers through price supports, security to wage workers through relief and recovery. Not liberty, not equality, but *security* was emerging as the pivotal concept of the New Deal.

As yet the remaking of the liberal state was far from complete. Roosevelt's forays in administering the capitalist economy were not much more successful than Hoover's in bringing economic recovery. The best that could be said at the end of 1934 was that things had stopped getting worse. Moreover, corporatist planning in conjunction with bankers, industrialists, and agribusinessmen had left vast segments of the social landscape—wage earners, consumers, the elderly—virtually unmapped. And no one had yet addressed the issues of gender or race. If the United States was going to preserve some semblance of democracy, the least it had to do was find some way to represent the interests of the majority.

10

Rendezvous with Destiny

Labor's New Millions

The ink was hardly dry on Roosevelt's recovery program before the New Deal was overtaken by an unexpected development: social movements awakened from their long slumber. From the grimy coal regions of Pennsylvania to the sultry bayous of Louisiana, the sleeping giants of labor, social justice, and populism snapped the cords that had tied them down in the early stages of the depression. As the earth began to shake with the tramp of strikes and rallies, there was a revitalization of radicalism and a resurgence of faith in the common people: Why not? Everything else seemed to have failed. Carl Sandburg captured the new mood in the title of his epic poem, *The People, Yes* (1936).

Ironically, the rebirth of social movements at the grass roots was in part the consequence of elite activities in Washington. The corporate planners and Brain Trusters of the early New Deal had found it necessary to penetrate ever deeper into the daily lives of ordinary Americans. As reported in a summer 1933 issue of the *Literary Digest*, "This central government of ours has now become the almoner to 12,000,000 unemployed and distressed people. It has become the guardian of middle-class investors, of the mortgaged-farm owner, of the mortgaged-home owner, of the bank depositor, and of the railway employee. It has become the partner of industry and of agriculture. And it has even become the friend of the beer maker and the beer drinker."[1]

The last thing New Dealers wanted was to have "distressed people" taking things into their own hands, but that is exactly what happened next. For the more the Roosevelt administration rationalized banking, industry, and agriculture, the more it raised expectations for government aid among workers, retirees, and the unemployed. Roosevelt had stumbled upon the law of unintended consequences, but anyone with a sense of the cunning of history could have seen it coming. Having cultivated the analogy between the depression "emergency" and the war "emergency," Roosevelt should not have been surprised when the people demanded delivery on the government promise of recovery, just as people had demanded that Wilson live up to his promise to "make the world safe for democracy."

Nothing better illustrated the unwritten law of unintended consequences than the way New Deal labor policy inadvertently mobilized workers. None of Roosevelt's inner circle could be accused of harboring a passion for organized labor, not even Secretary of Labor Frances Perkins, who was more of a progressive reformer than a trade unionist. The president betrayed his own indifference to the labor movement in remarking that he didn't care whether workers paid allegiance to a trade union, the Ahkoond of Swat, or the Royal Geographic Society. The fact that section 7a of the 1933 National Recovery Act piously declared that workers had the right to organize and bargain collectively "through representatives of their own choosing" did not mask any secret desire to rally workers to the union cause. It was simply a political bone thrown to the AFL in hopes of ending its support of a bill mandating a thirty-hour week, which the entire Roosevelt administration opposed.[2]

It took a canny opportunist such as John L. Lewis to ignore all this. The flamboyant autocrat of the United Mine Workers launched a membership drive under the slogan "The President wants you to organize." As tens of thousands of mine workers signed union cards, the spirit soon spread to workers in mass production. Together with the garment workers and a few other industrial unions, Lewis prepared to commit the greatest sin known to the labor movement—dual unionism—by breaking away from the AFL in 1935 to form the Committee (later Congress) of Industrial Organizations. It may have been all a misunderstanding, but by seeming to remove government objections to labor unions, section 7a contributed to the most significant mobilization of wage earners since the war.[3]

A dozen years of labor peace ended with a bang in 1934. From one end of the country to the other, industrial workers rediscovered a long-lost militancy. The textile industry was convulsed by the first nationwide general strike in its history, punctuated by company violence. In

San Francisco a longshoremen's strike against the indignities of the "shape-up" (in which foremen hired favorites from men herded together like cattle) escalated into a city wide general strike when police killed strikers. Similarly, teamsters brought truck transport to a halt in the vital entrepôt of Minneapolis, and, again, company thugs killed strikers. Communists and Trotskyists, respectively, played vital leadership roles in these strikes. Returning from a sojourn in the Soviet Union, Walter Reuther, future president of the United Auto Workers, was amazed at what he saw: "the NRA and the series of strikes and struggles of labor that followed ushered in a new epoch in America."[4]

Violence accompanied all the major strikes, and the reason was the same as always—business' hatred for unions. Although a handful of companies were prepared to recognize genuine unions, most fought as if there was no tomorrow. Turning section 7a to their own advantage, they set up company unions, or employee representation plans, which successfully forestalled independent trade unions in a host of places. At the same time, they brought in labor spies, hired thugs, private detectives, and "citizen" vigilantes, whose massive violations of civil liberties would soon be amply documented by a Senate investigating committee under Robert La Follette. A handful of so-called brass hats such as Tom Girdler of Republic Steel vowed never to accept collective bargaining. Girdler's intransigence led to the infamous Memorial Day Massacre of 1937, when ten members of a crowd of peaceful demonstrators were shot in the back by police. Although the number of strikes and the level of violence never reached that of the end of the First World War, industrial warfare was back.[5]

The difference was that this time unionism often came out on the winning side. Whereas the 1919 Seattle general strike had been crushed, the strikers of San Francisco and Minneapolis could justly claim victory. Whereas mass production and heavy industry had emerged union free from the postwar battles, organizing drives were now under way that would soon bring strong unions to the auto, meatpacking, electrical and steel industries; in short, to the entire heartland of modern capitalism. Whereas the craft unions of the AFL had lapsed into a lethargic "business unionism" during the 1920s, now the emerging industrial unions of the CIO rekindled a crusading spirit that brought in almost 3 million members and sparked an equivalent expansion in the ranks of the revitalized AFL.[6]

What explains this remarkable mobilization of "labor's new mil-

lions"? Once the trigger effect of the New Deal has been duly acknowledged, the upsurge should be understood in the context of the evolution of modern capitalism. Class relations were being reshaped by the
impersonal structures of mass society. In the realm of production, two
decades of technical rationalization and bureaucratic management had
homogenized the labor process so that workers in widely different settings had the sense that they were all parts of a single whole. By the
same token, in the realm of reproduction, the homogenizing impact of
mass culture—from advertising and chain stores to major league baseball and public schools—had lifted people out of their parochialism and
given them a common basis of communication across ethnic and religious boundaries. Everybody could root for the home team, and who
didn't love Charlie Chaplin?[7]

Taking these structural conditions as a given, real, flesh-and-blood
human beings brought about the rebirth of labor. Because the working
class spanned so many different cultures, the labor movement could
not count on a common set of values, and in almost every struggle
against the boss, there was a concurrent struggle for leadership within
the movement. In the case of New England textile workers, secular
radicals in the tradition of the French Revolution vied with devout
Catholic French-Canadians; and in the case of the electrical workers,
Communist fellow travelers competed with Catholic corporatists. The
divisions had always been there. The difference was that now the common struggle against the boss took precedence and drew these warring
factions together. In one of the most bizarre cases, an alliance arose
among New York transit workers between closet Communists and
Irish nationalists in the secret Clan Na Gael.[8]

That atheist lions could lie down with churchgoing lambs reflected
the change in climate in working-class communities. After years of
eclipse, visions of a just society were returning to the forefront. To
judge from the many testaments they left behind, labor organizers
were motivated as much by a desire to change society as by a desire for
power. Certainly, that was the case for Jewish garment workers, who
combined socialist ideals, *Yiddishkeit* (the transplanted culture of eastern
European Jews), and a sophisticated pursuit of political power that
eventually installed Sidney Hillman of the Amalgamated Clothing
Workers as one of President Roosevelt's many righthand men. And in
general, the advance of social consciousness helped revitalize the labor
movement and thrust it to the center of the historical stage.[9]

Signs of grass-roots activism sprouted on other fronts, as well. Impatient with Harry Hopkins' relief measures, the unemployed demanded a thoroughgoing program to combat unemployment. Novelist and journalist John Dos Passos captured the populist spirit at a national convention of unemployed councils in February 1934: "They are a real cross section of the U.S.A., not of the private U.S.A. of the Navy League and the Hamilton Fish and the Mellons and the Army Staff College, but the real shivering miserable and alive U.S.A. of the workers, farmers, producers, and would-be consumers, Whitman's and Lincoln's U.S.A."[10]

Inspired by the movements of the unemployed, social reformers raised anew the banners of social justice. Chastened by the Depression, the 1930s generation did not put its faith in moral uplift, but in a two-fisted combination of justice and power. The pages of old Progressive Era journals such as the *New Republic* and *Survey* once again bristled with bold ideas for economic planning and the cooperative commonwealth. Lewis Mumford's studies of urban planning emphasized the way civilization was shaped by the commandments of "technics," and in *Moral Man and Immoral Society* (1932) Reinhold Niebuhr threw over the progressive "social gospel" in favor of a blend of Christian ethics and Marxist interests he had developed as a Lutheran pastor in working-class Detroit. Niebuhr posited "equal social justice" as "the most rational ultimate objective for society" and insisted that to attain it the exploited must marshal power in their own interest.[11]

Many intellectuals felt the gravitational force of the working-class movement. In a bold departure from prevailing scholarship, W. E. B. DuBois portrayed *Black Reconstruction* (1935) in the South in terms of class conflicts. The works of Marxist economists such as Lewis Corey's *The Decline of American Capitalism* (1934) began to receive a hearing. A new breed of novelists invented "proletarian literature." By general agreement, the best of the genre was John Steinbeck's *The Grapes of Wrath* (1939), which retold in class-conscious terms the classic American epic of westward migration through the wanderings of the Joad family. Despite an undertone of sexual equality in some of the works, the more popular examples depicted working-class life through male eyes. For example, the hero of Robert Cantwell's *Land of Plenty* (1934) finds manhood in a spontaneous sit-down strike when his comrades initiate him into the fraternity of struggle and a factory girl initiates him into sex. Whereas much of Hollywood did its best to dance away the Depression in top-hatted musical extravaganzas, Charlie Chaplin caught the proletarian spirit and rebuked the alienation of factory work with typically disarming satire and boy-meets-girl romance in *Modern Times* (1936).[12]

Meanwhile, in the countryside, agrarian radicalism underwent something of a rebirth. In the upper Midwest, anger over dispossession had simmered all through the 1920s and now gave rise to renewed farmer-labor activity, while in the South, after three decades of decline, populism reemerged around the mercurial figure of Huey Long. Unlike race-baiting demagogues of the region, Louisiana's "Kingfish" stuck to economic issues in his Share Our Wealth campaign, which proposed to redistribute to every household in the land a $5,000 lump sum confiscated from the great fortunes. Claiming hundreds of thousands of followers, Long emblazoned his presidential ambitions in the unabashed title of *My First Years in the White House* (1935). Before his assassination by a political foe in 1935, he added a folksy, if reckless, voice to the growing chorus for the redistribution of wealth.[13]

Some of the radicalism of the era was neither of the left nor of the right, but of the hare-brained variety. No doubt the most popular of the crackpot panaceas was Dr. Francis Townsend's old-age pension scheme. Appealing to "the Bible Belt solid Americans," Townsend captured the attention of the elderly with his proposal to pay a $200 monthly pension to all retired persons on the condition that every penny be spent. His scheme enjoyed enough popular support to intimidate a significant number of congressmen into supporting it. In another vein, the "Radio Priest" Father Coughlin touted the virtues of silver inflation to millions of listeners in an increasingly vituperative, anti-Semitic attack on liberals and international bankers.[14]

The gathering forces of popular discontent forced redistributive ideas onto the political agenda. A case in point was aid to the unemployed. Veteran campaigner Abraham Epstein touted European models of compulsory tax-supported unemployment compensation, and Mary Van Kleeck, former head of the Women's Bureau, argued for massive government expenditure on the grounds that a "bold stroke that diverted frozen credit into consumers' purchasing power might, after all, be more effective as a means of 'recovery' than a balanced budget." Such proto-Keynesian ideas came to be embodied in the Lundeen Bill, introduced in February 1934, which called for universal unemployment compensation equivalent to 100 percent of wages lost, to be financed by progressive taxes on business and locally administered by councils of workers and farmers. For the first time since 1919–1920, dreams for social reconstruction were making political headway in Washington.[15]

The change was registered as populists and progressives became major players in the midterm elections of 1934. Upton Sinclair ran a creditable campaign for governor of California on watered-down socialism and the slogan "End poverty in California." Midwestern voters elected members of the Minnesota Farmer-Labor party, sent progressive Robert La Follette, Jr., to the Senate from Wisconsin, and revived the prairie populist ideas of the Non-Partisan League. Southern populism spoke through Huey Long's Share Our Wealth campaign, and southern progressives such as Hugo Black put aside states' rights and worry about race relations to support federal assistance to the poor. Contrary to the traditional pattern in midterm elections, voters further reduced the Republican contingent in Congress, and many of the new Democrats stood to the left of Roosevelt. For the first time in a decade of reversals, the labor movement actually gained friends in high office. Once the New Deal broke the logjam in American politics, a host of reformers came flooding through.[16]

In some respects, the new dynamic was comparable to the aftermath of the First World War. Then, the largest strike wave in American history, the onrushing women's movement, and the emergence of the New Negro confronted elites with a choice between progressive "reconstruction" that would co-opt these popular forces into a new governing system and top-down repression that would freeze things as they were. Although the Women's Suffrage Amendment was an example of co-optation, for the most part the Wilson and Harding administrations had chosen the path of repression. Nervous about Bolshevik revolution in Europe, they chose to crack down on strikers, incite the Red Scare, and abandon social reform in favor of laissez faire and immigration restriction.

Now, a decade and a half later, as the political initiative shifted from elites to masses, the Roosevelt administration faced a similar choice between repressing popular forces or co-opting them into some yet-undiscovered consensus. In the frame of international comparison, that choice translated into an ominous question of whether liberalism would be sacrificed to save capitalism. The question was posed most cruelly in Germany, where the Nazi seizure of power in 1933 had destroyed all semblance of civil liberties. If Germany could descend into fascism, was it possible that the United States would find its own road to repression?

The Great Compromise

Given all that was at stake, the choice facing the country in the mid-1930s was full of historical significance. For if the Roosevelt administration continued to take its cues from managerial liberals, and if, as seemed likely, its half-baked experiments in state planning failed to end the depression, then the inevitable protests would be met with troops and anticommunist hysteria. And if the lights of free expression were snuffed out in the land of liberty, how long could they remain lit elsewhere? If, on the other hand, the administration chose to reach out to the grass-roots movements, it would have to chart a new course for American politics. Since there were precious few precedents for incorporating wage earners in state policies, and since the interests of wage earners and capitalists were fundamentally at odds, it would not be easy to find the way.

In the event, the choice was for a new round of experiments in 1935 that became known as the Second New Deal. In what was the truly new part of the New Deal, the Roosevelt administration enacted a set of enduring reforms, including the National Labor Relations Act and the Social Security Act, that somehow reconciled capitalism and social reform, altered forever the relation between state and society in the United States, and stood as a beacon of liberal renewal to the entire world.

The original impetus for reform came not from corporate planners but from the popular movements for social justice and their allies in the administration and Congress. That fact was crystal clear in the more radical pieces of legislation, such as the Works Progress Administration (WPA). Responding to unemployed workers and social reformers, Harry Hopkins, a Chicago social worker in the Jane Addams tradition, devised a vast federal jobs program that spent over $2 billion at its peak in 1939 and had more than 3 million people on payroll doing everything from digging ditches to writing plays. Though ridiculed as "We Poke Along," it made lasting contributions in public works and even in public art through the heroic murals of people's struggle painted by the likes of Diego Rivera. To its supporters, WPA represented a rational system of production-for-use as against the chaos of production-for-profit. Verily, it prefigured the cooperative commonwealth.[17]

No doubt the most annoying burr in the saddle of privilege was the wealth tax. Roosevelt backed the "soak the rich" tax on capital stock, estates, gifts, and excess profits to recapture political ground lost to Long's Share Our Wealth campaign. Once enacted in 1935, the tax did not, in fact, soak the rich; econometric studies attribute most of whatever downward distribution of income occurred after 1929 to market forces or the impact of the Second World War. But nothing did more to provoke fear and loathing of the New Deal and "that man in the White House," and it marked the apogee of Roosevelt's swing toward redistributive ideas. Radicalism was also evident in TVA-style planned economy, WPA production-for-use, and the presence of agrarian reformers in Henry Wallace's Department of Agriculture. Thus for the first time since the border between progressivism and socialism had closed in 1917, Washington was open to influences from the left.[18]

The turn toward reform split the business community into pro– and anti–New Deal factions. A minority of corporate leaders such as Thomas Watson, head of International Business Machines, recognized the desirability, or at least the inevitability, of some social legislation. Rockefeller interests supported public pensions and unemployment assistance and sponsored a national tour by William Beveridge, who became the father of the British welfare state. When Secretary Perkins picked people associated with the well-connected American Association for Labor Legislation to work with the newly appointed Committee on Economic Security, the corporate-liberal wing of the business community knew it could count on Roosevelt to come up with a "sober" social insurance plan for the unemployed and the elderly. Managerial liberalism was not totally dead.[19]

Most businessmen, however, attacked public welfare as if it flew the red flag of socialism. At the first sign that social-democratic ideas were making headway in Washington, conservatives in the U.S. Chamber of Commerce deposed its pro–New Deal leader. Although the National Association of Manufacturers raised no serious objection to unemployment aid along the lines of the "Wisconsin Plan" (privately controlled employer reserves), it opposed anything that smacked of public control. In the face of 12 million unemployed, NAM commended individual "thrift and self-denial" as the answer to unemployment. NAM's Ohio affiliate denounced the "Ohio Plan" (compulsory group insurance) as "the greatest menace that has ever faced Ohio industry," and the Ohio Chamber of Commerce thundered against this "Bolshevik" proposal.[20]

That even mild social reforms looked like "creeping socialism" to most businessmen shows that they still saw the world in terms of nineteenth-century liberalism. Immersed in what a critic aptly called "the folklore of American capitalism," they reasoned that the best way to prevent poverty was for the husband to practice the old Protestant verities—"thrift, forethought, frugality, and individual initiative"—and thereby accumulate savings against a rainy day. Since wife and children were supposed to be dependent creatures, let the husband support his family. In cases of genuine destitution, private charity and the almshouse were in order for the deserving, and there was even a place for welfare capitalism. But there was to be no mollycoddling of malingerers at public expense.[21]

Beset by these political cross-pressures, Roosevelt was galvanized into launching the Second Hundred Days when the Supreme Court declared the National Recovery Act unconstitutional in the *Schechter* decision of May 1935. Shattering the centerpiece of Roosevelt's recovery program at a time of growing popular discontent, the Court's bombshell threatened to wreck the fragile public confidence that had returned in the preceding two years. Eager to experiment with ideas that might win votes, Roosevelt quickly shifted his labor policy. Having steadfastly ignored Senator Robert Wagner's bill for regulating labor relations, he now thrust it forward as a piece of essential legislation.[22]

With ties to both enlightened corporate leaders and labor progressives in his home state of New York, Senator Wagner espoused an "underconsumption" theory of the Depression and argued that collective bargaining was the route to recovery because it would raise "the purchasing power of wage earners." Wagner's aim was not to redistribute wealth from capital to labor but to rationalize the chaos of competition by smoothing out the peaks and valleys between boom and bust, large and small employers, and high- and low-wage industries. In an attempt to avoid running afoul of the Supreme Court, Wagner's bill employed a bit of legalistic legerdemain in making *individual* rights the legal basis for *collective* bargaining. In fact, the words *trade union* never appeared. All the same, the Wagner Act gave the new National Labor Relations Board power to halt "unfair labor practices," supervise representation elections, and certify duly chosen bargaining agents. Hoping to reap the advantage, the AFL put aside its traditional objections to state intervention and supported the bill, a move AFL leaders regretted when it turned out the CIO would be competing for the same harvest of union members.[23]

For all its labor sympathies, the Wagner Act did not fail to protect elite interests. Using their clout as committee chairmen, southern conservatives weakened the bill by excluding agricultural and casual laborers, thus leaving most of the Afro-American and Hispanic work force unprotected. The largely female occupations of domestic servants and retail clerks were also excluded. The friends of business, for their part, saw to it that the act confined "responsible" unions to a narrow range of bargaining issues, and, most important, it carefully avoided trenching upon the inner sanctum of managerial control over investment, product, and labor process. Freighted with such enfeeblements and exclusions, the bill passed overwhelmingly, with support from a majority of southern Democrats. Even the Supreme Court upheld the Wagner Act, granting its first approval to a major piece of New Deal legislation in the *Jones and Laughlin* decision (1937).[24]

All in all, it was a historic turnabout. The Wagner Act constituted labor as a great estate of the realm, not the peer of business or even agriculture, but in some sense a collective entity with legitimate interests deserving state protection. Although the intent of the framers was to promote recovery, the effect was to install the government as the patron of unionism and, in some measure, to redress the balance of power toward workers. But the beauty of the Second New Deal's expansion of interest-group liberalism was its exquisite compromise between mass interests and elite privileges. New Deal labor policy performed the amazing feat of raising the status of industrial workers while preserving their subordinate place in industry and society at large under the dominance of the modern corporation. In effect, state rationalization in the 1930s picked up where corporate rationalization in the 1920s had left off.[25]

If the New Deal was going to regulate production, it could hardly avoid also taking a greater hand in matters such as welfare that pertained to social reproduction. Having already gone into the business of emergency relief, New Dealers were determined to create a permanent and more rational welfare system. From one side, they were buffeted by a host of modern-day Robin Hoods who pushed a cartload of reforms—the Lundeen Bill on unemployment, Townsend's revolving pensions, and Long's Share Our Wealth—all of which quite openly aimed at the redistribution of wealth through confiscatory taxes on the rich. From the other side, New Dealers were pummeled by a shrill campaign financed by business against any system of government subsidies to the poor.

Walking a narrow path between redistribution and laissez faire, the President's Committee on Economic Security took private insurance plans as their guide. Legend has it that Secretary Perkins locked the committee in her dining room with a bottle of whiskey and instructions not to emerge until the legislation had been drafted. Seeking something that would block disorder and bolster purchasing power, the committee crafted a bill in early 1935 that provided security to industrial wage earners through a compulsory insurance system that contained unemployment compensation, disability pay, and old-age pensions. But because it was financed out of a regressive payroll tax, not out of general revenues, the bill did not put a dent in the fortunes of the rich.[26]

Artfully crafted to minimize conservative opposition, the Social Security Act exempted many of the groups that needed help the most. To placate southern planters, agribusinessmen, and economic conservatives in general, it denied protection to farm workers, domestics, and casual laborers, the very people whose low wages and irregular employment made them among the poorest in the land. Likewise, instead of setting a miminum national unemployment benefit, the system bowed to low-wage regions and allowed state officials to set the dollar level of unemployment checks. Thus with the same enfeeblements and exclusions found in the Wagner Act, Social Security easily passed through a Congress eager to show a humane face to the public that had lived through six grinding years of depression.[27]

As it went into operation, the rapidly growing welfare bureaucracy helped manage the family economy in ways appropriate to an age of mass reproduction. The goal was to even out extremes in the family earning cycle in the hope of stabilizing mass purchasing power, or, in Keynesian terms, maintaining aggregate demand. Thus unemployment compensation siphoned current income into a reserve against future loss through unemployment, just as old-age pensions set aside current income in an insurance fund for future retirement. In contrast to some European welfare states, what redistribution there was took place within the working class between present wage earners and future nonearners. To promote the consumer family's participation in the capitalist market, Social Security introduced neomercantilist regulation of family life on a scale not seen since the eighteenth century.

Ironically, it did all this while resolutely proclaiming the absolute virtue of the self-sufficient, nuclear family. The system was infused with the kind of ideal defined in Isaac Rubinow's manifesto for reform, *Quest for Security* (1934): "A father who works. A mother who tends house. Children who look to mother for care and to father for support." Through "family protection" provisions added to the system in 1939, the family became the channel for distributing benefits, and regardless of who earned the most, all members of the family, including working wives, were presumed to be the husband's dependents.[28]

The model of provider-husband/dependent-wife was also central to the design of Aid to Dependent Children. Growing out of the "mothers' pensions" of the Progressive Era, ADC (later AFDC) assisted female-headed families in which children would otherwise have become dependent on the state. Along with an explicit means test, eligibility was determined by an implicit sex-role test for woman's dependency. No matter how great the economic need, benefits were withheld from women with husbands or lovers on the grounds that these men were *supposed* to provide, whether they did so or not. On the strength of regulations that required a "suitable home" before aid was given, case workers could crack a moral whip over women's private lives. That attitude, plus the expectation in the South that black mothers should work, tended until the 1950s to confine benefits to orphans and white widows with children.[29]

Thus sexual inequality was built into every part of the welfare state. Constructed around the nuclear family ideal, the system favored lifelong homemakers over working wives and single women. Large groups of the lowest-paid female workers who needed protection the most were systematically excluded, including 3 million domestic servants; almost a third of all working women were thus deprived of unemployment and old-age benefits. In a compounding of women's predicament, divorced women were initially denied survivor's benefits, and young widows had to wait until retirement to collect. No one can say how a vital feminist movement would have changed all this, but it is clear that the absence of the kind of agitation that characterized the 1910s allowed these gender subordinations to go unchallenged.[30]

When it came to labor and capital, the architects of Social Security were quite explicit about their intention to buttress the ladder of wage inequality. Chief Administrator Arthur Altmeyer laid down the "fundamental principle" that benefits were not to exceed 80 percent of former wages. According to Edwin Witte, the main architect of the bill, "Only to a very minor degree does it modify the distribution of wealth and it does not alter at all the fundamentals of our capitalistic and individualistic economy. Nor does it relieve the individual of primary responsibility for his own support and that of his dependents." [31]

Reworking the Protestant ethic to suit the age of mass reproduction, the system also reaffirmed old prejudices toward the poor. Overseers of the poor had always worried that men would be emasculated if given a "dole." Now, even as the federal government doled out millions to jobless men, FDR was determined "to quit this business of relief." Instead of sheltering the destitute under the same roof as other aid recipients, the framers of the new system put "public assistance" in its own category. By separating aid to the destitute from aid to everybody else, they hoped to preserve the all-important boundary between dependence and independence. Thus in distinguishing between means-tested aid and contributory social insurance, the Social Security system managed to transpose the stigma once attached to "relief" under the old liberalism to "welfare" in the new. [32]

Contrary to common mythology, the poor and the working classes were not the only ones to receive welfare. The middle classes were also beneficiaries of massive state aid. For one thing, in the absence of a means test for old-age insurance, salaried white-collar workers were entitled to a federal pension. Although the old middle class of self-employed persons was initially exempt from the system, the fact that the new salaried middle class participated helped guarantee the political survival of Social Security through the thick and thin of successive liberal and conservative administrations in Washington. For another, small property owners also received the largesse of federal insurance on savings deposits and home loans. Tapping a deep vein of American folklore, Franklin Roosevelt proclaimed that "a nation of homeowners, of people who own a real share in their own land, is unconquerable." To stem the tide of mortgage foreclosures, in 1933 and 1934 the Roosevelt administration created the Home Owners Loan Corporation to refinance shaky mortgages, the Federal Savings and Loan Insurance Corporation to prop up wobbly financial institutions, and the Federal Housing Adminstration (FHA) to underwrite private loans for housing construction. Before long, the federal government held mortgages on fully one-tenth of all owner-occupied nonfarm residences in the United States. Working through Hoover's Home Loan Bank Board, the New Deal largely succeeded in repairing the bonds between middle-class families and capitalist institutions that had been ruptured by the Depression.[33]

The middle-class bias was evident in guidelines for home loans. The Home Owners Loan Corporation devised an invidious, four-tier, color-coded system for ranking neighborhoods in which, predictably, the top-ranked were composed of "American business and professional men" (that is, no Jews, blacks, or recent immigrants), while the bottom—coded red—were crowded slums or any neighborhood with a "rapidly increasing Negro population." This was the beginning of official federal sponsorship of redlining, or disinvestment in poorer urban neighborhoods, which did so much to devastate inner cities in the middle decades of the twentieth century. To its credit, the New Deal also subsidized low-income tenants through public housing, and it was the market, not the federal government, that created the slums. But in smoothing the transition from the productive farms and workshops of the old middle classes to the consumer homes of the new, Washington became the biggest single player in the housing market, and, as such, it did much to preserve the gap between "good" neighborhoods and "bad."[34]

The fact that New Deal reforms preserved social hierarchy does not mean the Wagner Act and Social Security were the result of a conspiracy of the rich or were devoid of humanitarian intent. Certainly, the New Deal had more than its share of humanitarian moments, including the abolition of child labor in the NRA codes and subsequently in the Fair Labor Standards Act of 1938.[35] But even as the New Deal responded to popular demands for social justice, it was careful not to infringe too much upon the privileges of wealth. By the end of the Second New Deal, the Roosevelt administration had crafted a compromise between privileged elites and subordinate groups that restrained liberty in the name of security without upending the social order.

It is possible in this remarkably fluid and dynamic situation to detect the restraining influence of the liberal inheritance. Standing in the path of more thoroughgoing reforms was a host of impediments—the absence of a great central bureaucracy or trained corps of professional civil servants ready to administer new government programs; the deep suspicion, long held by upper-class partisans of "good government," that massive state intervention would merely replenish the "pork barrels" of corrupt political machines; the tangle of checks and balances, especially the laissez-faire bias of the court system; the fragmented system of federalism. All these combined with the antistatism of industrialists and the anticentralism of southern elites to stack the deck against anything stronger than a liberal reform of corporate capitalism.[36]

Under a different balance of forces, there might have been some kind of social-democratic solution as in Sweden or, less likely, experiments in socialist redistribution of wealth and power. Or else, there might have been some kind of top-down, corporate regime, as seemed to be emerging in the initial managerial response to the Depression under Hoover and early in Roosevelt's administration. Instead, in response to pressures from below, the liberal legacy was transfigured by the incorporation of both social-democratic and corporatist elements.

There was no secret to what happened, no wily conservatives in left-wing masquerade, no conspiracy of judges and bureaucrats to draw the sting from radical legislation. The New Deal was just what it proclaimed itself to be, an effort to stabilize capitalist society by enhancing the security of all within it. Security was the very cornerstone of the New Deal—secure investments, secure bank accounts, secure jobs, secure mortgages, secure livelihood, secure retirement, and, transcending all, the emotional security of having a benevolent protector in Washington. Franklin Roosevelt's Four Freedoms spoke to the desire for economic security, as did his 1944 State of the Union Address: "We have come to a clear realization that true individual freedom cannot exist without economic security and independence. 'Necessitous men are not free men.' People who are hungry and out of a job are the stuff of which dictatorships are made."[37] Under such circumstances, security did not require an apology to be enshrined in the pantheon of virtues.

Even so, the turn toward security was a deflation of the liberal tradition in America. It was a far cry from the heroic age of the nineteenth century, when liberalism had gone from conquest to conquest over the continent, the Confederacy, discontented farmers, exploited workers, and the Spanish empire. Having been the battle cry of freedom in the Civil War, liberty retained its crusading fervor even down to the First World War. But the reign of unchained liberty came to an end in the twentieth century. It fell victim to wartime regulations, the challenges

The state played different roles while enforcing an unequal balance of social forces.

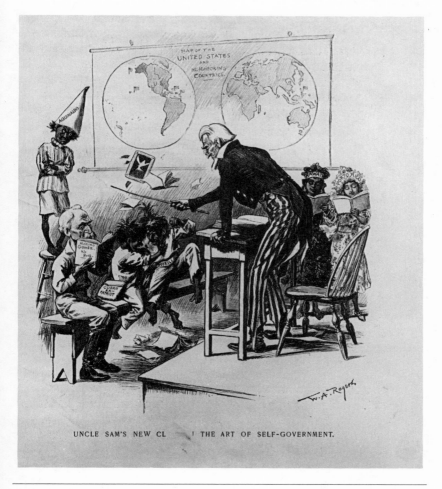

UNCLE SAM'S NEW CL   I THE ART OF SELF-GOVERNMENT.

Imperial disciplinarian: Uncle Sam administers the cane in "Uncle Sam's New Class in the Art of Self-Government," a W. A. Rogers cartoon in *Harper's Weekly*, August 27, 1898.

Educator: the Public Health Service warns doughboys of the dangers of venereal disease in *Fit to Win*, the first movie ever made by the U.S. government, 1918.

Repressor: the bayonets of the state militia confront textile strikers led by the Industrial Workers of the World in Lawrence, Massachusetts, 1912.

Mediator: Uncle Sam promotes industrial peace through the National Recovery
Administration in a Berryman cartoon, "The Spirit of the New Deal," 1933.

of the Bolshevik Revolution and the Great Depression, and the increasing dominance of the great corporations. By the 1930s old-fashioned liberty had lost its appeal in the world at large and also had to be sacrificed for the sake of stability at home. Watching a march in Tampa, Florida, that demanded nothing more than security, veteran progressive Margaret Robins was taken aback: "I cannot feel that 'Security' is a better slogan than 'Making the World Safe for Democracy' was."[38] Although democracy retained its ability to move masses, the days of revolutionary liberalism were done.

Limits of Reform

Standing before a cheering throng at the Democratic national convention in Philadelphia on June 27, 1936, Franklin Roosevelt summoned the crowd to a historic mission: "this generation of Americans has a rendezvous with destiny."[39] For once, campaign hyperbole struck close to the mark, for it was clear that a great transformation was taking place in American life. The generation that lived through the Great Depression had already worked a great change in the relation between state and society and was now preparing to turn the quadrennial ritual of national cohesion into a referendum on New Deal reforms.

Posing as the champion of the forgotten man against "economic royalists," Roosevelt metamorphosed from managerial liberal into rhetorical populist. In a memorable peroration on October 31 at Madison Square Garden, he tolled out the honor roll of the common people: "men at starvation wages," "women in sweatshops," "farmers whose acres yielded only bitterness, business men whose books were portents of disaster, home owners who were faced with eviction, frugal citizens whose savings were insecure." Gathering up this bedraggled army of the downtrodden, he promised to lead it into battle against business and financial monopoly. He brought down the house when he said: "I should like to have it said of my first Administration that in it the forces of selfishness and of lust for power met their *match*. I should like to have it said of my second Administration that in it these forces met their *master.*"[40]

Contradiction abounded in Roosevelt's newfound campaign posture. The Hudson River squire who had run as a fiscal conservative in 1932 and who had looked to big business in the First Hundred Days now proposed to lead a plebeian army against the patricians. In fairness, his

1936 election-year conversion was not all rank opportunism. There was some genuine populist substance to the wealth tax, WPA, and TVA. Roosevelt's supporters did not stretch the truth too far beyond credulity in saying that many New Deal agencies "put the protection of people ahead of that of property." Populist programs combined with FDR's ringing oratory and his radio magic to convince the little guy that the president was on his side. As one workingman said, "Mr. Roosevelt is the only man we ever had in the White House who would understand that my boss is a sonofabitch."[41]

Popular affection for FDR inhibited moves toward a third party. For the first time since the aftermath of the First World War, conditions seemed ripe for the emergence of a mass party of the left. Labor was on the march, and the persistence of hard times provided grist for the mills of radicalism. Progressives already held bases of real power in La Follette's Wisconsin and Governor Floyd Olson's Minnesota and were strong in California and Washington. Campaigning at the head of the Socialist ticket, Norman Thomas said the election came down to a contest of "Socialism versus Capitalism."[42]

Yet for all these signs of resurgence, no serious third party emerged on the left. Roosevelt's populist rhetoric and liberal reforms stole enough thunder to make the New Deal palatable to progressives, and, for the same reason, it began to look like a good way of blocking the authoritarian right. In a tardy response to the rise of fascism, the Communist International had announced support for a Popular Front at its Seventh World Congress in 1935, and American Communists eagerly tacked in the new direction. Having once compared the New Deal to fascism, they now portrayed Roosevelt's opponent Alf Landon as a tool of the "fascist-minded" Liberty League and the hysterical newspapers of press tycoon William Randolph Hearst. Contrary to the Socialists, they argued that the overriding contradiction of the moment was not between capitalism and socialism but between fascism and democracy. When fascism was on the march, it was not hard for Communists and left-progressives to justify joining hands with New Deal liberals.[43]

Although Landon himself was something of a midwestern progressive, some of his conservative supporters merited the "economic royalist" label pinned on them by the president. Stung by what they viewed as Roosevelt's treason to his class, upper-crust conservatives painted "that man in the White House" as a traitor to the republic. Presenting itself as the defender of constitutional liberties, the Liberty League railed against executive tyranny and government infringement of property rights. But the fact that their funding came from the likes of Alfred P. Sloan of General Motors, Sewell Avery of Montgomery Ward, and the du Pont family made the league look like a cabal of wealthy men taking refuge behind the flag to protect their profits from democratic reform. If that was not enough, their vitriol fueled the fires of prejudice. One nasty little ditty that made the rounds had Eleanor and Franklin singing a duet:

> You kiss the Negroes
> I'll kiss the Jews,
> We'll stay in the White House,
> As long as we choose.

But the more the conservatives impugned Roosevelt's patriotism, the more ordinary people believed they were the kind of scoundrels Roosevelt said they were, and Landon's campaign faltered.[44]

To judge from the rhetoric on both sides, the 1936 election was the closest thing to class politics since the farmers' revolt of the 1890s. A key constituent of the budding New Deal coalition was organized labor. John L. Lewis, a nominal Republican, spent $770,000 (an enormous sum for the time) of United Mine Workers money on the Democratic campaign and set up Labor's Non-Partisan League to squelch any move toward a farmer-labor party. A second key component was the urban ethnic groups that had begun their migration into the Democratic party with Al Smith's campaign and continued with the repeal of Prohibition. Once cool toward Roosevelt, big-city bosses warmed up in the sun of federal patronage—FDR appointed fifty-one Catholic judges; his three Republican predecessors had appointed eight in all—and turned out regiments of the party faithful.[45]

These changes in the composition of the Democratic party's voting base virtually compelled a thorough revision of the mythology of Americanism. Sloughing off the nativism that had made the Democratic party home to the KKK and immigration restrictionists in the 1920s, New Dealers began to move toward the ethnic pluralism that would emerge in the 1940s as the reigning ideology of a "nation of nations." Roosevelt's 1936 campaign speeches embraced Old World immigrants, particularly at the Statue of Liberty's fiftieth-anniversary ceremony. In a famous incident in his second term, Roosevelt did much to convince Poles, Italians, Jews, and other second-generation immigrants of his sincerity when he reminded a convention of the Daughters of the American Revolution that they were all "descended from immigrants." Attracted by the pluralist spirit and propelled by economic self-interest, the majority of urban ethnics and industrial workers streamed into the Democratic party, where they coexisted uneasily with the third major component of the New Deal coalition—Democrats of the mint-julep variety.[46]

Loved for his wealthy enemies and admired for his social programs, Roosevelt won reelection with a majority of historic proportions. Carrying all but two states (Maine and Vermont), he garnered 61 percent of the popular vote, and still higher percentages the further one moved down the ladder of income and occupation. According to contemporary polling data, he won 76 percent of lower-income votes and 81 percent of the unskilled, plus 84 percent of organized labor. Although the pattern did not really apply to the South (where everybody voted Democratic again after straying in 1928), and although the northern wing of the party included men of wealth such as Joseph Kennedy and Averill Harriman, all in all the election marked a degree of class polarization that had not been seen in decades. With their smashing victory, the Democrats finished the job of displacing the Republicans as the dominant party in national elections and went on to reign until the end of the 1960s.[47]

A few weeks after the election, the New Deal was confronted with a dramatic form of working-class struggle—the sit-down strike. Militants electrified the nation with a series of factory occupations that spread like wildfire in the winter of 1936–37, the most famous of which took place in Flint, Michigan. Waging a brilliant campaign for union recognition, the United Automobile Workers turned the tide in their battle with General Motors by seizing the strategic Chevrolet engine plant, paralyzing Chevy production lines everywhere. Hitherto, mass production had been the chief fortress of the open shop, but the sit-down proved that small groups of determined workers could cripple the whole system of rationalized production; the tactic revealed a gaping chink in the armor of managerial control over the shop floor.[48]

Under similar circumstances in the past, authorities had simply called out the militia and spilled whatever blood it took to reopen the plant. In the current climate, however, both Governor Frank Murphy of Michigan and President Roosevelt turned a deaf ear to pleas from GM officials to roust the sit-downers.[49] These eminently political decisions broke a chain of conquest that extended from Harding back through every president all the way to Hayes. Every one of those presidents had broken important strikes with the might of the U.S. Army, in some cases under far lesser provocations than this dramatic violation of the sacred rights of property. Clearly, the balance of power had shifted.

Congress responded to the new balance with the Fair Labor Standards Act of 1938, the final chapter of New Deal legislation. Like the Wagner Act, it was intended primarily as a recovery measure to stabilize wages, not to redistribute income from rich to poor. It established a national minimum wage, but pegged it so low (initially twenty-five cents per hour) and excluded so many of the lowest-paid workers—domestics, agricultural laborers, retail clerks—that only about 11 million of 48 million gainfully employed were covered, and few received any increase. The effect of other provisions outlawing child labor and setting maximum hours (initially forty-four per week) was much the same. That is, they brought marginal firms into conformity with industrywide standards, picking up where the NRA industrial committees had left off, but did little to redistribute wealth.[50]

Even the Supreme Court began to weigh in on the side of the New Deal. Frustrated by the obstructionism of the "nine old men," Roosevelt proposed in early 1937 to increase the number of justices to give himself a majority on the Court. Widely regarded as his major political blunder, the "Court-packing" scheme aroused fears of executive tyranny. At the same time, the Court demonstrated that it, too, knew how to read election returns. In a dramatic turnabout, the majority of justices withdrew their opposition to social legislation, having somehow found hitherto-undiscovered authority for state intervention under the commerce clause. This change in heart, known as "the switch in time that saved nine," brought the third branch of government into line behind the New Deal. From now on, checks and balances would modify the new governing system, but its basic hegemony was established.[51]

As the elements of a new governing system fell into place, the limits of liberal reform began to appear. For one, the racial hierarchy survived intact, in part because southerners held the Democratic party hostage to segregation. Support of segregation united pro–New Dealers such as Hugo Black of Alabama, who had been in the KKK for a short time, and anti–New Dealers such as Eugene Talmadge of Georgia, who gave out the opinion in the colorful idiom of the region that the New Deal was "a combination of wet nursin', frenzied finance, downright Communism, and plain dam-foolishness." Those in between supported the

New Deal out of loyalty to the party that was the alpha and omega of their political existence. Among these was Joseph Robinson, who as Senate majority leader was essential to the passage of New Deal legislation, in much the way that southern Democrats had been crucial to Woodrow Wilson's New Freedom. As the key to Democratic victory in national elections and to the passage of New Deal legislation, southerners exercised a veto on civil rights.[52]

Not that northerners had much inclination to purge the New Deal of racism. Instead of seeking to end the Afro-American predicament of being "the last hired and the first fired," the New Deal accommodated segregation at every turn. Southern relief workers gave out fewer dollars under FERA and forced black mothers into low-wage jobs by routinely withholding public assistance. The AAA gave out smaller crop allotments to black families, the Civilian Conservation Corps set up segregated bunkhouses, and the FHA accepted restrictive housing covenants as a matter of course. The fact that a disproportionate share of relief went to African-Americans was the result not of special solicitude, but of the fact the blacks were disproportionately poor to begin with.[53]

True, there were civil rights protests. Local struggles for fair employment converged in the March on Washington Movement, led by A. Philip Randolph, head of the Brotherhood of Sleeping Car Porters, and resulted in a presidential order for fair employment as the war approached in 1940. Likewise, Communists demanded "self-determination in the Black Belt," justice for the Scottsboro Boys, and racial integration in the CIO. It is also true that the New Deal provided more material aid in the form of relief, housing, and rural credits to the black community than had any previous administration, and that Eleanor Roosevelt and a few high officials championed racial equality against prevailing opinion. Such material and moral support went a long way toward explaining the historic shift of black voters from the party of Lincoln to the party of Franklin Roosevelt.[54]

Such changes were pregnant with implications for the civil rights movement, but for the time being white supremacy ruled. Perhaps the most glaring moral failure was Roosevelt's refusal to back an antilynching bill. After a spate of lynch-mob atrocities, the NAACP spearheaded a renewed drive for federal penalties. Through the good offices of Eleanor Roosevelt, Walter White, head of the NAACP, met with FDR to press the case in 1934. But the president demurred, claiming that his hands were tied by powerful southern committee chairs: "If I come out for the anti-lynching bill now, they will block every bill I ask Congress to pass to keep America from collapsing." Even after his program had passed, Roosevelt refused to intervene against a 1937 filibuster. Ducking the "race question" made it possible to continue to exclude African-Americans from the "nation of nations."[55]

In the South, as long as segregation stood in the way, social progress was slowed to a crawl. Although farm tenants of both races were caught in the web of dependency, black sharecroppers were especially entangled in the network of furnishing-merchants, local sheriffs, and hard-hearted landlords. Depression compounded the customary problems of regional backwardness as measured by substandard wage levels, low levels of literacy, and 1930 per capita income at 51 percent of the national average. Rural poverty fed into the dire cycle of urban poverty, segregation, and second-rate education.[56]

Racism and poverty were powerful impediments to lower-class organization. Tenants and landless laborers were notoriously hard to organize even under the best of conditions, and racial division made the task even harder. All the more remarkable, therefore, were organizations such as the Southern Tenant Farmers Union, an interracial union formed by Socialists. Echoing a long-dormant side of southern populism, a black member told a largely white crowd: "The same chain that holds my people holds your people." The problem of bridging the races had long stymied industrial unionists, and whatever success now came to the southern labor movement was largely a spillover from battles won in places such as Flint and Pittsburgh. Whereas the labor movement was beginning to win civil liberties in the North, southern authorities still wielded a brutal club, as in "Bloody Harlan," site of hard-fought Kentucky coal wars. As a result, the South emerged from the decade as the leading antiunion bastion in the country.[57]

Southern elites were thus in a good position to join with northern businessmen in reviving conservatism in the late 1930s. For every enlightened corporate liberal there were scores of so-called realists and brass hats fighting social legislation and union recognition to the bitter end. Conservative forces such as the National Association of Manufacturers and the Liberty League won new friends after Roosevelt's ill-fated Court-packing scheme and defeated a number of progressive candidates in the 1938 elections. Meanwhile, rabid anticommunism reappeared in many places, including the streets of New York, where the Catholic Front took to beating up trade unionists, and the chambers of Congress, where the House Un-American Activities Committee under Martin Dies of Texas held hearings aimed at tarring the New Deal with the red brush.[58]

Not all the checks on the New Deal came from its enemies. Among the most important came from within. In reality, the New Deal never intended an assault upon the inner citadels of elite power. Instead of going after the plutocrats, Roosevelt's first and still his foremost action had been the bank rescue. Summing up the president's early achievements, *Fortune* magazine observed that the New Deal "has had the preservation of capitalism at all times in view." A number of big businessmen remained loyal to the New Deal throughout, including A. P. Giannini of the Bank of America and IBM head Thomas Watson. In the 1936 campaign, Roosevelt himself complained of the ingratitude of big businessmen: "Business and industry were like a train which had gone off the rails into a ditch. It was this administration which saved the system of private profit and free enterprise after it had been dragged to the brink of ruin by these same leaders who now try to scare you." While the first New Deal tried to save the capitalist system *for* big business, the second tried to save it *from* big business.[59]

Another important limit was the boundary between the sexes. Although long-term changes in daily life continued, the "woman question" had paled into insignificance in comparison with the hot debates of yesteryear. Gone were the blood-stirring battles over eroticism, the militant marches for suffrage, the feminist manifestos for birth control. Now, gender issues were largely subsumed in economic ones. Influenced by economists' versions of liberal and Marxist theory, radicals forgot the ways they had once linked emancipation of the working class to sexual equality. Tracking the impact of depression on the family, a small army of psychologists and sociologists agreed on the need to shore up the sagging purchasing power of the consumer family and the authority of the jobless husband within it.[60]

To be sure, the decade was not a totally blank page. Here and there courts expanded the realm of sexual freedom by restricting the scope of obscenity statutes, as in a landmark 1933 decision allowing James Joyce's *Ulysses* into the country, and in other rulings that eased restrictions on birth control. These decisions helped bring the law into line with the social practice of sex for pleasure, whose extent is suggested in the statistic that condoms were mass produced at the rate of 1.5 million per day. But for the most part, public policymakers were able to duck issues of gender equality. By the same token, reformers had mixed success in pestering New Deal regulators about equal pay; female workers were often excluded from protection in the first place, and the emerging welfare state was molded at every point to fit the contours of women's economic dependency. Thus the reckoning around the issue of sexual equality was postponed to a later day.[61]

For all its limitations, the fact remains that by the time the New Deal was checkmated at the end of the 1930s, it had already altered the organic relation between the state and society. Responding to the resurgence of popular protest, the New Deal pushed through a social compromise between corporate elites and laboring masses that forever changed the dynamics of American civilization. In institutional terms, the state took a quantum leap into the business of regulating the market, so that virtually everyone from the Wall Street investor dealing with the Securities and Exchange Commission to the Pittsburgh steelworker voting in a union election supervised by the National Labor Relations Board, felt the power of some arm of the federal bureaucracy. In terms of legitimacy, the New Deal enshrined a new set of ruling values keyed to security, so that the mass of the population, from the small savings depositor trusting in the Federal Deposit Insurance Corporation to the retired couple relying on a pension from Social Security, felt as if the government cared about their welfare.

Although Roosevelt popularized his program with populist rhetoric, the new governing system did not redress the balance of class power or redistribute wealth so much as mediate social antagonisms by creating a new set of bureaucratic institutions. Building on Hoover's initiatives, Roosevelt's New Deal expanded state intervention in the market and launched a welfare state. None of these experiments in Keynesian economics ended the Depression; prosperity would not return until war orders started coming in. But the New Deal did succeed in restoring political balance to a system all out of kilter. The "fourth branch" of government, the New Deal coalition, and the ruling myths of security and pluralism renewed popular faith in the state and narrowed the gap between the state and modern society. Thus did the modern governing system take its place alongside the consumer family and corporate property as the third leg of the stool of political stability.

New Deal Liberalism/German Fascism

When Franklin Roosevelt became president on March 4, 1933, Adolf Hitler had been chancellor of Germany for less than five weeks. Having come to power through constitutional means, Hitler was now giving the world a foretaste of Nazi violence. Using the burning of the Reichstag as justification, he procured an emergency decree from the dottering President Hindenburg under which he suspended all civil liberties, arrested Communist deputies, and unleashed his Storm Troopers on hapless opponents. Less than three weeks later, on March 23, again observing constitutional formalities, Hitler procured the Enabling Law from the Reichstag, which authorized him to rule with the full powers of a dictator. Whatever remained of liberal democracy in Germany was dead by the time Roosevelt completed his First Hundred Days.[62]

The almost perfect coincidence of Roosevelt's and Hitler's accession to power cries out for close historical comparison. In the grand scale of world-historical events fascism and New Deal liberalism represented alternative solutions to the same problem of restoring political legitimacy undermined by the Great Depression. Since the two solutions were not hypothetical concoctions but lived realities, it is possible to learn a good deal about the actual forces propelling each country.

Given the extraordinary personalities of Roosevelt and Hitler, it is tempting to focus on the accidents of history, as unpredictable as genetic mutations, that prepare great figures to assume the role of hero or antihero. Undoubtedly something in the difference between Roosevelt's power brokering and Hitler's will to power helps explain the difference between New Deal democracy and Nazi dictatorship. But force of personality and quirks of fate are not adequate explanations of events of this magnitude.

At the opposite extreme, impersonal economic trends can not carry the burden of explanation, either. The United States and Germany were heartlands of corporate, or organized, capitalism, and of all that went with it in terms of rationalization, scientific management, and the conflicts between rising capitalists and the burgeoning industrial working class. Because of large-scale enterprise, the two countries were closer to each other in their industrial and occupational structures than either was to France, with its small-scale peasant and family enterprises, or to Britain, with its aging nineteenth-century industrial infrastructure. The historical destinies of the United States and Germany had collided head-on during the First World War, and afterward had coiled around each other like a double helix as American loans underwrote German reparations. Thus entwined, the world's two largest industrial economies plunged into the Great Depression at about the same time, with gross national product falling by about a third in both cases. When they hit bottom in the winter of 1932–33, unemployment stood at 25 percent in the United States and 30 percent in Germany.[63]

These events induced a crisis of confidence in both countries. Gone were the international financial stability and domestic business confidence of the mid-1920s, and gone, too, was popular confidence in the ability of existing governments to handle the situation. The longer the crisis dragged on, the clearer it became that restoring legitimacy would require deep changes in both countries. Yet, in retrospect, it is equally clear that the Depression itself did not determine what the changes would be. Similarity can never explain difference; therefore, the economic contours alone could not have caused such different political outcomes.[64]

Germany chose fascism in two stages. In the first, from 1929 through 1932, the Depression undermined confidence in the Weimar Republic and the Versailles Treaty, prompting elites to empty the State of its liberal content and to reject the Versailles system. On paper the Weimar constitution was a model of liberal democracy that substituted parliamentary authority, popular sovereignty, and universal suffrage for the old regime's imperial authority and property-weighted male suffrage. The key to Weimar's survival was a social compromise between industrialists and Social Democratic workers that had been blessed by the army in late 1918 to stave off socialist revolution. The compromise was embodied in corporatist policies that balanced the interests of capital and labor, including compulsory arbitration of labor-management disputes and social legislation (*Sozialpolitik*) that established an eight-hour day in large industry, plus unemployment insurance. This corporatist machinery was but the newest layer in two centuries of sedimentary deposits during which almost every aspect of German social life had been incorporated in the state. So long as the social compromise held, the republic was safe.[65]

Then came the Depression. With tax revenues and business profits falling, social legislation became a costly burden to both government and business. In fact, a dispute over unemployment compensation shattered the Grand Coalition that had presided from 1925 until 1930. Under the strain of depression, liberal corporatism fell victim to the very class antagonisms it was intended to override.[66]

Meanwhile, the Depression magnified German resentment over the limitations imposed by Versailles. German desire to avenge military defeat was breaking all bounds, but France and Britain had lost the will to hold it back. The cessation of U.S. loans further damaged the Versailles system. Under the Dawes and Young Plans, international stability had depended on the circular flow of capital from U.S. banks to Germany, then from German reparations to French and British coffers, and, finally, from French and British debt payments back to U.S. banks. Unfortunately, U.S. investors were caught short after the stock market crash and soon stopped lending overseas, while President Hoover's one-year moratorium on debt payments came too late to restore international confidence. With foreign powers losing the will to uphold the system, successive German governments from 1929 through 1932 unilaterally repealed so many of the reparations and arms limitations provisions of the Versailles Treaty that it was practically a dead letter by the time the Nazis took power.[67]

The collapse of Weimar did not automatically guarantee that a fascist regime would take its place. There were two other options to consider. Although no developed capitalist government had yet fallen to socialist revolution, the possibility could not be discounted. Together, Social Democrats and Communists amounted to some 40 percent of the Reichstag at their peak, and both had a devoted following; an extensive network of clubs, halls, and newspapers; and well-developed ideology, hagiography, and martyrology. Had the left been united, and had it been able to win over elements of the middle class, it could have governed the nation.[68]

Instead, Socialists and Communists were at each other's throats. Social Democrats had proved repeatedly that loyalty to nation came before loyalty to class. They had proved it upon the outbreak of war in 1914, and again in helping to put down the Communist "second revolution" in 1919. Then, having become a pillar of the Weimar Republic, they were ready to defend it even as it cut back social legislation. Tragically, however, in the hour of greatest peril to liberal democracy, the dead hand of the past reached out to prevent the left from uniting. Unable to forget the scars of 1919, Communists now deemed Socialists to be "social fascists" and refused to lift a finger to save the republic. By the time they rectified their folly in the Popular Front, it was too late.[69]

With the left occupied in internecine strife, this might well have been the moment for the second option. Traditional authority did its best to reassert itself. Although Germany preserved the outward form of a constitutional republic from 1930 through 1932, its inner life turned on the undemocratic machinations of upper-class conservatives. With the collapse of the Grand Coalition, President Hindenburg took the army's advice and appointed Heinrich Brüning, leader of the Catholic Center party, as the new chancellor. As head of a minority government, Brüning quickly took to ruling by decree, and some mark his appointment as the end of the German republic. In any case, he ran into stiff opposition when he proposed to investigate the state agricultural subsidies; the Junkers promptly denounced him for "agrarian bolshevism." Complying with their wishes, Hindenburg turned the offender out of office in May 1932 and replaced him with Fritz von Papen, an aristocratic conservative who quickly proved to be merely an incompetent Machiavellian.[70]

The search for ever-higher authority led finally to the army itself in the person of General Kurt von Schleicher. But Schleicher's scheming only worsened the crisis. The fact that he could not secure a parliamentary majority demonstrated what was by now painfully obvious—that traditional elites were unfit to govern modern Germany. At the very moment when Germany might have entrusted itself to "authority"— the army, the great industrialists, the estate owners—those forces were unable to unite among themselves or to rally a mass following. Capable only of destroying liberalism, they were incapable of putting anything else in its place.

Enter Hitler. His ascension to power in January 1933 was a charade in which the sworn enemy of constitutional liberties pretended to respect the now-meaningless liberal constitution. Surely, it was a "triumph of the will" that a lowborn megalomaniac who never won more than 37 percent of the popular vote became *Der Führer* to the high-caste gentlemen who had tried to make him their pawn. Forcing through a revolution from above, he pleased industrialists by destroying trade unions and leftist parties, made friends with the army by purging the more radical elements from the paramilitary Storm Troopers, and carried expansionists along on the dream of a thousand-year

Reich. Cementing alliances with old elites, however, did not make the Nazis a throwback to the old regime. As a modern-day mass movement they were not reactionaries but counterrevolutionaries in the double sense of the word: they were mortal enemies of socialist revolution but also of bourgeois liberalism.[71]

Although the Nazis drew from all layers of society, most of their followers came from the middling strata. Having watched inflation devalue their savings in the early 1920s, the middle classes distrusted the Weimar regime because it all but left them out of the system of corporatist bargaining. Acutely conscious of their position in a hierarchy of wealth and status, the new urban white-collar employees resented the favors that went to industrial workers. Suffering the effects of worldwide agricultural distress and the rise of industrial cartels, the old petty-bourgeois peasants and tradesmen saw liberal society as a cesspool of family breakup, salacious cabarets, and promiscuous mingling of the sexes.[72]

These middle ranks took seriously the injunction for women to be the guardians of home and morality. Among the large number of women counted as family assistants—wives or daughters of small property helping out in shops, farms, and families—the Nazi message of strengthening family life undoubtedly struck a resonant chord.[73] At least, the Nazis attracted a disproportionate share of women voters. It did not seem to matter that women were debarred from any significant role in the organization; the party could always trot out loyal women members such as Guida Diehl to warn that "Americanism, materialism and mammonism threatened to overwhelm *Volk*, God and Fatherland." Paeans to women's maternal virtue also won support from such groups as the German-Evangelical Women's League and even from the grandmother organization of German feminism, the League of German Women. To the extent that the Nazis built upon the values of family, *Volk*, and fatherland, they universalized the worldview of the lower middle classes.[74]

The fact that so many of the German bourgeoisie (including these middle layers) supported fascism casts doubt on a widely held notion about the links between class and ideology. Contrary to the common wisdom, there is no necessary historical connection between capitalism, the middle class, and liberal ideas. At all the critical junctures of German history—the revolution of 1848, the unification of 1871, the decision for war in 1914—the middle classes had kow-towed to king, aristocracy, and army.[75] Now, lacking deeply held constitutional scruples, they readily abandoned the Weimar republic in favor of authoritarian solutions. Seeking a new order, the forgotten men and women of Depression Germany were ripe for rapturous abandon in the fictive community of the imperial Teutonic nation.[76]

Breaking with the traditional politics of economic self-interest, Nazis constructed an ideology around racial nationalism. Lumping everyone together in a mythic "people's community" (*Volksgemeinschaft*), they subordinated everyone to the all-powerful state. Summed up in the slogan "ein Volk, ein Reich," Nazism offered the bogus "socialism" of rhetorical attacks on "international Jewish bankers" to a supposedly homogeneous Aryan race, unsullied by "lower" races (*Untermenschen*) of Slavs and Jews. And it whipped up German expansionism into an insatiable lust for room to live (*Lebensraum*) in the fit company of fascist Italy and imperial Japan.

Once race was taken as the founding myth of national identity, biology became destiny for men and women. Rejecting ideas of sexual equality that had gained a hearing during Weimar, Nazism incorporated a definition of gender that came to rest on extreme polar divisions between the sexes. Born to command, man was destined to lead the nation in battle, and so Nazism rang with the warrior ethic, especially in the hands of Storm Troopers and other paramilitary street fighters. Dripping with misogyny, Nazism was pathologically obsessed with violence and almost inherently sadistic. To men such as Heinrich Himmler, head of the Gestapo, the brotherhood of the trenches in the First World War was the model for the male comradeship of the Nazi movement, and that was, in turn, the germ of the male state (*Mannerstaat*), the very pinnacle of human achievement.[77]

Born to breed, woman was destined to produce offspring for the Reich. If the Aryan race was to remain pure, Aryan wombs must be kept under control. To increase the number of births to the master race, Nazis reversed the policies of Weimar governments and offered the carrot of family loans alongside the stick of criminal penalties restricting abortion and contraception. To prevent the master race from being contaminated by the *Untermenschen*, Nazis expanded on the preexisting movement for "race hygiene" to promote sterilization of "asocials," who included Jews, prostitutes and other "deviants," and the "feebleminded" among the lower classes. All manner of decadence and corruption was charged against the feminist idea of equality, which supposedly had compelled women to deviate from their true nature. The model of true womanhood was the the pregnant madonna, selflessly devoted to children, kitchen, and church (*Kinder, Kuche, Kirche*).[78] It is important to remember that even among those who embraced Nazi ideology, there was always a gap between myth and practice. For all the glorification of motherhood, fecundity did not increase, nor did women's participation in the labor force decline in the 1930s. But what few freedoms women may have retained came in the context of large oppressions.[79]

Taken as a whole, Nazism was the product of a historical conjuncture triggered by humiliating defeat in the First World War and economic anxiety in the Great Depression. The door to fascism was opened by traditional elites who eviscerated liberal democracy but who were themselves incapable of governing modern, capitalist societies. That created the opportunity for counterrevolutionaries to come storming through on the strength of a mass movement whose taproot lay in the lower middle class and whose appeal was built around a set of negations—anticommunism, anticonservatism, antiliberalism, antifeminsim, and anti-Semitism.[80] Invited into power by military and industrial elites who hoped to use the Nazi party as a mass base, the Nazis gave elites more than they had bargained for. Once in power, the Nazis imposed a brutal regime whose leading traits were capitalism by violence, racial nationalism, hypermasculinism, and imperial expansion. Having already conquered Italy under Mussolini, fascism now swept Germany and Austria, gained strength in eastern Europe, and found a close cousin in imperial Japan. Whereas in 1919 and 1920 the question of social revolution had hung over world affairs, the pertinent question after 1932 was whether counterrevolution might spread throughout the globe.

Did that possibility include the United States? That some type of authoritarian regime would emerge in the land of liberty did not seem out of the question at the time. Few could match John Dewey's credentials as an astute observer of the American scene, and in 1932 he was worried: "We have permitted business and financial autocracy to reach such a point that its logical political counterpart is a Mussolini, unless a violent revolution brings forth a Lenin." In fact, there were ominous signs of a corporatist regime in the state capitalism of Hoover and of Roosevelt in his first administration. Pointing to the fusion of capitalist titans and government bureaucrats in the RFC and NRA, Walter

Lippmann warned of "the dictatorship of casual oligarchs," while the *New Republic* described the early New Deal as an American-style "corporative state."[81]

In addition, many contemporaries saw militarist glimmerings in General Hugh Johnson's Blue Eagle and the Civilian Conservation Corps. Certainly, state repression was by no means foreign to America, as the labor movement, the Bonus Army, and generations of African-Americans could attest. No wonder some imaginations ran wild. Under the ironic title *It Can't Happen Here* (1935), Sinclair Lewis described the fictional seizure of power by an authoritarian regime backed by Wall Street, the Wasp establishment, and the military on the heels of a presidential victory by a bombastic demagogue bearing a strong resemblance to Huey Long.

If a repressive regime was going to develop in the United States, conservative elites would have to link up with a potent, right-wing mass movement. The fact that such a movement failed to emerge does not mean that the ingredients were altogether missing. America was no stranger to the class resentments and ethnic hatreds that fueled the revolt of the little guy in Germany. If anything could have become the basis for an American *Volksgemeinschaft*, it was white racism, and, in fact, the entire repertoire of unreason—racial bigotry, Christian anti-Semitism, nativist paranoia, anticommunism, and antifeminism—was tapped by hate groups such as the Ku Klux Klan and even by the more respectable Rotarians, American Legionnaires, and women's clubbers.[82]

The closest thing to a counterrevolutionary movement in the United States gathered around the figure of Father Charles Coughlin. A magnetic speaker who outdid FDR in the mastery of mass communications, the Detroit "Radio Priest" reached as many as 40 million listeners, and at its peak his National Union for Social Justice attracted perhaps 5 million members. Wrapping patriarchal and corporatist views in a quasi-populist cover, he portrayed an unholy conspiracy of bankers, Communists, and Jews. With the characteristic logic-chopping of the demagogue, he could pronounce that "the most dangerous communist is the wolf in the sheep's clothing of conservatism," and in ever more putrid rhetoric he excoriated "money changers" such as Andrew Mellon and Treasury Secretary Henry Morgenthau with their "Jewish cohorts."[83]

There was nothing unique in Coughlin's anticommunism, anticonservatism, and anti-Semitism, common elements in the underworld of American politics. Likewise, when he warned that birth control and premarital sex led to prostitution and socialism, his antifeminism was in keeping with the sentiments of a long line of purity crusaders. What was peculiar about Coughlin—and what linked him to European fascism—was his antiliberalism. Unlike most American rightists, he called for greater state control of the economy, including nationalization of the banks. Strongly influenced by the corporatist philosophy of social relations in Pope Pius XI's *Quadregesimo Anno* (1931), he urged a national welfare system. Just as the National Socialist party impersonated socialism, so his National Union for Social Justice impersonated social justice reform.[84]

If there was a threat of tyranny, it lay in the possibility that big business would join forces with the kind of mass bigotry represented by Coughlin. Given America's liberal inheritance, there was little likelihood of an all-powerful leviathan state, but there was a good deal of experience with the undemocratic power of business and the tyranny of the majority. In the frenzy of 100 percent Americanism after the First World War, the country got a taste of what a repressive regime might look like in a set of harsh measures ranging from the open shop to immigration restriction. In many ways, the choices confronting the country in the mid-1930s were quite similar. Would the response to popular discontent be social reform or the repression of another Red Scare? With the memory of postwar violations of civil liberties still fresh, the question was not whether fascism would spread to America, but whether the United States would pick up where it had left off in the early 1920s and develop a homegrown, repressive regime of its own.

Comparison with Germany illuminates the reasons why no such regime emerged. Perhaps the starkest contrast between the two countries lay in foreign policy. From the day the Versailles Treaty was signed, Germany was a revisionist power, and the fact that the United States was not goes a long way toward explaining why there was nothing to compare with the German impulse toward militarism. While the Nazis turned resentment over defeat in the First World War into a militarist crusade for *Lebensraum*, the United States was content to reap the harvest of economic exports and corporate diplomacy in the 1920s. Then in the 1930s the United States retreated into its shell. Signs of rising economic nationalism included the Smoot-Hawley Tariff of 1930, Roosevelt's "torpedo" of the 1933 London Economic Conference, and the Neutrality Acts (1935–1937), by which Congress pretended that the United States had no vital interests outside its borders. On the positive side, Roosevelt's Good Neighbor Policy toward Latin America foreswore armed intervention. But on the negative, the United States buried its head in the sand while fascist powers conquered Ethiopia, Spain, and Manchuria, only making the inevitable reckoning that much more devastating when it finally came in September 1939. Be that as it may, the spirit of neutrality allowed little room for the sort of bellicose nationalism that would have fostered a militarist regime in the United States.

On the domestic side, it is necessary, first of all, to credit popular social movements for revitalizing democratic traditions. Undoubtedly, the most important event in this regard was the resurgence of the labor movement as embodied in the newborn Congress of Industrial Organizations. Not only did the CIO seek to give workers a say in industry—that is, to make the Bill of Rights apply inside the factory gate—but CIO organizers were forced to combat ethnic hatred in order to unite the immigrant nationalities among the rank and file. The same pluralist imperative was imposed on political parties. Capitalizing on the popularity of the repeal of Prohibition, the Democrats brought urban ethnics into the New Deal coalition and prepared the way for general acceptance of the idea that the United States was a "nation of nations."

What was especially distinctive about democracy in the 1930s was that it came with a social twist. When social movements spilled over into electoral politics behind southern populists, midwestern progressives, and the occasional leftist, it became advantageous for politicians all the way up to the president to support social-democratic reforms such as the Wagner Act and Social Security. Roosevelt may have saved liberalism; he may have saved capitalism; but grass-roots social movements were the saviors of democracy.

Strangely enough, even when a spirit of cultural tolerance was absent, the diversity of the American population was an impediment to the formation of a mythic "people's community." Aside from the unifying role of white racism, it was hard for America's various ethnic and religious factions to feel close kinship with one another. The fact that Coughlin launched his radio career in response to a KKK cross-burning at his Church of the Little Flower points to the difficulty of forging a homogeneous community. In the same fashion, there was little love lost among America's self-professed fascists. The nativist Black Legion was comprised of Protestant blue-collar workers and had no truck with the German-American Bund or the Italian-American Black Shirts, both of whom imitated the fascist regalia of their respective homelands. In short, America's prejudices simply canceled one another out. If Americans had cause to be proud of their country for not succumbing to fascism, some of the reasons were not so flattering.[85]

Ideas of gender could not easily have been handmaidens to an authoritarian state, either. Again, although the elements of misogyny and ultramasculinity were present, they did not coalesce within a single mass movement. Comparison with Germany would suggest that the reasons had to do with such features of American society as the weakness of patriarchal institutions and the relative strength of the independent New Woman. Since German women worked in greater numbers and, if anything, were more prominent in politics (at least before the Nazis), the stronger sense of equality between the sexes in the United States was more a matter of general social values and manners. In America, everyone was supposed to be equal. In addition, the fact of ethnic pluralism made it virtually impossible to conceive of the nation as a single family writ large, while the pervasive distrust of centralized power made it unlikely for women willingly to submit their wombs to the service of the state.

Another obstacle was the inherited structure of the liberal state. American history was littered with the wreckage of centralizing impulses, from populism and prewar socialism to technocratic state planning of the sort embodied in the NRA. All of these had foundered on the liberal rocks of checks and balances, the separation of powers, and the three-tiered system of federalism. The same fragmentation of power—along with winner-take-all elections and the presidential (as opposed to parliamentary) system—made major political parties into amorphous agglomerations lacking clear ideological divisions.

What it came down to was the supremacy of American society over the state. Fascism was weak for the same reason that socialism was weak. Ever since the American Revolution, Americans have been deeply suspicious of state power. Given the tendency of power to become corrupt, that was undoubtedly a healthy suspicion. But too often, Americans threw the baby of organic community out with the bathwater of centralized power. It has often been said that when it came to the great trinity of liberty, equality, and fraternity, Americans refused to embrace the last. It is not that the values of community have been altogether missing from a culture steeped in liberal individualism. But every idea geared to commonwealth, every program of social solidarity, and every move toward public ownership had to swim upstream, because Americans had trouble conceiving of themselves as a genuine community in which the well-being of each was inseparable from the well-being of all.

Suspicion of state power was certainly evident among elites in the 1930s. The more the New Deal regulated the market, the more business turned against it. By 1936 the Du Pont–funded Liberty League was in full cry against the New Deal, and soon many Wall Streeters, provincial manufacturers, and southern Bourbons were coalescing into a conservative opposition. Unlike the traditional elites (landed, bureaucratic, military, clerical) of Germany, which had long supported a strong state, America's modern elites (corporate and professional) inherited a weak state and were eternally vigilant in guarding their liberty—that is, the prerogatives of class and culture—against encroachments from Washington.[86] Although businessmen soon learned to live with expanded state power—indeed, they embraced state capitalism from the start and never let go—they would have preferred a nexus of public-private authority to anything that smacked of a statist regime. Again, if tyranny had come to America, it would have worn the face not of state totalitarianism, but of corporate absolutism in league with mass conformity.

The failure of counterrevolution and the absence of authoritarian power permitted the United States to remain within the liberal frame even as it implemented a social compromise between capital and labor. If America in the 1930s was unlike Nazi Germany, it bore a strong resemblance to the Germany of the 1920s.[87] As in the case of Weimar, governing a modern society required social-democratic and corporatist practices that accorded a certain recognition to major social groups. Indeed, the press of events during the Depression overrode the die-hard resistance of laissez-faire liberals and, at long last, compelled some recognition of the collective interests of working people. Labor legislation and the welfare state studiously avoided the larger class goals of redistributing wealth and power but went just far enough to buy a large measure of mass loyalty.

That transformation, in turn, permitted liberal hegemony to continue. The persistence of liberalism was evident in a host of ways—the extension of the Bill of Rights to the factory floor; the continuation of checks and balances and federalism; the fact that the welfare state was designed to buttress the sagging institutions of the market and the nuclear family, not to transcend them; and the fact that special favors were never presented as "class" legislation, but as some kind of general benefit to all consumers. The persistence of liberalism was linked to the remarkable sway of the market in the United States in both fact and folklore. Where else could massive state intervention be justified as a way of strengthening the free-enterprise system? At the deepest level, then, the modern governing system was based not so much on corporatist groups—finance, agriculture, business, labor—as on atomized consumer families operating in state-regulated markets under the aegis of the modern corporation.

There is no doubt that a comparison of New Deal America and Nazi Germany makes the United States look good. Instead of pursuing militarist expansion abroad and a massacre of liberty at home, the United States coped with the seeming collapse of capitalism by enhancing civil liberty, expanding social programs, and refraining from imperial adventures. No doubt, there is justice in seeing all this as liberalism's finest hour. But what would not look good against the Nazis? Surely, there are higher hopes against which to measure the New Deal. Although social-democratic reforms undoubtedly humanized the rigors of life in the competitive marketplace, they barely trenched upon the dominance of corporate capital. And other aspects of social hierarchy—white supremacy and male dominance—were not even addressed in a serious fashion. New Deal liberalism was not the crusading liberalism of Woodrow Wilson (for which Latin America was thankful), nor was it the conquering liberalism of the nineteenth-century middle class (for which wage earners were grateful). It was, instead, a largely successful effort to stabilize a system that seemed to have gone haywire. In the end, America's rendezvous with destiny was not so much a heroic adventure on the high seas of freedom as a search for safe harbor in an insecure and dangerous world.

Conclusion

WHEN IT CAME time to celebrate the semicentennial of the Statue of Liberty on October 28, 1936, President Roosevelt was nearing the end of his first reelection campaign. Not one to pass up a chance for political advantage, he boated out to Liberty Island to rededicate the country's most hallowed public monument. Speaking over a nationwide radio hookup, he quoted President Cleveland's original dedication speech to say that the nation needed to renew its covenant with liberty, especially now after so many new immigrants had entered the country. Welcoming the huddled masses to the "place of the second chance," he boasted that the multitude of Old World cultures had finally found "their common destiny in America."[1]

Roosevelt's theme that day was as old as the republic. Like his ceremonial counterpart fifty years earlier, he looked to history for the common values that would unite a divided people. There was no doubt about the division. Even as he spoke, one-third of the nation still suffered the worst effects of the Great Depression, ethnic groups warily eyed one another, and labor and farmer movements demanded radical action against the rich. Seeking a way through these troubled times, Roosevelt called upon the tradition of Jefferson and Lincoln to give the current generation a sense of common destiny.

The great irony of renewing the covenant with liberty in the 1930s was that Roosevelt's New Deal had done more to change the liberal tradition than anything since the Revolution. Whether one looked at managerial institutions such as the National Recovery Administration or social reforms such as the Social Security system, it was clear that a new liberalism had come into being. Extensive government regulation of the market and the coming of the welfare state marked a permanent turn away from laissez faire.

Although it is impossible to speak about the "causes" of this transformation with anything like scientific precision, it is possible to say something about the central dynamics of American life. In one aspect, the dynamics arose out of internal contradictions among opposing social forces, and, in another, out of the imbalance between the changing life of the society and the existing form of the state. In either case, the growing incongruity between the way Americans lived and the way they were governed forced them into a reckoning with their traditional forms of liberty.

Tracing the matter to its roots, one is drawn deep into the subsoil of the material environment. From the relentless pace of Henry Ford's assembly line to the hustle and bustle of Montgomery Ward's home office, Americans were busy inventing new techniques of mass production and mass distribution and new forms of bureaucratic organization to manage them. Flocking to the roller-coaster thrills of Coney Island and the bewitching images of the silver screen, they also pioneered the development of mass culture. Indeed, they were changing the very way they handed down their way of life across the generations—that is, changing the way they *reproduced* in a social sense—as they patronized public schools, mass entertainments, and big city hospitals.

The fact that Americans increasingly worked and lived en masse did not make America a mass society of interchangeable individuals. To the contrary, the chasm of class and culture that separated the college-educated executive at a firm such as Armour & Company from the immigrant packinghouse workers of Upton Sinclair's *The Jungle* guaranteed that modern society would be divided against itself. As America rushed headlong through the second Industrial Revolution and as family capitalism gave way to corporate capitalism, the rift between corporate elites and working classes spread into every crevice of social life. With the social weight of industrial workers mounting to its all-time peak, it is not surprising that industrial conflict climaxed in 1919–1920 with the largest strike wave in all of American history. It is not too much to say that the tension between corporate elite and laboring mass was the main dynamic of social change in this period.

That is not to say it was the only one. The fact that every aspect of the society was changing at once was a measure of the depth of social transformation. Something as basic as the relation between the sexes was put on a new footing as increasing numbers of men and women threw over the ways of their Victorian forebears. Breaking free from her gilded cage, the New Woman claimed sexual equality as a human right against the more conventional assertion of women's special virtue and peculiar needs. As the middle-class family collapsed toward its nuclear core and as women increasingly entered the job market and public life, the old doctrine of separate spheres increasingly became an anachronism.

Another set of tensions swirled around the question of American identity. Passions ran high in bitter clashes between Protestant and Catholic, Anglo-Saxon and Jew, white supremacist and Negro nationalist, and a good deal of argument went to decide the best basis for a common national identity. The larger significance of this debate lay in its relation to the high-stakes game of wealth, power, and prestige. The fact that corporate elites were largely college-educated Yankee Protestants whereas the mass of urban wage earners were culturally diverse and poorly educated meant that the relative strength of the various groups hung in the balance around the outcome of political battles such as those over immigration restriction and Prohibition.

If the leading public issues of the day arose from the cockpits of social conflict, then the place to look for an explanation for the rise of the new liberalism is in the impact of contending social forces upon the governing system. For the more American society changed the more it outgrew the existing form of the liberal state. The old governing system—that is, legislatures and courts devoted to laissez faire, buttressed by Victorian forms of gender, and imbued with Social Darwinist myths of race—lost its capacity to govern.

The first inkling that a great transformation was in store came in the Progressive Era when social reformers first laid siege to laissez faire. According to the conventional wisdom, any meddling with the market to equalize social conditions inevitably curbed individual liberty. In other words, there was a choice between liberty and equality.

If so, progressive reformers were ready to restrain individual liberty for the good of society. In the springtime of the twentieth century, it was still possible to be full of optimism about human progress, and they mounted crusades for a new social conscience that made inroads on laissez faire upon which there was no turning back. When social consciousness revived in the 1930s, New Deal reformers only had to pick up where progressives had left off.

Not to be overlooked in the accounting, U.S. entrance onto the world stage laid heavy strains on the existing governing system. Even more than the acquisition of an overseas empire, the exigencies of the First World War proved that the old state structures were simply not up to the task of mobilizing, regulating, and propagandizing the civilian population. The Wilson administration's new battery of hastily improvised wartime administrations resembled the kind of corporatist institutions emerging in Europe in that they gave representation to broad interest groups—business, labor, the public—instead of to elected parliamentary representatives. Although the war ended before these exotic hothouse plants could develop into permanent state bureaucracies, they set an example that would be imitated in the response to depression in the 1930s.

The inadequacy of old-fashioned liberalism was also revealed in the aftermath of the war. Repelled by the unsettling turns of events in Versailles and Russia, the United States abandoned the spirit of crusading liberalism that had served it so well in the Spanish-American War and in the mobilization to "make the world safe for democracy." But Europe proved to be off-limits to the empire of liberty. Wilson's high hopes for a liberal world order as embodied in the Fourteen Points ran aground on the imperial ambitions of America's allies and were dealt another blow by the Bolshevik Revolution. Recoiling from the sticky entanglements of European power politics, crusading liberalism turned inward upon itself in the Red Scare and collapsed in a heap of isolationist reaction.

At home, the fact that liberal restoration could come only through repression showed a similar failing. In response to social tumult many progressives joined old-fashioned liberals to show their teeth in violent suppression of strikes and scandalous violations of the Bill of Rights. Frightened by the prospect of sexual emancipation, they set out to restore Victorian virtue through the discipline of Prohibition and the abolition of prostitution. Determined to restore the waning privileges of Anglo-Saxon Protestants, they closed the gates on Catholic and Jewish immigrants. If all this amounted to the revenge of nineteenth-century liberalism upon the twentieth century, the resort to vigilantism and state coercions only showed how far the old-time liberalism was out of step with the mass of the population. Thus in both foreign and domestic affairs, the country had not yet found the formula to restore the balance between the state and modern society.

By the time the Great Depression came along, the Gilded Age republic had become a hollow shell. So when political experiments resumed under the emergency conditions of economic collapse, Presidents Hoover and Roosevelt had no choice but to change the form of the state if they wished to regain consent of the governed to the governing system.

Even before the Depression, Hoover had begun to draw government into the affairs of the marketplace, and his pace only quickened in the face of economic calamity. Although he did not move nearly fast or far enough, he set the stage for many of the reforms enacted by his successor. Contrary to much worshipful mythology, Roosevelt began by following in his predecessor's managerial footsteps, and only when government-assisted corporate planning failed to end the Depression did he embark on new experiments of his own. Wedded to no particular philosophy, he supported the Wagner Act and Social Security, which, along with numerous other innovations, curbed private property and gave birth to a welfare state.

In terms of consequences, one must not expect mathematical exactitude, either. Much of what happened after the 1930s was not readily traceable to the New Deal or the New Era, and other influences would leave their mark on the years to come. Certainly, the Second World War had a major impact, as did such far-off events as the revolutions in China and Vietnam. Yet it is possible to say that the changes of the 1930s laid the foundation for a hegemonic system that lasted through the next four decades.

The New Deal reformed capitalism in ways that preserved both liberalism and capitalism. Never before had the federal government imposed so many restraints on the individual and so many curbs on private property; never again would the state absent itself from the market. State capitalism and the welfare state were here to stay. Yet somehow these changes were carried out in the name of preserving individual opportunity, and New Dealers stole the liberal banner from free-market conservatives.

Because the New Deal struck just the right political chord, its immense popularity went a long way toward replenishing the legitimacy that was slowly hemorrhaging away during the Depression. Out of the conflict of the depression-wracked 1930s came a new consensus.

In evaluating that achievement, there is something to be said for humanizing a system that, left to its own devices, invariably put profits ahead of people. The social-democratic reforms of liberalism undoubtedly improved the conditions of life for the majority of the working population, provided a certain dignity in retirement, and, for the first time, introduced a modicum of liberty inside the factory gate. Whereas crusading liberals at the time of the Red Scare had seen socialism as their mortal enemy, the new liberals of the "Red Decade" were willing to use watered-down socialist ideas against the would-be tyranny of archconservative industrialists. It may have been the case that the best in liberal values could no longer be realized within a capitalist society; even so, a more humane capitalism was better than a less humane one.[2]

If there was any doubt on that score, one had only to look at Germany. Certainly, a capitalism that honored liberal values was more benign than one that drew the fascist gun. Although the United States was not entirely free of the ugliness that characterized Germany's response to depression, it successfully resisted the strong pull of racial nationalism, masculine swagger, militarist expansion, and authoritarianism. Although the U.S. response to the rise of fascism can be faulted on many counts, including its head-in-the-sand diplomacy in the face of fascist aggression and its cold shoulder to many ordinary victims of Nazi persecution, the fact remains that America did not succumb to its own worst impulses.

But neither did it yield to its best impulses. The new liberalism incorporated privileges of gender and race that mocked the ideal of equality. With feminism at its lowest ebb since the turn of the century, the New Deal simply ducked the issue of equality between the sexes. Indeed, in excluding many of the poorest wage earners—often female—from state protection and in seeking to shore up the consumer family, it displaced many of the burdens of inequality onto women. With respect to race relations, although New Deal social programs won support from the black community, the New Deal never confronted "the American dilemma" head on. As a consequence, the unanswered questions of sex and race were left to become the burning issues of the 1960s.

For that matter, the New Deal's reform of liberty was never intended to usher in the reign of equality. Roosevelt was determined at all times to save the capitalist system, even if that meant saving it from the capitalists themselves. He certainly stopped far short of emancipating the working class for anything like full participation in social decision making. In truth, the aim was never to realize social equality but rather to promote social security.

That intent was summed up by Roosevelt himself in a revealing parable. Borrowing from Abraham Lincoln, the all-time master of the political parable, Roosevelt told the story of the shepherd (FDR) and the wolf (conservative businessmen of the Liberty League): "The shepherd drives the wolf from the sheep's throat, for which the sheep thanks the shepherd as his liberator, while the wolf denounces him for the same act, as the destroyer of liberty."[3] The parable speaks volumes about Roosevelt's conception of the federal government as the protector of a nation of sheep.

The new governing system that emerged by the eve of the Second World War was something more than the social programs associated with New Deal liberalism. Although it included safeguards and securities for the weak, it also incorporated protections for the strong. Whatever one may choose to call it—corporate liberalism, liberal capitalism, or interest-group liberalism—the fact was that the new system was more congruent with corporate dominance and the contending forces within American society than was the old.

The main proof of that fact lies in the longevity of the settlement. Having experimented for several decades with a variety of half-way solutions, the country settled down to live within the limits of the new hegemony for almost a half century. Although the 1960s witnessed profound challenges to the New Deal's acceptance of racial segregation and women's subordination, the rest of the system was simply taken for granted. While successive Democratic administrations from Truman's Fair Deal to Johnson's Great Society added new wings to the house the New Deal built, even Republican presidents from Eisenhower to Nixon and Ford were content to dwell within it. Indeed, the system built around state capitalism and the welfare state was so solid, even Ronald Reagan could not knock down the whole thing.

Today, in the waning years of the twentieth century, we are as far away in time from the 1930s as the New Deal was from the Gilded Age. In the interim, the relentless evolution of American society has radically altered material conditions to create computers, nuclear weapons, and other forms of hypertechnology unknown to previous generations. Great changes in production and reproduction have taken place, including a massive restructuring of the global economy, a tidal wave of women workers, and the growth of megalopolis. Their effect has been as significant as those of changes in the previous era.

The difference is that instead of going along with American ascendancy, they accompany American decline. Formerly the unchallenged colossus of world capitalism, the United States has shrunk relative to Japan and Germany. Once the world's leading creditor and prime exporter of industrial goods, it has become the world's largest debtor and a declining industrial power. Given the collapse of communism in Eastern Europe and the end of the Cold War, it has lost influence in what used to be called the "free world." With amazing speed, the "American Century" has come and gone, a casualty of deindustrialization, defeat in Vietnam, and the rise of Western Europe and Eastern Asia.

At home, the system built in response to the Great Depression has started to fall apart. New Deal policies that once stabilized the distribution of income gave way to policies under President Reagan that widened the gap between rich and poor. The removal of state regulations in the 1980s precipitated an orgy of speculation and the biggest rash of business failures since the 1930s. Even the core institutions of state capitalism became overburdened as a result of the crisis in banks and savings institutions. The loss of American hegemony in world affairs has been paralleled at home by the declining hegemony of the modern governing system.

Given these sharp discontinuities with the past, is there anything the earlier period has to say to the late twentieth century? Maybe not. Maybe the rusting factories and worn-out social programs from the era of industrial capitalism are just things of the past, and the long reckoning with liberty is merely a story to tell our grandchildren. And yet, surely there is something worth remembering in the way the Depression generation accepted its rendezvous with destiny and in the fact that common people played no lesser role in this than elites.

It still may be that the only lessons are negative ones. The twentieth century has become understandably engulfed in pessimism. After the cataclysmic events of the modern era, it was no longer possible to believe with all one's heart in the kind of limitless optimism about human progress that prevailed at the dawn of the century. American innocence has died many deaths, but none so convincing as those of the two world wars and the Great Depression.

And yet, why should that mean there was no progress at all? If one asks whether four decades of struggle humanized the harshest aspects of the competitive market, reaffirmed liberty against authoritarianism, and advanced the social goals of a truly human community—in short, if one asks whether there was social progress, then, surely, the answer ought to be yes.

CONCLUSION
⅋.

And what of the future? In the age of the "uncertainty principle," not even hard science is confident about prediction, so the Queen of the Humanities had best leave prediction to fortune tellers. Yet the inescapable fact is that understanding the past inevitably changes the future. People gain identity and purpose through individual and collective memory. They feel empowered by a sense of mission or destiny and may gain a certain power to shape a more rational future by understanding the logic of cause and effect. It may be impossible to predict the future, but it is equally certain that consciousness of the past affects the way people will shape it. They may not be able to shape it just as they please, but they can certainly judge for themselves what will make things better or worse and act accordingly.

Abbreviations

Selected Bibliography

Notes

Index

Abbreviations

HL   Hagley Library, Wilmington, Delaware
IHRC   Immigration History Research Center, University of Minnesota
LC   Library of Congress, Washington, D.C.
RG   Record Group, National Archives, Washington, D.C.
SL   Schlesinger Library, Radcliffe College
SHSW State Historical Society of Wisconsin, Madison
SWHA Social Welfare History Archives, University of Minnesota

Selected Bibliography

Manuscripts

Adjutant General's Office, RG 94 and 407
American Federation of Labor Papers, SHSW
American Social Health Association Papers, SWHA
Mary Anderson Papers, SL
Dorothy K. Brown Papers, SL
A. S. Burleson Papers, LC
Anthony Capraro Papers, IHRC
Chicago Foreign Language Press Survey, IHRC
Commission of Training Camp Activities, RG 165
George Creel Papers, LC
Ethel Sturges Dummer Papers, SL
DuPont Corporate Papers, HL
Federal Bureau of Investigation, RG 65
John Fitzpatrick Papers, Chicago Historical Society
Food Administration, RG 4
Felix Frankfurter Papers, LC
Herbert Hoover Presidential Papers, West Branch, Iowa
Harry Hopkins Papers, Franklin D. Roosevelt Library
Industrial Workers of the World Papers, Reuther Library, Wayne State University
Justice Department, RG 60
Harriet Laidlaw Papers, SL
Alexander Lincoln Papers, SL
Benjamin Lindsey Papers, LC
Military Intelligence Division, RG 165
National Association of Manufacturers Papers, HL
National Consumers League Papers, LC
National Industrial Conference Board Papers, HL
National League of Women Voters Papers, LC
National Women's Trade Union League Papers, LC
Donald Richberg Papers, LC
Raymond Robins Papers, SHSW

Elihu Root Papers, LC
Margaret Sanger Papers, LC
David Saposs Papers, SHSW
Sophia Smith Collection, Smith College
Special Conference Committee Papers, HL
Survey Associates Records, SWHA
Frank P. Walsh Papers, New York Public Library
Women's Rights Collection, SL
Leonard Wood Papers, LC

Published Government Documents

Attorney General of the United States. *Annual Report*, 1922. Washington, D.C., 1924.

Edwards, Alba. *Comparative Occupation Statistics for the United States, 1870–1940.* Sixteenth Census. Washington, D.C., 1943.

—— *A Social Economic Grouping of the Gainful Workers of the United States.* Washington, D.C., 1938.

New York Legislature [Lusk Committee]. *Revolutionary Radicalism.* 4 vols. Albany, 1920.

President's Conference on Home Building and Home Ownership. *Reports.* 12 vols. Washington, D.C., 1932.

Temporary National Economic Committee. *Final Report.* 77th Cong., 1st sess. Senate Doc. 35. Washington, D.C., 1941.

U.S. Bureau of the Census. *Historical Statistics of the United States from Colonial Times to 1957.* Washington, D.C., 1960.

—— *Tenth Census.* Vol. 20. Washington, D.C., 1886.

—— *Twelfth Census: Employees and Wages.* Washington, D.C., 1903.

—— *Thirteenth Census: Population.* Vol. 4. Washington, D.C., 1910.

—— *Fourteenth Census: Population.* Vol. 4. Washington, D.C., 1920.

—— *Fifteenth Census: Population.* Vol. 4. Washington, D.C., 1930.

U.S. Commission on Industrial Relations. *Final Report and Testimony.* 11 vols. 64th Cong., 1st sess. Senate Doc. 415. Washington, D.C., 1916.

U.S. Commissioner of Labor. *Annual Report.* Nos. 3, 10, and 16. Washington, D.C., 1888, 1896, and 1901.

U.S. Congress. *Reports of the Immigration Commission.* 41 vols. 61st Cong., 2d and 3d sess. Washington, D.C., 1911.

U.S. Industrial Commission. *Reports.* 9 vols. Washington, D.C., 1901–02.

U.S. Senate. *Bolshevik Propaganda: Hearings before a Subcommittee of the Committee on the Judiciary.* 65th Cong., 3d sess. Washington, D.C., 1919.

—— *Federal Aid in Domestic Disturbances.* 67th Cong., 2d sess. Washington, D.C., 1922.

—— *Hearings before the Committee on Education and Labor: West Virginia Coal Fields.* 67th Cong., 1st sess. Washington, D.C., 1922.

—— Committee on Education and Labor. *Documents Relating to Intelligence Bureau or Red Squad of Los Angeles Police Department.* 76th Cong., 3d sess. Washington, D.C., 1940.

—— *Violations of Free Speech.* 76th Cong., 1st sess. Washington, D.C., 1939.

—— Special Committee to Investigate the Munitions Industry. "Minutes of the War Industries Board," and "Minutes of the Council of National Defense." In *Senate Report 944*, 7 vols. 74th Cong., 1st and 2d sess. Washington, D.C., 1935–36.

White House Conference on Child Health and Protection. *Reports.* 35 vols. New York, 1931.

Books and Periodicals

Abbott, Edith. *Women in Industry: A Study in American Economic History.* New York: Arno Press, 1969; orig. 1910.

Adamic, Louis. *Dynamite: The Story of Class Violence in America.* Rev. ed. New York: Viking Press, 1934.

Addams, Jane. *Twenty Years at Hull House.* New York: Macmillan, 1910.

Allen, Frederick L. *Only Yesterday: An Informal History of the 1920s.* New York: Harper & Bros., 1931.

Anderson, Mary. *Women at Work: The Autobiography of Mary Anderson.* Minneapolis: University of Minnesota Press, 1951.

Anthony, Katherine. *The Endowment of Motherhood.* New York: B. W. Huebsch, 1920.

Bakke, E. Wright. *Citizens without Work: A Study of the Effects of Unemployment upon the Workers' Social Relations and Practices.* New Haven: Yale University Press, 1940.

Balch, Emily G. *Our Slavic Fellow Citizens.* New York: Charities Publication Committee, 1910.

Baruch, Bernard. *American Industry in the War.* New York: Prentice-Hall, 1941.

Berle, Adolf, and Gardiner Means. *The Modern Corporation and Private Property.* New York: Macmillan, 1932.

Berman, Edward. *Labor Disputes and the President.* New York: AMS Press, 1968; orig. 1924.

Bing, Alexander M. *War-Time Strikes and Their Adjustment.* New York: E. P. Dutton, 1921.

Bonnett, Clarence E. *Employers Associations in the United States.* New York: Macmillan, 1922.

Bourne, Randolph. *War and the Intellectuals: Essays by Randolph S. Bourne, 1915–1919*, edited by Carl Resek. New York: Harper & Row, 1964.

Brandeis, Louis. *Other People's Money*, edited by Richard Abrams. New York: Harper & Row, 1967; orig. 1914.

Brandeis, Louis, and Josephine Goldmark. *Women in Industry*. New York: National Consumers League, n.d.

Breckenridge, Sophonisba. *Women in the Twentieth Century*. New York: McGraw-Hill, 1933.

Budish, J. M., and George Soule. *The New Unionism in the Clothing Industry*. New York: 1920.

Byington, Margaret F. *Homestead: The Households of a Mill Town*. Pittsburgh: University of Pittsburgh Press, 1974; orig. 1910.

Chicago Commission of Race Relations. *The Negro in Chicago: A Study of Race Relations and a Race Riot*. Chicago: University of Chicago Press, 1922.

Claghorn, Kate. *The Immigrant's Day in Court*. New York: Arno Press, 1969; orig. 1923.

Clarkson, Grosvenor. *Industrial America in the World War: The Strategy behind the Line, 1917–1918*. Boston: Houghton Mifflin, 1923.

Committee of Fourteen. *Annual Report*. New York: 1917.

Corey, Lewis. *The Decline of American Capitalism*. New York: Covici, Friede Publishers, 1934.

Creel, George. *How We Advertised America*. New York: Harper, 1920.

Croly, Herbert. *The Promise of American Life*. New York: E. P. Dutton, 1963; orig. 1909.

Daniels, Josephus. *Cabinet Diaries of Josephus Daniels, 1913–1921*, edited by E. David Cronin. Lincoln: University of Nebraska Press, 1963.

Davis, Katherine B. *Factors in the Sex Life of Twenty-Two Hundred Women*. New York: Arno Press, 1972; orig. 1929.

Dell, Floyd. *Love in the Machine Age: A Psychological Study of the Transition from Patriarchal Society*. New York: Farrar & Rinehart, 1930.

Dennett, Mary. W. *Birth Control Laws*. New York: F. H. Hitchcock, 1926.

Dewey, John. *Democracy and Education*. New York: Macmillan, 1916.

———— *Reconstruction in Philosophy*. New York: Henry Holt, 1920.

Dos Passos, John. *Nineteen Nineteen*. New York: Grosset & Dunlap, 1937.

Dreiser, Theodore. *Sister Carrie*. New York: Bantam Books, 1958; orig. c. 1900.

DuBois, W. E. B. *Darkwater: Voices from Within the Veil*. New York: AMS Press, 1969; orig. 1920.

———— *Souls of Black Folk*. Chicago: A. C. McClurg, 1903.

The Fatherland.

Faulkner, William. *The Sound and the Fury*. New York: Random House, 1929.

Filene, Edward A. *Successful Living in the Machine Age.* New York: Simon & Schuster, 1923.

Fitzgerald, F. Scott. *The Great Gatsby.* New York: 1925.

Ford, Henry. *My Life and Work.* Garden City, N.Y.: Doubleday, Page, 1922.

Fosdick, Raymond. *American Police Systems.* Montclair, N.J.: Patterson Smith, 1969; orig. 1920.

Foster, William Z. *The Great Steel Strike.* New York: B. W. Huebsch, 1920.

Frederick, Christine. *Household Engineering: Scientific Management in the Home.* Chicago: American School of Home Economics, 1920; orig. 1915.

Gilbreth, Frank. *Motion Study.* New York: Van Nostrand, 1911.

Gilbreth, Lilian. *The Home-Maker and Her Job.* New York: D. Appleton, 1929.

Gilman, Charlotte Perkins. *Women and Economics.* New York: Harper & Row, 1966; orig. 1898.

Glueck, Sheldon, and Eleanor Glueck. *One Thousand Juvenile Delinquents and Their Treatment by Court and Clinic.* Cambridge, Mass.: Harvard University Press, 1934.

Goldman, Emma. *Living My Life.* New York: A. A. Knopf, 1931.

Goldmark, Josephine. *Fatigue and Efficiency: A Study in Industry.* New York: Survey Associates, 1913.

Gompers, Samuel. *Seventy Years of Life and Labor.* New York: Cornell University Press, 1984; orig. 1925.

Good Housekeeping.

Gould, Charles W. *America: A Family Matter.* New York: Charles Scribner's Sons, 1922.

Grant Madison. *The Passing of the Great Race.* New York: Charles Scribner's Sons, 1916.

Graves, William S. *America's Siberian Adventure: 1918–1920.* New York: Jonathan Cape and Harrison Smith, 1931.

Herring, Harriet. *Welfare Work in Mill Villages: The Story of Extra-Mill Activities in North Carolina.* Montclair, N.J.: Peter Smith, 1968; orig. c. 1929.

Hicks, Clarence. *My Life in Industrial Relations: Fifty Years in the Growth of a Profession.* New York: Harper & Bros., 1941.

Hoover, Herbert. *American Individualism.* Garden City, N.Y.: Doubleday, Page, 1922.

—— *Memoirs: 1874–1933.* 2 vols. New York: Macmillan, 1952.

Hourwich, Isaac A. *Immigration and Labor: The Economic Aspects of European Immigration to the United States.* Rev. ed. New York: B. W. Huebsch, 1922.

Howe, Frederic C. *The Confessions of a Reformer.* New York: Charles Scribner's Sons, 1925.

Hunter, Robert. *Poverty.* New York: Harper & Row, 1965; orig. c. 1904.

Interchurch World Movement. *Report on the Steel Strike of 1919.* New York: Harcourt, Brace & Howe, 1920.

Kallen, Horace. *Culture and Democracy in the United States.* New York: 1924.

Kelley, Florence. *Modern Industry in Relation to the Family, Health, Education, Morality.* New York: Longman's, Green, 1914.

Kellogg, Paul U., ed. *The Pittsburgh Survey.* 6 vols. New York: Charities Publication Committee, 1901–14.

Kellor, Frances. *Straight America: A Call to National Service.* New York: Macmillan, 1916.

Kinsey, Alfred C., et al. *Sexual Behavior in the Human Female.* Philadelphia: W. B. Saunders, 1953.

———— *Sexual Behavior in the Human Male.* Philadelphia: W. B. Saunders, 1948.

Kirchway, Freda. *Our Changing Morality: A Symposium.* New York: Boni, 1924.

Komarovsky, Mirra. *The Unemployed Man and His Family: The Effect of Unemployment upon the Status of the Man in Fifty-nine Families.* New York: Farrar, Straus, & Giroux, 1971; orig. 1940.

LaFollette, Suzanne. *Concerning Women.* New York: Arno Press, 1972; orig. 1926.

Lathrop, Julia. *The Child, the Clinic, and the Court.* New York: New Republic, 1927.

Lay, Wilfrid. *A Plea for Monogamy.* New York: Boni & Liveright, 1923.

Leiserson, William M. *Adjusting Immigration and Industry.* New York: Harper & Bros., 1924.

Lewis, Sinclair. *Babbitt.* New York: Harcourt, Brace, & World, 1922.

———— *It Can't Happen Here.* Garden City, N.Y.: Doubleday, 1935.

Life and Labor. 1920–1922.

Lindsey, Ben, and Wainwright Evans. *The Companionate Marriage.* New York: Boni & Liveright, 1927.

Lippmann, Walter. *Drift and Mastery: An Attempt to Diagnose the Current Unrest.* Englewood Cliffs, N.J.: Prentice-Hall, 1961; orig. 1914.

———— *A Preface to Morals.* New York: Macmillan, 1929.

———— *The New Imperative.* New York: Macmillan, 1935.

Locke, Alain, ed. *The New Negro.* New York: Albert and Charles Boni, 1925.

Machinists Monthly Journal. 1919–1920.

Madeleine: An Autobiography. New York: Harper & Bros., 1919.

Mason, Lucy Randolph. *Standards for Workers in Southern Industry.* New York: National Consumers League, 1931.

Mathewson, Stanley. *Restriction of Output among Unorganized Workers.* New York: 1931.

Maurer, James. *The American Cossack.* n.p., Pennsylvania Federal of Labor, n.d.

Mayo, Katherine. *Justice to All: The Story of the Pennsylvania State Police*. Boston: Houghton Mifflin, 1917.

McNeill, George E. *The Labor Movement: The Problem of To-Day*. Boston: A. M. Bridgman, 1887.

Moley, Raymond. *After Seven Years*. New York: Harper & Bros., 1939.

Mumford, Lewis. *Technics and Civilization*. New York: Harcourt Brace, 1934.

Myrdal, Gunnar. *An American Dilemma: The Negro Problem and Modern Democracy*. New York: Harper & Bros., 1944.

The Nation.

National Association of Manufacturers. Pamphlet series. New York, 1925–36.

National Bureau of Economic Research. *Income in the United States: Its Amount and Distribution, 1909–1919*, edited by W. C. Mitchell. 2 vols. New York: Harcourt, Brace, 1921–22.

National Industrial Conference Board. Pamphlet series. New York, 1917–32.
———— Memorandum series. New York, 1933.

National League of Women Votes. *Proceedings*. Annual conventions, 1920–24.

Nestor, Agnes. *Woman's Labor Leader: An Autobiography of Agnes Nestor*. Rockford, Ill.: Bellevue Books, 1954.

New Masses: An Anthology, edited by Joseph North. New York: International Publishers, 1969.

New Republic.

Parsons, Alice B. *Women's Dilemma*. New York: Thomas Crowell, 1926.

Parsons, Elsie C. *Social Freedom: A Study of the Conflicts between Social Classifications and Personality*. New York: G. P. Putnam's Sons, 1915.

Perkins, Frances. *The Roosevelt I Knew*. New York: Viking Press, 1946.

Railroad Trainman.

Rauschenbusch, Walter. *Christianity and the Social Crisis*. New York: Macmillan, 1907.

Recent Economic Changes in the United States. Report of the President's Commission. 2 vols. n.p., 1929.

Recent Social Trends in the United States. Report of the President's Commission. 2 vols. New York: McGraw-Hill, 1933.

Reckless, Walter C. *Vice in Chicago*. Chicago: University of Chicago Press, 1933.

Reed, John. *Insurgent Mexico*. New York: Greenwood Press, 1969; orig. 1914.

Roosevelt, Franklin D. *The Public Papers and Addresses of Franklin D. Roosevelt*, edited by Samuel Rosenman. 5 vols. New York: Random House, 1938.

Roosevelt, Theodore. *Fear God and Take Your Own Part*. New York: George H. Doran, 1916; orig. 1914.

Ross, Edward A. *Social Control: A Survey of the Foundations of Order*. Cleveland: Press of Case Western Reserve University, 1969; orig. 1901.

Sandburg, Carl. *Complete Poems.* New York: Harcourt, Brace, 1950.

Sanger, Margaret. *An Autobiography.* New York: W. W. Norton, 1938.

Saturday Evening Post.

Schiavo, Giovanni. *The Italians in Chicago: A Study in Americanization.* Chicago: Italian-American Publishing, 1928.

Shadwell, Arthur. *Industrial Efficiency: A Comparative Study of Industrial Life in England, Germany, and America.* London: Longman's, Green, 1920; orig. 1905.

Sinclair, Upton. *Boston.* 2 vols. New York: Albert and Charles Boni, 1928.

—— *The Jungle.* Urbana: University of Illinois Press, 1988; orig. 1906.

Sombart, Werner. *Why Is There No Socialism in the United States?* White Plains, N.Y.: International Arts and Sciences Press, 1976; orig. 1906.

Soule, George. *A Planned Society.* New York: Macmillan, 1932.

—— *The Future of Liberty.* New York: Macmillan, 1936.

Steffens, Lincoln. *The Shame of the Cities.* New York: Hill & Wang, 1957; orig. 1904.

The Survey.

Survey Graphic.

Taylor, Frederick W. *The Principles of Scientific Management.* New York: Harper & Bros., 1911.

Thomas, W. I., and Znaniecki, Florian. *The Polish Peasant in Europe and America.* 2 vols. New York: Dover Publications, 1958; orig. 1918–20.

Thompson, Warren S., and P. K. Whelpton. *Population Trends in the United States.* New York: McGraw-Hill, 1933.

Tumulty, Joseph. *Woodrow Wilson as I Know Him.* Garden City, N.Y.: Doubleday, Page, 1921.

Twelve Southerners. *I'll Take My Stand: The South and the Agrarian Tradition.* New York: Harper & Bros., 1930.

Upton, Emory. *The Military Policy of the United States.* New York: Greenwood Press, 1968; orig. 1904.

Van Waters, Miriam. *Youth in Conflict.* New York: Republic Publishing, 1925.

Veblen, Thorstein. *The Engineers and the Price System.* New York: Viking, 1921.

—— *The Theory of the Leisure Class: An Economic Study of Institutions.* New York: Modern Library, 1934; orig. 1899.

Vernier, Chester G. *American Family Laws: A Comparative Study of the Family Law of the Forty-eight American States.* 5 vols. Stanford: Stanford University Press, 1931.

Vice Commission of Chicago. *The Social Evil in Chicago.* Chicago, 1911.

Weyl, Walter E. *The New Democracy: An Essay on Certain Political and Economic Tendencies in the United States.* New York: Harper & Row, 1964; orig. 1912.

White, Walter. *A Man Called White.* New York: Viking, 1948.

White, William Allen. *The Autobiography of William Allen White*. New York: Macmillan, 1946.

Wilson, Woodrow. *The Public Papers of Woodrow Wilson*, edited by Ray Stannard Baker and William E. Dodd. New York: Harper & Bros., 1925.

Witte, Edwin E. *The Government in Labor Disputes*. New York: McGraw-Hill, 1932.

Notes

Introduction

1. The same doctrine that glorified equality of opportunity rejected equality of condition. William Graham Sumner, the leading Social Darwinist of his day, stated the prevailing view: "Let it be understood that we cannot go outside of this alternative: liberty, inequality, survival of the fittest; not-liberty, equality, survival of the unfittest"; quoted in Richard Hofstadter, *Social Darwinism in American Thought* (Boston, 1955; orig. 1944), 51.
2. In addition to *The Rise of American Civilization*, 2 vols. (New York, 1927), leading works include Charles Beard, *An Economic Interpretation of the Constitution of the United States* (New York, 1913); John R. Commons et al., *History of Labour in the United States*, 4 vols. (New York, 1918–1935); Mary Beard, *Woman as Force in History* (New York, 1946); Frederick Jackson Turner, *The Frontier in American History* (New York, 1962; orig. 1920). For a sympathetic account of the New History, see Morton White, *Social Thought in America: The Revolt against Formalism* (Boston, 1947). As with so many intellectuals of their generation, their argument with Marx was a battle with temptation. While flirting with socialism, young Walter Lippmann wrote: "Yet even if Karl Marx captured the secret of social evolution (which is doubtful) . . . the necessity still remains of showing concretely how that key unlocks the American difficulty"; Lippmann, *Drift and Mastery: An Attempt to Diagnose the Current Unrest* (Englewood Cliffs, N.J., 1961; orig. 1914), 168.
3. Perry Miller, *The New England Mind* (Cambridge, Mass., 1953); Henry Nash Smith, *Virgin Land: The American West as Symbol and Myth* (Cambridge, Mass., 1950); Louis Hartz, *The Liberal Tradition in America: An Interpretation of American Political Thought since the Revolution* (New York, 1955).
4. Uncritical celebration is found in Daniel Boorstin, *The Genius of American Politics* (Chicago, 1953); Oscar Handlin, *The Story of Liberty in America* (New York, 1986). Others are more critical, including Richard Hofstadter, *The American Political Tradition and the Men Who Made It* (New York, 1944) and *The Age of Reform* (New York, 1955).

5. The pioneer work of diplomatic revisionism was William Appleman Williams, *The Tragedy of American Diplomacy* (New York, 1959); other useful studies of early twentieth-century diplomacy include Lloyd C. Gardner, *Safe for Democracy: The Anglo-American Response to Revolution, 1913–1923* (New York, 1987); Friedrich Katz, *The Secret War in Mexico* (Chicago, 1981); N. Gordon Levin, *Woodrow Wilson and World Politics: America's Response to War and Revolution* (New York, 1968); Arno Mayer, *Political Origins of the New Diplomacy, 1917–1918* (New Haven, 1959); Klaus Schwabe, *Woodrow Wilson, Revolutionary Germany, and Peacemaking, 1918–1919: Missionary Diplomacy and the Realities of Power*, trans. Rita and Robert Kimber (Chapel Hill, N.C., 1985). For examples of pioneering works in social history, see Herbert Gutman, *Work, Culture, and Society in Industrializing America* (New York, 1976); Eugene Genovese, *Roll, Jordan, Roll: The World the Slaves Made* (New York, 1972); Ann Firor Scott, *The Southern Lady: From Pedestal to Politics, 1830–1930* (Chicago, 1970).

6. The lament of fragmentation was heard all through the 1980s. See, for example, Peter Novick, *That Noble Dream: The "Objectivity Question" and the American Historical Profession* (Cambridge, 1988). For a conservative critique of the entire run of social history, see Gertrude Himmelfarb, *The New Historians and the Old: Critical Essays and Reappraisals* (Cambridge, Mass., 1987).

7. Robert Wiebe, *The Search for Order, 1877–1920* (New York, 1967); Ellis Hawley, *The Great War and the Search for a Modern Order* (New York, 1979); idem, *The New Deal and the Problem of Monopoly: A Study in Economic Ambivalence* (Princeton, 1966); Louis Galambos and Joseph Pratt, *The Rise of the Corporate Commonwealth: U.S. Business and Public Policy in the Twentieth Century* (New York, 1988).

8. Immanuel Wallerstein, *The Modern World System* (New York, 1974); Joan Scott, *Gender and the Politics of History* (New York, 1988); Stuart Ewen, *All Consumer Images: The Politics of Style in Contemporary Culture* (New York, 1988). Currently there is great interest in French philosophers Michel Foucault and Jacques Derrida.

9. The method used here has been called historical materialism, but the term has been left aside because it excites so much misunderstanding. Suffice it to say that as it is actually practiced, historical materialism is both less than Marxism, because Marxism contains partisan political ideologies and official state doctrines that go beyond the pale of objective inquiry, and more than Marxism, because many who write what Eric Hobsbawm described as "the history of society" are not Marxists; Eric Hobsbawm, "From Social History to the History of Society," *Daedalus* 100 (Winter 1971), 20–45; for a dialectical approach in anthropology, see Eleanor Burke Leacock, Introduction to Friedrich Engels, *Origin of the Family, Pri-*

vate Property, and the State (New York, 1972); Eric Wolf, Peasant Wars of the Twentieth Century (New York, 1969). For a somewhat schematic depiction of feedback links in cultural evolution, see Charles Redman, The Rise of Urban Civilization (San Francisco, 1978), 11–14, 227, 230. British social history is exemplified in the work of Eric Hobsbawm, Christopher Hill, and Edward Thompson. On America's reluctance to come to terms with class, see William Appleman Williams, The Great Evasion: An Essay on the Contemporary Relevance of Karl Marx (Chicago, 1964); Ian Tyrell, The Absent Marx: Class Analysis and Liberal Historiography in Twentieth-Century America (New York, 1986). For a dialogue between pragmatism and Marxism, see Cornell West, The American Evasion of Philosophy: A Genealogy of Pragmatism (Madison, 1989).

10. The following are among the more useful works in early twentieth-century American social history: John Bodnar, Roger Simon, and Michael Weber, Lives of Their Own: Blacks, Italians, and Poles in Pittsburgh, 1900–1960 (Urbana, Ill., 1982); David Brody, Steelworkers in America: The Non-Union Era (New York, 1964; orig. 1960); Alfred Chandler, The Visible Hand: The Managerial Revolution in American Business (Cambridge, Mass., 1977); William Chafe, The American Woman: Her Changing Social, Economic, and Political Roles, 1920–1970 (London, 1972); Nancy Cott, The Grounding of Modern Feminism (New Haven, 1987); Pete Daniel, Standing at the Crossroads: Southern Life in the Twentieth Century (New York, 1986); Allen Davis, Spearheads for Reform: The Social Settlements and the Progressive Movement, 1890–1914 (New York, 1967); John D'Emilio and Estelle Freedman, Intimate Matters: A History of Sexuality in America (New York, 1988); Elizabeth Ewen, Immigrant Women in the Land of Dollars: Life and Culture on the Lower East Side, 1890–1925 (New York, 1985); Gary Gerstle, Working-Class Americanism: The Politics of Labor in a Textile City, 1914–1960 (Cambridge, 1989); David Gordon, Richard Edwards, and Michael Reich, Segmented Work, Divided Workers: The Historical Transformation of Labor in the United States (Cambridge, 1982); Linda Gordon, Woman's Body, Woman's Right (New York, 1976); John Higham, Strangers in the Land (New York, 1963); David Hogan, Class and Reform (Philadelphia, 1985); Kenneth Jackson, Crabgrass Frontier: The Suburbanization of the United States (New York, 1985); Dolores Janiewski, Sisterhood Denied: Race, Gender, and Class in a New South Community (Philadelphia, 1985); Alice Kessler-Harris, Out to Work: A History of Wage-Earning Women in the United States (New York, 1982); Roland Marchand, Advertising the American Dream: Making Way for Modernity, 1920–1940 (Berkeley, 1985); David Montgomery, The Fall of the House of Labor (Cambridge, 1987); Martin Sklar, The Corporate Reconstruction of American Capitalism, 1890–1916 (Cambridge, 1988); William Tuttle, Race Riot: Chicago in the Red Summer of 1919 (New York, 1970).

11. Eric Hobsbawm, *Industry and Empire* (New York, 1968), 128, estimates that "manual laboring classes" amounted to three-quarters of the population in 1867; Martin Kitchen, *The Political Economy of Germany, 1815–1914* (Montreal, 1978), notes that industrial employment passed agricultural between the censuses of 1882 and 1895; Jurgen Kuczynski, *A Short History of Labour Conditions under Industrial Capitalism* (London, 1947), 132, shows mining and manufacturing exceeding agricultural employment by 1910; Pierre Sorlin, *La société française 1890–1914* (Paris, 1969), 165, estimates that the industrial population approached parity with the agricultural after 1914, a view congruent with figures in Georges Dupeux, *La société française 1789–1960* (Paris, 1964), 168. Since the various national census takers did not use uniform categories, these figures should be taken as evidence of the trend, not as hard-and-fast comparisons.

12. The comparative method has proved fruitful in explaining such subjects as landlord-peasant relations from England to Japan: Barrington Moore, *Social Origins of Dictatorship and Democracy* (Boston, 1966); the causes of modern revolutions: Theda Skocpol, *States and Social Revolutions* (Cambridge, Mass., 1978); Crane Brinton, *Anatomy of Revolution* (New York, 1938); New World slavery: David B. Davis, *The Problem of Slavery in Western Culture* (Ithaca, N.Y., 1966); Frank Tannenbaum, *Slave and Citizen* (New York, 1946); and white supremacy: George Fredrickson, *White Supremacy: A Comparative Study in American and South African History* (New York, 1981), quote from p. xiv. Some basis of similarity must be established before meaningful differences can be drawn; without some causes in common, it is impossible to isolate the factors responsible for different effects. That is why, for example, it is easier to compare slave systems in the Western world, where so much was shared (Roman law, Christianity, monarchy, market economy), than "feudalism" in medieval Europe and Japan, where there were scarcely any common influences.

13. It is neither possible nor desirable to offer a hard-and-fast geographic definition of North, South, and West, since these labels are a kind of shorthand for historical and cultural differences, and since the borderlands are fluid—the classic Border states such as Kentucky and Tennessee were part northern, part southern, as the secession of West Virginia from Virginia vividly illustrates. Texas and Oklahoma were part southern, part western, just as the Dakotas were part northern, part western. Nonetheless, it is necessary to bow to cartography for clarity's sake. The North: New England, Middle Atlantic states, the Old Midwest, and the Northern Plains. The South: South Atlantic and East and West South Central states. The West: the Rocky Mountain states and the Pacific Coast.

14. There is little systematic comparison between the two countries; a pioneer work is Jurgen Kocka, *White Collar Workers in the United States, 1890–1940:*

A Social-Political History in International Perspective, trans. Maura Kealey (London, 1980).

15. The absence fallacy occupies a prominent place in Louis Hartz, *The Liberal Tradition in America* (New York, 1955); and Werner Sombart, *Why Is There No Socialism in the United States?* (White Plains, N.Y., 1976; orig. 1906). H.-J. Puhle provides an example on the German side: "the consequences of delayed state formation and delayed industrialization combined closely together with the effects of the absence of bourgeois revolution and the absence of parliamentarization to form the decisive brakes on political democraticization and social emancipation"; quoted in David Blackbourn and Geoff Eley, *The Peculiarities of German History* (New York, 1984), 49, which also calls attention to the way Ralf Dahrendorf put the question: "Why wasn't Germany England?" Blackbourn and Eley, 154, carve out an antiexceptionalism position in the *Sonderweg* (special path) debate: "it was not the absence of bourgeois revolution that forced a supine bourgeoisie into junior partnerships with a 'pre-industrial power elite,' but the particular form of Germany's bourgeois revolution (revolution from above under the aegis of the Prussian state through military unification) that combined with the accelerated character of Germany's capitalist transformation to impose a specific logic of class alliance."

16. Marc Bloch, *The Historian's Craft,* trans. Peter Putman (New York, 1953).

1. Gilded Age Liberty

1. Depew quoted in Hertha Pauli and E. B. Ashton, *I Lift My Lamp: The Way of a Symbol* (New York, 1948), 305.

2. Henry James, *Hawthorne* (Ithaca, N.Y., 1966; orig. 1879), 34.

3. Sumner quoted in Richard Hofstadter, *Social Darwinism in American Thought* (Boston, 1955; orig. 1944), 51.

4. Morris, *Signs of Change* (1888), quoted in E. P. Thompson, *William Morris: Romantic to Revolutionary* (London, 1977; orig. 1955), 507.

5. While economic and labor historians have hewed to the traditional line of division between "home" and "work," many social historians of women workers and family economy have noted that for domestic servants, home-workers, and housewives, home and workplace were one and the same, and that, in any case, it is necessary to see the seemingly separate realms of home and work, family and property, in terms of each other, not as hermetically sealed spheres of life. This approach is found in a growing number of monographic studies in social history, including Mary Ryan, *The Cradle of the Middle Class* (Cambridge, 1981); Nancy Cott, *The Bonds of Womanhood: "Woman's Sphere" in New England* (New Haven, 1977); Alice Kessler-Harris, *Out to Work: A History of Wage-Earning Women in the United*

States (New York, 1982); Tamara Hareven, *Family Time and Industrial Time* (Cambridge, 1982); Christine Stansell, *City of Women* (New York, 1986).

6. U.S. Bureau of the Census, *Historical Statistics of the United States from Colonial Times to 1957* (Washington, D.C., 1960; hereafter cited as *Historical Statistics*), 75–78.

7. The temperance movement is a favorite for frequent reinterpretation; for one linking drink and sex, see Barbara Epstein, *The Politics of Domesticity: Women, Evangelism, and Temperance in Nineteenth-Century America* (Middletown, Conn., 1981).

8. *Historical Statistics*, 75–78. For an analysis of the transition from agrarian to industrial forms of social reproduction, see Ryan, *Cradle of the Middle Class;* Susan Strasser, *Never Done: A History of American Housework* (New York, 1982).

9. John Mather Austin, *A Voice to the Married* (1841), quoted in Ryan, *Cradle of the Middle Class*, 189–190. Besides Ryan, the discussion of separate spheres draws upon Cott, *Bonds of Womanhood*, 63–100, and Barbara Welter, "The Cult of True Womanhood," *American Quarterly* 18 (Summer 1966), 151–174.

10. For an example of the domestic ideology, see Kathryn Kish Sklar, *Catharine Beecher* (New Haven, 1973); for attitudes on sexuality, see Nancy Cott, "Passionlessness: An Interpretation of Victorian Sexual Ideology, 1790–1851," in *A Heritage of Her Own*, ed. Nancy Cott and Elizabeth Pleck (New York, 1979), 162–181; and, in the same volume, Daniel Scott Smith, "Family Limitation, Sexual Control, and Domestic Feminism in Victorian America," 222–245. John D'Emilio and Estelle Freedman, *Intimate Matters: A History of Sexuality in America* (New York, 1988), 68–71, 166–179, argue that while a majority of the middle class in the late Victorian period accepted the position of social purists that sexuality should be confined to marriage and dedicated primarily to procreation, there was room for "intimacy," especially if male lust was bridled by female restraint.

11. Many writers emphasize feminine influence, including Ryan, *Cradle of the Middle Class*, 186–229.

12. On the Knights, see Leon Fink, *Workingmen's Democracy: The Knights of Labor in American Politics* (Urbana, Ill., 1983); Alan Dawley, *Class and Community: The Industrial Revolution in Lynn* (Cambridge, Mass., 1976); Daniel Walkowitz, *Worker City, Company Town* (Urbana, Ill., 1978). In hiding from contemporaries, secret societies were also kept hidden from posterity, so that little is known about all but the most notorious, such as the Mollie Maguires.

13. John Demos, *A Little Commonwealth: Family Life in Plymouth Colony* (London, 1970); Oscar Handlin and Mary Handlin, *Commonwealth: A Study in the Role of Government in the American Economy* (Cambridge, Mass., 1969);

Michael Grossberg, *Governing the Hearth: Law and the Family in Nineteenth-Century America* (Chapel Hill, N.C., 1985), 14–30; Eleanor Flexner, *Century of Struggle: The Woman's Rights Movement in the United States* (New York, 1970; orig. 1959), 7–8, 62–70.

14. Flexner, *Century of Struggle*, 161–178; Christopher Tomlins, *The State and the Unions: Labor Relations, Law, and the Organized Labor Movement in America, 1880–1960* (Cambridge, 1985), 44–52.

15. On gender and politics, see Paula Baker, *Gender and the Transformation of Politics: Public and Private Life in New York, 1870–1930* (New York, 1989); Ellen Dubois, *Feminism and Suffrage: The Emergence of an Independent Women's Movement in America, 1848–1869* (New York, 1978); Aileen Kraditor, *Ideas of the Women's Suffrage Movement, 1890–1920* (New York, 1920); Epstein, *Politics of Domesticity.*

16. Linda Gordon, *Woman's Body, Woman's Right: A Social History of Birth Control in America* (New York, 1976), 65–69; Ruth Rosen, *The Lost Sisterhood: Prostitution in America* (Baltimore, 1982).

17. Hale quoted in Cott, *Bonds of Womanhood*, 68; Welter, "The Cult of True Womanhood," 151–174; Gerda Lerner, "The Lady and the Mill Girl," in Cott and Pleck, *Heritage of Her Own*, 182–196; Rev. Joseph Cook, *Outlines of Music Hall Lectures on Factory Reform* (Boston, 1871); Barbara Werthei-mer, *We Were There: The Story of Working Women in America* (New York, 1977), 151–179, 180–191; Ann Douglas, *The Feminization of American Culture* (New York, 1977); Louisa May Alcott, *Work* (New York, 1977; orig. 1873).

18. Charlotte Perkins Gilman, *Women and Economics* (New York, 1966; orig. 1898), 151, 140, 217; idem, *The Home* (Urbana, Ill., 1972; orig. 1903), 108. For Gilman the key work of reform Darwinism was Lester Ward's *Dynamic Sociology* (1883).

19. David Katzman, *Seven Days a Week* (New York, 1978), 53, 66–80, 223–265; Beecher quoted in Carol Lasser, "The Domestic Balance of Power: Relations between Mistress and Maid in Nineteenth-Century New England," *Labor History* 28 (Winter 1987), 14–15. For a sociological study debunking "Bridget" and other ethnic stereotypes, see Stephan Steinberg, *The Ethnic Myth: Race, Ethnicity, and Class in America* (New York, 1981); for the impact of technology on service, see Strasser, *Never Done.*

20. David Montgomery, *Beyond Equality: Labor and the Radical Republicans, 1862–1872* (Urbana, Ill., 1981; orig. 1967), 448–452. The 10,402,000 blue-collar workers in 1900 were 57.3 percent of the nonagricultural labor force of 18,142,000, and 36 percent of the total 29,030,000; *Historical Statistics*, 75–78; see also Table 2.1 in Chapter 2.

21. Andrew Carnegie, "Wealth" (1889), reprinted in Andrew Carnegie, *The Gospel of Wealth and Other Timely Essays*, ed. E. C. Kirkland (Cambridge,

Mass., 1962); the capstone decision on liberty of contract was Allgeyer v. Louisiana (1897), which virtually equated state regulation with an unconstitutional deprivation of liberty; Bernard Schwartz, *The Reins of Power: A Constitutional History of the United States* (New York, 1963), 126–130; Tomlins, *The State and the Unions*, 48, citing, among other cases, Walker v. Cronin (1871); Old Dominion Steamship Company v. McKenna (1887); and Moore v. Bricklayers' Union (1890).

22. Quotes in this paragraph and the next are from Frank Watson, *The Charity Organization Movement* (New York, 1922), 218, 94.

23. E. W. Martin [J. W. McCabb], *The History of the Great Riots and of the Molly Maguires* (New York, 1971; orig. 1877). The definitive account of 1877 is Robert Bruce, *1877: Year of Violence* (Chicago, 1970; orig. 1959).

24. Frederick Jackson Turner, "The Significance of the Frontier in American History," in *The Frontier in American History* (New York, 1962; orig. 1920), 1–38; Turner's thesis is still under discussion almost a century later. For an astute analysis of the cultural meaning of the frontier myth, see Alan Trachtenberg, *The Incorporation of America: Culture and Society in the Gilded Age* (New York, 1982), chap. 1.

25. This cast of mind has been described in the title of William Appleman Williams' *The Great Evasion: An Essay on the Contemporary Relevance of Karl Marx* (Chicago, 1964). See also Hofstadter, *Social Darwinism*, 106–110, 178–179; H. H. Quint, *The Forging of American Socialism* (Columbia, S.C., 1953), 4–5, 78, 109–110.

26. Quoted in G. E. White, *The Eastern Establishment and the Western Experience* (New Haven, 1968), 109.

27. Roosevelt quoted in Trachtenberg, *Incorporation of America*, 33, 34; Patricia N. Limerick, *The Legacy of Conquest* (New York, 1987), 55–77, 197–200.

28. Limerick, *Legacy of Conquest*, 97–133. See also Mark Wyman, *Hard Rock Epic* (Berkeley, 1979); Ruth Allen, *The Southwest Strike* (n.p., 1942); Carlos Schwantes, *Racial Heritage: Labor, Socialism, and Reform in Washington and British Columbia, 1885–1917* (Seattle, 1979); Donald McMurry, *Coxey's Army: A Study of the Industrial Army Movement of 1894* (New York, 1970).

29. Alexander Saxton, *The Indispensable Enemy: Labor and the Anti-Chinese Movement in California* (Berkeley, 1971), 113–137; Chester Vernier, *American Family Laws* (Stanford, 1931), I, 206–208.

30. Louis Dumont, *Homo Hierarchicus: An Essay on the Caste System*, trans. M. Sainsbury (Chicago, 1970), develops the connections between egalitarianism and racism.

31. The names of the German coal and steel syndicates were, respectively, the Rheinische-Westfälische Kohlensyndikat and the Stahlwerksverband; Fritz Fischer, *War of Illusions: German Policies from 1911 to 1914*, trans. Marian Jackson (New York, 1975; orig. 1969), 4–5; Naomi Lamoreaux, *The Great Merger Movement in American Business, 1895–1904* (Cambridge, 1985), 1–12.

32. Fischer, *War of Illusions*, 5. The link between vertical integration and oligopoly is convincingly established in Alfred Chandler, *The Visible Hand: The Managerial Revolution in American Business* (Cambridge, Mass., 1977), 357–358. On national income, see Wesley C. Mitchell, *Income in the United States* (n.p., 1921), 145; on internal labor markets, see Sanford Jacoby, *Employing Bureaucracy: Managers, Unions, and the Transformation of Work in American Industry, 1900–1945* (New York, 1985).

33. Carnegie's essay "Wealth" is reprinted in Carnegie, *Gospel of Wealth*, 16–17; Sumner quoted in Hofstadter, *Social Darwinism*, 51.

34. David Blackbourn and Geoff Eley, *The Peculiarities of German History* (Oxford, 1984), 229–237.

35. Farm owners in this period ranged from a minimum of 32 percent of the total farm labor force in 1910 to a maximum of 37 percent in 1920; Stanley Lebergott, *Manpower in Economic Growth* (New York, 1964), table A–2, p. 511; farm owners' percentage of gainful workers is calculated from ibid. and *Historical Statistics*, 74.

36. Fred Shannon, *The Farmer's Last Frontier* (New York, 1945); Paul Glad, *McKinley, Bryan, and the People* (Philadelphia, 1964), 113–141; Lawrence Goodwyn, *The Populist Moment: A Short History of the Agrarian Revolt in America* (Oxford, 1978).

37. George McNeill, ed., *The Labor Movement: The Problem of To-day* (Boston 1887), 469.

38. Carter Goodrich, *The Miner's Freedom* (Boston, 1925); David Brody, *Workers in Industrial America* (New York, 1980), 1–9. See also David Montgomery, *Workers' Control in America* (Cambridge, 1979).

39. Heroism is evident in the statement "The iron workers are civilization's shock troops grappling with tyrannous nature"; this and other quotations are from James J. Davis, *The Iron Puddler: My Life in the Rolling Mills and What Came of It* (Indianapolis, 1922), 91, 114, 108, 88; Susan Hirsch, *Roots of the Industrial Working Class* (Philadelphia, 1978), 53–76.

40. Bruce, *1877*; a popular contemporary account is Martin, *History of the Great Riots*. For accounts of crowd action in 1885, see U.S. House of Representatives, *Investigation of Labor Troubles*, H.R. 4174 (Washington, D.C., 1887), 370–378. Material on train hijacking and the military response to Coxey's Army can be found in Justice Department Files, RG 60, file 4017–1894; see also McMurry, *Coxey's Army*.

41. Henry David, *The History of the Haymarket Affair* (New York, 1936); Michael Gordon, "The Labor Boycott in New York City," *Labor History* 16 (Spring 1975), 330–331, 311, 326. On the Knights, see Fink, *Workingmen's Democracy*; Dawley, *Class and Community*, 175–193; Walkowitz, *Worker City, Company Town*, 229–242.

42. Friedrich Engels, 1887 preface to *The Condition of the Working Class in England* (orig. 1844), trans. W. O. Henderson and W. H. Chaloner (Stanford,

1958); Edward Bellamy, *Looking Backward* (Boston, 1887); McNeill, *Labor Movement*.

43. Quoted in Anne Firor Scott, *The Southern Lady; From Pedestal to Politics, 1830–1930* (Chicago, 1970), 17.

44. Michael Johnson, *Toward a Patriarchal Republic: The Secession of Georgia* (Baton Rouge, 1977); Eric Foner, *Reconstruction: The Unfinished Revolution* (New York, 1988), 291–307. On emancipation as a social revolution, see Ira Berlin, Introduction to *Freedom: A Documentary History of Emancipation*, ed. Berlin et al. (New York, 1982). For a vivid narrative of the early experience of freedom, see Leon Litwack, *Been in the Storm So Long* (New York, 1979).

45. My own juxtaposition of hierarchical and egalitarian traditions in the South draws from both sides of the lively debate over the character of economy and society in the New South. For arguments on the hierarchical side, see Jonathan Weiner, *Social Origins of the New South: Alabama, 1860–1885* (Baton Rouge, 1970); for arguments on market competition, see Gavin Wright, *Old South, New South: Revolutions in the Southern Economy since the Civil War* (New York, 1986); for a review of the debate, see comments by Weiner, Robert Higgs, and Harold Woodman in *American Historical Review* 84 (October 1979), 970–1006.

46. Pete Daniel, *The Shadow of Slavery: Peonage in the South, 1901–1969* (Urbana, Ill., 1972), 3–5, 108–131; Jacquelyn Jones, *Labor of Love, Labor of Sorrow: Black Women, Work, and the Family from Slavery to the Present* (New York, 1985), 100. See also Jay Mandel, *The Roots of Black Poverty: The Southern Plantation Economy after the Civil War* (Durham, N.C., 1978).

47. Controversy over textile paternalism included a classic statement of owner benevolence by Broadus Mitchell, *The Rise of Cotton Mills in the South* (Baltimore, 1921). In contrast to these works of business history, labor historians have demonstrated both the harsher side of paternalist discipline and the extensive forms of resistance to subordination, which should forever banish the characterization of mill workers as "docile"; see Bess Beatty, "Textile Labor in the North Carolina Piedmont: Mill Owner Images and Mill Worker Response, 1830–1900," *Labor History* 25 (Fall 1984), 485–503. Philip Scranton, *Proprietary Capitalism* (Cambridge, Mass., 1983), shows that paternalist and impersonal forms of discipline coexisted in Philadelphia's textile industry.

48. Convict leases provided as much as one-third of total revenues in some states in the 1880s; Edward Ayers, *Vengeance and Justice: Crime and Punishment in the Nineteenth-Century American South* (New York, 1984), 196, 193, 210, 212–214, 221–222.

49. Wright, *Old South, New South*, 68–69, 163, 176–177, 187.

50. David B. Davis, "Slavery," in *The Comparative Approach to History*, ed. C.

Vann Woodward (New York, 1968), 126; Herbert Gutman, *The Black Family in Slavery and Freedom* (New York, 1976), 444, 445, 448.

51. The prominence of textiles has obscured the biracial character of southern industrial workers even to some otherwise careful scholars; see Joel Williamson "Southern Industrialization: For Whites Only," in *The Crucible of Race: Black-White Relations in the American South since Emancipation* (New York, 1984), 429–443; for compilations of census data on the biracial character of industrial employment in the South, see Wright, *Old South, New South*.

52. Peter Rachleff, *Labor in the South: Richmond, Virginia, 1865–1900* (Philadelphia, 1984); Jones, *Labor of Love*, 147; Oscar Ameringer, *If You Don't Weaken* (New York, 1940), 196–197.

53. W. E. B. DuBois, *Black Reconstruction in America, 1860–1880* (Cleveland, 1964; orig. 1935), 400–419, 441–449; Foner, *Reconstruction*, 291–307; see also Steven Hahn, *The Roots of Southern Populism: Yeoman Farmers and the Transformation of the Georgia Upcountry, 1850–1890* (New York, 1983).

54. Watson quoted in C. Vann Woodward, *The Strange Career of Jim Crow*, 3d rev. ed. (New York, 1974), 63.

55. Williamson, *Crucible of Race*, 135; as Woodward paraphrases the position of Tom Watson after his capitulation to racism, "the white men would have to unite before they could divide"; *Strange Career*, 90.

56. The family's "present degradation is chiefly ascribable" to woman's turpitude; quotes from Gutman, *The Black Family*, 534–538; see also George Fredrickson, *The Black Image in the White Mind* (New York, 1971); Forest Wood, *Black Scare: The Racist Response to Emancipation and Reconstruction* (Berkeley, 1970).

57. Tillman quoted in Williamson, *Crucible of Race*, 135.

58. Jacquelyn Hall, *Revolt against Chivalry: Jessie Daniel Ames and the Women's Campaign against Lynching* (New York, 1979), 129–157, 163. Ayers, *Vengeance and Justice*, presents the surge of lynching in this period as an aspect of the "crisis of the New South."

59. Vernier, *American Family Laws*, I, 204–209; Johnson quoted in Grossberg, *Governing the Hearth*, 136.

60. Dolores Janiewski, *Sisterhood Denied: Race, Class, and Gender in a New South Community* (Philadelphia, 1985), 52; Katzman, *Seven Days a Week*, 63, 289, shows that blacks accounted for 77 percent of southern female servants in 1900 and for 82 percent in 1920, with the shares in cities slightly higher; the foreign born accounted for only 3 percent in the South and 6.7 percent in the cities, compared with 37 percent in the North and as high as 60 percent in North Atlantic cities; *Chattanooga Times* quoted in Jones, *Labor of Love*, 149.

61. The chastity policy survived into the 1930s in Durham, North Carolina,

although less was expected of black women tobacco workers, according to Janiewski, *Sisterhood Denied*, 97–98; Wright, *Old South, New South;* Melton A. McLaurin, *Paternalism and Protest: Southern Cotton Mill Workers and Organized Labor* (Westport, Conn., 1971), 200, 206–207.

62. The most penetrating study of this pattern to date has been made for Durham tobacco factories by Janiewski, *Sisterhood Denied*. For a theory about rules of subordination, or "implicit principles," in a hierarchical context, see Pierre Bourdieu, *Outline of a Theory of Practice*, trans. Richard Nice (Cambridge, 1977).

63. J. Morgan Kousser, *The Shaping of Southern Politics: Suffrage Restriction and the Establishment of the One-Party South* (New Haven, 1974), 11–29, 224–225, 231–238. A number of political scientists following in V. O. Key's footsteps have developed compelling arguments fitting the one-party South into "the system of 1896"; see Walter Dean Burnham, *Critical Elections and the Mainsprings of American Politics* (New York, 1970).

64. Woodward, *Strange Career*, 97–102, 107, 108.

65. Lawrence Levine, *Black Culture and Black Consciousness: Afro-American Folk Thought from Slavery to Freedom* (Oxford, 1977), 371, 249, 251.

66. Booker T. Washington, *Up from Slavery* (Garden City, N.Y., 1901), 217–225.

67. W. E. B. DuBois, *Souls of Black Folk: Essays and Sketches* (Chicago, 1903), 42–54, 3–4.

68. Rockefeller quoted in Lloyd C. Gardner, Walter LaFeber, and Thomas McCormick, *Creation of the American Empire* (Chicago, 1973), 263; Martin Kitchen, *The Political Economy of Germany, 1815–1914* (London, 1978), 186–197, 228. Kitchen points out that Germany's direct trade with its own colonies amounted to less than 1 percent of exports/imports; Harry N. Scheiber, Harold G. Vatter, and Harold U. Faulkner, *American Economic History* (New York, 1976), 293; V. I. Lenin, *Imperialism: The Highest Stage of Capitalism* (New York, 1969; orig. 1905).

69. Kitchen, *Political Economy of Germany*, 232; quotations from Gardner, LaFeber, and McCormick, *Creation of the American Empire*, 264–265.

70. For an argument that racism was irrational displacement, see Kitchen, *Political Economy of Germany*, 196–197, 200–202, 210; but it would be a mistake to pass off *volk*ish nationalism, Social Darwinism, and anti-Semitism as merely the "dark and irrational drives" that filled the gap between rapidly industrializing social structures and unchanging structures of state power. To be sure, Germanic peasants who joined large estate owners in supporting the Agrarian League's call for Germanization and expulsion of Polish casual laborers undoubtedly gave in to irrational prejudice. But to understand why they scapegoated Jews and Poles, it is necessary to recognize that their fears for the future of the agrarian way of life had a cer-

tain rational basis. Sometime between the census of 1882 and 1895 industrial employment surpassed agrarian, a sure sign of the decline of the agricultural way of life. The wellsprings of racial nationalism were not to be found in some dark corner of German psychology, but at the center of social conflicts over trends in social reproduction.

71. Beveridge quoted in Hofstadter, *Social Darwinism*, 179–180.

72. For a realist argument against economic determinism, see Arthur Schlesinger, "America and Empire," in *The Cycles of American History* (Boston, 1986), 118–162; for a critique of moralism, see George F. Kennan, *American Diplomacy* (New York, 1951).

73. Gardner, LaFeber, and McCormick, *Creation of the American Empire*, 263; Richard Welch, Jr., *Response to Imperialism* (Chapel Hill, N.C., 1979), 49, 84–85. See Simeon Larson, *Labor and Foreign Policy: Gompers, the AFL, and the First World War, 1914–1918* (Rutherford, N.J., 1975).

74. Schlesinger, *Cycles of American History*, 69–86, 118–162; Gardner, LaFeber, and McCormick, *Creation of the American Empire*, 43, 260, 266, 274.

75. Welch, *Response to Imperialism*, 13–15.

76. Quoted in ibid., 40, 41.

77. Willard Gatewood, *Black Americans and the White Man's Burden, 1898–1903* (Urbana, Ill., 1975), 258–259, 224, 228–232, 240. DuBois, *Souls of Black Folk*, vii.

78. Williams, *Tragedy of American Diplomacy;* Fischer, *War of Illusions;* Gardner, LaFeber, and McCormick, *Creation of the American Empire*, 260–274.

79. Socialism was represented by German immigrants such as Marxist F. A. Sorge, undertaker for the faction-ridden and ineffectual First International Workingmen's Association when the organization was moved to New York in hopes it would become a corpse, and Johann Most, refugee from Bismarck's antisocialist laws. See Karl Marx, *On the First International*, ed. Saul K. Padover (New York, 1973); Quint, *Forging of American Socialism;* Paul Avrich, *The Haymarket Tragedy* (Princeton, 1984). On reform see Jane Addams, *Twenty Years At Hull House* (New York, 1910); Melvin Holli, *Reform in Detroit: Hazen Pingree and Urban Politics* (New York, 1969).

80. McNeill, *Labor Movement*, 459. This tradition was variously called "antimonopoly" by Selig Perlman, *A Theory of the Labor Movement* (New York, 1928); "equal rights" by Dawley, *Class and Community;* and labor "republicanism" by Sean Willentz, *Chants Democratic* (New York, 1984).

81. Jacob Burckhardt quoted in H.-U. Wehler, "Bismarck's Imperialism 1862–1890," in *Imperial Germany*, ed. James Sheehan (New York, 1976), 200.

82. It is clear that although patriarchy presupposed male dominance, the two were not the same thing. Patriarchy no longer occupied the core of Western societies, not even the agrarian sectors. But male dominance certainly

did. Therefore, if a single term must be used to cover the entire theoretical and historical ground from the dawn of civilization down through the twentieth century, then scholars might consider *andrarchy* instead of *patriarchy.*

83. Jurgen Kocka, *White Collar Workers in America, 1890–1940: A Social-Political History in International Perspective,* trans. Maura Kealey (Beverly Hills, 1980), 101–107; Blackbourn and Eley, *Peculiarities of German History,* 254–255.

84. Blackbourn and Eley, *Peculiarities of German History,* 191–192, 195–203, 229–237; Theodore Hamerow, *Restoration, Revolution, Reaction* (Princeton, 1958). On the nineteenth century as a period of bourgeois dominance, see Charles Moraze, *The Triumph of the Middle Class* (London, 1966); Eric Hobsbawm, *The Age of Capital, 1848–1875* (London, 1975); Roger Magraw, *France, 1815–1914: The Bourgeois Century* (New York, 1986).

85. East Elbe peasants tended to follow the landlords' lead in the Agrarian League; for a comprehensive account of the Prussian situation see E. J. Feuchtwanger, *Prussia: Myth and Reality* (Chicago, 1970); Ian Farr, "Populism in the Countryside: The Peasant Leagues in Bavaria in the 1890s," in *Society and Politics in Wilhelmine Germany,* ed. R. J. Evans (London, 1978), 136–159; Blackbourn and Eley, *Peculiarities of German History,* 269–272.

86. The example of imperial Germany was reconfirmed in the twentieth century by the proliferation of authoritarian regimes in the Third World. On this point, Blackbourn and Eley on Germany and writers such as James Cockburn on twentieth-century "national security states" in developing capitalist regions seem closer to the mark than those who, like Ralf Dahrendorf and Barrington Moore, argue the close association between the rise of capitalism, modernization, and parliamentary democracy.

87. C. Vann Woodward, *Reunion and Reaction: The Compromise of 1877 and the End of Reconstruction* (Boston, 1966; orig. 1951), 12–13, 204–216, showed the alliance of northern capital and southern elites that made for the Compromise of 1877, and the fusion of industrial and landed wealth in the South itself; a similar view appears in Barrington Moore, *Social Origins of Dictatorship and Democracy: Lord and Peasant in the Making of the Modern World* (Boston, 1966), which provides hints of a "Prussian path" in the South that are more fully developed in Weiner, *Social Origins of the New South.*

88. Hampton, writing in the *North American Review* (August 1894), quoted in C. E. Warne, ed., *The Pullman Boycott* (Lexington, Mass., 1955), 5.

89. Burnham, *Critical Elections;* Burnham compares the way industrial elites in the United States and Europe took steps to minimize the political influence of the emerging industrial working classes.

90. For a description of the election in roughly similar terms, see William Bar-

ney, *The Passage of the Republic: An Interdisciplinary History of Nineteenth-Century America* (Lexington, Mass., 1987), 420–423.

91. For a vivid portrait of an urban machine, see William Riordon, *Plunkitt of Tammany Hall* (New York, 1963; orig. 1905). Some historians stress the split between ethnic politics and economically generated class conflicts in industry; see, e.g., Ira Katznelson, *City Trenches: Urban Politics and the Patterning of Class in the United States* (New York, 1981). The ethno-cultural school of political history also stresses the absence of class conflicts from party organization, as in Richard Jensen, *The Winning of the Midwest* (Chicago, 1971); and Paul Kleppner, *The Cross of Culture* (New York, 1970). On the reformers, see Geoffrey Blodgett, *The Gentle Reformers* (Cambridge, Mass., 1966).

2. New Workers, New Women

1. The point of departure for many, if not most, formulations of this idea on the relation between consciousness and society is Karl Marx's preface to *A Contribution to the Critique of Political Economy* (Moscow, 1970; orig. 1859), 21: "The changes in the economic foundation lead sooner or later to the transformation of the whole immense superstructure. In studying such transformation it is always necessary to distinguish between the material transformation of the economic conditions of production, which can be determined with the precision of natural science, and the legal, political, religious, artistic or philosophic—in short, ideological forms in which men become conscious of this conflict and fight it out." British social historians have made especially fruitful contributions on this score, often at odds with Marx's economic emphasis, in particular R. H. Tawney on religion and the rise of capitalism, Christopher Hill on the Puritan revolution, and Edward Thompson on the making of the English working class.

2. Frederick Jackson Turner, "Social Forces in American History," in *The Frontier in American History* (New York, 1920), 323.

3. Carl Sandburg, *Complete Poems* (New York, 1950), 3.

4. U.S. Bureau of the Census, *Historical Statistics of the United States from Colonial Times to 1957* (Washington, D.C., 1960; hereafter cited as *Historical Statistics*), 23, 24, 16.

5. Judith W. Leavitt, *Brought to Bed: A History of Midwifery* (New York, 1986); Barbara Melosh, *"The Physician's Hand": Nurses and Nursing in the Twentieth Century* (Philadelphia, 1982); for the bizarre rituals and superstitions practiced by midwives, such as administering "rat pie" to their charges, see Carolyn C. van Blarcom, "Rat Pie: Among the Black Midwives of the South," *Harper's* 160 (February 1930), 322–332.

6. The main primary source on child labor is National Child Labor Commit-

tee Papers, LC; *Recent Social Trends in the United States,* Report of the President's Commission, 2 vols. (New York, 1933), I, 763, 327. Northern states, with more stringent compulsory education laws, were above the national average in school attendance; in Chicago, nearly everyone was in school through age fifteen, and even a majority of foreign-born sixteen-to-seventeen-year-olds were enrolled, up from only 13 percent in 1910; *Recent Social Trends,* I, 329; David Hogan, *Class and Reform* (Philadelphia, 1985), 121. Hogan provides an insightful look at the changing role of schools in social reproduction.

7. Dennis Hlastel quoted in Hogan, *Class and Reform,* 130–131, also 121, 123; *Recent Social Trends,* I, 329, 367.

8. Northern states far outpaced the South in spending for schooling: Wisconsin, for example, spent $76 per pupil in the 1920s, compared with Alabama's $26; *Recent Social Trends,* I, 375.

9. The democratic values of public school advocates receive emphasis in Merle Curti, *The Social Ideas of American Educators* (New York, 1935), and in the works of progressive educators themselves, such as John Dewey, *Democracy and Education* (New York, 1916); see also *Recent Social Trends,* I, 352–358. For a critique of the helping professions against the backdrop of a romanticized, Freudian model of the nineteenth-century bourgeois family, see Christopher Lasch on the onslaught of "experts" in *Haven in a Heartless World: The Family Besieged* (New York, 1977).

10. Stanley Schultz promotes the thesis of elite control over the children of nineteenth-century immigrant laborers in *The Culture Factory* (New York, 1973); some economists have seen changes in twentieth-century schooling as a reflex of the needs of the dominant class for a disciplined, trained work force: Samuel Bowles and Herbert Gintis, *Schooling in Capitalist America: Educational Reform and the Contradictions of Economic Life* (New York, 1976); a more complex analysis is presented by David Tyack, *The One Best System* (Cambridge, Mass., 1974).

11. John F. Kasson, *Amusing the Million: Coney Island at the Turn of the Century* (New York, 1978), 106–109.

12. Gilles Deleuze, "The Realm of 'the Social,'" introduction to Jacques Donzelot, *The Policing of Families,* trans. Robert Hurley (New York, 1979).

13. In the early twentieth century, Swift was slaughtering 8 million head a year, Durham tobacco factories were producing 3–5 billion cigarettes a year; Alfred Chandler, *The Visible Hand: The Managerial Revolution in American Business* (Cambridge, Mass., 1977), 392, 385. For an account of how Ford became a culture hero, see Warren I. Susman, *Culture as History: The Transformation of American Society in the Twentieth Century* (New York, 1984), 133–141.

14. Jurgen Kuczynski, *A Short History of Labour Conditions under Industrial Capitalism* (London, 1947), 163; *Historical Statistics*, 139; by the time the Great Depression hit bottom, it had temporarily wiped out most of that gain.

15. Siegfried Giedion, *Mechanization Takes Command* (New York, 1969; orig. 1948), 102–104; Robert Hughes, *The Shock of the New* (New York, 1981), 15–17; Lewis Mumford, *Technics and Civilization* (New York, 1963; orig. 1934), 342.

16. It is helpful to bear in mind the insight of British social historians that the stress of industrialization falls not just on technology and markets but on the entire culture. In the words of E. P. Thompson, the transition entailed "a severe restructuring of working habits—new disciplines, new incentives, and a new human nature upon which these incentives could bite effectively"; Thompson, "Time, Work Discipline, and Industrial Capitalism," *Past and Present* 38 (December 1967), 57.

17. Harry Braverman, *Labor and Monopoly Capital* (New York, 1974), 174; Frank Gilbreth, *Applied Motion Study* (New York, 1917), 36. Gilbreth subdivided a simple handgrasp into contact, pinch, wrap, and regrasp and along with his wife, Lilian, applied the chronocyclograph to the movements of bricklayers and shoebox wrappers. The inquisitive pair broke work motions down into their constituent parts to determine the ultimate in efficiency. First, regular motions were timed: "The timed units are then again subjected to motion study for more intensive study of method. Subdivided motions result. These are again timed, and so the process proceeds until the further possible saving will no longer warrant further study, or the available appropriation of time or money is exhausted" (p. 36).

18. Henry Ford, *My Life and Work* (Garden City, N.Y., 1922), 80.

19. Chandler, *Visible Hand*, 392.

20. Olive Schreiner, *Woman and Labor* (New York, 1911), 65, demanded for women "our share of honorable and socially useful human toil"; among writers of the era who worked within this framework was Alice B. Parsons, *Woman's Dilemma* (New York, 1926). The viewpoint has also influenced historians, such as Carl Degler, *At Odds: Women and the Family in America from the Revolution to the Present* (New York, 1980).

21. Thorstein Veblen, *The Engineers and the Price System* (New York, 1921) and *Theory of Business Enterprise* (New York, 1904), 39, 64. Beginning in the 1960s, Marxian economists and historians in Europe and the United States critiqued the hierarchical strategies of "scientific" management and examined struggles for power on the shop floor. By that time, leftist Keynesians had diagnosed unequal distribution of wealth and income as an inherent malady of the unregulated private enterprise system that led not just to a gap between rich and poor, but to the common ruin of depression. Repre-

sentative works include Braverman, *Labor and Monopoly Capital;* David Montgomery, *The Fall of the House of Labor* (Cambridge, 1987); John Kenneth Galbraith, *The Great Crash: 1929* (Boston, 1954).

22. William Kornhauser, *The Politics of Mass Society* (Glencoe, Ill., 1953).

23. For example, E. P. Thompson, "Eighteenth-Century English Society: Class Struggle without Class?" *Social History* 3 (March 1978), 133–165.

24. The leading figure in the pivot from horizontal to vertical axis was Alba Edwards, whose key book was *A Social and Economic Grouping of the Gainful Workers of the United States* (Washington, D.C., 1938).

25. The total proportion of blue- and white-collar wage earners grew to three-fifths by 1930, and the trend after that continued upward to reach as much as 70 percent of the population by the 1970s; Braverman, *Labor and Monopoly Capital,* 379.

26. Werner Sombart, *Why Is There No Socialism in the United States?* (White Plains, N.Y.; orig. 1906), provides the classic argument for American affluence. H. J. Habakkuk, *American and British Technology in the Nineteenth Century* (London, 1962), confirms that American manufacturers were more capital intensive than British because of the relative scarcity of labor.

27. Robert Hunter, *Poverty* (New York, 1965; orig. 1904), 59–60; Margaret Byington, *Homestead* (Pittsburgh, 1974; orig. 1910), 81–106, 139; Peter Shergold, *Working-Class Life: The American Standard in Comparative Perspective, 1899–1913* (Pittsburgh, 1982), 229–230.

28. Crystal Eastman, *Work Accidents and the Law* (New York, 1910), cited by Michael Nash, *Conflict and Accommodation* (Westport, Conn., 1982), 106; Alexander Keyssar, *Out of Work: The First Century of Unemployment in Massachusetts* (Cambridge, 1986), 50–51, 72–75.

29. Given conflicting evidence, the extent of poverty depended on how it was defined. The short-hours wing of the labor movement held that demand created supply—the higher the level of civilization, the greater the desire for consumption. Not content with such a subjective standard, progressive social engineers set out to create a scientific yardstick of the "minimum level of comfort" against which to measure need. Most businessmen opposed any such need-based definition and the trade union or state intervention they implied. Instead, the common business attitude was to insist on letting the "law of supply and demand" set the "prevailing standard," under which the spur of poverty was a positive incentive and want was the consequence of moral failing. At the same time, "scientific managers" modernized Manchester economics to argue a "productivity" theory of wages, which implied that poverty was the consequence of economic inefficiency. For the AFL's position, see George Gunton, *Wealth and Progress* (New York, 1887). Progressive arguments are laid out only to be rebutted by the conventional market view in National Industrial Conference Board (NICB), *Family Budgets of American Wage Earners* (New York, 1921), 60–

67, 86; the new productivity theory is critically examined by Robert Hoxie, *Scientific Management and Labor* (New York, 1915).

30. James T. Patterson, *America's Struggle against Poverty* (Cambridge, Mass., 1981), 21, 24–25.

31. Tamara Hareven, *Family Time and Industrial Time* (Cambridge, 1982); Virginia Yans-McLaughlin, *Family and Community: Italian Immigrants in Buffalo* (Urbana, Ill., 1982; orig. 1977); blacks, Italians, and Poles in Pittsburgh are compared in John Bodnar, Roger Simon, and Michael Weber, *Lives of Their Own: Blacks, Italians, and Poles in Pittsburgh, 1900–1960* (Urbana, Ill., 1982). See also Joseph Barton, *Peasants and Strangers: Italians, Rumanians, and Slovaks in an American City, 1890–1930* (Cambridge, Mass., 1975). Comparative studies such as Bodnar and Barton often employ ecological models whose lineage goes back to Durkheim via Robert Park, W. I. Thomas, and the Chicago School of sociology, even when the influence is unrecognized—a reason for historians to be more conscious about the ideas, theories, and methods within which they work.

32. NICB, *Family Budgets*, tables 1, 2; see also Ruth Schwartz Cowan, *More Work for Mother* (New York, 1983).

33. Heidi Hartmann, "Capitalism, Patriarchy, and Job Segregation by Sex," in *The Signs Reader*, ed. Elizabeth Abel and Emily Abel (Chicago, 1983); Alice Kessler-Harris, *Out to Work: A History of Wage-Earning Women in the United States* (New York, 1982), chap. 8, details the way employers used gender to shunt women into an unequal position even as their employment opportunities were expanding; David Katzman, *Seven Days a Week* (New York, 1978), 268; Susan Strasser, *Never Done: A History of American Housework* (New York, 1982), 176; Leslie Woodcock Tentler, *Wage-Earning Women* (New York, 1979), 85–114.

34. Quoted in Hogan, *Class and Reform*, 121; the estimate on child labor is derived from NICB, *Family Budgets*, tables 1, 2.

35. Jane Addams, *Twenty Years at Hull House* (New York, 1910), 162–163; Margaret Byington, *Homestead* (Pittsburgh, 1974; orig. 1910), 16, 114; formal and informal networks receive attention in Clarke Chambers, "Toward a Redefinition of Welfare History," *Journal of American History* 73 (September 1986), 407–433.

36. William L. Riordon, *Plunkitt of Tammany Hall* (New York, 1963; orig. 1905), 28.

37. Hogan, *Class and Reform*, 109; Bodnar, Simon, and Weber, *Lives of Their Own*, 48, 154; Dan Luria, "Wealth, Capital, and Power: The Social Meaning of Home Ownership," *Journal of Interdisciplinary History* 7 (Autumn 1976), 261–282.

38. Bodnar, Simon, and Weber, *Lives of Their Own*.

39. William H. Chafe, *The American Woman: Her Changing Social, Economic, and Political Roles, 1920–1970* (London, 1972), 55. Braverman, *Labor and Monop-*

oly Capital, 296, points out that in 1900 about three-quarters of the clerical jobs were held by men, and by 1970 the same share was held by women; Margerie Davies, *Women's Place Is at the Typewriter: Office Work and Office Workers, 1870–1930* (Philadelphia, 1982), recounts the "feminization" of office work.

40. Chandler, *Visible Hand*, 392.

41. Kessler-Harris, *Out to Work*. Some recent studies of women workers have suggested that women's family values were the *cause* of their being in lower positions; for example, Winifred Wandersee, *Women's Work and Family Values: 1920–1940* (Cambridge, Mass., 1981), leaves the impression that women preferred jobs that gave them maximum time with their families, but neglects to establish an analytic framework in which that claim could be tested. Other things being equal, it might be true; but only if women turned down real opportunities in order to be with their families would the case be plausible, and only if women who had no apparent family obligations also turned down such opportunities because of some cultural preference would it be convincing. Although some working women no doubt came to accept this state of affairs as unalterable and viewed upward mobility as impossible, there is no evidence that they "preferred" lower-level positions because of "family values."

42. Sanford Jacoby, *Employing Bureaucracy: Managers, Unions, and the Transformation of Work in American Industry, 1900–1945* (New York, 1985), 32–33, 21, 22; see also Daniel Nelson, *Managers and Workers: Origins of the New Factory System in the United States, 1880–1920* (Madison, Wis., 1975).

43. Scientific managers' pursuit of absolute power is the theme of Braverman, *Labor and Monopoly Capital;* Jacoby, *Employing Bureaucracy*, 65–132; Montgomery, *Fall of the House of Labor*, 238–244.

44. Robert Hoxie, *Scientific Management and Labor* (New York, 1976; orig. 1915), 78; the study concluded that the aim of the new incentive systems was to "lower the piece rate on labor cost as output and efficiency of the workers increase" (p. 78).

45. David Montgomery, *Workers' Control in America* (Cambridge, 1979), 122, 107–108, 113–138. The typographers' union prohibited a member from working "where a task, stint, or dead line is imposed by the employer"; George H. Barnett, *Chapters on Machinery and Labor* (Carbondale, Ill., 1969; orig. 1926), 24–25. See also Milton Nadworny, *Scientific Management and the Unions, 1900–1932* (Cambridge, Mass., 1955); Nelson, *Managers and Workers*. The introduction of the bonus system at the Bethlehem Steel mills in 1901 remained a bone of contention for two decades, highlighted by a War Labor Board order (largely ignored) abolishing it; information on the Bethlehem case is from *The Public*, August 10 and 26, 1918, in the scrapbook, vol. 40, of the Frank P. Walsh Papers, New York Public Library. Walsh was cochair of the War Labor Board.

46. Herbert Gutman, *Work, Culture, and Society in Industrializing America* (New York, 1976), 23–25; Rudolph Vecoli, *"Contadini* in Chicago," in *Many Pasts*, ed. Herbert Gutman and Gregory Kealey, vol. II (Englewood Cliffs, N.J., 1973); the opening passage of Upton Sinclair's *The Jungle* is an unforgettable rendition of a Lithuanian wedding celebration.

47. David Brody, *Steelworkers in America* (New York, 1969; orig. 1960); Gutman, *Work, Culture, and Society*, 24–25; Hareven, *Family Time and Industrial Time*, 85–119; Michael Piore, *Birds of Passage* (Cambridge, 1979).

48. James Barrett, "Immigrant Workers in Early Mass Production Industry," in *German Workers in Industrial Chicago* (De Kalb, Ill., 1983), 102–124; Upton Sinclair, *The Jungle*, ed. James Barrett (Urbana, Ill., 1988; orig. 1906), 39; James Barrett, "Unity and Fragmentation: Class, Race, and Ethnicity on Chicago's South Side, 1900–22," in *Struggle a Hard Battle*, ed. Dirk Hoerder (De Kalb, Ill., 1986), 229–253.

49. Edwin Fenton, "Immigrants and Unions" (Ph.D. diss., Harvard University, 1957), 574–576; unionist quoted in Barrett, "Unity and Fragmentation," 229–253.

50. Mary McDowell Papers, Chicago Historical Society, contain much material on packinghouse union struggles; transcript of testimony, Alschuler hearings, 1918, Alschuler Papers, Chicago Historical Society; William Tuttle, *Race Riot: Chicago in the Red Summer of 1919* (New York, 1970).

51. Brody, *Steelworkers in America;* Robert Christie, *Empire in Wood: A History of the Carpenters Union* (Ithaca, N.Y., 1956).

52. On the impact of "manliness," see Ava Baron, "Contested Terrain Revisited: Technology and Gender Definitions of Work in the Printing Industry, 1850–1920," in *Women, Work, and Technology: Transformations*, ed. Barbara Wright (Ann Arbor, 1987), 58–83; on the union as *padrone*, see Fenton, "Immigrants and Unions"; on union ties to municipal government and corruption, see Michael Kazin, *Barons of Labor: The San Francisco Building Trades and Union Power in the Progressive Era* (Urbana, Ill., 1987), 113–144.

53. The story of the Lawrence strike is a staple of labor history; for sample treatments see Sidney Lens, *The Labor Wars: From the Mollie Maguires to the Sitdowns* (Garden City, N.Y., 1973); Thomas Brooks, *Toil and Trouble* (New York, 1964), 118–123; James Green, *The World of the Worker* (New York, 1980), 84–87. New light is being shed on the subject by women's history, for example in the article by Ardis Cameron in *Women, Work, and Protest: A Century of United States Women's Labor History*, ed. Ruth Milkman (Boston, 1985). For Paterson, see Steve Golin, *The Fragile Bridge: The Paterson Silk Strike, 1913* (Philadelphia, 1988). For the IWW, see Melvyn Dubovsky, *We Shall Be All: The History of the I.W.W.* (New York, 1969).

54. Green, *World of the Worker*, 71–74. The definitive statistical portrait is P. K. Edwards, *Strikes in the United States, 1881–1974* (Oxford, 1981); for a

comprehensive account of industrial violence, see Louis Adamic, *Dynamite: The Story of Class Violence in America* (New York, 1934); for a contrary view minimizing industrial violence, see Rhodri Jeffreys-Jones, *Violence and Reform in American History* (New York, 1978).

55. Eugene Debs quoted in Montgomery, *Fall of the House of Labor*, 284; Debs, "The Socialist Party's Appeal," quoted in Jean Y. Tussey, *Eugene Debs Speaks* (New York, 1972), 110. See also J. M. Budish and George Soule, *The New Unionism in the Clothing Industry* (New York, 1920); Montgomery, *Fall*, 284–292.

56. Linda Gordon, *Woman's Body, Woman's Right: A Social History of Birth Control in America* (New York, 1976), 186–230; Kessler-Harris, *Out to Work*, 108–141.

57. The proportion of virgins continued to decline to 32 percent for those reaching their twenties in the 1930s, according to the Lewis Terman survey of premarital sex, reported in Susan Kellog and Steven Mintz, *Domestic Revolutions* (New York, 1988), 112; women born after 1900 were two or three times as likely to have premarital intercourse as women born before, according to Alfred Kinsey et al., *Sexual Behavior in the Human Female* (Philadelphia, 1953), 298–299. Survey data for Russian and Swedish women reported roughly similar changes in premarital intercourse in the cohort born after the turn of the century; ibid., 298 n. 17; Kinsey et al., *Sexual Behavior in the Human Male* (Philadelphia, 1948), 413.

58. Walter Lippmann, *Drift and Mastery: An Attempt to Diagnose the Current Unrest* (Englewood Cliffs, N.J., 1961; orig. 1914), 134.

59. Kathy Peiss, *Cheap Amusements: Working Women and Leisure in Turn-of-the-Century New York* (Philadelphia, 1986), 88, 95, 101–103, 110–111; Elizabeth Ewen, *Immigrant Women in the Land of Dollars* (New York, 1985), 218.

60. For a view of "the immorality of girls" as proof of immigrant "disorganization," see W. I. Thomas and Florian Znaniecki, *The Polish Peasant in Europe and America*, abr. ed. (Urbana, Ill., 1984; orig. 1918–1920), 256–290; for a fresh perspective on the Americanization of immigrant daughters as the winning of independence, see Ewen, *Immigrant Women*, 165–205; settlement house papers, such as those of the North Bennet Street Industrial School of Boston, SL, are full of censorious consternation about unwholesome entertainment.

61. Bourne and Schreiner quoted in Nancy Cott, *The Grounding of Modern Feminism* (New Haven, 1987), 35, 41. The relation between socialism and feminism receives definitive treatment in Mari Jo Buhle, *Women and American Socialism, 1870–1920* (Urbana, Ill., 1983).

62. Cott, *Grounding of Modern Feminism*, 53; Nancy Schrom Dye, *As Equals and as Sisters: Feminism, the Labor Movement, and the Women's Trade Union League of New York* (Columbia, Mo., 1980); Crystal Eastman, progressive social investigator, left-wing socialist, and independent thinker, personified fem-

inist panache and irreverence; see Blanche Wiesen Cook, *Crystal Eastman on Women and Revolution* (Oxford, 1978).

63. Quoted in Buhle, *Women and American Socialism,* 263.

64. Dell quoted in Ellen Kay Trimberger, "Feminism, Men, and Modern Love: Greenwich Village, 1900–1925," in *Powers of Desire: The Politics of Sexuality,* ed. Ann Snitow, Christine Stansell, and Sharon Thompson (New York, 1989), 131–152; Gordon, *Woman's Body, Woman's Right,* 186–206; Candace Falk, *Love, Anarchy, and Emma Goldman* (New York, 1984); see also John D'Emilio and Estelle Freedman, *Intimate Matters: A History of Sexuality in America* (New York, 1988).

65. Emma Goldman, "Victims of Morality" and "The Traffic in Women," in *Red Emma Speaks,* ed. Alix Kate Shulman (New York, 1972), 127, 149; Buhle, *Women and American Socialism,* 246–257.

66. *Woman Rebel* 1, no. 1 (March 1914); Alex Barkin, introduction to reprint edition (New York, 1976), i–xxii; on the birth control movement, see Gordon, *Woman's Body, Woman's Right.*

67. H. L. Mencken quoted in Henry F. May, *The End of American Innocence: A Study of the First Years of Our Own Time, 1912–1917* (New York, 1959), 339–340.

68. May, *End of Innocence,* 337–338; Eileen Southern, *The Music of Black Americans* (New York, 1971), 310–370; Frederick Lewis Allen, *Only Yesterday* (New York, 1931), first argued there was a sexual revolution in the 1920s, a position adopted by most historians, e.g., William Leuchtenburg, *The Perils of Prosperity, 1914–1932* (Chicago, 1958), until the arrival of women's history in the 1970s and the rediscovery of the origins of the new morality and cultural rebellion in the 1910s.

69. For an anthropological analysis of these matters, see Mary Douglass, *Purity and Danger: An Analysis of Concepts of Pollution and Taboo* (London, 1966).

70. Newton Hall's *Civic Righteousness and Civic Pride* (1914) is quoted and the city beautiful movement discussed in Paul Boyer, *Urban Masses and Moral Order in America, 1820–1920* (Cambridge, Mass., 1978), 201, 262–266; Charles Hudson of Chicago quoted in Hogan, *Class and Reform,* 67. Jane Addams, *A New Conscience and an Ancient Evil* (New York, 1912); Prince Morrow quoted in Michael Imber, "Analysis of a Curriculum Reform Movement: The American Social Hygiene Association Campaign for Sex Education, 1900–1930" (Ph.D. diss., Stanford University, 1980), 27.

71. Chicago Vice Commission quoted in Walter C. Reckless, *Vice in Chicago* (Chicago, 1969; orig. 1933), 32; Joseph Mayer, *The Regulation of Commercialized Vice: An Analysis of the Transition from Segregation to Repression in the United States* (New York, 1922), 24–25; Boyer, *Urban Masses,* 193–195.

72. Illinois Vice Committee, *Report* (Chicago, 1916), 24; Ruth Rosen, ed., *The*

Mamie Papers (New York, 1977); for contrasting interpretations of prostitution in the Progressive Era, see Ruth Rosen, *The Lost Sisterhood: Prostitution in America* (Baltimore, 1982), which depicts the "subculture" of the underworld and class tensions over prostitution; and Mark Connelly, *Fear, Anxiety, and Hope: The Response to Prostitution in the United States* (New Brunswick, N.J., 1977), which depicts prostitution through the eyes of anxious reformers seeking to salvage morality in the face of modernization.

73. Mrs. T. P. Curtis, "The Traffic in Women" (Woman Suffrage Party of Boston, n.d.), 8; *Woman Rebel* 1, no. 1 (March 1914).

74. New York *Sun*, December 6, 1913; for this and other press clippings on white slavery, see Harriet Laidlaw Papers, box 10, folders 156–158, SL.

75. William F. Snow, *1900–1915: Progress* (American Social Hygiene Association, n.d.), 2, pamphlet in American Social Hygiene Association Papers, box 1, folder 1, SWHA; Addams, *New Conscience*, 206.

76. The material on Jack Johnson in this and the next two paragraphs is from Randy Roberts, *Papa Jack: Jack Johnson and the Era of White Hopes* (New York, 1983), 6–7, 75, 122–123, 144–148, 152–153, 158–159, 178; Lawrence Levine, *Black Culture and Black Consciousness: Afro-American Folk Thought from Slavery to Freedom* (Oxford, 1977), 430.

77. A sampling of contemporary views appeared under the headline "Why Is the East Less Friendly to Woman Suffrage than the West?" in the *Boston Globe*, January 5, 1913; for an interpretation of suffrage as a form of social control associated with Yankee Protestant morality, nativism, and prohibition, see Alan P. Grimes, *The Puritan Ethic and Woman Suffrage* (New York, 1967). The coalition for equal suffrage in Colorado included male wage earners and populists; Elizabeth Jameson, "Women as Workers, Women as Civilizers: True Womanhood in the American West," in *The Women's West*, ed. S. Armitage and E. Jameson (Norman, Okla., 1987), 154–158. Tensions between working-class and elite influences in New York are explored in Ellen Dubois, "Working Women, Class Relations, and Suffrage Militance: Harriet Stanton Blatch and the New York Woman Suffrage Movement, 1894–1909," *Journal of American History* 74 (1987), 34–58.

78. Cott, *Grounding of Modern Feminism*, 16–20, 54–58, 35.

3. The Social Question

1. Eric Hobsbawm, *The Age of Empire, 1875–1914* (London, 1987), 276–301.

2. Jane Addams, *Twenty Years at Hull House* (New York, 1910); John Dewey, *Democracy and Education* (New York, 1916); Charles Beard, *An Economic Interpretation of the Constitution of the United States* (New York, 1913); Frederick Jackson Turner, "Social Forces in American History," in *The Frontier*

in American History (New York, 1962; orig. 1920); E. A. Ross, *Social Control: A Survey of the Foundations of Order* (New York, 1901); Mary Beard, *Woman as Force in History* (New York, 1946). The discovery of social forces altered the way all succeeding generations thought. It spawned a journal, *Social Forces*, and the most popular history text ever published in the United States, Charles and Mary Beard's *The Rise of American Civilization*, 2 vols. (New York, 1927). Morton White, *Social Thought in America: The Revolt against Formalism* (Boston, 1947), remains an insightful portrayal of key intellectuals. On the discovery of the realm of "the social," see Gilles Deleuze's introduction and the text of Jacques Donzelot, *The Policing of Families*, trans. Robert Hurley (New York, 1979).

3. J. H. M. Laslett, *Labor and the Left* (New York, 1970); H. H. Quint, *The Forging of American Socialism* (Columbia, S.C., 1953); Ira Kipnis, *The American Socialist Movement, 1897–1912* (New York, 1968; orig. 1952); James Green, *Grass-Roots Socialism: Radical Movements in the Southwest, 1895–1943* (Baton Rouge, 1978).

4. James Weinstein, *The Decline of Socialism in the United States* (New York, 1967), 93–118; Michael Nash, *Conflict and Accommodation: Coal Miners, Steel Workers, and Socialism, 1890–1920* (Westport, Conn., 1982).

5. Mari Jo Buhle, *Women and American Socialism, 1870–1920* (Urbana, Ill., 1983), 214–245, 249–257.

6. Elizabeth Gurley Flynn, *The Rebel Girl: An Autobiography* (New York, 1973; orig. 1955); Richard Drinnon, *Rebel in Paradise* (New York, 1976; orig. 1961).

7. Peter d'A. Jones, Introduction to Robert Hunter, *Poverty* (New York, 1965; orig. 1904), vi–xxiv; John Commons, "American Shoemakers, 1648–1895: A Sketch of Industrial Evolution," *Quarterly Journal of Economics* 24 (November 1909), 39–84, presents the theory of "bargaining classes" as an alternative to Marxian class struggle; James Kloppenberg, *Uncertain Victory: Social Democracy and Progressivism in European and American Thought, 1870–1920* (New York, 1896), 349–352.

8. Mary McDowell, testimony to the U.S. Commission on Industrial Relations, in *Final Report and Testimony* (Washington, D.C., 1915–16), IV, 3328–30; the Mary McDowell Papers, Chicago Historical Society, provide an intimate look at the life of a reformer wholly identified with the working class; Addams, *Twenty Years at Hull House*, gives a good account of her settlement; the North Bennet Industrial School Papers, SL, are another example. See also Allen Davis, *Spearheads for Reform: The Social Settlements and the Progressive Movement, 1890–1914* (New York, 1967).

9. Ben Lindsey, "My Lesson from the Juvenile Court," *Survey*, February 5, 1910, quoted in *Children and Youth in America: A Documentary History*, ed. Robert Bremner (Cambridge, Mass., 1971), II, 520; ibid., 439–441. For

the nineteenth century, see David J. Rothman, *The Discovery of the Asylum: Social Order and Disorder in the New Republic* (Boston, 1971). Michel Foucault, *Discipline and Punish: The Birth of the Prison*, trans. Alan Sheridan (New York, 1979), offers a stinging critique of the cruelties of Enlightenment rationalism as applied to criminal justice through solitary confinement and total surveillance. See also David J. Rothman, *Conscience and Convenience: The Asylum and Its Alternatives in Progressive America* (Boston, 1980).

10. Kelley's multifarious activities are reflected in the National Consumers League Papers, LC; Dorothy Rose Blumberg, *Florence Kelley: The Making of a Social Pioneer* (New York, 1966); Kathryn Kish Sklar's forthcoming biography of Kelley promises to shed important new light on the subject; Judith Mara Gutman, *Lewis W. Hine and the American Social Conscience* (New York, 1967).

11. Mary Ryan, *The Cradle of the Middle Class* (Cambridge, 1981); William L. O'Neill, *Everyone Was Brave: A History of Feminism in America* (New York, 1976; orig. 1971).

12. Alice Kessler-Harris, *Out to Work: A History of Wage-Earning Women in the United States* (New York, 1982), 180–214; Martha May, "The Historical Problem of the Family Wage: The Ford Motor Company and the Five Dollar Day," *Feminist Studies* 8 (Summer 1982), 399–424; Steve Meyer, *The Five-Dollar Day* (Albany, 1981).

13. Louis Brandeis and Josephine Goldmark, *Women in Industry* (New York, n.d.), 7; ironically, the plaintiff in *Muller* argued against state-regulated hours for women and in favor of the civil equality of a woman to contract freely under the Fourteenth Amendment as a *femme sole*, a position taken up in the 1920s by such different organizations as the National Women's party and the National Association of Manufacturers; women's minimum wages were upheld in Stettler v. O'Hara 243 U.S. 629 (1917).

14. Roy Lubove, *The Struggle for Social Security, 1900–1935* (Cambridge, Mass., 1968), 98–99, 101–103. Missouri passed the first law in 1911, and nineteen more states had followed suit by 1913. Lubove exaggerates in calling mothers' pensions "liberating"; their role in "enforcing patriarchal norms" is equally exaggerated in Mimi Abramovitz, *Regulating the Lives of Women: Social Welfare Policy from Colonial Times to the Present* (Boston, 1988), 200–206.

15. Elizabeth Brandeis, "Labor Legislation," in *History of Labor in the United States, 1896–1932*, ed. John Commons et al. (New York, 1966; orig. 1935), III, 546–547, 575; Ann Orloff, "The Political Origins of the Belated American Welfare State," in *The Politics of Social Policy in the United States*, ed. Ann Orloff, Margaret Weir, and Theda Skocpol (Princeton, 1988), 53–59; Lubove, *Struggle for Social Security;* Daniel Nelson, *Unemployment Insur-*

ance (Madison, Wis., 1969), shows the motives of business in supporting workmen's compensation, but the reform movement, not business, was the prime mover.

16. Eli Zaretsky, "The Place of the Family in the Origins of the Welfare State," in *Rethinking the Family*, ed. Barrie Thorne (New York, 1982), 188–219.

17. Orloff, "Political Origins of Welfare State," 55–59; Theda Skocpol and John Ikenberry, "The Political Formation of the American Welfare State in Historical and Comparative Perspective," *Comparative Social Research* 6 (1983), 87–148.

18. John D. Buenker, *Urban Liberalism and Progressive Reform* (New York, 1973), 204–206; Howe quoted in ibid., 211. Historians have used the term *urban liberalism* to describe the same phenomenon; the idea seems to have originated with J. Joseph Huthmacher, "Urban Liberalism and the Age of Reform," *Mississippi Valley Historical Review* 44 (1962), 321–341.

19. Hobsbawm, *Age of Empire*.

20. Harry Scheiber, Harold Vatter, and Harold V. Faulkner, *American Economic History* (New York, 1976), 293; Emily Rosenberg, *Spreading the American Dream: American Economic and Cultural Expansion, 1890–1945* (New York, 1982).

21. Michael Hunt, *Ideology and U.S. Foreign Policy* (New Haven, 1987), 80, 127; Richard Hofstadter, *Social Darwinism in American Thought* (Boston, 1955; orig. 1944), 179–196. The connection between cultural politics and foreign affairs is examined in Robert Dallek, *The American Style of Foreign Policy* (New York, 1983); slighting economic and ideological factors, Dallek sometimes reduces foreign relations to a reflex of domestic tensions, repeating the very error that is the target of criticism; e.g., p. 45: "Dominance in the Caribbean was a vicarious means of relieving frustrations over an unruly society at home."

22. Hofstadter, *Social Darwinism*, 179–196.

23. Lester D. Langley, *The United States and the Caribbean in the Twentieth Century* (Athens, Ga., 1980), 30–38, 25–29.

24. Roosevelt quoted in Howard K. Beale, *Theodore Roosevelt and the Rise of America to World Power* (Baltimore, 1956), 327, 328n6. Lloyd C. Gardner, Walter LaFeber, and Thomas McCormick, *Creation of the American Empire* (Chicago, 1973), 269–270; Hofstadter, *Social Darwinism*, 189–190.

25. Gardner, LaFeber, and McCormick, *Creation of the American Empire*, 291–294, 286–288. See also Harry F. Pringle, *The Life and Times of William Howard Taft* (New York, 1939).

26. One lesson of the unholy lexicon of "race" is to beware what might be called the categorical fallacy, the use of cultural fictions as analytic categories. It is not surprising that such fictions were invoked in service to one

cause or another in the cultural turbulence of the early twentieth century, but it is quite another matter when such inventions become part of the conceptual apparatus for studying the period. In the 1950s, "nationality" was thought to be a solidly objective category of analysis, just as "ethnicity" came to the fore in the 1970s. Obviously, since people group themselves into ethnic categories, it is necessary to examine the subject, but not from a vantage point within the fictions themselves. In such cases, Galileo's critics have a point; that is, what scholars may be seeing when they study "ethnic group behavior" are not spots on the sun, but spots on the telescope.

27. A 1916 eugenics textbook is quoted in Linda Gordon, *Woman's Body, Woman's Right: A Social History of Birth Control in America* (New York, 1976), 277; Mark Haller, *Eugenics: Hereditarian Attitudes in American Thought* (New Brunswick, N.J., 1963), 133–137; Hofstadter, *Social Darwinism*, 162–163; Michael Grossberg, *Governing the Hearth: Law and the Family in Nineteenth-Century America* (Chapel Hill, N.C., 1985), 149–151; Maldwyn A. Jones, *American Immigration* (Chicago, 1960), 262.

28. U.S. Bureau of the Census, *Historical Statistics of the United States from Colonial Times to 1957* (Washington, D.C., 1910; hereafter cited as *Historical Statistics*), 56; Virginia Yans-McLaughlin, *Family and Community: Italian Immigrants in Buffalo, 1880–1930* (Urbana, Ill., 1982; orig. 1977), 82–108. Three-fourths of second-generation Italians married other Italians; Polish and Russian immigrants had rates nearly as high, as did old-stock families; J. H. S. Bossard, "Nationality and Nativity as Factors in Marriage," *American Sociological Review*, December 1939, 796.

29. David Hogan, *Class and Reform* (Philadelphia, 1985), 127; the 1914 newspaper quoted in ibid., 131. Jozef Miaso, *The History of the Education of Polish Immigrants in the United States* (New York, 1977), reported that two-thirds of Polish children attended parochial schools, as cited by John Bukowczyk, "Mary the Messiah," *American Ethnic History* 4 (Spring 1985), 8.

30. Eric Hobsbawm and Terence Ranger, eds., *The Invention of Tradition* (Cambridge, 1984); John Bukowczyk, "Polish Rural Culture and Immigrant Working Class Formation, 1880–1914," *Polish American Studies* 41 (Autumn 1984), 23–44; Giovanni Schiavo, *The Italians in Chicago* (Chicago, 1928); Moses Rischin, *The Promised City* (Cambridge, Mass., 1977; orig. 1962), 95–111. For probing work on immigrant adaptation to and transformation of the New World, see the title essay in Herbert Gutman, *Work, Culture, and Society in Industrializing America* (New York, 1976).

31. A. A. Hopkins writing in 1906, quoted in Andrew Sinclair, *The Era of Excess: A Social History of the Prohibition Movement* (New York, 1964), 19.

32. Hunter, *Poverty*, 3–4.

33. U.S. Congress, *Report of the Immigration Commission*, 41 vols., 61st Cong.,

2d and 3d sess. (Washington, D.C., 1911); there quickly appeared a spirited rebuttal using Dillingham's own data: Isaac Hourwich, *Immigration and Labor: The Economic Aspects of European Immigration in the United States*, rev. ed. (New York, 1922). Historians have also discredited the notion that the new immigrants were at a significant disadvantage; for example, Rischin, *Promised City*.

34. Congressman Kelly of Pennsylvania in debate on the antiliquor Hobson resolution of December 1914, quoted in Sinclair, *Era of Excess*, 154–155.

35. Lincoln Steffens, *The Shame of the Cities* (New York, 1904).

36. Paul Boyer, *Urban Masses and Moral Order in America, 1820–1920* (Cambridge, Mass., 1978), 195–232, 277–283. The social engineers were akin to the French followers of Emil Durkheim insofar as they accepted the dictum "God is society."

37. Samuel Hays, "The Politics of Reform in Municipal Government," in *American Political History as Social Analysis* (Knoxville, 1980), 205–232; Robert Fogelson, *Big-City Police* (Cambridge, Mass., 1977), 32–34, 38–39; James J. Richardson, *Urban Police in the United States* (Port Washington, N.Y., 1974), 72, 77, 85; Samuel Walker, *Popular Justice: A History of American Criminal Justice* (New York, 1980), 127–135. For an example of the elite reform thought, see Raymond Fosdick, *American Police Systems* (Montclair, N.J., 1969; orig. 1920).

38. Herbert Croly, *The Promise of American Life* (New York, 1963; orig. 1909); James Weinstein, *The Corporate Ideal and the Liberal State, 1900–1918* (Boston, 1968); Marguerite Green, *The National Civic Federation and the American Labor Movement, 1900–1925* (Westport, Conn., 1973; orig. 1956). The shift to a new stage of American history was the pivot of Frederick Jackson Turner's frontier thesis in "The Significance of the Frontier in American History," an 1893 essay reprinted in Turner, *The Frontier in American History.*

39. Frances Kellor, *Straight America: A Call to National Service* (New York, 1916), 188; Gerd Korman, *Industrialization, Immigrants, and Americanization* (Madison, Wis., 1967), 153, 141–148.

40. John Higham, *Strangers in the Land* (New York, 1963), 234–263; Kellor, *Straight America*, 90, 188; Korman, *Industrialization, Immigrants, and Americanization*, 148–149; Gordon, *Woman's Body, Woman's Right*, 136–142.

41. William E. Leuchtenburg, "Progressivism and Imperialism: The Progressive Movement and American Foreign Policy, 1898–1916," *Mississippi Valley Historical Review* 39 (1952), 483–504; in this vein, see Jerry Israel, *Progressivism and the Open Door: America and China, 1905–1921* (Pittsburgh, 1971); for a contrary view, J. M. Cooper, "Progressivism and American Foreign Policy: A Reconsideration," *Mid-America* 51 (1969), 260–277.

42. The number of children under age five per 1,000 white women from ages

twenty to forty-four dropped from 624 in 1880 to 547 in 1890; *Historical Statistics*, 24. Atlanta had 249 servants or laundresses for every 1,000 families in 1920; by contrast, New York had 74 and Chicago 68; in fact, domestic service remained the primary employer of southern women, whereas industrial and commercial jobs were taking the lead in the North and West; David Katzman, *Seven Days a Week* (New York, 1978), 61.

43. Katzman, *Seven Days a Week*, 287, 290; Jacquelyn Jones, *Labor of Love, Labor of Sorrow: Black Women, Work, and the Family from Slavery to the Present* (New York, 1985), esp. chap. 4.

44. J. F. Clark, quoted in Sinclair, *Era of Excess*, 30; C. Vann Woodward, *Origins of the New South* (Baton Rouge, 1951), 389.

45. Giles Oakley, *The Devil's Music: A History of the Blues* (New York, 1976), 34; Paul Oliver, *The Story of the Blues* (Philadelphia, 1969).

46. Ray Stannard Baker, *Following the Color Line: American Negro Citizenship in the Progressive Era* (New York, 1964; orig. 1908), 4–7, 17–18; Walter White, *A Man Called White* (New York, 1948), 6–8.

47. See Jacquelyn Hall et al., *Like a Family: The Making of a Southern Cotton Mill World* (Chapel Hill, N.C., 1987).

48. Gavin Wright, *Old South, New South: Revolutions in the Southern Economy since the Civil War* (New York, 1986), 177–197.

49. Wright, *Old South, New South*, table 6.6, 179–180, and 71–77, also shows that only 2 percent of southerners were foreign born in 1910. Perhaps the heaviest employer of immigrant labor was the Alabama steel industry; roughly half the work force was white, and of these half were first- or second-generation immigrants, of which 43 percent were Russians, Slavs, Italians, and other "new" immigrants, or perhaps 20 percent of the total, compared with three or four times that proportion for northern steel workers; see Paul Worthman, "Working-Class Mobility in Birmingham, Alabama," in *Anonymous Americans*, ed. T. K. Hareven (Englewood Cliffs, N.J., 1971), 180.

50. Here and there a state mandated segregation in the textile factories, but these were exceptions proving the rule; for South Africa, see George Fredrickson, *White Supremacy* (New York, 1981), 212–238.

51. Wright, *Old South, New South*, table 6.6, 179–180; Dolores Janiewski, *Sisterhood Denied: Race, Class, and Gender in a New South Community* (Philadelphia, 1985), 104–105; Hall et al., *Like a Family*.

52. Janiewski, *Sisterhood Denied*, 102–103.

53. W. E. B. DuBois, "Economic Revolution in the South," in DuBois and Booker T. Washington, *The Negro in the South* (London, 1907), 114–115.

54. Oscar Ameringer, *If You Don't Weaken* (New York, 1940), 196–197.

55. George Tindall, *The Emergence of the New South, 1913–1945* (n.p., 1967), 76; the lion's share of southern textile spindles and lumber capital was in the

hands of southerners; these and related industries employed upward of 550,000 people in 1910, whereas the railroads and steel mills in the South were commonly owned by outsiders and employed fewer. Figures on combined employment in lumber and timber products, turpentine, fertilizers, furniture, cotton goods, and hosiery, and figures on productivity are in Wright, *Old South, New South*, table 6.2, 160–161; with respect to productivity, southern lumber and timber workers made up 43.8 percent of nationwide employment in the two industries, but only 38.5 percent of value-added.

56. Women clericals registered 13 percent of female workers in Mississippi, Alabama, and other East South Central states, the lowest in the nation. Among white males, 3.8 percent of the gainfully employed in the South Atlantic states were professionals, compared with 5.7 percent in the Middle Atlantic states; East South Central states had the highest proportion of proprietors, managers, and officials (38.7 percent), with West South Central second (36 percent); Alba Edwards, *Social Economic Grouping of the Gainful Workers of the United States* (Washington, D.C., 1938), 62.

57. Maurice Leven and W. I. King, *Income in the Various States: Its Sources and Distribution, 1919, 1920, and 1921* (New York, 1925), 264–267, cited in Woodward, *Origins of the New South*, 319. Long-range trends are mapped in Richard Easterlin, "Regional Income Trends, 1840–1950," in *American Economic History*, ed. S. E. Harris (New York, 1961), 528–529. See also Jeffrey Williamson and Peter Lindert, *American Inequality* (New York, 1980).

58. Woodward, *Origins of the New South*, 295, 296, 300–304, 315. Southern-bred executives included Samuel Spencer, head of the Southern Railroad, and George Crawford, head of Tennessee Coal and Iron. U. S. Steel sold Birmingham steel at the "Birmingham differential," i.e., the Pittsburgh price plus three dollars per ton plus freight from Birmingham; Alfred Chandler, *The Visible Hand: The Managerial Revolution in American Business* (Cambridge, Mass., 1977), 350–351; Tindall, *Emergence of the New South*, 81–82, 92.

59. Chandler, *Visible Hand*, 290–293, 382–391; Tindall, *Emergence of the New South*, 73–74; Janiewski, *Sisterhood Denied*, 72.

60. Woodward, *Origins of the New South*, 387; R. M. Brown, "The History of Vigilantism in America," in *Vigilante Politics*, ed. H. J. Rosenbaum and P. C. Sederberg (Philadelphia, 1976), 79–109; Green, *Grass-Roots Socialism*.

61. Sterling Spero and Abram Harris, *The Black Worker* (New York, 1969; orig. 1931), 332, 352–384; Tindall, *Emergence of the New South*, 164–165; for lumber workers see also Green, *Grass-Roots Socialism*; for the UMW in the 1890s, see Herbert Gutman, "The Negro and the United Mine Workers of America," in *Work, Culture, and Society*, 121–208.

62. Quoted in Leonard Dinnerstein, *The Leo Frank Case* (New York, 1968), 98, 10; Dinnerstein is the prime source for my account of the case.

63. Edward Ayers, *Vengeance and Justice: Crime and Punishment in the Nineteenth-Century American South* (New York, 1984), 274; Dinnerstein, *Leo Frank Case*, 10, 33.

64. Dinnerstein, *Leo Frank Case*, 118–119, 149–150; H. J. Rosenbaum, and P.C. Sederberg, "Vigilantism: An Analysis of Establishment Violence," in Rosenbaum and Sederberg, *Vigilante Politics*, 3–29. In the early 1980s, a witness who had been silent for seventy years came forward to implicate Conley. Ayers, *Vengeance and Justice*, 266, draws attention to the importance of sexual transgression to the jurisprudence of lawlessness; he quotes a Louisiana lawyer in 1906 to the effect that protection of women against rape, adultery, seduction, and "slander against chastity" were the first four justifications of personal violence.

65. White, *Social Thought in America*, 11–31.

66. For examples of works locating the wellsprings of progressivism in different social strata, see, for the elite: Hays, *American Political History as Social Analysis;* for the middle class: Richard Hofstadter, *The American Political Tradition and the Men Who Made It* (New York, 1944); George Mowry, *The California Progressives* (Chicago, 1963; orig. 1951); Robert Wiebe, *The Search for Order, 1877–1920* (New York, 1967); for the working class: Huthmacher, "Urban Liberalism and the Age of Reform"; Buenker, *Urban Liberalism and Progressive Reform.*

67. Peter Filene, "An Obituary for the Progressive Movement," *American Quarterly* 22 (1970), 20–34.

68. English politics were closest to American, and the "new liberalism" and the term *progressive* originated in the land of J. A. Hobson and the *Progressive Review;* but England was also giving birth to the Labour party, which would soon surpass the Liberals in giving the working class a political voice. German politics was further removed from American-style liberalism, and the list of German progressive intellectuals virtually starts and stops with Max Weber, Germany's nearest equivalent to John Dewey; on these points, see Kloppenberg, *Uncertain Victory,* 321–329. It is possible to find some kind of progressive reform at the municipal level, but at the national level there were no German counterparts to America's progressive leaders. There was a Progressive party in the Reichstag, but it was consigned to a narrow ledge of middle-class support, where it was content to be custodian of the remains of the failed liberal revolution of 1848. Contemporaries were inclined to ask, with Werner Sombart, "Why is there no socialism in the United States?" but it is equally pertinent to ask, why was there no progressivism in Germany?

69. Amy Hackett, "Helene Stöcker: Left-Wing Intellectual and Sex Re-

former," in *When Biology Became Destiny: Women in Weimar and Nazi Germany*, ed. Renate Bridenthal, Atima Grossman, and Marion Kaplan (New York, 1984), 109–130; R. J. Evans, "Liberalism and Society: The Feminist Movement and Social Change," in *Society and Politics in Wilhelmine Germany* (London, 1978), 187, 203.

70. Sigmund Freud, *Civilization and Its Discontents*, in *The Future of an Illusion, Civilization and Its Discontents, and Other Works*, trans. James Strachey (London, 1961).

71. The 1907 census recorded 36 percent of the paid labor force as female; Jean Quatert, *Reluctant Feminists in German Social Democracy, 1885–1917* (Princeton, 1979), 32–34; slightly different figures are reported in Jurgen Kocka, *White Collar Workers in the United States, 1890–1940: A Social-Political History in International Perspective*, trans. Maura Kealey (Beverly Hills, 1980), 67, 303n78, but he confirms both the trend of rising female employment and the wide gap between Germany and the United States.

72. Evans, "Liberalism and Society," 190–200; Katherine Anthony, *Feminism in Germany and Scandinavia* (New York, 1915), 192–196; Ute Frevert, *Women in German History: From Bourgeois Emancipation to Sexual Liberation*, trans. Stuart McKinnon-Evans (Oxford, 1988), 107–148.

73. O'Neill, *Everyone Was Brave;* Nancy Schrom Dye, *As Equals and as Sisters: Feminism, the Labor Movement, and the Women's Trade Union League of New York* (Columbia, Mo., 1980).

74. Richard L. McCormick, "The Discovery That Business Corrupts Politics: A Reappraisal of the Origins of Progressivism," *American Historical Review* 86 (April 1981), 247–274; Walter Lippmann, *Drift and Mastery: An Attempt to Diagnose the Current Unrest* (Englewood Cliffs, N.J., 1961; orig. 1914); Walter Dean Burnham, "The System of 1896: An Analysis," in *The Evolution of American Electoral Systems*, ed. Paul Kleppner (Westport, Conn., 1981), 196–197.

75. J. C. Hunt, "The Bourgeois Middle in German Politics, 1871–1933; Recent Literature," *Central European History* 11 (March 1978), 83–106; A. J. P. Taylor, *The Course of German History* (New York, 1962; orig. 1946), 156–158, 162; Hobsbawm, *Age of Empire*, 170; David Blackbourn and Geoff Eley, *The Peculiarities of German History* (Oxford, 1984); David Blackbourn, *Class, Religion, and Local Politics in Wilhelmine Germany: The Center Party in Wurttemberg before 1914* (Wiesbaden, 1980). As these sources suggest, the middle classes had gained predominance at all but the highest levels of the state. They dominated municipal government, wielded great influence in state legislatures, held sway in secondary schools and universities, chambers of commerce, and tradesmen's guilds, and became increasingly important in the parliamentary balance of power. The Progressives lent an air of national unity to the "Bulow bloc" (1906–1909), and their support

for direct taxes to fund the big military buildup in 1913 gave a "progressive" luster to Chancellor Bethmann-Hollweg's program.

76. Martin Kitchen, *The Political Economy of Germany, 1815–1914* (Montreal, 1978); Volker Berghahn, *Germany and the Approach of War in 1914* (New York, 1973); Geoff Eley, *From Unification to Nazism: Reinterpreting the German Past* (Boston, 1986), 42–60, 154–170.

77. Arnold J. Heidenheimer, "Education and Social Security Entitlements in Europe and America," in *The Development of Welfare States in Europe and America*, ed. A. J. Heidenheimer and Peter Flora (New Brunswick, N.J., 1981), 269–306.

78. Carl Schorske, *German Social Democracy, 1905–1917* (New York, 1970; orig. 1955), 49–53, 195–196, 224–226. The SPD accepted trade union autonomy in its Mannheim resolution of 1906; but, for all its class unity, the SPD had no record of significant reforms to show. The Reich Insurance Act of 1911, for example, fell far short of expectations for expanding the welfare state, and in any case, credit for reform accrued not to the socialists, but to the government as it sought to win consent of the workers by an end run around their chosen representatives, just as Bismarck had done in launching social insurance in the first place.

79. Ibid., 225, 228–234; B. R. Mitchell, *European Historical Statistics, 1750–1970* (New York, 1975), table C3, 174; Berghahn, *Germany and Approach of War.*

80. Werner Sombart, *Why Is There No Socialism in the United States?* (White Plains, N.Y., 1976; orig. 1906).

81. Marc Karson, *American Labor Unions and Politics, 1900–1918* (Carbondale, Ill., 1958); Stephan Thernstrom, *Poverty and Progress* (Cambridge, Mass., 1963); John Commons et al., eds., *History of Labor in the United States*, 4 vols. (New York, 1918–1935); Selig Perlman, *A Theory of the Labor Movement* (New York, 1949; orig. 1928); Aileen Kraditor, *The Radical Persuasion, 1890–1917* (Baton Route, 1981).

82. Baer and Roosevelt quoted in Richard Hofstadter, "Theodore Roosevelt: The Conservative as Progressive," in *The American Political Tradition* (New York, 1974; orig. 1948), 288, 289.

83. William A. White, *The Autobiography of William Allen White* (New York, 1946), 429–430, 465. For a dramatic overview of the period 1877–1919, see Nell Painter, *Standing at Armageddon* (New York, 1987).

84. Ira Kipnis, *The American Socialist Movement, 1897–1912* (New York, 1968; orig. 1952); Weinstein, *Decline of Socialism*, 93–103.

85. The socialist-progressive dialogue is plumbed in Martin Sklar, *The Corporate Reconstruction of American Capitalism, 1890–1916* (Cambridge, 1988), to whom I am indebted for the idea that progressivism "contained" socialism. According to Judith Anderson, *William Howard Taft: An Intimate History*

(New York, 1981), 21, Taft's inept leadership earned him the epithet "the blundering politician," although the problem was deeper than personal failing. Taft's later laissez-faire rulings as a member of the Supreme Court indicate that he was unable to make the transition from the nineteenth-century state of courts and parties to an administrative state of executive management.

86. Hofstadter, *American Political Tradition*, 327–337.

87. For an interpretation of progressivism as a conservative, elitist force, see Gabriel Kolko, *The Triumph of Conservatism: A Reinterpretation of American History, 1900–1916* (Chicago, 1963).

4. Progressive Statecraft

1. Lippmann, *Drift and Mastery: An Attempt to Diagnose the Current Unrest* (Englewood Cliffs, N.J., 1961; orig. 1914), 16.

2. Alfred Chandler, *The Visible Hand: The Managerial Revolution in American Business* (Cambridge, Mass., 1977), 357–358; Sanford Jacoby, *Employing Bureaucracy: Managers, Unions, and the Transformation of Work in American Industry, 1900–1945* (New York, 1985).

3. David Noble, *America by Design: Science, Technology, and the Rise of Corporate Capitalism* (New York, 1977), 1–32; Margerie Davies, *Women's Place Is at the Typewriter: Office Work and Office Workers, 1870–1930* (Philadelphia, 1982); Samuel Bowles and Herbert Gintis, *Schooling in Capitalist America: Educational Reform and the Contradictions of Economic Life* (New York, 1976).

4. National Industrial Conference Board (NICB), *A Graphic Analysis of the Census of Manufactures of the United States, 1849–1919* (New York, 1923), 113; figures on concentration of large-scale employers from Harry N. Scheiber, Harold G. Vatter, and Harold U. Faulkner, *American Economic History* (New York, 1976), table 15–3, 232; Robert Lampmann, *The Share of Top Wealth-Holders in National Wealth, 1922–1956* (Princeton, 1962), 206. Jeffrey Williamson and Peter Lindert, *American Inequality: A Macroeconomic History* (New York, 1980), 46–51, portray the era from the Civil War to the Great Depression as a high plateau of wealth inequality, in which the years around the First World War reduced inequality but the 1920s restored and perhaps increased the extremes; using figures from a Federal Trade Commission sampling of probated estates, they estimate that the top 5 percent of wealth holders owned from 77 to 80 percent of all wealth in 1912; as is the case with all such figures, these are estimates based on data and econometric assumptions that may or may not be valid.

5. Naomi Lamoreaux, *The Great Merger Movement in American Business, 1895–1904* (Cambridge, 1985), 1–4.

6. Thorstein Veblen, *Theory of Business Enterprise* (New York, 1904), 39, 64; idem, *The Engineers and the Price System* (New York, 1921). Veblen was the pivotal figure in the rise of "institutional" economics. More recent critics of big business include Marxist economists and historians who critique the hierarchical strategies of "scientific" management and examine struggles for power on the shop floor, such as Harry Braverman, *Labor and Monopoly Capital* (New York, 1974); David Montgomery, *The Fall of the House of Labor* (Cambridge, 1987). After the Great Depression, Keynesians diagnosed unequal distribution of wealth and income as an inherent malady of the unregulated private enterprise system that led not just to a gap between rich and poor, but to common ruin, as in the many works of John Kenneth Galbraith, including *The New Industrial State* (Boston, 1967) and *The Great Crash: 1929* (Boston, 1954).

7. Richard Abrams, introduction to Louis Brandeis, *Other People's Money* (New York, 1967; orig. 1914), vii–xliv.

8. George Mowry, *The Era of Theodore Roosevelt and the Birth of Modern America, 1900–1912* (New York, 1958).

9. Arthur Link, *Woodrow Wilson and the Progressive Era* (New York, 1954), 18–24.

10. Richard Hofstadter, *The American Political Tradition and the Men Who Made It* (New York, 1944), 256; Martin Sklar, *The Corporate Reconstruction of American Capitalism, 1890–1916* (Cambridge, 1988), 402–407, 418–419.

11. Link, *Wilson and the Progressive Era*, 36–43.

12. James Livingston, *Origins of the Federal Reserve System: Money, Class, and Corporate Capitalism, 1890–1913* (Ithaca, N.Y., 1986), 217; Brandeis, *Other People's Money*.

13. Link, *Wilson and the Progressive Era*, 44–53; Livingston, *Origins of Federal Reserve System*, 224, cites a letter from Irving Bush to Paul Warburg before the bill's passage saying, "in practice, the real banking operations of the country will be carried on under the direction of the officers and directors of the Federal Reserve banks."

14. Emily Rosenberg, *Spreading the American Dream: American Economic and Cultural Expansion, 1890–1945* (New York, 1982), 68–69.

15. In composing this picture of progressive aims, I have drawn on the very different interpretations in Hofstadter, *American Political Tradition*, 292–304, 327–338, which portrays Wilson as an Edwardian liberal in progressive clothing; and Sklar, *Corporate Reconstruction*, 402–404, 406–407, 418–419, which portrays Wilson as a corporate liberal and consistent proponent of government regulation.

16. Wilson quoted in Sklar, *Corporate Reconstruction*, 326.

17. Ibid., 226, 325–330, 420; Link, *Wilson and the Progressive Era*, 69–71, 72–73; the senator was James Reed.

18. Christopher Tomlins, *The State and the Unions: Labor Relations, Law, and the*

Organized Labor Movement in America, 1880–1960 (Cambridge, 1985), 65–67.

19. Link, *Wilson and the Progressive Era*, 73; Edwin Witte, *The Government in Labor Disputes* (New York, 1932), 70; hostile Supreme Court decisions include *Duplex Printing Press* (1921) and *Bedford Cut Stone* (1927), outlawing the secondary boycott, or sympathy strike; and *American Steel Foundries* (1921), against mass picketing.

20. Sklar, *Corporate Reconstruction*, 332; Livingston, *Origins of Federal Reserve System*, 215–234.

21. Lamoreaux, *Great Merger Movement*, 187–194; Morton Keller, "The Pluralist State," in *Regulation in Perspective*, ed. Thomas McCraw (Cambridge, Mass., 1981), 56–94.

22. George C. Suggs, *Colorado's War on Militant Unionism* (Detroit, 1972), 110–111, 118–119, 125–143, 150–151; Mark Wyman, *Hard Rock Epic* (Berkeley, 1979), 218–227; David Grover, *Debaters and Dynamiters: The Story of the Haywood Trial* (Corvalis, Ore., 1964), 52–56.

23. Howard Zinn, *The Politics of History* (Boston, 1970), 79–101; *The Military Occupation of the Coal Strike Zone of Colorado by the Colorado National Guard, 1913–14*, Report of the Commanding General (Denver, 1914), 36–37, 49–74; "Colorado Coal Strike," Adjutant General, RG 94, file 2154620–1,2,3; Justice Department, RG 60, file 168733.

24. D. W. Meinig, *Southwest: Three Peoples in Geographical Change* (New York, 1971), 66–71.

25. Robert D. Gregg, *The Influence of Border Troubles on the Relations between the United States and Mexico* (New York, 1970; orig. 1937); Karl Schmitt, *Mexico and the United States, 1821–1973* (New York, 1974); Eric Wolf, *Peasant Wars of the Twentieth Century* (New York, 1969), 21–23; Edward Berman, *Labor Disputes and the President* (New York, 1968; orig. 1924), 36–42, 60, 64–69; Frederick Wilson, *Federal Aid in Domestic Disturbances* (Washington, D.C., 1969; orig. 1903), 249; Adjutant General, RG 94, files 488494; 13/0155.

26. The most colorful of American labor movements, the Wobblies spawned a large literature; for a comprehensive treatment see Melvyn Dubovsky, *We Shall Be All: The History of the I.W.W.* (New York, 1969). Their lives made for high drama, as recounted in William D. Haywood, *The Autobiography of Big Bill Haywood* (New York, 1977; orig. 1929). The largest collection of IWW papers is housed at Reuther Library, Wayne State University. For obvious reasons, they also made it into Justice Department and Military Intelligence papers, housed at the National Archives.

27. Graham Adams, *Age of Industrial Violence, 1910–1915: The Activities and Findings of the United States Commission on Industrial Relations* (New York, 1966), 32, 40.

28. U.S. Senate, Commission on Industrial Relations, *Final Report*, 16 vols. (Washington, D.C., 1916), I, 2, 3–4; Adams, *Age of Industrial Violence*,

161–175; Frank P. Walsh Papers, New York Public Library, boxes 142–144.

29. Haywood, *Autobiography*, 190–222; Adams, *Age of Industrial Violence*, 1–24; for comparison to the role of courtroom theater in eighteenth-century England, see the essays in Douglas Hay, et al., eds., *Albion's Fatal Tree: Crime and Society in Eighteenth Century England* (New York, 1975).

30. For a discussion of labor and the law see Tomlins, *The State and the Unions.*

31. J. H. Cohen, *Law and Order in Industry: Five Years' Experience* (New York, 1916), 291–292; J. R. Commons and Florence Harriman, report in U.S. Senate, Commission on Industrial Relations, *Final Report*, I, 173–183; Herbert Croly, *The Promise of American Life* (New York, 1963; orig. 1909).

32. Alice Kessler-Harris, *Out to Work: A History of Wage-Earning Women in the United States* (New York, 1982), 202–214; John Higham, *Strangers in the Land* (New York, 1963), 112–163.

33. See Walter Trattner, *Crusade for the Children: A History of the National Child Labor Committee and Child Labor Reform in America* (Chicago, 1970).

34. Women's minimum wages were upheld in Stettler v. O'Hara 243 U.S. 629 (1917), only to be overturned in Adkins v. Children's Hospital 261 U.S. 525 (1923).

35. Montgomery, *Fall of the House of Labor*, 353–354; Daniel Nelson and Stuart Campbell, "Taylorism versus Welfare Work in American Industry: H. L. Gantt and the Bancrofts," *Business History Review* 46 (Spring 1972), 1–16. The multitude of NICB pamphlets and publications provides a running guide to managerial philosophy: see, for example, NICB, *Bulletin 1: Industrial Self-Government* (n.p., n.d.); NICB, *Health Service in Industry* (New York, 1921); NICB, *Industrial Pensions in the United States* (New York, 1925). See also Jacoby, *Employing Bureaucracy.*

36. Jacoby, *Employing Bureaucracy*, 49–52; report of the Sociological Committee at International Harvester, Cyrus McCormick Papers, box 42, SHSW.

37. Personnel Records, Pennsylvania Railroad YMCA, 1899–1927 and 1922–1960, HL; the quote is from about 1932; likewise, the purpose of the Reading Railroad's relief association was "greater co-operation and more harmonious relations."

38. Marguerite Green, *The National Civic Federation and the American Labor Movement, 1900–1925* (Westport, Conn., 1973; orig. 1956); Robert Ozanne, *A Century of Labor Management Relations at McCormick and International Harvester* (Madison, Wis., 1967); Daniel Nelson, "The New Factory System and the Unions: The National Cash Register Co. Dispute of 1901," *Labor History* 15 (Winter 1974), 163–178.

39. James Allen, *The Company Town in the American West* (Norman, Okla., 1966), 65–66; Adams, *Age of Industrial Violence*, 172.

40. Clarence J. Hicks, *My Life in Industrial Relations* (New York, 1941), 47–50, 80.

41. Frederick W. Taylor quoted in Samuel Haber, *Efficiency and Uplift: Scientific Management in the Progressive Era, 1890–1920* (Chicago, 1964), 27; ibid., 51–56. See also Frederick W. Taylor, *The Principles of Scientific Management* (New York, 1911).

42. Croly, *The Promise of American Life;* Josephine Goldmark, *Fatigue and Efficiency* (New York, 1913).

43. Richard A. Easterlin, "Regional Income Trends, 1840–1950," in *American Economic History*, ed. S. E. Harris (New York, 1961), 528; U.S. Bureau of the Census, *Statistical Abstract of the United States, 1933*, 259, cited in C. Vann Woodward, *Origins of the New South*, 319.

44. Lucy Randolph Mason of the YWCA was a southern Florence Kelley, as portrayed in Anne Firor Scott, *The Southern Lady: From Pedestal to Politics, 1830–1930* (Chicago, 1970), 192–197; see also Jacquelyn Hall, *Revolt against Chivalry: Jessie Daniel Ames and the Women's Campaign against Lynching* (New York, 1979).

45. George Tindall, *The Emergence of the New South, 1913–1945* (n.p., 1967), 17–18; Woodward, *Origins of the New South*, 371–380.

46. Walter Dean Burnham, *Critical Elections and the Mainsprings of American Politics* (New York, 1970), 78, 84, 80; J. M. Kousser, *The Shaping of Southern Politics: Suffrage Restriction and the Establishment of the One-Party South, 1880–1910* (New Haven, 1974), 224–225, 231–238; C. Vann Woodward, *Tom Watson: Agrarian Rebel* (New York, 1963; orig. 1938).

47. Tindall, *Emergence of the New South*, 17, 13–15; Pete Daniel, *Standing at the Crossroads* (New York, 1986), 73–74.

48. Tindall, *Emergence of the New South*, 143–144; Daniel, *Standing at the Crossroads*, 75–76; Robert Zangrando, *The NAACP Crusade against Lynching, 1909–1950* (Philadelphia, 1980), 33–34, 37–38.

49. Kearney quoted in Scott, *Southern Lady*, 182; Hall, *Revolt against Chivalry*, 35–38, 43.

50. Marshall Cushing to Charles Tuller, March 8, 1904, in National Association of Manufacturers Papers, series 1, box 43, HL.

51. Tindall, *Emergence of the New South*, 16n50, 20, 321–322.

52. For a discussion of liberal democracy as the political expression of a balance between capitalists and the working class, see Alan Wolfe, *The Limits of Legitimacy: Political Contradictions of Contemporary Capitalism* (New York, 1977).

53. Frank Koester, "The Greatest Secret of German Progress," *The Fatherland*, December 16, 1914, 5.

54. Arnold J. Heidenheimer, "Education and Social Security Entitlements in Europe and America," in *The Development of Welfare States in Europe and America*, ed. A. J. Heidenheimer and Peter Flora (New Brunswick, N.J., 1981), 269–306.

55. Koester, "The Greatest Secret of German Progress," *The Fatherland*, De-

cember 23, 1914, 7; and January 13, 1915, 9; Molly Nolan, *Social Democracy and Society: Working-Class Radicalism in Dusseldorf, 1890–1920* (Cambridge, Mass., 1981); Geoff Eley, "Joining Two Histories," in *From Unification to Nazism: Reinterpreting the German Past* (Boston, 1986), 180–186; Jurgen Kocka, *Facing Total War: German Society, 1914–1918*, trans. Barbara Weinberger (Cambridge, Mass., 1984), 77–83; Heidenheimer and Flora, *Development of Welfare States*, 17–36, 269–304.

56. Arthur Shadwell, *Industrial Efficiency: A Comparative Study of Industrial Life in England, Germany and America* (London, 1920; orig. 1905), 424; Carl Schorske, *German Social Democracy, 1905–1917* (New York, 1970; orig. 1955), 225, described prewar Germany as a case of "stagnation on the surface, tension and ferment beneath it." Strike statistics offer some support for this view: after peaking in 1905 at 966,000, the number of strikers fell to a low of 281,000 in 1908 and then climbed again to the prewar high of 1,031,000 in 1912; B. R. Mitchell, *European Historical Statistics, 1750–1970* (New York, 1975), table C3, 174.

57. Jean Quatert, *Reluctant Feminists in German Social Democracy, 1885–1917* (Princeton, 1979), 24–26; Katherine Anthony, *Feminism in Germany and Scandinavia* (New York, 1915), 173–179; see also Ute Frevert, *Women in German History: From Bourgeois Emancipation to Sexual Liberation*, trans. Stuart McKinnon-Evans (Oxford, 1988).

58. Norway was arguably home to the world's first feminist, Henrik Ibsen's Nora, and at the start of the First World War Norway gave out-of-wedlock children the same rights as legitimate children; Norway and Sweden permitted divorce by mutual consent; and Swedish writer Ellen Key's *Renaissance of Motherhood* rejected monogamy as the sole legitimate sexual union; Anthony, *Feminism in Germany and Scandinavia*, 95–96, 147–158. Norway, Sweden, and Finland all adopted women's suffrage before the war; see Ross Evans Paulson, *Women's Suffrage and Prohibition: A Comparative Study of Equality and Social Control* (Glenview, Ill., 1973), 153–154, 154 n. 23.

59. Anthony, *Feminism in Germany and Scandinavia*, 117–133.

60. Shadwell, *Industrial Efficiency*, 33–35, 331, 457.

61. Koester, "Greatest Secret of German Progress"; Koester was a civil engineer who wrote about city planning; John Dewey, *Reconstruction in Philosophy* (New York, 1920), 208; Croly, *The Promise of American Life*, 249–52.

62. There were short-term redistributive effects from the First World War, after which inequality more or less recovered in the 1920s to the point that the top 5 percent received on the order of 30 percent of national income in 1929; results of several studies are combined in Williamson and Lindert, *American Inequality*, 75–80. The distribution of national wealth was considerably more skewed, and the time bomb of uneven distribution finally went off in 1929.

5. The Dynamics of Total War

1. Wilson, Baltimore address, April 6, 1918, *Harper Book of American Quotations*, ed. Gorton Carruth and Eugene Ehrlich (New York, 1988), 237.
2. Eric Hobsbawm, *The Age of Empire, 1875–1900* (London, 1987), 315–323. The argument that Germany went to war to overcome internal division was put forward by Fritz Fischer, *German Aims in the First World War* (New York, 1967); the same argument is found in Volker Berghahn, *Germany and the Approach of War in 1914* (New York, 1973).
3. Wilson quoted in William Leuchtenburg, *The Perils of Prosperity, 1914–1932*, (Chicago, 1958), 18. See ibid., 12–34; also Ernest R. May, *World War and American Isolation, 1914–1917* (Cambridge, Mass., 1959).
4. Henry F. May, *The End of American Innocence: A Study of the First Years of Our Own Time, 1912–1917* (New York, 1959), 366–368, 393–395; Linda Gordon, *Woman's Body, Woman's Right: A Social History of Birth Control in America* (New York, 1976), 186–230; Nancy Cott, *The Grounding of Modern Feminism* (New Haven, 1987), 12–50; Elliot Shore, *Talkin' Socialism* (Lawrence, Kans., 1988); J. M. Budish and George Soule, *The New Unionism in the Clothing Industry* (New York, 1920).
5. UMW president John White quoted in David Montgomery, *The Fall of the House of Labor*, (Cambridge, 1987), 363; C. Roland Marchand, *The American Peace Movement and Social Reform, 1898–1918* (Princeton, 1973), xii–xv; Jane Addams, *Peace and Bread in Time of War* (New York, 1945).
6. This analysis suggests that Wilson was less successful in fusing peace to progressivism than Arthur Link claims, *Woodrow Wilson and the Progressive Era* (New York, 1963; orig. 1954), 247–251.
7. Walter Millis, *Arms and Men: A Study in American Military History* (New Brunswick, N.J., 1981; orig. 1956), 225–233; Martha Derthik, *The National Guard in Politics* (Cambridge, Mass., 1965), 29–30, 33–35.
8. John P. Finnegan, *Against the Specter of a Dragon: The American Campaign for Military Preparedness, 1914–1917* (Westport, Conn., 1974), 111, 105; John Higham, *Strangers in the Land* (New York, 1963), 199–200; Frances Kellor, *Straight America: A Call to National Service* (New York, 1916).
9. Arthur Link, *Woodrow Wilson and the Progressive Era* (New York, 1954), 239–251; David M. Kennedy, *Over Here: The First World War and American Society* (New York, 1980), 148–149. On Republican dominance and the "system of 1896," see Walter Dean Burnham, *Critical Elections and the Mainsprings of American Politics* (New York, 1970).
10. Lloyd C. Gardner, Walter LaFeber, and Thomas McCormick, *Creation of the American Empire* (Chicago, 1973), 305.
11. Eric Wolf, *Peasant Wars of the Twentieth Century* (New York, 1969); John Womack, *Zapata and the Mexican Revolution* (New York, 1967); for an ac-

count that vividly captures the chaos and upheaval, see John Reed, *Insurgent Mexico* (New York, 1914); on the world-historical significance of the Mexican Revolution, see Hobsbawm, *Age of Empire*, 286.

12. Wilson quoted in Link, *Wilson and the Progressive Era*, 119, 111–113; Lane quoted in R. F. Smith, *The United States and Revolutionary Nationalism in Mexico, 1916–1932* (Chicago, 1972), 90; Lloyd C. Gardner, *Safe for Democracy: The Anglo-American Response to Revolution, 1913–23* (New York, 1984), 62.

13. Link, *Wilson and the Progressive Era*, 123; Karl Schmitt, *Mexico and the United States, 1821–1973* (New York, 1974), 147–149.

14. Joseph Tumulty, *Woodrow Wilson as I Knew Him* (New York, 1921), 159, quoted in Friedrich Katz, *The Secret War in Mexico* (Chicago, 1981), 311. As early as October 1915 Secretary Robert Lansing had said: "Our possible relations with Germany must be our first consideration: and all our intercourse with Mexico must be regulated accordingly"; quoted in ibid., 302.

15. Link, *Wilson and the Progressive Era*, 271; Gardner, *Safe for Democracy*, 122–139.

16. Lansing's recollection of Wilson's statement is quoted in N. Gordon Levin, *Woodrow Wilson and World Politics: America's Response to War and Revolution* (New York, 1968), 25; Leuchtenburg, *Perils of Prosperity*, 14–16; the Anglo-American special relationship is the subject of Gardner, *Safe for Democracy*.

17. Wilson, "Peace Without Victory," *The Public Papers of Woodrow Wilson*, 6 vols. (New York, 1925–27), II, 407–414; Link, *Wilson and the Progressive Era*, 261–264.

18. Katz, *Secret War*, 350, notes that Germany's decision had been made on January 7, 1917; Leuchtenburg, *Perils of Prosperity*, 31–32; Link, *Wilson and the Progressive Era*, 278–281.

19. Link, *Wilson and the Progressive Era*, 276, 279.

20. Wilson, address to Congress, April 2, 1917, in *Public Papers*, I, 6–16.

21. Norris quoted in Kennedy, *Over Here*, 21; Randolph Bourne quoted in Leuchtenburg, *Perils of Prosperity*, 46; see also Bourne, "The State," in *War and the Intellectuals*, ed. Carl Resek (New York, 1964); James Weinstein, *The Decline of Socialism in America* (New York, 1967), 145–159; Theodore Saloutos and John Hicks, *Twentieth-Century Populism* (Lincoln, Neb., 1951), 179; Link, *Wilson and the Progressive Era*, 282.

22. Hobsbawm, *Age of Empire*, 324–327; Kennedy, *Over Here*, 3–4.

23. Bourne, "The State," 71.

24. Wilson quoted by *New York World* journalist Frank Cobb, in Hofstadter, *The American Political Tradition and the Men Who Made It* (New York, 1944), 352; Frederick Luebke, *Bonds of Loyalty: German Americans and World War I*

(De Kalb, Ill., 1974); Carl Wittke, *German-Americans and the World War* (Columbus, 1936).

25. John Higham, *Strangers in the Land* (New York, 1963), 164.

26. Florette Henri, *Black Migration Movement North, 1900–1920* (Garden City, N.Y., 1975); Elliot Rudwick, *Race Riot at East St. Louis* (Cardondale, Ill., 1964), 16–19, 75, 217–218; Pete Daniel, *Standing at the Crossroads* (New York, 1986), 61–63, 77–79.

27. Vernon Jensen, *Heritage of Conflict* (New York, 1968; orig. 1950), 384–385; James Green, *Grass-Roots Socialism: Radical Movements in the Southwest, 1895–1943* (Baton Rouge, 1978), 357–360; Evan Anders, "Boss Rule and Constituent Interests: South Texas Politics during the Progressive Era," *Southwestern Historical Quarterly* 84 (January 1981), 280; Clarence Clendenen, *The United States and Pancho Villa* (Port Washington, N.Y., 1972; orig. 1961), 286–287; President's Mediation Commission, transcript of Bisbee sessions, November 1–5, 1917, RG 174, entry 8; William D. Haywood, *Bill Haywood's Book* (New York, 1929), 298, 301; Melvyn Dubovsky, *We Shall Be All: The History of the I.W.W.* (New York, 1969), 391–392.

28. Weinstein, *Decline of Socialism;* Marchand, *American Peace Movement,* 308–309.

29. William Preston, *Aliens and Dissenters: Federal Suppression of Radicals, 1903–1933* (Cambridge, Mass., 1963), 119, 145–147. The goal of criminalizing dissenting ideas was manifest in the rash of "criminal syndicalism" statutes, such as the one passed in California that outlawed any doctrine *advocating* sabotage "as a means of accomplishing a change in industrial ownership or control," according to R. W. Henderson, *Constructive Conspiracy* (San Francisco, n.d.), 6; U.S. Spruce Production Corporation, *History of Spruce Production Division* (n.d., n.p.), 1–11, 16, 19; Secretary William Wilson to Newton Baker, December 14, 1917, February 21 and March 2, 1918, Glasser Files, Justice Department, RG 60; report of C. O. Young, August 2, 1918, ibid; see also Harold Hyman, *Soldiers and Spruce: Origins of the Loyal Legion of Loggers and Lumbermen* (Los Angeles, 1963); Eldridge F. Dowell, *A History of Criminal Syndicalism Legislation in the United States* (New York, 1969; orig. 1939).

30. Kennedy, *Over Here,* 83–86; Ray Ginger, *The Bending Cross: A Biography of Eugene V. Debs* (New Brunswick, N.J., 1949), 353–376. See also Zechariah Chaffee, *Free Speech in the United States* (Cambridge, Mass., 1941).

31. Millis, *Arms and Men,* 211–213; Russell Weigley, *The American Way of War* (New York, 1973), 192–200; for a general interpretation of the relation between war and society, see Stanislav Andreski, *Military Organization and Society* (Berkeley, 1968).

32. George Creel, *How We Advertised America* (New York, 1920), 94, 125–129, 459; for the Polish rally, see *Dziennik Zwiazkowy,* September 24 and 27,

1918, reel 51, Chicago Foreign Language Press Service (hereafter CFLPS); see also *Daily Jewish Courier*, June 14, 1918, May 1, 1919, reel 34, CFLPS; for similar evidence about Italian-Americans, see John Duff, "The Italians," in *The Immigrants' Influence on Wilson's Peace Policies*, ed. Joseph O'Grady (Lexington, Ky., 1967), 114.

33. John McClymer, *War and Welfare: Social Engineering in America, 1890–1925* (Westport, Conn., 1980), 29–30; Kellor, *Straight America*, 188; U.S. Bureau of Education, *Americanization Bulletin*, September 15, 1918, 7; for example, photographs of flag-raising ceremonies at Westinghouse on August 20, 1918, show the multiethnic work force assembled in the steam turbine shed, as if in steerage aboard ship, beneath a patriotic display of half a dozen little European flags surmounted by one imposingly large Old Glory; Photo Collection, HL; Creel, *How We Advertised America*, 200–207.

34. Antonio Gramsci stressed the "educative" role of the state in developing a ruling consensus or *egemonia;* see Gwynne Williams, "Gramsci's Concept of *Egemonia,*" *Journal of the History of Ideas* 21 (October–December 1960), 586–599. Elizabeth Ewen, *Immigrant Women in the Land of Dollars* (New York, 1985), 76–92; McClymer, *War and Welfare*, 29–40. Denying that America was a "melting pot," one Jewish editor wrote: "America is a gathering of peoples in the family of one nation"; *Daily Jewish Courier*, June 5, 1918; Horace Kallen, *Culture and Democracy in the United States* (New York, 1924), is the best exposition of cultural pluralism.

35. Samuel Gompers, *Seventy Years of Life and Labor* (New York, 1984; orig. 1925), 203–206. On the AFL's efforts against the Stockholm plan, see Ronald Radosh, *American Labor and United States Foreign Policy* (New York, 1969); the papers of one of the members, John Frey Papers, LC; Elihu Root to S. Menken, February 16, 1918, Elihu Root Papers, box 136, LC; Weigley, *American Way of War*, 202–203; Robert Leckie, *The Wars of America*, rev. ed. (New York, 1981), 642–655.

36. U.S. Bureau of the Census, *Historical Statistics of the United States from Colonial Times to 1957* (Washington, D.C., 1960; hereafter cited as *Historical Statistics*), 427–429, 356–357, 416. Only in the years 1942–1948 did coal production exceed the First World War level.

37. Millis, *Arms and Men*, 236–238; Weigley, *American Way of War*, 192–200.

38. Kennedy, *Over Here*, 195–196, 98–105; Link, *Wilson and the Progressive Era*, 228.

39. The prophet of a professional army was Emory Upton, *The Military Policy of the United States* (New York, 1968; orig. 1904); Weigley, *American Way of War*, 201. Millis, *Arms and Men*, emphasizes the changes wrought by the managerial revolution, while Stephen Skowronek, *Building a New American State* (Cambridge, Mass., 1982), emphasizes the extent to which things remained the same.

40. Food Administration pamphlets, RG 287, boxes Y772–773; Harold Tobin and Percy Bidwell, *Mobilizing Civilian America* (New York, 1940), 12–13; Lewis P. Todd, *Wartime Relations of the Federal Government and the Public Schools, 1917–1918* (New York, 1945), 14–15; Young Men's Christian Association, *Summary of the World War Work of the American YMCA* (n.p., 1920).

41. *New Republic* quoted in Kennedy, *Over Here*, 40; Robert Cuff, *The War Industries Board: Business Government Relations during World War I* (Baltimore, 1973); Bernard Baruch, *American Industry in the War* (New York, 1941); Grosvenor Clarkson, *Industrial America in the World War* (Boston, 1923).

42. Kennedy, *Over Here*, 130–137; 118–122; Ellis Hawley, *The Great War and the Search for a Modern Order* (New York, 1979), 20–27.

43. Amos Pinchot, "Patriots and Profits," *International Socialist Review* 18 (January 1918), 350–351. In the 1930s the Nye Committee investigated profiteering as part of the campaign to secure neutrality legislation and published forty volumes of hearings as well as seven volumes of reports; U.S. Senate, Special Committee to Investigate the Munitions Industry, *Report*, 7 vols., 74th Cong. 1st sess. (Washington, D.C., 1935–1936).

44. Wilson quoted by Newton Baker, *American Chronicle*, in Nell Painter, *Standing at Armageddon: The United States, 1877–1919* (New York, 1987), 328; Lippmann quoted in Kennedy, *Over Here*, 39.

45. On the effect of the war on prewar social polarization, see Georges Haupt, *Socialism and the Great War: The Collapse of the Second International* (Oxford, 1972); Carl Schorske, *German Social Democracy, 1905–1917* (New York, 1970; orig. 1955); Jurgen Kocka, *Facing Total War: German Society, 1914–1918*, trans. Barbara Weinberg (Cambridge, 1984).

46. Gerald Feldman, *Army, Industry, and Labor in Germany, 1914–1918* (Princeton, 1966), 3–38; Robert Armeson, *Total Warfare and Compulsory Labor* (The Hague, 1964), 57–60; see also Kocka, *Facing Total War*.

47. Charles Tilly, Louise Tilly, and Richard Tilly, *The Rebellious Century, 1830–1930* (Cambridge, Mass., 1975), 245–246, shows that only Italy experienced large-scale internal collective violence during the war; James Hinton, *The First Shop Stewards' Movement* (London, 1973).

48. Montgomery, *Fall of the House of Labor*, 374–375, notes that the AFL Executive Committee repudiated the "no-strike" pledge; Kennedy, *Over Here*, 45–92, emphasizes the public relations aspect of mobilization, as, of course, does Creel, *How We Advertised America*.

49. Wilson quoted in Edward Berman, *Labor Disputes and the President* (New York, 1968; orig. 1924), 118–119; Mark Wiseman, *Keeping the Peace with Labor* (New York, 1920), 11. Felix Frankfurter at the newly created War Labor Policies Board crafted a cohesive set of rules on hours and labor standards; the Frankfurter Papers, LC, are a rich source for the War Labor

Policies Board. Innovations in mediation receive emphasis in numerous accounts of the Wilson years, as in Melvyn Dubovsky, "Abortive Reform," in *Work, Community, and Power: The Experience of Labor in Europe and America,* ed. J. E. Cronin and Carmen Sirianni (Philadelphia, 1983), 207–213; Valerie Jean Conner, *The National War Labor Board* (Chapel Hill, N.C., 1983), 18–34; Montgomery, *Fall of the House of Labor,* 354–356. In addition, the four-year-old Federal Mediation Commission was revved up.

50. Frank Grubbs, *The Struggle for Labor Loyalty: Gompers, the A.F. of L., and the Pacifists, 1917–1920* (Durham, N.C., 1968), details the AALD; Gompers to Robert Maisel, July 31 and September 29, 1917, AFL Records, boxes 25 and 26, respectively, SHSW; boxes 25–27 in this collection are a crucial resource for studying the AALD, including its role in the power struggle within the AFL between Gompers and socialist opponents such as James Maurer, leader of the Pennsylvania State Federation; Samuel Gompers, *American Labor and the War* (New York, 1919), reprints Gompers' tub-thumping prowar addresses before such groups as the National Security League and the American Alliance for Labor and Democracy.

51. David Montgomery, *Workers' Control in America* (Cambridge, 1979), 97, reports the number of workers on strike throughout the country for the following years: 1915: 640,000; 1916: 1,600,000; 1917: 1,227,000; 1918: 1,240,000; 1919: 4,160,000; 1920: 1,463,000; 1921: 1,099,000; 1922: 1,613,000; 1923: 757,000.

52. Montgomery, *Workers' Control,* 91–108, 332; strike data from Florence Petersen, *Strikes in the United States,* U.S. Department of Labor Bulletin, no. 651 (Washington, D.C., 1938), 21; Fred Mooney, *Struggle in the Coal Fields* (Morgantown, W.Va., 1967); U.S. Senate, Hearings, *West Virginia Coal Fields,* 67th Cong., 1st sess. (Washington, D.C., 1923); on the battles in Mingo County, see Adjutant General's Office, RG 94, Project File, W.Va., files 370.6 and 370.61; P. K. Edwards, *Strikes in the United States* (New York, 1981).

53. *Historical Statistics,* 126; similarly, the Douglass cost-of-living index went from 139 in 1914 to 286 in 1920; ibid., 127.

54. Quoted in Dana Frank, "Housewives, Socialists, and the Politics of Food: The 1917 New York Cost of Living Protests," *Feminist Studies* 11 (Summer 1985), 255–286.

55. Montgomery, *Workers' Control,* 97; Stanley Lebergott, *Manpower in Economic Growth* (New York, 1964), 512; minutes of Du Pont plant managers, Parlin and Haskell, New Jersey, Du Pont Corporate Papers, accession 500, box 134, HL; *Historical Statistics,* 91, 127; see also U.S. Bureau of the Census, *Biennial Census of Manufacturers, 1923* (Washington, D.C., 1926), 1150, which shows 12 percent of the labor force working forty-eight hours per week or less in 1914, compared with 49 percent in 1919.

56. The definitive story on federal suppression is Preston, *Aliens and Dissenters;* the president made an example of striking munitions workers by threatening to blacklist them and strip them of deferments unless they acceded to a War Labor Board order. Alexander Bing, *Wartime Strikes and Their Adjustment* (New York, 1921), 79; Interchurch World Movement, *Report on the Steel Strike of 1919* (New York, 1920), 229–231; Steven Meyer, *The Five-Dollar Day* (Albany, 1981), 169–194; Henry Landau, *The Enemy Within* (New York, 1937), 112–113; Joan Jensen, *The Price of Vigilance* (Chicago, 1968), 117–119; Leonard Wood, diary, November 12, 1919, Leonard Wood Papers, LC; Higham, *Strangers in the Land*, 280; Walter Sweeney, *Military Intelligence: A New Weapon in War* (New York, 1924), 95–96.

57. Green, *Grass-Roots Socialism*, 329–344; Edward Levinson, *I Break Strikes!* (New York, 1969; orig. 1935), 200, 207.

58. Federal Revised Statutes, secs. 5297, 5298, 5300; Berman, *Labor Disputes*, 59–62.

59. The main source on troop use is Adjutant General's Office, RG 407, Decimal Files, files 381 and 370.6; most of this material, and much else besides, was collected in the mid-1930s by Justice Department lawyer Abraham Glasser, and the Glasser Files are an incomparable resource, in perennial danger of being closed by the FBI, as they were for fifteen years in the 1960s and 1970s. War Department cables, June and July 1917, box 8, Glasser Files, reveal the "public utilities" doctrine and the emergency directive for direct response to governors' requests; this was modified November 20, 1917, to have requests referred to the adjutant general, but the requirement of a presidential proclamation was not reinstated until June 8, 1922; cf. unfinished manuscript of Glasser Report, box 10, Glasser Files. Preston, *Aliens and Dissenters*, 106 and passim, has made extensive use of these files and is a definitive guide.

60. Capt. James Hornbrook to War Department, July 12 and 16, 1917, Glasser Files, box 7. Glasser Files, box 7, contains copies of Adjutant General's Office, file 370.61, with the relevant material on the copper disturbances, including incoming correspondence of Newton Baker, July 2–5 and 8, 1917; Maicopa Co. Loyalty League to Commander Southern Department, July 20, 1917; Baker to Governor Campbell, July 24, 1917. The frustrations of the President's Mediation Commission in the copper industry are amply detailed in RG 174, entry 8, 3 vols., 1 box, and in Glasser Files, box 8. On the role of U.S. troops, see General Liggett to Adjutant General, July 19, 1917, ibid; Attorney General Gregory to Baker, October 23, 1918, ibid., box 7; Preston, *Aliens and Dissenters*, 113–114. Philip Taft, "The Bisbee Deportation," *Labor History* 13 (Winter 1972), 3–40, lacks mention of military intelligence.

61. Taft, "Bisbee Deportation," 13; W. H. Rogers to Secretary Wilson, June 26, 1917, Glasser Files, box 3, notes Rankin's objection. See also Rankin

to Woodrow Wilson, December 8, 1917, ibid. Assistant Secretary of Labor Louis Post impeded the Justice Department's deportation proceedings; Higham, *Strangers in the Land*, 231–232.

62. H. J. Rosenbaum and P. C. Sederberg, "Vigilantism: An Analysis of Establishment Violence," in *Vigilante Politics*, ed. Rosenbaum and Sederberg (Philadelphia, 1976), 3–29; and, in the same volume, Richard M. Brown, "The History of Vigilantism in America," 79–109.

63. Frank Walsh, Labor Day speech, 1918, Frank P. Walsh Papers, scrapbook 41, New York Public Library.

64. Hywel Davies to Felix Frankfurter, July 20, 1918, Labor Department File 33-1730, Glasser Files, box 3.

65. The theme of war and gender is the subject of Margaret Higonnet, ed., *Behind the Lines: Gender and the Two World Wars* (New Haven, 1987).

66. For a general account of organized women, pro- and antisuffrage, see Barbara Steinson, *American Women's Activism and World War I* (New York, 1982).

67. Cott, *Grounding of Modern Feminism*, 59–61; Eleanor Flexnor, *Century of Struggle: The Woman's Rights Movement in the United States* (New York, 1970; orig. 1959), 82–90.

68. Alicia Kessler-Harris, *Out to Work: A History of Wage-Earning Women in the United States* (New York, 1982), 171; see also Nancy Schrom Dye, *As Equals and as Sisters: Feminism, the Labor Movement, and the Woman's Trade Union League of New York* (Columbia, Mo., 1980); Maureen Greenwald, *Women, War, and Work: The Impact of World War I on Women Workers in the United States* (Westport, Conn., 1980).

69. Eli Zaretsky, "The Place of the Family in the Origins of the Welfare State," in *Rethinking the Family*, ed. Barrie Thorne (New York, 1982), 188–219.

70. On child labor, see Walter Trattner, *Crusade for Children: A History of the National Child Labor Committee and Child Labor Reform in America* (Chicago, 1970); National Child Labor Committee Papers, scrapbooks, boxes 42–44, LC; Allen Davis, "Welfare, Reform, and World War I," *American Quarterly* 19 (1967), 522–524.

71. Conner, *National War Labor Board*, 142–157. In celebrated cases involving women streetcar conductors, the Labor Board decided according to circumstances, first ordering women discharged in Cleveland because of male workers' objections, then reversing itself to order only current women employees reinstated, locking out future women employees. It never accepted the principle of equal employment opportunity. Greenwald, *Women, War, and Work*, 97, 107, 113.

72. [William A. Snow] to Rockefeller, January 7, 1919, copy in American Social Hygiene Association (ASHA) Papers, box 25 folder 9, SWHA.

73. Social Hygiene Division, War Department, "Venereal Diseases," n.d., RG 165, box 246; Allan Brandt, *No Magic Bullet* (New York, 1985), 52–65, 68. The Commission on Training Camp Activities admonished the troops: "A man who is thinking below the belt is not efficient"; ibid., 64.

74. Brandt, *No Magic Bullet*, 75, 72, 77; Joseph Mayer, *The Regulation of Commercialized Vice: An Analysis of the Transition from Segregation to Repression in the United States* (New York, 1922), 9; ASHA, *Legislation Manual* (n.p., 1920), 7.

75. Gompers quoted in Brandt, *No Magic Bullet*, 67; Baker quoted in "Welfare, Reform, and World War I," 531.

76. Ethel Sturges Dummer Papers, box 24, folder 381, SL; "The Venereal Menace," ASHA Papers, box 177; Mayer, *Regulation of Commercial Vice*, 1–9; Ruth Rosen, *The Lost Sisterhood: Prostitution in America* (Baltimore, 1982), 69–111. For primary material on reconstructing gender in wartime, see "Committee on Protective Work for Girls," Ethel Sturges Dummer Papers, box 24, folders 378 and 381; War Department, General and Special Staffs, Commission on Training Camp Activities and Social Hygiene Division, RG 165, entry 399, boxes 232–246; also Kathy Peiss, *Cheap Amusements: Working Women and Leisure in Turn-of-the-Century New York* (Philadelphia, 1986).

77. "Keeping Fit," ASHA Papers, box 178; Davis, "Welfare, Reform, and World War I," 528–530.

78. Brandt, *No Magic Bullet*, 66.

79. The observations on Germany are drawn primarily from the following sources: Kocka, *Facing Total War*; Arno Mayer, *The Persistence of the Old Regime: Europe to the Great War* (New York, 1981); Feldman, *Army, Industry, and Labor*; David Blackbourn and Geoff Eley, *The Peculiarities of German History* (Oxford, 1984).

80. See Arthur Marwick, *War and Social Change in the Twentieth Century* (London, 1974); Renate Bridenthal, Atina Grossman, and Marion Kaplan, eds., *When Biology Became Destiny: Women in Weimar and Nazi Germany* (New York, 1984), 1–5; Ute Frevert, *Women in German History: From Bourgeois Emancipation to Sexual Liberation*, trans. Stuart McKinnon-Evans (Oxford, 1988), 151–167; Feldman, *Army, Industry, and Labor*.

81. Rural Protestant animus toward the city is emphasized in Paul Boyer, *Urban Masses and Moral Order in America, 1820–1920* (Cambridge, Mass., 1978); Andrew Sinclair, *The Era of Excess: A Social History of the Prohibition Movement* (New York, 1964); Richard Hofstadter, *The Age of Reform* (New York, 1955). The gender component is discussed in Barbara Epstein, *The Politics of Domesticity: Women, Evangelism, and Temperance in Nineteenth Century America* (Middletown, Conn., 1981); spiritual ambiguity is emphasized in Joseph Gusfield, *Symbolic Crusade: Status Politics and the American*

Temperance Movement (Urbana, Ill., 1963); progressive social engineers receive attention in James Timberlake, *Prohibition and the Progressive Movement, 1900–1920* (New York, 1970).

82. See Sinclair, *Era of Excess*, 161.

83. See Section on Women and Girls, Commission on Training Camp Activities, "Monthly Text Reports" for 1918, RG 165, box 232; "Committee on Protective Work for Girls," Ethel Sturges Dummer Papers, box 24, folder 381.

84. Steinson, *American Women's Activism*, 299–309.

85. Frederick Howe, *The Confessions of a Reformer*, (New York, 1925), 267; Creel to Wilson, November 8, 1918, George Creel Papers, box 2, LC.

6. Response to Revolution

1. Wilson quoted in C. Gardner, *Safe for Democracy: The Anglo-American Response to Revolution, 1913–1923* (New York, 1984), 1.

2. The revolution occurred in October under the old Julian calendar; when the Bolsheviks replaced it with the Gregorian calendar, the date became November.

3. Arno Mayer, *Wilson v. Lenin* (New York, 1967; orig. 1959), 264–265, 276, 334–339; N. Gordon Levin, *Woodrow Wilson and World Politics: America's Response to War and Revolution* (New York, 1968), 55–56, 82–87.

4. Examples of scholarship associated with these respective interpretations include: (1) state breakdown: Theda Skocpol, *States and Social Revolutions: A Comparative Analysis of France, Russia, and China* (Cambridge, 1979); (2) class antagonism: V. I. Lenin, *The State and Revolution* (Peking, 1973; orig. 1917); and, with a Weberian inflection, Barrington Moore, *Social Origins of Dictatorship and Democracy: Lord and Peasant in the Making of the Modern World* (Boston, 1966); (3) resistance of the oppressed: Eric Wolf, *Peasant Wars of the Twentieth Century* (New York, 1969); Frantz Fanon, *The Wretched of the Earth*, trans. Constance Farrington (New York, 1966; orig. 1963).

5. F. L. Carsten, *Revolution in Central Europe, 1918–1919* (Berkeley, 1972), 323–335; Klaus Schwabe, *Woodrow Wilson, Revolutionary Germany, and Peacemaking* (Chapel Hill, N.C., 1985), 59, 120–121; Kocka, *Facing Total War: German Society, 1914–1918*, trans. Barbara Weinberger (Cambridge, Mass., 1984), 155–161.

6. The vast library on the Bolshevik Revolution includes E. H. Carr, *The Bolshevik Revolution*, 3 vols. (London, 1950–1953); Leon Trotsky, *The Russian Revolution* (New York, 1959; orig. 1932); and, for a less sympathetic treatment, Roger V. Daniels, *Red October: The Bolshevik Revolution of 1917* (New York, 1967).

7. Perry Anderson, "The Antinomies of Antonio Gramsci," *New Left Review*

100 (January 1977), 5–80. Georges Haupt, *Socialism and the Great War: The Collapse of the Second International* (Oxford, 1972), 249, argues: "In this context, the revolutions of 1917–19 would not appear as an incident inserted artificially in the history of the Great War or as a violent catastrophe interrupting long-term developments, but as a process in which the war acted as a delaying or a deviating force and not as a catalyst." See Antonio Gramsci, *Selections from the Prison Notebooks*, ed. Quentin Hoare and G. N. Smith (New York, 1971).

8. Strong support for U.S. intervention in Russia came from Wilson's cabinet, including the archly antiradical Postmaster General Albert Burleson. Relying on reports sent from State Department emissary J. B. Wright, Burleson sent a memo to Wilson on June 17, 1918, urging that a U.S. police force be dispatched to Siberia; copy in A. S. Burleson Papers, vol. 21, LC; the Allies' dual motives for the intervention—to bolster the war against Germany and "to resist the spread of Bolshevistic ideas"—are noted by the commander of the U.S. Siberian forces, William S. Graves, *America's Siberian Adventure: 1918–1920* (New York, 1931), 69; the two motives are discussed by George F. Kennan in *Soviet-American Relations, 1917–1920: The Decision to Intervene*, vol. II (Princeton, 1958), and in *Russia and the West under Lenin and Stalin* (New York, 1960). Peter G. Filene, *Americans and the Soviet Experiment, 1917–1933* (Cambridge, Mass., 1967), 20–21, 41–46; Committee on Public Information, *The German-Bolshevik Conspiracy* (Washington, D.C., 1918), copy in George Creel Papers, box 23; although a panel of distinguished historians confirmed the authenticity of the "Sisson documents," they soon came to be regarded as forgeries; see correspondence between Ambassador Francis and the State Department in U.S. Department of State, *Foreign Relations: 1918, Russia*, vol. I (Washington, D.C., 1931).

9. James Cronin, "Labor Insurgency and Class Formation," in *Work, Community, and Power: The Experience of Labor in Europe and America*, ed. J. E. Cronin and Carmen Sirianni (Philadelphia, 1983), 20–48; Carsten, *Revolution in Central Europe*. For a perspective that plays down the insurgent spirit in Germany, see Stanley Weintraub, *A Stillness Heard round the World: The End of the Great War* (New York, 1918), 378–406.

10. Lansing and Hoover quoted in Schwabe, *Wilson, Revolutionary Germany, and Peacemaking*, 76, 151–152; Wilson quoted in Lloyd C. Gardner, Walter LaFeber, and Thomas McCormick, *Creation of the American Empire* (Chicago, 1973), 343.

11. Scheidemann quoted in Schwabe, *Wilson, Revolutionary Germany, and Peacemaking*, 108; Dick Geary, "Radicalism and the Worker: Metalworkers and the Revolution, 1914–23," in *Society and Politics in Wilhelmine Germany*, ed. R. J. Evans (London, 1978), 267; Mary Nolan, "Workers and Revolu-

tion in Germany, 1918–1919: The Urban Dimension," in Cronin and Sirianni, *Work, Community, and Power*, 117–142.

12. Schwabe, *Wilson, Revolutionary Germany, and Peacemaking*, 99; Kocka, *Facing Total War*, 155–161; Renate Bridenthal, Atina Grossmann, and Marion Kaplan, eds., *When Biology Became Destiny: Women in Weimar and Nazi Germany* (New York, 1984), 6–7, 10.

13. Gerald Feldman, *Army, Industry, and Labor in Germany, 1914–1918* (Princeton, 1966), 523–531; Charles Maier, *Recasting Bourgeois Europe: Stabilization in France, Germany, and Italy in the Decade after World War I* (Princeton, 1975), 77–79, 512.

14. Gardner, LaFeber, and McCormick, *Creation of the American Empire*, 340–347.

15. Ralph Stone, *The Irreconcilables: The Fight against the League of Nations* (Lexington, Ky., 1970), 81–112.

16. Reed quoted in ibid., 81; Thomas Bailey, *Woodrow Wilson and the Great Betrayal* (Chicago, 1963; orig. 1945), 190, 195.

17. Wilson, "The Fourteen Points," address to Congress January 8, 1918, in *Documents of American History*, ed. H. S. Commager, 5th ed. (New York, 1949), 319.

18. George F. Kennan, *American Diplomacy* (New York, 1951), 50–65, forcefully argues this position; in rejoinder, William Appleman Williams, *The Tragedy of American Diplomacy* (New York, 1959), began the intellectual effort to come to terms with a revolutionary world.

19. *New York Times* quoted in E. A. Ross, *The Russian Soviet Republic* (New York, 1923), 269. Christopher Lasch, *The American Liberals and the Russian Revolution* (New York, 1962), xiv–xv, 94–96; Filene, *Americans and the Soviet Experiment*, 29–31, 57–82; Raymond Robins, ms. statement on Russian mission, Raymond Robins Papers, box 14, folder 8, SHSW; Robins to Theodore Roosevelt, August 24, 1918, ibid., folder 5; Robins testimony before U.S. Senate, Hearings, *Bolshevik Propaganda*, 65th Cong., 3d sess. (Washington, D.C., 1919), 763–896, esp. 784–786. Progressives were not always clear-eyed themselves: Lincoln Colcord pressed the idea upon Wilson that by supporting Lenin and Trotsky in order to manipulate them, "the Russian situation could be turned into a triumph of democracy"; Colcord to President Wilson, July 7, 1918; copy in Raymond Robins Papers, box 14, folder 5.

20. Mary Drier, *Margaret Drier Robins: Her Life, Letters, and Work* (New York, 1950), 43; John Dewey, *Reconstruction in Philosophy* (New York, 1920), 203; Herbert Hoover, "Address before the Federated American Engineering Societies," November 19, 1920, p. 12; copy in Herbert Hoover Presidential Library, West Branch, Iowa; courtesy of James Cebula.

21. G. S. Watkins, *Labor Problems and Labor Administration in the United States*

during the World War (Urbana, Ill., 1920); Frank P. Walsh Papers, scrapbooks 82–85, New York Public Library; Valerie Jean Conner, *The National War Labor Board* (Chapel Hill, N.C., 1983), 35–49; Mary Anderson, *Women at Work: The Autobiography of Mary Anderson* (Minneapolis, 1951); Drier, *Margaret Drier Robins*, 142–145; International Congress of Working Women, "Proceedings," typescript in Mary Anderson Papers, SL.

22. For the thesis of nativist "social control," see Alan P. Grimes, *The Puritan Ethic and Woman Suffrage* (New York, 1967), 142–145; Ross Evans Paulson, *Women's Suffrage and Prohibition: A Comparative Study of Equality and Social Control* (Glenview, Ill., 1973); for an emphasis on the women's movement see Eleanor Flexner, *Century of Struggle: The Woman's Rights Movement in the United States* (New York, 1970; orig. 1959), 276–324; Nancy Cott, *The Grounding of Modern Feminism* (New Haven, 1987), 60–62.

23. *Amsterdam News* quoted in Judith Stein, *The World of Marcus Garvey* (Baton Rouge, 1986), 58, 52; *Messenger* quoted in Nathan Huggins, *Harlem Renaissance* (New York, 1971), 53.

24. Alain Locke, ed., *The New Negro* (New York, 1925), 12; this volume was an expanded version of the Harlem issue of the March 1925 *Survey Graphic*, the leading organ of progressive thought in the 1920s; see Alexis de Tocqueville, *Democracy in America* (New York, 1963; orig. 1835); Gunnar Myrdal, *An American Dilemma* (New York, 1944).

25. Elsie Parsons, "Changes in Sex Relations," in *Our Changing Morality*, ed. Freda Kirchwey (New York, 1924), 46: "Birth control makes possible such clear-cut distinctions between mating and parenthood that it might be expected to produce radical changes in theories of sex attitude or relationship, forcing the discard of many an argument for personal suppression for the good of the children or the honor of the family, and forcing redefinition of concepts of honor and sincerity between the sexes." Parsons also argued that "reciprocity takes the place of proprietorship" and "mating and parenthood are seen to be theoretically distinguishable," to which she added, somewhat overconfidently, "The introduction of contraceptives has made acceptance [of the distinction] inevitable;" Parsons, *Social Freedom* (New York, 1915), 31–32; Ben Lindsey and Wainwright Evans, *The Companionate Marriage* (New York, 1927).

26. Mary Dennett, *Birth Control Laws* (New York, 1926), 198–199; idem, *The Sex Side of Life: An Explanation for Young People*, pamphlet reprinted from the 1918 *Medical Review of Reviews*.

27. Every "business" couple in Muncie, Indiana, practiced birth control, according to Robert Lynd and Helen Lynd, *Middletown* (New York, 1929), 123; among college women surveyed, three-quarters practiced birth control and two-thirds masturbated, according to Katherine Bement Davis, *Factors in the Sex Life of Twenty-two Hundred Women* (New York, 1929), 14,

97; similar results were recorded for this age cohort in Alfred Kinsey et al., *Sexual Behavior in the Human Male* (Philadelphia, 1948) and *Sexual Behavior in the Human Female* (Philadelphia, 1953).

28. *Recent Social Trends in the United States,* Report of the President's Commission, 2 vols. (New York, 1933), II, 1444, and I, 694, 692.

29. Suzanne LaFollette, *Concerning Women* (New York, 1972; orig. 1926), 47–48.

30. Quoted in Theodore Draper, *American Communism and Soviet Russia* (New York, 1977), 9.

31. Theodore Draper, *The Roots of American Communism* (New York, 1957), 176–209.

32. Robert L. Friedheim, *The Seattle General Strike* (Seattle, 1964); Samuel Heber, *Efficiency and Uplift: Scientific Management in the Progressive Era, 1890–1920* (Chicago, 1964).

33. McKay quoted in Huggins, *Harlem Renaissance,* 71; Chicago Commission on Race Relations, *The Negro in Chicago* (Chicago, 1922).

34. Agnes Nestor, *Woman's Labor Leader* (Rockford, Ill., 1954), 225.

35. Basil Manly, "The Present Situation and the Outlook," in National Conference of Social Work, *Proceedings: 1919* (Chicago, 1920), 433; David Montgomery, *Workers' Control in America* (Cambridge, 1979), 97; P. K. Edwards, *Strikes in the United States, 1881–1974* (Oxford, 1981), 16; William Leiserson, *Adjusting Immigration and Industry* (New York, 1924).

36. Lewis Mumford, *Technics and Civilization* (New York, 1963; orig. 1934), 156–158; Jurgen Kuczynski, *A Short History of Labour Conditions under Industrial Capitalism* (London, 1947), 132; blue-collar workers are defined as craftsmen, operatives, laborers (40.2 percent) plus farm laborers (11.7 percent) plus household and other service workers (7.8 percent); U.S. Bureau of the Census, *Historical Statistics of the United States from Colonial Times to 1957* (Washington, D.C., 1960), 75–78; Alba Edwards, *Comparative Occupation Statistics for the United States, 1870–1940* (Washington, D.C., 1943), 63–72, 187.

37. Clarence Bonnett, *Employers' Associations in the United States* (New York, 1922), 506–509 and passim; David Montgomery, *The Fall of the House of Labor* (Cambridge, 1987), 438–439.

38. David Parry quoted in Marguerite Green, *The National Civic Federation and the American Labor Movement, 1900–1925* (Westport, Conn., 1973; orig. 1956), 90; Mr. Dooley's sardonic observation was widely quoted, e.g., in Paul Blanshard, *The Open Shop Movement* (New York, n.d.), 4, an Amalgamated Clothing Workers pamphlet opposing open shop; Robert Murray, *Red Scare: A Study in National Hysteria, 1919–1920* (New York, 1955), 268, 92–93; Edwin Witte, *The Government in Labor Disputes* (New York, 1932),

120, 220–231; NAM, *Open Shop Bulletin*, nos. 1–5, November 1920–June 1921.

39. Edward Levinson, *I Break Strikes!* (New York, 1969; orig. 1935).

40. Feldman, *Army, Industry, and Labor*, 519–533; David Abraham, *The Collapse of the Weimar Republic* (Princeton, 1981), chap. 1; Feldman's work on the war and Abraham's on Weimar complement each other so well that it is possible to speak of the "Feldman-Abraham thesis" on German political stability; for Britain, see Keith Middlemas, *Politics in Industrial Society: The Experience of the British System since 1911* (London, 1979).

41. Special Conference Committee, unpublished report on labor conditions, May 16, 1919, app. D, 8–9, Du Pont Corporate Papers, HL; The *Open Shop Bulletin* and other evidence on the open shop drive can be found in National Association of Manufacturers Papers, boxes 243, 250, 251, HL; Clarence J. Hicks, *My Life in Industrial Relations* (New York, 1941), 78; on the Conference Board, see Sanford Jacoby, *Employing Bureaucracy: Managers, Unions, and the Transformation of Work in American Industry, 1900–1945* (New York, 1985). On the limitations imposed by the liberal tradition, see Stephen Skowronek, *Building a New American State: The Expansion of National Administrative Capacities, 1877–1920* (Cambridge, Mass., 1982).

42. On this period see Burle Noggle, *Into the Twenties: The United States from Armistice to Normalcy* (Urbana, Ill., 1974).

43. Josephus Daniels, *Cabinet Diaries*, ed. E. David Cronin (Lincoln, Neb., 1963), 444; Bernard Baruch, "Report of Public Group," Department of Labor, RG 174, folder 13/160, NA; Leonard Wood, diary, January 1–December 31, 1919, Leonard Wood Papers, LC; Secretary of War, *Annual Report: 1920*, vol. I (Washington, D.C., 1921); see also Jack C. Lane, *Armed Progressive: General Leonard Wood* (San Rafael, Calif., 1978).

44. Even after wielding the stick of an injunction in the coal strike, the administration held out the carrot of a coal commission, an account of which can be pieced together from correspondence in the Robert Lansing Papers, LC, including Gompers to Lansing, November 22, 1919; Fuel Administrator H. A. Garfield to Lansing, January 13, 1920; Garfield to Woodrow Wilson, December 5 and 11, 1919; and William Green to Lansing, December 2, 1919. Apparently, Palmer and presidential aide Joseph Tumulty were the prime movers in this fruitless maneuvering. Mediation was failing at the local level, as well. For example, with a textile strike in full swing in Lawrence, Massachusetts, a steering committee of the state's progressive reformers vainly offered their services as mediators, as recorded in Massachusetts Joint Committee, minutes, March 1919, Consumers League of Massachusetts Papers, box 25, folder 416, SL.

45. Baker quoted in *New York Times*, October 16, 1919; Stanley Coben, *A.*

Mitchell Palmer: Politician (New York, 1963), 210–214; William Preston, *Aliens and Dissenters: Federal Suppression of Radicals, 1903–1933* (Cambridge, Mass., 1963), 104–105; Secretary of War, *Annual Report: 1920.* The best documentary source on federal coercion in labor disputes is Glasser Files, Department of Justice, RG 60.

46. Attorney General of the United States, *Annual Report: 1922* (Washington, D.C., 1923), app., 20–21; Robert Zeiger, *Republicans and Labor* (Lexington, Ky., 1969), 109–143; Witte, *Government in Labor Disputes,* 84, 191–192; on the violent suppression of the strike, see the voluminous appendix to the attorney general's 1922 annual report.

47. *New Republic,* July 19, 1919, 310, quoted in Coben, *A. Mitchell Palmer,* 172.

48. Evidence on race riots is drawn primarily from William Tuttle, *Race Riot: Chicago in the Red Summer of 1919* (New York, 1970), 6–7, 21, 32, 43, 65–66, 182. A similar pattern existed in the 1917 riot in East St. Louis; see Elliot Rudwick, *Race Riot at East St. Louis* (Carbondale, Ill., 1964), 16–19, 75, 217–218; the strength of a "rape-lynch complex" underlying southern lynching is shown in Jacquelyn Hall, *Revolt against Chivalry: Jessie Daniel Ames and the Campaign against Lynching* (New York, 1979), 129–150, esp. 149. For the link between sex and southern riots, see the turgid account of the 1906 Atlanta riot in Ray Stannard Baker, *Following the Color Line,* (New York, 1964; orig. 1908), 4–7. For similar evidence on postwar riots in Omaha, Washington, D.C., Longview, Texas, and Ellsville, Miss., see Tuttle, *Race Riot,* 23–30.

49. On the isolation of black workers, see Sterling Spero and Abram Harris, *The Black Worker: The Negro and the Labor Movement* (New York, 1969; orig. 1931), 250–263.

50. On law and suffrage, see Flexner, *Century of Struggle;* on women in the public square, see Paula Baker, "The Domestication of Politics: Women and American Political Society, 1780–1920," *American Historical Review* 89 (June 1984), 620–647.

51. Linda Gordon, *Woman's Body, Woman's Right: A Social History of Birth Control in America* (New York, 1976); Mark Haller, *Eugenics: Hereditarian Attitudes in American Thought* (New Brunswick, N.J., 1963); Allan Chase, *The Legacy of Malthus: The Social Costs of the New Scientific Racism* (New York, 1977), 432–447; Andrew Sinclair, *The Era of Excess: A Social History of the Prohibition Movement* (New York, 1964).

52. Kennan, *Russia and the West,* minimizes the extent of anticommunism; Lansing is evidence to the contrary, quoted in Coben, *A. Mitchell Palmer,* 210; see also Graves, *America's Siberian Adventure.*

53. Friedheim, *Seattle General Strike,* 1–12; William Preston, *Aliens and Dissent-*

ers: *Federal Suppression of Radicals, 1903–1933* (Cambridge, Mass., 1963), 165–166; Interchurch World Movement, *Report on the Steel Strike of 1919* (New York, 1920), 20–43.

54. Wilson quoted in Coben, A. *Mitchell Palmer*, 204, 211; Higham, *Strangers in the Land*, 222–233; for suggestive anthropological ideas, see Mary Douglass, *Purity and Danger: An Analysis of Concepts of Pollution and Taboo* (London, 1966).

55. Stevenson testimony in U.S. Senate, *Bolshevik Propaganda*, 13; New York Legislature, *Revolutionary Radicalism*, 4 vols. (Albany, 1920), also known as the Lusk Committee; several former YMCA agents in Russia testified against the Bolsheviks, including R. B. Dennis *(Bolshevik Propaganda*, 163–193), R. F. Leonard (194–228), and R. M. Storey (229–234).

56. Bryant testimony in U.S. Senate, *Bolshevik Propaganda*, 532, 540–547. According to Beatrice Farnsworth, *Aleksandra Kollontai: Socialism, Feminism, and the Bolshevik Revolution* (Stanford, 1980), 127–172, Kollontai envisioned a nuclear family with prime child-rearing responsibility combined with the socialization of housework in communal kitchens and laundries, a position close to the ideas of Charlotte Perkins Gilman despite the overlay of Marxist ideas; Filene, *Americans and the Soviet Experience*, 46, cites accounts from October 1918 in the *New York Times;* upon hearing of women doing manual labor, Senator Overman gasped, "They have no respect for the educated lady of property?" U.S. Senate, *Bolshevik Propaganda*, 233.

57. The quote is from the masthead of the *Woman Patriot; Organizing Revolution through Women and Children*, pamphlet reprinted from *Woman Patriot*, September 15, 1922, Mary Anderson Papers, box 4, folder 83; see also Samuel Saloman, *The Red War on the Family* (New York, 1922).

58. On patriarchal values, see Virginia Yans-McLaughlin, *Family and Community: Italian Immigrants in Buffalo, 1880–1930* (Urbana, Ill., 1982; orig. 1977); on ethnic polarization, Carl Ross, *The Finn Factor* (New York, 1977); on ethnic radicalism, Paul Buhle, *Marxism in the U.S.A.* (London, 1988).

59. For Gomper's view of bolshevism, see *New York World*, June 26, 1924; Murray, *Red Scare*, 93; the whole subject of the impact of anticommunism on the working class begs for investigation.

60. Baker quoted in *New York Times*, October 16, 1919.

61. Preston, *Aliens and Dissenters*, 223; Murray, *Red Scare*, 190–222; the cartoon is in *The Liberator* 3 (February 1920), 4; Draper, *Roots of American Communism*, 204–209.

62. Murray, *Red Scare*, 242; Coben, A. *Mitchell Palmer*, 235.

63. For documentation on army contingency plans for waging counterrevolution at home see RG 165, Military Intelligence Division, War Plans White, 212-E, box 242-13, 6th Corps Area, app. 2.

64. Ibid., 3rd Corps Area; on state police, Katherine Mayo, *Justice to All: The Story of the Pennsylvania State Police* (Boston, 1917), 57; see also Lane, *Armed Progressive.*

65. Entries in Leonard Wood's diary in the spring and summer of 1920 show he believed his command of troops to suppress the steel strike and other civil disorders would help propel him to the nomination; Lane, *Armed Progressive,* 230–239.

66. John Hicks, *Republican Ascendancy, 1921–1933* (New York, 1960), 24, 25.

67. Lincoln Steffens, *The Autobiography of Lincoln Steffens* (New York, 1931), 799; Ross, *Russian Soviet Republic;* Weyl quoted in Lasch, *American Liberals and Russian Revolution,* 132–133; Lasch takes a sour view of liberal sympathizers with the Bolshevik revolution.

7. Restoration by Repression

1. On the connection between economic opportunity and the rise of slavery, see Edmund Morgan, *American Slavery/American Freedom: The Ordeal of Colonial Virginia* (New York, 1975); on the logical connection between the Enlightenment idea of formal equality and the idea of race, Louis Dumont, *Homo Hierarchicus: An Essay on the Caste System,* trans. M. Sainsbury (Chicago, 1970; orig. 1966); on the paradox of racism within the "American creed," Gunnar Myrdal, *An American Dilemma* (New York, 1944).

2. Warren S. Thompson and P. K. Whelpton, *Population Trends in the United States* (New York, 1933), table 27, p. 91; these authors use 94,821,000 for the white population in 1920; subsequent revisions increased that number to 95,511,000, as reported in U.S. Bureau of the Census, *Historical Statistics of the United States from Colonial Times to 1957* (Washington, D.C., 1960; hereafter cited as *Historical Statistics);* the percentages of the various ethnic groupings are derived from Thompson and Whelpton's percentage estimates for the white population calculated upon the total population (white and nonwhite) of 106,466,000.

3. *Historical Statistics,* 56, 64, reports 123,522 emigrants and 141,132 immigrants.

4. William Miller, ed., *Men in Business: Essays on the Historical Role of the Entrepreneur* (New York, 1962; orig. 1952), 333, calculates that 79 percent of a group of 190 top businessmen in the first decade of the twentieth century traced their ancestry to England, Wales, Scotland, Northern Ireland, Canada, or the British Empire; these groups may have made up 47 percent of the white population in 1920 according to Thompson and Whelpton, *Population Trends,* table 27, p. 91; although all calculations of ethnic "stock" are fraught with ideological biases and numerical murkiness, applying

rough estimates to the total population of 106,466,000 in 1920 yields the result reported.

5. William Leiserson, *Adjusting Immigration and Industry* (New York, 1924), 7–14; author's tabulations with the assistance of Sean Thorne from U.S. Bureau of the Census, *Fourteenth Census: 1920* (Washington, D.C., 1921–1923), vol. IV, *Population*, 941–945, 982–983, 1004–05. First- and second-generation immigrants had always made up the bulk of industrial labor, as proved in Herman Gutman and Ira Berlin, "Class Composition and the Development of the American Working Class, 1840–1890," in *Power and Culture*, ed. Ira Berlin (New York, 1987), 380–394.

6. Maldwyn Allen Jones, *American Immigration* (Chicago, 1960), 262; John Higham, *Strangers in the Land* (New York, 1963), 250–254, 258–259; Frances Kellor took up the work of the Inter-Racial Council. The Carnegie Endowment spoke for the new generation of corporate managers in proffering a social-scientific approach to Americanization through improvements in immigrant housing, health, home economics, and criminal justice; it even touted AFL-style trade unionism as a positive engine of Americanization, and funded David Saposs, who conducted scores of probing interviews with trade union leaders whose militancy was toned down for publication in Leiserson, *Adjusting Immigration and Industry*. The Carnegie studies were characterized by a dual concern for the hardships of the immigrants and their rapid Americanization, as in Kate Claghorn, *The Immigrant's Day in Court* (New York, 1969; orig. 1923).

7. Robins quoted in Elizabeth Payne, *Reform, Labor, and Feminism: Margaret Drier Robins and the Women's Trade Union League* (Urbana, Ill., 1988), 167.

8. Nancy Cott, *The Grounding of Modern Feminism* (New Haven, 1987), 125.

9. Dewey quoted by Kallen, *Culture and Democracy*, excerpted in Stanley Coben, ed., *Reform, War, and Reaction: 1912–1932* (New York, 1972), 191–192, 188–206; *Daily Jewish Courier*, June 5, 1918, reel 33, Chicago Foreign Language Press Survey.

10. Basil Manly, "The Present Situation," in National Conference of Social Work, *Proceedings: 1919* (Chicago, 1920), 433; evidence on the use of foreign-language organizers is in interviews with trade union leaders, 1918–1920, David Saposs Papers, SHSW.

11. New York Legislature, *Revolutionary Radicalism* (Albany, 1920); John McClymer, *War and Welfare: Social Engineering in America, 1890–1925* (Westport, Conn., 1980), 40; Higham, *Strangers in the Land,* 255, 260–262; see also John McClymer, "The Federal Government and the Americanization Movement," *Prologue,* Spring 1978, 23–41; Gerd Korman, *Industrialization, Immigrants, and Americanization: The View from Milwaukee* (Madison, Wis., 1967).

12. Higham, *Strangers in the Land*, 265; this book remains the best guide to the history of nativism.

13. Madison Grant, *The Passing of the Great Race* (New York, 1916), 6, 1–8; see also Kenneth Roberts, *Why Europe Leaves Home* (n.p., 1922), 50.

14. Charles Gould, *America: A Family Matter* (New York, 1922), 26; Sinclair Lewis, *Babbitt* (New York, 1922).

15. Kenneth Jackson, *The Ku Klux Klan in the City, 1915–1930* (New York, 1967).

16. Hiram Evans, "The Klan's Fight for Americanism," *North American Review* 223 (March 1926), 33–63, excerpted in Coben, *Reform, War, and Reaction*, 217–232.

17. Grant quoted in Evans, "The Klan's Fight for Americanism," 223.

18. Charles Lydecker, National Security League, press release, October 6, 1919, Elihu Root Papers, box 137, LC.

19. Gordon Hostetter and Thomas Beesley, *It's a Racket!* (1929), 170, quoted in Dwight Smith, *The Mafia Mystique* (New York, 1975), 68; Robert K. Merton quoted in Giovanni Schiavo, *The Truth about the Mafia* (New York, 1962), 191–192; see also Daniel Bell, "Crime as an American Way of Life," in *The End of Ideology: On the Exhaustion of Political Ideas in the Fifties* (New York, 1960), 127–150.

20. John Kobler, *Capone* (New York, 1971), 36–37.

21. Kallen quoted in Coben, *Reform, War, and Reaction*, 198.

22. RG 165, Military Intelligence Division, War Plans White, 212-E, box 242-13, 3rd Corps Area.

23. Lothrop Stoddard, *Revolt against Civilization: The Menace of the Under Man*, quoted in Warren I. Susman, *Culture as History: The Transformation of American Society in the Twentieth Century* (New York, 1984), 117; Gould, *America*, 29.

24. Mark Haller, *Eugenics: Hereditarian Attitudes in American Thought* (New Brunswick, N.J., 1963); Allen Chase, *The Legacy of Malthus: The Social Costs of the New Scientific Racism* (New York, 1977), 295–308.

25. W. R. Bowie, "Is Prohibition a National Benefit?" *Good Housekeeping*, October 1928.

26. Holmes quoted in Chase, *Legacy of Malthus*, 315; Haller, *Eugenics*, 133–137; Paul Popenoe and R H. Johnson, *Applied Eugenics* (New York, 1923; orig. 1918), 180–182; Michael Grossberg, *Governing the Hearth: Law and the Family in Nineteenth-Century America* (Chapel Hill, N.C., 1985), 149–151.

27. Laughlin's testimony quoted in Chase, *Legacy of Malthus*, 293.

28. John Roach Straton, letter to the prosecution, quoted in Mary Dennett, *Who's Obscene?* (New York, 1930), 102–107, also 123–124.

29. Paul Boyer, *Purity in Print: The Vice-Society Movement and Book Censorship in America* (New York, 1968); Dennett, *Who's Obscene?* 123–124.

30. Osborn quoted in Chase, *Legacy of Malthus*, 278.

31. Cornelia James Cannon, "American Misgivings," *Atlantic Monthly*, February 1922, 154; Michael F. Guyer, "Eugenics," in *Our Present Knowledge of Heredity* (Philadelphia, 1925), 242; copies of both supplied to author by Allan Chase.

32. Karl Marx, *The Eighteenth Brumaire of Louis Bonaparte* (New York, 1964; orig. 1852), 15; Susman, *Culture as History*, 115–119.

33. W. E. B. DuBois, *Souls of Black Folk: Essays and Sketches* (Chicago, 1903), vii; Lothrop Stoddard, *The Rising Tide of Color against White World Supremacy* (New York, 1920); Gould, *America*, 28–29.

34. The psychic tangle of race as an implicit barrier to modernization is explored in Joel Williamson, *The Crucible of Race: Black-White Relations in the American South since Emancipation* (New York, 1984).

35. Jackson, *The Klan in the City*, 27, 31, 82. Though close in spirit to small property, the Klan included plenty of wage earners, in some cases industrial workers, as in the railroad town of Knoxville, Tennessee, where about two-thirds of the members were from blue-collar occupations, especially railwaymen; ibid., 62–63, 240–242.

36. George Tindall, *The Emergence of the New South, 1913–1945* (n.p., 1967), 333–334, 339.

37. Norman Furniss, *The Fundamentalist Controversy* (Hamden, Conn., 1963), 11–13.

38. Ibid., quoting a Mississippi legislator, 34, and quoting J. E. Conant, *The Church, the Schools, and Evolution* (1922), 22.

39. In Arkansas, when science-minded officials balked, a popular referendum pushed it through; Furniss, *Fundamentalist Controversy*, 78–95.

40. Ibid., 44, 85; and Ray Ginger, *Six Days or Forever* (Boston, 1958), 33.

41. Leon Litwick, *North of Slavery: The Negro in the Free States, 1790–1860* (Chicago, 1961), 64–112; Stanley Lieberson, *A Piece of the Pie: Blacks and White Immigrants since 1880* (Berkeley, 1980), 313–322, tables 10.7–10.9.

42. In 1930 11 percent of Chicago black families owned homes, versus 42 percent of the foreign born; U.S. Bureau of the Census, *Fifteenth Census: 1930* Washington, D.C., 1931–1933), *Families*, 357 and passim. John Bodnar, Roger Simon, and Michael Weber, *Lives of Their Own: Blacks, Italians, and Poles in Pittsburgh, 1900–1960* (Urbana, Ill., 1982), 179, contend that the census overestimated the gap, but confirm a sizable differential between Pittsburgh blacks, on the one hand, and Poles and Italians, on the other.

43. Sociology has provided the bulk of the argument for the "last of the immigrants" thesis, as in Nathan Glazer and Daniel Patrick Moynihan, *Beyond the Melting Pot* (Cambridge, Mass., 1963), 16–20; for a powerful rebuttal see Stephan Steinberg, *The Ethnic Myth: Race, Ethnicity, and Class in America* (New York, 1891); Lieberson, *Piece of the Pie*; Stephan Thern-

strom, *The Other Bostonians: Poverty and Progress in the American Metropolis* (Cambridge, Mass., 1973), 194. Among the numerous works on the ghetto are Allan Spear, *Black Chicago* (Chicago, 1967), and Kenneth Kusmer, *A Ghetto Takes Shape: Black Cleveland, 1870–1930* (Urbana, Ill., 1976).

44. Kusmer, *A Ghetto Takes Shape*, 230–233; see also Amy Jacques-Garvey, ed., *Philosophy and Opinions of Marcus Garvey*, 2 vols. (New York, 1969; orig. 1923).

45. Kusmer, *A Ghetto Takes Shape*, 231.

46. Judith Stein, *The World of Marcus Garvey: Race and Class in Modern Society* (Baton Rouge, 1986), 61–88, 162, 157–158.

47. Ibid., 196–201, 207–108.

48. Gino Speranza, "The Immigration Peril," *World's Work*, April 1924, 646; supposed proof of foreign meddling came before Congress when several European governments protested the discriminatory aspects of American immigration policy; see the congressional objections against Italian and Romanian protests in U.S. Department of State, *Foreign Relations of the United States*, 1922, II, 579; ibid., 1924, I, 224–226; U.S. House of Representatives, Committee on Immigration, Hearings, *Restriction of Immigration*, H.R. 350 (Washington, D.C., 1924), 603.

49. Alan P. Grimes, *The Puritan and Woman Suffrage* (New York, 1967), 141.

50. The lobbies were analyzed by J. J. Spengler in 1958, quoted by Marion T. Bennett, *American Immigration Policies: A History* (Washington, D.C., 1963), 53; Special Conference Committee (SCC), *Report* (n.p., 1922), 3, copy in HL; see also the comments of Cyrus Ching, head of U.S. Rubber, who spoke for the executives of several major corporations in arguing for "carefully selected Europeans who fit the American social structure" in preference to "undesirable" Latin American and Negro migration; SCC minutes, November 7, 1923, National Industrial Conference Board (NICB) Papers, HL. In 1925 the SCC mentioned no shortage of labor in its minutes and annual report.

51. Gompers' views reported in *New York World*, June 26, 1924; Bennett, *American Immigration Policies*, 53.

52. *Congressional Record*, 66th Cong., 1st sess., May 1919–November 1919, 4564.

53. For background on nativism and racism in the working class, see Alexander Saxton, *The Indispensable Enemy: Labor and the Anti-Chinese Movement in California* (Berkeley, 1971); Gwendolyn Mink, *Old Labor and New Immigrants in American Political Development* (Ithaca, 1986).

54. Edwin Witte, *The Government in Labor Disputes* (New York, 1932); Robert Zeiger, *Republicans and Labor, 1919–1929* (Lexington, Ky., 1969).

55. Jones, *American Immigration*, 262.

56. William S. Bernard, *American Immigration Policy: A Reappraisal* (Port

Washington, N.Y., 1969; orig. 1950), 48–49; Yugoslav petitions, March 1924, Senate Committee on Immigration, Committee Files 68A–J27, National Archives.

57. State Department report, U.S. Senate, Committee on Immigration, Hearings, *Emergency Immigration Legislation* (Washington, D.C., 1921), 11–12.

58. *Congressional Record*, 68th Cong., 1st sess., December 1923–June 1925, 4742, 5673; Coolidge message to Congress, December 6, 1923, U.S. Department of State, *Foreign Relations*, 1923, I, xviii; Higham, *Strangers in the Land*, 316–324.

59. Walter Trattner, *Crusade for the Children: A History of the National Child Labor Committee and Child Labor Reform in America* (Chicago 1970), 119–144, 163–188; John A. Ryan, *The Proposed Child Labor Amendment* (n.p., [1924]), 10–13; Children's Bureau, "Child Labor," in *Annual Report* (Washington, D.C., 1922). Key documents on the battle over child labor can be found in the National Child Labor Committee Papers, esp. boxes 8 and 42; National Consumers League Papers, esp. reels 82 and 83; National League of Women Voters Papers, esp. series I, boxes 3 and 7, series II, box 85; all in LC. *Bailey v. Drexel* held that the Tenth ("states' rights") Amendment prohibited a federal tax on the products of child labor in interstate commerce.

60. Trattner, *Crusade for the Children*, 170–179, 184; National Association of Manufacturers (NAM), *13 Leading Questions*, pamphlet (n.p., 1926), copy in HL; Alonzo B. See to Jane Addams, July 10, 1924, National Consumers League Papers, reel 83; statement in opposition to Child Labor Amendment, Alexander Lincoln Papers, folder 15, SL.

61. Dorothy K. Brown Papers, scrapbook, box 3, folder 69, and box 2, SL; Alexander Lincoln Papers, boxes 1–3, folders 14–18; National Consumers League Papers, reel 48.

62. NAM, *Protective Legislation for Women*, pamphlet (n.p., 1927); undated press release, NAM Papers, box 251, HL; Adkins v. Children's Hospital 261 U.S. 525 (1923).

63. NICB, *Unemployment Insurance in Theory and Practice* (New York, 1922), 127 and passim; SCC, statement on unemployment insurance, March 11, 1921, accession 473, folder 279, HL; see also SCC, *Annual Report*, 1923 and 1931. The NICB also agitated against compulsory health insurance on the grounds that sickness was best left to the family, supplemented by private group insurance; see the NICB pamphlets *Is Compulsory Health Insurance Desirable?* (New York, 1919), *Health Service in Industry* (New York, 1921), *Industrial Group Insurance* (New York, 1927), *Health and Accident Group Insurance* (New York, 1927).

64. NAM, *Public Old Age Pensions* (New York, 1930), 67; NICB, *Industrial Pensions in the U.S.* (New York, 1925), ix, 4–5.

65. Herbert Hoover, *American Individualism* (Garden City, N.Y., 1922), 62.

66. Charles Maier, *Recasting Bourgeois Europe: Stabilization in France, Germany, and Italy in the Decade after World War I* (Princeton, 1975), 3–15; Gerald Feldman, *Army, Industry, and Labor in Germany, 1914–1918* (Princeton, 1966); Barbel Schrader and Jurgen Schebera, *The "Golden Twenties": Art and Literature in the Weimar Republic* (New Haven, 1988).

67. Geoff Eley, "The German Right, 1880–1945: How It Changed," in *From Unification to Nazism: Reinterpreting the German Past* (Boston, 1986), 231–253; Arno Mayer, *Dynamics of Counterrevolution in Europe, 1870–1956* (New York, 1971).

68. Ambassador Alanson Houghton quoted in Frank Costigliola, *Awkward Dominion: American Political, Economic, and Cultural Relations with Europe, 1919–1933* (Ithaca, 1984), 115.

69. Warren I. Cohen, *Empire without Tears: American Foreign Relations, 1921–1933* (New York, 1987), 46–54.

70. John Hicks, *Republican Ascendancy, 1921–1933* (New York, 1960), 90–105. As progressivism disintegrated on the shoals of social conflict, its various elements scattered to other points along the political spectrum. Anglo-Saxon moralists such as Hiram Johnson who supported Prohibition and immigration restriction commonly wound up as conservative critics of the New Deal. But the main progressive legacy was on the left. A small group of onetime state managers such as Felix Frankfurter and Donald Richberg played important roles in the New Deal. Likewise, a hardy band of progressive lobbyists in such groups as the National Consumers League and labor progressives around unions such as the Amalgamated Clothing Workers also carried the torch in the Progressive party campaign of 1924 and on through the Great Depression to experience rebirth in the New Deal. It is this last contingent that defined the term *progressive* as left of center and bequeathed this legacy to New Dealers, Henry Wallace's Progressive party, and later generations of social reformers.

71. The clash is captured best in the scintillating retrospective by Frederick Lewis Allen, *Only Yesterday: An Informal History of the 1920s* (New York, 1931); and in the vibrant narrative by William Leuchtenburg, *The Perils of Prosperity, 1914–1932* (Chicago, 1958).

72. William Young and David Kaiser, *Postmortem: New Evidence in the Case of Sacco and Vanzetti* (Amherst, Mass., 1985), 14–26; Luigi Galleani, leader of the group, had actually been held for deportation as early as May 1918, before the Red Scare, and was deported in 1919 around the time postal bombs were sent to Palmer and other prominent figures.

73. Felix Frankfurter, *The Case of Sacco and Vanzetti* (New York, 1962; orig. 1927), 64; John Dos Passos, *Facing the Chair: The Story of the Americanization of Two Foreign Born Workmen* (Boston, 1927). Contemporary opinion remains divided over the guilt of the accused; Francis Russell, *Tragedy in*

Dedham: The Story of the Sacco-Vanzetti Case (New York, 1971), argues that ballistics tests showed that Sacco's revolver was used in the murder, but an exhaustive examination of the evidence leads Young and Kaiser, *Postmortem*, 164, 9, to conclude that there is an "overwhelming probability" that the bullet was substituted by police and Sacco and Vanzetti were "two innocent men, most probably framed for a murder they did not commit."

74. Upton Sinclair, *Boston*, vol. II (New York, 1928), 749–752; Roberta Feuerlicht, *Justice Crucified: The Story of Sacco and Vanzetti* (New York, 1977), 412–413.

75. House Committee on Immigration, *Restriction of Immigration*, 16.

76. Bernard, *America's Immigration Policy*, 26, 48–53.

77. Higham, *Strangers in the Land*, 264–299.

78. Ginger, *Six Days or Forever*, 181, 183, 171.

8. The New Era of Corporate Capitalism

1. "Organizational" historians have led the effort to come to terms with large-scale bureaucracy; key works include Robert Wiebe, *The Search for Order, 1877–1920* (New York, 1967), and Ellis Hawley, *The Great War and the Search for a Modern Order* (New York, 1979). The Weberian foundation of the organizational school is revealed by Louis Galambos, *The Public Image of Big Business in America, 1880–1940* (Baltimore, 1975), 15–21, 246–249; here, as for Weber, the final adversary is Marx and class analysis in general.

2. Adolf Berle and Gardner Means, *The Modern Corporation and Private Property* (New York, 1932), 353, 9; Charles Beard and Mary Beard, *The Rise of American Civilization*, 2 vols. (New York, 1927), 197, compare the corporations to the great Roman seigneurs.

3. Berle and Means, *Modern Corporation*, 32, 21–23.

4. Ibid., 59–60, 74; see also Alfred Chandler, *The Visible Hand: The Managerial Revolution in American Business* (Cambridge, Mass., 1977).

5. Louis Galambos, *Competition and Cooperation: The Emergence of a National Trade Association* (Baltimore, 1966); Ellis Hawley, "Herbert Hoover," in *Herbert Hoover and the Crisis of American Capitalism*, ed. J. J. Huthmacher and W. I. Susman (Cambridge, Mass., 1973), 1–27. For contemporary accounts, see P. G. Agnew, "Step toward Industrial Self-Government," *New Republic*, March 17, 1920; E. Clark, "Industry Is Setting Up Its Own Government," *New York Times*, March 21, 1926; National Industrial Conference Board (NICB), *Industrial Self-Government*, pamphlet (n.p., n.d.), copy in HL.

6. Walter Lippmann, *A Preface to Morals* (New York, 1929), 255, 256.

7. Special Conference Committee (SCC), "Methods of Wage Payment" (1927), typescripts of reports on ten large industrial corporations, acces-

sion 1699, box 241, HL; Sanford Jacoby, "The Origins of Internal Labor Markets in American Manufacturing Firms, 1910–1940" (Ph.D. diss., University of California, Berkeley, 1981), 469.

8. SCC, "Methods of Wage Payment," report on AT&T, p. 7; on raising productivity without raising wages, see esp. the SCC report on Bethlehem Steel, ibid. Evidence on workers' resistance was gathered by Stanley Mathewson, *Restriction of Output among Unorganized Workers* (New York, 1931).

9. Robert S. McElvaine, *The Great Depression: America, 1929–2941* (New York, 1984), 39.

10. E. A. Filene and T. N. Carver, *The Present Economic Revolution in the United States* (1924), quoted in Lewis Corey, *The Decline of American Capitalism* (New York, 1934), 19.

11. Irving Bernstein, *The Lean Years: A History of the American Worker, 1920–1933* (Boston, 1960), 187, views "avoidance of trade unions" as the prime purpose of welfare capitalism; the same view pervades the most comprehensive study of the subject, Stuart Brandes, *American Welfare Capitalism* (Chicago, 1976); the view is contested by David Brody, *Workers in Industrial America: Essays on the Twentieth-Century Struggle* (New York, 1980), 48–81, who argues that welfare capitalism sprang from the needs of the modern economy and gained a degree of real support among workers.

12. NICB, *Health Service in Industry* (New York, 1921), 3; other pertinent NICB publications include *Industrial Relations: Administration of Policies and Programs* (New York, 1931); *Industrial Relations Programs in Small Plants* (New York, 1929).

13. Evidence of ties of dependency in industrial districts pervades the interviews with Polish, Russian, Croatian, and other immigrant workers in John Bodnar, *Worker's World: Kinship, Community, and Protest in an Industrial Society, 1900–1940* (Baltimore, 1982), 77–79 and passim.

14. Frey quoted in Brody, *Workers in Industrial America*, 78; on the subject of reciprocity between the weak and the strong, see James Scott, *The Moral Economy of the Peasant* (New Haven, 1976).

15. Marc Karson, *American Labor Unions and Politics, 1900–1918* (Carbondale, Ill., 1958); on the influence of Catholic corporatism, see Ronald Schatz, *The Electrical Workers: A History of Labor at General Electric and Westinghouse, 1923–1960* (Urbana, Ill., 1983); with a few exceptions, parish priests opposed the 1919 steel strike, according to oral testimony in the Carnegie Americanization Study, David Saposs Papers, SHSW; most priests appear to have been enmeshed with the nonunion status quo, to judge from interviews in Bodnar, *Worker's World;* on the reform tradition, see David M. Byers, ed., *Justice in the Marketplace: Collected Statements of the Vatican and the U.S. Catholic Bishops on Economic Policy, 1891–1984* (Washington,

D.C., 1985); the same tradition is expanded in the bishops' pastoral letter *Economic Justice for All* (Washington, D.C., 1986).

16. NICB, *Health Service in Industry*, 3; NICB, *Economic Status of the Wage Earner in New York and Other States* (New York, 1928), 62–75, reports only 14 percent of employees covered under health and accident plans; see also NICB, *Health and Accident Group Insurance* (New York, 1927) and *Industrial Group Insurance* (New York, 1927).

17. Berle and Means, *Modern Corporation*, 59, estimate that 800,000 employees owned stock in their companies; given that the total number of stockholders in 1929 probably did not exceed 7 million, according to Berle and Means, 60, the estimate of Brandes, *American Welfare Capitalism*, 84, that 6.5 million wage earners held stock is certainly too high; a tiny fraction of workers—perhaps 2 percent in 1929—received private pensions when they retired, and scarcely any more enjoyed paid vacations; Brody, *Workers in Industrial America*, 60, cites an NICB study to the effect that one in five companies had pension plans; but for more conservative estimates, see Brandes, 141–142; Sanford Jacoby, "Origins of Internal Labor Markets," 477, 478; idem, *Employing Bureaucracy: Managers, Unions, and the Transformation of Work in American Industry, 1900–1945* (New York, 1985), 196–199.

18. SCC, statement of March 11, 1921, and minutes, February 4, 1926, accession 473, file 279, HL.

19. Frederick Lewis Allen, *Only Yesterday: An Informal History of the 1920s* (New York, 1931), 3–8, begins with just such a portrait.

20. Helen Lynd and Robert Lynd, *Middletown: A Study in Modern American Culture* (New York, 1929).

21. *Recent Social Trends in the United States*, Report of the President's Commission, 2 vols. (New York, 1933), I, 668; ladies' magazines such as *Good Housekeeping* were the prime outlet for such advertising.

22. Edward A. Filene, *Successful Living in the Machine Age* (New York, 1932), 98; Allen, *Only Yesterday*, 175–181; Roland Marchand, *Advertising the American Dream: Making Way for Modernity, 1920–1940* (Berkeley, 1985), 206, 217–222, 8.

23. Allen, *Only Yesterday*, 161–164; Warren I. Susman, *Culture as History: The Transformation of American Society in the Twentieth Century* (New York, 1984), 131–141; Marchand, *Advertising the American Dream*, 7.

24. Hoover address to White House Conference on Home Building, December 2, 1931, Herbert Hoover Papers, Herbert Hoover Presidential Library, West Branch, Iowa; Kenneth T. Jackson, *Crabgrass Frontier* (New York, 1985), 184–187; report of J. M. Gries in "Better Homes," James S. Taylor Papers, Hoover Library; Lewis Mumford indicted suburbia for its lack of integrated home and community planning: "In the suburb one might live and die without marring the image of an innocent world. Thus

the suburb served as an asylum for the preservation of an illusion. Here domesticity could flourish, forgetful of the exploitation on which so much of it was based. Here individuality could prosper, oblivious of the pervasive regimentation beyond"; Mumford, *The City in History* (New York, 1961), 494; see also Mumford, "The Chance for Civilized Housing," *New Republic*, September 17, 1930, 115–117.

25. Among the few studies of advertising that make this connection between consumer culture and corporate power is Stuart Ewen, *Captains of Consciousness: Advertising and the Social Roots of the Consumer Culture* (New York, 1976); among the many that do not is Marchand, *Advertising the American Dream*.

26. National Bureau of Economic Research, *Income in the United States: Its Amount and Distribution, 1909–1919*, ed. W. C. Mitchell (New York, 1921), 143–145; Brookings Institution, *America's Capacity to Consume* (1932), cited in McElvaine, *The Great Depression*, 38–39. If Americans were troubled about the high degree of inequality, Mitchell's international comparisons reassured them that U.S. per capita income was some 50 percent more than Britain's and more than twice that of Germany. Beginning with Mitchell, the National Bureau of Economic Research pioneered research on income distribution that culminated in Simon Kuznets, *Shares of Upper Income Groups in Income and Savings* (New York, 1953).

27. William H. Chafe, *The American Woman: Her Changing Social, Economic, and Political Roles, 1920–1970* (London, 1972), 103; Christine Frederick, *Household Engineering* (Chicago, 1920). On housework, see Susan Strasser, *Never Done: A History of American Housework* (New York, 1982); Ruth Schwartz Cowan, *More Work for Mother* (New York, 1983); Joann Vanek, "Time Spent in Housework," in *A Heritage of Her Own: Toward a New Social History of American Women*, ed. Nancy Cott and Elizabeth Pleck (New York, 1979). In answer to the seemingly provocative question "Should Wives Be Paid Wages?" *Good Housekeeping* (March 1925) replied: "Any man who has a good wife and doesn't pay her a salary . . . isn't a good business man."

28. E. W. Burgess, "The Family," in *American Society in Wartime*, ed. W. F. Ogburn (Chicago, 1943), 17–39. E. R. Mower, *Family Disorganization* (Chicago, 1926); *Recent Social Trends*, I, 421–432, 693; Robert S. Lynd and Helen M. Lynd, *Middletown in Transition* (New York, 1936), 544; Ben Lindsey and Wainwright Evans, *The Companionate Marriage* (New York, 1927).

29. On marital obligations, see Nancy Cott, *The Grounding of Modern Feminism* (New Haven, 1987), 187; Strasser, *Never Done*, presents a convincing analysis of corporate dominance over twentieth-century housework; meanwhile, corporations were grooming their own internal images, as revealed in David Nye, *Image Worlds: Corporate Identities at General Electric* (Cambridge, Mass., 1986).

30. Paradoxically, desire to improve the home motivated wives to earn income

outside, according to Lynn Weiner, *From Working Girl to Working Mother* (Chapel Hill, N.C., 1985), 84–88; Lorine Pruitt in an article in *American Annals of Social and Political Science* (1929), quoted in Cott, *Grounding of Modern Feminism*, 184. On the double bind, Margaret Mead said she was forced to choose between being "a woman and therefore less of an achieving individual, or an achieving individual and therefore less a woman"; quoted in Chafe, *American Woman*, 100.

31. David Hogan, *Class and Reform* (Philadelphia, 1985), 119–120, estimates that 15 percent of Chicago wives earned wages outside the home, while the proportion of Chicago families with foreign-born heads that kept boarders and lodgers declined from 37 percent in 1907 to 11 percent in 1930; Leslie Woodcock Tentler, *Wage-Earning Women* (New York, 1979), 85, estimates that 20 percent of working-class wives earned wages; the most convenient summary of women's labor force participation for the country as a whole is in Chafe, *American Woman*, which relies heavily on Janet Hooks, *Women's Occupations through Seven Decades*, Women's Bureau Publication no. 232 (Washington, D.C., 1951), and which notes, pp. 55–56, the slight increase in the proportion of females who held jobs, from 20.4 percent in 1900 to 24.3 percent in 1930. See also the studies of white-collar women by the Bureau of Vocational Information, a private organization in Massachusetts whose papers are in SL; studies included "The Woman Secretary" and Virginia Collier, *Marriage and Careers* (1926).

32. Alice B. Parsons, *Women's Dilemma* (New York, 1926), 284.

33. Alice Kessler-Harris, *Out to Work: A History of Wage-Earning Women in the United States* (New York, 1982), chap. 8, details the way employers used gender to shunt women into unequal positions even as their employment opportunities were expanding; Susan P. Benson, *Counter Cultures: Saleswomen, Managers, and Customers in American Department Stores, 1890–1940* (Urbana, Ill., 1986), describes the nuances of class and gender in the department store; Tentler, *Wage-Earning Women*, 85–114, emphasizes the subordinations of women in the marketplace; Winifred Wandersee, *Women's Work and Family Values: 1920–1940* (Cambridge, Mass., 1981), argues unconvincingly that most women were satisfied with their marriages, worked primarily to satisfy family needs, and accepted subordination, with the result that the relation between home and work "remained constant" (p. 106); for an alternative view, see Lois Scharf, *To Work and to Wed: Female Employment, Feminism, and the Great Depression* (Westport, Conn., 1980); Joan Scott and Louise Tilly, *Women, Work, and the Family* (New York, 1978), critique the notion that factory work would liberate women from patriarchal families, an idea mistakenly ascribed to Engels (who actually believed that capitalist advance was a precondition, not a solution, for equality between the sexes) and twentieth-century modernization theorists such as Wilbert Moore.

34. David Tyack, *The One Best System: A History of American Urban Education* (Cambridge, Mass., 1974), 268; Judith Walzer Leavitt, *Brought to Bed: Childbearing in America, 1750–1950* (New York, 1986), 179–195. The effects of hospital birth on maternal and child health were at best equivocal. Although infant mortality declined for the country as a whole in this period, statistical evidence suggests that hospital delivery was less important than such other causes as improved nutrition and general health. Maternal mortality actually increased in many big-city hospitals. Feminists and health reformers who had played St. George to the dragon of unsanitary home birth were caught defenseless before the dragon of professionalism; for documentation, see *Recent Social Trends*, II, 762–763; Neal Devitt, "The Statistical Case for Elimination of the Midwife: Fact versus Prejudice, 1890–1935, Part 2," *Women and Health* 4 (Summer 1979), 169–186.

35. Carole Shammas, *Inheritance in America from Colonial Times to the Present* (New Brunswick, N.J., 1987), 212–213; Daniel Luria, "Wealth, Capital and Power: The Social Meaning of Home Ownership," *Journal of Interdisciplinary History* 7 (Autumn 1976), 262–282; Natalie Rogoff, *Recent Trends in Occupational Mobility* (Glencoe, Ill., 1953), 106–111, used Indianapolis marriage certificates from 1910 to 1940 and found that although a son was more likely to be in his father's occupation than in any other single category, 70 percent were in different categories.

36. American Social Hygiene Association (ASHA), "Report," 1928, ASHA Papers, box 7, folder 5, SWHA; William Snow to John D. Rockefeller, June 6, 1924, and Gertrude R. Luce to Rockefeller, August 29, 1924, ibid., box 25, folder 10; ASHA, "Report," 1919, ibid., box 25, folder 9; see also Allan Brandt, *No Magic Bullet* (New York, 1985).

37. Philip van Ingen, *The Story of the American Child Health Association* (n.p., 1935), 15–30; David Burner, *Herbert Hoover: A Public Life* (New York, 1979), 221–222; Katherine Glover, *The Story of May Day* (New York, 1929), 35; see American Child Health Association, *May Day Festivals* and *May Day Festival Book*, pamphlets in American Child Health Association Papers, box 19, folder "May Day," Hoover Library; see also White House Conference on Child Health and Protection, *The Home and the Child* (New York, 1931).

38. Modernization theory informed a good deal of work on family history, including such pioneering works as Peter Laslett, *The World We Have Lost* (New York, 1965), and the controversial Edward Shorter, *The Making of the Modern Family* (New York, 1975); for a critique of these and an alternative approach relying on class analysis and an evolutionary view of social reproduction, see Stephanie Coontz, *The Social Origins of Private Life: A History of American Families, 1600–1900* (London, 1988), 7–40, 348–354. Betty Friedan, *The Feminine Mystique* (New York, 1963).

39. NICB, *Family Budgets of American Wage Earners* (New York, 1921).

40. For parallels in Europe, see Robert Hughes, *The Shock of the New* (New York, 1981).

41. Edward T. James et al., eds., *Notable American Women, 1607–1950,* 3 vols. (Cambridge, Mass., 1971), III, 185–187; see Nelson Aldrich, *Old Money: The Mythology of America's Upper Middle Class* (New York, 1988).

42. Susman, *Culture as History,* 141–149; Elizabeth Ewen, *Immigrant Women in the Land of Dollars* (New York, 1985), 216–224.

43. Francis Couvares, "The Triumph of Commerce: Class Culture and Mass Culture in Pittsburgh," in *Working Class America,* ed. Michael Frisch and Daniel Walkowitz (Urbana, Ill., 1983); Pete Daniel, *Standing at the Crossroads* (New York, 1986), 99–103.

44. The 1925 novel *Porgy* was written by proper Charlestonian DuBose Heyward; Langston Hughes, *The Langston Hughes Reader* (New York, 1958), 368–391.

45. Frederick Thrasher, *The Gang: A Study of 1313 Gangs in Chicago* (Chicago, 1927), 221–237.

46. Kathy Peiss, *Cheap Amusements: Working Women and Leisure in Turn-of-the-Century New York* (Philadelphia, 1986); Ewen, *Immigrant Women,* 208–224; Susan Kellogg and Steven Mintz, *Domestic Revolutions: A Social History of the American Family* (New York, 1988), 113–119.

47. This point is central to the arguments of otherwise different interpretations in Cott, *Grounding of Modern Feminism,* and J. Stanley Lemons, *The Woman Citizen: Social Feminism in the 1920s* (Urbana, Ill., 1973).

48. Filene, *Successful Living in Machine Age,* 96; Ewen, *Captains of Consciousness,* 160–161; Edward Bernays, *Biography of an Idea* (New York, 1965), 387–389. See also Rayna Rapp and Ellen Ross, "The Twenties' Backlash: Compulsory Heterosexuality, the Consumer Family, and the Waning of Feminism," in *Class, Race, and Sex: The Dynamics of Control,* ed. Amy Swerdlow and Hanna Lessinger (Boston, 1983), 93–107; and Estelle B. Freedman, "The New Woman: Changing Views of Women in the 1920s," in *Setting a Course: American Women in the 1920s,* ed. D. M. Brown (Boston, 1987), 21–37.

49. On the domestication of the New Woman see Barbara Epstein, "Family, Sexual Morality, and Popular Movements in Turn-of-the-Century America," in *Powers of Desire,* ed., Ann Snitow et al. (New York, 1983), 117–129; Floyd Dell, *Love in the Machine Age* (New York, 1930); see also Dell, *The Outline of Marriage* (New York, 1926), written for Sanger's American Birth Control League.

50. Wilfred Lay, *Plea for Monogamy* (New York, 1923), 277, 294; Anne Koedt, "The Myth of the Vaginal Orgasm," in *Voices from Women's Liberation,* ed. Leslie B. Tanner (New York, 1970), 157–165; Susan Lydon, "The Politics

of Orgasm," in *Sisterhood is Powerful*, ed. Robin Morgan (New York, 1970), 197–205; see also John D'Emilio and Estelle Freedman, *Intimate Matters: A History of Sexuality in America* (New York, 1988).

51. Katherine B. Davis, *Factors in the Sex Life of Twenty-two Hundred Women* (New York, 1972; orig. 1929), 97, 247; Alfred Kinsey et al., *Sexual Behavior in the Human Female* (Philadelphia, 1953); Kinsey et al., *Sexual Behavior in the Human Male* (Philadelphia, 1948).

52. Only the Women's Trade Union League, which drew the line between involuntary motherhood and workers' subordination, supported Dennett's bill; Mary Dennett, *Birth Control Laws* (New York, 1926), 198–199.

53. Nancy Wolloch, *Women and the American Experience* (New York, 1984), 412–418; Dennett, *Birth Control Laws*, 203–05; Margaret Sanger, *An Autobiography* (New York, 1938); Lynd and Lynd, *Middletown*, 123, report that while all "business class" couples surveyed used birth control, only half the working-class couples used artificial or natural methods.

54. George Tindall, *Emergence of the New South, 1913–1945* (n.p., 1967), 232; Richard Easterlin, "Regional Income Trends, 1840–1950," in *American Economic History*, ed. S. E. Harris (New York, 1961), 528.

55. Donald Davidson, *The Attack on Leviathan* (Chapel Hill, N.C., 1938), quoted in Tindall, *Emergence of the New South*, 216.

56. Twelve Southerners, *I'll Take My Stand: The South and the Agrarian Tradition* (New York, 1962; orig. 1930), 139–141, 246–264; Smith quoted in Daniel, *Standing at the Crossroads*, 132; Theodore Saloutos, *Farmer Movements in the South, 1865–1933* (Lincoln, Neb., 1964; orig. 1960), v–vi.

57. Faulkner's pessimism shaded over into the macabre; in a story worthy of Poe, "A Rose for Emily," the mad relic of an old southern lineage beds down every night with the decayed corpse of the northern construction foreman she has poisoned.

58. Lawrence Levine, *Black Culture and Black Consciousness* (Oxford, 1977), 407–420, 421–429.

59. Herbert Hoover, *American Individualism* (Garden City, N.Y., 1922), 4–13; Hoover's link to progressivism is emphasized in Joan Hoff Wilson, *Herbert Hoover: Forgotten Progressive* (Boston, 1975), and in Hoover's own admiring biography of Wilson, *The Ordeal of Woodrow Wilson* (New York, 1958); Ellis Hawley is the one historian who has done most to explore Hoover's "associational" philosophy; see, for example, his essay "Herbert Hoover and American Corporatism" in *The Hoover Presidency: A Reappraisal*, ed. Martin Fausold (Albany, 1974).

60. Hawley, "Herbert Hoover"; F. M. Feiker, "The Cooperation of the Department of Commerce and Private Business in Simplifying Standards of Manufacture," in National Conference of Social Work, *Proceedings: 1928* (Chicago, 1928), 390–395.

61. John D. Hicks, *Republican Ascendancy, 1921–1933* (New York, 1960), 53; see

also Harvey O'Connor, *Mellon's Millions: The Biography of a Fortune* (New York, 1933).

62. Hicks, *Republican Ascendancy*, 62–64; Theodore Saloutos and John Hicks, *Twentieth Century Populism: Agricultural Discontent in the Middle West, 1900–1939* (Lincoln, Neb., 1951), 404–407.

63. Young quoted in Frank Costigliola, *Awkward Dominion: American Political, Economic, and Cultural Relations with Europe, 1919–1933* (Ithaca, 1984), 63. Revision of the view of the 1920s as isolationist began with William Appleman Williams, *The Tragedy of American Diplomacy* (New York, 1959), and went on to become the prevailing wisdom in such works as Joan Hoff Wilson, *American Business and Foreign Policy, 1920–1933* (Lexington, Ky., 1971); Carl Parinni, *Heir to Empire: United States Economic Diplomacy, 1916–1923* (New York, 1969), Michael Hogan, *Informal Entente: The Private Structure of Cooperation in Anglo-American Economic Diplomacy, 1918–1929* (New York, 1977).

64. Atina Grossmann, "The New Woman and the Rationalization of Sexuality in Weimar Germany," in Snitow et al., *Powers of Desire*, 153–176.

65. Quoted in Emily S. Rosenberg, *Spreading the American Dream: American Economic and Cultural Expansion, 1890–1945* (New York, 1982), 92–93, 100.

66. Ludwell Denny, *America Conquers Britain* (New York, 1930), quoted in Costigliola, *Awkward Dominion*, 140; Warren I. Cohen, *Empire without Tears: America's Foreign Relations, 1921–1933* (New York, 1987), 24.

67. Cohen, *Empire without Tears*, 6, 7–8, 19–21, 28–29.

68. Rosenberg, *Spreading the American Dream*, 130–136, 138–140; Cohen, *Empire without Tears*, 63–75; see also Herbert Feis, *The Diplomacy of the Dollar, 1919–1932* (New York, 1950).

69. Warren I Cohen, *Empire without Tears: America's Foreign Relations, 1921–1923* (New York, 1987), 21–22; Robert Zieger, *Republicans and Labor 1919–29* (Lexington, Ky., 1969), 76–77.

70. Charles Maier, *Recasting Bourgeois Europe: Stabilization in France, Germany, and Italy in the Decade after World War I* (Princeton, 1975), 483–488.

71. Costigliola, *Awkward Dominion*, 61–63; Maier, *Recasting Bourgeois Europe*, 543, 501.

72. *Findings of the Conference on the Cause and Cure of War* (Washington, D.C., 18–24, 1925); significant was the participation of such labor progressives as Selma Borchardt, whose papers are at Wayne State University.

73. Cohen, *Empire without Tears*, 59–62; see also the running critique of progressivism in U.S. foreign relations by Robert Dallek, *The American Style of Foreign Policy: Cultural Politics and Foreign Affairs* (New York, 1983); the fact that hardheaded realists and corporate diplomats, not progressives, were the main architects of illusion in U.S. foreign relations deprives Dallek's critique of its sting.

74. This picture of Weimar Germany relies primarily on Gerald Feldman,

Army, Industry, and Labor in Germany, 1914–1918 (Princeton, 1966); David Abraham, *The Collapse of the Weimar Republic: Political Economy and Crisis* (Princeton, 1981); Maier, *Recasting Bourgeois Europe;* Renate Bridenthal, Atina Grossmann, and Marion Kaplan, eds., *When Biology Became Destiny: Women in Weimar and Nazi Germany* (New York, 1984); Ute Frevert, *Women in German History: From Bourgeois Emancipation to Sexual Liberation,* trans. Stuart McKinnon-Evans (Oxford, 1988).

75. Susan Lehrer, *Origins of Protective Labor Legislation for Women, 1905–1925* (Albany, 1987), 3–18, 227–240; Frevert, *Women in German History,* 170–171, 179–180.

76. David Noble, *Forces of Production: A Social History of Industrial Automation* (New York, 1984); Guy Alchon, *The Invisible Hand of Planning: Capitalism, Social Science, and the State in the 1920s* (Princeton, 1985), 48–52.

77. Social work should be a "strong hoop around the barrel which was falling to pieces," according to Rowland Hayes, "The Contribution of the Community Chest to Community Welfare Planning," in National Conference of Social Work, *Proceedings: 1928,* 410. R. M. Mennel, *Thorns and Thistles: Juvenile Delinquents in the United States, 1825–1940* (Hanover, N.H., 1973), 158–195, argues that the emphasis shifted in the 1920s to individual psychology, following the lead of works such as William Healey, *The Individual Delinquent* (1915). It would appear that the focus shifted to individuals not because social causes were ignored, but because it was assumed that the social matrix could not be changed while "maladjusted" individuals could be; social causes were examined by those influenced by the Chicago School, including W. I. Thomas, *The Unadjusted Girl* (1923); Thrasher, *The Gang;* and Clifford Shaw and Henry McKay, *Social Factors in Juvenile Delinquency* (1931). On delinquency, see Miriam Van Waters, *Youth in Conflict* (New York, 1925); on probation, see Ethel Sturges Dummer Papers, boxes 24–25, SL, for correspondence about the National Probation Association and copies of the *Probation Bulletin;* thanks in part to the Commonwealth Fund of New York, the number of child guidance clinics increased to 232 in 1931; *Recent Social Trends,* II, 772–774.

78. Addams quoted in John Ehrenreich, *The Altruistic Imagination: A History of Social Work and Social Policy in the United States* (Ithaca, 1985), 82–83; National Social Work Council, monthly minutes, 1927, National Social Work Council Papers, box 3, folders 19–26, SWHA; Walter Trattner, *From Poor Law to Welfare State* (New York, 1974), 217; Feiker, "Cooperation of Department of Commerce and Private Business."

79. See Jurgen Kocka, *White Collar Workers in America, 1890–1940: A Social-Political History in International Perspective,* trans. Maura Kealey (London, 1980).

80. For an analysis along these lines, see Alan Dawley, "Workers, Capital, and

the State in the Twentieth Century," in *Perspectives on American Labor History*, ed. Carroll Moody and Alice Kessler-Harris (De Kalb, Ill., 1990).

81. Charles Mitchell, in a 1928 advertising bulletin, *New Market News*, quoted in Corey, *Decline of American Capitalism*, 16.

82. Walter Lippmann, *A Preface to Morals*, (New York, 1929), 258; Filene quoted in Corey, *Decline of American Capitalism*, 19.

83. T. N. Carver, *The Present Economic Revolution in the United States* (1925), quoted in Corey, *Decline of American Capitalism*, 19.

84. Mencken quoted in Leuchtenburg, *Perils of Prosperity*, 152; F. Scott Fitzgerald, *The Great Gatsby* (New York, 1925). To Fitzgerald, Gatsby was "great" in pursuing a pure dream, the fair Daisy, but met a tragic fall through the foul means of ill-gotten wealth acquired in corrupt business dealings with East Coast Jews.

85. John Dos Passos, *Facing the Chair: The Story of the Americanization of Two Foreign-Born Workmen* (Boston, 1927); Theodore Draper, *Roots of American Communism* (New York, 1957); William Z. Foster, *American Trade Unionism* (New York, 1947); Suzanne LaFollette, *Concerning Women* (New York, 1972; orig. 1926), 47–48; Paul Buhle, *Marxism in the United States: Remapping the History of the American Left* (New York, 1987).

86. Tindall, *Emergence of the New South*, 224, 259, 262, 283, 276–282.

87. Edward Ayers, *Vengeance and Justice: Crime and Punishment in the American South* (New York, 1984), 221–222; the leading Durham mill owner liked to be called "Daddy" Erwin, and a study of white tenant farmers found that a "patriarchal ideal" still prevailed in the 1930s; Margaret Hagood, *Mothers of the South* (Chapel Hill, N.C., 1939), cited by Dolores Janiewski, *Sisterhood Denied: Race, Class, and Gender in a New South Community* (Philadelphia, 1985), 28n5. On the decline of paternalism, see Harriet Herring, *Welfare Work in Mill Villages* (Montclair, N.J., 1968; orig. 1929), 122–123; Tindall, *Emergence of the New South*, 340–341; Janiewski, *Sisterhood Denied*, 75–77, 116, 122, 153; Jacquelyn Hall et al., *Like a Family: The Making of a Southern Cotton Mill World* (Chapel Hill, N.C., 1987), 268–271, 310.

88. Tindall, *Emergence of the New South*, 275; Daniel, *Standing at the Crossroads*, 89–93; Robert Zangrando, *The NAACP Crusade against Lynching, 1909–1950* (Philadelphia, 1980); Richard Wright, *Uncle Tom's Children* (New York, 1940; orig. 1936), 54–102.

89. Tindall, *Emergence of the New South*, 302–305; Janiewski, *Sisterhood Denied*, 124; Bernstein, *Lean Years;* Jacquelyn Hall et al., "Cotton Mill People: Work, Community and Protest in the Textile South, 1880–1940," *American Historical Review* 91 (April 1986), 245–286.

90. Hoover quoted in Allen, *Only Yesterday*, 303.

91. Like tea leaves, election returns are open to conflicting interpretations. Walter Dean Burnham, "The System of 1896: An Analysis," in *The Evo-

lution of American Electoral Systems, ed. Paul Kleppner (Westport, Conn., 1981), 193–195, portrays the election as the beginning of the great electoral realignment culminating in 1936 with the Democrats supplanting the Republicans as the party of national government. A number of political scientists following V. O. Key and Samuel Lubell see 1928 as the ideological harbinger of the "urban liberalism" of the New Deal coalition. In rebuttal, Allan Lichtman, *Prejudice and the Old Politics: The Presidential Election of 1928* (Chapel Hill, N.C., 1979), 197–198, 228–245, argues tellingly that the roots of New Deal ideology are more visible in the 1924 protest candidacy of Robert La Follette. In any case, the Democrats did not offer an ideological alternative on economic issues in 1928, leaving the election to turn largely on religious affiliation.

92. Details on the Empire State Building in this and succeeding paragraphs are from Theodore James, Jr., *The Empire State Building* (New York, 1975). For a biting analysis of modern architecture as an expression of political power, see Hughes, *Shock of the New*.

9. Managing the Depression

1. A pioneering oral history of the Depression is Studs Terkel, *Hard Times: An Oral History of the Great Depression* (New York, 1970); a glimpse of mass consciousness is available in Robert S. McElvaine, *Down and Out in the Great Depression: Letters from the "Forgotten Man,"* (Chapel Hill, N.C., 1983); of workers, in Gerald Markowitz, *"Slaves of the Depression"* (Ithaca, 1987).

2. "No One Has Starved," *Fortune* 6 (1932), 21–24, reprinted in William Leuchtenburg, ed., *The New Deal: A Documentary History* (New York, 1968), 6–9; Keynes quoted in Albert Romasco, *The Poverty of Abundance: Hoover, the Nation, and the Depression* (New York, 1965), 3; Frank Friedel, "The New Deal in Historical Perspective," in *The New Deal: Analysis and Interpretation*, ed. Alonzo Hamby (New York, 1969), 13.

3. Most of these theories are summarized in Robert S. McElvaine, *The Great Depression: America, 1929–1941* (New York, 1984), 28.

4. Herbert Hoover, *Memoirs, 1874–1933*, 2 vols. (New York, 1952), I, 4; Warren I. Cohen, *Empire without Tears: America's Foreign Relations, 1921–1933* (New York, 1987), 24–36, 40–41, 102–104; Charles Kindleberger, *The World in Depression, 1929–1939* (Berkeley, 1973).

5. Kindleberger, *World in Depression*, 127, 106, 131–135, 291.

6. An unsurpassed introductory guide to economic ideas is Robert Heilbroner, *The Worldly Philosophers*, 3d ed. (New York, 1967; orig. 1953); for an evolutionary framework adopted from Joseph Schumpeter, see Michael A. Bernstein, "Why the Great Depression Was Great: Toward a New Understanding of the Interwar Economic Crisis in the United States," in

The Rise and Fall of the New Deal Order, 1930–1980, ed. Steven Fraser and Gary Gerstle (Princeton, 1989), 32–54.

7. Eric Hobsbawm, *The Age of Capital, 1848–1875* (London, 1975), 34–50.
8. Chase Manhattan banker Benjamin Anderson quoted in Albert Romasco, *The Politics of Recovery: Roosevelt's New Deal* (New York, 1983), 21; *Recent Economic Changes in the United States*, Report of the President's Commission, 2 vols. (n.p., 1929), xxi–xxii; Irving Fischer quoted in John Galbraith, *The Great Crash*, 3d ed. (Boston, 1954), 75; on utopian capitalists, see the section on the subject in Chapter 8 of this volume.
9. George Soule, *A Planned Society* (New York, 1932), 237–239; Pew quoted in August Giebelhaus, *Business and Government in the Oil Industry: A Case Study of Sun Oil, 1876–1945* (Greenwich, Conn., 1980), 91–92; a parade of corporate executives from coal, oil, and banking plus the director of the Taylor Society joined in a symposium in 1930 that produced Scoville Hamlin, ed., *The Menace of Overproduction: Its Cause, Extent, and Cure* (Freeport, N.Y. 1969; orig. 1930).
10. Brookings Institution, *America's Capacity to Consume* (Washington, D.C., 1934), cited in McElvaine, *The Great Depression*, 38–39; Adolf Berle and Gardner Means, *The Modern Corporation and Private Property* (New York, 1932), 32; E. S. Mason, *Economic Concentration and the Monopoly Problem* (Cambridge, Mass., 1954), 25–26, 28–29; the pattern is confirmed in Jeffrey Williamson and Peter Lindert, *American Inequality: A Macroeconomic History* (New York, 1980).
11. Productivity is an elusive figure; output per worker is from McElvaine, *The Great Depression*, 39; output per man-hour in manufacturing rose even faster from 1919 to 1929, by 72 percent, as reported in Irving Bernstein, *The Lean Years: A History of the American Worker, 1920–1933* (Boston, 1960), 54; GNP from U.S. Bureau of the Census, *Historical Statistics of the United States from Colonial Times to 1957* (Washington, D.C., 1960), 139 (hereafter cited as *Historical Statistics*).
12. Hourly earnings in McElvaine, *The Great Depression*, 39; weekly earnings in 1923–1928 rose by only 2.5 percent, as reported in Bernstein, *Lean Years*, 67; John D. Hicks, *Republican Ascendancy, 1921–1933* (New York, 1960), 193–201, 230.
13. Hoover, *Memoirs*, I, 3–4; Galbraith, *The Great Crash*, 174–176, 186–187, and passim; Paul Baran and Paul Sweezy, *Monopoly Capital* (New York, 1966), 243–244; Jim Potter, *The American Economy between the Wars* (New York, 1974), 95.
14. Potter, *American Economy*, 93; business failures calculated from *Historical Statistics*, 570; Baran and Sweezy, *Monopoly Capital*, 243–244; Sumner Schlichter, "A Dole for Employers," *New Republic*, December 31, 1930, 181–183.
15. Potter, *American Economy*, 95; Clarke Chambers, *Seedtime of Reform: Ameri-*

can Social Service and Social Action, 1918–1933 (Minneapolis, 1963), 178. Unemployment figures are not reliable, but according to Bernstein, *Lean Years*, 59, unemployment ranged from 5 to 13 percent in 1924–1928, although the lower figure is likely to be closer to the average; F. Stricker, "Affluence for Whom?—Another Look at Prosperity and the Working Class in the 1920s," *Labor History* 24 (Winter 1983), 5–33.

16. Coal mine operatives and laborers: 982,000 in 1920 compared with 887,000 in 1930; steam railroad workers: 1,132,000 in 1920 compared with 1,038,000 in 1930; Alba Edwards, *Comparative Occupation Statistics for the United States, 1870–1940* (Washington, D.C., 1943), 60. Cotton textile labor force age ten and over: 450,000 in 1920 compared with 372,000 in 1930; Stanley Lebergott, *Manpower in Economic Growth* (New York, 1964), 510. Coal, gas, and oil production from *Historical Statistics*, 355; John Bodnar, Roger Simon, and Michael Weber, *Lives of Their Own: Blacks, Italians, and Poles in Pittsburgh, 1900–1960* (Urbana, Ill., 1982), 185–187.

17. Chambers, *Seedtime of Reform*, 176–177; James Patterson, *America's Struggle against Poverty, 1900–1980* (Cambridge, Mass., 1981), 20–34.

18. Stanley Mathewson, *Restriction of Output among Unorganized Workers* (New York, 1931), 86–90.

19. Helen Lynd and Robert Lynd, *Middletown in Transition* (New York, 1937), 166–167, 151; Alice Kessler-Harris, *Out to Work: A History of Wage-Earning Women in the United States* (New York, 1982), 252; Clarke Chambers, "Toward a Redefinition of Welfare History," *Journal of American History* 73 (September 1986), 407–433; interview with Stacia Treski, in John Bodnar, *Workers' World* (Baltimore, 1982), 22; Chambers, *Seedtime of Reform*, 201.

20. Lewis Corey, *The Decline of American Capitalism* (New York, 1934), 192; Karl Marx, *Capital*, vol. I (New York, 1967; orig. 1867), 685.

21. Dreiser quoted in John Garraty, *The Great Depression* (Garden City, N.Y., 1987), 170.

22. Karl Polanyi, *The Great Transformation* (Boston, 1957; orig. 1944); Roosevelt has been well served by an extremely able band of biographers, notably Arthur Schlesinger, Jr., *The Age of Roosevelt*, 3 vols. (Boston, 1957–1960); William Leuchtenburg, *Franklin D. Roosevelt and the New Deal* (New York, 1963); Richard Hofstadter, *The American Political Tradition and the Men Who Made It* (New York, 1974; orig. 1948).

23. Among those responsible for the reassessment of Hoover are Ellis Hawley, "Herbert Hoover," in *Herbert Hoover and the Crisis of American Capitalism*, ed. J. J. Huthmacher and W. I. Susman (Cambridge, Mass., 1973); Joan Hoff Wilson, *Herbert Hoover: Forgotten Progressive* (Boston, 1975); David Burner, *Herbert Hoover: A Public Life* (New York, 1979); and Martin Fausold, *The Presidency of Herbert C. Hoover* (Lawrence, Kans., 1987).

24. Hoover, speech in Des Moines, October 4, 1932, in *Public Papers, 1932–33* (Washington, D.C., 1977), 460–463; Burner, *Herbert Hoover*, 3–11.
25. Herbert Hoover, *American Individualism* (Garden City, N.Y., 1922), 62.
26. Quoted in Frederick Lewis Allen, *Only Yesterday: An Informal History of the 1920s* (New York, 1931), 303.
27. *Historical Statistics*, 540; David B. Danbom, *The Resisted Revolution: Urban America and the Industrialization of Agriculture, 1900–1930* (Ames, Iowa, 1979), 128–130.
28. Danbom, *Resisted Revolution*, 125–133.
29. Lebergott, *Manpower in Economic Growth*, table A-2, p. 511, shows that in 1890 33 percent of farmers (excluding laborers) were tenants, compared with 47 percent in 1930; according to U.S. Bureau of the Census, *Fifteenth Census: 1930* (Washington, 1931–1933), *Agriculture*, vol. II. pt. 2, 35, 31, and *Population*, vol. IV, 118, 443–444 65 percent of Alabama farms were tenant operated, as were some 40 percent in Illinois; farm population figures are from *Historical Statistics*, 284–285.
30. For an in-depth exploration of California agribusiness, see Linda Majka and Theo Majka, *Farm Workers, Agribusiness, and the State* (Philadelphia, 1982); on Latino labor, see Carey McWilliams, *North from Mexico: The Spanish Speaking People of the United States* (Philadelphia, 1949); *Historical Statistics*, 280, reports 3.4 million hired workers at the peak in 1929, when they constituted 26.6 of total farm employment, declining to 2.7 million in 1939, when they constituted 23.8 percent, trends that continued well past the Second World War.
31. *Historical Statistics*, 288; Danbom, *Resisted Revolution*, 134–135.
32. Theodore Saloutos and John Hicks, *Twentieth Century Populism* (Lincoln, Neb., 1951), 407, 404, 433; Fausold, *Presidency of Hoover*, 106–112.
33. Fausold, *Presidency of Hoover*, 106, finds Hoover's farm policies "the best illustration of his presidency's corporatist formulas"; see also Ellis Hawley, "Herbert Hoover and American Corporatism," in *The Hoover Presidency: A Reappraisal*, ed. Martin Fausold (Albany, 1974), 107.
34. James Olson, *Saving Capitalism: The Reconstruction Finance Corporation and the New Deal* (Princeton, 1988), 15–16, 21, 28–30; Potter, *American Economy*, 98–99; Romasco, *Politics of Recovery*, 10–11.
35. Romasco, *Politics of Recovery*, 21, 16–25; Hoover, *Memoirs*, II, 30, gives a good account of the "liquidationists."
36. President's Conference on Home Building and Home Ownership, *Report*, 12 vols. (Washington, D.C., 1932), x, xi; material on Hoover's housing policies is in Presidential Papers, Better Homes files, Herbert Hoover Presidential Library, West Branch, Iowa; Kenneth T. Jackson, *Crabgrass Frontier* (New York, 1985), 193.
37. Hoover, *Memoirs*, I, 257; II, 111–115.

38. Ibid., II, 48; Burner, *Herbert Hoover*, 268–269; Olson, *Saving Capitalism*, 21. On the Anglo-Hispanic divisions built into the labor market, see Mario Barrera, *Race and Class in the Southwest: A Theory of Racial Inequality* (Notre Dame, Ind., 1979).

39. Hoover, *Memoirs*, I, 30–31, 45; Stuart Brandes, *American Welfare Capitalism* (Chicago, 1976), 142; Potter, *American Economy*, 93; Sanford Jacoby, *Employing Bureaucracy: Managers, Unions, and the Transformation of Work in American Industry, 1900–1945* (New York, 1985), 207–209.

40. *Outline of the Share the Work Movement*, pamphlet, Du Pont Corporate Papers, Harrington Collection, box 12, folder 17, HL; "History of the Six Hour Day Movement," Personnel Papers, Pennsylvania Railroad, HL; Lamont du Pont to B. M. May, October 31, 1931, and L. A. Yerkes to L. du Pont, November 13, 1931, Du Pont Corporate Papers 1662, box 71; *Business Week*, April 22, 1931; Potter, *American Economy*.

41. Hoover's voluntarist philosophy is evident in his State of the Union Message, December 2, 1930, in Herbert Hoover, *The State Papers and Other Public Writings, 1929–1933*, ed. William Myers (Garden City, N.Y., 1934), vol. I, 510; White House Statement, January 18, 1931, ibid., 28; E. P. Hayes, *Activities of the President's Emergency Committee for Unemployment* (Concord, N.H., 1936); Walter Gifford, who headed the President's Organization on Unemployment Relief, is quoted in Frances Fox Piven and Richard Cloward, *Regulating the Poor: The Functions of Public Welfare* (New York, 1971), 52.

42. Burner, *Herbert Hoover*, 268–269, 264; Romasco, *Poverty of Abundance*, 129, 131–132.

43. Interview with Orville Rice, in Bodnar, *Worker's World*, 146–147.

44. Benet quoted in Leuchtenburg, *The New Deal*, 3.

45. "No One Has Starved" and Charles R. Walker, "Relief and Revolution," *The Forum*, 1932, quoted in Leuchtenburg, *The New Deal*, 9, 11.

46. Louis Adamic, *Dynamite: The Story of Class Violence in America* (New York, 1934), 439, 325–372, 438–442; David Brody, *Workers in Industrial America: Essays on the Twentieth-Century Struggle* (New York, 1980), 82; see also Bernstein, *Lean Years*.

47. Edwin Witte, *The Government in Labor Disputes* (New York, 1932), 276–282, 298–302; Christopher Tomlins, *The State and the Unions: Labor Relations, Law and the Organized Labor Movement in America, 1880–1960* (Cambridge, 1985), 117–118.

48. Saloutos and Hicks, *Twentieth Century Populism*, 443.

49. Ibid., quote 448, 441–449.

50. Roger Daniels, *The Bonus March: An Episode of the Great Depression* (Westport, Conn., 1971), 91; Terkel, *Hard Times*, 27–33. See also Donald Lisio, *The President and Protest: Hoover, Conspiracy, and the Bonus Riot* (Columbia, Mo., 1974).

51. Richard Maxwell Brown, "The History of Vigilantism in America," in *Vigilante Politics*, ed. H. J. Rosembaum and P. C. Sederberg (Philadelphia, 1976), 79–109.
52. Daniels, *Bonus March*, 102, 161–163.
53. Leuchtenburg, *Franklin D. Roosevelt*, 15.
54. A Chicago march of the unemployed on October 31, 1932, drew 20,000, and although Communists played the leading role, factional battles with Socialists were intense; Edmund Wilson, *New Republic*, January 25, 1933, 287–290. The return of fear over the red menace among midwestern businessmen is recounted in Lynd and Lynd, *Middletown in Transition*, 110–117. The Illinois national guard's "Emergency Plans for Domestic Disturbances," issued in December 1931, were an outgrowth of military intelligence's 1919–20 War Plans White. For left-wing protests about their political bias, see Norman Thomas, *New Republic*, January 27, 1932, 280; Oscar Ameringer, testimony in U.S. House of Representatives, Subcommittee of the Committee on Labor Hearings, *Unemployment in the United States*, 72d Cong., 1st sess. (Washington, D.C., 1932), in David Shannon, ed., *The Great Depression* (Englewood Cliffs, N.J., 1960), 123.
55. Hoover, quoted in National Commission on Law Observance and Enforcement (Wickersham Commission), *Report*, 71st Cong., 3d sess., House Doc. 722 (Washington, D.C., 1931), iii, 54–55, took note of working-class resentment: "Laboring men resent the insistence of employers who drink that their employees be kept from temptation"; Burner, *Herbert Hoover*, 218–220; David Kyvig, *Repealing National Prohibition* (Chicago, 1979), 45–49, 119–123.
56. Dewey quoted in Leuchtenburg, *Franklin D. Roosevelt*, 9.
57. Roosevelt quoted in ibid., 11.
58. Hoover quoted in Olson, *Saving Capitalism*, 16; Hoover speech at Valley Forge, May 30, 1931, *Memoirs*, vol. II.
59. Roosevelt speech, Atlanta, May 22, 1932, *The Public Papers of Franklin D. Roosevelt*, ed. Samuel Rosenman (New York, 1938) vol. I, 639–646; Hofstadter, *American Political Tradition*, 410–432.
60. Roosevelt, speech at Commonwealth Club, quoted in Hofstadter, *American Political Tradition*, 429–431.
61. Roosevelt, speech, Atlanta, Ga., May 22, 1932, quoted in Howard Zinn, ed., *New Deal Thought* (Indianapolis, 1966), 83.
62. Agnes Meyer quoted in Leuchtenburg, *Franklin D. Roosevelt*, 39; Herbert Hoover, *The Ordeal of Woodrow Wilson* (New York, 1958), 301–302.
63. Quote from Lillian Symes, "Blunder on the Left: The Revolution and the American Scene," *Harper's*, December 1933, in Shannon, *The Great Depression*, 128. The "revolutionary" view of the New Deal is found in Carl Degler, *Out of Our Past* (New York, 1959), 416; and Degler, "What Was the New Deal?" in *The New Deal*, ed. Degler (Chicago, 1970), 24–25; the key

scholarly work in fixing the image of the First Hundred Days is Arthur Schlesinger, Jr., *The Coming of the New Deal* (Boston, 1958), vol. 2 of *The Age of Roosevelt.*

64. Baran and Sweezy, *Monopoly Capital*, 244; Potter, *American Economy*, 95; Ruth McKenney, *Industrial Valley* (New York, 1939), quoted in Leuchtenburg, *The New Deal*, 21.

65. J. Frederick Essary, "The New Deal for Nearly Four Months," *Literary Digest*, 116 (1933), quoted in Leuchtenburg, *The New Deal*, 25. Liberal historians have kept the legend alive; see Schlesinger, *The Age of Roosevelt.*

66. Donald Richberg, speech at Faneuil Hall, Boston, December 27, 1933, Donald Richberg Papers, box 45, LC; Barton Bernstein, "The New Deal: The Conservative Achievements of Liberal Reform," in *Towards a New Past: Dissenting Essays in American History*, ed. Bernstein (New York, 1968), 263–288.

67. Quoted in Hofstadter, *American Political Tradition*, 430; William Leuchtenburg, "The New Deal and the Analogue of War," *Change and Continuity in Twentieth Century America*, ed. John Braeman, Robert Bremner, and Ronald Walters (Columbus, Ohio, 1964).

68. Raymond Moley, *After Seven Years* (New York, 1939), 155; Olson, *Saving Capitalism*, 30–41.

69. Adolf Berle, "The Social Economics of the New Deal," *New York Times Magazine*, October 29, 1933, quoted in Leuchtenburg, *The New Deal*, 38; Olson, *Saving Capitalism*, 44–45.

70. Romasco, *Politics of Recovery*, 16–25, 35–51.

71. Louis Galambos, *Competition and Cooperation: The Emergence of a National Trade Association* (Baltimore, 1966), 167–169; Hawley, "Herbert Hoover and American Corporatism," 111–112.

72. Soule, *A Planned Society*, 184–203, 206–207, 231, 252; Charles Beard, "The Myth of Rugged Individualism," *Harper's*, December 1931, 13–22; Stuart Chase, "The Age of Distribution," *The Nation*, July 25, 1934, 93–96; Rexford Tugwell, "The Principle of Planning and the Institution of Laissez Faire," *American Economic Review* 22, supp. (March 1932), 75–92; Walter Polakov, "How Efficient Are the Russians?" *Harper's*, December 1931, 37–47; David Lilienthal, *TVA: Democracy on the March* (New York, 1944.

73. Elizabeth Brandeis, "Protective Legislation," in *History of Labor in the United States, 1896–1933*, ed. John Commons et al. (New York, 1966; orig. 1935), III, 200–202; Irving Bernstein, *The Turbulent Years* (Boston, 1970), 24–27; Ronald Schatz, *The Electrical Workers: A History of Labor at General Electric and Westinghouse* (Urbana, Ill., 1983), 59–60; Jacoby, *Employing Bureaucracy*, 211–213; NICB, *The Service Letter on Industrial Relations* (n.p., 1932); Tamara Hareven, *Family Time and Industrial Time: The Relationship*

between Family and Work in a New England Industrial Community (Cambridge, Mass., 1982), 342–354.

74. Ellis Hawley, *The New Deal and the Problem of Monopoly* (Princeton, 1966), 53–71; the language of 7a was taken from the 1926 Railway Labor Act, one of whose drafters, Donald Richberg, also played a key role in drafting the NIRA; see "Labor Provisions of N.I.R.A.," undated memo [September–October 1933], Richberg Papers, box 45; it is too much to read into 7a a grand corporatist design, as does Fausold, *Presidency of Hoover*, 122–124.

75. NICB, *Memorandum 11: The NIRA: Analysis of Approved Codes* (New York, 1933), 12–14; Hawley, *New Deal and Monopoly*, 56; NICB/NAM, Bulletin 1: Industrial Self-government (New York, 1934), 1.

76. Donald Richberg, speech at Faneuil Hall, December 7, 1933, copy in Richberg Papers, box 45; Richberg followed a common trajectory for many Progressives. Starting as a Bull Mooser, he wrote the Railway Labor Act of 1926, helped devise and then headed the NRA, but wound up in the 1950s an archconservative critic of his former friends in the labor movement, which he denounced in *Labor Union Monopoly* (1957).

77. Walter Lippmann, *The Method of Freedom* (New York, 1934), 26; Hawley, *New Deal and Monopoly*, 43–46, 62, 91–93.

78. Steven Mintz and Susan Kellogg, *Domestic Revolutions: A Social History of American Family Life* (New York, 1988), 139, 134. The Depression may have accelerated trends toward lower birthrates and marriage rates, but it did not change long-range demographic trends, according to Lynd and Lynd, *Middletown in Transition*, 181; Roland C. Marchand, *Advertising the American Dream: Making Way for Modernity, 1920–1940* (Berkeley, 1985), 196–197, 290–291, 293.

79. Susan Ware, *Beyond Suffrage: Women in the New Deal* (Cambridge, Mass., 1981), 87–96; Lois Scharf, *To Work and to Wed* (Westport, Conn., 1980), 111–114. See also Kessler-Harris, *Out to Work*, 262–263.

80. Fausold, *Presidency of Hoover*, 112; Saloutos and Hicks, *Twentieth Century Populism*, 469–472.

81. Pete Daniel, *Standing at the Crossroads: Southern Life in the Twentieth Century* (New York, 1986), 121–122; because of its favoritism to planters in the South, the Department of Agriculture was the target of picketing by the Southern Tenant Farmers Union, which made some New Dealers squirm, as in the case of "Beanie" Baldwin, in Terkel, *Hard Times*, 293–302.

82. Herbert Hoover, message of December 2, 1930, *Presidential Papers 1930*, 510; Burner, *Herbert Hoover*, 268–269; Piven and Cloward, *Regulating the Poor*, 52. Private cash assistance rose from $10 million in 1929 to $56 million in 1933; Chambers, *Seedtime of Reform*, 192. Total local, state, and federal government expenditures rose from $100 million annually to $208

million in 1932; Patterson, *America's Struggle against Poverty*, 56–57. On family and communal relief networks, see Chambers, "Toward a Redefinition of Welfare History," 407–433.

83. Patterson, *America's Struggle against Poverty*, 56–57; Frances Perkins, *The Roosevelt I Knew* (New York, 1946), 184–187; Lynd and Lynd, *Middletown in Transition*, 120–122; Russell E. Smith and Dorothy Zietz, *American Social Welfare Institutions* (New York, 1970), 82, 88–90.

84. Burner, *Herbert Hoover*, 316; Kyvig, *Repealing National Prohibition*, 134–135, 158–162, 177–180; Leuchtenburg, *Franklin D. Roosevelt*, 116.

85. Henry S. Commager, *The Growth of the American Republic* (New York, 1962), 708–709; Bernard Schwartz, *The Reigns of Power* (New York, 1963), 149.

86. Hoover, *Memoirs*, II, 36.

87. Hawley, *New Deal and Monopoly*, 96; Darrow, "Supplement to Report," quoted in Hugh Johnson, memorandum May 17, 1934, Richberg Papers, box 45, folder NRA; George Soule, *The Coming American Revolution* (New York, 1934), 294–295; John Dewey, 1935 lectures, quoted in Zinn, *New Deal Thought*, xxvii; Corey, *Decline of American Capitalism*; E. Wright Bakke, *Citizens without Work* (New Haven, 1940), 56, reports a mock auction staged by the New Haven John Reed Club in which an the American worker is sold to the NRA after bids for "starvation wages, Fascism, paternalistic soft soap, wages cuts."

88. Richberg, speech at Faneuil Hall, December 27, 1933; Walter Lippmann, *The New Imperative* (New York, 1935), 1–7; idem, *Method of Freedom*, 50–52.

10. Rendezvous with Destiny

1. J. Frederick Essary, "The New Deal for Nearly Four Months," *Literary Digest* 116 (1933), quoted in William Leuchtenburg, ed., *The New Deal: A Documentary History* (New York, 1968), 29.

2. William Leuchtenburg, *Franklin D. Roosevelt and the New Deal* (New York, 1963), 108; Irving Bernstein, *The Turbulent Years* (Boston, 1970), 24–27; Elizabeth Brandeis, "Protective Legislation," in *History of Labor in the United States, 1896–1932*, ed. John Commons et al. (New York, 1966; orig. 1935), 200–208.

3. Robert H. Zieger, *American Workers, American Unions, 1920–1985* (Baltimore, 1986), 29; Bernstein, *Turbulent Years*, 352–431; see also Walter Galenson, *The CIO Challenge to the AFL* (Cambridge, Mass., 1960); Melvin Dubovsky and Warren Van Tine, *John L. Lewis: A Biography* (New York, 1977).

4. Walter Reuther, letter to Victor Reuther, May 1936, quoted in Kevin Boyle, "Building the Vanguard," *Labor History* 30 (Summer 1989), 446;

Bernstein, *Turbulent Years*, 273–298; Sidney Lens, *The Labor Wars: From the Mollie Maguires to the Sitdowns* (Garden City, N.Y., 1973); Art Preis, *Labor's Giant Step* (New York, 1972), 19–30.

5. NICB, *Individual and Collective Bargaining under the NIRA* (New York, 1933), 5–6; NICB, *The Effect of the Depression on Industrial Relations Programs* (New York, 1934), 6–8; U.S. Senate Committee on Education and Labor. *Violations of Free Speech*, 76th Cong., 1st sess. (Washington, D.C., 1939); Jerold Auerbach, *Labor and Liberty: The La Follette Committee and the New Deal* (Indianapolis, 1966): Leo Huberman, *The Labor Spy Racket* (New York, 1966; orig. 1937); Howell Harris, *The Right to Manage* (Madison, Wis., 1982), chap. 1.

6. In 1941 the CIO had about 2,654,000 members, roughly as many as the AFL in 1933, which had grown to 5,179,000 by 1941; Bernstein, *Turbulent Years*, 400–424, 773–774.

7. Mary Heaton Vorse, *Labor's New Millions* (New York, 1938). The process of homogenization is outlined in David Gordon, Richard Edwards, and Michael Reich, *Segmented Work, Divided Workers: The Historical Transformation of Labor in the United States* (Cambridge, 1982); see also Harry Braverman, *Labor and Monopoly Capital* (New York, 1974); Richard Edwards, *Contested Terrain: The Transformation of the Workplace in the Twentieth Century* (New York, 1979). On mass culture, see, e.g., Robert Lynd and Helen Lynd, *Middletown* (New York, 1929); Ronald Edsforth, *Class Conflict and Cultural Consensus: The Making of a Mass Consumer Society in Flint, Michigan* (New York, 1987); Elizabeth Ewen, *Immigrant Women in the Land of Dollars* (New York, 1985); Stuart Ewen, *Captains of Consciousness: Advertising and the Social Roots of Consumer Culture* (New York, 1976).

8. Gary Gerstle, *Working-Class Americanism: The Politics of Labor in a Textile City, 1914–1960* (Cambridge, 1989), 78–91, 120–126; Ronald Schatz, *The Electrical Workers: A History of Labor at General Electric and Westinghouse, 1923–1960* (Urbana, Ill., 1983), 29, 92–99; Joshua Freeman, "Catholics, Communists, and Republicans: Irish Workers and the Organization of the Transport Workers Union," in *Working Class America*, ed. Michael Frisch and Daniel Walkowitz (Urbana, Ill., 1983), 256–277; and idem, *In Transit: The Transport Workers Union in New York City, 1933–1966* (New York, 1989).

9. Among the multitude of autobiographical accounts, see Wyndham Mortimer, *Organize! My Life as a Union Man* (Boston, 1971); Rose Pesotta, *Bread upon the Waters* (New York, 1944); Alice Lynd and Staughton Lynd, eds., *Rank and File* (Boston, 1973). On the rise of Hillman, see Steve Fraser, "The Labor Question," in *The Rise and Fall of the New Deal Order, 1930–1980*, ed. Gary Gerstle and Steve Fraser (Princeton, 1989), 55–84; and Matthew Josephson, *Sidney Hillman* (Garden City, N.Y., 1952).

10. John Dos Passos, excerpt from the *New Masses*, February 13, 1934, in *The*

New Masses: An Anthology of the Rebel Thirties, ed. Joseph North (New York, 1969), 143.

11. Reinhold Niebuhr, *Moral Man and Immoral Society* (New York, 1932), 234–237; Lewis Mumford, *Technics and Civilization* (New York, 1934).

12. Richard Pells, *Radical Visions and American Dreams* (New York, 1973), 202–219; among the "proletarian" novels with strong female characters are Tillie Olsen, *Yonnondio* (n.p., 1974; begun 1934); and Thomas Bell, *Out of This Furnace* (Pittsburgh, 1976; orig. 1941). For a somewhat jaundiced view of the culture of the 1930s, see Warren I. Susman, *Culture as History: The Transformation of American Society in the Twentieth Century* (New York, 1984), 150–183.

13. T. Harry Williams, *Huey Long* (New York, 1969), 693–697; Alan Brinkley, *Voices of Protest: Huey Long, Father Coughlin, and the Great Depression* (New York, 1982), 11, 63, 72–73.

14. Leuchtenburg, *Franklin D. Roosevelt*, 103–106; Geoffrey S. Smith, *To Save a Nation: American Countersubversives, the New Deal, and the Coming of World War II* (New York, 1973), 28.

15. Mary Van Kleeck, "Security for Americans," *New Republic*, December 1934, quoted in Theda Skocpol and John Ikenberry, "The Political Formation of the American Welfare State," *Comparative Social Research* 6 (1983), 123; Daniel Nelson, *Unemployment Insurance: The American Experience, 1915–1935* (Madison, Wis., 1969), 193, 195, 203.

16. Leuchtenburg, *Franklin D. Roosevelt*, 116–117.

17. Frances Perkins, *The Roosevelt I Knew* (New York, 1946), 186–188; Hopkins emphasized the virtue of work over relief in announcing WPA at a press conference on May 16, 1935, Hopkins Papers, box 30, Franklin D. Roosevelt Library, Hyde Park, New York; James Patterson, *America's Struggle against Poverty, 1900–1980* (Cambridge, Mass., 1981), 45–50, 63–67.

18. The classic study of income distribution is Simon Kuznets, *Shares of Upper-Income Groups* (New York, 1950); see also Gabriel Kolko, *Wealth and Power in America* (New York, 1962), 30–36; Leuchtenburg, *Franklin D. Roosevelt*, 152–154; among the radicals at Agriculture were Rexford Tugwell and his subordinates C. B. Baldwin, whose Farm Security Administration hired Dorothea Lange and Walker Evans to document rural poverty, and John Beecher, who helped run a federal camp for impoverished southern laborers; see their interviews in Studs Terkel, *Hard Times: An Oral History of the Great Depression* (New York, 1970), 293–301, 319–324.

19. Perkins, *The Roosevelt I Knew*, 278–281; Ann Orloff, "The Political Origins of America's Belated Welfare State," in *Politics of Social Policy in the United States*, ed. Margaret Weir (Princeton, 1988), 58, 69–76; the key figure in the Committee on Economic Security was Edwin Witte, a protégé of John

Commons and a strong advocate of cooperation among business, labor, and government; Witte prepared the initial blueprints for the Social Security bill, which centered on rationalizing the market economy to reduce insecurity and betrayed no redistributive intent; key documents include Committee on Economic Security, "First Tentative Outline," August 16, 1934, and idem, "Preliminary Report," September 1934, Hopkins Papers, box 48.

20. The Employment Relations Committee, minutes, June 13, 1934, National Association of Manufacturers (NAM) Papers, box HL; Ohio Manufacturers Association, letter of December 20, 1932, and "Practical Plans . . . to Defeat Unemployment Insurance," NAM Papers, box 250; NAM Social Security Meetings, minutes, November 30, 1935–June 18, 1936, NAM Papers, box 1; Nelson, *Unemployment Insurance*, 217; Roy Lubove, *The Struggle for Social Security, 1900–1935* (Pittsburgh, 1986), 172.

21. Thurman Arnold, *The Folklore of American Capitalism* (New Haven, 1937); NAM, *Public Old Age Pensions* (New York, 1930), 3, 78–82, 67.

22. Leuchtenburg, *Franklin D. Roosevelt*, 150–151; Stanley Vittoz, *New Deal Labor Policy and the American Industrial Economy* (Chapel Hill, N.C., 1987).

23. Theda Skocpol, "Political Response to Capitalist Crisis: New-Marxist Theories of the State and the Case of the New Deal," *Politics and Society* 10 (1980), 155–201; the economic views of Wagner and William Leiserson are quoted in Christopher Tomlins, *The State and the Unions: Labor Relations, Law, and the Organized Labor Movement in America, 1880–1960* (Cambridge, 1985), 99–100, 122, 132; similar views of the Wagner Act's chief drafter are in Kenneth Casebeer, "Holder of the Pen: An Interview with Leon Keyserling on Drafting the Wagner Act," *University of Miami Law Review* 42 (November 1987), 285–363; Bernstein, *Turbulent Years*, 336–343. The AFL switched positions, however, when it discovered that the Wagner Act also promoted the growth of the CIO, whereupon the AFL joined NAM in opposition.

24. George Tindall, *The Emergence of the New South, 1913–1945* (n.p., 1987), 513; Tomlins, *The State and the Unions*, 124, 143, 148–150, 160; National Labor Relations Board v. Jones and Laughlin Steel Corporation 301 U.S. 1 (1937); see also Stanley Vittoz, *New Deal Labor Policy and the American Industrial Economy* (Chapel Hill, N.C., 1987).

25. Interest-group liberalism had begun with Hoover's farm policy, described by some historians as corporatist; for example, Martin Fausold, *The Presidency of Herbert C. Hoover* (Lawrence, Kan., 1987); for a general analysis of interest groups, see Grant McConnell, *Private Power and American Democracy* (New York, 1966); David Montgomery, *Workers' Control in America* (Cambridge, 1979), 161–166; Edwards, *Contested Terrain*, 182–185; in the *Fansteel* decision the Court outlawed sit-down strikes in the interests of

industrial peace under a definition of public order that restored the lion's share of control on the factory floor to management; see Karl Klare, "Judicial Deradicalization of the Wagner Act and the Origins of Modern Legal Consciousness, 1937–1941," *Minnesota Law Review* 62 (March 1978), 265–341.

26. Skocpol and Ikenberry, "Political Formation," 126–131; Susan Ware, *Beyond Suffrage: Women in the New Deal* (Cambridge, Mass., 1981), 99; Clarke Chambers, *Seedtime of Reform: American Social Service and Social Action, 1918–1933* (Minneapolis, 1963), 217; Lubove, *Struggle for Social Security*, 175.

27. Gaston Rimlinger, *Welfare Policy and Industrialization in Europe, America, and Russia* (New York, 1971), 223–225; Orloff, "Political Origins," 76–78.

28. Rubinow quoted in Chambers, *Seedtime of Reform*, 218; Rimlinger, *Welfare Policy and Industrialization*, 233.

29. By 1930 forty-four states provided aid for 250,000 children, in addition to the same number placed in foster care, according to *Recent Social Trends in the United States*, Report of the President's Commission, 2 vols. (New York, 1933), II, 770–771; Mimi Abramovitz, *Regulating the Lives of Women: Social Welfare Policy from Colonial Times to the Present* (Boston, 1988), 314–319.

30. Lois Scharf, *To Work and to Wed: Female Employment, Feminism, and the Great Depression* (Westport, Conn., 1980), 128–129. The census counted 3,180,251 domestic and personal servants in a total of 10,752,116 females gainfully employed in 1930; U.S. Bureau of the Census, *Abstract of the Fifteenth Census of the United States* (Washington, D.C., 1933), tables 5, 7, 322, 324; Abramovitz, *Regulating the Lives of Women*, 253, 262–266.

31. Edwin Witte quoted in Jerry Cates, *Insuring Inequality: Administrative Leadership in Social Security, 1935–1954* (Ann Arbor, 1983), 14, 39–49, 151; the general argument that Social Security propped up class inequality is found in Frances Fox Piven and Richard Cloward, *Regulating the Poor: The Functions of Public Welfare* (New York, 1971).

32. Lynd and Lynd, *Middletown in Transition*, 143, quote a newspaper announcement to able-bodied men: "We'll see that your wife and children are cared for, but you either work or starve"; Patterson, *America's Struggle against Poverty*, 59–60.

33. Roosevelt quoted in Kenneth T. Jackson, *Crabgrass Frontier: The Suburbanization of the United States* (New York, 1985), 190, 195–196.

34. Ibid., 197, 198–218.

35. Contrary to two previous decisions, the Supreme Court upheld the prohibition on child labor in a tardy act of mercy in U.S. v. Darby 312 U.S. 100 (1941); Ware, *Beyond Suffrage*, 103.

36. The position taken here, that the New Deal transformed the liberal state in significant ways, does an end run around the question of whether the New Deal was a revolutionary departure, as emphasized in works by Carl Degler and Arthur Schlesinger, Jr., or a moment of liberal continuity, as emphasized by Skocpol and Ikenberry, "Political Formation," 139–141, and Barry Karl, *The Uneasy State: The United States from 1915 to 1945* (Chicago, 1983), which depicts a perennial tension between individualism and nationalism through which the New Deal muddled. For an argument that the New Deal was essentially conservative, see Barton Bernstein, "The New Deal: The Conservative Achievements of Liberal Reform," in *Towards a New Past: Dissenting Essays in American History*, ed. Bernstein (New York, 1968), 263–288. The constraints of liberalism in an earlier period are examined by Stephen Skowronek, *Building a New American State* (Cambridge, Mass., 1982).

37. Roosevelt quoted in Chambers, *Seedtime of Reform*, 182.

38. Margaret Robins quoted in Elizabeth A. Payne, *Reform, Labor, and Feminism: Margaret Drier Robins and the Women's Trade Union League* (Urbana, Ill., 1988), 169.

39. Franklin D. Roosevelt, *The Public Papers and Addresses*, ed. Samuel Rosenman, 5 vols. (New York, 1938), V, 232–233.

40. Ibid., 568–569; emphasis added.

41. Stanley High, "I Vote for Roosevelt!" *Christian Century*, September 16, 1936, 1219–21; worker quoted in Leuchtenburg, *Franklin D. Roosevelt*, 189; for other samples of ordinary Americans who felt they had a friend in the White House to whom they could write personal letters, see Robert S. McElvaine, *Down and Out in the Great Depression: Letters from the "Forgotten Man"* (Chapel Hill, N.C., 1983).

42. Norman Thomas, "Vote Socialist!" *Christian Century*, September 30, 1936, 1283; David Montgomery, "The Minnesota Farmer-Labor Party," in *Working for Democracy*, ed. Paul Buhle and Alan Dawley (De Kalb, Ill., 1985), 73–81; Mike Davis, *Prisoners of the American Dream* (London, 1986), 65–69.

43. Harvey Klehr, *The Heyday of American Communism: The Depression Decade* (New York, 1984), 193–195; Pells, *Radical Visions*, 292–302.

44. David Kyvig, *Repealing National Prohibition* (Chicago, 1979), 191–193; Arthur Schlesinger, *The Coming of the New Deal* (Boston, 1958), 479, 486–487, 568. Schlesinger quotes Ogden Mills, former secretary of the treasury, on p. 479: "We can have a free country or a socialistic one." Mills added: "There is no middle ground between governing and being governed, between absolute sovereignty and liberty, between tyranny and freedom." The 1936 election also had a Union party, whose standard-bearer, North

Dakota's Senator Lemke, railed against the New Deal as an unholy conspiracy of bankers, Communists, and Jews. From the front ranks of this quasi-fascist party, Father Coughlin vowed: "As I was instrumental in removing Herbert Hoover from the White House so help me God I will be instrumental in taking a Communist from the chair once occupied by Washington"; quoted in Leuchtenburg, *Franklin D. Roosevelt*, 182; see also ibid., 105; Smith, *To Save a Nation*, 26–28.

45. William Leuchtenburg, "The Election of 1936," in *History of American Presidential Elections, 1789–1968*, ed. Arthur Schlesinger, Jr., vol. III (New York, 1973), 2830–34; on the entrance of ethnic workers into the CIO and thence the Democratic party, see John Bodnar, *Immigration and Industrialization: Ethnicity in an American Mill Town, 1870–1940* (Pittsburgh, 1977), 144–49.

46. Roosevelt; Washington, D.C. address, April 21, 1938, *Public Papers*, VII, 259; Richard Weiss, "Ethnicity and Reform: Minorities and the Ambience of the Depression Years," *Journal of American History* 66 (December 1979), 566–585; Ronald H. Bayor, *Neighbors in Conflict: The Irish, Germans, Jews, and Italians of New York City, 1929–1941* (Baltimore, 1978), 30–56.

47. Leuchtenburg, "The Election of 1936," 2842–46; Walter Dean Burnham, *Critical Elections and the Mainsprings of American Politics* (New York, 1970), 59. The 1936 pattern was more or less replicated in 1940. Jurgen Kocka, *White Collar Workers in America, 1890–1940: A Social-Political History in International Perspective*, trans. Maura Kelley (London, 1980), 244, reports the following percentages for Roosevelt in 1940: proprietors, 26 percent; professionals, 28 percent; skilled workers, 49 percent; unskilled workers, 69 percent.

48. Edward Levinson, *Labor on the March* (New York, 1938), 169–176; Sidney Fine, *Sitdown: The General Motors Strike of 1936–1937* (Ann Arbor, 1969); Henry Kraus, *The Many and the Few* (Los Angeles, 1947), 209–226; Edwards, *Contested Terrain*, 127–128; elsewhere, Akron rubber workers staged spontaneous sit-downs against the stretch-out and changes in piece rates, and Detroit autoworkers engaged in "quickie" strikes in protest of the pace of the assembly line.

49. Kraus, *The Many and the Few*, 227–229, 266–278; Edsforth, *Class Conflict*, 170–176.

50. John Forsythe, "Legislative History of the Fair Labor Standards Act," *Law and Contemporary Problems* 6 (Summer 1939), 464–490; Carroll Daugherty, "Economic Coverage of the Fair Labor Standards Act: A Statistical Study," ibid., 406–415. The maximum work week was really a device to force employers to pay overtime, and since many of the larger employers were already doing so, the effect was to standardize the practice throughout industry.

51. The Wagner Act was upheld by the *Jones and Laughlin* (1937) decision, and the Fair Labor Standards Act was upheld in U.S. v. Darby 312 U.S. 100 (1941); see Bernard Schwartz, *The Reins of Power: A Constitutional History of the United States* (New York, 1963); the new decisions overturned decades of laissez faire under the interstate commerce and due process clauses of the Fifth and Fourteenth Amendments going back through *Adkins v. Children's Hospital* (1922), *Hammer v. Dagenhart* (1918), and *Lochner v. New York* (1905), to *E. C. Knight* (1895).

52. Tindall, *Emergence of the New South*, 607–611; Talmadge quoted on 617.

53. Ibid., 544–548; Abramovitz, *Regulating the Lives of Women*, 319; Jackson, *Crabgrass Frontier*, 178, 208.

54. Tindall, *Emergence of the New South*, 546–549; for some black sharecroppers, federal credits broke the stranglehold of white furnishing merchants, as in the case of Nate Shaw, the subject of Theodore Rosengarten, *All God's Dangers* (New York, 1974), 302. Joseph P. Lash, *Eleanor and Franklin* (New York, 1971), 525–527, notes that the First Lady resigned from the Daughters of the American Revolution in 1939 to protest their exclusion from Washington concert halls of the noted contralto Marian Anderson, who sang instead at the Lincoln Memorial. On the general subject, see Harvard Sitkoff, *A New Deal for Blacks: The Emergence of Civil Rights as a National Issue* (New York, 1978).

55. Roosevelt quoted in Lash, *Eleanor and Franklin*, 516; Robert Zangrando, *The NAACP Crusade against Lynching, 1909–1950* (Philadelphia, 1980); Walter White, *A Man Called White* (New York, 1948), 179–180; Tindall, *Emergence of the New South*, 552–555.

56. Douglas Dowd, "Comparative Analysis of Economic Development in the American West and South," *Journal of Economic History* 16 (1956), 558–574; Pete Daniel, *Standing at the Crossroads: Southern Life in the Twentieth Century* (New York, 1986), 120–124. Tindall, *Emergence of the New South*, 409, reports that half the white farmers were tenants, compared with two-thirds of the Negro farmers. For background, see Gavin Wright, *Old South, New South: Revolutions in the Southern Economy since the Civil War* (1986), and James C. Cobb, *Industrialization and Southern Society, 1877–1984* (Chicago, 1984).

57. Unionist quoted in Tindall, *Emergence of the New South*, 417; ibid., 420, 514–515, 527, 618–619; Rosengarten, *All God's Dangers*, 323; Bernstein, *Turbulent Years*.

58. Tindall, *Emergence of the New South*, 620–625; Howell Harris, *The Right to Manage: Industrial Relations Policies of American Business in the 1940s* (Madison, Wis., 1982), chap. 1; Bayor, *Neighbors in Conflict*, 97–104.

59. *Fortune* quoted in Schlesinger, *Coming of the New Deal*, 494; Roosevelt in *Public Papers*, V, 487.

60. Lynd and Lynd, *Middletown in Transition*, 177; Mirra Komarovsky, *The Unemployed Man and His Family* (New York, 1971; orig. 1940), 23–48; Ruth S. Cavan and Katherine Rauck, *The Family and the Depression: A Study of One Hundred Chicago Families* (Freeport, N.Y., 1969; orig. 1938), 55–75; E. Wright Bakke, *Citizens without Work: A Study of the Effects of Unemployment upon the Workers' Social Relations and Practices* (New Haven, 1940), 120–152, 236.

61. In the foreword to the first American edition of James Joyce's *Ulysses* (New York, 1934), v–xii, Morris Ernst quotes the 1933 decision of U.S. District Judge John Woolsey finding *Ulysses* not obscene and, therefore, admissible to the United States; Linda Gordon, *Woman's Body, Woman's Right: A Social History of Birth Control in America* (New York, 1976), 315–317, 321, 339–340. Some of the millions of condoms were undoubtedly for export; David Kennedy, *Birth Control in America: The Career of Margaret Sanger* (New Haven, 1970), 240–250; Alice Kessler-Harris, *Out to Work: A History of Wage-Earning Women in the United States* (New York, 1982), 269–272.

62. Alan Bullock, *Hitler: A Study in Tyranny*, rev. ed. (New York, 1962), 263–270.

63. Kocka, *White Collar Workers*, 194; Kindleberger, *World in Depression*, 116–117, 124–125.

64. For a contrary interpretation that stresses the similarity between New Deal and Nazi governing policies (though not political behavior), see John Garraty, *The Great Depression* (Garden City, N.Y., 1987), chap. 8.

65. Gerald Feldman, *Army, Industry, and Labor in Germany, 1914–1918* (Princeton, 1966), 523–531; Charles Maier, *Recasting Bourgeois Europe: Stabilization in France, Germany, and Italy in the Decade after World War I* (Princeton, 1975), 77–79, 512; David Abraham, *Collapse of the Weimar Republic: Political Economy and Crisis* (Princeton, 1981), 240–242.

66. Rimlinger, *Welfare Policy and Industrialization*, 131–133; Abraham, *Collapse of the Weimar Republic*, 29, 249.

67. Kindleberger, *World in Depression*, 108–109, 306; Warren I. Cohen, *Empire without Tears: America's Foreign Relations, 1921–1933* (New York, 1987), 28–29; A. J. P. Taylor, *The Course of German History* (New York, 1962; orig. 1946), 207–208, 210.

68. Although capitalist influences had penetrated agriculture and set up textiles and railroads, Russia in 1917 was still an overwhelmingly peasant society steeped in patriarchal practices and religious obscurantism. Even after the March revolution overthrew the czar and the bourgeoisie gained ground, the country remained in the grip of traditional elites. Although the Bolsheviks made use of strategically placed workers' soviets in seizing power, they did not rule through the working class, because the working class was not the life blood of the society until after Stalin's forced industrialization. See Eric Wolf, *Peasant Wars of the Twentieth Century* (New

York, 1969); Barrington Moore, *Social Origins of Dictatorship and Democracy: Lord and Peasant in the Making of the Modern World* (Boston, 1966). German leftist parties actually peaked in 1928 with 40.7 percent in the voting for the Reichstag, while the center parties accounted for 28.8 percent and the right for 29.9 percent. In 1932 the Communists increased their share to 17 percent, the Socialist Democrats declined slightly to 20.3 percent, and the Nazis went from 2.6 percent in 1928 to 33 percent in 1933; see Abraham, *Collapse of the Weimar Republic*, 32, 33. With the collapse of Weimar, three alternatives confronted Germany: concessions from ruling groups to workers and the middle classes, socialism, or imperialist expansion; see Franz Neumann, *Behemoth: The Structure and Practices of National Socialism* (New York, 1942), 34.

69. Bullock, *Hitler*, 230–231; Taylor, *Course of German History*, 205–206, 212–213.

70. Bullock, *Hitler*, 236–237, 246–250; Taylor, *Course of German History*, 203–204, 209; Abraham, *Collapse of the Weimar Republic*, 297.

71. *Triumph of the Will* is the title of Leni Riefenstahl's masterpiece of film propaganda; Bullock, *Hitler*, 217, 230–231, 246–250. For an extended discussion of counterrevolution, see Arno Mayer, *Dynamics of Counterrevolution in Europe, 1870–1956* (New York, 1971), esp. 59–85.

72. Maier, *Recasting Bourgeois Europe*, 514–515; Kocka, *White Collar Workers*, 262–267; Geoff Eley, "The German Right," in *From Unification to Nazism: Reinterpreting the German Past* (Boston, 1986), 231–253; Ute Frevert, *Women in German History: From Bourgeois Emancipation to Sexual Liberation*, trans. Stuart McKinnon-Evans (Oxford, 1988), 207–209.

73. In 1939, women employed by families (family assistants) accounted for 36.3 percent of all economically active women; another 10.5 percent were domestic servants; David Schoenbaum, *Hitler's Social Revolution* (Garden City, N.Y., 1966), 188. The overall percentage of female workers is partly a matter of definition: Renate Bridenthal and Claudia Koonz, "Beyond *Kinder, Kuche, Kirche*," in *When Biology Became Destiny: Women in Weimar and Nazi Germany*, ed. Renate Bridenthal, Atina Grossman, and Marion Kaplan (New York, 1984), 45, report 36 percent of the female population "gainfully employed" in 1925; Tim Mason, "Women in Germany, 1925–1940," *History Workshop*, Autumn 1976, 11, reports 46.9 percent of women aged fourteen to sixty-four "economically active." But in either case the proportion of female workers was considerably higher than the 20–25 percent of adult women in the United States. Part of the gap may have been the result of different accounting; it appears that U.S. census takers did not count "family assistants" as scrupulously as their German counterparts; farm wives, for example, were almost never counted as gainfully employed farmers.

74. Bridenthal and Koonz, "Beyond *Kinder, Kuche, Kirche*," 34; and Claudia

Koonz, "The Competition for a Women's Lebensraum, 1928–34," in Bridenthal, Grossman, and Kaplan, *When Biology Became Destiny*, 222, 223, 214.

75. After the Second World War, leading German historians such as Fritz Fischer, Ralf Dahrendorf, Henry Winkler, and Jurgen Kocka spread the view of German exceptionalism in which Germany's middle classes were seen as repeatedly failing to live up to their liberal destiny, a notion made somewhat plausible by comparison to the history of the United States, and perhaps more popular by virtue of U.S. postwar hegemony in Western Europe. The comparison between the German and American middle classes is made explicit in Kocka, *White Collar Workers*. Third World authoritarian regimes in the capitalist world economy offer further refutation of the idea that capitalism inevitably produces liberal regimes whose prime support comes from the middle class.

76. On mass psychology, see Hans Fallada, *Little Man, What Now?* (New York, 1933); Joachim Fest captured the fusion of the individual with the mass: "The collective feelings, the fascination of the vast mass, of which each individual could feel himself a part, gave people a sense of power which they had long lacked and which found fulfillment in Hitler's rhetoric in the atmosphere of rapturous emotion: extreme self-elevation was brought about by extreme self-surrender"; quoted in Garraty, *The Great Depression*, 186.

77. George Mosse, *Nationalism and Sexuality* (New York, 1985), 162–180.

78. Frevert, *Women in German History*, 229–231; Gisela Bock, "Racism and Sexism in Nazi Germany: Motherhood, Compulsory Sterilization, and the State," in Bridenthal, Grossman, and Kaplan, *When Biology Became Destiny*, 274–275, 279–289; see also Claudia Koonz, *Mothers in the Fatherland: Women, the Family, and Nazi Politics* (New York, 1987).

79. Seeking to demonstrate that women were not just victims of Nazi ideology, some works come perilously close to arguing that women's social condition was not set back under the Nazis; for example, Schoenbaum, *Hitler's Social Revolution*, 201, argues that the initial impetus failed, and by the end Nazis had to accommodate "a new status of relative if unconventional equality"; Frevert, *Women in German History*, 251–252, says that for the majority of women, life was acceptable. These miss the point.

80. Part of the key to fascism is its opposition to liberalism, communism, and conservatism; the idea of these "negations" as defining characteristics is spelled out in Stanley G. Payne, *Fascism: Comparison and Definition* (Madison, Wis., 1980), although he neglects the crucial quotient of antifeminism; for a similar definition, see Ernst Nolte, *Three Faces of Fascism: Action Française, Italian Fascism, National Socialism*, trans. L. Vennewitz (New York, 1969; orig. 1965).

81. John Dewey, *The Nation*, July 27, 1932; Walter Lippmann, "Planning in an Economy of Abundance," *Atlantic Monthly*, 159 (1937), 39–46; George Soule, *The Coming American Revolution* (New York, 1934), 294–295; many New Dealers thought they were forestalling fascism or communism, as is evident in Donald Richberg, speech at Faneuil Hall, December 27, 1933, copy in Donald Richberg Papers, box 45, LC.

82. Kenneth Jackson, *The Ku Klux Klan in the City* (New York, 1967), portrays at least the urban Klan as the sociological counterpart of European fascists.

83. Coughlin quoted in Smith, *To Save a Nation*, 26, 28; Brinkley, *Voices of Protest*, 95; Bayor, *Neighbors in Conflict*, 97–104.

84. Smith, *To Save a Nation*, 13, quotes from Coughlin's linkage between immorality and socialism: "Christian parents, do you want your daughter to be the breeder of some lustful person's desire, when the rose of her youth has withered, to be thrown upon the highway of Socialism? It is either the marriage feast of Cana or the brothel of Lenin!" Brinkley, *Voices of Protest*, see Coughlin and Huey Long as right-wing populists, close to European fascists, but liberal rather than antiliberal; this view is convincing neither for Coughlin, because of his antiliberalism, nor for Long, because of his leftist ideas on redistributing wealth.

85. Brinkley, *Voices of Protest*, 82; Kocka, *White Collar Workers*, 237–240, catalogues various U.S. fascist groups without basing his conclusion in their culturally based mutual animosity.

86. Moore, *Social Origins*, argues that the route to dictatorship lay in a convergence of landed elites trying to make up for economic decline by pulling political levers and a weak urban middle class trying to strengthen its hand; Jurgen Kocka puts even greater stress on traditional elites, including "the great power of the Junkers in industrial Germany and the feudalizing tendencies in the big bourgeoisie; the extraordinary power of the bureaucracy and the army in a state that had never experienced a successful bourgeois revolution and which was unified from above; the social and political alliance of the rising bourgeoisie and the ever-resilient agrarian nobility against the sharply demarcated proletariat; the closely related antiparliamentarian, anti-democratic, and anti-liberal alignment of large parts of the German ruling strata"; quoted in Eley, *From Unification to Nazism*, 257; such explanations automatically rule out fascism in liberal-democratic regimes such as the United States.

87. If the United States was well behind Europe in the development of the welfare state, it was more than a generation ahead in mass education. Germany may have pioneered social insurance, but higher education was restricted to a tiny stratum of bureaucratic mandarins drawn from the upper classes, and even secondary schooling in the *Gymnasium* was highly exclusive. Whereas German education reflected well-defined social status,

American schooling was touted as a great engine of equal opportunity; Arnold Heidenheimer, "Education and Social Security Entitlements in Europe and America," in *The Development of Welfare States in Europe and America*, ed. Peter Flora and Arnold Heidenheimer (New Brunswick, N.J., 1981), 269–304.

Conclusion

1. Roosevelt quoted in Hertha Pauli and E. B. Ashton, *I Lift My Lamp: The Way of a Symbol* (New York, 1948), 316–334.
2. Noting the incompatibility between individual freedom and collectivized economy under private control, John Dewey wrote in 1936 that "social control, especially of economic forces, is necessary in order to render secure the liberties of the individual, including civil liberties"; quoted in Richard Pells, *Radical Visions and American Dreams* (New York, 1973), 113; George Soule, *The Future of Liberty* (New York, 1936), 180–182. See also George Seldes, *You Can't Do That: A Survey of the Forces Attempting in the Name of Patriotism to Make a Desert of the Bill of Rights* (New York, 1938).
3. Franklin D. Roosevelt, *Public Papers and Addresses*, ed. Samuel Rosenman, 5 vols. (New York, 1938), V, 557–558.

Index